Thy Faith Hath Made Thee Whole

Thy Faith Hath Made Thee Whole

The *Integrity* Years (1946–1956)

CAROL ROBINSON'S
COLLECTED WORKS

Foreword by Alan Fimister, Ph.D

AROUCA PRESS

Integrity Inc., New York (1946–1956)
Copyright © by Arouca Press 2021
Foreword © Alan Fimister 2021

All rights reserved:
No part of this book may be reproduced or transmitted,
in any form or by any means, without permission

ISBN: 978-1-7770523-0-0 (pbk)
ISBN: 978-1-989905-78-4 (hc)

*This is the fifth book in the collected works series.
New editor's footnotes included throughout the book.
Illustrations in Chapter 3 by Ed Willock.
The articles with a "†" have never been republished.*

Arouca Press
PO Box 55003
Bridgeport PO
Waterloo, ON N2J 3G0
Canada
www.aroucapress.com
Send inquiries to info@aroucapress.com

Cover illustration
by Matt Livermore

"But Jesus turning and seeing her, said:
Be of good heart, daughter, thy faith hath made thee whole.
And the woman was made whole from that hour."
—Matt. 9:22

CONTENTS

EDITOR'S NOTE xi
FOREWORD xiii
PREFACE xvii

1946 1
   1. The Frustration of the Incarnation 3
   2. The Leaven 14

1947 27
   3. A Christian Abnormal Psychology 29
   4. Contemporary American Protestantism 76
   5. I'd Rather Be a Menial in the House of the Lord, than to Dwell Among Princes 90
   6. Man's Providence† 103
   7. Sins of Flesh and Commerce 110
   8. The Thirst for Theology† 121
   9. Secular Education—Some Years After† 133
  10. Why Aren't Americans Contemplative? 144
  11. The Pertinence of Penance 154
  12. The Death of Western Society 162

1948 169
  13. Job Hunting and Vocation 171
  14. The Good News—Plain and Sugared† 178
  15. The Science of Temptation 185
  16. The Evolution of Social Work 194
  17. How Modern Man Became Merry† 205
  18. The Impotence of Money Today† 210
  19. The Age of Lay Sanctity 218
  20. The Tragedy of Modern Woman† 227

1949 237
  21. The Two Enemies of the Church† 239
  22. The Problem of the Newman Club† 251
  23. Christian Vocational Guidance 262
  24. The Unity of the World† 271

1950 279
    25. Catholic Action and Responsibility. 281
    26. It All Goes Together 289
    27. The Rainmakers† 304
    28. The Servant Problem† 316

1951 323
    29. Did We Never Have It So Good? 325
    30. About Television 335
    31. Religious Fanaticism† 350
    32. The Crisis. 364

1952 401
    33. Optimism† 403
    34. The 100 Neediest Cases† 412

BOOK REVIEWS 419
EDITORIALS (October 1951–March 1952) 573

EDITOR'S NOTE

THY FAITH HATH MADE THEE WHOLE INCLUDES ALL OF the articles Carol Jackson Robinson (1911–2002) wrote for *Integrity*, the magazine she co-founded with Ed Willock and others in 1946. A collection of many of her articles was published by The Angelus Press in the book, *My Life with Thomas Aquinas*, in two editions (1992 & 1995).

This volume not only includes all of her articles for *Integrity* but also all her book reviews and editorials (October 1951–March 1952). The preface has been taken from an article she wrote in 1962 in which she reflects on her work as editor of *Integrity*. In the preface, she stated: "...we were essentially right all the way across the board, but these are no longer burning issues." We beg to differ and believe that many of the issues she raises in this book are still of concern for any thinking Catholic, so much has the world been taken in by a technocratic, liberal, impersonal, and un-Christian spirit. For Carol Robinson, mammon had replaced what should be the true object of our love and worship. As rational creatures we have as a natural end the perfection of our souls, and as baptized Christians, the Beatific Vision. Our lives are not meant to be lived on the purely natural level but on one which takes cognizance of grace. It is grace that will re-orient our lives towards God and, as a consequence, will re-orient the social order. Our priorities no longer lie where they should.

This volume will give the reader a greater insight into Carol Robinson's prodigious mind, nourished as it was by the thought of St. Thomas Aquinas. Hers was a naturally inquisitive mind, formed by grace and her experience and later rejection of her bourgeois upbringing. It seemed as if her conversion to the Faith in 1941 lit a fire in her mind and heart.

This volume shows forth a relentless determination to see *all of life* in the light of eternity and Christ's redemptive mission as continued through the Catholic Church. If she seems brazen at times, it is because of her total commitment to and conviction of the absolute truths of the Catholic Faith, which she refused to lock away in a tidy corner of sentimental devotion without any consequence for the realities of modern life.

Particular attention should be made to her book reviews, which indicate analyses not often found in many of her articles. It shows an even greater love for the thinking of St. Thomas, and especially of the great Thomistic commentator, Fr. Reginald Garrigou-Lagrange, O. P., whom she read throughout her long life.

These articles will challenge the reader to rethink some of the assumptions he has about life. Although written over 60 years ago, we believe that there are general principles that can be extrapolated and questions that we can still ask today. Is the current economic and political system conducive to an authentic Christian life? Is it easier *to practice virtue?* What can we do? What is our role as laity? The world—she argued—must be won over for Christ, and not remain for the secularists and rationalists to reshape according to their image and likeness. She makes great demands on the laity to be apostolic, not out of a desire to replace the mission of the ministerial priesthood, but because she believed that they must be in the front lines of the defense against secularism's onslaught against the Church and society: "Christ has been thrust out of the *layman's* domain; hence the logical instrument by which He will be reinstated is the layman. That is the reason for the lay apostolate, which is not just another good thing, but is of supreme importance." (*The Two Enemies of the Church*, June 1949)

Some of the terminology and turns of phrase are particular to the time period, so we beg the reader's indulgence for any infelicities he may encounter in reading the book.

The hope is that the reader will wrestle with the arguments she makes and at least be open to the claim that she was one of the most original and insightful of American Catholic authors of the past 60 years.

We would like to give a special acknowledgment to all those who helped with this book in any way. The inclusion of Matt Livermore's original linocut for the front cover hearkens back to the great Arts and Crafts period during the time of *Integrity's* publication and for this we are deeply grateful. Additional acknowledgement is extended to Alan Fimister who kindly agreed to write the foreword.

FOREWORD

ALAN FIMISTER

THE PRESENT VOLUME COMPRISES THE WRITINGS OF Carol Jackson Robinson in the magazine *Integrity* of which she was the co-founder in the second half of the 1940s and the beginning of the 1950s. These texts are a profoundly significant witness to the discernment of a faithful and intellectually well-formed Catholic of the 'signs of the times' in a vital period between the end of the Second World War and the opening of the Second Vatican Council. She would later lament that her grasp of St. Thomas was at this time less perfect than in the period after the Council but, in a way, this makes the historical significance of these writings even greater.

Despite the continuous expansion of the Church between the sixteenth and twentieth centuries in missionary territories, her fortunes declined in regions where the faith had been established prior to the voyages of discovery. Culture and then public and private law were progressively secularised until we reached the darkness of the present times where not only divine but now also natural law is being banished from the civil order of those nations which once composed Christendom.

However, this sorry tale of decline, the 'long defeat' as J. R. R. Tolkien called it in 1956,[1] was interrupted by a sample or glimpse of final victory in the period 1878–1958. This period, the Leonine Era, was initiated by the policy of Pope Leo XIII (1878–1903). Leo's strategy was to distinguish the cause of the Gospel from that of the royal houses who were the target and victims of the revolutionary movement of 1789. He laid out, in the nine principle acts of his pontificate, a programme for the reconstitution of Christendom, drawn from abstract first principles identified and elaborated by St. Thomas Aquinas the revival of whose works and the exaltation of whose Christian philosophy he decreed in 1879.[2]

---

[1] "Letter to Amy Ronald, 15 December 1956" in H. Carpenter, *The Letters of J. R. R. Tolkien* (Boston: Houghton Mifflin, 1981), 195.
[2] Forthcoming publication: Etienne Gilson, ed., *The Church Speaks to the Modern World: The Social Teachings of Leo XIII*. With a new foreword by Thomas Storck, (Waterloo, ON, Arouca Press: 2021).

Carol Jackson Robinson was, to her bones, a product of this project. It was a project which transformed a catastrophic cultural and political situation in 1878 into one in which by 1958 every one of the apostate polities of mainland western Europe was governed by Catholics and the position of the Church in Britain and the United States was strengthening at an even faster rate than these former heartlands. It almost seemed as if a new Christendom was a real possibility.

And yet, this brief renaissance would collapse utterly in the succeeding decades in the greatest abandonment of the Catholic faith and priesthood that the Church has ever experienced. Our understanding of this period is inevitably coloured by the catastrophe that followed. Carol Jackson Robinson wrote of it later with a clarity of vision that she did not possess in these pages[3]. But, again, that is what makes this volume so valuable.

By the time the texts collected here were written the decline was already underway although that would not have been entirely clear to Catholics at the time. The intellectual apogee of the Leonine revival came between the two wars. Totalitarian monsters of left and right demanded the whole person and liberal capitalism was discredited in Europe and after 1929 everywhere. Catholicism stood out as the authentic champion of Western Civilisation and its true spiritual foundation.

> News that shook [...] a dozen capitals brought deep peace to one English heart. Now, splendidly, everything had become clear. The enemy at last was plain in view, huge and hateful, all disguise cast off. It was the Modern Age in arms. Whatever the outcome there was a place for him in that battle.[4]

Suddenly in 1945 the cause of liberal capitalism was renewed and the only alternative seemed to be Marxism. The Church was popular once more but her popularity was tied to the fatal expectation that

---

[3] "The early *Integrity* couldn't last because the editors did not have sufficient backlog of learning. In the years since we collapsed, I have studied St Thomas and filled in so far as I could the substance of his thought." Carol Jackson Robinson, *My Life With Thomas Aquinas* (Kansas City: Angelus Press, 1995), 4–5. See her forthcoming book from Arouca Press: *An Embattled Mind: In Defense of St. Thomas: Collected Works (The Wanderer Years, 1971–1987)*. With an introduction by Gregorio Montejo.

[4] Evelyn Waugh, *Men at Arms* (New York: Alfred A. Knopf, 1994), 10.

Foreword

she would throw in her cause with the plutocracy. The position so carefully established by Leo XIII apart from and untainted by these errors was badly compromised. Whatever the difficulties with the St. Benedict Center's radicalism the horror with which its WASPy converts were greeted by the US Bishops (a question which is touched upon in the pages that follow) marks an ominous bourgeoisification of the Church.[5]

Our protagonist writes as a citizen of the newly crowned hegemonic power in the west—the victorious United States. She sees the potential for total cultural transformation and is profoundly preoccupied with the possibility that Catholic Action might effect this transformation but she sees everywhere the omens and presages of doom. She hears in her heart (although the text remained sealed-up somewhere in Vatican City until 1960 and for most of us until the year 2000) the cry of the angel in the Third Secret of Fatima: 'Penitência, penitência, penitência'![6]

But she also hears the siren voices that she would later reject in horror after witnessing the collapse. She is impressed by Thomas Merton. She worries about integralism. She even thinks the faithful might cooperate in a secular reform of society first and achieve conversion later. This is not the chastened and implacable woman who faces us in later volumes in this series. And yet, this is even more valuable. As Auden would put it in 1941,

> Listen with attentiveness
> To her life-story: unless
> You become acquainted now
> With each refuge that tries to
> Counterfeit Atlantis, how
> Will you recognise the true?[7]

Bishops, priests and laypeople bought into these false versions of Catholicism and acted upon them with passion in the years following the death of Pius XII. A bishop on the floor of the Council warned

---

5   B. Harrison "Feeney, Leonard (1897–1978)" in Michael L. Coulter, *et al* (eds.), *Encyclopedia of Catholic Social Thought, Social Science and Social Policy* Vol. 1. (Laneham: The Scarecrow Press, 2007), 416-417.
6   Congregation for the Doctrine of the Faith, *The Message of Fatima* (Rome, 2000).
7   'Atlantis' in Wystan Hugh Auden, *Selected Poems* (New York: Vintage Books, 2007), 125.

his brethren that the Church had already suffered too much from ignoring the insights of Marx, Darwin and Freud, and she could not afford to spurn those of Pierre Teilhard de Chardin.[8] Carol was not so deluded as this.[9] As the reader will see, she knew communism for the peril it was, she trembled at the thought that America's power was born in the flames of Hiroshima and Nagasaki, she was profoundly sceptical of psychology, she despised the acquisitive commercial civilisation born of victory but more truly of the Protestant ethic. Not every proposal she makes may sound credible nor did every (any?) project in which she placed her hopes bear fruit but she strove to live as a stranger and sojourner, a high-born exile on earth[10] in an era in which complacency was fattening up her coreligionists for disaster. Now we have no choice but to live as strangers and sojourners in a world which barely conceals its desire to wipe the Gospel from the face of the earth and as such we can profit much from the hope and perseverance of Carol Jackson Robinson.

---

8   Roberto de Mattei, *The Second Vatican Council: An Unwritten Story*, (Fitzwilliam: Loreto Publications, 2010), 452.
9   J. P. Slattery, 'Dangerous Tendancies of Cosmic Theology: The Untold Legacy of Teilhard de Chardin' in *Philosophy and Theology* 29, 1 (2017): 69-82.
10 St Augustine, *Enarr. in Ps.* 136, 13.

PREFACE

Shortly before we started *Integrity* I was urged to consult a man said to be wise about adventures such as ours. Among other things, he advised it would be folly for us to begin publishing without the first six issues clearly planned and the articles for the first three in hand.

Of course we had no such thing. We had no writers except ourselves, no potential writers except our friends, no staff except two friends as foolish as ourselves, no money, no office and no experience. The editors hardly knew one another and Ed Willock lived in Boston, where he barely managed to feed a burgeoning family by unloading trucks of Planter's Peanuts.

What we did have was a sharp, intense and intuitive realization that at every turn the Church and the secular world were inimical, and the certitude that truth was on the side of the Church. We had an unfeigned horror of the efforts of some Catholics to serve two masters.

The only time in my life I ever desperately clutched my rosary in prayer was at a conference of religious high school teachers we "cased" in the Bronx. This was an assemblage of Sisters and Brothers who taught business courses. In all innocence, I suppose, their dedicated zeal was making their classrooms into mock white-collar factories. It seemed to us as though this was preparing victims for sacrifice to Mammon under the auspices of the salesmen of business machines and equipment. We could almost see St. Peter's toppling.

ED WILLOCK'S HUMOR

Fortunately, my own nakedly apocalyptic view of the situation was tempered by Ed Willocks' sense of humor. For one thing, he had lived with the situation longer. He used to tell us about the night he discovered some priests weren't interested in religion. It was only one priest at the time, but to understand the mental attitude with which we started *Integrity*, you must realize that we found it hair-raising and nearly incredible that even one priest should be more interested in baseball than the apostolate.

Ed was with the *Catholic Worker* in Worcester, Mass., at the time, waiting for a train back to Boston where his family lived. When he saw a priest also waiting he struck up a conversation about matters he thought would be of mutual interest, and it was quite a while before he realized the priest actually couldn't care less.

Ed and I had almost nothing in common except the essential view of the world which characterized *Integrity*. There was also a mutual esteem and fondness which we shared with Doreen O'Sullivan and John Murphy who founded the magazine with us, and similar feelings toward those who joined us later. All this harmony and jollity wore thin to the breaking point later on, but the friendships were not permanently severed.

Ed came from a Boston Irish Catholic family which had vicissitudes of its own in addition to the Great Depression through which it suffered in his youth. Someone put him on to Catholic social writers during his high school days. He was self-educated, but wonderfully educated, in a parish library. It is not too much to say that his mind was actually formed by G. K. Chesterton, even to his style of writing.

He also spent a couple of years in the wards of a public hospital waiting to die of a kidney injury suffered in football. This was a remote cause of his death at the age of 44 in 1959. His partial recovery in youth was an effect of Extreme Unction.

If it were not for this illness he would have taken some kind of menial work to help support his family, but he taught himself to draw in the hospital. And but for this illness he would have tried to become a priest. As it was he fell in with Peter Maurin and the Catholic Worker movement and completed his education in Houses of Hospitality in Boston and Worchester.

HEROIC TRUST IN GOD

When Ed married Dorothy Brophy (a Worchester Catholic Worker volunteer) he had only $40 in the world. When he died he was the father of 12 children and had long been incapacitated from a series of strokes.

Many people said he had no right to have so many children in his circumstances, but if Ed had measured his activities by natural prudence he would never have married, much less had any children, and we would never have started *Integrity*. He lived by heroic trust in God.

I had been a Catholic about five years when we started the magazine. Mine was a "bourgeois" background, with no religious training (on account of the mixed marriage of my parents), and a degree in

Preface

philosophy from Wellesley. It was all the wrong philosophy and the Church was the first positive thing in my life. I saw it as the answer to everything.

It was my good fortune that I met the Dominicans. My personal debt to Father Francis N. Wendell, O. P., is inestimable. He instructed me in the Faith. For several years I was his secretary and learned much doctrine from him while keeping him from his work. He was also my spiritual director, and in these matters I started considerably below scratch, misshapen and neurotic.

FATHERS WENDELL AND EGAN

Father Wendell was editor of the *Torch*, where Ed and I and just about everyone else in the lay apostolate got started writing. He is responsible for the founding of *Integrity* because he brought the editors together. At the time, I was living in a tenement on 64th Street washing dishes part-time for a living, trying to write, and talking at random about starting a magazine. When Father Wendell met Ed in Boston he saw a similarity in our thinking and started us corresponding.

Integrity also would have been impossible without the help of another Dominican, Father James Mark Egan, O. P., who is now head of the school of theology at St. Mary's, Notre Dame, but was then chaplain of the Dominican Sisters' motherhouse in Sparkill, New York. He censored the magazine and helped us with our theology during the entire span of its publication. He was the ideal censor; a superb theologian who knew exactly what doctrine or principle was relevant to a problem, who never once tried to press his own views about the temporal matters we were analyzing, inexhaustibly humble, patient and kind. People used to tear their hair at the things that appeared in *Integrity*, but nobody ever convicted us of doctrinal error, nor could they.

JOE MCQUADE AND OTHER FRIENDS

There are several other people without whom *Integrity* would have been impossible. Chief among them was the late Joseph M. McQuade, whom we always regarded as a saint. Unlike us, whose financial acumen was nil, Joe knew exactly what he was doing, and what folly it was, when he undertook to print *Integrity*. I believe this heroic deed was connected with other personal matters, about which I know little and can say nothing. I still owe him money. May he rest in peace.

A Capuchin priest, Father Martin de Porres, now a missionary in the Pacific, financed *Integrity's* beginning with $1,500 which he gave to Father Wendell to dispose of when he left the New York Fire Department to study for the priesthood. He was a friend of Joe McQuade's.

Frank Sheed, always our friend and in any number of ways our helper, let us use the Sheed and Ward mailing list to send out advance promotion.

We began work in the late summer of 1946, when the housing shortage was at its worst. Ed put an ad in the *Catholic News* in New York ("Undesirable family needs shelter") which produced a very suitable little house in the upper Bronx for a modest rent. Fortunately I had my three-room, $18.50-a-month tenement, while John and Doreen lived with their families.

In August we rented the front half of a coal cellar on York Avenue near 82nd Street for $20 a month, our one-room office for the next two years. We had hardly set up shop when the local gangsters appeared to offer us protection (from themselves) at a price, but we assured them we had already put ourselves under the protection and patronage of the saints.

Our promotion brought us 1,100 advance subscriptions at $3 a year. Our first issue—October, 1946—had for its cover Ed's drawing of air foam Christianity (a Catholic curled up asleep on a padded cross) and the first set of his jingles with drawings:

> *Mr. Business went to Mass*
> *Every single Sunday;*
> *Mr. Business went to Hell*
> *For what he did on Monday.*

A PARTICULAR TOPIC

In each issue we had four or five articles, an editorial and some book reviews, plus the jingles and cartoons. We devoted each issue after the first to a particular topic in the manner of *Blackfriars*; the subjects very often and quite coincidentally paralleled those of the English magazine. Since we were nobody and we paid very little (three-quarters of a cent a word), we looked mostly to unknowns who had something to say. This was also a matter of principle, because we thought the popular Catholic writers were done to death.

Preface

Quite a few of our writers were at first readers who started corresponding with us about their ideas, or came in to see us. Some, like Mary Reed Newland, Norma Krause Herzfeld and Marion Stancioff, wrote for us and other papers frequently thereafter; others wrote once only on the basis of special knowledge or experience.

We thought anybody could write what he knew from personal experience and felt strongly about, and this seemed to work out. However, we were much more interested in ideas than in style. All things considered, the literary level was quite high. Ed wrote well and sometimes brilliantly.

The circulation, mostly in subscriptions, ran about 13,000 to 15,000 during most of the life of the magazine. Renewals were exceptionally high. About 50% of the copies went to priests and religious. There was no homogeneity among the lay subscribers. We always considered our readers "people who think," and it seemed to us that this had nothing to do with their educational level.

No matter what the topic we were treating in the magazine we always tried to see it in the light of Christian principle, solidly based on St. Thomas, whom we never found wanting in criteria. "The relation of religion and life" in our own day was our tireless thesis, whether we were dealing with social work, television, psychiatry, advertising, death, art or medicine.

We did not present both sides of our subjects because we didn't think there were two sides on the level were discussing them. We were searching for the essential truth of their operation in the light of Christian norms.

Our enthusiastic readers, and most of our readers were enthusiastic, seldom expressed their gratitude for instruction, but rather for the reassurance we gave them about truths they saw themselves.

Once, when Ed and I were discussing how we arrived at these views, we were forced to admit it ourselves that ours was in the first place an intuitive knowledge. We were somewhat ashamed of it at the time, because we thought it lowered our intellectual prestige, but it was, after all, a kind of contemplative gift. Either you see it or you don't, but if you do you have a chance of leading others to the same view.

'FRENZIED OPPOSITION'

This "gift" then, plus our Thomism, met with a certain amount of frenzied opposition. We said that TV just then beginning to mushroom, was an opiate and would have an all-over deadening effect, no matter what you did about it. They said it was a box, a scientific invention, a something that depended for its morality on how it was used.

We said that modern advertising was based on, and inseparable from, the science of inciting concupiscence. They saw nothing wrong in it unless there were pictures of sexy girls in the ads. Our wars, semi-amicable, were chiefly with *America, Commonweal,* and the *Christophers* (there was a time when Father James Keller[1] and I followed one another around the country nullifying the effects of each other's lectures), and for quite a while we had a running war with the Catholic social work schools.

Our contention here was they had swallowed whole the secular techniques based mostly on Freud, and certainly not on charity and the Christian view of man.

LOST ALL THE WARS

We lost all these wars, at least so far as affecting the course of events or convincing our opponents. Yet periodically the old problems are raised again by Catholic magazines and discussed inconclusively on a superficial level. I am not aware of anyone who is now pressing these issues on a deeper level. As far as the particular issues are concerned I think it does not much matter.

My present opinion is that we were essentially right all the way across the board, but these are no longer burning issues. Television is part of the American way of life now; let those who can, modify its effects or use it for occasional good. No one will ever be able to measure the mediocrity of which it has been the occasion. *Integrity* probably helped strengthen an elite of non-viewers.

As far as social work is concerned, the opportunity to Christianize even the Catholic contribution has long since been lost. The Church still has an immense bureaucratic-administrative responsibility in welfare, which has negative importance, but the great surges of supernatural charity are finding other channels.

---

[1] Fr. James Keller (1900–1977), a Maryknoll priest, founded *The Christophers* in 1945.—*Ed.*

TOO LITTLE TOO LATE

It is even possible that our efforts were too little and too late. Yet our major themes, concerning the necessity for a responsible and integrated laity, has certainly gained momentum. We didn't dream this idea up ourselves of course, so we were only one of many forces in this movement which will be solidly grounded only after the Ecumenical Council.

Integrity took a pretty dim view of the Catholic Press, and especially of the diocesan press. On the whole this was heartily reciprocated. A southern bishop, for instance, wrote one editor to ask if he ought to encourage a young woman to join our staff, and was advised against it.

During our first five years we refused to join the Catholic Press Association as a matter of principle. We were horrified because the main subjects of discussion at national conventions seemed to be How-to-Get-National-Advertising, and we thought it ought to have been How-to-Improve-the-Diocesan-Papers. We also objected, rather puritanically, to the "worldliness" of the conventions. In return the Catholic Press Association pretended we didn't exist. I have often wondered how they could refrain from giving Ed Willock awards for his cartoons. He was surely the best Catholic cartoonist we have yet seen in America.

The "first period" of *Integrity*, during which Ed and I were co-editors, lasted from 1946 to 1951. Ed left the magazine and very shortly afterwards had the first of his strokes. I took over for several months, came within a hairsbreadth of cracking up, and had to leave. Dorothy Dohen then took over for five years until publication finally ceased in 1956.

Of the latter period I am not qualified to speak, but it is clear in retrospect of the first period that we simply ran out of capital of all kinds. We did some fatally imprudent things, but they were probably the consequence of failures elsewhere rather than causes in themselves.

OUR WATERLOOS

Chiefly, our intellectual capital gave out. We gave *Integrity* the fruit of years of thinking, without having the leisure to keep the storehouse full. One result was tension between the editors, for we tended to opposite views. The final result of "trying to give what we didn't have,"[2] was the revolt of our brains. Ed had his stroke, and it was several years before I could even read a book.

Subordinately, we got involved in practical affairs where our competence was limited or nil and which bred all sorts of dissensions.

To provide housing and community for his by now much larger family, Ed joined with some other fathers to build Marycrest, a housing community on the other side of the Hudson. Unfortunately, Marycrest also started without capital of any sort, including know-how and group formation.

Our other Waterloo was in the business and circulation affairs of *Integrity* itself. Neither of us had any management ability but we erred in opposite directions. We didn't really think we had any competence in business affairs but we thought we had a responsibility to direct them, and even to Christianize them.

The worse things became (through our fault, although this was not clear to us at the time), the more responsibility we felt. It seems to be a law of outraged nature for people to act this way. There are some worn-out television figures who don't know enough to quit, who have my sympathetic understanding.

In the light of what happened I can even appreciate the six-issues-in-advance approach to magazine editing. Certainly the atmosphere seems to have changed in that direction. Apostolic ventures now pride themselves on paying a living wage, whereas we operated according to the tradition of voluntary poverty. There seems to be plenty of room at the top now, for cream-of-the-cream honor students starting at high salaries.

All around, publishing has become much more sane. But surely also, much less fun. For those early years on *Integrity* were wonderful.

Carol Jackson Robinson
Catholic Press Annual 1962

---

2   *Nemo dat quod non habet* (scholastic axiom) — *Ed.*

1946

1
The Frustration of the Incarnation
OR
The Need for a Reintegration of the Natural and the Supernatural Orders[1]

OCTOBER 1946

ASK ALMOST ANY NON-CATHOLIC WHAT HE THINKS "supernatural" means and he will refer vaguely to crystal gazing and ghost stories. Ask him for his concept of a holy man and he will blush slightly, restate the question to refer to a "good" man and describe an ideal not essentially different from the ancient pagan ideal of a just and virtuous man. His highest admiration is reserved for Abraham Lincoln; he would be scandalized by St. Catherine of Siena or Benedict-Joseph Labre. In short, outside the Catholic Church the presence of Divine Life in the world has been almost totally forgotten. A surprising number of people have never even heard of the Holy Eucharist. The words "mystery" and "mysticism" have fallen into discredit. Penance awakens a shudder, sacrifice is misdirected, miracles are disbelieved *a priori*, and the Gospels are grossly distorted. This state of affairs has gone so far that a book like "The Human Life of Jesus" by John Erskine (which is blasphemous) can be chosen as "The Religious Book of the Month."

This situation is reflected in the Church by an artificial separation by the faithful of the supernatural order and the natural order; a separation of their sacramental lives from their daily lives and work. It is the true contemporary schizophrenia.

---

[1] The following informal distinction can be made between the several orders: *Natural* is what is proper to anything in the created order. (examples: reason, as natural to men; nutrition as natural to men and animals) *Supernatural* (above the natural) refers to God's nature, present in the world through grace, because of the Incarnation.

A further distinction is made in theology. *Preternatural* (beyond the natural) designates what is natural to the angels (including the fallen ones), but which is ordinarily beyond us. Our first parents had some preternatural gifts (integrity, immortality and impassivity), but men do not now have such powers, save exceptionally (as levitations).

From this source flows the popular chant, "what's wrong with *that?*" which is used for a justification for everything from jukeboxes to taking a job purely for the financial rewards involved. The assumption back of this popular gauge of morality is that the only connection between the natural and supernatural is one of remote and general intention. The exponents of this theory reason that as long as what they do is naturally good (often enough it is naturally bad and the Catholic does not know it), and as long as they make a morning offering, everything they do is meritorious and they are leading supernatural lives. It is true that such actions when they are good, being formally directed to a supernatural end, are in so far useful for salvation. They remain, however, intrinsically natural. A religious life which stops there is frustrating the Incarnation. It is as though one were to say, "I will do my eating for God, but it isn't possible that that could make any difference in my diet," or, "I'll offer my work to Christ, but the fact that Christ became man is irrelevant to the telephone company I work for."

Another obvious effect of our separation of the natural and the supernatural is prevalent in social action. We tend overly to preach the natural law, especially in matters of social reform and economic planning. The reasons are obvious. In the first place, all men, whether Catholic or not, are bound by the natural law and capable of discerning it. Therefore, it forms a basis on which we can operate with non-Catholics in matters economic, political and social. Certainly we need to cooperate with all men of good will, even before we succeed in converting them, if we do. But it seems that the harder we urge the natural law, the more difficult it becomes to get all men to agree on it. See, for instance, how many men fail to discern the necessity of private property, or the existence of the soul.

Another obvious reason for preaching the natural law is the urgent necessity for reform in the purely natural order. The papal social encyclicals deal at length with social justice, universal human rights, economic reorganization and other problems on the natural plane. Yet not one of them rests matters on the natural level; all urgently advocate the fullness of Christian life. The great encyclicals, for instance, say over and over again, "Seek ye *first* the kingdom of heaven and its justice," yet one seldom hears it quoted when speaking of these letters. Or again, have we forgotten that Pius XI, in *Quadragesimo Anno*, goes out of his way to explain that we cannot be one with the earth-bound Socialists, even when they happen to be right on a particular issue?

"Those who wish to be apostles amongst the Socialists should preach the Christian truth *whole and entire,* openly and sincerely, without any connivance with error."

IT IS EASILY POSSIBLE to overemphasize the natural order, so that the Catholic Church becomes known as the Church that recommends a corporate state, or that defends private property, or that urges a living wage, or favors the land movement. All these things the heathen do also, and often better than we. The most successful folk dances in New York are run by the Communists. Cooperatives are still the glory of the Danes, and credit unions are anyone's baby. In what sense is a program *Catholic* which can be subscribed to as well by Socialist agnostics and followers of Gandhi? It may be good, and yet not good enough either to bring us finally to God or to save an earthly society.

And what about our propaganda with non-Catholics? Are we trying to convert them to the Church via private property and the natural dignity of human being? What right have we to assume that they are not aching rather for the remission of their sins and a share in the Divine Life, and that these might now prove a much greater attraction?

In any case, we are badly in need of considering the natural and the supernatural orders to see if their relationship is not closer than, and different from, that which we ordinarily think.

THE SUPERNATURAL IS NOT THE CULMINATION OF THE NATURAL

The natural order does not get any nearer to the supernatural order, no matter how splendid it becomes. A man does not, by becoming more and more zealous in the practice of natural virtue, grow into supernatural life. Whether or not he disposes himself for supernatural life is another matter in which natural virtue's role is only the negative one of removing implements. If he does, supernatural life comes not through his own efforts, but through baptism, by water, blood or desire. Who can say whether a Vassar graduate is a more likely candidate for grace than an Alcoholic Anonymous? Who can say that a learned man is nearer to Divine Life than an ignorant one? Or that life in the suburbs disposes more for grace than life in the slums? Or that a strong-willed matron is a better candidate for conversion than a weak-willed financial failure? One can argue that, other things being equal, what is naturally good forms a better basis for leading the life of grace, once grace has been received, but not that it of itself pulls heaven earthward. The natural as natural has no claim whatever on super-nature and does not even lead in the direction of it. In the matter of disposing oneself to receive grace it cannot even be argued that good natural conditions of life are especially valuable, because the supreme disposing condition is humility, and humility does not ordinarily characterize worldly success. As a matter of fact, natural despair is very close to supernatural hope, in the sense that it is a disposing agent. Alcoholics Anonymous makes use of this fact without being aware of the theology involved. They like to catch their drunks when under the humiliation of an especially disastrous bout, and remind them of how powerless their own good intentions are. "Cast yourself on God, or what you know as God," is their recommendation. "Admit that you cannot reform of yourself and ask God to do it for you."

Another example of the power of humility to receive grace is given by Leon Bloy[2] in the case of his one-time mistress. He tells that she was converted from a life of prostitution to a high degree of sanctity in a very short time, owing to her complete abandonment to the will of God.

WHAT IS TRUE OF INDIVIDUALS is also true of society. Higher wages, clean washrooms, just laws for Negroes, good housing, farm life, folk dancing, washing machines, parks and clean government, do not *of themselves* tend to Christianize society. They are just good things which improve society in the natural order. The very thought of a society in which these things were regarded as the *summum bonum*, as ends in themselves, and in which they had been largely achieved, would make one yawn or reach for a drink, according to one's temperament. Life would be hygienic boredom in a garden suburb. It would be partial living and quiet desperation. Wherever a semblance of this has been achieved; wherever men have regarded material niceties as ends in themselves and have achieved a comfortable modicum of them, the same phenomena have been observed. Whether in pre-war Scandinavia, in American suburbia, or in a grandiose housing project, behind the lifeless façade of material luxury, is drunkenness, insanity and suicide, going up and up.

---

2 French author (1846–1917) and Catholic convert whose works were instrumental in the conversions of Jacques Maritain, Joris-Karl Huysmans, and George Roualt. Some of his novels include *Despairing* (1887) and *The Woman Who Was Poor* (1897). — *Ed.*

All the department stores and cancer committees and country clubs and refrigerators lumped together will not bring us eternal life. In the absence of these things we hope in them. In the possession of these things we know our own despair. Herein lies the explanation for Communism's appeal to the rich and intellectual (those classes with a surfeit of natural goods). Men have a passion for the absolute. Communism is an absolute, a religion. It is not a new egg beater, but a cause to die for. It does not demand five dollars down and ten dollars a week, but blind and unswerving loyalty.

EVEN WHAT IS NATURALLY GOOD CANNOT BE NATURALLY OBTAINED

An earthly paradise is not for us fallen creatures. Because of original sin we cannot attain it; because of grace and redemption, it would not satisfy us if we could.

For the individual human being (unbaptized) who has reached the age of reason there is no such thing as an extended state of natural goodness. Not being in the state of grace, he will inevitably fall into mortal sin before very long. This is one of the Church's official teachings on grace. "Man in the state of fallen nature, not healed by habitual grace, cannot long remain without mortal sin."[3] Catholics are not affected by this, of course, because since they are validly baptized, they are not candidates for *natural* goodness anyhow. They have been healed by habitual grace, at least once. But what about our non-Catholic friends, whom we blithely assume to be as good as gold and ready candidates for Heaven (which, incidentally, relieves us of the necessity of being apostolic among them)? Few of them are validly baptized these days, since the proper intention is lacking among liberal Protestant ministers. Therefore, they cannot be assumed at random to possess supernatural life or, in view of the above pronouncement, to be naturally good. What chance is there, then, that they will be able to produce a naturally good society? For you can extend the principle. What one man cannot do without the light and help of grace cannot be done by an aggregate of men with a similar deficiency.

We could have derived the same conclusion from a look around us. We know that naturalism has long been the predominant philosophy of Western society and now prevails almost universally. No one can deny

---

3   II Council of Milene, can 3. (Denz., No. 103), Coelestine I, "Indiculus" (Denz., No. 132).

that Western society is in an unprecedented mess. Isn't this because we have been trying to run it without grace?

We no longer open our peace conferences "in the Name of the Father and of the Son and of the Holy Ghost." From having made an unjust and unwise peace after the last war, we are quite unable to make peace at all after this one. We no longer count marriage a sacrament, and cannot even preserve contractual marriage. It is considered indecent to talk about eternal truths, so we have the curious phenomenon of having nothing really important to say, with magnificent instruments for saying it. Considering health an end in itself, we are quite unhealthy. Refusing to fast, we haven't the strength to resist black markets. Every single branch of our society is sick.

There are a few voices calling for a return to God and to the life of grace. Most reforming voices, however, are still crying for a reform in the natural order. Let's re-arrange this, elect him, divide the spoils this way, and build better school buildings. *Let's appropriate ten million dollars for psychiatrists, and three million for brotherhood, and eight million for cancer. Let's build ten thousand housing projects and set up a commission for holding down excess profits, and examine the kitchen sinks of all restaurants, and clean the teeth free for all school children under ten.*

Americans are full of good will and zeal and plans. They are also more devoid than most people of a sense of the supernatural. The salvation of America will depend not on converting Americans to the idea of goodness and unselfishness. They take to it quite readily. But they must be converted to a sense of the life of grace, a desire to do penance, a love of solitude and quiet, a respect for contemplation.

GRACE PERFECTS NATURE

The statement that grace perfects nature does not mean that nature has to be made perfect before you can top it off with grace. It means that the perfection of nature is only to be obtained, and preserved, through the action of grace. Natural remedies for natural defects will be effective locally and occasionally, as witness the salutary effect of army discipline on weak-willed young men, up to a point. But without grace, what is naturally good tends to become naturally bad, and what is naturally bad tends to become perverted. Without grace men fall into sexual license and, when that is widespread, into unnatural practices. And when whole cities are sunk in lust, as is now the case, how can widespread purity be restored? Only through grace. It *looks* as though it would be sufficient to clean up the news stands, censor the movies, warn about venereal disease and increase the police force. It isn't. Only grace can restore the harmony of our natures. Only with supernatural help can we control our concupiscence. The natural remedies follow along, but by themselves are insufficient.

It all goes back to Adam and Eve. The harmony of their natures prior to the fall was contingent on the fact that they were subject to God and possessed supernatural life. Because of this, their lower natures (and lower nature generally) were subordinate to their higher natures. It was when they disobeyed God that everything got out of hand. Consequently, the key to our control of ourselves and the world is our corporate subordination to God.

The further men get away from God, the worse become our troubles. The worse our troubles become, the more irrelevant God seems, whereas the truth of the matter is that the more imperative it has become to have His help. We may soon reach the point where it will be too late to save all those naturally good things we cling to with such persistence, when we can only save ourselves by the mass manufacture of hair shirts.

SOME MISTAKEN NOTIONS

It must be borne in mind that the supernatural life is not wholly identical with the pious life. It is hard for some people to see how grace can save the world because they think of grace as something apart from, and not affecting, daily life. This is mostly because of stopping short at the "there-is-nothing-wrong-in-what-I-do-and-I-make-my-morning-offering" sort of religious life. We do not let grace course though us into social life, we do not take our inspiration from the Holy Ghost. The multiplication of devotions, even daily Mass and Communion, will not tell in the life of society unless grace is allowed to mold our *whole* lives. How does one express grace? In everything. The Catholic cathedrals of Europe are grace caught and expressed in stone. Radio City is the spirit of commercialism and man's fancied omnipotence, fashioned in steel and concrete.

A further misconception is that the supernatural has to work within the present social and economic framework. There has been built up a dogma, a sort of phobia, that the present social and economic structure is here to stay; a feeling that God must supernaturalize file-clerking, and wouldn't dare destroy the files; a conviction that democracy is at least as inviolable as Christianity and possibly more so. Under this conception, we Christians are the sprinklers of holy water, who must repair all the little things and query none of the big ones. We must get rid of this phobia so that it will not stand in the way of the Holy Ghost's inspiration. Let us be ready for anything, so long as God wills it.

Another, and worse, error is the supposition that we can save our own souls apart from society. We have corporately sinned by directing society to ends irrespective of, and often inimical to, God. We need corporate as well as individual reform. Furthermore, we are all in the same boat, a very leaky one materially speaking. Strangely enough Catholics don't, but they should, feel at home in this vessel, as the barque of Peter was never an individualist's paradise. If God intends us to be apostles in the modern world, we shall not be abundantly favored by grace if we run away from it.

REFORM THROUGH THE SUPERNATURAL

A strong injection of the supernatural at any point will act to renew society. But supernatural grace will have to be allowed to do its transforming work. It is most often not allowed in our society. Take the imaginary instance of a relief administrator in the state of grace. Suppose he refuses help to a needy man owing to a residential technicality bound up with the relief law. He may have to observe his rules, but he is certainly not exercising his supernatural gift of charity (unless, of course, he makes his private gesture), and therefore cannot be said to be injecting the supernatural into society just because he is in society and supernatural life is in him.

Suppose the supernatural is allowed to express itself in us, and consequently in society. What would happen? Who can say exactly? The effects of Divine Life are always unpredictably lovely and are forever beyond the capacity of "planners" to anticipate (if they were, by chance, to take such things into account). Besides, it is not for us to inquire too deeply into the workings of God's Providence, for fear of presuming to understand what is essentially a mystery. Still, it does no harm to point out some of the probable consequences in obvious cases.

LET US TAKE PENANCE, as a timely subject. If we could not figure out ourselves that a wave of penance were in order, we could learn as much from Our Lady, for it has been the burden of her several messages within the last century. We are obviously going to do penance, whether voluntarily or not. Europe is undergoing an unprecedented fast, which might be regarded as imposed penance which God has allowed those countries to suffer. If so, we can look forward to something of the sort ourselves, since so far we have done nothing to warrant exemption.

It might conceivably happen that presently, under the terror of atomic bombing, and urged by holy and fiery preachers, possibly over the radio, several million Americans would take to the traditional sackcloth and ashes. It would be an edifying sight. Imagine an army of Franciscan-like penitents filling the highways from coast to coast and refusing to eat anything more tasty than the scraps of old hot dogs left by the Sunday picnickers. Converted psychiatrists might form a special elite of flagellants, scourging themselves constantly for their sins, the while repenting their foolish talk about masochism. There would be bonfires in every city, into which the frenzied citizens could throw their lipsticks, nylons, comic books and cheap literature. The Radio City choruses, clad in long and formless garments, would perform penitential dances to the *Attende Domine,* with the entire audience bursting forth on *quia peccavimus tibi.*

One can easily imagine that such a change of American hearts might move God to the use of extraordinary means to save our country. A legion of anti-aircraft angels, for instance.

However, let us suppose for the moment that we were to do penance less spectacularly and without waiting until the zero hour. It is easy to show that any appreciable amount of mortification could not help but transform the economic and social structure.

Fasting is an elementary and very efficacious form of penance. The Church theoretically demands a considerable amount of it from every able-bodied Catholic. Most Catholics are excused, for one reason or another; and the Protestants have lost the very notion of fasting. One never hears of the food stocks fluctuating during Lent or on Ember Days. They would, though, if even the faithful denied themselves on the specified occasions. Proof is that the fishing industry attunes itself to the Friday abstinence, which we do observe pretty conscientiously.

If we were to fast, first of all there would be less food consumed. That would mean more food for Europe. That would mean better health for us, because as a nation we overeat.

Two slices of bread is the specified fasting breakfast. You cannot work on two slices of the denatured white bread that is currently extolled in the advertisements and grocery stores. The quality of bread and other foods would have to improve, and this improvement would eventually be reflected in a decrease of degenerative diseases.

YET OUR SPIRITUAL HEALTH IS WHAT will primarily benefit from fasting. We would see conspicuous improvements. Take the matter of black markets. They are scandalous in America. They are obviously not the handiwork of a few depraved individuals, but bear testimony rather to the self-indulgence of millions of housewives. Mrs. X likes butter. Butter disappears. Mrs. X is tempted to satisfy her longing for butter through illegitimate channels. Mrs. X succumbs. However, if Mrs. X put in fifty or sixty days annually of eating less than she desired, it would be pretty easy for her to pass up gastronomic gratification in deference to the common good. If Americans were able to resist black markets, the economic order would be profoundly affected. Similarly, we would be able voluntarily to eat less on the whole so that other nations could eat more. Who can deny that that would affect international amity? It is useless to pretend that we can do these things for purely natural motives of altruism or enlightened self-interest. The religious motive has the strongest appeal and, therefore, the best chance of succeeding. Lesser motives are currently failing ignominiously.

Fasting has indirect results too. The will, once strengthened, is primed to resist a variety of temptations. For instance, one who fasts does much to overcome temptations to impurity. Jacinta (one of the children who saw the apparition at Fatima) was told by Our Lady in the hospital that it was the sin of impurity that would ruin the greatest number of souls. Any return to purity would have enormous repercussions; it would restore the dignity of women, strengthen the family, and consequently, the state, etc. We are concerned here only to point out that penance is an approach to the problem of restoring purity.

Another simple form of penance is the practice of custody of the eyes; the practice of deliberately not looking at everything that offers. This may sound like a silly or a trivial mortification, but it was obviously suggested by the fact that the eyes are a major avenue of temptation. Practically the whole advertising business rests on that fact. What if women decided, in consequential numbers, not to look at any of the advertisements in the *Saturday Evening Post?* What if all the Catholics in New York gave up reading subway car cards and instead read pious books or said their rosaries going back and forth to work?

What if several hundred thousand women declined, say as an offering for peace, to look in any store window during Advent? What if all pious societies of men refused for a year to look at any women's legs? What would happen to the sale of nylons? Very much of this sort of thing and the whole economic system would be threatened.

AND SO IT GOES. Penance might become popular. People might cut down on the number of clothes they exposed, throw away half their furniture, take the rugs up from the floor, glory in china that doesn't exactly match. They might do all these things if they discovered that it would free their minds for much more important spiritual things. It is just barely possible that they might. And if they did, the whole direction of our society would be changed.

2

The Leaven

NOVEMBER 1946

How to reconvert a post-christian western world to Catholicism? This seems to be the most important question in the Church, to which all other problems are related. Where is there mission territory so distant as not to be subject to influences arising in Europe and America? Our political quarrels, our wars, our radios, our denatured food, our second-rate movies, our pornographic magazines, the split in Christendom which is the Protestant heresy, our immodest dress, our culture, such as it is; all reach to the far corners of the world. How can we hope that Orientals or African Negroes will carry on if we fail? We are obviously bent on dragging the whole world with us to destruction. Whether we like it or not, we have to attack the very difficult problem of self-reform, for it seems that in us circumstances have placed the present hope of the world.

We must see the United States as missionary territory. There is a revival of apostolic spirit (which is a measure of the health of the Faith) going on. It is evident, for instance, in the over-crowded novitiates of Maryknoll. What is late in arriving is an intensely apostolic spirit on the home territory, an earnest hope for the soul of the girl at the next desk or the local politician.

If our problem were to introduce Christianity into some new planet recently discovered, we could proceed on simple lines. The Church has a pattern for this sort of apostolic work: a pattern of the formal presentation of the Good News, and of nasty, but fruitful, martyrdoms. What we now need is a pattern for the reconversion of a once-Christian society which thinks the Good News old stuff, and wherein the Christians themselves have absorbed large amounts of their pagan environment.

To date there has been just one really revolutionary technique offered for making this type of conquest; a technique which is adequate to the circumstances, which has had some startling successes, and which represents a flowering in experience and practice of the doctrine of the Mystical Body. This is Specialized Catholic Action. It is new, and little understood, in the United States. Many people are trying to learn the techniques, but few are able to see the woods for the trees. This article will attempt to explain major Catholic Action methods, not in detail, but as they relate to the problems at hand.

THE IDEA OF THE LEAVEN

Specialization is the one absolutely basic and essential characteristic of Catholic Action.[1] It is the idea of like by like. The once-Christian world is to be reconverted from within by simultaneous apostolic effort in every stratum of society, every professional, vocational, age or other distinctive group, by the Catholics who do already find themselves there. Gathering spiritual strength from the Eucharist, Catholics are to be as yeast in the dough of society, acting as a leaven to raise society to God. The font of strength, which is grace, will be the same for all; as will the ultimate objective, the salvation of souls. The means will vary according to circumstances, but each Christian will be an apostle to his own kind. Doctors will be apostles to fellow doctors; clerks to other clerks; laborers to fellow laborers, intellectuals to intellectuals.

There may not, at first glance, seem to be anything very revolutionary about the idea of specialization. But consider how it cuts across most of our present concepts and methods.

An ingrained prejudice that must go is that of patronization, the idea of the salvation of the lower classes by the upper, of the ungifted by the gifted. There is a certain reciprocity of gifts owing in the nature of society, a necessary trading of talents. But it does not need to extend between classes and groups in the matter of the salvation of souls. The rich owe their superabundant wealth to the poor; but one poor man will do better in converting his neighbor to Christ than will the rich man who doesn't "speak their language." Intellectuals have a certain, not unimportant function to perform in society. But in the matter of turning men again to God, let the intellectuals persuade

---

[1] Catholic Action never really operates except under bishop's mandate. That is why Catholic Action is defined as "the participation of the laity in the apostolate of the Church's hierarchy."

This article omits discussion of the relationship of Catholic Action and the hierarchy of the Church. The necessity of subordination to the hierarchy stems not from the nature of Catholic Action, which we are here discussing, but from the nature of the Church. Every form of public apostolate must be exercised under the "hierarchy of jurisdiction." Catholic Action has also a special dependence, as being auxiliary and official; publicly proclaimed so by Pius XI.

their fellow intellectuals rather than make plans for the conversion of the laboring masses, who are (as the Jocists have proved) capable of effecting their own resurrection. These two classes represent the two great apostasies of recent centuries. The intellectuals will do their greatest good turn for the workers by converting fellow intellectuals, and so stopping the stream of atheistic and pornographic matter now channeled in the direction of the laboring classes.

AMERICANS MAY OBJECT that specialization will have the effect of formalizing class and other distinctions between peoples, and so be "anti-democratic." But distinctions are good so long as they represent a wholesome diversity among people. The universality of Catholicism can unite on a higher level people with differences of national customs, of temperament, of intellectual power and of income. It is safer for most people's salvation that they live within a traditional pattern, so long only as it is good. When we are all saints we can mingle freely without envy or covetousness.

Preserving distinctions, however, does not mean preserving unhealthy ones. There will be a lot of individual readjustment going on because of the present disorder in society. Catholic Action ought to help this by stimulating intellectual and spiritual life. When we see worldly young men turning to the priesthood, Hollywoodish glamour girls discovering that they are really not ashamed of their immigrant parents and "foreign" neighborhood; when we see the "get-ahead" boys practicing voluntary poverty, college graduates choosing manual labor, and manual laborers taking to the study of St. Thomas; then we will know that society is struggling toward form and order. Each will find his own functional place in order to work there for the apostolate.

Specialization will check another unfortunate tendency here. After society has broken down very far (as now) it can only be saved by a universal improvement in morality. We often urge, instead, a system of undue checks and balances to try to prevent, by legislation or pressure groups, the growing indifference to the common good. Rather than hope for more integrity among doctors, we begin to think it might be well to put undue checks on doctors to insure their maintaining professional standards. We even (Heaven help us!) think patients might form pressure groups to protect themselves against malpractice. And socialized medicine (which is the same tendency in its most acute form) hangs over our heads. Yet obviously what is needed is a reform of the medical profession by medics.

Similarly, we despair of virtue among tradesmen, and place our hope now in legislation against them, now in consumer pressure groups (some cooperatives amount to as much as this). Yet the grocery business, or the drug business, should be reformed by grocers or druggists, through whatever associations are suitable, and certainly accompanied by the widespread diminution of avarice and an increase in moral responsibility.

STAY IN THE DOUGH

Inherent in the idea of specialization is the corollary that the yeast must stay in the dough. From without it cannot leaven. Catholic Action is action from within; not a going out into the dessert, not a leaving of society. From this follows the very firm conviction of Catholic Action adherents that it is not for the Church today to leave the rottenness of western society but to transform it. They are opposed to all of what they would call "escapist" movements; all efforts at flight away from our sick brethren into a cleaner atmosphere.

Some internal controversies in Catholic Action rage around this point. The subject is far too difficult to treat here; we shall at another time. However, several things everyone would agree on are:

1) That no Christian can in good conscience flee the problems of the day in order to save himself. If he goes away (to the land for instance), it must be for a purpose related to the salvation of his city brethren.

2) Staying in society doesn't mean approving it. A figure sometimes used is that of goldfish in a bowl of dirty water. We are not to take the fish out, but to change the water. So staying in the mess means changing it, and the real quarrels arise over how drastic a change is necessary.

3) There are two directions of action. One is the personal stimulation of one's neighbor to a deeper spiritual level (or to a state of grace), which will make reform of society possible. Without good men you cannot have a good society. The other direction is the reformation of the institutions of society, in order to make it easier for men to save their souls. The two actions develop progressively the one encouraging the other. It is in the matter of the second that there is a difference of opinion about the direction which it should take. As an obvious example of the problem, what sort of an economic order shall we work toward? One day *Integrity* will thrash out these matters.

THE CELL TECHNIQUE

Besides the all-important specialization, there are certain Catholic Action techniques which, if not always absolutely essential, are generally considered integral to the movement. The three most important are Cell Organization, Inquiry Method, and Services (or Campaigns).

The cell is mere common sense. In its essence it is organized cooperation. It is in the nature of the organism, which is the Mystical Body, for its parts to cohere. If we want to work as Christians in the apostolate, it is imperative that we work together. The most efficient way to work is in small, effective units.

Isolated individuals cannot renew our highly centralized and very pagan society. They must unite to give society form, unite to increase their influence, unite to strengthen their own faith. This should be clear to everyone by now. Even an especially gifted doctor, whose personal influence is enormous, cannot do effective work in the apostolate without some organization with his fellow Catholic doctors. The good a single doctor can do is largely a matter of personal good in particular cases. The need today goes beyond this. Medical ethics are themselves in danger of turning completely against Christian practice. It is not enough for a doctor to observe the Church's medical laws himself. If he is to save the medical profession, he must work with a guild of doctors or with a Catholic group within the American Medical Association toward a reform of medicine by doctors. The example of doctors is particularly apt because we lack in the United States any effective Catholic influence in the medical profession, despite there having been great Catholic doctors of tremendous personal, and Catholic influence within a secular framework. The late Dr. James Joseph Walsh is an example in point. Admired and respected by Catholics and non-Catholics alike, his excellent Christian ideas about medicine are already nearly forgotten, for lack of a body of doctors to perpetuate and add to them.

THERE ARE A FEW INSTANCES in which the cell technique might prove a hindrance rather than a help. Writing, for instance, is a solitary profession which does not ordinarily lend itself to group effort. A Catholic writer would not get far without keeping in close personal touch with the lay apostolic movement, but he is hard to organize and it seems on the whole inadvisable to organize him.

The cell need not be too formalized for certain highly educated groups, but it should be compact, small (not more than a dozen members at the most), disciplined and meet regularly and frequently. It is the basic operational unit of Catholic Action. Cells should multiply rapidly once Catholic Action gets under way, there being no limit to their potential number.

Anyone who doubts the wisdom of the cell technique should consider the alternatives. Especially in the large worker and student groups, the tendency of modern society is to deal with unindividuated masses. This is a dangerous procedure. It is quite possible to sway masses of men and women by appealing to their passions; no one has yet found them particularly responsive to reason. Even relatively small, homogeneous groups of two and three hundred do not lend themselves so much to formation as to obedience. Perhaps it is the temper of the time. We certainly see it in colleges today, where students are turned out as though by rubber stamp. Thinking comes hard and the small group with everyone a responsible member seems to be the necessary condition of breaking up our irresponsibility.

THE INQUIRY METHOD

The Inquiry Method, which forms the bulk of a cell meeting, and is the Catholic Action method of procedure, is again a technique which can exceptionally be dispensed with as to formal use. However, it too is rooted in the nature of things. SEE, JUDGE and ACT, its three parts, follow the normal process of reasoning. Lawyers, or college presidents, might telescope or elaborate the steps, but without eliminating them. SEE could take the form of a nationwide, sociological survey, JUDGE represent ten years of theological study, and ACT be the formulation of national legislative policy over a period of years. It still amounts to the same thing in essence, as one-meeting inquiry on classroom cheating.

The best way to get a simple view of the Inquiry (so often made stilted and complex by the slavish following of a misunderstood formula) is to contrast it with an alternative method of mental training, the sermon, whether as heard in church or in a sodality meeting. The sermon could easily be more wise and penetrating in content than are the apostles' own inquiry findings, yet fail to move them. To make them *think*, as contrasted with making them enthusiastic about someone else's ideas, is the purpose and accomplishment of the Inquiry. In the end you really do get people who can think; people who are responsible; people who have formed Catholic minds; people in whom the Church can well hope. But the effort has to be there.

One way or another (usually through study days) it is the priest-director of a Catholic Action cell who guarantees the JUDGE material the Christian standard in the matter. The other two parts belong to the lay members, and it is from them that the priest learns the actual condition of the world from which he is largely shut off today by secularism.

The making of inquiries is not so difficult as is sometimes thought. When Catholic Action is highly organized there will probably be need for simultaneous study and action on major problems throughout the country. Then the inquiry might be centrally made and adapted locally to each milieu. In the beginnings, however, the inquiries should be made locally, and should concern problems which are immediately at hand for the cell in question.

There is a point (which is not the beginning) at which the making of inquiries becomes difficult. Obviously, the direction of Catholic Action will be determined by the subjects of the inquiries. How long should students inquire into campus morality and communal life before asking whether or not they are really getting an education? How long should clerical workers in an advertising agency work on problems of office morality and procedure before querying the morality of modern advertising? This is not subject for the present discussion, but it is important. Technique, however excellent, is merely technique. A philosophy will have to develop along with it if the resultant action is to be fruitful.

SERVICES

Services are organizations or functions which develop, on a more or less permanent basis, to solve the problems studied in the inquiries. When the problem can be solved by a one-time effort, campaigns are used. Catholic Action cells go on making more inquiries and do not themselves grow into services, but as the movement progresses it is constantly enriched by these auxiliaries which are, second only to the quality of the Catholic Action leaders themselves, the true measure of the movement's effectiveness. What might constitute a service? A credit union, a weekly folk dance, a newspaper, a magazine, a system of rehabilitating juvenile delinquents, a summer camp, a marriage preparation course, anything. The collective power of the members to finance and staff such services becomes tremendous. Herein lies the great power of Catholic Action to change the social order. Unlike mere political power, it is dynamic because it is the organic expression of a body of formed Christians. Catholic Action has the potential power to settle thousands of families on the land, should it seem wise to do so. It has the potential power to control the direction of industry, when it decides what is to be the proper direction.

CATHOLIC ACTION IN THE UNITED STATES

The beginning of Catholic Action can be found in nearly every center of consequence in the United States. There are cells operating, or in the formative stages, in New York, Chicago, Boston, Rochester, San Francisco, San Antonio, Detroit, Woonsocket, South Bend, and dozens of other places. The movement has begun, or is beginning, in high schools, colleges, parishes, offices, factories, among girls, boys, married women and professional men. Nearly all the groups are feeling their way, training leaders and trying out methods. Very few are officially operating under bishop's mandate. There is communication between cells in different cities, but no coordinated action so far, and not a little disagreement about the true nature of Catholic Action and the philosophy which is to accompany it.

Corporate study of Catholic Action techniques on the part of interested priests is a little further advanced. An annual study week for priest takes place in Chicago, and a priests' bulletin is regularly published from that city.

Seminarians were slower getting started in their interest, but it is increasing fast. The first seminarians' study week was held at Notre Dame this past summer.

CANON CARDIJN'S VISIT

The founder of Jocism is Canon Cardijn. His was the genius which developed Catholic Action techniques out of compassion for the masses of workers lost to the Church. Canon Cardijn is a dynamic and saintly Flemish-Belgian priest who has suffered at German hands now in two wars. He admits he feels his sixty-some years, yet can summon vitality sufficient to exhaust companions half his age. Last summer he made a whirlwind trip up and down and across North, Central and South America, chiefly to prepare a first hand report on the lay apostolate for the Holy Father. During the trip he spoke to Catholic Action laity and interested priests in various parts of the

United States. Since he is not only the supreme authority on Catholic Action but also the embodiment of its spirit, his visit had an enormous effect, both in setting our embryonic movement on correct paths and in encouraging first beginnings.

The Canon made some interesting and emphatic observations. For one thing he kept deploring the dearth of young men in the movement. This has long been a subject of regret anyhow. It has seemed that on the whole girls were more zealous and apostolic than boys and that, however desirable it might be to have masculine leadership in the abstract, in the concrete it looked as though women were going to take the initiative in restoring all things in Christ. Canon Cardijn thinks it is impossible for the movement to succeed on that basis, since he places his greatest hope in a whole generation of new and Christian families. And how can you have really Christian families if only the girls are formed Christians? Indeed it is not a new problem. Yet some would not agree with Canon Cardijn. Perhaps, they say, it is for the women to remake American men in our day, even if this is contrary to the normal order. Another case of God using the weak things of the world. Anyhow, now that the war is over, male leaders may be forthcoming.

ANOTHER INSISTENCE OF CANON CARDIJN is on getting the movement rooted in industry. So far Catholic Action is confined largely to white collar workers and students, and not to the laboring man. One difficulty here is that boys do not go into industry at the early age that they go into it abroad. At the time which is psychologically best for attracting them to a Catholic Action movement, they are still in school. School is not a particularly good setting for Catholic Action because the problems there are not sufficiently vital. Almost the only industrial beginnings of Catholic Action so far have been among the workers of French descent in New England, where the inspiration of French Canada prevails. It cannot be said to be a typically American effort.

Most interesting of all was the Canon's insistence on the importance of the United States in the North American movement. Since Catholic Action is highly organized and effective in Canada to the north of us, in Mexico and some other Latin American countries to the south of us, why should we, in our fumbling, be the hope of the movement? Yet Father Villeneuve of Montreal, who accompanied the Canon, held to the same thesis. The Canadian Jocists, he said, have

St. John the Baptist as their patron saint. Like the Precursor, they consider themselves the presages of a much greater movement in the United States, to which they would willingly be subsidiary.

If we are to be the American leaders of Catholic Action, it is certainly not because we have so far deserved it. It must be, as in political affairs, because of our natural, industrial and technical wealth and power which we can use for good or for evil. Hollywood movies too tenth-rate to make the grade in the United States, serve to degrade the peoples of many a Latin American country. Our worst pulp magazines, our cheapest clothes, our most primitive and erotic jazz music, are all passed on to the south, where political instability usually allows entry. In Quebec to the north, the Church is powerful enough still to hold the dam against a flood of our sexy advertisements and extremes of women's dresses, but for how long? If we could clean up the source of evil, our neighbors would have a much better chance of Christianizing their own lands.

Canon Cardijn always sees Catholic Action as a world movement. In his opinion only a world movement is sufficiently powerful and universal to overcome Communism. He foresees an international organization even before the movement is highly organized nationally. And, indeed, there is that sense of international unity already in Catholic Action. Two Chicago girls attended an international congress in Paris last summer. The New York Catholic Action cell's guest apartment is quite accustomed to visitors who do not speak English. There is a free exchange of literature from various countries, and many a cell member regrets not having studied French more assiduously in high school.

WARNINGS

Specialized Catholic Action, as we hope this article has made clear, allows for considerable adaptation according to circumstance. While using the major techniques, the movement ought normally to develop differently for each country. How it will develop in the United States is still problematical, but it ought not to be formed into European mold. Americans ought to study their own problems very closely and ought to distinguish and preserve what is peculiar to the American temperament, as long as it is good. The Belgians take to mass, semi-military enthusiasm and demonstrations. Perhaps that is not our temper. Once we grasp the essentials and the spirit of Jocism, we ought not to hesitate to strike out as befits our own circumstances.

On the other hand, there is a false Americanism running through the lay organizations of the Church, a bling worship of American ideals as set forth by Coco-cola advertisements and the National Association of Manufacturers. We Catholics in general have conformed so to commercial ideals that we accept a shocking and gross materialism without question. Most Catholic societies have fallen into mediocrity and ineffectiveness because of their reluctance to question these "immutable" standards. It is precisely these things which Catholic Actionists must hold up to the light of Christian judgment. Yet sometimes they identify them with the American spirit, and so fail at the start. There are cells which are reluctant even to consider as possibly un-Christian, current women's fashions, the seemingly endless pursuit of "a higher standard of living," industrialism, liberal colleges, hot swing music, dating, and large cities. They end up wanting only to change the insides of people and not society, or to improve sexual morals in disregard of the occasions of sin thereof, and in disregard of the other commandments.

RATHER SIMILAR, and equally disastrous, is a powerful anti-intellectualism which runs through young Catholics. It may have honorable roots in a detestation of the academic aridity produced in scholars by liberal education. But thinking is itself honorable, and has never been more needed. It has been said of the Jocist leaders (laboring young men) in the suburbs of Paris before the war that they had the keenest understanding of their times and their environments of any men of their day. Contrast that with the oft-heard exclamation among Young Christian Workers here: "Thank goodness, I'm no intellectual!" There literally is no hope for Catholic Action in the United States unless the movement produces some good thinkers and has a great respect for the intelligence. The philosophy that is going along with Catholic Action, for instance, is not susceptible of solution on the emotional or intuitional level. It awaits hard thinking on everyone's part.

Catholic Action should form integrated Catholics, and this should be a prelude to a high sanctity in the midst of the world. It may well be dangerous for lay people to be overly "pious" if they are not going to be integrated. But providing their spiritual life is not on the merely devotional level and is not combined with a sort of blindness in regard to the true nature of secular society, the holier the better. A girl who does not wish to conform to pagan mores is usually shuttled off to a convent someplace, wherein it is considered decent to aspire to contemplation. But those in Catholic Action are spiritually ambitious, and rightly so. Their conquest of the world will ultimately succeed only in the measure that supernatural charity overflows in them, and in the measure that the gift of Wisdom lights their way. There are contemplatives, not infrequently, in the movement elsewhere. There must be contemplatives here. One problem is to find spiritual directors who are able and willing to help the development of the spiritual life of members.

Catholic Action, especially among workers, gives rise to a "mystique," a certain characteristic spirit which is the same everywhere. It is a spirit of conquest, of contagious confidence in their ability, through Christ's power, really to change the face of society and the course of history. The vitality of Catholic Action contrasts sharply with the despair-born enervation still pervading our secular culture. It is challenged only by the Communist mystique, which it will overcome by an ever-increasing outpouring of Charity.

1947

3
A Christian Abnormal Psychology
JANUARY 1947

THE BANKRUPTCY OF MODERN PSYCHIATRY

Of all modern problems none is more serious than the alarming growth of mental disorders, slight and not so slight. Asylums are packed, psychoanalysts are doing a lucrative business, psychiatrists have taken on a new dignity, and psychology is a popular field of graduate and undergraduate study. A demented relative used to be a closet skeleton. No longer. Uncle Alexander, but yesterday carted off (by the combined force of ten strong men) to a "psychoneurotic institution" is only "sick." It's just like a cold, but a little more inconvenient. Especially for Uncle Alexander.

How we kid ourselves! It's like pretending that there is no atom bomb, or that we can get along amicably with atheistic Russia, or that there always was as much cancer as now only we didn't recognize it. And so we manage to pretend that the loss of reason, that the terrible, unbearable, mental and spiritual torture of thousands doesn't really hurt. What's worse, we try to pretend that this "just happened," and that it has nothing to do with our decline of morals, our cult of luxury, our liberal education, our disdain of discipline, and our all-pervading, wanton disregard of God.

An army of experts has arisen to deal with the situation. They are working in the dark. It is curious that we have so long tolerated their groping; that we are impressed by the curious vocabulary they have made up for themselves; that we pay such enormous sums to them and are content with so little in return. A psychiatrist enjoys the prerogatives of the undertaker: we are grateful to each for taking over an unsavory job; and we are more than willing that the details of the operation remain a mystery.

Would it be impertinent to inquire about the ideal toward which psychiatry is presumably working; would it be presumptuous to demand that abnormal psychologists specify their norm? Here is the opening sentence in a current college text of abnormal psychology:

> In all of the treatises on abnormal psychology there arises the problem of determining what activities are normal and what activities are abnormal.... The fact that no solution has been reached (on this) is due in a large measure to our lack of knowledge of the normal individual.

It is as though a medical doctor had no idea what health was and might be misled into thinking that a dead person had recovered, merely because his convulsions had ceased.

The root of the difficulty is this matter of the norm, and the reason is that the science of psychiatry arose in the post-Christian era, after the truth about the nature and purpose of man had been lost, lost at least to the fathers of that science.

Most references to "medieval" treatment of the insane in textbooks are wildly inaccurate. Snake pits were a device of the ancients; the chained inmates of Bedlam were a post-Reformation scandal; and diabolism as an all-pervasive explanation was 17th century. True history does honor to the Church. The admirable Gheel system of allowing freedom of the village to harmless lunatics was started by a cult to St. Dymphna, and still persists. Medieval references to the care of the insane were simple and salutary, including such advice as playing music to cheer the melancholy. Above all what honors the Church is that mental disease never became a major problem while the world still lived within the framework which She made.

Freud is the father of modern psychiatry. His philosophy has a pervasive influence even where his technique is rejected. Freud did not know what a man is, much less what a normal man is; or what the purpose of life is; or that God exists. His standard of a "cure" is that a neurotic patient should achieve a satisfactory sex life.

Not everyone agrees with Freud, but all take him as a standard of reference, good or bad. The reason for his influence is that he did offer some sort of comprehensive explanation of mental disease, even though the explanation is materialistic, atheistic, and sensual. The real alternative to Freud is another comprehensive explanation, not just a modification or criticism of his system. Freud is not accidentally wrong; he is essentially wrong. Accidentally and occasionally he is right. He had his insights, but his explanations were off-center.

You can't build a rival system to Freud's starting experimentally. Freud didn't build his system experimentally either. He already had a philosophy in the light of which he made up his principles.

A Christian Abnormal Psychology

The first work on a Christian abnormal psychology must be to build a comprehensive general explanation rooted in truths that we do certainly know. Then in the light of this, let us explain the abnormalities and work out the cures. This paper proposes a rough framework.

PART I. THE NORM

Ought a man to adjust himself to his environment, or conspire to make over or escape from his environment? A neurotic is usually conspicuously out of step or is he, perhaps, the only one in step? How can you know unless you have objective standards as to what constitutes a good environment? The normal man cannot be studied in isolation from his normal habitat because his mental balance is affected by his environment.

Because we live in cities which are ugly and disordered, and made by men, we lose sight of the harmony of the universe as made by God. God designed everything harmoniously. There is a rhythm in the movement of the planets, an order within atoms; there is a procession in the season, an ebb and flow in tides, a balance of elements in the soil and a reciprocal relationship among members of a family. There are little things and big things, and all sizes in between. There are organic things and inorganic things. There are material things and spiritual things.

Is man little or big? Neither. He is the measure of the little and the big. He is the standard of reference of maximal and minimal. Within the macrocosm which is the universe, he is a microcosm, a little universe, containing within himself all gradations of material being while he is himself the most complex organic structure in the universe.

All other material things are made for man. He is king pin of the visible universe, even if not its absolute master. Only when men's thinking is warped do they fancy themselves inferior and subordinate to the material universe.

There is a whole invisible universe above man, in which he also shares. In relation to it he is on the bottom rung. The unique position of man in the universe is that it is he alone who bridges the material and spiritual orders, with one foot in each. He is highest in the material order by virtue of the complexity of his organism; lowest in the spiritual order because of the cumbersome way he attains knowledge, through his senses and through reason.

The world isn't just a jumble of things; it's an ordered and very intricate arrangement of things. God makes a synthesis of things. He doesn't just put them together; He also supplies a principle of operation. Not just planets but also a law of gravity, an internal tendency according to a certain mode of physical attraction of forces. Not just animals, but animals with instincts which lead them to do what they are made to do. The whole universe is like that; filled with principles by which they operate. Everything operates according to reason — only it is God's reason, reflected in the thing by instinct or law.

The catch is man. He too is a synthesis, more intricate than all the others. He, too, has a vital principle, his soul. But he has the power to understand what he ought to do and he has the free will to do it, or not to do it. This is how it comes about that man is in the moral order, and that a new law, the moral law, is operative in regard to him. Man's freedom makes it possible for him to be upset and possibly destroy the harmony of the universe.

Man may soon succeed in destroying the harmony of the physical universe, which will be the end of him and it. He has already considerably upset the balance of nature. He has created chaos in his relationships with his own kind, chaos which we know as world war. He can destroy himself and he sometimes does. When he kills his body, it is suicide. When he turns away from God, it is mortal sin. When he destroys the harmony of his own nature, it is insanity.

All things are made for man, but man is made for God. Man preserves the harmony of the universe and operates within it only so long as he himself is ordered to God and respects God's laws on the various levels. The great sin of our time is presumptuous disregard of God's natural, moral and physical laws. We set ourselves up as gods and try to create a harmony of our own, ordered to our own pleasure. That is why, in every field, there is profound disorder.

Insofar as the harmony of the sub-human world is disturbed, it redounds on man and creates a tension in his nature too. For instance, enormous cities are a strain on most men, if only because they surround men with cement and steel, from which men are remote in the scale of being, and separate them from the organic world with which they have a closer natural relationship. It is not strange that gardening, that farm animals and pets, and that all the manifold changes of the seasons, should have a soothing effect on men. These things (and not subways and skyscrapers) form their natural habitat.

However, most of the strains on human nature come from disordered human relationships. Here too, there are organic laws which must be observed. The arrangement of society is not arbitrary in its fundamentals, but only in its accidentals. One thing that *is* arbitrary is the form of government. It is silly to attach an exaggerated importance to democracy, while permitting divorce. The family is a matter of necessity; democracy is a matter of preference.

There are four elements essential to an ordered society: the family, the community, authority, a functional nature. We shall treat of each briefly, only insofar as it relates to mental disorders.

The family. The basic unit of society is the family, and not the individual, as liberal economics would have it. The practical necessity for the family is the bearing and rearing of children; but the practical necessities of nature are all reflected in the psychological make-up of human beings. Men and women are not really whole individuals in a psychological sense, but meant to complement each other in a permanent stable, family unit. Children need the security of parental love as much as they need the physical care of adults. These things are all pretty obvious and the greatest effort in history to dispense with the family, the Russian experiment, failed dismally. We still have the family, but I wonder if we appreciate how much we owe to it for whatever stability we do have in society.

However, our families are not healthy, and this is reflected almost immediately in mental disorders. Marriage is not stable, thanks to the possibility of divorce, which affects all marriages and carries a threat to all women. Further, even where there is no immediate threat of divorce, domestic unhappiness is rife, and this can be traced to all sorts of factors, chief among which is the unholiness of family life. The practice of birth control is another serious disorder, for what marriage can survive on the basis of adolescent romanticism?

The Community. There needs to be a community life beyond the family. Men especially need a little world where they are known by their first names, where they are accepted for what they are, where people care whether they live or die, are happy or unhappy. It should be an organic community, like a village or a really active parish, or a self-contained small town. But organic communities have nearly disappeared with over-centralization. Five hundred people rushed together in the same subway train, packed into the same Broadway nightclub, decorously arranged in the same suburb, or lined up in rows in the same insurance office, are not a community. Ten mothers of infant babies in the same park, an alumni association, an air-raid warden crew, or the local chapter of the Knights of Columbus, are only faintly so.

In place of community we are offered "one world." It is too big. Even half a world is too big. It does not matter psychologically how the large nations are apportioned, so long only as a man can carry on his ordinary affairs in a pint-sized puddle to which he has some relevance. Let there be a million such puddles compromising one state, if only each man has his own puddle and doesn't have to crack his brain to comprehend Japanese affairs of state, or Indonesian economics. The man who prefers the kitchen gossip of the tabloids to a full account of the proceedings of the United Nations Assembly is at least biting off something he can chew. Perhaps he would lift his intellectual level to politics and economics if these were small-scale enough.

Loneliness reflects the absence of community life, and also the absence of a healthy family life of the sort which can embrace aging grandparents and indigent great uncles. It is all too common in large cities, especially among unmarried women and old people. If you really face the truth of the problem you have to admit that most loneliness should never have been in the first place. Unless a woman brings social ostracism upon herself by some terrible deed or deficiency, she should be accepted and at home someplace with all her eccentricities (of which she would have much fewer) and faults. Both the usual diagnosis (that lonely Miss X has a personality defect that can probably be remedied by a charm school or psychoanalysis) and the usually recommended cure (attendance at artificial gatherings full of other forlorn souls), is calloused, uncomprehending, and unlikely to succeed.

Authority and function. Christianity teaches that every man has a particular job to do in the world and that he will be judged according to how well he does it. The corollary proposition is that it takes all kinds to make a world and that there is indeed a natural diversity among men. Not all men are fit to rule; not all men are fit to contemplate.

Here contemporary American society is at its greatest odds with the Church. Anyone can be president of the United States; anyone can make a million dollars; and all people ought to desire both. In consequence we have a society in which very intelligent men are doing stupid work (because only a handful of people run everything), which is a strain on them; in which many stupid men (through graft or inheritance) are doing work far beyond their intelligent capacity, which is a strain on *them*; in which a very few intelligent men have vast responsibilities, and die early of coronary thrombosis. We have a society in which the president is hopelessly overburdened and where every last clerk and truck driver feels duty bound to decide all matters of state along with him. Nobody has security. Everybody suffers from envy. No one is contented with his state of life (and, indeed, few people can boast a state in life). Avarice is universal. This is background for thousands upon thousands of neuroses and psychoses which would never have occurred in a simpler and more reasonable society.

THE NORMAL MAN

Man is composed of body and soul, in a substantial unity. Psycho-somatic medicine (which is the last but one fad in psychological circles) is an elegant way of saying the same thing. The psyche is the soul (divested usually of its true spiritual nature) and the somatic part refers to the body. One influences the other, as doctors are rediscovering. However, the relationship between body and soul is one of true unity, not just of mutual influence. The philosophical way of putting it is that the soul is the *substantial form* of the body. Without a soul the body cannot operate, and soon corrupts, as is evident in death which is the separation of soul and body. The soul is the vital principle of operation in the whole man. The body is the soul's avenue of knowledge and the vehicle of much of its operation.

In most cases the body and soul operate as a unit. It is not surprising then that a man down with the flu is depressed in spirits, or that a man habitually lost in lust will lose his mind.

THE NORMAL MAN IS THE HIERACHICAL MAN, OF WHOM THE EXEMPLAR IS THE SAINT.

The pictures below give a rough illustration of the hierarchical man and his disordered opposite. In this crude presentation the hierarchical man is grossly oversimplified, while his opposite is unnecessarily chaotic. In reality certain localized defects, if severe, would suffice for a mental breakdown.

The important thing to note in the pictures is that a man's balance depends on the right ordering of all his parts; the lower subordinate to and governed by the higher. Thus the passions (emotions) should be subject to reason. The reason, in turn, should be subject itself to God.

There are two sorts of spiritual disorders in man: mental disease and sin. Mortal sin is a matter specifically of the will's direction. Mental

THE HIERARCHICAL MAN

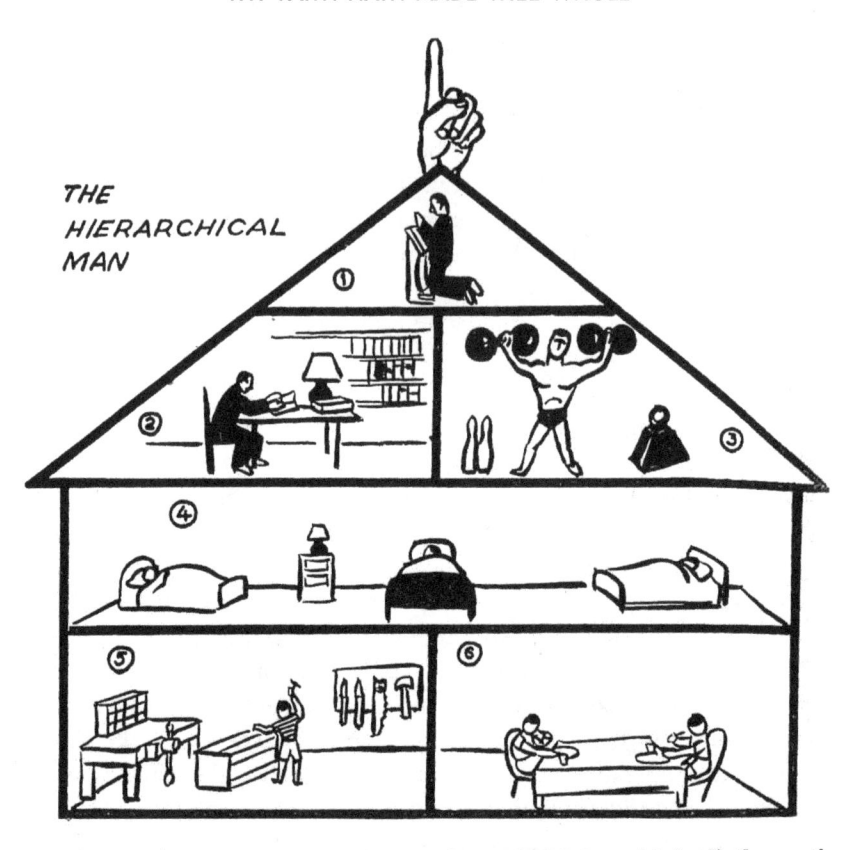

This is a man compared to a household in which, 1) the entire activity is ordered to GOD. The spiritual faculties: 2) the INTELLECT meditates so that it may make true judgments, 3) the WILL grows strong so as to make decisions, and control the PASSIONS, 4) of which some are dormant, while some are operating in an orderly way. 5) & 6) disease may mean a disorder in the functioning of the mind or of the will, or it may mean failure of the reason to govern the passions.

Sin and insanity are related disorders but not parallel disorders. The saint is the most sane of men, because the concept of sanctity includes perfect sanity. That is why peace is the fruit of holiness, because peace is defined as the tranquility of order, which tranquility consists in all the appetitive movements in one man being set at rest together. Otherwise the two disorders are not necessarily coincidental. A man can be grievously proud, yet sane. A demented man can be in the state of grace.

THE
DISORDERED
MAN

This is a man compared to a disordered household, which 1) ignores God, The PASSIONS run wild 2) making true judgments impossible. 3) & 4) The WILL grows flabby and the INTELLECT does not operate. 5) There is no work, but destruction. 6) Worship is toward SENSE PLEASURES.

DIFFERENCES IN PEOPLE

1. Differences in Intellectual Capacity

Other things being equal, the simple-minded and the very intelligent men are the most easily unbalanced. A simple intellect cannot handle complex and subtle ideas because it is unable to resolve seeming contraries and make subtle distinctions. There are quite a few simple people in the world. For their own happiness, sanity and sanctity, they should lead simple, peaceful, ordered lives according to truths authoritatively given them by others. The Catholic Church has always guarded the simple, and the near-simple. She has protected them when she could from religious controversy (while the wise could debate about such matters publicly), from reading harmful books, and even from the mental and moral tangles of Hollywood. When She made a society the simple were mostly on the land, close to animals and fields, folk-music and dancing, and their guardian the Church. Even today the mildly demented among them can occasionally find sanctuary working in peace, silence, and simplicity for a monastery or convent.

Heaven help the simple today! The schools want them to make up their own minds about the gravest problems of life and eternity. The newspapers and radio invite them to consider matters too difficult for international statesmen to settle. Everyone has to have an opinion about everything, whether or not it is within his province or competence.

The very intelligent have a different problem, peculiar to societies like ours. Intelligence drives the mind to the discovery of basic principles, to correlating, comparing, weighing, testing. A philosophical genius could easily go mad in Harvard or Yale, where every professor consciously or unconsciously contradicts his colleagues, to say nothing of the internal inconsistencies in his own theories. In a world devoid of fundamental certainties, and even implicitly denying the possibility of discovering truth, its best brains are tempted to blow themselves out. When high intellectual quality is combined, as it often soon is, with escape via the sense pleasures, the hazards are even greater. Again it is the Church which could have saved them, and would have in another age. The mind driven to distraction by Nietzsche and Hegel would have found rest, joy and adventure in the certainty of the Faith and the lucidity of the *Summa Theologica*.

2. Sex Differences

Men and women, being made to complement each other, have sort of half-natures. What one lacks the other is meant to supply. It works out neatly when they pair off to start families, as was intended. The man stands on his own two feet and goes about taking care of the welfare of his family and society. He is given to manliness, courage and enterprise. He is objective in his reasoning, usually accurate in his judgments, and not much interested in personalities. His wife's intelligence is more diffuse. Her judgments are made with the spontaneous assistance of her heart and her senses. They are often more penetrating than her husband's, but sometimes not so accurate. She is subject to moods and depressions traceable to physiological sources and considerably modified by the presence of a loving husband. She cheerfully will give herself entirely for her husband and children.

The very possibility of divorce unsettles all marriages. It is the woman who suffers chiefly from the prospect of impermanence in marriage, since hers is the dependent nature. Her normal womanliness, domesticity and tenderness can be twisted into instability, emotionalism and vacillation, fertile grounds for neuroses. Current ideals of married love as reflected in movies, magazine stories and divorce courts, are completely cock-eyed morally and psychologically. The ideal woman as portrayed therein just doesn't exist. She is radiantly and persistently beautiful. She never becomes old. She never becomes pregnant. She falls in love only with worthy and devastatingly handsome men, who reciprocate an hundredfold. It is all very adolescent and imaginary. In real life not all girls are beautiful, but all of them are aching for a totality of devotion to someone. They ought to expend their generosity in a secure domestic situation. If a woman's marriage is not secure or if she is not married her need for devotion will find another outlet, which ought to be in piety. There is sound psychological basis for calling women "the devout female sex." Psychologically, if one may say so, they need God more than men do, because their nature demands that they give themselves. Here it is interesting parenthetically to note that God does really supply much of what is wanting in the natural order, such as fulfillment to a woman's nature and solace to the afflicted.

A woman's mental balance is related to her necessity of self-giving. Even the selfish, gold-digger type of woman cannot escape her own nature, and usually ends up hopelessly devoted to some quite worthless member of the opposite sex. As for most women, their happiness, and often their mental balance, depends on what they choose to worship. A husband, securely held by bonds other than adolescent physical charms, plus a house-full of children in constant need of attention, is the safest environment for the majority of women. The alternative is the convent, which supplies a framework for selfless devotion to a high ideal, and does in fact provide most of its nuns with a full, joyful life of serenity. One of the greatest lacks among most non-Catholics is a framework, like a community of nuns within which to lead selfless life. Even the works of mercy have become professionalized, so that a girl who wants to spend herself as a nurse or social worker usually finds herself instead making rather a good thing of a career to which the sick and the poor are incidental. This is the fundamental reason for the discontent among nurses and social workers. They are unhappy not so much because they are underpaid, but because they are paid.

Unmarried girls who go in for business careers are in a much worse state. There is nothing satisfactory about giving yourself wholly to International Business Machines or R. H. Macy. It is usually only possible to bring yourself to spend yourself for their causes via a personal devotion, whether from afar or all too dangerously near, to the first vice president, or the section manager or the supervisor of the filing department. This fact is well recognized in shrewd personnel practice, and accounts for the unusual charm found among the company's representatives whose special duty it is to persuade office girls to work overtime. Never mind the disorder it may cause in the affections of plain little Miss Brown, whose life seems so drab on the exterior, but whose day dreams are wildly exciting and not a little adulterous.

There is another grave tension on the modern woman, and that is the strain of trying to be like a man. Its most pronounced manifestations are found among successful business women. They are either calloused and hard (much more unattractively so than men who are calloused and hard), or they are strained to the point of, or beyond, a nervous breakdown. Self-sufficiency and objectivity, which are necessary in high positions in our competitive society, are not natural feminine characteristics.

Women trying to imitate men is at its worst in matters of sex. Traditional morals, double standard and all, are consistent with the psychology of the sexes. A man's passions are distinct from his intellectual judgment and he can be promiscuous without involving his whole nature. He does not fall in love with every girl he makes love to. It is not so with women. Their hearts go right along with their feelings, and drag the intellect after, causing no end of trouble, and possibly unbalancing them. Nor do women who try to be calloused about these things (possibly at the behest of a psychoanalyst whom Heaven forgive!) succeed in becoming like men. Rather are they degraded to something below the human species.

Men's mental balance stands more strain in personal and domestic affairs than does women's, because men are more objective and

A Christian Abnormal Psychology

self-sufficient, in general less sensitive. For unbalance in men one should look to other factors. The war is the most important factor now. In it men were brutalized and demoralized, shocked and paralyzed with fear. Another common and general cause is industrialism, which frustrates the initiative, responsibility and creativity of men, and carries the constant threat of insecurity. Not having a functional, secure place in the world of affairs puts a man in roughly the same position as a woman who is insecure in her home.

3. Temperamental Differences

Four basic temperaments have been recognized since ancient times. Most modern efforts to classify people according to bodily structure or the bumps on their heads or some other physical factors are efforts to discover a measurable basis for temperamental differences and have so far been unsuccessful. Evidently the differences of temperament of the body rather than of the soul (and therefore inheritable) are diffuse.

Knowledge of temperament provides a guide as to how to treat different people; whether to console a person or be harsh with him; whether to spank a child or gently reprimand him. Temperamental differences are very important in relation to sanity. Why is only one child out of six neurotic as a result of identical home conditions? Why does one girl on the assembly line have hysterics after two days and the next girl remain placid after five years? Usually temperament is the deciding factor.

Certain factors modify or cloud one's native temperament. You cannot easily discern the temperament of a holy person, because he will have overcome the defects of it. Gross sinners are so much alike that temperament is not evident. Mental disease also can blur temperamental distinctions.

The four basic temperaments[1] are the choleric, melancholic, sanguine and phlegmatic. Most people are a mixture of two temperaments one modifying the other.

The Choleric is the executive type, with great drive, ambition and capability; with powers of organization and a love of commanding. He has two minds and no heart, very little human sympathy. He has

---

[1] For an admirable and more detailed description of the temperaments, see *The Four Temperaments*, by the Rev. Conrad Hock. Bruce Publishing Company, Milwaukee, Wisconsin.

great pride and is given to anger. Choleric people direct the great enterprises of the world. In our day that means big business. The handful of men who direct our gigantic commercial enterprises are mostly choleric. This type rarely goes insane because, despite strong passions, the choleric operate chiefly by intellect and will. These men do a superhuman amount of work. They break down physically rather than mentally, usually from heart trouble.

The Melancholic is more the thoughtful type. His temperament is the most unfortunate from the point of view of mental balance. Melancholic people react slowly, feel deeply, and tend excessively to the passion of sorrow. They naturally see the dark side of things, often to the point of warping their judgments. When they go overboard in their sorrow they are candidates for involutional melancholia, a madness of despair with suicidal tendencies.

Melancholic people are naturally reflective, serious, passive, reserved, irresolute, diffident, pusillanimous, given to solitude and easily falling into day dreaming. For all that many saints and great creative thinkers have been melancholic.

People of this temperament need God more than others. When they are "emotionally unbalanced" their need for religion is acute, and indeed it is doubtful if anything else can help them. Excessive talking about their troubles, as in psychoanalysis, can only aggravate the difficulty. Naturally speaking it is almost impossible to restore a melancholic to mental balance once he has reached the psychotic stage.

The Sanguine is charming and superficial. These people have weak passions but are quick. They have great optimism, usually unfounded; love fine clothes and good manners, are cheerful and vain. Except in that they are unstable they are proof against mental disorders. However their instability, if increased by careless upbringing or by unstable economic and domestic conditions, can eventually cause a breakdown.

The Phlegmatic is slow but not deep. People of this temperament have weak passions. They are the office workers who seem to have an infinite capacity for being bored, who can do the same monotonous work for years on end with solicitude only for a full lunch hour. These are the children it is quite safe to spank and even then you won't make much as an impression.

It takes a lot to unbalance a phlegmatic person. However should he lose his mental balance, it will be almost impossible for him to recover, because of the difficulty of arousing him to make an effort.

PART II. DISORDERS SEATED IN THE INTELLECT

Functional mental disorders involve the spiritual nature of man. They are disorders either within the mind itself (defective operation of the intellectual faculty or the will) or of the mind's jurisdiction over the passions (emotions).

The three elements chiefly involved are the intellect, the will and the passions. The inter-relationship of these three elements is very close. Nevertheless we shall make logical distinction between them for purposes of orderly discussion. This division will be useful in explaining the origin of mental disorders although it may have no clinical value.

The Nature of the Intellectual Faculty

The intellect is not simply a faculty for knowing but a faculty for knowing *truth*. It is determined as to universal truth, but not as to particular truths. That means that in the presence of the Beatific Vision the mind can no longer be deceived. Here on earth the mind can accept error for the grain of truth that is usually in it. Nothing, as erroneous, can be accepted by the mind. So, for instance, self-contradictory statements are instantly rejected. The fact that the mind is made to know truth is the reason why what really is true always seems to put the mind at rest, seems to correspond with something already in the mind.

The way the mind works is just the opposite from the way of the senses. The senses are concerned with particulars; *this* rose, and *that* bottle of scotch. The mind's first concern is with universals. The mind has to have some universal goal or objective before it can even begin to operate. You have to know you are going to Chicago before you can decide which route to take. It is as simple as that. The way it is put philosophically is that the end is the last in the order of execution, first in order of intention, and that you have to have the first general intention before you can make lesser particular intentions.

This means that nobody can live without a purpose in life, and that there can be only one last end, although a man can have a lot of proximate ends so long as they are ordered somehow to the final goal.

Now the mental disorders which we are going to consider as chiefly in the intellectual faculty are all related to this matter of the last end. If a man cannot find a last end he is incapable of mature operation; if his last end is false he will suffer more or less; if his last end is vague and indistinct he will not be able to derive secondary principles of operation from it.

God and False Gods

Our last end and perfect happiness is God. As St. Augustine has said: "Thou hast made us for Thyself, O Lord, and our hearts are restless till they rest in Thee."

If we set up something else as our final goal that something else becomes a god to us. This fact is quite often striking, so that we say, for instance, that a man *worships* his belly when is life is devoted to fine eating. All final ends have a sort of infinity about them. Thus, not the ambition to have enough clothes to cover our nakedness, which could easily be arranged; but to be well dressed, which tends toward infinity. So also not to make a hundred dollars a week, unless this goal be very remote; but to make a million dollars or just to make money in general. You have to take your last end seriously, worship it, even to the extent of sacrificing for it, and let it give order to your life.

Here we come upon the question of sanctity and sanity again. Mortal sin is the deliberate turning away from God as one's last end, and the consequent turning to another last end. Because of the deliberate element, however, the sin is in the will rather than in the intellect. It is possible through ignorance to have a badly distorted view of God as your last end, and yet not be in mortal sin. This is especially the case in inculpable paganism and material heresy. However, most false gods do indicate a distorted will, even if not an incipient mental disorder. The road to Hell is not necessarily via the insane asylum.

On the other hand, you are in a bad way if you have no final goal at all, a state which is not uncommon today. You can vacillate only so long before you slow down to a full stop. A person who hesitates to accept the goals currently offered by a materialistic world, yet lacks opportunity or drive to discover better, may well be in a better state spiritually than his eager-beaver confreres. It sometimes seems almost as though God allowed some to lose their sanity as a merciful escape from an intolerable situation in which they declined to compromise. These are the people who would have found God if we had made God known in the market-place as we ought. Perhaps they will recover their sanity again, and sanctity too, if we go out and minister to them in charity.

From a purely psychological point of view (which is not the final criterion) it is better to have a false end than no end at all. Almost any end will preserve a hierarchy within one's nature even if it is distorted a bit. This doesn't mean you can choose a final end at random. You

A Christian Abnormal Psychology

have to have some conviction about it or it's as good as no end at all.

From the final goal derives the first intention, and from that all the secondary goals and secondary intentions. Let us say that a man has decided his goal is making money. How neat it is. Everything falls into place. He moves to the suburbs, buys his wife a fur coat, chooses a dark-blue tie, joins the Masons, and sends his son to Yale, all as remotely or directly auxiliary to the accumulation of wealth. Such a man will keep his sanity up unto the very gates of Hell unless he loses confidence in his goal, or despairs of reaching it. Since the making of money has no natural limit but can continue to infinity, it is a good goal for keeping up one's interest. There is little danger that it will be realized and the emptiness of it seen. On the other hand, in these times of economic uncertainty, there is the prospect of despair. A bad stock market crash might send our man insane. But we shall come to despair presently. One more word about our example. Notice that he will practice austerity in the pursuit of his ideal. If he really believes, he will not be a jolly drunkard or waste money on wild women. The austerity will increase his chances of sanity on the whole, as it will keep his emotions in order. Hitler and Stalin have not been conspicuously sullied by lust and carousing in their steadfast pursuit of power. Maybe this explains why they have not gone mad in their madness. Sense indulgence can be very debilitating.

Psychologically, esoteric religions like theosophy are useful, if you can bring yourself to believe them. They preserve the sense of mystery which really does shroud God. It is more restful to the mind to consider too many things mysterious and above it, than to try to analyze and dissect the sort of god liberal education usually

Harvard man with world on his shoulders.

45

offers: a god at once responsible for the entire universe and yet capable of our complete comprehension, some sort of a mathematical formula perhaps. Clearly such a god is no god at all, since blind forces and mathematical formulae are considerably inferior to the men who are, in the concepts of the same liberal school, the finest emergent evolution types yet: the contemporary gods. What such thinking resolves itself into is that we are god, and therefore we are our own last end. It's a sort of egomania, a madness per se. Self-worship is by all odds the worst form of worship, save only Devil worship. Even unaccompanied by malice it is a menace to sanity, especially to those who think or feel deeply. Many a college graduate is wandering around with mental indigestion from trying to figure out, comprehend, coordinate and encompass the world of which he appears to himself to be the focal point. It leads to headaches and swelling of the brain; then to mental torment, and possibly to madness. If our student has a strong moral sense he is also carrying the world around on his shoulders: a very heavy, sometimes crushing load. His to wipe out venereal disease, his to put an end to war, and all the time he may be a person of no influence or position whatever even for initiating such crusades. It's not so much a matter of pride as of having been maneuvered into the control position of the universe through having unfortunately attended the best colleges. What a relief it would be to learn that God's Providence presides over all things. It would even be a relief to believe that the goddess of the Atlantic Ocean will wipe out all suffering if only men go about their daily business with confidence and blow kisses oceanward each day at high noon.

Of the many possibilities for false worship there is one more which ought to be mentioned and that is worship of another person. This most tempting form of false worship can be recognized by the fact that one orders one's life to the person in question; just as Hitler's youth directed their whole lives to the Feuhrer. We have the same unhealthy element in our love affairs. Our popular songs tend more to "I worship and I adore you," than to "You are so beautiful."

We have said before that melancholic people especially need a strong religion to balance their despondent nature. Lacking it they are the ones most likely to go overboard in false worship of another person. Especially is this true of melancholic women when they fall in love. Since men find it wearing to play the dual role of love and god, the women's hearts are often broken. They then easily fall into despair and sometimes want to kill themselves.

A Christian Abnormal Psychology

Freud had a misdirected insight into this problem. He saw the tendency of some women to expect mere men to be more than husbands and lovers and guessed the women were looking for fathers, which sounds plausible because of the fatherliness of God. To explain it Freud cooked up a theory about how every young girl has to go through a period of falling in love with her father before she can fall in love properly with young men. It is like Freud to have made fathers (who are handy, to be sure) suddenly dispensable to the psychical development of their daughters, while waving away a traditional prejudice in favor of God's indispensability.

What's Wrong With True Worship?

Since Catholics know the only true God and have their last end all set and certain, they should be marvelously well balanced, at least spiritually. One can understand how bad Catholics might run into trouble but when pious Catholics have nervous breakdowns, when even nuns and priests go insane, does it not call for some explanation? We think it does, despite the fact that deeply religious people have the lowest insanity rate.

You need not only to have a final end, but to have one from which distinct secondary principles can be derived. The true final end, and the most universal one is God but it is also the farthest away in a sense, because it really is the final end, and many are the paths which lead to God, according to the nature and work and temperament and circumstances of every man. In between a man and his final end of God there is a complicated maze which he must tread according to certain derivative principles. Otherwise God is meaningless as a final end. All right, where are the principles? There are the ten commandments, largely prohibitory, except for the injunction to love God with our whole hearts (which in turn needs a multitude of derivative applications as regards daily life). There are the precepts of the Church, which have limited application. But where are the guiding principles for choosing a job? For a social life? For much of professional life, and for many other spheres of activity? For the most part they have not been worked out in regard to our society, for we live in a society which the Church did not make, which is not built on Catholic foundations, or even on the foundations of the natural law. There is that wide gap between religion and daily life which INTEGRITY is always talking about, and which is creating a terrific tension in all our lives.

This is probably the root reason why lay Catholics have mental breakdowns. The more penetrating and sensitive they are the more sharply they feel the contrast between the nobility of their religion and the sordidness of their economic aspirations; between the intensity of their spiritual life and the dullness of mechanical work and play. But if they do not recognize it as a tension, they lead double lives and feel it dimly. Most of them are trying to serve both God and Mammon. It is impossible, psychologically and on the authority of revelation. To do so would be to have two final ends contradicting each other. They are in this spot. They have a distant goal, which is God, but no precise rules, other than prohibitory and devotional, for getting there. Meanwhile they have a temporal life to live. So they accept the working principles of Mammon, and shift to a godly economy for devotional purposes. Or they try to make a synthesis between spiritual progress and worldly success. Now the Protestants can do this because in a sense they are responsible for the underlying principles of our economic order. *Catholics cannot, because their religion continually confronts them with the antithesis which exists between the spirit of the world and the spirit of God.* When Catholics attempt a synthesis they merely try to lead Catholic lives within a secular framework by the vigorous practice of minor virtues; try to fit God into a Mammon

scheme of things. They are like a man who, having taken a bride, sees her only clandestinely, while daily appearing in public with another woman. Besides the scandal, it is a strain, and one which could easily provoke a nervous breakdown.

With religious the situation is a little different, but comparable. They don't need temporal principles so much as lay people do. What they

Young man lacking a final end.

need, and what they frequently do not get, is theology. They need not only to aim at God, but to know how to progress toward Him in prayer and sanctification, and they need to know this pretty specifically. The same thing holds for pious souls in the world who are engaged in works of mercy or are otherwise removed from the usual temporal activities. They are starved from lack of religious instruction commensurate with their fervor and desire. They need dogma, spiritual direction, instruction in advancing in prayer, and liturgy. Instead they usually get, or fall into, either mediocrity or sentimentality or both. Mediocrity means a lessening of fervor, a deadening of the ideal. Sentimentality means reducing religious practice to the sense level of feeling. Devotionalism is an exploitation of the emotions, which is dangerous for one's spiritual health, and sometimes leads to a crazed state. The more intelligent a person is, the more dangerous it is to feed him pious fluff in religion because humility keeps a pious person from discarding what his intelligence tells him is nonsense. Instead he tries to erect a system without substance, to mull over and reflect on and live by, ideas which are too puny for him. Such a person often falls into scrupulosity.

No Life Without Purpose

It isn't always easy to find a last end, and sometimes it is impossible. In that case the person is bogged down completely and literally cannot operate. You cannot do the first things unless you have a last end. You cannot, for instance, keep your room clean, or yourself neat, or get to appointments on time, or read the latest book, or look for a job, if you are unable to decide what is the purpose of life. It is quite irrational of parents to say to their neurotic children, "Take your mind out of the clouds and at least clean your room. That's easy enough." It isn't easy. It's impossible if you don't see any reason for living anyhow. It may be hard to save a person who is headed for what will presently be diagnosed as schizophrenia, but the only real cure is to provide an ultimate reason for living. The victim is often enough an idealistic adolescent who declines to accept the drab commercial future envisioned by his parents, and yet has not had sufficient contact with vital religion to give credence to his noble feelings. His idealism ought to be caught up and encouraged (and could easily be by religion, or by the pseudo-religion which is Communism). But the conservative world wants to make him settle down to being worldly; to bow to commercialism and defer to the omnipotence of respectability. When they fail, he makes his exit from the rational world; when they succeed he takes his place in a humdrum office, and may never again become "unbalanced." It is not for us to measure the spiritual cost of his compromise, but sometimes when reading case histories of psychiatric "cures," you have an oppressive sense that the doctor has been the devil's advocate.

Marking Time

For the person who is not able to find a final end, because none of those offered tempt to belief or desirability, there are two ways to stave off slowing down to a full stop, or losing control of a confused mind. Both are temporary measures, but given time, what cannot a man discover?

The one way out is to postpone the necessity of choosing a final end, which always involves postponing one's full maturity. The army offers a convenient respite, for instance. It has its own mysterious ends, which one can generally presume to be good. All you have to do is obey. The purpose of life can wait. Who knows if one will come back alive? How many young men were at loose ends in regard to their lives' purpose and work is evidenced by the general lethargy among returned veterans, for the army is not a likely place to discover the purpose of life if you don't know it already. Many of them are falling into another temporary groove: education. Education for what? Education to prepare for a life that you don't know the purpose of, in many cases. You vaguely hope that college will tell you the purpose of life. But that is the last thing a modern college will tell you. So get a B. A. you go on to your M. A., still hoping. Then you get your Ph.D. and have a nervous breakdown, which can gracefully be attributed to overwork.

Or you can escape via the senses. We shall discuss this outlet under the passions, because there are several different

Girl foreshortening her final end.

ways of being precipitated into it. One thing only we would like to point out here. Sense pleasures really can be set up as final ends, by drastic foreshortening of life. "I decline to look beyond midnight tonight, and my one ambition until then is to get drunk."

PART III. DISORDERS SEATED IN THE WILL

Psychiatry can never be an exact science because of the freedom of the will. The will is the only really capricious element in the universe. Men may justifiably hope to be able exactly to predict the weather, but not human conduct. There are two factors involved which are essentially beyond their powers of prognostication: free will and the grace of God. Many psychiatrists deny the existence of both. The wonder is that they have any success at all.

Realize that the will is a blind faculty. It desires, but it cannot desire what it does not know. Therefore it is tied absolutely to the intellect. This does not mean that it is governed by the intellect, but rather the reverse, although the influence is mutual. Nevertheless it is dependent for its knowledge, and were the knowledge to be entirely cut off, the will would be impotent and the person mad.

The intellect moves the will as presenting its object to it. The will desires good and it is determined to the universal good. But short of God, who is the universal good the will can choose any particular thing as good, so long only as the intellect can be brought to present the good side so the will can choose it. Short of God everything has its good and bad aspects (just as all errors have a grain of truth); the only thing is that the will has to choose something *as good*. This is verified over and over again in common experience.

The good thing about castor oil is that it may make you well. The bad thing is the awful taste. As long as you think about the bad taste you can't take the medicine. But if you want to get well badly enough you may be able to bring yourself to act. Exterior influences on the will always have to modify the intellectual stalemate which prevents action. They bring pressure to bear. They rush up reserve arguments, to twist the intellectual judgment and move the will. That's why fear is so useful. A mother's threat of a spanking may make the prospect of taking castor oil attractive by contrast with the alternative.

Things done through fear are truly voluntary, though under some pressure. It is otherwise with coercion. If you force medicine down the throat of the screaming and protesting child, the act of taking castor oil is completely involuntary, however effective medicinally.

The will and intellect cooperate only in practical judgments and not in speculative matters. The act is simultaneous, neither will nor intellect having chronological primacy. But there is a primacy of knowledge on the part of the intellect; a primacy of election on the part of the will. Once the judgment has been formed the will has to follow along, but it is the will which moves the intellect to make the judgment.

The Matter of the Guilty Conscience

When the practical judgment of the intellect is a moral one, the conscience is involved. The conscience isn't a special faculty, it's simply the name for the practical moral judgment of the intellect. But it has a particular insistence about it which gives it almost a personality.

It will be useful to recall here that man belongs to the moral order, since he has a free will. It is a matter of indifference which subway you take home (because that is not a moral question) but it is not a matter of indifference whether or not you steal money. Animals have instincts to lead them to do what they ought to do. We have a conscience which merely informs us. Nor do we have to obey, because we have free wills. But just disobey and see what trouble you get into. First of all, it's a sin ever to go against your conscience. Often enough it's also neurotic trouble. Here's how the conscience operates:

A Christian Abnormal Psychology

CONSCIENCE --- SPURNED --- REMORSE

By the time conscience has become remorse of conscience the disorder which is sin has set in and the disorder which is lack of peace is swinging into operation.

The cure for remorse of conscience is absolution which literally does wipe the slate clean, restore peace and grace. Absolution (it comes from God of course, who else could do these things?) is normally and most easily obtained in the confessional, but obtainable extraordinarily with perfect contrition, by direct recourse to God.

The alternatives to absolution are hardness (which is a building up of resistance to, a dulling of, the conscience), or some sort of nervous disorder, minor or major.

It is not strange that today, when the moral order is so largely ignored or denied, that there should be many disorders and derangements stemming from tortured and twisted consciences. Anyone who has had any contact with the insane can testify to the overt manifestation of this. Men's instincts are better in this regard than much formal education. The drive to confess and be forgiven seeks curious outlets, but it has a healthy origin. It accounts for the appeal of revivalist Protestantism, with its mass meetings at which "sinners" are urged to publicly to manifest their sorrow and change of heart. Whoever has seen the sordid, undignified, and over-emotional exhibition put on by evangelists cannot, even so, help but feel that the humiliation endured by the repentant sinners abundantly suffices for perfect contrition and perhaps often does indeed win them the absolution which comes so easily to Catholics. Amid more luxurious surroundings, the Oxford Group provides a confessional for the better heeled. Alcoholics Anonymous has a similar provision, treated somewhat gingerly by members, who seem to prefer to relate their colorful misdeeds on public lecture platforms. Even blurting out one's tale at random helps, insofar as it relieves the tension. Most such accounts do contain contrition of a sort anyhow, what with the frequent expression of "I ought not to have," "What a fool I was," "My weakness was so great," etc. Any such recital is beneficial to a person's mental health, at least the first time. The danger is that what verges on indecent spiritual exposure to begin with will become a habit and the person may easily come to brag about what he formerly recited with shame. Then he is in the same spot as those who never had any contrition but were loose-tongued about their immorality only to show what virile fellows they were: a state morally grave and mentally dangerous.

Is it odd that pent-up remorse of conscience should seek a physical outlet? There is a real unity between our bodies and souls. An intensity which is frustrated spiritually will seek relief physically, and usually an appropriate one. When a moral cleansing is in order it may find expression in physical cleansing; in washing hands all the time, or bathing with undo frequency. A neurotic's new year's resolutions are often about bathing, or laundering or neatness. They are the physical parallel of the Catholic penitent's post-confession resolutions to be careful about morning and evening prayers and to receive the sacraments more frequently. Look at our society. There never was such a mania for cleanliness, such a preoccupation with plumbing, such an interest in bathrooms. Can this be unrelated to our unrelieved guilty consciences?

Some consciences are naturally stronger than others. All men have a moral sense, but some men show little evidence of it, while others seem driven by theirs.

Those of lax conscience are known to confessors as recidivists. They are the people who confess the same sins over and over again without much contrition and with no real effort at amendment. Pathological personalities are their psychological counterpart. They are the people who persistently steal or forge checks or commit other crimes without noticeable remorse. They usually have a background of lax upbringing which serves to aggravate their native defects. These are really moral problems. They fall into psychiatric hands partly through the sentimentality which says that all bad people are really only sick.

The ultra-sensitive consciences provide fertile material for sanctity under proper spiritual guidance. Otherwise they fall into scrupulosity. A person with a "New England conscience" who hasn't very specific objective moral standards is excellent potential neurotic material.

A Christian Abnormal Psychology

The Matter of an Erroneous Conscience

A conscience may be wrong, either in a vacillating, uncertain way, or triumphantly.

The first case is pretty general in this day of moral chaos. A person has to make his moral judgements catch at catch can, because the conscience keeps on working even in a semi-vacuum, just as the speculative intellect, starved for substantial food, will keep trying to understand and philosophize about the monotonous work the person is doing, or the petty affairs of his associates. One basis of conscience formation is whispered gutter confidences, usually about sex, and almost always fantastically wrong. Another is what other people think and do—a very fluctuating standard. The movies set the standard now, with advertisements a close second. "Inner feelings" are another poor criterion. What are "inner feelings"? Something you ate, or idle phantasms passing through the imagination. A vague conscience looking into itself for moral standards will get awfully confused. The person will not be able to distinguish between temptation and sin (the consent of the will). Just because a person idly thinks that his brother may be killed in the war does not mean that he wishes his brother were dead. It does not follow from a passing physical attraction that you have consented to the idea of fornication. Here is the trouble with scrupulous people. They cannot distinguish between temptation and sin.

It is interesting to note here that the Freudians hasten to accuse where the Church insistently absolves and hastens to console. The former doesn't hesitate to say: "You really wish he were dead." "You really hate your mother, don't you?" "You are secretly in love with your brother's wife and that is why you put salt in your brother's coffee. You wanted to poison him."

But a priest would remind you that what pops up in your imagination doesn't constitute sin unless consented to, and he would forbid you to worry about inadvertently putting salt in your brother's coffee just because you were lost in admiration of his wife's fresh beauty in her new blue dress.

Or, again, you form your conscience by your sense of shame. A sense of shame is a good thing, but it can be wrong too. Sex as such often seems shameful to people because they have come by their sex information surreptitiously, or not at all. The Catholics of the last generation have been almost as remiss as non-Catholics, thanks to Puritan influence in both cases, in the matter of sex instruction. Sins of omission in this regard do really account for much mental torture. Now the pendulum has swung and the mental torture is from excesses in the other direction. For a brief moment we had a generation immodest, promiscuous, appallingly outspoken, carefree and gay. The immodesty and promiscuity linger on; tongues continue unrestrained, but the whole business has lost its air of innocence. What happened to the sense of shame? It is still missing, but it will return automatically in its proper role, with a return of a balanced view of sex and the cultivation of the virtue of modesty.

What about consciences which are conscientiously wrong? What about people who are sure they are right, only they are not? What about those who practice birth control as their civic duty, divorce their wives in the spirit of self-sacrifice, put their cancerous aunts painlessly to death, and practice cannibalism with religious fervor? Well, they won't have guilty consciences. Most non-Catholics who practice birth control, for instance, really feel quite virtuous about it. And, as a matter of fact, they really are not sinning as long as they are sincere in their ignorance. They can, however, be guiltless in the sight of God without getting the slightest sympathy from nature, which always takes its toll. So if their practices are against nature, unnatural, they can expect to suffer natural consequences, the grief or the loneliness or the nervous disorders which they bring upon themselves. Birth control, for instance, is a much greater threat to mental health than a nursery full of children is to physical health. It also indirectly undermines the stability of marriage and the security of a woman's position. The possibilities of unhappiness and neurosis as the result of practicing homosexuality are far greater, because it is a graver perversion of nature. Other practices, like cannibalism and euthanasia, cause social disorders perhaps along with psychological ones.

What's in the Unconscious?

It is interesting to consider the unconscious in connection with the conscience. There seems no doubt but that the deeps of our nature are not readily accessible to our scrutiny and that they might contain matter in conflict with our conscious life.

The moral judgment which we call the conscious is not under our control but operates according to certain moral considerations of its own. One thing the conscience is very strong and insistent about: that good must be done and evil avoided. We would like here to make the hypothesis that the conscience also has, but dimly, all the natural moral laws as regards the human person, as part of its initial equipment. So, for instance, if you could isolate a person from any sort of moral instruction, he would instinctively react against lying (which is an unnatural abuse of the power of speech), against homosexuality, against birth control, etc. No doubt he would soon become corrupted, or his progeny would (owing to original sin and the insistence of the passions). But the right rules would continue to lie deep within him. If this hypothesis is true then there is deep-set conflict within people who are following the dictates of an erroneous conscience in good faith. The corollary is that peace, that blessed interior peace that comes from being completely at one with yourself, is the prerogative of the just. It would mean, for instance, that people who practice birth control are dimly disturbed in their unconscious. It would mean that all Communist party members are potential neurotics, if only because of their deliberate denial of the objective criterion of truth.

Here seems a good place to discuss psychoanalysis, which dabbles in the unconscious.

Psychoanalysis

Psychoanalysis is a method without a very coherent, or generally agreed upon philosophy. It supposes that causes of mental disease lie deep in the personality, in the unconscious, and that they can be brought into the conscious mind by prolonged, uninhibited talking. Freud is the father and hero of psychoanalysis.

How can psychoanalysis cure conflicts? Conflicts involve conscience and morality. But psychoanalysis is an amoral process at best, at frequent worst it has sort of an inverse morality. Where there is an express conflict of conscience the psychoanalyst will grant absolution, of his sort. It is done by denying the conscience, not the guilt. Nothing is evil to the Freudians; it's only your *attitude* that matters.

In the case of the conflicts mentioned above, where the conscience is making feeble protest from below against its own conscious operation on false information, one has the feeling that the very heart of the conscience is being run down and destroyed by psychoanalysis for it even goes so far in extreme cases at to try to destroy the basic principle that good must be done and evil avoided. At this point psychoanalysis, and any other form of psychiatry that goes along with

THY FAITH HATH MADE THEE WHOLE

it, is no longer fit subject for joking, but very close to, and possibly involved in, diabolical activity.

One of Gertrud von le Fort's novels, *The Veil of Veronica*[2], treats of this matter. Veronica's Aunt Edelgart hesitates to join the Church for twenty years. Finally she takes instructions and then refused to make her confession. After a period of intense spiritual suffering, she tries to find a cure by going to a psychiatrist. From him she obtains a sort of peace, followed by diabolical disturbances. She is finally freed, not without violence, and enters the Church, making a public confession on her death bed, of which this is an excerpt:

> With my sense of guilt I still believed in God. But a sense of guilt is not the last form of Faith; the last form of Faith begins when one can no longer bear the sense of guilt, when its torments becomes so excruciating that one is driven to hate it. At this time, I thrust away from me everything that could remind me of God: Crucifix and Rosary and Missal, for the sight of them was like a devouring fire. And this is the last form of Faith. Only when his hatred of God is extinguished, does man become a complete unbeliever. And here the truly awful derision in which he, who had me in his power, held me, begins to show itself; I, now in my fear unlocked myself to mortal man — not however to man in his compassion, but to man in his presumption. To this presumption I exposed those deeps of my soul which God alone has reserved to Himself the power to adjust. Instead of flying to the Sacrament, I fled to science: I confessed to the doctor, and I received from him the only absolution which the world has power to give, namely the absolution of the psychiatrist, in the eyes of which there is no sin that cannot be forgiven, because, there being no such thing as the soul, it cannot refuse itself to God. And this absolution conferred on me that terrible peace in which thousands live today whose disease is simply this, that they have despised the peace of God! For even those who are furthest away from Him have an Either-Or in relation to God, otherwise they would not be living.

---

2   Sheed and Ward, 1934. This quotation is taken from pages 297 and 298.

> From that day forward, I no longer believed in anything, not even in him in whose hands I was—the doctor had soon talked me out of my belief in him. Nor was I any longer animated by feelings of hatred towards God, but on the contrary I started going to Church again—the doctor had likewise advised this, albeit in moderation. I suffered no more from an inner conflict and sadness, but I ate and drank and slept. I ceased to have struggles or temptations, for the simple reason that he in whom I no longer believed, from now on paid no further attention to me, but cast me aside like a worm or a lump of earth. And I myself did not regard myself as other than such. For as what else could I regard myself—there was nothing anywhere but that in the whole universe there was nothing left but matter alone grey, blind matter!

To return to the psychoanalytic technique as such. It presupposes that you cannot cure a spiritual trouble of which you do not know all the sordid details. That is not true. For one thing, it should not be hard to guess the trouble, for people are much alike and there are only a certain number of things that bother them. A good confessor can guess pretty accurately what is tying the tongue of his unseen penitent, because he knows men. If the psychiatrist is long in doubt it is because he does not know men, and he has an erroneous theory he has to fit the facts into. If a psychiatrist does know the truth about life and men, and can guess what the trouble is with his patient, what is wrong with handing out some information that might be helpful? Let the doctor, or a priest, supply data to a patient tormented by metaphysical problems. Likewise on the matter of sex. Or, if the doctor suspects the person to be tormented with good reason, let him tell about the mercy of God and how to make acts of contrition. These things are, of course, common sense, and likely often done. But they are contrary to the psychoanalytic theory which would persist in airing a person's dirty laundry, and probably much soiled linen as well that wasn't there to begin with, because concentration on sex matters sends the imagination into tail spins.

Let's leave the unconscious alone. Aren't we trying to invent a science of darkness where we ought to be availing ourselves of mystical theology instead? Our earthy and less than earthy parallel to what happens in high spiritual states is suspicious, for the devil imitates.

How differently God deals with our unconscious (or if you want to call it that). In the first place He accepts our relationship on the conscious level and only holds us accountable for what we knowingly do. If the enormity of our pride is so near to us that we cannot see it, God waits, and he keeps pouring grace through the sacraments into that same depth of our being in which Freud discovers so much that is vile. Only after a long time (until we can bear it?) does God set out to purify our innermost nature. He does not trust us to direct the process, but he does it to us, we only suffering it to be done. This is the dark night that mystical theology talks about. The end result is high sanctity. What have the psychoanalysts to show for their efforts? Is it sometimes the death of the soul? They say one of the fruits of psychoanalysis is self-knowledge. But is it? Truly to know yourself is to know what the saints know, which is that you are nothing. You learn it through knowing God, that He is everything.

Diabolism

There is regular chant in psychiatric textbooks to the effect that the Catholic Church for many ages obscured problems of mental disease because of the superstitious belief in the devil. They are wrong twice. The Church never did attribute all insanity to diabolism. And there is really a devil. He does obsess and possess people. Even today.

Quite often one hears of experiences in insane asylums which can only be explained preternaturally. For instance, patients have been known to become very violent when the Blessed Sacrament was brought into their section of the hospital, even though they did not see the priest and had no way of knowing he had entered.

Evidently some of the insanity today is not insanity at all, but diabolical possession. How much? Probably not very much. This is the last explanation which must be given when all others fail (and if the conditions indicate it). Purely natural factors are quite sufficient to account for the undue amount of insanity today, quite apart from this explanation. On the other hand, there are two factors which would lead one to look for diabolical activity. First is the fact that around seventy percent of Americans are now unbaptized, which means the devil has a certain jurisdiction over them. The other is that Freudian psychiatrists are providing grist for the mill.

Diabolical possession means that the devil (or a number of devils) takes possession and control of a person's body; during which time the person himself is usually unconscious, although he may be dimly aware of what is going on. There are intervals, usually violent, when the devil thus takes over. There are other intervals of calm and lucidity when the devil, still evidently remaining, does not interfere with a person's normal functioning.

If you wanted to find diabolical possession in America, the obvious place to look is among the mentally diseased, since that is what possession would look like to our secular minds. The next stop would be to find a classification of patients corresponding to the known characteristics. As it happens, there is such a classification. It is known as multiple personality and its chief mark is the alternating possession of the same body by distinctly different persons. It is a rare and spectacular "disease," about which physicians have sundry conflicting theories. The public is acquainted with it chiefly in Dr. Jekyll and Mr. Hyde. Treatment is attempted with analysis, hypnosis and other methods. If it really is diabolical possession, how futile and yet how dangerous to the doctors, are their efforts. The devil is driven out forcibly by the exorcism of those having the power, or is persuaded to leave by particular friends.

PART IV. DISORDERS ARISING THROUGH THE PASSIONS

Here is where emotional difficulties come in. A passion has no necessary connection with torrid love stories, but is roughly equivalent to an emotion (if strong) or a feeling (if weak). It is an act of the sensitive appetite, a desire on the sense or animal level, of men.

The passions represent joint action of our psychical and physiological natures (as when blood rushes to the head in anger). A lot of contemporary effort is being wasted trying to account for emotional difficulties solely on the physiological level, which is like trying to account for murder by metabolism.

Our passions, though not the highest sphere of our lives, are in a sense the predominant sphere. The idea is to regulate them by reason. To the degree that we do subject our passions to reason we are truly human, we preserve our hierarchical nature, our balance, our sanity. On the other hand, when our passions get out of control we are for that very reason in a bad way. Disordered passions can cause trouble all the way up to and including insanity depending on to what extent they cloud or distort the intellect and so pervert the will. When the passions take over and obliterate the reason, there is madness simply.

Disorders of sin and insanity run a close parallel in the matter of the passions. All the sins of weakness belong to the order of uncontrolled passions and the correspondence between the degree of material sin and the degree of nervous disorder is often startling. So here again we are reminded that religion is the guardian of sanity. As a matter of fact the Church retains a full understanding of man's nature in regard to the passions. It is intended in man that the passions should be governed by reason, but there is a certain conflict of ends between the two. ("The spirit is willing, but the flesh is weak.") It was to correct this internal warfare that God gave us the gift of integrity, which we lost by original sin. It is to regain some semblance of integrity that discipline and mortification are necessary in our lives.

The world is completely at odds with the Church in this matter of mortification. Whereas we gain control of ourselves only with difficulty in any case, the world with its false compassion is raising havoc with our natures. A philosophy of self-indulgence runs all through education. Advertising exploits our passions on a gigantic and scientific scale. Advertising and mortification work on exactly the same principles toward different ends. "Feast! Save yourself labor! Buy our cigarettes which show you pictures of such luscious girls!" cry the advertisements. "Fast! Be diligent! Keep your mind pure!" says the Church. No wonder religion is unpopular in these days of ascendant commercialism. Advertising wants to perfect everything except man. Incidentally, a very good case can be made on these grounds for the essential immorality of modern advertising.

The ultimate effect of all this stimulation of sense desires (Heaven help us it is even called "The American Way of Life.") is the multiplication of sorrows. Material things, attractive at first, eventually pall and provoke despair. Spiritual things at first repel then attract and satisfy.

Inhibitions

You might argue that advertising corrupts people only as incidental to its own profit and not from deliberate denial of man's nature. The same cannot be said about some psychiatry which is intent on glorifying the passions at the expense of the reason. According to this notion, it is unhealthy to restrain the passions; and if restrained there will be neurotic manifestations. Hence the popular idea that it is unhygienic to be without sex life.

The truth of the matter of inhibitions is this: every passion involves some bodily change, as counterpart to the spiritual effect. An inhibition is an attempted suppression of the physical part of the passion rather than of the passion itself. It is the suppression not of anger, but of the appearance of anger. It is the presence of aplomb to hide the reality of embarrassment. But you cannot suppress the physical element in passion and you only succeed in diverting it elsewhere, into ulcers or tics. Inhibitions are usually charged in regard to sex passions, but this is true only insofar as people entertain sex desires which circumstances prevent their satisfying. It is not true in the case of people who for reasons of a higher good, decline to entertain this passion at all. Here again the Church's moral teaching is consonant with our nature: purity of thought is essential to chastity.

Looking at the matter in a large perspective however, it is true that the intensity of human nature is suppressed in the modern world. Human nature is intense. Vitality is its mark. Yet all the way down the line the intensity is frustrated. Our souls are denied a noble cause. Our love is denied worthy objects. Our intellects are deadened, especially in our work. Our creativity is stultified. Our marriages are barren. Our bodies grow flabby from overstuffed furniture and super-comfortable automobiles. We can't even play games and invent amusements. We are passive. We are spectators. We are robots.

But vitality will out. Some people stand up and scream. Some get drunk. Some go in for sex. Some read the tabloids, getting their daily dose of violent death, execution, rape, murder, and all the rest. How near is mass violence to the surface of American life?

Sentimentality, Sex and Lust

Love is basic to all the other passions. Ultimately all human action springs from love. This accounts for the plausibility of the Freudian theory. Freud could not have explained so much by, for instance, hope, as he did by sex, because sex is the most vehement form of this basic passion of love.

Besides the love which is a passion, there is also a rational love seated in our will. It is with this rational love that we love God, and other men for God's sake. We also with this love cherish people in that love of friendship which seeks to give itself and not to possess. When love which belong on this rational level because of its object, drops to the sense level, you have a disorder known as sentimentality. We Americans are maudlin in our sentimentality.

This dropping of love from the rational to the sense level has happened often in religion. It comes from an overemphasis on devotional matters. It is characteristic of the "love is my only dogma" type of liberal Protestantism, which tries to solve all its problems by "love" in the absence of principles. What else can this love be but feeling, and chiefly, as it has turned out, the feeling of pity. Pity is a good enough feeling, but needs the guidance of reason. Sentimental pity (more often than malice) is back of the enthusiasm for birth control and euthanasia. Sentimentalists lose full control of their reason. They are fuzzy thinkers of the "how heartless you are to let this poor woman suffer so from cancer," school. They shudder at the mention of Hell. Naturally it does not fit in with their doctrine of love, because it doesn't appeal to their feelings.

All of us are infected with fuzzy thinking and sentimentality to some degree. It is at least a remote cause of mental disorder, and it makes the cure of neurotics enormously more difficult than it would be otherwise. There is nothing left for it but patiently to instruct and discipline the sloppy modern mind.

Sex is the most vehement form of passionate love since it has to insure, from the natural point of view, that we carry on the race. Although sex is on the sense level it is capable of being caught up with the love of friendship on the rational level, and even divinized through the *sacrament* of matrimony. It is in this way that Christianity has exalted sex. It is wonderful to meditate on the fact that God has not despised our animal nature but has transformed it. He has done the same thing with eating, which is a rather ludicrous procedure considered in itself. On the human level, however, it is a social as well as a biological function.

Passions under control. . . .

And since the Eucharistic banquet was initiated, eating itself has been elevated to something of a ceremony.

During the decline of the Roman Empire, the primary passions were grossly disordered, with lust and gluttony especially prevalent.

A Christian Abnormal Psychology

Pagan rites included revolting obscenities and sex symbols were everywhere. It took centuries of Christian austerity to restore simple goodness to simple natural phenomena, and to purify the minds of men.

It seems as though the Freudians are bent on making everything obscene again. Freud even has a whole set of sex symbols for the interpretation of dreams. Many people's minds are already so diseased that they cannot see a tall building or a vegetable stand without sex associations.

Instead of lifting sex up to a holy familial love, our age is ruthlessly pulling it down to sheer lust, which is sex from which as much reason as possible has been eliminated.

Nothings so distorts the intellect as lust. The imagination keeps feeding the intellect images calculated to distort the judgment. And it is no easy matter to purify a mind of lust once it has been saturated; in fact it is very difficult to get such a person to want to rise out of his mire. Where there is any will to recover, the Church's method is the emergency treatment: constant and continuous attendance at the sacraments, penance as often as one falls, and daily Communion. When a man is beyond self-help God will lift him up so long as he merely consents. The world's methods are quite other. The world invites the mind to the consideration of lust, now everywhere in books, magazines, advertisements, and even radio jokes. Some psychiatrists do the worst possible thing. They urge as a remedy for preoccupation with sex, still more preoccupation with it.

Another reason for sex disorders lies in the fact that people confined by their philosophies to the physical level, the materialists, sometimes have messianic expectations in regard to sex. It's like having a deep yearning which is really for a college education and a house in the country, but which you hope to satisfy with chocolate pecan sundaes (because everyone assures you that houses in the country and college educations don't really exist and that chocolate pecan sundaes are the highest good). Under these circumstances your appetite for chocolate pecan sundaes is insatiable. Maybe nymphomaniacs can be accounted for here.

Passions in control.

THY FAITH HATH MADE THEE WHOLE

Fear and Insecurity

Fear chills and paralyzes. This is its physiological aspect. In extreme cases it can turn the hair white, cause more or less permanent shock or amnesia. There were a lot of cases of this during the war. The diagnosis is simple enough. And because the effects are chiefly bodily, physical measures are effective in the cure.

Fear is a special problem today in its aspect of widespread insecurity. It is popular to talk about insecurity as though it were a problem inherent in economics instead of a fear inherent in men, and to try to cure it by guaranteed annual wages and such. This is an exact parallel to our trying to cure unhappiness among nurses by raising their wages, without bothering to account for the fact that they were much happier when they were paid less. There is hardly a contemporary problem which is not now basically and blatantly spiritual. Insecurity is one of them.

Mr. Roosevelt's "We have nothing to fear but fear itself," is a very inaccurate statement. There are a lot things to be afraid of: atomic bombs, death, economic ruin, starvation, cancer, and the rest. They all fulfill the conditions for exciting the passion of fear: they are evil; they threaten; they are not yet upon us. We are falling all over ourselves to eliminate these causes of fear, but without self-reform. The only way to eliminate many of them (all of them can't be eliminated) is for our society to turn again to God and right itself. This doesn't have much popular appeal. Instead we plan to guarantee security where there is no security. We try long and patiently to get Russia to sign a treaty, although we have no reason to suppose that she will honor it. We try to guarantee wages without regard to the economic balance of the industry. We pile up insurance in the face of currency inflation. We huddle together in large cities where we make excellent targets. We tend toward socialist government, by way of assembling all our bad eggs in one basket.

Meanwhile our lives are utterly in God's hands, as always, whether we face the fact or not. As long as we do God's Will things will work out well. Since we pretend He isn't there we continue to suffer the consequences of our own muddling.

Where insecurity is an individual psychological problem there is no cure short of trust in God. People who are worried at 18 about job security at 60 should not be taken seriously on an economic plane. They are in the same boat with people who are afraid to cross streets or walk over bridges. There is only one condition under which they can be freed, not from fear itself (which is often a good thing and is taken care of by the virtue of courage), but from morbid fear. Trust in God. "No harm can come to a good man." "In the sight of the unwise they seemed to die, but they are at peace. Alleluia." All sorts of things may happen to us. But that ultimately it will all turn out all right, and that God will give us grace to sustain us in trials, are certainties of faith. Without these certainties who can cure fear? Men will kill themselves for fear of death (for such is the paradoxical character of the human animal).

Despair

Despair is a little further along the road that fear travels. Evil is already upon you in despair, and the sorrow it causes by its presence threatens to overwhelm. The sudden tension and semi-paralysis caused by fear is replaced by deep bodily as well as spiritual depression. People who despair are always tired, weighted down quite literally by their own depression. They want to sleep all the time. Neurasthenia is the name usually given them. Doctors who fail to take into account spiritual realities try all sorts of cures. One doctor's remedy for this was simply prolonged rest, during which his patients were not even allowed to feed themselves. Since despair usually carries a wave of self-pity along with it, it is hard to suppose he helped them.

Despair is the prevailing mood of western civilization. It is not the sin against hope kind of despair, which directly doubts God's power to save. In America it is usually natural despair; the despair of making a million dollars, of settling in Westchester, of obtaining international peace, of finding a husband, or of advancing in the social scale, or of buying love and happiness. We brought it on ourselves by placing our hope in materialistic things. Of itself our despair has nothing to do with God, but it might lead to humility which is good ground for grace.

To commit a crime is to kill the soul, but to despair is to fall into Hell. The truth of this old saying will be echoed by anyone who has ever tasted despair. Despair is not just painful. It is intolerable. The antidote is hope, or anything that gives pleasure and will encourage the vital elements of the body. Warm baths, rest, wine, music, friends, all the ordinary consolations are in order. But if the despair runs deep more drastic measures are in order. Suicide is the logical conclusion of despair. Many people try to escape it via intense sensual pleasures, of which sex and alcohol especially recommend themselves. Here again is a precipitating point of escape mechanisms. But in the case of despair the senses are not only an escape from it, they also precipitate you into it.

The alternative to suicide and/or madness on the one hand, and to forced revelry on the other, is hope, the only real cure for despair. If the despair is deep the hope must be strong, which is to say that it must rest in God. This is the more essential the worse the mess people are in or the more melancholic their temperament.

It can be said categorically that people of pronounced melancholic temperament will only find consolation in God and *must* therefore have a strong religious life. Otherwise they will despair and their sorrow will itself lead to madness. Involutional melancholia has always been recognized as a distinct form of insanity which tempts to suicide and is hard to cure. It is very bad for melancholic people to talk too much, and they should avoid any sort of analysis.

Opiates Are the Religion of the People

We are a nation of escapists. We run from our own despair, from the meaninglessness of our lives, from sorrow, from fear, from the spectacle of our own mediocrity.

It is on the whole a wise move. It is nature making one last effort at self-preservation. So it is wise not to remove the props, however unsteady, from under a man poised on the brink of despair, until you are prepared to support him otherwise.

Will you drown yourself in pleasure in disregard of the day of reckoning? Try sex or alcohol (not both; they are incompatible in the long run). The sins of the flesh will divert you for a while. Then what? Something may turn up to make it worthwhile to return to respectability. It won't be easy to return, but it will be possible up to a point. And if not, or if I can't return? Madness. If you live long enough and drink hard enough your brain will deteriorate. Lust may get you functionally. Or it, too, may destroy your mind organically through disease.

Perhaps it would be better just to keep too busy to think. Join committees like mad. Be an eager-beaver. Read everything. Go out every night. Never be alone. Never think a serious thought. But it's hard to keep up the pace. Something will happen that you will have to think about. Or you'll have a physical breakdown. Or more likely a nervous breakdown.

A Christian Abnormal Psychology

Opiates are the religion of the people.

Try oblivion if you're sure you never want to recover. It's done with drugs.

If none of the above suit you, or if they are too expensive or disgraceful, the thing for you is daydreaming. Doesn't cost a cent. Can be done under the very noses of a vigilant family. It gets progressively more interesting. As you become more adept at it, the pain of your circumstances eases. Who cannot invent a better world than this one? Maybe you will be able to cast off from reality entirely.

What Is Reality?

Most people are living in two unreal worlds. There is the ordinary humdrum world. It would be gross flattery to call this reality. It is unredeemed. Its values are all wrong. It does not consider God. It is the secularist nightmare. In it the millionaire's palace is as false as the slum tenement. As a matter of fact suicide comes easier amid material splendor, or on lovely sunny days. It is the contrast between one's aching heart and the riches and beauty which cannot assuage or satisfy that makes things especially intolerable. But to get back. There are tenements. There is almost universal ugliness. There is domestic strife, stupid jobs and all the rest. Only love can make it endurable, and only God can make it really real. The facts are always there: the irritation at the breakfast table, the fifty pounds overweight, the ten dollars a week, the spot on the carpet. But the world is a nightmare of meaningless without God, or without love (love is the most godlike thing among us, and whenever it reaches a selfless spiritual degree it has a power to transform things).

The other unreality is the world of the movies, the advertisements, the radio and the magazines. This is the world in which everything in the kitchen matches and everyone dresses like Hollywood stars. This is the world of tawdry glamour, of hypocrisy and pretense.

So with two unrealities already, why not a third? The advantage of the world of daydreams is that you yourself can be the central character, a sort of composite of all ideal qualities. Daydreaming absorbs the imagination, which should be busy supplying the intellect with data about daily life. That's why daydreamers are abstracted. You can daydream a lot before your imagination starts handing over daydream world data as the real stuff. But there is abundant opportunity for practice in the ordinary life. With many girls their work is an invitation to daydream, and their evenings are spent at the movies, gathering new material. It can be laid down as a general rule that something is always going to be going on in the brain. Where people will not think their imagination will take over.

Daydreamers are regularly classified as schizophrenics and almost certainly given shock treatments. What is the point in forcing persons by drastic means back into a grim unreality that they have been trying to escape from all their lives?

PART V. THE WAY OUT

We cannot repeat it too often. The world will do anything but reform itself. We'll spend a million dollars any day rather than make a radical change in our way of thinking. So long as we are committed to such a philosophy, we'll assuage our consciences with superficialities in regard to mental disease. We probably feel very virtuous now that we've lately stirred up a lot of indignation about the physical care of the spiritually tortured. But the physical structure of insane asylums is accidental to the problem of mental disease whereas the prevailing philosophy of psychiatrists is of the essence of the problem. Who has led a crusade against Freud? Who has campaigned for exorcists in asylums or for trained chaplains?

The fact that should be most obvious from this paper is that there is no hope for remedying the general condition of widespread mental breakdown without a spiritual transformation of society. If we don't reform we'll all be locked up, unless we are blown to bits first. If we keep on trying to wipe out venereal disease apart from morality, if we keep on trying to cure cancer without questioning the food industry, there just is no hope for us anyhow.

Having said that, there remains the problem of helping those who are the victims of our disordered society.

Relevance of Religion to Mental Disorders

Some indication has been given in this paper of the continual interweaving of religious considerations with those of mental health. We have barely touched on the stabilizing effect of objective "authoritarian" moral standards. We have discussed the matter of a troubled conscience and the therapeutic effects of absolution. We have mentioned the unbalancing propensities of sins of the flesh, and the mental torment of metaphysical uncertainty. For lack of space we have neglected until now any real mention of grace in this connection, although this is most important of all.

The synthesis that has to be made psychologically between religion and mental disorders centers about this question of grace, and it has not been made yet so far as we know. St. Thomas was not concerned with it, but elaborated a *rational* psychology which does not include the supernatural.

We usually think of mystical theology in connection with devout people well advanced in the spiritual life, and not in connection with neurotics and dypsomaniacs [alcoholics]. Unconsciously we assume that progress toward God lies through the acquisition of natural virtue, forgetting that supernatural life is gratuitous and forever beyond our deserts, and forgetting also that the only disposing condition is humility.

It is the dypsomaniacs who have rediscovered in practice the approach to God through humility alone, although they don't know quite what to do with it. Natural despair is fertile ground for supernatural hope. Alcoholics Anonymous, who are drawn mostly from the spiritually underprivileged classes, work on this theory. They don't try the old tack of urging a drunk to make a man of himself. Instead they approach him at his humblest (just recovering from a disastrous bout) and urge him to admit his own impotence to reform and beg God to do for him what he cannot do for himself. It works, even among people who can't seem to go on from there theologically.

Why should it work, apart from the rather vague explanation that God is good. It works because those in a state of grace can, if they will allow it, shift over from a natural to a supernatural economy of operation. The supernatural gifts and virtues operate as habits paralleling our natural psychological equipment for human operation. Take a single example. Our control of the passions is accomplished partly through the natural virtue of temperance, which is markedly absent in habitual drunks and others snowed under by the sins of the flesh. Through humble and complete abandonment one predisposes oneself for a shift to the supernatural economy where virtues, including the virtue of temperance, operate in us through no direct effort on our part. It is rather as though a man were a puppet lying twisted in a heap, who consenting to be lifted up by God, is therefore raised up and untwisted in one process. Actually supernatural grace carries natural perfection in its wake. A neurotic who was converted to the Church and started going to daily Communion would feel the sanctifying and healing effects of grace at the same time, as though he were being at once lifted up and straightened out. He would feel as though he were being drawn upward to God for a long time in a spiral motion before proceeding in a straight line.

The shift from the natural to the supernatural economy is the only way out of bad breakdowns, persona and social. It is the "reaching for the stars in order to get out of the mire" technique. To use it means to offer a neurotic not a less trying life, or a less exacting goal, but to commission him to make over the world. Neurotics need to lose themselves in a great cause and complete dependence on God. We usually preoccupy them instead with their own mediocrity.

The Practical Problem

The practical problem in relation to functional mental disorders is that of how to combine spiritual assistance and psychiatric care. There are other problems of course: problems of money, physical care, etc., but this is the broad general problem to which the others are subordinate. It has three levels, that of prevention, the level of slight disorders, and the level of insanity.

Preventative Measures

As we have said, the only generally effective preventative measure would be the spiritual transformation of society. However, there are a few specific things that might be effective within the present society. They are all spiritual things; psychiatry is not necessary on this level, although it has tried to work here. There is a lot of talk of "mental health" measures, usually involving wholesale distribution of sex information. It is spiritual training that is needed.

Catholics would be spared many a nervous breakdown if good spiritual direction were more generally available and if confessors were trained to help penitents with problems and advance in holiness. It is shocking how many Catholics wouldn't dream of discussing with confessors problems which have a considerable bearing on their spiritual life and mental health.

Non-Catholics are out on a limb completely. It is a ticklish matter, and not for us to decide, but would it be possible for priests to take over the sort of burden currently falling on Mr. Anthony? Could the Church make available, discretely, certain priests who could be consulted by anyone desiring a straight, authoritative answer to a moral problem? "Father, shall I leave my husband or shall I stay on for the sake of the children, and how shall I treat such a problem?" "Father, is it right that we do such and such in our office?" Certainty and moral encouragement would make it possible for many a person to endure heroically circumstances which would otherwise be crushing. Curiously enough, most people would accept a priest's authority without question. It might not occur to them for five or six years to join the Church whose authority they accept, but such is human nature.

On the Level of Neuroses

On this level the burden should fall mostly on the psychiatrist, as handling neurotics demands more time and patience than is ordinarily available for the priest. Yet almost none of the contemporary psychiatrists have any understanding or appreciation of religion. They tend rather to overemphasize, since they are medical doctors, the physical and physiological aspects of nervous breakdowns. We need psychiatrists with spiritual, philosophical and theological training, who have as much knowledge of the faith as they currently have of Freud, Jung and Adler; psychiatrists who can intelligently discuss the metaphysical aspects of their patients' problems and who have some ideal of a Christian norm.

Such a psychiatrist would work in harmony with a priest spiritual director in the case of his Catholic patients. With his non-Catholic patients he would not keep silent on the subject of religion, because God is not irrelevant to mental disease. That does not mean he would proselytize, but that he would explain things in the light of moral considerations, treat a guilty conscience as such, etc. Rudolf Allers said in one of his books that he knew of no cure for neurosis except sanctity or the desire for sanctity. We hold to the same general thesis. People are not seriously unbalanced by trivialities, and what is not trivial in the spiritual realm, very much involves God.

At present, in lieu of such psychiatrists, the few priests who are competent spiritual directors are carrying, often successfully, a psychiatric as well as spiritual burden.

On the Level of Insanity

At what point does a neurosis become insanity? At the point, hard to discern exactly, at which the person loses the principle of recovery. He may be deeply melancholic while yet cherishing a ray of hope; when that is gone he is oriented to despair. A girl may daydream a long time before stepping into the world of phantasms. When the principle of recovery is lost it is usually the person's will which breaks free of control, and with it the hope of recovery through the appeal of right reason.

Therefore the problem of the insane is partly the problem of reaching them (whereas with neurotics it is more a problem of gaining their cooperation). Here grace should be invaluable. We would even venture the hypothesis that a mentally deranged person is more sensitive to supernatural influence than a normal person and would respond in time to great supernatural charity on the part of an attendant when nothing else could touch him. This is in line with a general principle, which is true, that the worse our plight the more we need God.

In relation to the practical problem, the integration of psychiatric and spiritual treatment, it would be wonderful if they could be combined in holy nurses. But we mean more than that. We mean to suggest possibly even an order of psychiatrist-priests who might even also do nursing work. The idea seems foreign to our modern ears, but it is not without precedence in the Church

The Catholic Duty

It is really shocking that Catholics have so far neglected the great work of mercy in our day. There are only a handful of Catholic asylums in the whole country and most of these are to care for religious. There is no general sense of duty toward non-Catholics who have had mental breakdowns. There has practically been no opposition to the prevailing philosophies. We have chaplains in public institutions but no special training is afforded them.

It isn't necessarily a question of money. Catholics would have no difficulty nursing the insane in public institutions, state hospitals and the like. They probably could do it in a body, taking over whole sections and instituting their own methods, subject to state supervision. This is one field in which there would probably be only gratitude. There would opposition from the Freudian doctors who are now largely in control, but who are not as well-entrenched or as highly thought of as they might wish.

There is probably no harder work than the care of the insane. It is much too much for most people. Those who did the work would have to be very holy indeed. It is useful to remember that one reason God allows terrible things to happen to some is so that the rest of us can exercise charity toward them.

4

Contemporary American Protestantism

FEBRUARY 1947

IS AMERICA PROTESTANT?

The usual answer to a question of this sort is given statistically, and it proves practically nothing. There were, at the time of the 1936 census (notoriously unreliable in this regard) 31,000,000 avowed Protestants in the United States, as against 20,000,000 Catholics and 70,000,000 unchurched. The Protestants comprised over 250 sects, quite a number of which can be considered "Christian" only by stretching the imagination.

A better index to the times is gained from the personal sampling of the spiritual atmosphere of the newsstands, hotels, churches, suburbs, movies, radio and by taking careful note of what has happened to home town friends and college classmates. The vitality of a civilization is spiritual, and spiritual temper cannot be reduced to statistics. On this basis then, of a clue here, and a clue there, plus our own powers of discernment, the following appears to be the situation.

The period of Protestant ascendancy was finished a generation ago. The country is now in the grip of no intense spiritual force, nor is there any all-over general direction in which we are heading. An uncommon number of our present leaders get their vitality from a residual Protestantism, but are not themselves Protestant and are not passing on their heritage. Just as the country has for a long time been feeding the cities its own best vitality, so has the traditional Protestant home, steeped in Bible reading, been providing men and women of strong character. Often the two sources of vitality coincided. Rural America has now been drained of vitality. The traditional Protestant home life was progressively abandoned by the laity, then the ministers, and now even the missionaries. Dorothy Thompson, Henry Luce, Robert Hutchins, and many other prominent figures (note that they are articulate America, not America fatted on mercantile profits) came from ministers' and missionaries' homes. Does anyone expect that a childhood of Superman and progressive schools will produce citizens of like caliber?

Anyhow, we are now coasting along on a residual strength, which is not being renewed, or even acknowledged. We are living in a post-Protestant age, turning barbarian. We are in a moment of indecision, waiting for a new source of vitality, ready otherwise to retrogress rapidly. Two strong forces are coming up, from sharply opposed directions: Catholicism and Atheistic Communism. It seems unlikely that Protestantism, modernized and mild as it is, will prove a serious contender for tomorrow's America, but we shall examine the potentialities in this regard presently. The average man of today is a neo-pagan, frustrated in his directionlessness. Some of them are being converted to Catholicism. Some are falling prey to Communism. In between is a large area of neurosis and alcoholism, laying waste much of our country's best blood and natural gifts.

Why the loss of Protestant supremacy? It is useless to look to external conditions for its present weakness, for it had a clear field in the building up of America. Protestantism must either have inadvertently pulled its house down on top of itself (as, for instance, in its unfortunate and now lamented support of secular education) or be suffering from internal disorders. Let us first examine the internal malady.

DISEASES OF PROTESTANTISM: SENILITY

The 400th anniversary of Luther's death was commemorated last year. It is four centuries then, since the Reformation breach in Christendom; a schism which broke the floodgates which might have held back the rising tide of uncontrolled humanism and commercialism. It has taken 400 years for the unleashed forces to run their course to the breakdown of western civilization. 400 years to undermine the mental ability, the health, the hope, the peace, the happiness, the common morality of man. 400 years to destroy the beauty of the face of the earth, the upset the balance of fertility in the soil, nearly to exhaust the natural resources of the earth. 400 years to pervert knowledge to the total service of destruction. 400 years to go from an ideal of self-discipline to an unashamed commercial exploitation of the passions. 400 years to twist men's minds to an acceptance of the perversions of birth control, homosexuality, abortion and euthanasia. 400 years from an ordered society with respect for authority to a hideous alternation of pressure-group democracy and fanatic dictatorship. 400 years from a civilization built and permeated by the Church to a monstrous scientific barbarism untouched by Christ. In that 400 years what has happened to the branch which broke off from the vine? Has it withered yet? Nearly. It is certainly senile, and the best measure of its senility is the prevalence of religious indifferentism. Future ages, if any, will look with horror upon the time when men by the millions disregarded God, when schools and courts and hospitals and jails and insane asylums and day nurseries neglected to pay homage to God. They will read that the more or less established religion "played" to almost empty houses, while thousands upon thousands of men gathered to watch nine men play baseball. They will learn that whole sections of newspapers recorded the minutia of money trading while little or no space was given to religion. They may even learn that men sank so low mentally and spiritually as to try to identify, in a muddled sort of fellowship, creeds not only diverse but contradictory.

DISEASES OF PROTESTANTISM: DISINTEGRATION

Protestantism keeps falling apart, subdividing like an amoeba. Every time someone is displeased he can, and he often does, start a new sect. There are now some 250, without the process' having been stemmed. The reunion effort of the Federal Council of Churches does not check the disease, but merely arranges for cooperation among the diseased parts. The disease itself if of the essence of Protestantism, rooted in its rejection of authority. It was a serious and terrible thing for the original reformers to break the unity of Christendom and reject the rightful authority of the Church. After that, however, Protestantism had no ground on which to object to further fissure. It is like marriage. If you stand on the ground that it is indissoluble, and allow no divorce, you have a tenable position. If you deny the indissolubility you undermine the whole structure of marriage and inevitably let yourself in for a string of divorces. The only way to stop the disintegrating process and its unlovely consequences, is to return to the initial tenable position. This Protestantism is still reluctant to do, both in the matter of itself and its views on marriage.

Protestantism clung to the "right of private judgment," as they call it, which is really an indirect way of saying that there is no objective truth. It is consistently foreign to the Protestant temper to search for a truth external to the individual and binding on all men. Instead the tendency is to search one's own mind to determine the credibility of a doctrine. This may explain why the word "humility," which to a

Catholic suggests an ever so desirable virtue, has a distasteful, servile connotation in common American parlance. The rejection of authority and the lack of humility is a Protestant characteristic which has been engrafted on the American temper. Our country was populated, someone has said, not just by Protestants but by Protestants who couldn't get along with other Protestants. Once here the disgruntled or avaricious could always proceed westward. Over a period of several hundred years this tendency has produced its exemplar in the rugged individualist of recent unlamented memory. You couldn't make a society out of him, so he is at length disappearing. His progeny are much less splendid. They are just plain undisciplined in every way.

If protest against authority (and chiefly, of course, against papal authority) is of the essence of Protestantism, one ought not to wonder at the present hew and cry against the rising tide of Catholicism. The ordinary non-Catholic citizen responds instinctively and unreasoningly with a shudder to the prospect of authority, especially when it is called "authoritarianism."

But men get tired of following their own rule, just as children get tired of doing as they please. Anyone with half an eye can see that the United States is spoiling for strong, unhesitant, leadership. In the political field the danger of dictatorship lies in the mood of the people rather than in the strong-armed tactics of... of whom? The miracle is that no one has yet set upon such easy prey.

In the religious sphere, official Protestantism is making one last barrage attack against the Church which, having authority, has stood firm on the same ground since the breach. Some of it is hysterical. Most of it is pelting with marshmallows. In the spirit of reconciliation Protestants and other non-Catholics keep making friendly overtures to the Church, involving slight compromises. Unbend a little on birth control, concede a few points on mixed marriages (by contrast the Anglican Archbishop of York is lately getting scrupulous in reverse on the matter of mixed marriages. Is the tide of their usual effect turning, or is it a revenge move?). but most of all we are besought one way and another to admit that one religion is as good as another. Were it not for our obstinacy in this regard all Christians (and Jews, Buddhists and others) could join in a splendid spiritual fellowship.

With so much genuine good will on both sides, and so little personal enmity, now that vast rivers of water have run under the bridge, it is just possible that the obdurate position of the true Church may suddenly be seen for what it is, and that the Protestants may begin to appreciate the magnificent strength with which Catholicism has held to the fullness of truth which alone can restore society. They may even look up and see the Church's outstretched arms of welcome.

Their alternative is to return to the tyranny of petty authority. "Jesus, I was certain," said Rev. Dr. Harry Emerson Fosdick in his farewell address to the Riverside congregation, "would not be in the least intent on such a ritual detail (as baptism by immersion)... and I had decided that I would never be a minister of a church where all Christians, devoted to our Lord, could not freely enter on equal terms with what form of baptism—or none—their Christian heritage made sacred to them." How do you know, Dr. Fosdick? By what authority do you presume to read God's mind?

DISEASES OF PROTESTANTISM: SELF-CONTRADICTION

Eventual self-contradiction is the invariable mark of heresy. The true Church preserves all the intensities of Christianity in delicate balance. Heresy, by denying some truths, or exaggerating some at the expense of the others, destroys the balance, so that its adherents become extremists in one direction, and then swing to the opposite extreme by way of reaction, always without finding the stabilizing center. This process if very clearly marked in Protestantism, the more so now that the process has run its course in a half-dozen different aspects. Protestantism has swung from the gloomy despair of Calvinism (man, being especially corrupted by original sin, cannot please God) to the presumption of liberalism and modernism (there never was any original sin, there is no Hell, and if there is a Heaven I shall certainly arrive there without effort.) It is starting to swing now from an exaggerated confidence in the temporal order and man's reason to an exaggerated and phony mysticism. Its morality has ranged all the way from "no fun on Sunday" to the solemn and sentimental endorsement of euthanasia. It has swung from an excessive individualism into the yawning Russian jaws of collectivism. This pendulum swing accounts for the phenomenon which attracted Chesterton to the Church: Protestantism alternately criticizes the Catholic Church on diametrically opposite grounds; now for being too other-worldly, now for being too this-worldly. But the Catholic Church hasn't moved from dead center. It is her critics who are revolving.

Two major reversals warrant particular attention:

FAITH AND GOOD WORKS

It pleased Martin Luther to declare good works useless for salvation, even though he had to discredit St. James' Epistle to do so. The effect of his doctrine of salvation by faith alone was a local and immediate abandonment of charitable works; indirectly, and with other contributing factors (such as the greed of the political arm) it meant the virtual wiping out of the works of mercy in the Protestant countries of the western hemisphere. Nothing is more disguised and misrepresented in our textbooks than this appalling fact. There was, under a united Catholic Europe, a magnificent network of good works, ranging from universities to orphan asylums, from hospitals to burial societies. They were operated by the Church, not the state, and were mostly under the auspices of religious orders. They were manned by thousands and thousands of nuns and monks, leading heroic, dedicated lives of piety and poverty. In one Protestant country after another the properties belonging to the charities were usurped, that is, stolen, by politicians for ignoble reasons, and the lot of the poor and the weak was reduced to intolerable, unalleviated misery. Protestantism lost the Catholic idea of works of mercy, that Christ was to be seen in our weak brothers. It has never recovered that idea, although the pendulum has now swung over to social service Christianity. The change began with pharisaical, patronizing philanthropy, which still faintly lingers in our society. The rich helped the poor without impoverishing themselves; pried into the lives of those whose benefactors (and often exploiters) they were, judged and managed, and tried to make the poor clean like themselves.

Now the whole of Protestantism is permeated with the spirit of good works. Faith is irrelevant and salvation unimportant. Never mind if poor Mr. X goes to Heaven or Hell, the important thing is to get his teeth fixed. Who cares about the morality of abortion; it is economically advisable. This social service Protestantism is usually now just social service, and never mind the Protestantism. The child it bore had repudiated its mother. But within Protestantism the social service spirit is still rife. When sincere, earnest Protestants want to intensify the practice of their religion, they do not go on retreats or make corporate acts of faith; they go down to the Italian section of town and help empty the garbage. They form colonies of college students to build houses for mine workers, or groups to do occupational therapy in mental hospitals. This is even, and especially, true of the Quakers whose attraction is usually reputed to be their emphasis on the contemplative.

We associate Communism with Russia, but it had its birth in Protestant Europe and gathered momentum from the absence of good works in a society bred on salvation by faith alone. In a sense Communism, social security legislation and the curious material messianism of some of the United Nations committees, represent a final, extra-religious exaggeration of the emphasis on good works apart from faith.

Now the pendulum is trying to reverse itself again, but the effort is deceased and diffuse. The emphasis is no longer chiefly on the temporal welfare of people but on their "emotional" welfare, with Freudianism and sentimentality muddling around in everything.

THE BIBLE

The Protestant somersault in regard to scripture is a sad commentary on the waywardness of dissidents. The Bible is the inspired work of God, completely true but neither the sole nor the primary authority for Christianity. Protestants having left the Church (which is the supreme authority), were more or less forced to regard the Bible as the sole and comprehensive religious guide. Since the Bible is not easily interpreted, they were further reduced to specifying the literal meaning as a criterion (after some convenient changes in the original text had been made by the reformers).

Bible literalists still plentifully exist in America. The control movement of Protestantism, however, has swung over to a denial not only of the authority, but even of the *authenticity* of the Bible. They derive their position from some 19th century German scholars, the "higher critics," who questioned traditional dates and texts. Although the most credible scholars among the higher critics came to eat most of their own words, in favor of the traditional teachings, Protestants seem not have heard of this. Even, and especially, in the major Protestant seminaries (which have been liberalized) a view of the Bible is taught which entirely discredits it. It goes like this: the gospel of John is of late date and not apostolic. The other three, synoptic, gospels are all variations of an original manuscript, possibly Mark, plus some other sayings. Mark is the most authentic gospel. It contains no account of the Virgin Birth (which is anyhow common religious folklore) which therefore never took place. The end which treats of the Resurrection is a later interpolation in the text. Christ died in agony and despair. The miracles were exaggerations, lies, epileptic fits; anyhow, not miracles. Christ didn't think himself divine; it was pinned on him later. Judas was a well-meaning zealot whose plans went awry. Etc. It is essentially the same account of Our Savior which is found in the Jewish Encyclopedia.

Incredible though it may seem, this sort of stuff is not only taught, but is even considered edifying. "How much more inspiring Christianity is, now that it is shorn of its superstitious coating," is the sort of double-talk by which it is justified. This is similar to another common trick of speech, wherein one first denies that men have souls and then talks about their sacred personalities. The students with better minds, those who can follow through a premise to its conclusion, understandably resign from Protestantism to join Alcoholic Anonymous.

It is well to keep this scriptural aberration in mind when considering Protestant plans to restore the teaching of religion to secular colleges. Unless Protestantism suffers a change of heart, this is what they are going to be handing out. Wellesley College has been teaching this sort of "religion" for years in a required course, without conspicuous increase in student piety.

DISEASES OF PROTESTANTISM: THE THEOLOGICAL VOID

A galaxy of churches, millions of members, wealth incalculable, good will in abundance, the blessings of the political wing, and every other material and social advantage cannot perpetuate Protestantism in a theological void. If Protestantism doesn't believe in anything it isn't anything. Creeds are of the essence of religions. Liberal Protestantism has abandoned creeds. The result is sound and fury signifying nothing. Protestantism is always expending a lot of money and effort to start something which tomorrow will still be there but will not still be Protestant. It will be secular. Protestants are now fearful of the threat of secularism, but they brought it upon themselves. There is hardly a one of what are now the "best" colleges: Harvard, Wellesley, Yale, etc. which is not of pious Protestant formation, and usually for the training of ministers. Now they are secular. What is Presbyterian about the Presbyterian Medical Center in New York? Nothing. The universities and hospitals founded at great expense by the Protestant missionaries in the Far East were almost immediately secularized. Protestants keep pouring missionaries and money into China and Japan, but with very little *Protestant* effect.

This all stems from theological deficiencies. One of its most pathetic manifestations is due to the absence of *moral* theology. Modern irreligious psychiatry is threatening to fill this void. For instance, Protestant chaplains in state mental hospitals (often admirable men) are actually learning from psychiatrists how to minister spiritually to the patients.

It is curious to the point of absurdity, how strenuously Protestants avoid theological criteria. The current upheaval in the Episcopal Church is illustrative. This church, which encompasses within itself all shades and degrees of personal belief, is considering whether or not to merge with the Presbyterian Church. One can search the accounts of the debate in vain for the slightest inquiry as to whether Presbyterianism or Episcopalianism, if either, is *true*. A very daring person might bring up the question of the validity of orders, but theology is verboten.

Protestantism is formally split into fundamentalism and modernism, representing (characteristically) two untenable positions at opposite extremes. The fundamentalists are Bible literalists who accept the major Christian dogmas, with an exaggerated emphasis on Christ's imminent second coming. Their adherents are mostly from the lower middle classes. Fundamentalism produced the good living, good willing, sincere and believing Protestant that Catholics have in mind when they talk about how certain it is that Protestants will go to Heaven. How many of these typical, sincere Christians with a grossly over-simplified religion remain? They are said to be legion in the south; yet closer investigation reveals that southern churches are strong on social life, but not conspicuous for the piety of their members. Then there is the Negro, who lent his own particular dignity and grace to a shorn Christianity. The rapidity with which the Negro is being de-Christianized is scandalous, and not pertinent to this discussion. The third great repository of middle-class Protestantism is in the middle-west, where simple goodness and godly talk is hard-pressed by the radio, movies and "an ever-increasing standard of living." Many of the new sects are lunatic-fringe offshoots of fundamentalism.

Let us now observe what has happened to the modernist, liberal wing of Protestantism. Dr. Fosdick exemplifies it in his own career. He is a Baptist minister who had to give up his Fifth Avenue pastorate in the twenties because, chiefly under the influence of the current evolutionary doctrines, he could not believe fundamentalist dogmas. Rockefeller built him the imposing Riverside Church, where he could preach as he pleased. In this church, adjacent to International House, the Union Theological Seminary and Columbia University, Fosdick developed to its fullest the liberal positionless position. The liberals seemed at first to have chosen the part of reason and science. The irony is that they ended up with sentimentality and double-talk. They are prey to every passing secular aberration, hastily readjusting their tenets to the latest findings of this and that. The capitulation of liberal Protestant leadership and pseudo-science is complete and abject. They deny the divinity of Christ, more or less deny immortality, hold no objective moral standards, concede divorce, recommend birth control (indeed, sponsor it) and now endorse euthanasia (at least, some of the prominent ones, including Fosdick, have done so).

The liberals control organizational Protestantism. They rule the seminaries, control the Federal Council of Churches, get written about in the papers, run the leading Protestant magazines, and occupy the city pulpits. Do they also have a majority following? Quite likely not. It sounds silly, but they may well be self-appointed shepherds with precious few sheep. For one thing, as we pointed out, their followers tend logically to drift altogether away from religion.

A word about the sacraments. Liberal Protestants are thoroughly unsacramental. They have dispensed with the two sacraments which Protestantism in general did retain for some time; matrimony, no longer considered binding, and baptism. Some sort of baptismal rite is usually performed in liberal churches, but it is regarded as merely symbolic, and therefore is invalid. To "join" a liberal Protestant church you need only signify your belief in Jesus Christ, not specifying what you believe about Him.

WILL THERE BE A PROTESTANT RESURGENCE?

We cannot pretend to measure accurately the residual vitality of Protestantism, but we shall indicate some of the places where it is to be found.

The respectable, conservative, monied element of American life is still nominally Protestant, but it is not true that they still hold the reins of our national life. Leadership has fallen to propagandists and labor leaders, the lower classes, the poorly educated and the mercantile owners. Few of any of these groups are Protestant. So the upper-middle class affiliation is not the asset it might at first appear to be.

A better gauge of Protestant strength is the spiritual strength of its members. How is that determined? It is not necessarily reflected in the leaders or in the official publications; there are no religious orders to flower from it. The best place to look is among the rather old, or among the young laity and clergy. And here and there you find it; an isolated man or woman of saintly character, an occasional godly family. Among the young you find groups forming to do works of mercy, to go to the missions, to restore rural community life, or to think out religious problems. The Christian Students League has considerable vitality. The more conspicuous Youth for Christ movement we would be inclined to disregard. It puts on a good show, but it is a bit on the hysterical side for accomplishing permanent results. Protestantism is subject to revivalist waves which always catch up men's goodness and desire for religion, without being able to sustain them. The Oxford Group was an evidence of this.

To sustain such vitality as remains in Protestantism there must be theological food; else it is sheer emotionalism. It is true, as we said before, that Protestant theology in America is conspicuous by its absence. This is not true of Europe where there is renewed interest in theology. One movement, which has followers in this country, is backwards to neo-orthodoxy. Here and there you will find people who have returned to the original Calvinist or Lutheran position (some Lutheran sects have never departed from the teachings of their founder and stand apart from the usual Protestant federations). Then there are contemporary European theologians who are attracting a lot of attention, but whose influence in this country is still limited to the intense groups: earnest young lay people and theological students. Brunner[1] is one such. He is straining toward a theology which will synthesize religion and life. Most famous, however, is Karl Barth who holds to a position of exaggerated supernaturalism. He catches Protestants on their pendulum swing back to the supernatural and the mystical. The same tendency accounts for the attraction of the young to the Quakers, some of whose leaders have borrowed heavily, and quite indiscriminately, from mystics, Catholic and pagan. They are rediscovering the potentialities of prayer, silence, solicitude, and the inner life in general. There is also in most of the Protestant sects a groping for a return to the sacramental life. Especially marked is the renewed emphasis on the Lord's Supper, long reduced to symbolism and grape juice (of course without powers of consecration). There is a sort of liturgical movement in process too; a renewed interest in

---

[1] Heinrich Emil Brunner (1889-1966) was a Swiss Reformed theologian who, along with Karl Barth, was part of the neo-orthodox or dialectical theology movement within Protestantism. — *Ed.*

good Church music, including Gregorian chant, and a borrowing of ritual from the Episcopalians and the Orthodox.

Ritually speaking, the upward movement is most pronounced among the high Episcopalians (who decline to call themselves Protestants at all, but consider that they are one of the three Catholic branches of Christianity[2]—the third is the Orthodox Church. TIME, whose managing editor is Episcopalian, has lately taken a dogmatic stance on this point for his magazine usage). They smother in incense, have elaborate and very beautiful services, increasingly favor clerical celibacy, and stress the sacraments. They hold (contrary to the opinion of the Holy See) that their orders are valid. Devout Episcopalians receive "communion" every morning.

There is a less lovely variety, of a sort, within Protestantism which consists in residual hatred of the Catholic Church. This provides a rallying point (it is, after all, the common element in historical Protestantism) for diverse elements. It is very outspoken where it exists, but on an hysterical, low intellectual level. We are not referring to the fulminations of the Jehovah's Witnesses, who can hardly be classed as Protestants, but of such people as Bishop Oxnam.[3] These people see horrible portents in Myron C. Taylor's[4] mission to the Vatican. Among other Protestants outspoken antagonism is not very common. There is a vestigial, instinctive, horror of Catholicism that is fairly common, but usually it is beneath the surface. There is a growing good will of the "some of my best friends are Catholic" sort. It is impossible to estimate how much of an anti-Catholic conflagration could be started in a crisis.

These, then, are the main reservoirs of Protestant strength. They do not seem strong enough to affect a resurgence from within. It seems as though Protestantism is losing more ground than it gains. There remains to be considered whether or not its life may be prolonged artificially from outside, notably through the support of some strong political force.

---

2 The so-called "Branch Theory" of ecclesiology as formulated first by High Anglicans in the 19th century.—*Ed.*
3 Garfield Bromley Oxnam (1891–1963) was a social reformer and bishop of the Methodist Episcopal Church.—*Ed.*
4 Myron C. Taylor (1874–1959), an American industrialist who served as the US ambassador to the Holy See from 1940 to 1950. His appointment was condemned by many Protestants as incompatible with the American idea of separation of Church and State.—*Ed.*

PROTESTANTISM AND COMMUNISM

Nothing is too absurd for it to happen in this age of drastic changes and strange bedfellows. It might conceivably suit Communism to affect a resurgence of American Protestantism for its own ends; and it might be able to do so. The middle minds of liberal Protestants would be opening enough.

We do not say that this will happen, nor even that it has begun; but only that it might happen, and that there are some evidences of a beginning here and there. The strongest indication of the possibility, however, lies in the general situation of the world today. This is a time of growing absolutism in which there are two strong forces and a handful of weakfish factors. Protestantism is weak as compared both with Catholicism, which stands like a rock in her 2,000 year old position; and as compared with Communism, which drives relentlessly from the opposite pole. It is weak not so much materially as in the sense of wishy-washy; weak in the sense of being diluted or fragmentary Christianity. How can it hold out in the face of these forces? If it stands by its original position of protest against Catholicism it may well find itself in the Communist camp.

What are the signs? There is the "Red Dean" in England. There is the conspicuous presence of the Russian Orthodox clergy at solemn Episcopal functions; a clergy under strong pressure from the Kremlin. There is the protest against Myron C. Taylor, which is at least useful to Russia. There is the militant immorality of the liberals with their birth control, euthanasia and abortion. There is the tendency of the clergy of affiliated Protestant churches to busy themselves with political and international issues, in which they could easily be duped.

The hysterical anti-Catholic element in Protestantism hugs the Communist party line, but whether inadvertently or advisedly is not clear. Not only is this true of *The Protestant*, which is not quite a reputable magazine, but also, for instance of *The Churchman*, an Episcopalian magazine which is lay and not official, but in sufficiently good standing to give a dinner for Eisenhower at the Waldorf-Astoria. The Churchman has lately run a series on the Stepinac trials, written by the Yugoslav Ambassador. It took a pro-Wallace stand on the cabinet upheaval. It devotes much of each issue to tirades against the Catholic Church.

WILL PROTESTANTISM RE-UNITE WITH ROME?

Anything can happen today, but reunion seems very unlikely. We pray for it in the Church Unity Octave and this is probably the most effective single measure that can be taken. What separates Catholics and Protestants now is almost a matter of temperament; something which can be healed by prayer, or by common suffering, by mutual love or by explanation (rather than debate). Certainly individual Protestants are much nearer, and much more receptive to Catholicism than in all the long past history of bitter schism.

However, in point of fact, those who are finding their way home to the Catholic Church are post-Protestants who have gone through a period of doubt and suffering. The trend is not so much from Protestantism direct. The one exception is in the case of the High Anglican Church where there have been group conversions, and might conceivably be a mass conversion.

There is something besides ignorance which keeps Protestants from becoming Catholics. There are now quite a number of educated Protestants who have a fairly accurate idea of Catholicism (except that they do not see the Church as Christ), and view it with repugnance. Union Theological Seminary in New York (Liberal Protestant) has an excellent collection of Catholic books for instance. But Protestants can read Max Weber's indictment of the concept of a "worldly calling" without considering it unflattering. They can look on the civilization which they have largely made, and like it. They are still scandalized by dirt (more than sin), and poverty, and beggars, and Latin Americans who had rather sit in the sun than work on an assembly line, and nuns who "waste" their lives in contemplation, and wives who have more babies than they can afford, and bingo which looks so much like gambling and so little like banking. Worst of all, they continue to glorify the search for truth at the expense of finding the truth, so shutting themselves off from the joy, and humility, of certainty.

Perhaps this explains why our world has come to such a pass. The worst punishment men can suffer is that which they bring upon themselves by preferring their own to God's way.

5
I'd Rather Be a Menial in the House of the Lord, than to Dwell Among Princes

MARCH 1947

THE PSALMIST HAS EXPRESSED EXACTLY THE LONGING of today's idealist, caught up in huge commercial financial and military enterprises, when all he wants is to spend himself, however humbly, for a great cause. He'd rather be a buck private in a conflict which really is a crusade than be a major general in a trade war. He'd rather tend the fires of the modest concern making good soap to supply local human needs than to be on the board of directors of the international soap cartel. He'd rather sweep the floors of the Vatican than be managing director of Radio City. It isn't that serving God necessarily involves waste of talents or gross self-abnegation (indeed, usually quite the reverse), but just that serving God is so much more delightful than serving Mammon that all other factors involved pale by consequence. It's just that the *end* of our work is primary. It overshadows the means and conditions and remuneration. Its dignity is our dignity; its goodness is our goodness. It measures our stature.

WHAT CONSTITUTES A GOOD ACT

The morality of an act is determined chiefly by its end. This theological principle offers the clue to the understanding of the moral problems of our time relating to our life work. It can be applied to the military, to show that the lack of great purpose in our modern wars has robbed soldiers of heroic stature. It can be applied to politics to show that statesmen have lost dignity and honor because expediency has replaced the ideal of the common good. We shall apply it to economics. We shall show, presently that our economic system as a whole is directed toward money-making and not God as a final end, and that this fact degrades all the millions of us who are caught up in the system.

An act can be considered in respect of its natural species or in respect of its moral species. When considered in respect of its natural species, morality is accidental (so the act of typewriting a page is not a moral act as such. Morality comes in accidentally, as in what it is that is being typed on the page or — to a much lesser extent — as to how accurate the typing is). Conversely, when an act is considered in respect of its moral species, as in spreading truth or untruth, the natural species (whether the matter is typed, mimeographed or printed) is accidental. Now it is not an arbitrary matter whether you regard things according to their natural or their moral species. We are obliged to regard them according to their moral species, because we are human beings and, as such, moral creatures. There are no acts in the concrete which are not morally good or bad. There are no typists typing blank pages. They all have something on them, and that something determines, largely, the morality of the act of typing.

From this distinction between natural and moral species it is immediately clear that in our society most of us have our eyes riveted on the natural species of acts. We trained to be typists, accountants, file clerks, salesmen. The morality of our future work will be determined chiefly by what we type, what we account for, what we file, what we sell. It is understood by us that this crucial matter of WHAT is to be determined, not by us, but by our future employers. If the WHAT is evil, untrue, trivial or unworthy, our work is going to be bad, or stupid, or both,[1] while an increase of accuracy, punctuality, efficiency and speed on our part can only aggravate the trouble.

There are other factors involved in the determination of the morality of acts. Almost as important as the end is the question of the means. A good end does not justify bad means. But if the end is bad no means whatsoever can justify it. Often enough, but not always, bad means are the result of a bad end (as when a mechanic fixes your car poorly because he wants the money you will have to pay for periodic repairs).

---

1   It is possible to separate our ends from the ends our employers have in mind, providing we cooperate only materially, and that the operation we perform is not bad in itself, and there is a good and serious reason for our staying in that job. So a man in a menial capacity can work *in order to support his family*, or a Jocist in like capacity can work *to do an apostolate among his fellow-workers*. However, you cannot in practice nowadays will as your end to provide people with shoes if you are in the employ of a shoe manufacturer who wills as his end to make money, because you will find all the messages are geared to his end and you will be impotent to carry out the implications of your desire. Furthermore, wherever there is material cooperation you cannot sanctify yourself wholeheartedly through your work, but almost in spite of it.

The *means* of modern work have been thoroughly explored by such keen thinkers as Eric Gill and Dorothy Day. The monotony, frustration, waste, regimentation, and impersonality of modern work have been brought to light. Many people say that industrial capitalism must be condemned on this score, because the nature of the work destroys human personality. No doubt these grounds are sufficient to condemn it, but it would be more sound to shift the attack to the end, maintaining that the system must be abandoned (progressively, of course, to prevent worse suffering) because it is not ordered to God. By striving to order the ends of the economic system to God instead of to Mammon, the nature of the work itself will be transformed. On the contrary, concentration on the means will not rectify the end and consequently will not make what is bad good. Craft production (which would transform the means) can be ordained to Mammon too; indeed (because it is a better way of making things) the few crafts that are left are just this under our present economy. Only the rich have hand-made shoes, custom-made dresses and suits, hand-hammered silverware and Rolls-Royces.

Much less important than the *means* is the matter of the *conditions* of work: such things as nice washrooms. Conditions have an accidental relationship to the problem of the morality of acts and therefore of our work. They seriously affect the morality only if they are very bad. Really serious overcrowding of offices, very dirty washrooms and exceedingly long hours can make otherwise good jobs bad. But that we can tolerate a lot of deficiency in regard to conditions is obvious from the sacrifices we make for things we really want. We gather in crowds for Mass, dispense entirely with washrooms on camping vacations, and the whole family works eighteen hours a day to run a small Italian grocery store; all good things. What is happening today is that *magnificent conditions* are being offered as a camouflage for the indignity, the immorality, and the monotony of our work. The more regimented office and factory work is, the more magnificent the washrooms; the more meaningless the work, the more necessary it is to dangle the leisure state in front of us; the less a stenographer has to use her head, the more gadgets she will find on her typewriter. What we need is not a three-hour day of meaninglessness, followed by cocktails and culture, but an eighteen-hour day building a new world founded in Christ. We are spoiling for a great release of energy, not for idle corruption under the southern sun.

The *remuneration* also has a sort of accidental relationship to work (actually it is almost irrelevant, but this is too big a subject to discuss here), and becomes important only through gross abuse. We could be handsomely paid and still be slaves, as is evident now that many industries and businesses do pay handsomely. Through disregard of the entirety of what the Holy Fathers said in their encyclicals, and through uncritical admiration of secular trade unions, we have failed to notice that we neglected to affect the peaceful revolution the popes had in mind. It was their idea that men were to band together to get some breathing space, some little leisure and some excess cash *eventually to buy productive property and escape from the system.* Where workmen have obtained the leisure and the cash they have settled down to an ever-increasing standard of living. What they needed also, and did not get, was a spiritual revolution. They were formally caught up helplessly in a system ordered to Mammon. Now they are themselves ordered to Mammon.

THE END JUSTIFIES THE MEANNESS

Let us make it quite clear. The industrial and financial capitalistic system of which we are almost all a part has concentrated our whole economy into one highly intricate and inter-dependent whole, ordered to Mammon. Mammon is just another word for money. Money is the final end, the ultimate criterion, the measure of everything.

At the center of the system are the banks. We like to think that banks are primarily places for the safe-keeping of money. It would be more accurate to think of them as establishments for making loans at interest. Because these loans are not necessarily, or even primarily productive loans, it would also be quite accurate to call bankers "usurers,"[2] although it would make them much less acceptable socially.

Just off-center is the stock exchange, which likes to pose as a beneficent organization which provides the capital to launch worthwhile industrial enterprises. Like the banks, the stock exchange is mixed up with usury, but not always, and there are also other accounts against

---

[2] St. Thomas' and Aristotle's definition of usury is any interest at all taken on an unproductive loan (one which does not bring about an increase of natural wealth) and its condemnation is rooted in the true nature of money, that it does not fructify. If usury is permitted, by a normal process the wealth of a society will accumulate in the hands of the usurer. This accounts for the enormous power of the banks.

it. It increasingly resembles a large-scale gambling establishment, as one broker in New York recently was so obtuse as to say quite flatly. An increasing number of "investors" behave like people playing the numbers racket. These facts are discreditable, but perhaps not as discreditable as the highly respected conduct of the "conservative" brokers who have practically eliminated the risk of investment (risk is inherent in a productive loan). To have come through a general depression without financial loss (as they often boast of doing) is like coming fatted through famine.

Manufacturing (this is by and large) is a matter of concentrating machines and machine workers under the control of a certain organization for the end of enriching the owners thereof. Now this is important: the thing that is produced (let it be shoes or sheets or sleds) is, in our system, the *by-product* of manufacturing. The *end* is profit. It should be the other way around. A man should be a producer of sheets for the human need of sheets, and his living be incidental, be in the nature of a reward for, this production. It is because money is the last end that we have large factories and concentration of Industry. Take shoes, for instance. The machinery used to make shoes (all rented, incidentally, from a monopoly company) is rather simple, and needs only a few men. A shoe factory contains over and over again the same unit, whereas each unit could be better separately owned and decentralized. The only reason for duplication is so that *one* man or *one* group of men can grow fat on very many men's labor.

The money goal also accounts for this frequent phenomenon: that a given company makes highly diverse products. If the Dromedary Company only furnished us with dates we might have some romantic notion that they were date men, devoted for generations to the skillful cultivation and careful transportation of this exotic food. But when they also sell us gingerbread we begin to suspect that they are trafficking in anything that is profitable. We cannot avoid this accusation in a case of companies like General Foods. Indeed, it is taken for granted and considered honorable. The thing is that when you take your eye off the product itself (which really could hold your interest) you think in terms of mechanization and organization; and once you have an organization and all sorts of equipment and trained salesman and reduced advertising rates and accumulating capital, you might as well branch out. So R. H. Macy, the most over-swollen of department stores, sells cows and cars and airplanes now, although it started out to sell dry goods, and there is no real reason, on our present principles, why it should not take over all the retail distribution of goods in the United States and even in the world. There is no natural limit to the desire to make money.

The National Association of Manufacturers would not exist in a rational, Christian society. It is composed of a group of factory owners whose aim is to make money by the use of machines and the labor of other men. They have a common problem because they have a common interest: money-making. In a rational, vocational, functional society not order to profit, but to the common good, and ultimately to God, you would have associations of cobblers, of linen weavers, of watchmakers and winemakers. These groups would readily have common problems and not just a common greed.

Advertising is not an embellishment of our system, it is an integral part of it, a naturally monstrous growth on the parent stem. The advertising profession began within living memory. It started at a time when men's normal needs (that is, the needs of men who could pay to have them filled — nobody cares about the needs of poor or destitute men) were largely satisfied, and its function was (and is) to create new needs for the enrichment of merchants and manufacturers.

Radio is an interesting example of Capitalism's unselfish interest in the advancement of scientific discovery. When it first came to light that men could transmit sound by radio waves nobody was interested, because it did not seem to be an invention from which profit could be derived. Only after radio's advertising potentialities came into view did men's interest quicken. It would be edifying to know how many useful inventions have been suppressed, how many patents bought up in order to ensure their *disuse*, in an economy which pretends to foster science.

Financial Capitalism has made money out of money (more accurately, out of credit). Industrial Capitalism has made money out of our needs, real and artificial. But our system went further. With truly remarkable ingenuity we have devised ways of profiting by men's deaths and misfortunes. Insurance is the prime example, with life insurance especially interesting. It should be seen as an inverse work of mercy. How can a life insurance company claim to exist in the interests of widows and children (its clients) while foreclosing mortgages on thousands of other widows and children (as was done during the depression)! How can it claim to be solicitous on behalf of those who die prematurely when the very people to whom insurance is denied are those who seem likely to die prematurely? The natural Christian instinct in the matter would have been to form a society, rooted in charity, to take care of the most needy. Were charity fluid in society it would not be necessary for everyone to insure against every eventuality of God's Providence.

Hospitalization plans follow along the same charity-less pattern, the same mercenary ideal cloaked in beneficence. They are non-profit organizations which exist that hospitals may get their bills paid—in advance. As in insurance, the system works by getting the healthy to pay the bills of the sick; not as charity (which would be meritorious) but as self-interest (in which there is no virtue, unless worldly prudence is a virtue). It is interesting to trace the course of these schemes. As in life insurance, they avoid taking on those who are in imminent need of their services. Usually they start on a group basis, taking a given number of people from a certain office where average health can be presumed. However, there is a renewal privilege clause on an individual basis. What happened was that the unhealthy renewed the insurance, the healthy often let it lapse (and reasonably enough, for hospitalization should be a very rare occurrence in a man's life). So the rates went up. What is interesting to note is that this and other things are calculated to destroy the charity of the one outstandingly Christian institution left amongst us, the hospital.

Lastly, in this brief survey, the whole publishing field bears sad testimony to the ordering of society to Mammon. Within comparatively recent memory nearly all our magazine and book Publications have turned from editorial criteria (worn thin to be sure, from loss of respect for objective truth) to financial criteria and standards. Now writers write for money and editors buy what will sell, and it is only occasionally that this turns out to be something true and useful.

THE PRESENT SITUATION

Capitalism is not in its youth but in its senescence. One consequence of this is that we cannot presume much discrepancy to exist between the Capitalistic system and those involved in it. The greed which characterized the leaders of early Capitalism is now universal and respectable. Americans by the millions take it for granted that all other considerations defer to the profit motive, that everything is to be measured in money. Furthermore, our educational system has been diverted from the pursuit of truth to the preparation for money-making. This is even true (one is sometimes tempted to say especially true) of Catholic schools. That is a chief reason why the Church is frustrated in Her proper work of today, the making over of the temporal order. Catholic colleges are not pouring our learned Sir Galahads; they are belching forth aspiring business men and career girls, with a side course of apologetics. It is almost hopeless to look among them for men and women to lead us out of the money markets. Saddest of all is the spectacle of nuns who have dedicated their lives to the service of God, founding and staffing shiny new business schools with accelerated courses, so they can pop innocent, fresh young Catholic girls into the steel catacombs of insurance companies and banks. Surely they know not what they do. There is a whole world to be made over, and we keep providing grist for the Capitalist mill.

THE PRIMACY OF THE SPIRITUAL

Anyhow, what matters it now if the system *is* finished. So are we. We are all ordered to Mammon too. Therefore it first behooves us to reorient our own selves. *Nothing* can be made better now without better people. An increase in holiness will not of itself rectify things, but it is the prerequisite. By an increase in holiness we mean a turning again to God as the end, and not a continuation of worldly ends accompanied by an increase in devotional piety. If God is to be preferred above all things *then* we will break the chains that bind us to the ever-increasing standard of living, to our $300 radios, our sensitivity to the pulse of fashion, our cult of pleasure, our lust after new automobiles and our worship of glamour and pretension. This will be the sign of a spiritual revival in our time, a turning to asceticism and penance. It is our *only* hope, and there is no real sign of its beginning anywhere. One reason may be because we entertain false hopes of saving ourselves otherwise.

Within a materialistic framework, what could we possibly hype to achieve? The trade unions are excellent examples of the failure of reform where it remains within the material order. After all the effort and sacrifice they expended against cupidity, they have arrived in a like state. It is doubtful if their material condition has permanently improved, considering the change in the value of money, the frequent incidence of strikes, and the possibility of a new depression. They have substituted collective insecurity for individual insecurity. Furthermore, although we like to pretend otherwise, it is doubtful if the spiritual condition of the workman has improved either. It is better to be ground down by greed than to be greedy. The labor unions might have been the vehicle of our economic salvation. They have failed for not having been godly.

Or, take another example: socialism. Socialism is what Capitalism turns into, left to itself. It is only more of the same thing; just as materialistic, but even more concentrated, even more regimented, even more dull, and hopeless. It is just another palliative in the material order.

In this vale of tears good does not ordinarily grow out of evil, unless it is God who draws it out. Let all Christians beware of falling for schemes by which indifference is supposed to work itself out into good. They say, for instance, that the advent of electrical power (which is adapted to small unit use) will more or less automatically decentralize industry, allow us to finally live in the country and make things locally. But we lived in the country and made things locally to begin with. We only centralized, and urbanized, and industrialized, and mechanized and materialized, out of love of money. The only thing that can save us is to despise money.

If anyone doubts that it is cupidity which perpetuates our system, let him imagine the mortal effect which would result from a change of heart. A wave of penance and mortification would ruin advertising. But advertising is integral to the system, and production would largely collapse if it failed. Again, widespread dependence on God's Providence, or practice of fraternal charity would ruin insurance companies, and considering that their financial entanglements are colossal, there is no doubt but that repercussions would be heard throughout the land. How terrible, you say? No, that would not be terrible. What is terrible is that we have an economy which could not stand up under the genuine practice of Christianity. A penitential movement so widespread as to affect these collapses suddenly is so unlikely, and would be so wonderful, so pleasing to God, that we wouldn't have to worry about laws of economics during the interim period of adjustment. We might be fed manna, who knows?

However, reform, if reform there is to be, is more likely to be gradual. There are beginnings everywhere, but to our mind the movements appear to bog down because they do not see their temporal goals clearly enough in the light of their final end. Catholic Action is committed to restoring all things in Christ but many engaged in it seem not yet to have realized how radical a restoration is necessary in the economic order.

THE NEW ORDER

If God is the final end, what are the proximate ends which must be considered? The proper goal of economics as a whole is *the prosperity of all the people.* Clearly Capitalism sharply violates this principle by enriching some at the expense of others. Hence it comes about that men will produce luxuries, which can be made profitable through advertising, while millions are starving for lack of enough to eat. In reorienting the economic order we must first, therefore lend our energy to a vital project rather than aspiring to get in on a new field on the ground floor. One of the most naturally gifted young Catholic men we know is planning to establish a helicopter service, and he wants to apply all the papal principles to his relations with his employees. He would do better to apply Catholic principles to his choice of occupation. There is, as yet, no crying demand for helicopters. We seem to have heard that there *is* for housing, for statesmen of integrity, for someone to facilitate the return of industrial workers to organic farming. You cannot justify going into the sachet business where there are not enough people growing potatoes. You ought not to take up straightening of teeth when there is no one to fill cavities. Catholics cannot justifiably gravitate toward the sidelines where there is a major battle for a new world to be fought.

An appalling number of us are doing nothing really useful. We are transporting back and forth across the country, goods which would be better made locally. We are filing minutiae, or adding up figures which will be cleverly misrepresented on the annual statement. We are retouching photographs of $8.98 dresses, counting the number of women who pass a corner in tan stockings, indexing foolish books, recording batting averages and making copies in triplicate of inter-office memoranda.

So for many of us, the problem is not how to Christianize the work we are in, but how to get enough courage to think our way out of our jobs. It isn't easy to reason the ground out from under you, especially if you have put in several years of graduate work and have professional standing. That is why an almost heroic sanctity is needed, and a great trust in God's Providence.

PARTICULAR ENDS

All legitimate economic projects have distinctive proximate ends from which a whole set of principles of operation can be derived. This is the field in which Catholics should make detailed studies, especially Catholic Action groups. It is complex and technical to make these studies, but it is not difficult or vague; the principles all fall in line once you get started. Courage is needed, and heroic objectivity. It is not usually a question of minor repairs. Here we will give only a brief indication of the framework of such inquiries. They cannot be made exhaustively anyhow except by the people actively engaged in the field. *The Professions* have as their proximate ends the works of justice and mercy. While most of them are corrupt and deteriorated at the moment, the Christian framework is still visible.

Production of basic human necessities is where the drastic change is necessary, because here is the heart of industrialism. In this category we include the making of shoes, dresses, sheets, houses and other necessities. The general criterion is the *right making of things.* The product has become a by-product; let it become the end. Clothes rightly made are custom-made and not subject to fluctuation of fashion, nor shoddily made. Things rightly made are made to last, to fit, to nourish, to be suitable, to be beautiful, etc. If any inquiry such as this is pursued, it will likely turn out that most necessary things are better eventually made by craft-type production, combined with refinements made possible by the increase of scientific knowledge. It is very hard to make things by craft skill in an economy ordered to large-scale manufacturing, just as it is very difficult to serve as a small shop-owner in an era of mammoth department stores; but if giant department stores are economic monstrosities, then we must try to start a movement in the other direction. It will gain momentum as it goes along. It is a question as to whether things are done according to God or not. If they are not, as now, we just cannot decide to put up with them; morality is involved. We have got to order our ends toward God somehow. If it takes ingenuity, then we have to become ingenious. If it involves hardship, then we must brace ourselves for hardships; if it needs mass movements, then we must have mass movements.

People are disheartened when they begin to suspect that we have to change the whole manner of making things. Actually, the fact that most things are better made in comparatively small units will probably be our salvation. It is true that it is better to have shoddy shoes machine-made, than to go barefoot. But if we stimulate young men who wish to be cobblers to drop out of industrialism and start supplying local needs on small scale, then when the shoe factories collapse (as they will) we shall still be shod. The whole idea is to build up, with small beginnings everywhere, an economy which can take over when industrialization collapses. As Christians who understand what is going on we have a duty to build for the future. There are plenty of others who will perpetuate the present system as long as we need it. The Jocist idea of cooperating materially in Capitalistic enterprise, in order to save souls by a personal apostolate there, is quite another matter. There are two sides to the apostolate; the spiritual leavening, and the reordering of the institutions of society to God. Some people are called more to one than to the other. Let leaders infiltrate into the factories by all means; but let them also send out a stream of rejuvenated people to make new beginnings.

Transportation Units such as automobiles and airplanes are not strictly basic human needs, so whereas they should be well made, it is legitimate to work toward making few of them if that seems to be the common good. They are not good in themselves (except materially) but according to the use to which they are put. Planes have so far overwhelmingly served the use of war and commercial exploitation; whereas automobiles have made it possible for men to live far from their places of work and recreation, and have also served good uses. It is true that these things, and telephones, typewriters and the rest, are necessary under our present economy, and especially in view of international unrest. The chances are that an ordered society would make only moderate use of them and that it might be more practical to make them then in semi-skilled fashion. It would be worth looking into whether the Rolls-Royce might not be a more economical vehicle in the long run than the Ford.

Catholics should realize that they are perfectly entitled to use automobiles, airplanes, typewriters, power presses and all the rest of things which are materially good, even if they should be plotting to do away with them eventually. St. Augustine could not exonerate Rome from the evil involved in her conquests. Yet God used a united, peaceful Roman Empire in which to become Incarnate, the Roman highways on which to spread the Gospel; and Rome itself as Peter's See. The boycott idea must be of non-Catholic origin, because it can rarely be used in a healthy way. We are not meant so much to withdraw from society as to walk unscathed in the midst of evil. This does not mean that we should perpetuate, or even prop up disordered things which can be put to good use. No matter what happens, God is not frustrated. And it is our duty to promote what is good with all our strength.

Agriculture is the field in which the manner of operation is most clearly indicated by God's natural laws. The present mechanized commercial farming will have us all starving if it continues much longer. The key to proper farming is that it should be *organic,* operating in regard to the balance and rhythm of nature. It will be difficult to reorientate farming, but not because it is impossible to find out the rules. We need to apply the real rules, and we need many more farmers.

* * *

The need of more people on the land is just one of the many indications of the fact that most of us cannot begin to restore society where we are, but must first find our proper places in it. A machine-worker in a shoe factory is not necessarily a frustrated cobbler; he might be meant by God to be a farmer or a newspaper editor.

So in a way the first problem is to straighten out our own ends. The beginning is a divine discontent: "I'd rather be a menial in the house of the Lord, than to dwell among princes."

6

Man's Providence

APRIL 1947

A RECENTLY PUBLISHED BOOK ON THE METROPOLITAN Life Insurance Company[1] provides an excellent opportunity to examine in detail the insurance phenomenon.

As insurance is one of the institutions which industrial capitalism indirectly brought into being it needs viewing in the floodlight of Christian teaching. When men strayed off the Christian center after the Reformation, things didn't work so well. They declined to retrace their steps. Instead they invented new, makeshift arrangements to cover up their errors. Eventually the makeshift arrangements occasioned new disorders. This is the familiar pattern of our unrepentant society. Insurance is one of the makeshift arrangements. Let us examine it. The Metropolitan is a splendid specimen; not because it is a bad company, but because it is such a good company. We are not looking for accidental chicanery, but for structural defects.

In our society Big Business is playing Santa Claus, Psychiatry is playing Priest, but Insurance is playing God.

THE MET

The Metropolitan Life is the largest insurance company in the world. It represents the largest concentration of private money (over 7 ½ billion dollars) in the world. Hence its omnipotence.

It began business along with other pioneer life insurance companies in the middle of the last century, as a frankly commercial enterprise (which compares well with some other companies which were swindles, and which met an early demise). That life insurance caught on at all was undoubtedly due to the fact that industrial capitalism had so far separated men from small ownership and broken down their sense of community, that they turned with relief to this new offer of security.

What accounted for Metropolitan's rather sensational rise to first place in the insurance business? Even highly imperfect things like

---

[1] *The Metropolitan Life, a Study in Business Growth*, by Marquis James, Viking Press

unhappy marriages flourish with the practice of virtue. So it was with Metropolitan. An institution in itself unfortunate (as we shall see) rose to its present position of esteem and prosperity not by shrewd business practice so much as by a certain integrity and benevolence it exercised. First of all it issued industrial insurance in tiny policies to the dispossessed multitudes of industrial wage slaves. Although its motives for inaugurating industrial insurance were mixed, at least the company was visiting the poor with a sort of compassion, instead of vying with other companies for the privilege of "protecting" the rich. It prospered. From 1919 to 1929 Metropolitan had as president a man named Haley Fiske, who was a sort of humanitarian saint. He was also a gifted insurance man (in the trade use of the term), but he appears to have acted as often *first* to seek the Kingdom of Heaven and its justice, as he saw it (a compassionate, but not a blinding vision), as from the principles of expediency. Other presidents and high officials, though of lesser stature than Haley Fiske, exhibited the characteristics of men seriously devoted to the welfare of society in preference to their own selfish interests. In several major investigations the outstanding integrity of the company was brought to light. From the financial point of view (not the Christian now, but according to the best capitalist ethics), the Metropolitan has not only been phenomenally sound and prudent, but also has shown brilliant initiative. Its handling of farm mortgages during and after the depression, and its vast real estate projects of recent years, are notable examples of financial acumen. More about them anon.

What then can be said against a company so obviously admirable? Really nothing derogatory can be said by anyone who accepts the fundamental presuppositions of the society in which this institution grew. Even the TNEC Inquiry of the Franklin Roosevelt administration (with it socialist tendencies) couldn't make an indictment. They said the Metropolitan was too big (as it is), but as they only had it up their sleeves to make it yet larger, their criticism fell a little flat. They too were materialists, secularists, humanitarians, and so were wasting their time. It is only from the Christian Center, the Catholic Church, that the Metropolitan really shows itself for the curious and abnormal growth that it is.

INSURANCE SUBSTITUTES FOR CHARITY

All insurance is simply this, in its essence: it is a system of getting the fortunate to contribute to the welfare of the unfortunate, but without charity. All insurance calculations are based on statistical averages. Of a given 1000 men 35 years old, 3 or 4 (or however many it is) will die this year. Of 1000 factory workers, 6 or 7 will hurt themselves at work. Let the living undertake the support of the widows of the dead; let the able-bodied pay the doctors' bills of the injured, through the intermediary services of the insurance company. Now as Christians we are bound to help each other anyhow, for the love of God.

There are three major differences between the one and the other method of distributing largesse.

The first is that it costs more to do it the insurance way because you have to pay all the insurance people for the red tape and investigation that is involved.

The second difference is that the insurance plan benefits only those who can pay dividends, whereas the Christian plan benefits especially those who cannot (and therefore need it most).

The third difference is that the Christian scheme of things encourages the flow of the virtue of charity, which is the oil of society, whereas the insurance plan tends to destroy charity. A man buys insurance for selfish reasons (vide the advertisements. How far would insurance get by advertising: "A man is run over. It might be *your neighbor*." Oh no. The ads read: "It might be *you*."), or at least for reasons of a love not extending beyond his own family, and this despite the fact that he does participate, by buying it, in a group plan by which his money is distributed to help others. Insurance is a way of effecting the material results of charity without charity, and therefore without merit in the sight of God. This situation was occasionally eased in the case of the Metropolitan, as we said. The system in itself cuts out person-to-person charity but the company itself exercised a certain charity when small policy holders were pressed by showing a leniency to which they were not bound by contract. The company is so set up that this could be done almost entirely at the will of one man at the top, but all of the thousands of agents and clerks participated a little in the merits that flowed from it. We see here very clearly the advantage of capitalism over socialism, as going not quite so far in the same direction. Capitalism allows the free exercise of virtue in one's work to only the top few, but socialism would allow it to no one. A Christian social order would make it generally possible. The Christian should not deplore the exercise of charity by the few who are able (and therefore withhold a genuine admiration for the Metropolitan officials), but rather work to make the practice of charity more generally possible.

There is a story attributed to the Baroness de Hueck. It describes the instinctive reaction of a solidly Christian, Russian (pre-Soviet) woman to life insurance. A young man of a certain village went to the city, where he became a life insurance salesman. Returning to the village he pressed his wares upon one of the native women. The first time he explained the workings of insurance to her she didn't understand what he was talking about. He tried again. This time she understood.

"You mean," she said, "that if I pay you a certain amount of money every month, that if my husband dies you will take care of me and my children?"

"Yes, that's it," he answered.

"But why," she said, "should I deprive my friends and relatives of the privilege?"

INSURANCE IMITATES GOD'S PROVIDENCE

To listen to insurance salesmen you would almost think that insurance would protect you against every eventuality of God's Providence. Death holds no terrors to a man adequately covered, while theft or fire can be positively a boon.

A Christian lives by faith, which means, for one thing, that he frankly faces his utter dependency on God. Of course he is utterly dependent on God whether he faces it or not, but few men can stand naked and dependent as did St. Francis. It used to be clear that God provided through nature and the weather. Industrialism blurred that fact. Man found himself in a precarious position, in which he was especially vulnerable to the solicitations of insurance agents. So it came about that God's Providence was to operate through a man-made, mechanical, system rather than organically through nature, and with that it came about that men shifted their faith in God's Providence to faith in men's providence through the regular payment of premiums.

Some day we shall learn why the Irish fell for this in droves. That they were poor and dispossessed is part of the reason, but hardly all. They developed a positive mania for insurance (and civil service jobs), to the point of indecency for Christians who have been assured that under certain circumstances all things will be added unto them.

THE OMNIPOTENCE OF INSURANCE

The omnipotence of insurance companies is something which, as the investigators pointed out, tends to snowball. It's worse than they thought, however. The key is usury.

Let us go back to the original simplification of insurance. We said that it was a matter of getting a group of people to share a risk which would prove fatal to only several of their number. The reader may have wondered about life insurance, which in the long run proves fatal to all of them. Life insurance represents the same principles as originally stated, with added complications. It still is based on group age statistics, but let us consider another aspect. Any one man making out life insurance, even though he live to be very old indeed, never pays the full amount which his heirs can claim. Where does the difference come from? It come from the compound interest on the investments of the insurance companies.

A man should risk losing his money in order to deserve getting interest on it. He should at the very least risk getting no returns in the way of dividends. Insurance investments (according to their own concerted efforts, and also to government regulations) are notoriously unrisky. Specifically they go in for bonds, preferred stocks and mortgages, all of which are usurious[2] according to Church teaching and the natural law. They are usurious because they entitle the investor to interest, whether or not business makes a profit. (Common stock, by contrast, pays dividends only when business warrants — in other words, it increases the investor's wealth only when there has actually been an increase in real wealth. At least this is the theory. There are other counts against common stock at the moment, and these might have contributed to Metropolitan's vigorous opposition to a recent proposal to rescind the existing prohibition against insurance companies' investment in common stock.)

This is what happens when people practice usury: bad times inevitably come, when interest is not deserved. Those who pay it have to scrape it up from their general wealth somewhere and eventually, if times are hard enough, all the debtor's wealth gravitates to the usurer. This is what happened to the Metropolitan's farm mortgages. When the farmers fell upon prolonged hard times in the thirties,

---

2   Usury is here used in the technical, not the popular sense. It does not mean charging exorbitant interest, but charging any interest at all on unproductive loans, and it is rooted in the truth that money does not fructify.

Metropolitan had vast mortgage holdings. As long as they could they adjusted policies and extended payment dates instead of foreclosing. Strictly from a Christian point of view they had no right to do either. They were exacting their pound of flesh and the longer they took interest (where there was not money to pay interest) the less kind, not the more kind (as some farmers pointed out) they were.

Well, in the end they did foreclose, and to such an extent that Metropolitan became the largest single owner of farm properties in the country. They then hired an executive with agricultural training, and invested large sums of money to recondition the farms (which had been exhausted partly in an effort to meet their own exactions). Eventually they sold the improved farms, often back to the original farmers whom they had kept on as tenants.

Note the gross injustice of the whole process according to true economics. Metropolitan would argue that it had a sacred trust, etc., but actually Metropolitan's policy holders (it is a mutual company) are not entitled to bleed farmers out of all their possessions on any account. Why are policy holders more sacred than land owners?

There are two interesting side-lights to this affair which serve to show that the best interests of the Metropolitan Life Insurance Company are not always synonymous, or even harmonious, with the common good. The stable kind of farming, the kind that would have saved the farmers, is subsistence farming or the growing of what one needs first, and then selling the surplus. Metropolitan knows this. Yet subsistence farming was not in fact encouraged at a time when the company, through its propaganda and local agents, in addition to its temporary ownership, could have done much to change the commercial nature of American farming. Was this because subsistence farming is no way to keep up mortgage payments?

The other interesting point is that Metropolitan was reluctant to have the mortgages finally paid off and to sell the farms. That a man should be independent and debt free is not a beautiful sight to a usurer.

With city mortgages the story was similar. Metropolitan almost had to take over the Empire State Building at one time, but eased its interest rate in order not to destroy the goose which was laying it golden eggs.

Of another evil, there is only the faintest hint. Yet who has not observed it? Life insurance has made it possible for almost everyone to have a $500 funeral, and in so doing has been accessory to changing the undertaking business from a reasonable facsimile of a work of mercy, to a racket.

THE FUTURE

Goodness knows what will happen to insurance. It ought progressively to cease to exist, but this is impossible to it (did it wish to, which it doesn't), as the payments which will fall due are to be paid in part our of new policy premiums. Indeed, the Metropolitan must not only stay large, but also (according to its president) continue to grow. When you set out to be Providence, you can't help seeing that it would be easier if you were also Omnipotence.

Were an atomic bomb to fall on New York that would probably finish the Metropolitan. Even if its own structure were to survive, the claims would be ruinous. You can provide for most contingencies, but you can't provide for universal disaster.

A less noisy sort of atomic bomb is inflation. Companies don't like to mention this, but they keep urging the general populace not to buy *things* but to *save* money and pay insurance premiums (while they, along with other shrewd financiers, invest heavily in real estate, which is the only bulwark against inflation). Severe inflation would certainly ruin insurance, and us too. Still it would be poetic justice of a sort—something like "those who live by the sword shall perish by the sword."

The third alternative is that the government take over insurance. This is not imminent at the moment (although they have already done so in part with social security). There is this to be said for the government's controlling insurance: the government would include the less good risks (like the Negroes, whom the Metropolitan has rejected with some vigor), if only because governments are allowed to operate at a deficit whereas insurance companies are not.

There is this to be said against the government: It isn't God either. It might be bigger and more omnipotent, but it is considerably less efficient than private companies. If the Metropolitan can't take care of us all and balance the budget, much less will the government be able to do so.

Can it be that the virtue of charity could have done the job economically? Can it be that the cost of red tape and executive brainpower represents *the precise uneconomic factor?* If so, then one way or another we have to return to the simple practice of personal charity.

7
Sins of Flesh and Commerce

MAY 1947

SOCIOLOGY IS THE WOULD-BE-SCIENCE OF EXPEDIENCY, and fittingly honored in an age which has abandoned morality for expediency. We no longer act according to objective moral principles, doing things because they are *good*; rather we do things because they seem to be *expedient*, even if that involves transgression of the moral law. Sociology purports to explain to college students what will be expedient. When expediency is carried into practice on a wide-spread, pre-meditated scale, it is called planning.

The irony of the situation is that the moral law indicates precisely what will be expedient, on the authority of One Person Who really knows, God. It is exactly insofar as we observe the moral law that things will turn out right. We can never calculate this exactly in advance because it depends largely on the grace of God and the free-will of men, and these are not humanly predictable factors. Sociology has to deny, in effect, that these factors exist, and then make its predictions in accordance with purely materialistic considerations. So sociology decides that education will improve with an appropriation of five billion dollars, and that criminals will soften up if the jails have better facilities, and that we shall have no more wars if we only practice birth control. The more we follow the principles of expediency, the worse mess we get into, materially and morally. Were it not that men's blindness increases in proportion to their folly, this would long since have become evident. To those who still have eyes to see, the true expediency of morality becomes increasingly evident. Even to the myopic it must be evident that the past performance of expediency leaves something to be desired. Another thing that becomes increasingly evident to the observant Christian is the unity of morality, the absolute impossibility of observing anything short of the totality of the moral law. Particularly obvious it is that the sins of the flesh cannot be separated from the sins of commerce. It is irrational to condemn Margaret Sanger and defer to the advertising profession.

One of the pre-occupations of sociology is the matter of population. It is also a pre-occupation of morality. The fruits of sociological probings are the expedient laws for the regulation of population, chiefly the law of the necessity of practicing contraception, and the law (gradually gaining acceptance) of the advisability of imposing euthanasia.

The moral law has lately been struggling along (firmly, but losing ground in practice) on one wheel. It has affirmed in a loud voice that we shall not practice contraception. It has been relatively silent in regard to the commercial sins which have been accessory to the crime of race suicide. It will be useful to show the profound relationship that exists between the sins of the flesh and the sins of commerce.

THE LAWS OF FERTILITY

Fertility is the measure of fecundity. It varies according to laws which are not wholly fathomable, at least at this point. Many a birth-controller is discovering that it is not really in our power mechanically to regulate the quantity of human beings who walk this earth, much less their quality. There are not a few unhappy modernists who have found that years of conscientious contraception have evidently been quite unnecessary, for they are sterile. Here are some of the real laws of fertility:

I. Under conditions of hardship nature will preserve the species at the expense of the individual.

This law is readily observable in plant life. It also applies to the human species. If you are growing carrots and there is a drought, the carrots will absorb the last moisture in the soil, using it *not* to become bigger and better carrots, but to go to seed, i.e. to preserve the species carrot.

So it is with human being. One obvious example is furnished by the pregnant woman and her child. If there is not enough calcium for the two of them, the fetus will get its full quota of calcium, and never mind the mother's teeth.

However, the law works much more generally than that. If undue hardship is put upon a people, they will have more children than they would otherwise have had. The classic example of this is the case of the Israelites whom the Egyptians hoped to exterminate by oppression. The worse the Egyptians treated them, the more they increased in numbers, as the Egyptians themselves observed and lamented. See the first chapter of Exodus for details. Incidentally, the sociologists and other modern law-givers might learn quite a few things from the Bible. For instance, the whole theory of "rhythm" is contained in the Book of Leviticus, whereas modern "scientists" had it completely backwards until recently. Needless to say, the concern of the Old Law was in the interests of fertility, rather than vice versa. The fact that the Jews observed this law, together with the recurring persecutions they have suffered, probably furnishes the natural explanation of the survival of that race.

But one need not go back to Egypt to observe the workings of the law that a hard-pressed people will have more children than usual. It was the commonly observed phenomenon of the industrial system that the poor were always having too many babies.

And from the law certain simple deductions are obvious. The first is that you don't have to press contraception on the poor; if you just give them more to eat (that is to say, if you just practice a little justice and charity) they will oblige by having fewer children anyhow. The next is that we and God ae not of one mind in the matter of species versus individual. After all, God it is Who made the laws of nature, Who arranged that the species should be preferred to the individual. Whenever we get a chance, we decree just the opposite. Most all family limitation schemes are based on solicitude for the well-being and comfort of those already here. Abortion, of course, is a gross imposition of our preference, even at the expense of committing murder. So also is the custom of choosing whether the mother or the child shall live in a case of difficult childbirth. No human being has the right to make the choice. Non-Catholic doctors do make it though, and customarily in favor of the mother. Were the choice put to a truly Christian mother, she would certainly decide otherwise.

II. The birth rate fluctuates with the death rate.

Increasingly enough, (and characteristically) the sociologists have this law backwards. They are always trying to show that if you fix up the birth rate (by contraception) the death rate will go down. This is the old story about it being better to have *one* healthy child than *five* unhealthy children who will die young. But children do not die of having too many brothers and sisters, they die of tuberculosis or diphtheria or something, which may come partly from being poor. The causal relationship is between poverty and death, not between large families and death, and the obvious thing to do is to treat the poverty.

However, the law does work the other way around. Changes in the death rate tend to be reflected in the birth rate. Taking the matter in the large, it appears that throughout nature the birth rates of species have adjusted to their chances of survival. That is why some species have abundant fertility (the conger eel lays fifteen million eggs a year) while others, whose chance of death are slight, reproduce slowly (the fulmar petrel lays one egg a year). It is because of this tendency to adjust that a balance in nature is obtained and the world is not over-run by two or three conquering species of animal or insect. It is devotedly to be hoped that the advent of D. D. T. and its possible irresponsible use will not, by too sudden changes, upset the balance nature has established.

Within limits the birth rate can adjust itself to changes in the death rate. When salmon are preyed upon heavily one year they return the next year fairly bursting with eggs. When human beings make wars, the carnage thereof seems to be followed by an increase in the birth rate which cannot be entirely attributed to the more loving nature of veterans.

Note that this law works in both directions. If there is an increase in the death rate, there is liable to be a corresponding increase in the birthrate (as shown, for instance, in the tremendous increase in the population of Ireland during the famine years. It is useful to note here how God uses our sins for His own purposes. This tremendous increase in population among the Irish forced them to migrate, and served to carry the Faith to many places).

On the other hand, if you bring the death rate down, the birth rate lowers of itself. There was a striking example of this in the Suez Canal area during the early years of this century. Owing to malarial conditions in the region surrounding the Canal there was a very high death rate. Officials hesitated to improve living conditions by a drainage project for fear that then the population, which also had a very high birth rate, would outstrip its food supply and end up in yet more suffering. Nevertheless, they did drain the area. The death rate dropped as anticipated, but to their surprise, the birth rate fell correspondingly *of its own accord.*

The moral of this law is that nothing but good will come of our pursuing a virtuous course in reducing death rates, as notably through modern medical advances, but that we should stop interfering artificially in the matter of births.

III. Fertility decreases with luxurious living.

It is because of the operation of this law that the rich tend to have fewer children than they would normally, and this even apart from contraception, which greatly aggravates the situation.

There seem to be two main causes. This first is purely physical. Luxury means soft living, food in excess, and food which makes for fat rather than sinew. Besides there is the important factor of a lessening of exercise on the part of the rich, which further adds to the softness and detracts from the fertility of the body.

The second factor is psychological. Life which is too easy is a breeding ground for neuroses, which mitigates against fertility quite often.

To take a calloused view of the situation, it appears that extravagance and riches ill become the human race, and so nature goes through cycles of sloughing off those who have become parasitical drains on society. Indeed, it is a well-observed fact that the "best families" are prone to decadence much more than the laboring classes who really don't have time. We are in a period now in which both the quantity and quality of our erstwhile leading families is suffering diminution, and we are still awaiting new leaders with sufficient vitality to lead and save us. Society does not suffer too much from the recurrent renewal of its vitality from below. But see what has happened in our own day. There seems to be no real reservoir of vitality left in America. Why? Because from the physical point of view (the important point of view is not physical but spiritual; however spiritual debility parallels the physical pretty well in this case) we are all "enjoying" luxurious living, and our vitality and fertility is correspondingly drained. For this we can thank the industrial-capitalist system which, as its admirers love to reiterate, has raised the general standard of living in industrial countries to a level unknown in history. We are now all privileged to live in crowded cities, sit hours in the movies, and days in office chairs, eat white bread, drink pasteurized milk and get jelly doughnuts from the bakery. We can all have neuroses too. Only a malcontent would remind us that there is not beauty anywhere, that we have no space and no fresh air, that our jobs are meaningless and dull, and that maybe there would have been more joy in a baby than in a radio. We know better. We have equality. Sterility is no longer the prerogative of the rich.

Sins of Flesh and Commerce

IV. Populations tend to stabilize within enclosed areas.

All the old birth-controllers' arguments were based on the theory that if you just went on having children the race would increase geometrically by leaps and bounds until very shortly there wouldn't be room for us all, much less food for us all. As a matter of fact, under relatively good conditions, and in a closed economy, the population tends to stabilize itself. This may have something to do with the fact that people living in closed economies do not eat exotic food, I don't know.

The outstanding example of this law is Japan, where the population remained just about stationary between the years 1723 and 1846. This was the period during which Japan shut her doors to all outside interference, especially from western civilization. There was no overcrowding during this time, and a good standard of living (not the American way of life, of course; we speak now of essentials, not luxuries) prevailed. There was an agrarian-craft economy. No birth-control was practiced. There were no major wars, no grievous natural catastrophes, no plagues. At the end of the period, as at the beginning, the population was about 27 million. After this period Japan rapidly became a "civilized" and then an industrial power. With industrialization the mass of people became poorer, and then the population soared. By 1934 it was, with her dependencies, 84 million. One has only to reflect that the underlying natural cause of the late war in the Far East was the over-population of Japan, to have another example of the marvelous benefits which flow from industrial capitalism.

V. God provides a natural spacing between babies in the period of lactation.

All the modern talk about baby spacing (it was up to four-year intervals a while ago, but appears to be coming down) neglects to consider the fact that nature normally provides an interval between children, and that that interval is the period of lactation (which with the period of pregnancy would usually make the children two years or so apart). This fact has been part of the folk wisdom of the race up until now. It has been variously used. Women who wished to avoid pregnancy have nursed their children scandalously long. Chinese women who have sometimes wished to speed up propagation have given their newborn out to wet nurses so that they themselves might become pregnant soon again.

The late Alexis Carrel set down this law categorically in the *Readers Digest* some years ago in an article about the advisability of nursing babies. However, there are probably many doctors who would deny that there is such a natural law, on the grounds that it no longer can be counted on to operate in regard to modern American women. As a matter of fact, deft inquiry among nurses, mothers and grandmothers usually results in a flat denial of the law by young nurses, assent among grandmothers, and a qualified statement from mothers of grown children to the effect that, "Oh yes, that used to work, but it doesn't anymore."

Someone ought to make a study as to why it doesn't work anymore. Such a study would be complicated by the fact that many women are physically unable to nurse their babies anyhow.

THE CONCATENATION OF SINS

As every liar knows, one lie leads to an ever-increasing number of other lies to cover up the first one. So it is with social expediency. You break the moral law once, and then you have to do it again and again and again and again. There is no end short of a return to the moral law. It is wise to keep this in mind, because the current evils of birth control and euthanasia and abortion are really the latest manifestations of a chain of sins in the service of expediency. It is not so much that anyone desires them of themselves, as that they are more or less inevitable, given the circumstances which occasion them. Let us examine the chain. It will take us back to England, where the industrial revolution began.

Be it noted, first of all, that the population of England and Wales remained almost stationary during the 14th to the 16th centuries, at a little less than 2 ½ million people. As far as we can determine, there was never an increase during that period of more than 3% per ten-year period. This was the Merrie England which we so love to represent on our Christmas cards and assiduously avoid imitating in our daily life (if it were still possible, which of course it isn't — the face of the earth has changed from a Sherwood Forest to the wasteland of industrialism.)

The chain of circumstances which started with the Reformation and culminated in the industrial revolution, profoundly changed England. There is no need to go in the well-known details here. First there was the confiscation of the monastic lands, which was followed in time by the enclosure laws and wholesale evictions. Meanwhile the widespread pauperization occasioned by the dissolution of the monasteries (it broke the whole framework of charity, and in addition set the religious in vagabondage) was dealt with first by inhuman laws against beggary and then by Poor Laws which were not any good either. Meanwhile small farms (through evictions) were consolidated into large farms, two or three families sufficing where formerly there had been several hundred, and arable land became pasture. Country people were forced into the city, where they lived wretchedly and where they became grist for the mills of industrialism, which was just then unfortunately beginning. One can scarcely read the account of the industrial beginnings in England (which have finally culminated in the evils which beset that unfortunate country today, not to mention the ills and ugliness which have spread to the far corners of the earth from it) without weeping. Still, it is the purpose of this paper not to lament but to note the effects on population. *The most notable effect of the industrial revolution was a tremendous increase in population.* There are some people so misled that they would like to make out that this shows how good the industrial revolution was.

Note these increases:

Prior to 1751	never more than 3% increase in population in any ten-year period.
1751–1761	6% increase
1761–1771	6% increase
1771–1781	6% increase
1781–1791	9% increase
1791–1801	11% increase
1801–1811	14% increase
1811–1821	18% increase

During the years between 1800 and 1820 there were famine conditions in England. After 1821 a vast emigration set in, so that 18% represents the peak increase percentage.

During the early period of industrialism children were welcomed because they were useful in the factories when they were as young as four years old. It is better to pass over this period swiftly.

In time industrialism began to regret the high birth rate. Technical improvements in machinery made child-labor unnecessary, as also a lot of adult labor. Periods of unemployment were setting in.

Over-production was at first compensated for by exploiting all the unindustrialized countries of the world, but as other countries became industrialized themselves, the consequences of over-production caused more and more misery on the home front.

It was at this period that a few advanced and far-seeing souls started to see the advantage of contraception. Basically the advocates of contraception have always argued in the same way: Here we have a situation which is inevitable and cannot be changed (why not?), and therefore we have to go on to show mercy (or protect our own financial interests) through birth control. It is one of the mysteries of iniquity that industrial capitalism has always been considered immutable. Legion are the immoralities which have been perpetuated to the chant of "industrial capitalism is here to stay."

The next stage of industrialism, which is the one we are still in, is the stage in which it was realized by the capitalists that the worker is also the consumer, and that he must buy the luxuries he makes, even if he has to go without the necessities to do so. Here is where advertising comes in, which now surrounds all of us, inciting our concupiscence in every direction. Now the worker is willing to practice birth control, because he has to cut down somewhere and the advertisements will not let him cut down on clothes, extravagant food, amusements or labor-saving devices. Besides, his wife is usually working to help keep up the new standard of life.

But if a man does not practice birth control, he is still in a rather bad way as regards propagating the race. First of all, there is the danger of sterility from luxurious living and neuroses. But besides that there is the fact that his wife will have children with increasing difficulty.

It has been shown that soft, luxurious, depleted modern foods make childbirth increasingly difficult, through nutritional deficiencies which narrow the pelvic girdle. The increased difficulty leads in turn to increased need for hospitalization, more expense and elaborate anesthesia, etc.

All the way along the line, from the dissolution of the monasteries (which marked the destruction of the Catholic Church in England and its moral authority), all the way along from the banishing of the priests to the turning out of the cottagers, to the crowding in the cities, to the poverty, the materialism, the introduction of contraception, all the way down to the Raleigh cigarette ads of our own glorious day, an increased sexual license has accompanied the process. The birth control people may not be in favor of high school delinquency, but they are certainly fostering it. So and so, who has a 40-million dollar factory may not personally like adultery, but he is certainly providing a breeding ground for it, if only because of the dullness and uncreativity of the jobs in his plant. Do advertisers regret that they have to break down our will power in order to make their pretentious livings? One has not heard it.

THE FUTURE

It is evident now that we are in the crescendo part of the development herein outlined. In the cities there is a rapid intensification of all the evils: overcrowding, adulteration, pretension, pornography, despair, luxury. There is no sign of repentance, no sign of a reversal of direction. Take, for instance, the persistent efforts of city people to prevent decentralization. Consider the curious circumstance under which the United Nations' Headquarters came to choose a site in the heart of New York City. It looked for a while as though the United Nations was going to settle in Philadelphia, but the Rockefellers stopped that at a cost to themselves of, as I remember, some eight million dollars. Now obviously peace can be deliberated as well in the City of Brotherly Love as in New York. Why is it worth eight million dollars to the Rockefellers to keep the United Nations in an already hopelessly congested area? Can it be to protect their real estate interests?

In the country the situation is comparable. Large holdings and commercial farming are the rule. This tends to depopulate the country and so lessen the yield per acre (although it increases, temporarily, the yield per farmer).

The birth rate has been falling in England since 1900, and is in a bad way here (although temporarily buoyed up by a post-war boom in babies). With a falling birth rate you get a preponderancy of old people, who must be supported by a decreasing number of young people. Hence, our preoccupation with social security. It would normally be quite a burden for the young to care for preponderantly large numbers of old. Who dares say that this does not present a temptation to the practice of euthanasia?

Even the Planned Parenthood Association is now concerned about the lack of fertility in its clients. It is expediency again, and not a return to morality. It will presently be expedient, especially if we get a dictator and are going to have another war, for the state to pay double for illegitimate children. By then we shall have committed just about all the sins it is possible for us to commit from having departed from the laws of objective morality.

THE REMEDY

The only remedy, of course, is to start immediate, strict observance of the *entire* moral law. Let those who marry have children as God sends them. It will comfort them to remember that God is not bound by the laws of a bad economic system, and that He will provide, somehow, extra (extra rooms and extra food) for the children He sends. It will take an heroic faith to act upon this principle, and a willingness to sacrifice a materialistic way of life. It is characteristic of our day that nothing less than an heroic faith will suffice. But there is no alternative, the mediocre will go under.

There will have to accompany this heroic trust in God's Providence, a general spiritual revolution against the materialism of our time. Let us preach the *un*importance of being well-dressed. Let it be bruited about that it is a sin to incite concupiscence, whether it be a lust for an all-electric kitchen, incited through the courtesy of the *Saturday Evening Post* and the advertising agencies; or whether it be smart pornography in fashionable night clubs. Let us somehow or other leave the cities, somehow or other get wholesome food again.

Let us forget about the American Way of Life, and start the Godly Way of Life, which will bring down graces upon us to rectify all the messes we have made of things.

8
The Thirst for Theology
JUNE 1947

WE LIVE IN AN INTELLECTUAL HODGE-PODGE, IN a society that can't see the woods for the trees, but that has corps of "experts" out in the forest studying the bark, watching the moss grow, and counting the leaves. Suppose you were to go to one of these experts, or even to the president of one of the colleges at which he was trained, and ask a simple question such as: "Tell me, on what principle do you decide which trees to cut down and which to allow to grow?" or "What are woods for, and who made them?" or "What is the significance of the fact (as you have determined after a life study) that oak trees thirty years old average 46,501 leaves a season as compared with 65,834 in elm trees? Suppose you were to ask these questions, and suppose you got in return nothing but puzzled looks. Would you not suppose you were in a nation of slightly crazed men?

What we need is not more detail, but some perspective; not yet more facts (as often as not erroneous ones), but some principles; we need some last ends, some first directives, some clear light, some *meaning*. We are thirsting, in a word, for theology. Theology is the science which will give us the last ends, the first principles, the meanings, the clarity and the directions which alone will make sense of the world and ourselves.

But theology is the one science which is generally withheld from us. This is due to the taint of liberalism, which has even affected Catholics. The liberal view is that it is not cricket to be told the answers and to go on from there, and that it is positively unmanly to have any certainty. It is all right to *look* for the final answers, only you must do so blindfolded, and *never, never* find them. So the liberal world goes groping about, while we Catholics often neglect to use the fullness of our revealed truth out of mistaken deference to those who cannot accept revelation because they cannot figure it out themselves. Instead of theology we have been feeding on the insufficient food of philosophy, apologetics and devotionalism.

THE INADEQUACY OF PHILOSOPHY

Both theology and philosophy deal with the last things; the former as we know them in the blinding light of revelation, the latter as we can partially and inadequately discern them through the exercise of our own reason. They are the same last things in either case and therefore there is no incompatibility between the two sciences. Moreover, each is a legitimate and necessary science. It is only when philosophy, which is the lesser of the two, is over-emphasized at the expense of (or exclusion of) theology that a disorder is created.

The philosopher is a man lost in the dense, dark forest jungles who, if he is sufficiently clever and his mind is not warped by intellectual pride, may conceivably deduce the existence of the sun from the life of the trees around him, although, of course, he would know very little about the sun. The theologian, on the other hand (be he erudite or a simple Christian versed in the catechism) is a man seated on the mountain overlooking the forest, who has only to open his eyes to know far more than the most clever philosopher can ever deduce.

Philosophy is useful as auxiliary to theology; it is in no way a substitute for theology. When we are thirsting for the fullness of truth it is painful to set back into an intellectual framework approximating that of the Greek, pre-Christian philosophers. Philosophy belongs to the natural order, while all our problems are in desperate need of supernatural light. Now that Christ has redeemed us it is impossible to rationalize all our problems as though there had been no Redemption. The more we try to do so, the more we come out with the wrong answers to our problems. Only so much can be deduced from the natural law, and among the things that cannot be deduced is the all-important fact of grace. Too much straining with the intellect in disregard of Faith, and you have a picture of the good life which includes the right to collective bargaining, to a living wage, good health, etc., etc., but which has no place for the folly of the Cross. We have no right to build a picture of life or of society confined to the natural law, to the philosophical level; to do so is, in effect, to postulate a this-worldly end for man. Such an approach completely misses the paradoxical nature of Christianity. If we had been able to figure out philosophically that we would have to die to ourselves in order to live, we would not have needed the light of Faith by which seeming contradictions such as this grow ever more luminous.

Naturalism is one of the great heresies of the day. The secular world is intent on bringing about the millennium within the natural sphere; we are always besought to lend help to schemes for replacing the *bad* natural with the *good* natural, but it is naturalism itself (not nature) which has to be replaced by a consideration of man's supernatural end, and the understanding and use of the supernatural gifts whereby it is to be obtained.

One frequently finds among Catholic college graduates this over-balance of philosophy. They will have spent a whole semester on the proofs for the existence of God (which was, in a sense, unnecessary for them, since they already believe in God by Faith), yet have no working knowledge at all of, say, God's Providence.

With the non-Catholic we tend to make the same error; to instruct him on his own natural level instead of introducing him to the fact of supernatural life. It is a rare non-Catholic who doesn't know that the Catholic Church forbids contraception (a not very inviting piece of knowledge from his point of view); but a surprising number, even of college graduates, have never even heard of the Blessed Sacrament.

THE OBSOLESCENCE OF APOLOGETICS

Apologetics, which is the science of explaining and defending the Faith, is in itself honorable, and has been very useful in its day. But it is now obsolescent. Nobody ever asks the questions to which apologetics is prepared to reply.

Apologetics characterizes a defensive church, and the Church is no longer defensive. The real enemies of the Church today are not muck-raking the Church's past, but are fabricating lies out of whole cloth. One is faced with the alternatives of ignoring them or denying them flatly. Meanwhile the majority of Americans are not so much enemies of as strangers to the Church.

Both Hitler and Stalin have developed to its highest point the art of the lie. So have their fellow-travelers in America. If you try to argue with them you will find yourself completely at a loss to establish a rational basis for discussion. Would you like to argue your interpretation of the facts of the case against their interpretation of the facts of the case? It is impossible, because you will not even be able to agree as to what are the facts of the case. There will be two sets of facts, the true set and theirs. This is what is happening with Russia in the U. N. and in the Big Four attempts at making a peace. You cannot argue with Russia about whether or not she ought to remove her troops from such and such a territory if she flatly denies having troops there.

The same sort of thing happens here, with people who are not necessarily Communist. Msgr. Sheen gave a talk on the godlessness of psychoanalysis. But now, it appears from indignant letters in the public press, that the psychoanalysts have been much maligned. Either they do not take after Freud, or else they and Freud both revere the human personality, are profoundly respectful of religion, etc., etc. You can't argue with them on that basis. And they will not argue with you on the basis of, say, setting forth their beliefs in regard to God, the human soul, or the meaning of happiness.

Our learned opponents are also indifferent to the law of contradiction. If you pointed out to them that they have contradicted themselves several times in the same conversation, they would only say, "What difference does that make?" With such men you do not argue.

Among the less learned you find, even where they have good will, that they are so ignorant and their minds are so warped by sentimentality, that here again the art of apologetics is wasted energy. Usually they just do not even ask the questions which the apologist is prepared to answer, and if they do, they do not mean it seriously. If someone says "You Catholics have bad popes," the best thing to do is to say, "Name three." Then, after they have failed to name even one, and mutter something about having heard about it somewhere, you can favor them with a comparison between our present Holy Father and all the statesmen of the western hemisphere rolled into one.

Mr. Sheed has often pointed out the futility of apologetics. You wear yourself out, as he says, proving that God exists, and then your audience walks away muttering, "so what." They do not even know what God means. In the darkness and despair of our godless society they have not even dreamed that there could be Someone Who loves them and cares one iota whether they die or live, whether they sin or behave themselves.

DEVOTIONALISM

It is a dangerous thing to substitute devotionalism for a sound understanding of theology. Devotionalism is here used to mean feverish attendance at novenas, plus an accumulation of pious external devotions, which is fed not with the solid food of doctrine but with exhortations on the emotional level. The more energy with which devotionalism is pursued, the more dangerous it becomes. At best it degenerates into a gross sentimentality, at worst into madness.

When devotionalism concentrates, as it so easily can, on the charismatic aspects of religion, it can easily degenerate into superstition. It is not unusual to find people seemingly pious, who can converse endlessly about this or that mysterious or miraculous happening, yet who are not conspicuously virtuous and who evidently are devoid of a real interior life.

THEOLOGY FOR THE LAITY

Since, then, there is such a general need for theology, what is the best way in which it can be supplied to the laity?

The important thing about theology for the laity is that they should not get a watered-down course in seminary theology, much less a full course in seminary theology. The laity are not supposed to be diminutive theologians. To suppose so would be an error analogous to that which would have pious laity become little monks and nuns in the world, adopting conventual practice in so far as possible. We are called to be saints, but the path to sanctity must be according to our states in life. We are all called to know God, but here again there are different approaches to the same Truth. To suppose otherwise is to feel that the clergy or religious are somehow more a part of the Church than are the laity. But we are all equally members of the same Body; some eyes, some ears, some hands.

The difference is one of function, and it is according to the difference of function between the clergy and the laity that theology should be differently learned by each.

The similarity between the clergy and the laity as regards theology is this, that it is the same truth in either case, and should in both cases, since it is truth about God, be auxiliary to one's sanctification. The difference between the two cases is that the clergy must learn theology also in order to teach it as such, whereas the laity learn it chiefly for practical application in their personal and daily lives. From this difference spring the chief characteristics of theology for the laity:

> 1. The laity will have what might be called the "psychological" approach to theology rather than approaching it from the internal order of the science itself. For the laity the *Summa Theologica* will be a reference book rather than a textbook. They will not start at the beginning of it, but

wherever they can find principles which apply to the problem which they are considering. The Benziger publishing house is going to publish an English edition of the *Summa* with an index which will give detailed references to theological problems such as come up in different professions. It ought to be very useful.

Since the laity's interest in theology will be pre-eminently practical, they will not be under the necessity of remembering it so much as of absorbing it. The layman does not, for instance, have to remember all the daughters of sloth or pride, but only such as interfere with his own sanctification. As a matter of fact, one can informally observe that the laity are much more vulnerable to pride and to sterile pedantry in their theological knowledge than are clerical theologians.

2. It follows as a corollary to the above that the laity will always have to lean on the clergy for theological guidance. Those who claim the right to pick and choose the theology they will study, will never lose their dependence on those who have the fullness of theology, nor is it fitting that they should, since the laity are dependent upon and subordinate to the clergy in the hierarchical structure of the Church. This does not mean that a lay person cannot study by himself (indeed he is obliged to study according to his state in life), but only that he must seek guidance from his confessor or an advisor from time to time, the more so if he engages in any public use of theology.

3. It should be clearly understood that if the layman's theology is to be partial in regard to extension, it must nevertheless be deep. In fact, it is impossible to have too much understanding of the theological principles which apply to one's state in life. All too little is known about the Sacrament of Matrimony by many a husband and wife, whereas they ought continuously to grow, if not in study of it, surely in understanding of it. Catholic doctors have to know sharply the Church's teaching as it pertains to their profession, and in general this knowledge is readily available on the technical level, more generally ignored now on the broader level of professional obligations to charity, modesty, etc. The psychiatrist and psychologist, on the other hand, will need some intensive study of St. Thomas' treatise on man, not to mention books on ascetical and

mystical theology. Theology pertaining to economics and the social order is still *terra incognita* for the most part, despite the papal encyclicals. It is our habit to seize upon the natural principles set forth by the popes in disregard of their theological admonitions, so ending up at one with the liberal and other curious bedfellows.

SYSTEMS OF THEOLOGY FOR THE LAITY

To say that the laity can pick and choose is not to suppose that their study of theology must be hit or miss, but only that it does not follow the scientific order of the theological science. It normally should follow an organic order of its own, and this it can do in several ways.

LITURGY

The liturgy, which marks the rhythm of the life of the religious must also be a background influence in the life of the laity, teaching them the Church's great mysteries through the seasons of the Church year, and great spiritual principles through the psalms, for such of the laity who have time to read part or all of the Divine Office or one of the Little Offices. This is not to mention the Mass, which is the great teacher, but in another sense than we are here considering. But unless one has an exceptional lay vocation it is impossible to lead any sort of *full* liturgical life in an urban society geared to commercialism. What can be done with the liturgy in a closed, intensely Christian, rural community, is well exemplified by the Grail. On its farm in Loveland, Ohio, the Grail builds the whole pattern of its life around the liturgy, following not only the rhythm of the Church year, but also using the blessings and sacramentals, as well as holding up saint after saint for emulation and admiration.

One thing especially obvious at the Grail is the richness of the liturgy which provides far more than enough material with which to plan a community program. I once visited a Catholic camp where a well-meaning but inept attempt was made to provide not very well instructed children with a sense of Christian observance by mechanical rather than organic reference to the liturgy. So Christmas was "celebrated" in the first week of August, Easter in the second week, and so on. The camp directors would have taught the children much more had they just relaxed and taken the Church season as they found it, amplifying the day's liturgy by fitting drama and practices. Three days at the Grail would have been a revelation to them.

SCRIPTURE

Learning theology through scripture is learning it the way Christ first taught it, by parable, by admonition, by principle, and overwhelmingly by His own life. And so it is learned by the legions of those whose excellent custom it is to read a little every day from the Bible. The problem here is whether scripture can be used as a group instruction method. Its obvious use is, of course, in parish sermons. But apart from that, is it a suitable basis for a study club or college class?

There have been but few attempts, and most of them have not been notably successful. The difficulty is not so much in the scriptures as in finding a suitable priest director of the group or course. Owing to the rationalist attacks on the Bible, seminary courses in scripture have had no concentrate on the refutation of rationalist heresies, on sundry historical and technical studies valuable in themselves but not conducive to simplicity in approaching the word of God. What the layman needs to know is how to interpret the words of Christ in his own life.

Our danger today is not that we shall too literally interpret the scriptures (following the fundamentalist Protestants) but that we shall not take the Bible seriously enough, believing that when God says, for instance, that it is hard for rich people to be saved, that He means it is hard for rich people to be saved, and not that He means that it is hard for nasty rich people to be saved except in capitalistic America.

There are many new and useful helps to the study of scripture. One way and another they throw into unfamiliar perspective the words which have, through over-familiarity without meditation and practice, come to be taken for granted. Msgr. Knox's translations are very useful in this regard. So also is Fr. Stedman's little manual of daily readings, which is a re-arrangement of the order of the text.

CATHOLIC ACTION

The genius of Catholic Action lies in the fact that it is organic. It is not so much something which has been invented, as something which has been discovered. The thing that is organic about Catholic Action is that it follows the natural process of reasoning: see, judge and act. Therefore it is, to over-simplify, a way of learning practical theology, with the immediate purpose of putting it to use. The "act" part of the inquiry technique is made possible because Catholic Action begins with the most obvious and pressing problems which confront its members, and therefore keeps the study in the realm of their own personal lives. It also automatically adjusts the dose to the capacity of the people concerned.

Catholic Action suggests the study group by way of contrast. The reason that study groups are over and over again failures is not because they do not teach theology (and often more of it and more clearly than Catholic Action) but because their approach is not organic, and therefore the study either fails to interest people, or makes the students academic and their study unfruitful. A Catholic Action cell must be homogeneous, which guarantees common problems and allows for common action. Study groups are all too often not homogeneous, or if they are they do not take advantage of their homogeneity.

Another contrast is between the passivity of the study group and the activist participation of those in Catholic Action. The activity of study groups is usually on the part of the clergy, and the passivity on the part of the laity. The result is that the outstanding fault of the Catholic laity is the lack of initiative.

Another familiar sin of study groups is their tendency to concentrate on other people's shortcomings. What good does it do housewives to study euthanasia? They might better be studying Christian home life. Meanwhile the doctors, who might well be studying Communism, eyes averted from the sins of industrial-capitalism. When will we learn that the world problem has to be solved locally?

THEOLOGY IN HIGHER EDUCATION

How should theology be taught in college? It is already the consensus of opinion that it should be taught and a number of experiments are being made. I would like to suggest that the key is not advanced catechetical studies, or a diluted seminary course, but integration. There is such a tension already between secular courses of study and religion, even in Catholic colleges, that students have shown conspicuous resentment when God is mentioned in the so-called ordinary courses. Because of the separation of the departments of religion and other studies, students have lost the feeling that God is relevant to His creation. The synthesis must be restored. This cannot be done for the saying so, because there are not many teachers who can teach integrated courses, but it looks like the only answer, and therefore something will have to be done about it. An integrated college course is the only realistic way of teaching today.

How do you integrate religion with secular course? It will not be done on a superficial level, but on the most profound level. Take history, for instance. Who since Bossuet has really attempted to show history as the unraveling of God's Providence? Yet is it not so? Is not the Incarnation the overwhelmingly most important of all *historical* events? It may even be well not to teach Church history separately any more in colleges, in the interest of showing that the Catholic Church is not a side issue in history, but the focal point of history. In order to do the integrating job in history we will need scholar-saints, who will take account of all the facts, yet always see the undiminished brilliance of Christ in His Church. If the Church really is Christ it will always look like Christ unless there are defects in the beholder, and this in the midst of recurrent crucifixions and betrayals. Catholic college graduates are more given to explaining how none of our sins really reflect on the Church than they are to the much more profound view that even our sins contribute mysteriously to God's greater glory and to that of His Church.

Economics is a subject which is crying for religious light. Garrigou-Lagrange, speaking of spiritual blindness, remarks that it makes people look for the explanation of our ills in economic cycles or over-production instead of seeing them truly as God's punishment upon us because large numbers of men have turned away from God as their last end and placed their last end in money or material prosperity. It is in this light that the economic system should be seen, as the invention of men who have turned away from God. It would be folly, therefore, to teach that economics is just the way things work, to which morality is irrelevant. Rather let us show that the law of supply and demand is not law whatever, and is in fact reversed in practice (we create demands so as to get rich by supplying them). Let the college students look clearly at the fact of almost universal economic ruin. Let them see the sharp contradiction which exists between economic endeavor and Christian ideals of detachment and mortification. Let them go to the roots of true economics to see that it is God Who gives real wealth and that our practices should be harmonious with His laws.

Even *English composition* would be considerably changed in an integrated college course. Writing is now a glamour profession at which you can get enormously rich if you have the facility of style which you are willing to put at the service of contentlessness. Catholic colleges have no honorable course but to turn their back on current practice and teach writing as an apostolate, putting the major emphasis on what is being said rather than on superficialities of style.

If Catholic colleges are going to teach *Sociology* they will have to transform the usual contents of such a subject. If the descriptive part is really to be valid, it will be necessary, besides describing the sordid living conditions of the poor, to describe the sordid living conditions of the rich. Then it might become apparent that what is really terrible is universal materialism and loss of religion.

Psychology is another subject which will require drastic transformation. This should be seen as the study of the soul, taken from a certain point of view, showing the spiritual organism, and how it is meant to work and what happens when, as frequently now, its nature is violated.

And so also with the other courses. It does not so much matter what framework of teaching is employed (whether the tutorial system, or through great books, or through certain courses as at present), so long as the integration is there. The integration will first of all have to be in the teachers and then, if such a system is used, in the textbooks. One sign of returning health in education will be the re-emphasis on perfecting the *teacher*. The cursory suggestions given above for accomplishing the integration should not be taken to indicate that the process is obvious and easy, but that it is largely *terra incognita*, awaiting exploration in the direction indicated.

One cannot imagine that a Catholic college with a truly integrated curriculum would be accredited by a secular system of accreditation. That would be just as well, because that would spare the college the necessity of sending its teachers to schools where they would be taught useless and erroneous things. Maybe if someone would dare to take the lead, Catholics would soon be setting the pace in education matters. To date all the daring educational experiments have been made by non-Catholics and are doomed to failure despite the sincerity of the experiments, because they lack the first principles.

Of the religion course which should be taught in addition to an integrated curriculum, there just is not space to treat here.

RETREATS AND SPIRITUAL DIRECTION

The theology which is most important to everyone has been left until last. It is the theology which pertains directly to one's own sanctification. Apart from reading spiritual books on one's own, this theology is chiefly gained from spiritual direction and retreats. As things are at present both of these sources are somewhat wanting. It is hard to find a spiritual director who will seriously undertake to help one to become a saint. Even retreats are ordinarily on the cozy side. One gets a warm glow of satisfaction from having set aside a day or two for God, but the stimulation is largely emotional. The usual retreat is geared low, like the parish mission, for those in a state of mortal sin, or nearly so. The few theological retreats that are given, whether Catholic Action or other, are far more fruitful. These abound in real solid principles of what the spiritual life consists in, and how necessary it is for salvation and a fruitful life. Not a few people's lives have been completely transformed by such retreats.

THE SWORD OF THE SPIRIT

One of the most hopeful signs in the Church is the growing army of laymen who are armed with the sword of the spirit, which is the word of God. One finds them in offices, in factories, on street corners and at cocktail parties, explaining and defending the Faith. It is largely owing to theological instruction of one or another sort that this army is supplanting the mute, unapostolic Catholic laity of former days.

9

Secular Education—
Some Years After

JUNE 1947

I SEE BY THE PAPERS THAT MY ALMA MATER IS RAISING some many millions of dollars. A new library. A new dormitory. Some running expenses. It costs a lot to run Wellesley. I myself, or rather my father, paid $1,000 a year for four years so that I could be educated there, and that was only about half what it cost the college to put me through my paces. If you add to that the cost of unlearning what they taught me—but you can't add that, because it was largely a spiritual cost.

It is not that I don't have a certain gratitude to my college. It is gratitude for what was intended to be kindness, but turned out to be unkindness; for seeming light that turned out to be darkness; for guidance by the halt and the blind.

But before I beat Wellesley's breast (because it has not yet itself received the grace to view its own sins with humility and horror), let me beat my own. If Wellesley is no credit to me, neither am I any credit to it. Nor was I its joy as an undergraduate. There were nobler, brighter, more diligent students at every hand. The seeds the college sowed were bad, but the ground they fell on was as bad or worse. Neither my home training nor my previous schooling nor my own virtue provided auspicious foundation on which to implant a higher education, so if the higher education wasn't so high after all, it is yet not fully responsible for the end product.

I did not study very hard at college, so I was guilty of sinning by sloth. If I had studied harder I would have learned more untruths. It has been useful for me to reflect on this dilemma, as I have seen it repeated a thousand times since, in my own life and in the lives of my friends. If your job is selling cheap, badly-made and unnecessary dresses, the better salesman you are the more you sin by deceit and by adding some more materialism to a materialistic world. But if you are a poor salesman and lacking in diligence, you take money under false pretenses. Or suppose it is your job to file correspondence about comic strips. The more seriously you take your job the more the fool you are; the less seriously you take it, so much the less do you deserve the salary which you think you must have in order to eat.

Now I see that it is the devil who has maneuvered so many of us into such untenable positions, and that the only way out is God's way, which is to strike out in the direction of His righteousness, letting one's daily bread follow as it will. The answer to the Wellesley dilemma (had I known it) would have been to leave and to seek truth elsewhere. It was what I came to in the end, but only after a wasted youth, out of which only God could bring good.

ON THE CREDIT SIDE

Wellesley has plenty of minor virtues. It is breathtakingly beautiful, both in its natural surroundings and in its semi-monastic architecture. It is not bourgeois. Wealth is neither paraded nor worshipped; luxurious comfort is not held up as an ideal. The college has, or had, a tradition of scholarship. We obtained our information at first hand (from Spinoza himself and not someone's comments on, or condensations of, Spinoza). There were no courses in such non-academic subjects as feeding babies or department-store buying. There was still a lingering admiration for Philosophy and Greek majors, despite the fact that they were a handful compared with the hordes of those majoring in Psychology (which was then largely a matter of memory work). No one ever dreamt of teaching shorthand, typing, or indeed any subject bearing on gainful employment, the contention being that Wellesley undertook to train the mind and that anyone who could manage somehow to scrape together money enough for four years of it could find enough more money for three months at a secretarial school.

Wellesley students came largely from upper middle class, professional families. They were healthy and intelligent, usually possessed of high humanitarian ideals. The college had a definite religious foundation, in consequence of which it attracted the daughters of Protestant missionaries, as well as a sprinkling of their Chinese and Japanese converts. In my day the college motto, "Non ministrari sed ministrare," was still jokingly translated, "Not to be ministers but to be ministers' wives," yet the religious strain had worn a bit thin and the joke was no longer very funny. Every year one girl was chosen as "most typical of Wellesley," which really meant that she represented the ideal rather than the typical. It was a very high ideal, naturally speaking:

wholesome, self-possessed, extrovert and gracious; without affectation and with marked nobility of character. There were always a few Negro girls in school and no noticeable race prejudice. One of the student's parents used as a matter of course to entertain Negro friends at their Bronxville home, a fact which caused but little comment at college.

THE DEBIT ACCOUNT

Despite these advantages, and many others, I was more nearly finished by than graduated from Wellesley. Four years left me with:

> A vague but persistent feeling of superiority.
> An intellectual curiosity run riot.
> A militant immorality.
> A set of wholly erroneous convictions.
> No plans for the future.
> A mind closed to the supernatural.
> A profound ignorance of the purpose of life, the existence and nature of God, and all the rest of the really essential truths.
> A growing despair (unacknowledged).

I cannot absolve my alma mater from responsibility for this state of affairs, even after due allowance is made for other contributing factors and my own exceeding lack of intellectual and moral virtues. I shall show in part how it came about.

RELIGION AT WELLESLEY

Wellesley is not so much a secular college as a sectarian college which has ceased to be Christian. It is of pious Protestant origin, as are most New England colleges, and its charter insists on the compulsory study of the Bible. In my day the clash between what the founder had in mind and the ultra-liberal religion of the faculty had reached an uncomfortable stage. Grace was still said at meals, but chapel attendance was no longer compulsory; the personal lives of the teachers continued to follow the Christian pattern in which they had been reared, while they themselves directly or indirectly undermined the whole of Christian ethics in the classroom. The required study of the Bible was in process of being telescoped into insignificance, after having first been completely perverted.

Wellesley fell hook, line and sinker for the higher biblical critics. It was not until long afterwards that I discovered most of the higher critics had then already eaten their words, unbeknownst to Wellesley.

If you want to damn religion by indirection the thing to do is to study it from a literary point of view, or anthropologically, or historically. We studied the Bible historically. All I remember from one year on the Old Testament is that the Pentateuch was said to have been written by a number of different people designated by letters of the alphabet and that this was supposed to have invalidated it somehow. No mention that I recall was made of original sin, of the singular mission of the Jewish race, of the nobility of the patriarchs, of the foreshadowing character of Old Testament events, or of the messianic prophesies. One could have spent one's time more valuably in a Baptist Sunday school.

The New Testament course was Wellesley's masterpiece, on a par with the "Man and Nature" course at the University of Wisconsin in the production of atheists. We studied only the synoptic gospels, Matthew, Mark and Luke, as John was supposed to have been written by someone else at a far later date. All we heard of St. Paul in the required course was that he was the publicity agent responsible for the phenomenal spread of the teachings, not in themselves singular, of an obscure Jewish prophet named Jesus Christ.

The synoptic gospels were first reduced to St. Mark, as being (so they said) the earliest, most matter of fact, and therefore the most accurate. Mark does not describe Christ's birth: therefore there is nothing extraordinary about it. The miracles are then explained away; all diseases being reduced to epilepsy or neuroses, while such tales as the multiplication of the loaves and fishes became illustrations of the disciples' tendency to exaggerate. Christ's teachings were then twisted to support a theory of narrow Judaic preoccupation. By this time we had reached the triumphal entry of Palm Sunday (really so insignificant as to have caused no stir in Jerusalem and only seemingly important in retrospect). The Passion of Our Lord was considered the tragic end of blunderings and miscalculations, and the whole story ends abruptly as Christ dies in desolation on the Cross. And what of the Resurrection? It's a made-up story, later interpolated into the manuscripts.

A very pious Quakeress taught us these things. She opened every class with a prayer and frequently pointed to the nobility of Christian teaching, now that it was shorn of superstitious coating. Pretending to praise that which you have just destroyed is a common technique these days. You find it used in the popular expositions of the wonders of sex: three hundred pages of carnality, every fiftieth of which bows and says, "Love is so wonderful, especially married love." Its use is also flagrant in the standard obstetrical textbooks for nurses (Catholic and non-Catholic), which treat of woman as a biological exhibit, while carefully inserting periodic praise of motherhood.

For the most part Wellesley students succumbed to the enlightenment without protest. Who were we to argue with "the reading in the original Hebrew is...," and "all present-day scholars agree that..."? Besides, our previous religious training usually amounted to a dubious baptism, some Sunday school stories, a dash of sentimentality and a dose of adolescent idealism. I took part in what was probably the most famous protest. Our teacher had been explaining away the Last Supper. It was, of course, an uneventful celebration of the Jewish Passover, to which sentiment later attached significance. Someone had been so foolish in the morning class as to have defied this interpretation because it clashed with what she had always been taught and firmly believed. There was a recent convert to Catholicism in our class who arose in her defense, defying the whole historical method. I joined her, but only for the love of a good fight, since I was already an atheist. The brightest girl in school, a Jewess of amazing intelligence, chimed in and the uproar lasted until the teacher walked out white with rage, long after the closing bell had rung.

Nothing I learned at college stuck with me so long and clearly as did the fourteen reasons why Christ wasn't divine, according to the Gospel of St. Mark. In the end it took a large miracle of grace to get me to reconsider Christianity at all. I sometimes wonder if that convert's prayers were instrumental in getting me another chance. She talked to me a lot and even took me to Boston to Mass, but I was a million miles away and impenetrable. Meanwhile the Quakeress was revealing the heartening news that a Dutch scholar was on the brink of actually being able to *prove* that Christ had really lived. "You know," she said, "we really have no proof now, in case we are challenged."

PHILOSOPHY AT WELLESLEY

Now that the supernatural order had been explained away, I in my folly went on to the destruction of the natural order. I majored in Philosophy.

We studied every major philosopher from the pre-Socratics to John Dewey, except all Christian philosophers. It was as though human thought had been suspended during the 1900-year interval separating Aristotle and Descartes. Indeed, that was the precise opinion of the head of the Philosophy department, who put it thus: "When you are ready to give up thinking, become a Catholic."

Philosophy was taught cafeteria style. All the philosophers were presented to our view and no reason was given why one should be preferred to another. I didn't realize this at first and spent a miserable afternoon in consequence. The dean was conducting a seminar in modern philosophy. The very few students attracted to this study were sitting around the dean's dining room table while one student read a paper on John Dewey. The rest of them were taking copious notes so that on an examination they would be able to say: "John Dewey says so and so." I made the mistake of listening critically and discovered that Dewey's idea of the purpose of life was the pursuit of certain "ends" until they opened up new "ends," which would in time reveal still more "ends," etc. At the end of the reading I burst out with, "But that doesn't make sense!" There followed an argument, which was concluded by the dean's icy: "I would hardly say that the greatest living philosopher is talking nonsense."

I was miserable all through tea and only in later years discovered how right I had been.

As I said earlier, we were scholarly at Wellesley and read our text in the original. A list of our philosophy books would read like an extract from the Roman Index. Nothing pleases me more than to be forbidden ever again to share the intellectual writhings of post-Christian thinkers. I spent the better part of two weeks once in a beer parlor in Natick trying, with another girl, to make head or tail of Hegel. "Being is non-being, and the union of the two is becoming...."

Still, the big things I learned in Philosophy came not so much from books as from teachers. Foremost was that there is no truth. This one was well hidden under verbiage about the love of truth and the nobility of searching for it; but we were never to find it. You have only to scratch any secular college graduate to find him infected with this same conviction; indeed it is held by the whole of secular society. The fact that she claims to know the truth is really the stock objection to the Catholic Church in America today, made by people who are so far from having disproved her claim that they actually do not know what the claims are, but only that they are to certainties and not to opinions, prejudices or possibilities.

Secular Education—Some Years After

The next important thing I learned in Philosophy was that there is no free will. I'm ashamed to have picked up this error because it was presented quite baldly and I could easily have used my brain in support of my common sense. Psychology and science students were persuaded more subtly, but the same determinism infected almost everybody. Its most popular form of expression was either the sentimental "You must not call these people bad, but sick," or the useful, "I couldn't help it because I was so badly brought up." One would be very mistaken to suppose that our theoretical determinism eliminated harsh judgments in the practical order.

I also picked up a certain working philosophy of life, a sort of courageous despair, amoral and rather on the sentimental side. I bore a much stronger resemblance to the Professor of Philosophy than to any of the philosophical systems we studied, most of which were in the purely speculative plane anyhow.

Lest anyone suppose that my Philosophy professor was a uniquely vicious man, let me hasten to assure them that he was by no means either vicious or singular. Indeed, it was because of his personal charm and exceeding kindness that his erroneous ideas were taken so to heart and did so much harm. He was a devout admirer of Alfred North Whitehead, whom I understand to have the same sort of soul-devastating effect on his Harvard students. The late Morris R. Cohen, famous Philosophy Professor at C. C. N. Y., who wrote "The Faith of a Liberal," is the exact counterpart of my teacher. Now there is another book out by a disciple of Professors Cohen and Whitehead. It is "Nature and Man," by Paul Weiss, who is Professor of Philosophy at Yale, and it follows the tortuous mental twists of Whitehead. I quote:

> The past conditions the future as a limited but not yet determinate realm within which a range of occurrences can take place. A concrete course in time is necessary in order to determine and thereby realize the future. The result can be known in advance as a possibility, not as an actuality.

My personal conclusion on this type of thing has long been that these erudite gentlemen are trying, in their intellectual pride, to invent the doctrine of God's Providence, but on the natural level.

It was not a pleasure to read of the death of Morris Cohen. I searched the obituary in vain for any sign that he had at last humbled himself before God.

CONTRASTS

You would misunderstand the curious nature of our instruction if you did not take into account the example set us by our superiors, which was on the whole exemplary. So far as I knew the faculty, I admired them. One of my teachers practiced voluntary poverty. Another bore with great patience the arthritic pains with which she was racked. It would not at all surprise me to learn that many other faculty members led lives of heroic personal sacrifice.

Furthermore, there may have been Catholic influence making itself felt here and there. Vida Scudder, who was to me only an illustrious retired member of the faculty, was, as I have since discovered, the great American authority on St. Catherine of Siena. A curious saint to preoccupy a non-Catholic. My art professor had influential ecclesiastical connections through which she was admitted to a view of the papal robes. How far beyond liturgical beauty her admiration for the Church extended I do not know. She may even have been trying to inculcate us with a pre-Raphaelite bias in art for all I managed to grasp of that subject. The college choir was partial to Gregorian Chant, which it sang without integral relation to the Sunday church service, of course. There were also a few Catholic teachers, mostly in the foreign language departments, with a consequent limited influence.

While the faculty continued their exemplary lives of noble pagan stoicism, or even of Catholic gropings, the student body took to heart their teachings and was noticeably degenerating. The students' favorite subject of private discussion was that of moral principles, which was argued endlessly. Under the circumstances the only argument for high moral principles was expediency, although the argument was given a hundred different ways. Expediency is the least strong deterrent of immorality and my informal observation was that it lost ground at an alarming rate.

At about this time the college took on a psychiatrist as advisor on student problems. Up until then the official attitude toward moral problems was non-existent, but could have been presumed to favor conventional Protestant moral standards. With psychiatry entered Freud and the all-explanatory sex. Rumors were that the psychiatrist was working to remove the inhibitions of the college girls.

THE VOCABULARY OF AN EX-CHRISTIAN

The commonly accepted connotation of certain key words will furnish an excellent indication of the spiritual state which underlay the polite Protestant covering of our lives at Wellesley:

SIN was a word which was never used, except facetiously or historically. When we did in fact sin, we had "done something wrong" or "made a mistake." The idea of sin as an offense against God would not have occurred to most of us, as we found ourselves unable to conceive a "personal" God. It goes without saying that anything we found ourselves unable to conceive of therefore didn't exist.

MODESTY, in the usual Christian sense, was another word missing from our vocabulary. It is quite true, as I have since read in ecclesiastical writings, that those outside the Catholic faith are incapable of understanding the delicacy of conscience involved in the Christian virtue of modesty. We might, in an extreme case, have labelled a costume indecent, but we would only have mocked a dress to call it modest. Our campus clothes were pretty modest, as a matter of fact, but we were not modest. We had long since lost our sense of shame, and nudity, whether informally in the dormitory or officially at the elaborate physical examinations presided over by the hygiene department, was more or less taken for granted.

SUPERNATURAL meant phony psychic phenomena, like crystal gazing. We were strict naturalists. If there was a higher intelligence than ours in the universe, it was of the same sorts as ours. But generally we credited what higher powers there might be with having lower intelligences than ours: blind force, or energy, or chance. So much for God. As for angels, it never crossed our minds that they might really exist, fallen or otherwise.

All the words which are more or less related to the supernatural went by the board with it. Sacrament, grace, mystical: they were words which we seldom heard and to which we attached no meaning. "God is Love" was written conspicuously over the choir of the chapel and was given as the designation of a special autumn Sunday. Still, the idea of the theological virtue of charity was certainly lacking to almost all students.

HUMILITY was no virtue to us, whether in practice (for the most part) or in theory. It suggested to us a sort of base groveling, a lack of the ever-desirable self-confidence. Instead of humility we used the word modesty to indicate a person who doesn't brag about his attainments. We would have thought St Thérèse of Lisieux was lacking in modesty for saying "I was made for great things." We had never heard that humility does not involve the denial of good qualities but the acknowledgment of them as from God.

SANCTITY was an unfamiliar word, and certainly not an ideal of character. Our ideal characters were strictly on the natural plane of greatness. We admired Abraham Lincoln, Florence Nightingale and Walt Whitman, and we would have gone right along with those who say St. Teresa of Avila was a prize psychoneurotic. That is, we would have if we had ever heard of her.

Our ideals of conduct were on the natural level too. We thought it would be a wonderful thing to find a cure for cancer and to give money to reputable charities. We were scrupulously honest according to our conception of honesty. There was practically no cheating at college and theft was limited to an occasional kleptomaniac. Most of us came from families which wouldn't have dreamt of taking anything not theirs and would have been disgraced to accept relief if jobs could still be had scrubbing floors. Yet most of our fathers were responsibly involved in banking, corporations, railroads, insurance companies and Wall Street, places where (it is said) robbery on a large scale sometimes takes place. That curious clinging to what might be called "petty honesty" is still a conspicuous "virtue" of the graduates of our best colleges, especially those engaged in such business as publicity, radio and publishing. The Harvard graduate who assures us that X-AX [sic] is gentle and harmless, feels he preserves his integrity by freely admitting in the bosom of his closest friends that the stuff is probably poison.

Some of our natural ideals of conduct were far less attractive. We were coming around to the idea that no fair-minded wife would force her husband to continue living with her after he had lost his love (romantic lust) for her. We rather thought it would be unfeeling to bring children into a world not fully prepared (financially) to take care of them. There was even a growing admiration for the man she loves to marry her for any other reason than pure romantic love (lust) at a time suited to his convenience.

RESULTS

So after four years we were turned out into a world which had, on the whole, even worse ideas that we had. It was a world desperately in need of salvation, but we were in no position to save it.

Secular Education—Some Years After

What happened to most of my friends was that they spent the next several years adjusting themselves downward to a world they couldn't lift up.

What's the point of studying English literature in order to spend your life reading unbelievably bad manuscripts for a publishing house with quite other than literary ambitions?

Why master higher mathematics in order to measure the capricious ups and downs of the stock market?

Had we disciplined our minds in order to do what was called "advertising research" but was really counting by ones?

Why had we bothered so with our brains if we were going to end up exhibiting our physical charms as Powers models?

The only thing ruthless commercialism had in common with our academic past was the irrelevancy of God to both types of life.

It is no wonder that none of my collegemates I know now lead a joyous, purposeful life. Some have married, some not. Some have made money, some not. One killed herself. Most have reached a working compromise (not very stable) with circumstances as they found them.

Only a few remain actively tormented by the contrast between the mediocrity and materialism to which the world invites them, and the hollow in their hearts which aches for God.

M. B. W.[1]

---

[1] This was almost certainly written by Carol Robinson since she graduated from Wellesley College and referred to things that she often mentioned in her other works. — *Ed.*

10
Why Aren't Americans Contemplative?

JULY 1947

WHEN MOTHER MARY MAGDALEN BENTIVOGLIO, foundress of the Poor Clares in the United States, applied for permission to make a foundation in Philadelphia in 1876, the diocesan council refused on the grounds that such a convent was "not in conformity with the spirit of the people."

That was over a century ago, and an isolated instance, but it expresses an antipathy to the contemplative life which persists, affecting both the Catholic and non-Catholic population, although differently. We like our saints to be "normal people." We prefer Thomas More sans hair shirt and St. Francis minus the stigmata. Contraception does not seem unnatural, even to many Catholics who refrain from it, but contemplative nuns do seem unnatural. We are more at ease with an aspirant millionaire than with one who hopes to become a saint.

"Why aren't Americans contemplative?" is not an idle question, like "Why do Americans prefer coffee to tea?" It isn't a matter of idiosyncrasy, or national temperament or genius; it is much the same as saying, "Why aren't Americans godly people?" A distaste for contemplation is at the root of the so-called "American Heresy," of modernism and of naturalism.

We hope to show in this paper that there is a real antagonism between the American Way of Life as commonly understood and practiced, and sanctity.

The likely saints in America's past (with some notable exceptions such as Mother Seton) have not been conspicuous in the mainstream of our country's development. Most were early missionaries; nearly all were foreign born. Mother Cabrini certainly led a hidden life in New York and Chicago where everyone had heard of her contemporary, J. P. Morgan. Americans until now have been supremely anti-mystical. It looks as though the tide is changing, both among the Catholics and the non- Catholics (who, when they do not find the Church, go in for a false mysticism, jumbling up Theosophy with St. John of the Cross, or deep breathing with Dr. Emmet Fox). It is good to see an ex-Communist poet leave the New Yorker staff for a Trappist monastery. It is good to learn of the ordination of another Trappist who has a background of Judaism, Psychiatry and the University of Chicago. Among those in the lay apostolate, there is the conviction that all things will not be restored in Christ unless they themselves advance toward contemplation. With these signs it is not unreasonable to hope that we shall one day as a nation realize that to be anti-contemplative is to be truly un- American.

WHAT IS CONTEMPLATION?

The reason that it is so important that contemplation not be considered "un-American" is that contemplation is the normal process of salvation, so that he who will have none of it, in reality refuses to approach God. Contemplation is the beginning here on earth of the Beatific Vision. It is a simple, intuitive grasp of the religious order of things, and it admits of many degrees between its beginning, early in the life of prayer, and its end in the Beatific Vision.

Salvation is not a matter of doing good deeds or of avoiding mortal sin; it is a matter of sharing God's Life. Thomistic theologians, like Garrigou-Lagrange, teach that the development of the interior life as described by St. John of the Cross is in essence (though not in degree) the same and equally necessary for everyone, so that if we neglect to begin it here and yet manage to save our souls, we are going to have a long period of purification in purgatory. Furthermore, if the body of Christians on earth fails to cultivate the interior life and to advance seriously on the road toward God, the strength of that body will be negligible, and the spiritual health of the nation will be adversely affected. Indeed our spiritual state is reflected in our national conduct. We are the nation which dropped the atomic bomb (and has not yet repented it). We are the nation which characteristically operates on principles of expediency rather than morality. We are the nation which is famous not for the Cross, but for the dollar sign.

THE ACTIVE LIFE AND THE CONTEMPLATIVE LIFE

The reason why we Americans are not contemplative is usually put this way, that Americans are active people (we get things done) and that activists are the opposite of contemplative.

Certain temperaments, such as the melancholic, incline more by nature than others to the life of the spirit and therefore to contemplation. Conversely, the "shallow" temperaments are more given to things of the body than to things of the mind; to things of the world than to things of the spirit. Superficially it seems as though Americans incline by national temperament to the earthy, but the influence is more than likely not temperament but the prevailing materialism. We are not racially or temperamentally homogeneous.

On the road to salvation, grace, not temperament, is the all-important factor. Physically energetic people are as touched by grace as those who like to sit around and think. God must become progressively and equally insistently the center of everyone's life.

However, the active and contemplative types will manifest differently the divine life within them. The difference will be marked not by the degree of charity each attains, nor by the fact that one will pray and the other not (both will pray, although the contemplative will spend more time at it). The real difference will be marked by the difference in the gifts of the Holy Ghost which will predominate in each. In the contemplative the gifts of wisdom and understanding will be especially prominent; in the active person it will be the gifts of fortitude, counsel and knowledge which will be uppermost. This predominance of different gifts is what marks the difference between the sanctity of a Don Bosco and the sanctity of a St. Teresa. It is what should mark the difference between a saintly statesman, nurse or teacher, and a Trappist. The comparison is more clearly seen in those advanced in prayer and holiness because their lives are more noticeably under the guidance of the Holy Ghost.

ARE AMERICANS REALLY ACTIVE?

There is another relationship between activity and contemplation which applies especially to beginners. A truly active life on the natural level prepares for contemplation, which in turn will give rise to better activity.

What is this truly active life? It is activity according to moral virtue, as opposed to what St. Thomas calls the active life of pleasure, or life according to the senses. One cannot escape the realization that much of our American activity is the active life according to sensibility and pleasure. For instance, all the frantic haste and energy which goes into moneymaking as a last end is activity of this type; all the way from running for the 8:17 train to the business conference in the afternoon. The much-vaunted American efficiency fits into the same category, and that is really why we tend to despise it. So much punctuality, so much exactitude, so much precision-for what? Then consider the energy Americans give to sports when they really go in for sports. The tennis match and the golf game are the active life of pleasure, although they may be meritorious if accessory to a life of moral virtue, though apparently they seldom are. Take, finally, the energy we devote to expediency, that contemporary substitute for moral virtue. What a lot of energy has gone into Planned Parenthood! What a lot of racing back and forth in airplanes there is among statesmen who cannot be said to proceed with international affairs along the path of moral virtue.

On the other hand, in some ways Americans are not even active, but shockingly passive.

We never walk if we can ride. We have gadgets to keep from developing skills, elevators to eliminate the necessity of climbing stairs, spectator sports, radios instead of musicians. Our passivity is most conspicuous and deplorable in the intellectual sphere. We work at jobs without ever thinking, and indeed there is usually nothing to think about. We passively accept all our opinions predigested.

WHERE INTEGRATION COMES IN

This is where integration comes in. When we say that Catholics should have an integrated life we are really saying that they should exchange a passive life, or an active life of pleasure or sensibility, for an active life according to the moral virtues, and that this life according to the moral virtues will put them in line for contemplation, which is the route that they should be traveling toward God.

The basis of an active life according to moral virtue is an intellectual comprehension of the relationship between religion and work, family, recreation, reading and all the other phases of daily life. If there is no synthesis between religion and life a man will be blundering around in the dark, and will save his soul only through ignorance of the undone duty (if he can still manage an invincible ignorance). Meanwhile our country will not be appreciably bettered by such negative candidates for heaven.

IS PIETY CONTEMPLATION?

There is no doubt but that American Catholics are pious. They stream in and out of churches, are very devotional. The number of Communions is impressive.

Piety, in the popular sense, is largely a matter of external activity-vocal prayer and pious exercises. It is good, of course. But of itself it stands in the relation of peripheral activity to the real interior life. Contemplation does not usually begin until after a period of meditation, and most devout Catholics have not yet even learned to meditate. The fact that many Americans seem to prefer a novena to Mass is indicative that their piety really is on the external and sensible level. You get out of devotions what you put into them, whereas the sacraments give grace of themselves and are therefore much to be preferred. As for the Americans who frequent Communion and yet do not develop an interior life, their difficulty lies chiefly in that lack of integration which prevents the full exercise of the moral virtues.

WHY AREN'T AMERICANS CONTEMPLATIVE?

1. Materialism

Looked at from the underside, the advance toward God is a progressive detachment from creatures. The "dark nights" of which the mystics speak are purifications in this regard which God arranges. They are for people who are already on the contemplative road. Those who have not yet reached the beginnings of contemplation have to do the first and obvious detaching themselves. They have to mortify themselves in order to lift themselves up from a life bound to the senses so that their spiritual life can get started. This is really the first step: we have to stop loving the things of this world.

Now it is right here that religion and the American Way of Life are at odds. "We're spoiled, thank God," say the advertisements. Don't thank God, thank the devil. God it is Who gave us abundance, but it is the devil who has encouraged us to waste it, to wallow in it, or talk endlessly about it, to forget Who gave it to us, to cherish it and to lay up treasures of it on earth which may prevent our getting to heaven.

Every man has his own struggle against concupiscence. What is vicious in America as presently constituted is that our way of life heaps temptations in a man's path, whereas a godly society, recognizing man's weakness and looking to his salvation, would forbid the exploitation of concupiscence in the interests of avarice. Advertising is the ordinary and most flagrant instrument of our temptations, but advertising is not an isolated phenomenon, it is only the instrument of an industrial-capitalist system which has had to turn to the home market. It cajoles us into buying what we don't need and what is harmful to the salvation of our souls. It cajoles, and that works, but every once in a while one senses the iron hand of force behind the velvet glove of invitation. It is almost as though we were being made to consume in order to keep feeding a monstrously destructive system. As long as our economic system (the tentacles of which are twisted around everything from politics to publishing) is ordered to money as its last end, so long will the spirit of contemplation and the American Way of Life be at odds. There are not enough people yet who have declined to be exploited, so as to disturb the profiteers. But if there were a widespread wave of penance then we would see people showing their colors.

II. Spiritual Blindness

Spiritual blindness is a disease of intellectuals, those people who are the most likely to have escaped the lure of materialism. It is about the worst thing that could happen to those whose lives center in the mind.

First, what is it? It is a punishment inflicted by God for intellectual sins. The sins are intellectual curiosity and pride. The punishment consists in this: that God takes away His light from the minds of those who do not wish to receive it, abandoning them to the darkness which original sin and their own sins pull down upon them. Spiritual blindness is characterized not by ignorance of facts (which is a relatively clear and easily remediable state), nor by native stupidity, but by confusion of thought and defect of judgment. Those who suffer from it are the blind guides of Scripture, who strain out a gnat and swallow a camel, who have every comma in place in an article rife with internal inconsistencies, who concentrate on the artistic elements in pornographic statuary, who feature the delivery of morally bad poetry, and worry about only the medical aspects of venereal disease. Garrigou-Lagrange says of spiritual blindness: "It takes all penetration away from us and leaves us in a state of spiritual dullness, which is like the loss of all higher intelligence."

There are several ways of recognizing spiritual blindness. It is chiefly marked by mental confusion and the inability to recognize implications and contradictions. It also consists in a preference for discussing the trivial over the important, the material rather than the spiritual. It is common among teachers in secular colleges, among liberal Protestant clergymen, among Catholic intellectuals who have higher degrees in social studies, and among Catholics generally who try to serve God and Mammon. It is the obvious punishment of those who lightly disregard the Church's prohibition in the matter of books and movies.

Let us take a gross example of spiritual blindness. Several years ago an interfaith organization had a brotherhood campaign. They proposed to raise several million dollars to establish a research project to determine the bases of brotherhood (money and research discovered the atomic bomb, why not brotherhood?), after which they were going to arrange to have the same taught in colleges. Now there may exist some simple child of a scientific age so ignorant of religion as to suppose that brotherhood is a fit subject for a research project, or to suppose that the basis of brotherhood has not long since been known and ignored, but such cannot be said of the clergy. "Woe to you, blind guides!"

Evidence of spiritual blindness is at every hand. The double-talk of the radio. The nonsense written in most magazines. The learned palaver of the schools. The fine speeches of statesmen.

Spiritual blindness is the inverse, the opposite of contemplation. As contemplation is characterized by a simple intellectual grasp of truth, so this blindness is marked by multiplicity. It accounts, for instance, for the rash of facts and statistics gathered in contemporary America. Vast amounts of money and energy have been channeled in this direction without adding to anyone's wisdom. People given to this collect thousands of uncorrelated, mechanically arranged facts. They have a lust for stuffing more and more information into already overcrowded memories, without ever going to the heart of any matter. Instead of the passivity of the contemplative gaze, the spiritually blind are always restless in their pursuit of knowledge, reading magazines, attending lectures, weighing the latest theory propounded by the latest paper read at the latest assemblage of experts, joining the book-of-the-month club, keeping up with this and that.

Let us examine the sins which precipitate the punishment of spiritual blindness. They are two: curiosity and pride.

Why Aren't Americans Contemplative?

Curiosity

Curiosity is a defect of our mind, which inclines us with eagerness and precipitation toward the consideration and study of less useful subjects, making us neglect the things of God and our salvation... whereas people who have little learning but are nourished with the Gospel possess great rectitude of judgment, there are others who, far from nourishing themselves profoundly with the great Christian truths, spend a great part of their time carefully storing up useless, or at least only slightly useful, knowledge which does not at all form the judgment. They are afflicted with almost a mania for collecting. Theirs is an accumulation of knowledge mechanically arranged and unorganized, somewhat as if it were in a dictionary. This type of work, instead of training the mind, smothers it, as too much wood smothers a fire. Under this jumble of accumulated knowledge, they can no longer see the light of first principles, which alone could bring order out of all this material and lift up their souls even to God, the Beginning and End of all things.

That's what St. Thomas had to say about curiosity.[1] It will come as a shock to many to learn that it is a sin, since intellectual curiosity is exalted by the liberalism which prevails in our "best" colleges. It is not a greed for knowledge, but a thirst for truth, which is virtuous. The man who has a thirst for truth is forever seeking to know first principles, to find God. He may be way off the beam at a given moment, taken in by Freud or Yogi, but if he maintains his search and his good will, he will find the ultimate truth. (Here we cannot help but remark on the difference between a pagan searching for truth and seeing, for instance, the glimmer of truth in Freud, and the Catholic who admires Freud in disregard of the fullness of truth which he has and which he has neglected to explore. The former comes through almost untarnished, the latter is a candidate for spiritual blindness.) The curious man, on the other hand, sticks to second, third, tenth and trivial things. He would do well on Information Please, or as a Professor of Sociology at Hunter College, or compiling another volume of "strange facts."

---

[1] This quote was mistakenly attributed to St. Thomas but is from Volume 1 of *The Three Ages of The Interior Life* by Fr. Reginald Garrigou-Lagrange. —*Ed.*

Most Americans don't know (or seem to care) if God exists; which, if any, is the Church Christ founded; what the purpose of life is; and what will happen to them after they die. What they must know is whether the Brooklyn Dodgers won, if U. S. Steel is off 1/2, the weather report, a five-letter word meaning "to steal," and so on. "Ought we to have a Third Party in the United States?" Town Hall asks. But Town Hall has not committed itself for or against the existence of the Deity, or even ventured to investigate the morality of contraception. And the truth of the matter is that if Town Hall concerned itself with anything really important the radio would frown upon it. Because we Americans originally disagreed about fundamentals, we have come to assume that there is no truth about them.

This mental busyness, this superficial accumulation of facts, this "don't miss anything" attitude which causes Americans to break out in a rash of newspapers and digests, deserves to be punished by spiritual blindness. God is trying to show us, through circumstances, how dangerous our condition is. We are like men who won't look up from the latest work on "How to Make Hatchets" long enough to see the axe descending on our own heads. What wonder then that God takes light away, so that if we should chance to look up, we would only see the unusual contour of the axe handle, or want to measure the wind's resistance to its descent.

Pride

The chief condition of learning truth is humility, a certain docility to light from above, a certain mistrust of one's own powers of discernment. But we Americans have even lost the correct meaning of the word humility, and we have striven to set ourselves up as gods. We have self-confidence, self-assurance. We are self-made. All these are reflections of the fact that we no longer look to God but to ourselves. Now the hero of American academic circles is the agnostic, the skeptic, the liberal philosopher. He is the man of tolerance, who regards only one thing with horror, and that is dogmatism. The American liberal exactly fits Ernest Hello's description of The Mediocre Man "...who considers every affirmation insolent, because every affirmation excludes the contradictory proposition." These people are usually gentle by nature, and therefore escape the censure which they richly deserve. We have glorified them, whereas in truth they have done incalculable harm to souls.

Academic pride has given rise to the factory system of teacher-training, to the Ph.D. assembly lines, to the accreditation system and the mania for experts and footnotes in America. Everybody is talking at once, and nobody has truth. You can ask anybody from the ten-cent store clerk to the president of the university this simple question: "What is the purpose of life?" and not get an answer, unless someone has chanced to read it in a catechism. The situation is at once ludicrous and tragic.

Intellectual pride does not seem to have affected the ordinary man directly, but only to characterize his blind university guides. He is more likely to have curiosity. Anyhow, between the two vices, there is widespread spiritual blindness, and almost universal materialism. Why aren't there more miracles around? Where are the saints? You might find them in the byways, but don't look for them in the highways. The American Way of Life does not conduce to their production.

CAN AMERICANS BECOME CONTEMPLATIVE?

"We need a St. Francis of Assisi in America," one frequently hears. Indeed we do. What a delight it would be to have a great barefoot saint helping us to extricate ourselves from the chains of materialism which bind us to the consideration of earthly things.

But we also need a St. Dominic. We need someone who dares shout what we scarcely dare whisper, that everywhere youths are going to college and being graduated as bewildered fools who do not even know the purpose of life. We need someone to give us courage to disregard the latest expert in deference to The First Expert. Then we shall take to our knees and light will be given to us.

11

The Pertinence of Penance

OCTOBER 1947

EITHER THE U.N. IS WRONG, OR OUR LADY IS WRONG. The U.N. (and the League of Nations and the Marshall Plan and the Yalta Agreement and all the rest of them) proposes to remedy the undiagnosed and mortal disease of society with sundry economic and political nostrums. They increasingly favor research and committees and plans, on the theory that the situation is vastly more complicated than at first was thought, and also on the unconscious pre-supposition that once the facts are known the remedy will be obvious. Our Lady, on the contrary, grossly "oversimplifies" things. Her message is brief, always the same (whether at La Salette, Lourdes, Fatima, or Heede), and it is more and more insistent: *Do penance.*

Now, as nothing has been said about penance at the U. N., so far as I know, it is possible that men do not think Our Lady's advice is very practical. The purpose of this article is to suggest that maybe it is much more practical than they think.

IRRELEVANT TO WHAT?

What are we trying to do anyhow? Are we trying to save democracy? It isn't very important whether we save democracy or not except insofar as the existence of democracy conduces to some greater end beyond itself. Men have been happy under kings as well as councils. Democracy is not an end in itself and (being a particularly unromantic form of government really, and not to say vague at the moment) there is little likelihood that there will be a successful crusade on behalf of it.

Or are we trying to bring about some sort of materialistic millennium? Obviously, if this is our goal, penance does seem a little absurd. The probability is that most people who are trying to fix up the world have some globular housing project or garden suburb in mind by way of eventual beatitude.

Here is where they break sharply with Our Lady, who says the goal is the salvation of souls and the Beatific Vision. The framework of reference in the two cases is entirely different. If you accept the secular

The Pertinence of Penance

view, which does not look beyond death, or even at death, then penance doesn't pertain. If, however, you accept the Christian structure, which places this life as a time of trial, sees Hell yawning and the sight of God inviting, then it can immediately be seen that penance has some relevance to our present mess. All the materialists' and secularists' strength consists in keeping people's eyes focused on their false framework of life. Otherwise they would have no real power. Doesn't it seem as though some of the credit for our narrowed vision belongs to the Devil? Possibly this is his greatest triumph, that he has set the modern problems in terms which cannot but turn out to his advantage. If people have jam on their bread, and peace in which to pursue their money-making without the hazards of war, they are his. And if they fail of peace and are bombed to death, they are still his, but maybe sooner. How crude of Our Lady to have shown the Fatima children a vision of Hell! It is so obvious then that the real issue is the salvation of souls.

HOW DID WE GET IN THIS MESS?

Here again Our Lady would "oversimplify." She would simply say, in complete disregard of all interesting studies of sociologists, the vast researches of statisticians, and the new discoveries that are being made every day, that we sinned against God. We broke the rules (the moral law, that is) so *of course* everything went wrong, and this is our punishment, which nothing can mitigate, save we are sorry and beseech God to help us.

The only alternative explanation of our predicament is that of our Russian friends, whose theory is that it is the inevitable result of inexorable economic laws, working through increasing chaos to a classless millennium.

Our statesmen in general refuse to accept this determinist position, and scorn Our Lady's verdict if they have heard of it. This leaves them shaking their heads and saying that the matter is vastly too complex to be understood without vastly more research. Withal they keep sliding toward the Communist position.

It will be useful to examine Our Lady's hypothesis to see if facts do bear it out.

WHO SINNED AND WHAT SINS?

The hypothesis is that we're in our mess, of instability, war and threats of war, famine and all the rest of it, because we have sinned.

We certainly must have sinned on a vast scale to have warranted such a vast and tragic disorder. And so it appears.

In the first place, there is a universality about sin which is unprecedented in Christian history. It once was that the poor remained virtuous while the courts disported themselves. Infidelity, immodesty in dress, avarice, love of luxury and all the rest are now nearly as indigenous to the tenements as to Park Avenue. We have really attained a sort of equality, if only an equal guilt.

So it is also with countries. We like to fancy that our American hands are cleaner than some in Europe and Asia, but we are the ones who have committed some of the worst national crimes. Who dropped the atomic bomb? President Truman has not repented, and neither have we. We Americans also were responsible for some of the most ghastly air raids in Europe, not to mention looting, rape and black markets. We are the greatest materialists in the world. We have legalized divorce, are the chief promoters of birth control, increasingly favor euthanasia and conscientiously keep the mention of Christ out of our schools. Need one go on? The air is heavy with iniquity and commercialism, with worse vapors threatening. So Our Lady is right at least in her diagnosis. Now what about the prescription?

WHAT IS PENANCE?

Penance is sorrow and satisfaction for sins. It means first of all an acknowledgement to God that we have sinned against Him. That means confession on a personal basis. On a national basis it would mean something like a day set apart for sackcloth and ashes, or flags at half-mast during congressional beating of breasts, as representing the citizens at large. It would mean in consequence a shift back to the morality economy (where good is done for its own sake) from expediency (where good and bad are done indifferently according to whether or not it will pay).

As for the classification for sin, that means simply doing something distasteful to make up for sins, let it be anything from accepting cancer patiently to giving up cigarettes or eating spinach, or going without a new Nash.

WASTED SUFFERING

One of the most ironic things about today is that the amount and degree of suffering is enormous (has it ever been greater?), and it is virtually wasted. It is not wasted in this sense, that it satisfies God's justice (for it is punishment for sin, most of it). It may also serve to show men their folly and cause them to turn again to God and so save their souls. But is this usually the case? The suffering is too severe for the softened and weakened nature on which it falls. Cancer has not provoked a return to religion, nor do the majority of European sufferers seem so much chastened as bitter. But suffering far less than ours, if patiently accepted and offered to God in contrition, could be enormously efficacious.

It is the same way with our good deeds. Just as we have made suffering useless to our salvation because of our impatience, so even our virtuous acts are unmeritorious because of the motive. Things done for reasons of expediency do not help to win Heaven. If you give a million dollars to the poor out of vainglory, or loan money to Britain in order to save your own economy, or are honest because it is the best policy, there is no virtue in it, nor does much permanent good come of it even here on earth.

MORTIFICATION AND FREEDOM

Now let us look at another aspect of penance, the effect it has on our own spiritual nature. All penance has the indirect effect of mortifying our desires because it involves willingly denying them satisfaction.

The world's chaos is miniatured in each of us. There is a certain hierarchical order of our faculties which we only achieve (thanks to original sin) after patient self-discipline and self-denial. If instead of mortifying ourselves we go in for self-indulgence, we encourage our passions to revolt against the control of reason. Thus we become progressively enslaved to our lower natures and there is neither peace nor order within men. Naturally this is reflected in the condition of the world at large.

We love to exalt freedom and democracy but what good is political freedom to men who already are enslaved to themselves? What good is liberty if we are not masters of ourselves? It is like giving a drunkard the keys to the city.

What good are noble ideas if you can't carry them out? Modern American man is like a general who glibly promises to rush reinforcements into a breach and then finds his troops only laugh at his orders and continue their card playing. Or rather he is like a young man who cannot pass the acid test of manhood in order to wed the fair lady, or save his city, or win the crown of martyrdom, when the acid test consists in going without a cigarette for twenty-four hours. It's not that he prefers a cigarette to a fair lady and the rest, but just that when he comes to give orders to himself he discovers a mighty insurrection has taken place. Isn't penance relevant to this state of affairs?

PENANCE AND BOURGEOIS SOCIETY

The austerity of life which the spirit of penance fosters has its exact opposite in what is known as bourgeois living. It is the way you and I live. Of its essence are comfort, ease, mediocrity, labor-saving devices, pretensions. It is the social ideal of an all-pervading commercialism, the beatitude reflected by the advertisements. It used to be rare and limited to the comfortable, merchant middle class, but now bourgeois living has spread over all, especially in America.

The way you incite a Communist against the Western democracies is to point with scorn at our bourgeois softness. It can almost be said that the strength of the dictators, whether Communist or Fascist, lies in their fairly accurate condemnation of our vulnerable softness. They sometimes lie and often exaggerate, but the basis is really there.

The paradox of the situation is that our Fascist and Communist enemies really cherish the ideal they pretend to scorn. Karl Marx had enormous respect and admiration for the achievements of bourgeois capitalist society. The real grievance is that the Communists do not share in our luxurious living and they hold it out as a goal to their subjects, while asking them to despise it meanwhile in the interests of sacrifice to the state. One of the most pitiful aspects of Hitler was revealed after his death. He was not a fanatic, tragic, selfless madman. He was a petty bourgeois man who loved overstuffed furniture and geegaws[1] in too great abundance and deplorable taste.

So our bourgeois living both attracts and repels our Communist enemies who are in a sense, comrades behind the imitation-oriental-rug-beside-the-Benedix-automatic-washing-machine façade. As long as we cherish comfort and ease and pretension we are at their mercy. If they do not win us by force, they will win us be peaceful suasion. Is penance pertinent?

---

1 A showy, but valueless trinket. — *Ed.*

OUR LADY AND PENANCE

What has penance to do with Our Lady, and why is she God's emissary in this crisis? Well, it appears to be because of her role as Mediatrix of All Graces. That explains the apparitions. "I can scarcely restrain the arm of my Son," she said at La Salette, weeping. She is interceding for mercy for us and to get us a little more time to repent, whereas we have long since deserved complete disaster for our sins against God. If we had listened at Fatima, and done penance, we would have staved off the recent war and the terrible suffering continuing from it. We were warned of this at Fatima and reminded of it at Heede.

As Mediatrix of Graces, Mary has the power to increase the merit of voluntary sufferings and to distribute the graces that are earned by them. This is the burden of St. Louis de Montfort's teaching, that we should give to Mary all our satisfactions to distribute as she will. This is what she asked of the children of Fatima, that they make sacrifices for sinners, so that she would have more graces to distribute. The advantage of having Mary distribute the graces is not only that they are increased through her mediation, but also because she knows, as we cannot, how best to use them to avert universal disaster, and she has made it clear that her use of them will be, in a way she alone knows, conducive to the conversion of Russia, which will in turn stop the propagation of errors which cause the loss of very many souls.

THE UNEQUAL BURDEN

In a world of dog-eat-dog and eye-for-an-eye, we have forgotten the sacrificial nature of Christianity. Who is to do penance? Is each man to do it in proportion to his sins? Or are only the evil to do penance? Of course not! It is almost the other way around. Those who are the most pure and the least sinful are to do the most penance. "Make sacrifices for sinners," Our Lady demanded of three innocent children at Fatima. Christianity has always been an "unfair" arrangement in this regard, even since the Sinless One offered up His life for all of us who sin from the beginning to the end of the world.

OUR LADY AND RUSSIA

Mary specifically mentioned Russia at Fatima. Why is Russia so crucially important? The fate of the world doesn't hang on what happens in Holland and Greece, so why Russia? Obviously this mystery is bound up with the fact that Russia is the seat and source of

Communism. In fact, Our Lady's appearances at Fatima coincided with the Marxist coup d'etat in Russia and she knew it for the menace it was, before the world even took the matter very seriously.

There is something unique about Communism in comparison with other ills which beset mankind. Is it possibly this, that it represents the Devil's fully organized attack on what was once Christendom? The advent of Communism was preceded by several hundred years in which manifold errors in increasingly coalesced into systems. In the last century there arose Freemasonry, a secret society which gave form to the errors of the rationalists, and was a medium for an organized and seemingly diabolical attack on the Church. Indeed, this was the setting of the apparitions both at Fatima and at Lourdes. Communism seems to have superseded Freemasonry as an instrument of occult powers. Now it is in the open, has absolute political control, which is at the same time complete economic control. It is highly organized and persistently universal. Its propaganda tentacles are everywhere, and everywhere also antithetical to the Faith.

If this thesis is correct, and Communism does represent a major foothold of the Devil in world affairs, then Our Lady's intercession is vitally necessary for it is she who will crush the Serpent (that is to say, the Devil), to whom she was never subject because she was immaculately conceived.

If our struggle is against preternatural powers, then the U. N. is going to be pretty impotent, and we are going to need Mary's help badly. It is also obvious, if this is the case, why Russia will have to be converted. You can defeat a nation, but the Devil you can only exorcise. Once he has got this far he will take advantage of our every weakness (and certainly he outsmart us, for he has an angelic intellect) to spread his influence everywhere for his own ends. The naivete of statesmen will but play into the hands of the enemy.

From the secular point of view Russia doesn't seem at all consistent, and even the wisest among us cannot predict her next move. Now she tells the truth, now she doesn't. One minute she is conciliatory, the next obstinate. Why? What is Russia driving at? The whole thing makes sense only in the light of one end, and that the destruction of souls. Only Lucifer, Our Lady and the Church understand the real issue of our times.

"This kind can be cast out only by prayer and fasting." Again our role becomes clear. Penance is of the essence.

RUSSIA WILL BE CONVERTED

Our Lady of Fatima said that in the end Russia will be converted. If we do not do penance the errors of Communism will spread to every country in the world, but in the end Russia will be converted. How that will be if we don't do penance, has not been revealed. Obviously it will only come about after terrible suffering.

But there is no reason why we shouldn't do penance. If Our Lady chooses to use the graces that way, the sufferings of one cancer victim lovingly accepted might mean the conversion and salvation of Stalin. And heaven knows what might happen if Catholic office girls dressed poorly for Our Lady's sake and for the sake of the salvation of souls ("Christians ought not to follow the fashions," said Jacinta shortly before her death).

To those who believe, it should be obvious that the burden of righting the world situation lies chiefly with them.

12
The Death of Western Society
NOVEMBER 1947

I T IS ONLY WHEN YOU SEE OUR WESTERN SOCIETY AS dying that you can make any sense of it. If the contemporary scene is viewed as a deathbed scene, things fall into their right perspective, all the way down to the death rattle contributed by the ignorant but voluble optimists.

This is not an original idea, of course. The obsequies of the West have been celebrated by many a modern thinker. The trouble with most the learned diagnosticians is the same as the trouble which affects many a medical doctor these days—they do not realize that they are in on the death of what has been redeemed by Christ. They are always comparing ours with the dead civilizations of the modern world, which inevitably corrupted and died, inevitably and mysteriously. Much of the mystery and all of the inevitableness of our plight vanishes if you see that we are attending the last hours, not just of a splendid civilization, but of *Christendom*. The proper comparison is not with Rome or Egypt or even Babylon (despite many a similarity); it is with the Christian man. Societies are not men, and they don't have immortal souls; they will not go to heaven or hell. Nevertheless a striking analogy can be seen between the death of a Christian and the death of Christendom.

THE ALL-IMPORTANT MOMENT

The most important thing about death is that it is the final decisive moment of a man's life. Our life-paths are marked by temptations to mortal sin (the only real crises), at each of which a man turns decisively toward God or away from God. At death he has the final choice and so, no matter how the world may choose to gloss over the end of a man, that moment is not ignored by those who know its true significance. God and the Devil contend then for a man's soul. The Devil puts up quite a fight, unless he has long had the case sewed up. But God provides special graces that are even more powerful. In the natural order God has provided the "fear of death" which comes over a man in his last illness, presaging the end. It brings even the most superficial and worldly people (indeed especially these people) sharply to the consideration of eternal things and moral judgment. It is a last-ditch opportunity to turn to God's mercy through fear, if one has failed heretofore to seek Him through love. For many it is the last opportunity to save their souls.

Quite different and far greater is the supernatural help Christ has provided in the Sacrament of Extreme Unction, which along with Confession and Viaticum prepare a person for a holy departure from this life, and give graces to resist the Devil's temptations. The last anointing also restores health if it is for the good of the soul.

There is one other Christian aid to dying and that is, as traditionally taught by the Church, that Our Lady intercedes especially at that time—"Holy Mary, Mother of God, pray for us sinners now and *at the hour of our death.*"

THE DEVIL AND MODERN DEATH

In view of all the assistance god gives the dying man, the Devil is relatively powerless because all he can do is present temptations to the imagination. Yet working subtly (when will we learn that the Devil is much cleverer than we are?) and indirectly, Satan has arranged to win the deathbed battle without even bothering to be present. This is how it is done. First of all he has arranged for a conspiracy of silence about the impending death, under the guise of virtue. Produced as we all are today of a sentimental, residual humanitarianism, it is almost universally considered dastardly to allow a person to prepare to meet God. You must not tell him he's dying because it might kill him, is the curious line of reasoning that is taken. Yet for millions of materialists sodden with self-indulgence, what could be more salutary in the light of eternity than to spend several weeks contemplating the certainty of dying (provided, of course, that the love of God and the prospect of heaven are also made known). It would be enough to sanctify very mediocre material. As long, however, as hospitals and doctors and families continue dogmatically to hold their secular views, the Devil can take a vacation.

There is also the little matter of sudden death. The chances of a man's dying in an automobile accident or an airplane crash or by bombing, atomic or otherwise, are very good today—vastly greater than ever before. If we were all holy people it wouldn't matter if we were caught unawares, but the likelihood is that some of us could use a few minutes for an act of contrition, and so, at present, sudden death plays into the Devil's hands. Indeed, he may have helped invent some of the instruments thereof.

Finally, we find modern man lavishly provided with opiates to ease the pain of dying. This is no simple situation. There appears to be a great increase in suffering (notably cancer) combined with a loss of the ability, physical and spiritual, to accept it. It would indeed be cruel to take away a cancer patient's morphine.

Yet morphine, besides killing pain, gives people a false sense of well-being. A man who is, in fact, about to die feels that his demise is remote. That "fear of death" which God provided in our very nature, as a last salutary warning, just doesn't operate. Does it make very much difference? I have heard of a nurse whose cancer patient was in great physical anguish and even greater moral peril, highly unrepentant and openly contemptuous of God. There was no way of reaching the woman through the pleasant haze of morphine, so the nurse stopped giving morphine, merely going through the motions as larger and larger doses were ordered by the doctor in response to the woman's complaints. As soon as the morphine wore off, the fear of death penetrated even the pain. The patient repented, made her peace with God, and then was given morphine again to ease the last few hours. What this nurse did (her moral duty) would be considered a shockingly cruel and professionally unethical thing. To allow pain for the salvation of a soul is considered immoral—by people who are beginning to commit murder as the latest in pain-killers.

THE MISSPENT LATTER DAYS OF WESTERN SOCIETY

Let us now get to our analogy. Like men, societies die; also like men they sin mortally (that is, men collectively turn against God). Our society has committed more and more serious sins. There was a terrible break with God when Christendom split and half of it fell into heresy. But a sort of recovery was made. There was another bad break following the Industrial Revolution when men turned their hearts to the accumulation of wealth. But we marched on down the wrong road, still far from its dead end, still able to turn back. Then we turned God out of peace conferences and we turned fervently nationalistic. Again and again we drove out the religious, confiscating their monasteries. The going got tougher, what with a succession of wars. And we got desperate in sinning, using incendiary and finally atomic bombs. All along the way until now there has been the possibility of repentance and recovery. But nothing is different. Christendom is dying.

The patient has cancer. It is riddled with it. It is diseased in almost every cell. This being so, the disease may be studied locally. An X-ray of the local cancers of Kansas City or Miami would be almost as revealing as one done in Budapest or Chicago or Moscow. The remedy can also be applied locally—but we'll come to that. Our society is dying and is in a state of mortal sin.

OUR LADY

That's why Our Lady keeps appearing. It is the hour of our death, so she comes to tell us that she is interceding for us, and pouring graces upon us. She says what you say to a dying man: Repent, do penance, pray, turn again to God. You don't approach a dying banker with a new loan system or a dying mayor with plans for a housing project. You don't suggest to a dying not-so-good housewife that she try a new vacuum cleaner, or approach the dying drunk for membership in AA. It is too late for new beginnings in the temporal order. Nothing remains except to repent and make your peace with God. The Blessed Virgin is the only one giving sensible advice these days.

THE FEAR OF DEATH

God is trying to give us the fear of death too, by showing us as clearly as possible that we are dying and that we have sinned. Everything men touch fails these days. Men can't make peace. Men can't stop divorce. Men can't cure or prevent insanity. Men can't distribute the world's goods properly. The financial world is a mess; the economic world is a mess; the political world is a mess. And the atom bomb hovers over us. But why go on? Our heart is failing; our lungs are almost finished. Everywhere there are aches and sores.

God's mercy in our days wears a disguise to the ordinary man. Just as the fear of death is merciful in the case of the dying man (because it is a help to salvation), even if it isn't pleasant, so God is gracious now in allowing our plans to fail. Were we only sick, or even healthy, He would show His love in good harvests and soft rain. But in the hour of death, supreme mercy is to defeat man's hope whenever he seeks it where there is no hope; so that in the end he may turn to his Only Hope.

US AND THE DEVIL

What's happened to the Devil? He's taking a vacation someplace, because he has everyone working for him.

First he has all the doctors and relatives around to assure us we'll be up and about in a week or two. All those newspaper men, teachers, public officials and professional statesmen who make a life work of reassuring us, belong in this group.

Then the Devil is tempting us to sins of the flesh and unbelief on a colossal scale. His major helpers here are the advertising men who thrust upon us a multiplicity of luxuries to tempt us to sins of the flesh. As long as we are drowned in the comforts and gadgets of materialism we will be too stupid to see how late it is. But should we try to rise to the intellectual level we shall only encounter the stupidities and inanities of a decadent and diseased liberalism, calculated to drive us all into the oblivion of dementia.

But the Devil's big work is in opiates. We are doped with spiritual morphine until we have developed a shocking unconcern, a false sense of security. It is done with movies, radio, mass circulation magazines, comic strips. A man need never think, be silent, come face to face with the God Who will so soon judge him.

HYPODERMIC NEEDLES

When a man is dying a nurse will often startle him back into a few minutes of life with a hypodermic needle. In a way fascism and communism are like hypodermic needles. In a dying, lethargic people they stimulate momentarily a little life through force and emotional fervor. It looks strong, but it can't last because it is an artificial stimulation. Yet we who hate these tyrannic movements had better see them for what they are — an unlovely alternative to death. What have we to offer in their place?

THE LAST SACRAMENTS

It is too late for any purely economic or political nostrum, even a good one. It is interesting to speculate as to whether Belloc's and Chesterton's Distributism (which was essentially an economic scheme) might have saved England and possibly Europe, if it had been applied in, say the 1920's. One wonders if some correction of the ills of usury wouldn't have mended many matters once. Quite possibly so. While we were still suffering from acute mortal sin there was the possibility of turning back, and whereas it would have to be accompanied by a turning back to God also, it could possibly have started with economic reform. Chesterton's insistence that we go back to where we took the wrong road, and his insistence also that it had to be done very quickly, were probably quite correct at that time. It was the eleventh hour. We didn't turn back. Now it is midnight and we are dying!

There is only one hope for society now, and that is hope in the supernatural. The doctors have failed. Let the priests take over, including the lay priesthood of Catholic Action.

First of all there must be penance, as is beginning to happen as men are turned by grace from sinning and worldliness to beg for forgiveness. This includes the converts, and the cradle Catholics who are being converted from mediocrity to some comprehension of the meaning of their Faith.

After the turning away from evil to God comes the strengthening of the Eucharist, which more and more people are receiving daily.

And finally, then, these people who have turned away from a corrupt world to purify themselves by the Sacraments, administer to our dying society a sort of Extreme Unction in the form of Catholic Action. Whether it uses the Jocist technique or some other integrating form, this Catholic action must have the effect of dynamically restoring supernatural grace to our dying world. Therefore all purely natural efforts will fall infinitely short of the vitality necessary. When a billing machine operator invites the engaged girl at the next desk to an explanation of the Sacrament of Matrimony, she is applying a bit of the holy unction, as is the contemplative nun doing penance for the world, and the Belgian Jocist restoring purity to a factory, and the Mexican Catholic Action girl teaching catechism in a remote, priest-less province, and the Hungarian martyr before the forces of communism, and the mother who starts the family rosary.

But the man, whoever he may be, who goes all out for the Republican Party, or rests his hope in a planned society or in our banks, or International Business Machines, or free milk at ten o'clock in the morning, or the Marshall Plan, or what not, is impotent to help dying Christendom and probably will hasten its corruption. And Grover Whalen, with his plan for New York City's Golden Jubilee, is only fiddling while Rome burns.

All men ought to love God with their whole hearts but at this crucial point no one ought to make his religion a subsidiary or part-time occupation. The only people who can save society are those who give their whole lives to doing so. In the midst of secular occupations the prime concern will be to speak of God to those with whom they are associated and to try to turn the institutions of society once more Christ-ward.

IF IT IS FOR THE GOOD OF THE SOUL

If our analogy holds, that something like Extreme Unction is being applied to our dying society by Catholic Action and other vital movements, then the patient should recover its health, *if it is for the good of its soul*. That must mean that if the effect is strong enough and successful enough and soon enough to turn men and institutions decisively Godward, we shall be spared. There would be no point in saving Western society if it only meant a continued increase in the population of hell—just as there is no point in having children if they are to lose their souls.

How much has to be done to make it worthwhile to save us? No one knows, but it isn't just a matter of numbers—one person in a state of grace plus another person in a state of grace, etc. There is also the matter of re-directing society, which means reintegrating life with religious principles. If then, health is restored, it will come about naturally, as in Extreme Unction, and naturally in this case means through a new synthesis.

Let us therefore make haste, using all our energy to restore things in Christ. Let those who think we are not in a final crisis consider if they are not enjoying a false peace, opium induced. And let us not be like the social workers and nurses (whom may heaven help) who hide the fact of impending death because the patient is "psychologically unprepared" to face it. God does not wait on our good pleasure, let alone our folly.

1948

13
Job Hunting and Vocation
JANUARY 1948

Nothing could be more unnatural by way of discovering one's life-work than the current, debasing system of "job-hunting." It would be more dignified and nearer the true ideal, to be born a slave who grows up to take his place on his master's plantation. At least such a one *has a place*. Back of today's perusal of the want-ad columns, back of today's dreary trek from employment agency to employment agency, back even of the scheming and conniving through one's father's friends for "pull," is the terrifying assumption that one is extraneous to the world's affairs, that there is no place waiting but that an opening has to be hacked out in a desperate competitive effort at survival. The Christian idea and the currently accepted method are poles apart. The Christian idea is *vocation*; our commercial reality is *job-hunting*.

We speak of vocations to the religious life and the priesthood. Doesn't God call us also to tasks in the world? Yes He does, but the idea that one's daily work is a vocation is an idea that was lost through a perversion of it by Protestantism. Calvinism combined with industrialism to try to induce a religious fervor into what were not really vocations, but just jobs. We still have traces of that today, even among Catholics. "This is the job you have," they say, "therefore it is obviously the will of God—so consecrate yourself to it." The catch is that people do not find themselves in these jobs—they go hunting for them. There is no real evidence that they are doing the will of God, although of course God has allowed them to be there. Historically, this false, Calvinistic concept of vocation led to a single-minded intense devotion to money-making as the final end. It was one of the major factors in bringing about our industrial-capitalistic economic system. The great men of the modern world have been the saints and monks of business, for whom no sacrifice was too great. They were led by the beatific vision of Infinite Wealth. They gave a religious devotion to their lifework of building up a fortune.

The Calvinist error was not so much in advocating devotion to one's calling. It was in considering a job, or an opportunistic avaricious move, a "calling." The same thing holds today. Did God call you into the public relations field? Or were you maneuvered in that direction by your own desire to earn a lot of money with minimum effort and maximum glamor? Has God planned from all eternity for you to throw away the natural gifts He gave you and suppress all your natural affections, in the interest of filing insurance policies accurately? If you are quite sure that He willed it so, then you can proceed in this purgatorial way of salvation. If you are not following God's will, but your own inertia or craven love of material security, beware! Every talent will have to be accounted for.

THE MECHANISM AND THE ORGANISM

There are two kinds of societies. The organic society (a Christian society will always be organic) is one in which each man has a *functional* place, no two doing exactly the same work (as the eye doesn't do what the ear does) but all contributing to the proper functioning of the whole, and each one necessary in some real way.

A mechanical society (as is industrial capitalism) rides roughshod over the delicate functional differences in men. It does not care to foster each man's unique talent. It is not interested in developing initiative and responsibility. It ignores one's brains and mind, preferring to regiment us under someone else's direction. This sort of society always tends toward total centralization and concentration of all forces, with fewer and fewer men at the top directing serried ranks of de-rationalized men. In addition to the men (a handful of men) who guide a mechanized society, there is a small intellectual coterie who subserve them. These are the engineers, inventors, scientists, etc. All these people use their brains and talents to the bursting point. Nobody else uses them at all. The work is accomplished by a lot of machines, but the whole system is a vast machine, in which the ordinary man is a mere unthinking mechanical part.

How do you find your place in such a set-up? You just go looking around until you find an opening. It doesn't matter much where, because your talents and desires are irrelevant to almost all the jobs. There is no reason why you should have this job rather than someone else, except that you got there first, or your Uncle Jim is the employment manager. Every once in a while the vast machine, which is the system, expands or contracts for reasons having to do with its own basic lack of conformity to the true nature of things. Then machine

Job Hunting and Vocation

parts called men are let out or taken on in droves. This being wanted or not being wanted, being useful or useless, is again something you suffer through no fault or action of your own — unless it be your share in the gigantic sin of omission which is the neglect to change the system.

A mechanical society is never in itself conformable to God's will, because it is not erected on man's rational nature, since it denies each man the use of his own reason and his own gifts in his daily work. It regiments men in a way fitted for termites, so it is wrong at its beginning. A good society, a Christian one, may take many accidental forms, but it will always be organic, and in the main, functional. It may use machines. That isn't the point. It will not make of society one vast machine.

TODAY'S DILEMMA

Since a mechanistic society is *of itself* not conformed to God's will, how can we do God's will working within it? The answer is that we can't, as such. People who are conformed to God's will in such a society will participate in the structure of society accidentally. A girl will spend fifty years filing or adding or sorting to support an invalid mother, and in so doing can become a saint. But the structure of society is accidental to her noble purpose. God looks to her sacrifice and not to the end of the work she is doing, because her sacrifice is the reason for her accepting a life of drudgery.[1] If our heroine had not been under the necessity of supporting her mother, but merely under the necessity of supporting herself, the case would be different. Could she be sure that God wanted her to follow the path of least resistance when there are things of God's work which need doing?

As a general principle, if one's life work is considered in itself, and not in relation to some accidental reason or necessity, then it is impossible for a person to find his *vocation* (to do God's calling) in a mechanical society. He has to be in a functional, organic society, because that is the only society which allows for true vocation.

GOD'S ECONOMY IS ALWAYS PRESENT

The answer to that dilemma is that God has a functional economy which operates regardless of how much we men mess up the economic

---

[1] Of course she couldn't do evil even for her mother's sake, but this is the case of the person so remote from evil in which she might be cooperating as not to share in its immorality.

and political order of things. If we can't be farmers or blacksmiths or artists (which were *vocations* in the essentially functional society of the Middle Ages), we can be apostles, and street speakers and textbook writers and holy attendants at insane asylums and contemplatives in a monastery or elsewhere, which are some of the functional positions in God's contemporary organic society.

There are two economies today. There is the mechanical one in the material order, and there is God's economy in, shall we say, the supernatural order, which is related to the world's economy at all sorts of odd points, but the two are really antagonistic, because our mechanistic society is what men have conjured up out of their godlessness.

GOD'S ECONOMY

God's economy is directed toward the salvation of souls, both immediately and through changing the world's economy so that it will conduce to the salvation instead of the destruction of souls. The keynote of God's economy is that it is apostolic. There are two main directions. First there is the general leavening process, the turning of men's hearts, one by one, away from avarice and materialism and sin to God. This is to be done within that other system which is so bad because the people are there who have to be leavened. It is this apostolic purpose which is sufficient reason (if it seems to be God's will) for Jane and Alice and Tom and Harry to remain at their filing and their benches — to bring their fellow workers to Christ. God can work organically within the mechanical monster which wants to destroy us. The other direction is the re-orientation of the institutions of society, which usually must be done with a certain amount of freedom of action, and therefore at a certain distance from the present order. The important thing to remember is that God does have an organic society which transcends a mechanical one, and in God's pattern each of us has a special functional place.

THE UNIQUE NATURE OF TODAY'S VOCATIONS

There is no point in crying over spilt milk or sighing for a more ordered society. You ought not to wish that you were a gently-bred English aristocrat instead of a New York City office girl with a Brooklyn accent. We are called to be saints, not culture vultures; and Brooklynese, previous personal experience as an alcoholic, night-school at Hunger College, and still-unmarried-at-twenty-eight, may prove to be more useful states in the economy of today's salvation than a perfect command of the French language, classical features, or a Ph.D. in Psychology. It certainly would have been unseemly of Joan of Arc to have refused to command an army on the grounds that woman's place is in the kitchen. The important thing is to do the will of God, to allow ourselves to be called to the vocations which God wishes, and for which we may find we were remotely preparing (according to the mysterious economy of God's Providence) even in the midst of heartache and darkness. We may not want to live in our own time, but God is always operating in the present, nor can it truthfully be said that we are unfortunate in the choice of our generation. Pius XI thought it a singular privilege to live in such exciting times. And so it is. It is a time for saints. The thing which is hard today, which is virtually impossible, is to muddle along.

Certain generalizations can be made about today's vocations, just from viewing the times. Certain it is that you will not be swimming with the crowd. You will definitely be going against the tide — at least until we succeed in changing the direction of the current. That is why job-hunting is so futile. The sorts of jobs that are open are all jobs within the system, but we have to change the system, and most of the work will not be done from within. This is also why the educational system is off the beam. In general it is preparing us to *fit in*, where it ought to be preparing us to *make over*.

There will be, and in fact there already is, an increase in religious vocations to the contemplative life. The Trappist monasteries, and the Carmels, are filling up, or are already full. The penance and prayer therein will form the basis of the work of those whose vocations are in the world. There will also be an increase in vocations of suffering in the world. There certainly is an increase in suffering, which seems to indicate (to the cancer victims, the starving and the oppressed) a vocation to suffer willingly that the world may turn again to God.

There are no real secular vocations today, that is, vocations to do the work of the world (which could be good in itself, of course) without regard to religious considerations. This is especially true among the young, and it is what is meant by a general call to the lay apostolate. Today's street cleaner will have to work to convert his fellow street cleaners; today's doctor will have to restore Christian ideals of medicine; today's millionaire will have to start, for example, a movie company to tell of God; today's mother will have to raise saints (and stop undue worry about health, education, and manners); today's writer will have to write the Good News; and vast numbers of us will have to get out of what we are doing or what we are trained to do, in order to initiate or cooperate with some other work we haven't yet dreamt of.

Now the basic reason for this change from secularism is that all the problems that are important problems today are spiritual problems at their roots, and we Catholics have to attack the problems at their roots. That means that not only must we have religious motives and spiritual development, but what we are doing must have as its discernable end the restoration of all things in Christ.

HOW TO FIND YOUR VOCATION

As I have tried to show, the difference between a Christian and a secular society does not lie in the fact that there are vocations in the former and not in the latter, but in the fact that in a secular society vocations (as contrasted with jobs) transcend the established economic or political order. Since such is the case one will not easily fall into one's vocation; the less easily the more one is a materialist. This is why a secular society is advantageous to the Devil. It is harder to save your soul if you have not found your rightful place in society (as anyone can testify who is married to the wrong husband or who is typing when she wants to paint, or writing advertising copy when he wants to build houses). And it is much harder to find your vocation in a secular society. The Popes have put it this way: today it is impossible to be mediocre. They mean that if you are mediocre, if you only make a half-hearted effort, you will be carried off by the trend of the times into the loss of your soul.

Most people fail to find their vocations through lack of spiritual development. A vocation is a calling from God, which means you have to be near enough to hear God above the din of worldliness. The most practical advice that can be given to a young man or woman in search of a lifework is to go to Mass and Communion every morning and learn how to pray. The great saints reached so great intimacy with God that they were almost directed from within by the prompting of the Holy Ghost. You won't have to reach that stage before you find your vocation, but increased holiness means increased docility to the Holy Ghost acting through the gifts which we all have latently. However, in general a deepened spiritual life will make you spiritually sensitive and you will begin to see God's order of things, the order into which you will fit.

Since today's vocations are, because of the nature of the Church's situation, apostolic, the more one develops an apostolic sense the closer one will approach one's vocation. It is important to realize this. Some people think it is enough that work be good in itself for them to do it. It is a good thing to dust furniture, but not when the house is on fire. It is a good thing to sit on the grass and drink lemonade, but not while a child is drowning in the lake in front of you.

If you use your head and deepen your spiritual life, God will show you your vocation. It will be indicated through circumstances, through reason and through your talents, which will soon begin asserting themselves.

When you have found your rightful path, it will probably be an odd one and even a mysterious one, but you will have that sense of peace which comes from being in harmony with God's will and which is at the opposite pole from that resignation which comes upon mechanized slaves who have ceased to protest. There will also be a blessed relief from the temptation to envy. People richer, more famous, better dressed, healthier, even doing nobler things will leave you unmoved, save sincerely to wish them well. In God's economy each man knows he has only to perform his own function well. Does the ear envy the eye? Neither will we envy and emulate millionaires and movie actresses when we have found our vocations in God's functional order.

14

The Good News— Plain and Sugared

FEBRUARY 1948

> If he had overcome his flesh, if he had mortified his appetite, if he had chosen the austerities that refine like a pure flame, he would still have something of the power, purity, of a child. He would still be able to effect a communion with heaven, through his contact on earth. Perhaps his wife would not have left him, *if his caress had not lost the power to communicate love.*

SO SAYS CARYLL HOUSELANDER ABOUT ONE OF THE CHAR-acters in *The Dry Wood.*

If we abuse the gifts and talents and faculties God has given us, corrupting them with habits of insincerity, our faculties will not prove suitable instruments for a changed will and a new sincerity. This is as true as applied to intellectual and creative gifts as it is applied to physical faculties. If we use our oratorical or literary or poetic or artistic gifts insincerely (giving people what they want, which is not what they ought to want, or shuffling relative values, or writing someone else's ideas which are not also our ideas, or subordinate our gifts to an advertiser's end), then our gifts are not fit instruments for noble and sincere purposes. Those who have been writing singing commercials needn't try a hymn to Our Lady. Those who have been drawing pretty girls should refrain from immediate transfer of their talents to the Stations of the Cross. Don't think that because someone writes well for Coca Cola, or contributes to *The Saturday Evening Post*, or edits *The Reader's Digest*, that he can write the Gospel according to N. B. C.

The generality of contemporary artists and writers has so prostituted its talents that it is better to look among amateurs for someone to convey a great message. This is not because lack of polish is in itself a virtue but because freshness and purity can at least convey a great idea, whereas abused powers cannot.

All this philosophizing has its application in the field of religious radio. It helps explain why a much-lauded program, *The Greatest Story*

Ever Told, is very bad, and why another, less-auspiciously launched, *The Hour of St. Francis*, is very excellent indeed.

THE TWO PROGRAMS

The Greatest Story Ever Told is a half-hour Sunday evening coast-to-coast network dramatization of the Gospels. It is sponsored by Goodyear Tires, which omits its commercial, and is written by Fulton Oursler, who is at present a senior editor of *The Reader's Digest*. He is a convert to the Catholic Church of several years standing.

The Hour of St. Francis is an apostolic venture conceived and executed by a Franciscan priest. It is a fifteen-minute dramatic program, showing the ideals of Saint Francis in their application to modern life. Recorded in Hollywood, it is offered as a sustaining program by well over one hundred local stations in the United States and Canada. The expense is carried by members of the Third Order of Saint Francis. Ideas for the program came from Franciscan priests and members of the Third Order, and are written in script form by several professional Hollywood writers who have a facility for grasping the ideas, and by several tertiaries without previous script-writing experience. Before each recording the actors and actresses kneel and pray, so we can suppose that they regard this assignment as more than a chance to make money. Their acting is excellent.

THE VERNACULAR AND THE VULGAR

Both these programs want to popularize religion. One understands how this must be done in our day, the other does not.

It can be laid down as a general rule almost without exception that the *historical* Christ, as historical, will not win contemporary hearts. Religious drama that is heavy with Palestinian lore, bearded men and flowing garb, merely confirms men's suspicion that Christianity is an old and dead thing, a musty relic in a bright new day of progress. What men must be shown is the *living* Christ: Christ Who is present in the Macy's which ignores Him (and can kindle the fire of His love there), Christ present to and in the derelicts of the Bowery, and the elbow of the Park Avenue divorcee, Christ redeeming and saving and loving and transforming in the midst of a secular world.

The Franciscans have caught this principle exactly. Almost all their settings are contemporary and true to life. They build their programs around such characters as a thirty-nine-year old secretary, single and lonely, a couple of atom bomb scientists at work in a desert shed at night, a successful businessman coming into Grand Central Station on the Twentieth Century Limited, or a fussy housekeeper who doesn't want to take care of a cancerous relative. Once in a while a script is set in thirteenth-century Assisi, but usually even then with a modern note. One such was about the Gallepo Poll conducted by the star reporter of the *Assisi Blade* to increase circulation. In 1181 he asked: Who is the most popular man in Assisi? Unanimous answer: Francis Bernardoni. A year later he asked: Who is the most unpopular man in Assisi? and go the same answer (Francis had just become a beggar). Twenty years later the new widely-circulated *Blade* inquired far and wide for the most popular man in the world—who turned out to be, of course, Francis of Assisi.

But in general the scripts hug the contemporary scene. The authors are especially to be commended about the thirty-nine-year old secretary, lonely and weary of life, whose name might be legion. This one makes her way to the roof of the office building to kill herself and there meets Saint Francis (he conveniently appears and disappears as ragged Brother Francis in these scripts) who explains that she would do well to lose her life but not in the way she's contemplating.

There is none of this intense relevance to modern life in *The Greatest Story Ever Told*. When we encounter the man with a superabundance of grain whose life is about to be required of him he is just a two-thousand-year old Semite with shades of nineteenth century religious art and the magazine section of the Hearst Sunday papers. Yet how easily he might have been a successful stockbroker about to retire from margin dealings.

Where Fulton Oursler has failed to contemporize he has tried to popularize by putting some of the conversation in the vernacular. Now if he really had put modern conversation into the mouths of ancient characters the effect would have been weird. He has done worse than that. He has speckled his scripts with the hackneyed phrases and cheap clichés of the soap opera and the feature article. In consequence, he has been justly accused of vulgarization. A few phrases will suffice to show how ludicrous it is. Imagine Saint Joseph speaking to Mary about "your baby and my baby," or telling her "Oh, it's good to see you smile!" See what indignity is visited on Anne and Joachim by having them say, "The Angel Gabriel appearing to *my* daughter! Will we ever get used to it?" It's corn, straight out of the soap opera.

Fulton Oursler doesn't mean to be vulgar, or sentimental or almost blasphemous in his familiarity (as it sometimes seems). There is no reason to doubt his sincerity. But he has spent a lifetime with Grade B novels, with magazine articles calculated to attract circulation and with the Rotarian sentimentality of the digest magazines. His pen falls into the hackneyed groove by the irresistible pull of long habit, as yet unpurged by literary austerity. He cannot express the reverence and sincerity he undoubtedly feels.

SENTIMENT AND SENTIMENTALITY

Emotion is useful for raising our hearts to God and, when properly subordinated to the spiritual meaning of a drama, can increase our understanding of holy things. The difference between sentiment and sentimentality is that the former is proper feeling, the latter disordered feeling. Sentimentality is emotionalism for its own sake, or in excess of what the situation demands, or even as a substitute for the spiritual or intellectual.

Sentimentality pervades *The Greatest Story Ever Told*. It is sentiment definitely disordered and illegitimately aroused. Like *The Reader's Digest* it leaves its audience in a state of emotional exhaustion. Emotion is aroused not so much by what is said as by how. Most of the actors are panting all the time, which is meant to convey the intense excitement which is going on. All the cheap acting tricks of the soap opera are used. One is the initial stutter: "I...I...." "Mary...Mary...." "Ezra...Ezra, don't...." That sort of thing. Another trick is jerky speech. Here is Mary saying the Magnificat: "My soul (deep breath) doth magnify (pause, pause) the Lord (deep breath)." Then there is slow talking (to express holiness) and a lot of exclamations. Every scene is played for all it is worth, indeed for much more than it's worth at the level of the spiritual comprehension of the dialogue.

The Hour of Saint Francis (blessed relief) is played straight. No one's voice sounds like an exaggerated moan. The meaning and writing, plus the situation, raise feelings without the necessity of resorting to anything besides good acting. The openings and closings of the scripts are sharp and clean; the conclusion is always restrained. This is even true with episodes which are charged with emotional possibilities. There was one in which Saint Francis' humility and charity in caring for a leper effected a miraculous cure of leprosy. Every effort was obviously made to put restraint into that script, and it ended almost abruptly, as soon as the climax was passed.

INSPIRATION AND FORMULA

One way to tell a hackneyed radio program is to see if it is written to formula. Formula means that the pattern is so set and standardized that, given the weekly or daily theme, any hack could write the script automatically. With programs like *Corliss Archer* one sometimes suspects that any intelligent listener could write the next program, so neat and inevitable is the sequence of events.

The Greatest Story is written to the least inspired of all formulas: simple chronology. It begins. It plods from event to event in natural sequence. It comes at long last to a halt. Sometimes there is not even a well-defined climax.

The Franciscan programs are uniquely without formula. They transmit the ideals of Saint Francis with a constant freshness. Not only are they without formula but they also cast aside (successfully) some of the sacred canons of radio. One script is about "what God looks like" in which a father reads aloud as he writes a letter to his young son. It is practically a fifteen-minute monologue. Now everyone in radio knows that two or three minutes is the longest single speech the audience will tolerate. Yet this went on, with two short episodic interruptions, for a whole script, on a very difficult subject, and held attention.

Radio should take note of these Franciscan programs because they illustrate the freedom and variation which result from having a solid grasp of a subject. The contrast in this respect between our two programs was especially evident at Christmas because they treated the same subject completely differently. Fulton Oursler, as might be expected, labored through a detailed chronological account of the birth of Christ, with a few interpolations of his own (the shepherds hunting all over Bethlehem for the stable).

The Franciscans plunged right in, cleanly as always (They have a sort of an O. Henry way of giving the whole setting in an opening sentence.): "Night has fallen over the City of Commerce and Thomas Berkeley...." There you are immediately in New York or Chicago or in any American town on Christmas Eve, with Christ about to be born again to us. Just as in Bethlehem so in the City of Commerce the simple and the learned hastened to adore at the Crib. Thomas Berkeley, a prominent businessman, is one with the people in Bethlehem who slept through that night, who through all the glory lay in comfort and indifference. And so the story proceeds, showing how difficult it is for the mediocre to adore — and yet not impossible.

COMPROMISE AND CLARITY

Each script of *The Greatest Story Ever Told* is said to be censored by a Protestant minister, a Jewish rabbi, and a Catholic priest. If you think this leads to ambiguity of doctrine you are quite right. It does indeed. Christ becomes a sort of emasculated "Master" (with a prolonged broad "a"). How could it be otherwise under commercial sponsorship? It is interesting to watch the effect of this on the program content. Is Christ man or God-man? Well, that issue is carefully avoided. On one program the necessity was mentioned of "being born again of the Holy Ghost" (not of water and the Holy Ghost). The angels at Christmas sang "Peace on earth and good will among men," in the popular Protestant version. The Lord's Prayer, oddly, doesn't go beyond the first few phrases. The only moral lessons driven home with any vigor are the vaguish humanitarian ones. Here's religion with lots of emotional content, no supernatural reference, and without any definite dogma. Is that why so many people like the program?

The Franciscans, by pleasant contrast, are precise on their dogma, precise on their moral law. The above-mentioned script about what God looks like was a masterpiece of clarity. It told how nature reflects God without once muddling it with pantheism. As for moral questions, they are met head on. The Franciscans don't even promise people they can have their cake and eat it too. They give them straight stuff. One story is about the governess (Frances) of a child whose mother is insane. The husband falls in love with the governess and proposes. She loves him too. Most of the fifteen minutes is taken up with her tormented thoughts during the night she makes her decision. Here is part of it:

> Frances: (Tries to pray) Arches — empty arches, long, white rows of them....
> Voice: I fled him down the arches of the years.
> Frances: I read that somewhere. The arches of the years.... These are the arches of the years — stretching out before me, cold and barren and endless, the years without him....

Voice: It's wrong.
Frances: I can't help it. I love him!
Voice: It's wrong.
Frances: I can't go on without him!
Voice: He has a wife — she's still alive.
Frances: She might as well be dead. She's insane. She'll never be better.
Voice: She is still his wife.
Frances: He loves me now. He'll get a divorce.
Voice: You can't marry a man when his wife is living. It's a sin.
Frances: Is love a sin? I could make him happy — him and the child. I could be happy. Is that a sin?
Voice: "Whom God has joined together...."

Incidentally, that is good technical use of the radio, which can do tricks with voices impossible to other media.

THE RADIO APOSTOLATE

The analysis of these two programs indicates much about the use of radio for the apostolate. It shows the primacy of the spiritual. Without holy people, spiritually formed, we can do nothing in the radio apostolate. With them money, prestige, form and all the other secondary things are easily obtained. We have become so overawed by large concentrations of money and economic power that we underestimate the power of the spirit.

Another lesson we ought to learn (we should have learned it long ago) is that big names and popularity and lots of listeners can be as so much sounding brass. The progress of the Church is not measured in fanfare but in foolishness, not in money but in martyrs. All the comfortable bourgeois citizens who have divided their lives neatly between God and mammon may listen to and applaud a program which has no spiritually transforming effect whatever.

A last conclusion is that we ought not to complain unduly about religion's being slighted on the radio until we have learned to purify our own motives and make proper and apostolic use of the radio opportunities we have.

15
The Science of Temptation

APRIL 1948

THE PHENOMENON OF MODERN ADVERTISING RESTS increasingly on a coherent set of underlying principles which together form the Science of Temptation. As a leading advertising man once put it: "Our business is to get people to buy things they don't need, don't want and can't afford." Books on advertising try to explain how this is done in a scientific manner. They could be much more exact and comprehensive about their explanations if they would read Saint Thomas Aquinas. The art of temptation is not new. The novelty lies in men's considering it honorable.

THE DEVIL'S PSYCHOLOGY

Unmoral man is an abstraction. Saint Thomas says that anything we do, in the concrete, is either good or bad, not neutral. Walking is neither good nor bad, considered in itself, but any particular walk takes on moral color from its destination and circumstances. Similarly, there is no such thing as an unmoral psychology. Rational Psychology, which merely describes what the will is like, what the intellect is like and so forth, can only exist as an abstract study. Let psychology deal with cases and it enters the moral realm, either directly or indirectly. The intellect understands — but does it understand truly or not? The will chooses, but rightly or wrongly? The passions operate, but are they in accordance with right reason, or are they swaying the reason because they are out of control?

Theology (first moral, and then ascetical and mystical) analyzes the progressive workings of the soul on its way upward to God. Incidental to this it discusses the temptations, the vices and deceits to which the soul is liable, and which would deflect it from its proper course. Today it has been found profitable to categorize these temptations, not, strangely enough, so that they might be avoided, but that they might be exploited. The knowledge of man's tendencies to vice is used to pull him toward indulgence rather than away from the danger. This Devil's Psychology which forms the basis for modern advertising we shall call the Science of Temptation.

There is only one perfection suitable to our nature. Our reason must be subject to God, and our lower nature (emotional and carnal) brought under the subjection of reason. The main effort of our lives should be directed to the establishment of this hierarchical order in ourselves. It is not easy. Because we are both body and soul there is an inevitable struggle between the flesh and the spirit. Because of original and subsequent sin there is also a struggle in the soul itself, against the spiritual sins such as pride, envy, malice and rancor. With the help of grace, good will and long hard work, we can hope finally to harmonize our nature under God's jurisdiction.

The Science of Temptation is calculated not to heal the wounds in our nature, but to exploit them. It sets passion against reason, the flesh against the spirit, and even creates disorder in the purely spiritual part of man. Whatever may be the immediate excuse for exploiting man's weaknesses (in the case of advertising it is profit), it is evident that the natural end of the Science of Temptation itself is precisely the damnation of souls. That is why it is called accurately "The Devil's Psychology."

WHAT ADVERTISING IS

Most people who defend advertising do it according to their own definition. This is not legitimate. They cannot define advertising as it pleases them, but must consider the phenomenon as it exists. It is not an activity that can be traced back to ancient Egypt, but a business which scarcely antedates the year 1900. It is bound up integrally with a bad economic system and a godless philosophy.

Many would like to hold that advertising is just a technique, neither good nor bad in itself but capable of being used for good or bad ends. They imply that it is only a matter of time before advertising will be made to serve man's spiritual and material perfection. This is not true. We will show that it cannot be instrumental in man's true progress. Let us first plan an advertising campaign directed to good spiritual ends. Let us take the best end, the salvation of souls.

It is easy to imagine a very lively series of advertisements for the salvation-of-souls campaign. Just as advertisers stress the importance of repetition, so masters of the spiritual life tell us that thinking often on death serves to keep people concentrating on their last end. Therefore, we should plan the first several advertisements on the death, decay and damnation theme, and run them during Lent. The opening ad would

The Science of Temptation

present simply the thesis: "Remember man that thou art dust, and unto dust thou shalt return!" This would be featured on billboards throughout the nation, with a picture of a young man on one side and a new grave on the other. It would be a spot advertisement on the coast-to-coast radio on Ash Wednesday. The following ad would show damned souls enduring the torments of hell. Then there would be an accusatory one: "Are you sure you will be alive tomorrow?" followed by a statistical variation, "386 of you will die during the night," ending up with a funeral scene and the reminder that "this might be *you!*"

It would be well to follow the death series with something more cheerful, say a series on beatitude (There's no cancer in heaven! San Moritz is beautiful, but not half so lovely as paradise! He is only a street cleaner here but he will have a high place in the hereafter!). Then a series on the virtues would be useful (Perseverance does it! You *too* can be patient! Have you examined your conscience yet today?).

But why go on? We know it couldn't happen. The reason it couldn't happen is that it would entail a constant and enormous financial drain on whoever chose to promote it. Advertising spiritually good things, on which it is impossible by their nature to realize a dollar-and-cents return, is like walking up a down escalator. It is a constant drain on our energy, physical or financial, which can only end in exhaustion. It is possible to run a religious advertisement now and again, just as we can walk up a down escalator awhile. But it does not prove that advertising is good, or neutral, if at great sacrifice its paraphernalia can be turned to an occasional good use. (As witness the excellent "ads" being run by the Knights of Columbus; good in themselves, but again, going against the grain of the advertising business.) Its normal, natural use doesn't involve sacrifice at all, but only rewards. Advertising men, agencies, books, courses and clubs exist in virtue of the advertising that pays. If we want to know the true nature of advertising, this is where we must look. This real advertising has as its reason for being the creation of demands for material goods. To put it theologically, advertising exists to incite concupiscence (to arouse desire for material things).[1] If we want to know whether advertising is moral or not, we have to examine the morality of inciting concupiscence.

---

[1] Strictly speaking, advertising is an adjunct to a decadent industrial-capitalism, and this accounts for its having come into being so recently. Industrial-capitalism can only exist if it sells more and more goods. First it exhausted the ready home market for its new products. Then it preyed upon the peoples

THE AMERICAN WAY OF LIFE

We have a higher standard of living here in America than is to be found anywhere else in the world. This high standard is owing in considerable measure to advertising. Therefore, we ought to say nothing against advertising. This is the way the argument runs. What is there in it?

It is true that we have the highest standard of living in the world if you measure it by material luxuries. We do not have the highest moral standard, the highest spiritual standard, or the highest cultural standard! We do not even have the highest material standard as judged by fundamentals; nor the highest standard of health (positively measured), or of beauty in natural and architectural surroundings, or of air, light, and space. But we have the highest standard in convenience, luxury, ease: bathtubs, radios and Bendixes.

It is true, too, that advertising is a strong auxiliary to our standard of living, although it is not the sole influence. To hear some people talk, bathtubs would never have got around without advertising men. But good things, and especially necessary things, can spread without benefit of the copy writer, and in the days when shopkeepers were responsible socially, we could use their knowledge and integrity in lieu of a brand name as guide to quality — not that brand names are guides to quality.

Advertising is not so much an adjunct to good living as it is to *better and better living*, as measured in luxuries. This is what is really meant by the American Way of Life: a bourgeois standard of comfort and ease, tending to infinity.

The key to the whole thing is that the standard tends to infinity. When we look through *McCall's* magazine where the ads are concentrated in categories, we are struck by this ever-receding ideal.[2]

---

of unindustrialized states. Then it was forced to return to the home territory for intensified selling, that is to sell more goods per capita than even the fallen nature of each capita would normally take. Here is where advertising came in. Those who are determined to defend industrial-capitalism must defend advertising, because the former can no longer exist without the latter. Incidentally, it is interesting to note what advertising has done to the so-called "law of supply and demand." Now we create the demand in order to supply it at profit.

2 Do not be put off by the fact that many advertisements are concerned chiefly with the competitive angle. The don't say "smoke more cigarettes" but "change to our cigarettes," not "more coffee" but "our coffee." This is because they have already stretched our concupiscence to the limit and have only to fight over the spoils. Where we are not yet "educated" to the habit

Page after page pictures table delicacies, each more luscious than the one before, with the editorial copy planned and so interspersed as to heighten the appeal of the ads. The whole is an overwhelming temptation to gluttony, of both the quantity and quality sorts. Eat more and more, and better and better, it says. Naturally none of the copy writers says "worship your belly," nor probably even thinks it. Yet this is the precise invitation that is given.

It is the same thing in the women's clothes section. How well is well-dressed? Here again it is a receding ideal, tending of itself to infinity. The extent and variety of an American woman's wardrobe is limited only by the accidental factor of the amount beyond which she can't manage to go in debt to buy more clothes.

Even houses tend to be infinitely well furnished. No matter how good our kitchen is, it can always be better—either more convenient or more beautiful, or more in accordance with the latest fashions.

With ease and comfort it is the same thing. The mattresses get softer and softer, the chairs get deeper and deeper, the cars ride smoother and smoother. Everything tends to be done by merely pressing a button.

All spiritual writers teach that the advance toward God, our goal, is marked by a progressive detachment from creatures. The spirit soars in proportion as it is freed from the tyranny of the body. We cannot do without material goods, but we must learn to be indifferent to them, to use them as though we used them not. The precise passion which we must war against is concupiscence, the desire for material things.

The essence of advertising, which is to incite concupiscence, is the antithesis of spiritual progress, which is marked in its beginning stages by the overcoming of concupiscence. In the spiritual life we cannot stand still. We either go up or down. Which way are we Americans going?

HOW MUCH IS ENOUGH?

The ideal of infinite (or indefinite) progress is compatible with Christianity only insofar as it refers to spiritual progress. When infinity is attached to material things it becomes idolatry, which is strictly what our materialism has become. We do not just *use* material things. We *worship* them! It is therefore beside the point to argue that material things are good in themselves. Of course they are (most of them), but that does not justify a disordered regard for them.

---

which will increase profits (note the current campaign to have wine with our dinner), the brand name takes second place.

We cannot love God too much, but we can be too well-dressed, too well-fed, have too much ease, too much comfort, too much money and too many possessions. Where do we draw the line between enough and too much?

It is possible really to determine a right measure of material things. We should live frugally according to our states of life. The mayor and the bootblack should live differently from each other, but not as differently as nowadays. (The manor house of medieval England was nicer, but not terribly much nicer, than the villager's cottage. The contrast between the vast estate and the mean tenement came with industrial capitalism.) Each should live frugally, now and again feasting for the glory of God, and sometimes fasting for the good of their souls.

The right measure is not mathematically exact, but it is an obtainable ideal. It is opposed diametrically to the ever-increasing standard of living which is the stock-in-trade of the modern advertiser.

THE DEVIL'S HARVEST

We are so used to reflecting on our material progress that if this ideal of infinite material advance were to be taken from us it is hard to see how we would allocate our energies. What is there to do in the world if we are not busy harnessing the physical resources of the earth to man's use and pleasure?

God gives each man a certain talent which he can use in a variety of ways, though not in all ways. Because of the materialistic orientation of our civilization men have turned to the construction of skyscrapers the gifts which might have been used for building cathedrals; they have devised housing projects when they might have been designing homes. A director of a large corporation, with marvelous executive ability, singleness of purpose and austerity of life, might under other circumstances have made an excellent Father Abbot. What copy writer has not felt his talent ought to be turned to nobler ends?

If men had not so far forgotten their least end as to fall into idolatry, if they had set out to master themselves for God, instead of mastering the earth for their bodies' sakes, would it have made so very much difference? Cathedrals and systems of theology, books about the spiritual life, and liturgical vestments have their just measure too, and are subordinate to spiritual ends. The real work of the world is the sanctification of souls. Each generation might have been busy (as the humanists say so glibly) making the world a better place to live in.

The Science of Temptation

If better were taken to mean "easier to save our souls in," we would have no quite a different world. But more than that, each generation might have practiced more virtue, exercised more charity. The number of souls who each year went to hell might have been fewer. Since we do not know the population of hell we shall have to wait until some time later to discover what harvest the devil has reaper from our materialism, and how helpful advertising has been in the matter.

The more "scientific" advertising becomes the more clearly it reveals its diabolical intent. Messrs. Batten, Barton, Rubicam and the rest begin to reveal themselves as front men (whether innocently or not is here beside the point) for a chief executive dressed in red.

Advertising concentrates its biggest guns on our imaginations, following the hackneyed and successful technique of the devil. That is why advertising is most pictures, to which copy is secondary. This is also the principle behind the singing commercial. Music has a stronger effect on the imagination and memory than does the spoken word. If the imagination is worked on long enough it can distort the intellect and so move the will to make a choice that it wouldn't have made otherwise. As the theologians put it, the idea is to make something seem good which isn't good.

One of the principles of advertising is that people can be reached better when they are tired (standing up in a crowded subway car at the end of a day, with nothing to do but stare vacantly at the car card advertisement in front of them), or when they are in an unintellectual mood (such as during the emotional fervor following on soap opera), than when they are awake, alert and calculating. What the advertisers mean to say is that their products can be foisted on us better in our least human moments. The devil thought that up long ago, too.

When copy writers talk about the "appeal to reason" they mean usually the appeal to rationalization—here they are concerned to help their victims justify themselves for doing something which is not advisable. We rationalize our misdeeds because our will can choose something only as good. If the picture of the $79.95 spring suit, or the extra-fine flavored wine does not sufficiently overcome budgetary considerations, the devil (in the person of the copy writer) will whisper in our ear, "Only three cents a day" or "It pays to have the best."

And so it goes. We could make a list of the seven capital sins and their progeny and collect advertisements to fit each case. The advertising textbooks are not as skillful at analyzing the appeals as a moral theologian would be, but all the temptations have been used even if they haven't all been catalogued. Let us consider here only one of them: lust.

People who think in moral terms would be shocked at the naivete with which advertisers consider the use of "sex appeal" in their advertisements. "Sex always attracts attention," is one of their principles. They go on from there (even while loudly defending the honor of their profession) to discuss, not whether it is moral to use sex appeal, but the difficulties of turning sex attraction into sales of an irrelevant product. While thus concentrating on the almighty dollar the advertisers have gone far in the last several years toward becoming large-scale purveyors of pornography.

LEGITIMATE "ADVERTISING"

Not everything that looks like advertising is advertising as we have defined it, that is, a business or "profession" which exists to create new desires for material goods. This new thing, the pioneer millionaires of which are not yet old men, is the hypodermic needle which has produced a sudden flush of life in a dying capitalism. It brought into existence the advertising man, the advertising agency, the courses in advertising and the painstaking development of the Science of Temptation.

There is another thing which is neither new nor reprehensible. We shall call it "announcing." It is this which dates back to ancient Egypt and which advertising books try to identify with modern advertising. But announcing is specifically different from modern advertising, because its end is different. It wants to "let people know" that Bill Smith is opening a dentist's office or that such-and-such a ship is sailing next week and can take passengers. It doesn't try to make us buy what we "don't need, don't want and can't afford." Announcing is moral if what is announced conforms to the laws of morality and needs to be made known. Normally, announcing demands merely simplicity and clarity, and can be taken care of by the head bookkeeper or the third vice-president. Of itself, it would never have given rise to a "profession" of any appreciable size.

The need for announcing has continued with the advent of advertising. Furthermore, since advertising has set up such a clamor, announcing has to compete a little with it just in order to be heard. This causes confusion in the popular mind, but it oughtn't to confuse us very much. About the only advertising which is essentially pure (it may have accidental evils) is the advertising of Catholic books and magazines. The appeal here is to truth and spiritual progress, neither of which can possibly be the object of the passion of concupiscence. With secular books, distinctions have to be made. No one can deny that the most blatant appeal in publishers' advertisements, even in the *New York Times*, is to juicy passages, that is, lust. Still, considerable book advertising, especially of technical books, is not suspect. In fact, legitimate advertising is limited generally to the technical fields and even there it is sometimes illegitimate. There is another field of "mixed" good and bad advertising. The steamship lines come in here. They have a perfect right to announce their sailings but their ad appeal (and their ships) often exceed a due measure in respect of luxury. Store advertising is also of the mixed variety. The local grocer's ad in the evening paper (usually little more than a price list) is much more legitimate than the canner's luscious display ads in the women's magazines. Department store advertising is most of the concupiscence sort, though there is a small element of announcing. Neither Macy's nor Gimbels could stave off bankruptcy if they were to cease advertising, even for a short time. Their profit must therefore rest on the selling of unnecessary things for which there is no spontaneous desire.

What we are trying to show in this article is not that Mr. X or Mr. Y has no right to advertise his product. Let each manufacturer or store owner or insurance company examine its own conscience in the matter. We are more concerned to show the shaky foundations on which advertising rests (as a profession or a business). Young men and women who aspire to become account executives or copy writers would do well to turn their talents to more godly uses. It is hard to see how they could justify offering their services to the ordinary advertising agency. Most whose aspirations lie along those lines start out without any misgivings because advertising is considered generally an acceptable, indeed an especially desirable, career. It is only afterwards that consciences begin to be troubled. Many who feel vague misgivings are unable to ferret out the root evil. This article is written especially for them. If advertising is ordered against God, then no one has a vocation to pursue it, and learning that it is wrong may be a step in the direction of a Christian career, which measures success in conformity to God's will.

16
The Evolution of Social Work
MAY 1948

SHOULD ANY OF THE ONE HUNDRED THOUSAND OR so social workers in the United States feel a vague but persistent malaise in respect of their work, they would have a hard time diagnosing their difficulty. What's wrong with social work is now a case of an ill within an ill within an ill. Specious reasoning, bad history, ignorance of human nature, and apparent inevitability are all tangled up with mixed motives and even much goodness. Clarification is easier through historical analysis than by a frontal approach to the contemporary situation.

Social work is an outgrowth of that branch of human activity roughly covered by the phrase, "the works of mercy." For our purposes the different historical approaches to the works of mercy can be divided into three periods: charity, philanthropy and sociology.

THE FIRST PERIOD: CHARITY

It is characteristic of pagan societies that they neglect (often despise) their weak members. The Greeks and Romans exposed their unwanted children, African tribes have killed their old people, Hindus used to burn widows, and pagan Chinese to this day stone lepers. The fact that we shudder at these things testifies to the Christian conscience which is residual in us. For it was Christianity that really initiated the works of mercy, and at the highest possible level.

The Christian saw in the beggar, the leper, the sick, the poor and the insane, what no pagan could ever see: Christ. "I was hungry and you fed me, naked and you clothed me.... Inasmuch as you did it unto one of these my least brethren, you did it unto me." With the Christian it is wholly a supernatural matter. Christ is seen by the eyes of faith, and loved with the love of God—supernatural charity.

One can scarcely think of the Christian ideal of charity without a burning in one's heart, so beautiful is this love which Christ brought into the world. Even the pagan stands in respect and awe before Saint Francis of Assisi, who kissed and served the lepers, and who has become a sort of symbol of the charity which was repeated over and over again (and still is) by saints who ransomed captives, nursed the sick, tended the insane, instructed the orphans, protected the aged, and dressed the wounds of the cancerous. They did it (and they still do it) with a tenderness, a joy and a reverence. It was not an onerous duty, but a rare privilege, for it was always the same person they were serving, Christ.

The characteristic institution of the age of charity was the religious order. The duties of hospitality, almsgiving and personal service were recognized as universal, but an abundance of religious institutions sprang up to meet the needs more effectively. The work of the religious orders was done by a multitude of dedicated men and women whose lives were rooted in prayer (which fostered the charity that was the principle of their action) and who stripped themselves of all worldly possessions and preoccupations in order the better to serve God in their fellow men.

Gradually these religious institutions formed a whole network of charity which covered Europe. The monasteries were the poor man's inn (now we have Bowery flop houses), hospitals abounded (there were seven hundred in England in the thirteenth century), the lepers were segregated and cared for, and almsgiving was a universal and honored custom. At that time men gave money (tithes) to the Church which was the mother of all these charities, as we now pay taxes to the government (which is becoming the mother of today's good works), only in the former case the giving was more likely to be meritorious and the total cost was certainly less, since the ministers of charity were vowed to voluntary poverty. This poverty combined with obedience and chastity to make for a tremendous economy of effort. Further, although these multitudinous works were all under the Church, there was the minimum of centralization, each local convent or monastery, or each religious order, exercising a certain autonomy under its approved rule.

Not all the religious in this period of charity were saints, but nevertheless the saint was the exemplar, the characteristic person devoted to the works of mercy. The training of religious was chiefly spiritual, since the primary motivation of the whole thing was the love of God. The Ages of Faith were realistic. They didn't have any millennial complexes about the eradication of poverty, disease and human unhappiness (yet they rid Europe of leprosy with their quarantines and were never visited with our major problems of divorce, juvenile delinquency, widespread unemployment and general neurosis). They saw God's purposes in suffering and, while working with tremendous personal sacrifice to alleviate it, knew that sin, not suffering, was the worst evil, and that perfect justice and joy were to be found only in heaven.

THE BREAKDOWN OF CHARITY

The system of charity built up by the Church worked very well. The excellence with which it was administered varied in proportion to the holiness of the nuns, brothers, monks and priests who administered it (and also according to their number, which was seriously depleted by the plagues). Religious institutes fell now and again into laxity or worldliness, but they had, as they still have, power to recuperate. They were essentially sound, and well fitted for their purposes.

Why, then, did this network of charity disappear? Why was it superseded by something else?

We shall consider here only the situation in England. In Catholic countries the system never quite vanished, or did so only recently, but our tradition stems from the Protestant countries. In England the whole system disappeared virtually overnight because Henry VIII confiscated the monastic lands and set most of the religious at large, and without provision. Henry's reasons had to do with his own marital problems and his defiance of the Pope. The fact that he destroyed the institutions of charity was incidental to his main purpose and had nothing to do with whether they were operating well or poorly. This is a pattern we shall see repeated, and the lesson to learn from it is that how men treat their poor and weak brothers is always a by-product of something else, spiritual, political or economic. Anyhow, Henry VIII, in confiscating the monastic lands and destroying the religious foundations, wiped out the whole system of charity. He also (because the land holdings were large and rich — but used overwhelmingly in the interests of the poor, despite occasional abuses) disrupted the whole economy of England, with far-reaching consequences even until today. Because the seized land passed rapidly to the nobles, in return for favors granted in supporting Henry, the balance of power in England swung heavily on the side of the nobles and the king has remained more or less putty in their hands to this day. One consequence has been the impotence of the king to defend the poor against the abuses of the rich. However, be that as it may, it only indirectly affects this discussion.

THE TRANSITIONAL PERIOD

After Henry there followed a transitional period. At first the poor and the weak were not cared for at all, and their numbers were greatly augmented by the indigent religious. Extremely harsh laws were instituted to quell the resultant disorders. It was during this time that picking pockets was a crime punishable by burning at the stake. But people went on picking pockets and the rest because they really had no alternative. Gradually a system was evolved whereby the responsibility for the indigent was fixed by law on the parishes of what was now the Church of England. The regulations are contained in the famous "Poor Laws," and they are harsh and unfeeling. It is odd that one history of social work after another will trace the care of the poor back to these infamous Poor Laws, but none will go yet further back to investigate the circumstances under which the Poor Laws came into existence. It is much more flattering to modern social work to choose this darkest hour with which to contrast its own "enlightenment", than to remember Saint Elizabeth of Hungary, Saint Camillus de Lellis, Saint John of God and Saint Catherine of Siena.

In the Middle Ages there was a hospital for the insane in London, called Bethlehem (from which comes our word "bedlam"). It was manned by religious, of course, and was quite famous for its enlightened and humane treatment of its patients. The mildly insane were released in the custody of the general public wearing the hospital badges which won them such kind treatment that these badges were coveted and stolen by beggars. Now this hospital was shut down with the confiscation, and for awhile there was no one to care for the insane. But since the necessity was so great for such an institution, it was perforce opened again after the Reformation with the lowest type of paid attendant. Then it was that the insane were exhibited like monkeys, and the public could observe their misery for a small fee. They were also chained, ill-fed and often cold. Modern people shudder to think of the inhumanity with which the insane were visited in the "Middle Ages." Let them continue to shudder, but for the abuses of the post-reformation period, and let them correct their textbooks.

ENTER INDUSTRIALISM

The Poor Laws remained in effect for a long time and were a grievous burden to the poor. That was the era of the work house and the debtor's prison. But things were to get worse before they got better.

The advent of industrialism in the late eighteenth and early nineteenth centuries was immediately preceded in England by the enclosure laws, whereby multitudes of independent farmers lost their land and were forced to the city, forming there a semi-vagrant population which readily succumbed to the exploitation of the early, wholly unprincipled industrialist. It was during this period of the early and middle nineteenth century in England and in America (a little later here) that the foundations of the great modern fortunes were laid. Industrialism, which enabled one man to profit readily by the exploitation of many, was one factor. Capitalism, with its paper money and opportunities for usury, was another. To these must be added in America the magnificent natural wealth of our country, which was so quickly and wantonly despoiled and also the legitimate development opportunities, illegitimately exploited, of which the chief example is the railroads.

The net result of all this, insofar as it concerns us here, is that the gap between the rich and the poor widened enormously. The poor were worse off than ever they had been while free men and independent owners, and were also increasingly numerous. The really rich were rich as Croesus, and with a type of wealth which (given the legality of usury) tended of itself to multiply prodigiously.

THE SECOND PERIOD: PHILANTHROPY

For a variety of reasons, ranging anywhere from embarrassment of riches to trying to retrieve a good name, or possibly twinges of conscience, these rich began to take on the burden of the relief of the poor. They did it by giving large sums of money to foundations of one sort or another (The Rockefeller, Carnegie and Russel Sage Foundations in our own day are residual examples) which distributed and administered the funds. The intermediaries between the rich and the poor were at first well-bred, educated women of the wealthy or middle classes, working on a volunteer basis; subsequently the paid, "professional" social workers.

By the time philanthropy had become the characteristic mode of administering the works of mercy (which was roughly by the turn of the last century) there had been an entire change in man's attitude toward man. Philanthropy is Greek for "love of man," whereas charity means the love of *God*. The prevailing philosophy was now humanitarianism, or love of man for his own sake and his own natural

The Evolution of Social Work

ends. The prevailing mood was now pity, which expressed at once the greatness and the weakness in the humanistic position. It is good to pity the sufferings of one's fellows, but pity which is not subordinate to, and ordered by, supernatural faith and love, is bound to become diseased. We see what it has degenerated to in our own day: the pity that kills, with euthanasia and birth control and sterilization on the one hand, and the ineffectual sentimentality on the other hand. But this is to get ahead of our story.

Philanthropy was preoccupied with man for his own sake. Almost inevitably it concentrated on natural reforms, and especially cleanliness. Nothing appalled the early social worker so much about the poor man as the fact that he was dirty. Since she didn't see with the eyes of faith, she neither saw Christ, nor the possibilities of beatitude; but she only saw dirt, and bad manners, smelled garbage and shivered in cold flats. The characteristic good works of the social worker (ante-Freud) were free dental clinics, summer camps, T. B. sanatoriums, maternity clinics and budgeted almsgiving.

Social workers were very zealous about minor reforms and were instrumental in obtaining fire regulations for tenements, school lunches and that sort of thing. Characteristically they never attacked root evils, such as industrial capitalism itself, or the existence of monstrous cities, or the lack of small private ownership of the means of production. They could not very well have challenged these things as they were distributing the largess of the very men who had been partly responsible for these evils and whose continued affluence depended on the *status quo*. But the social workers, too, came from (and for the most part remained in) the privileged classes and so it probably never occurred to them to challenge the system.

The early philanthropic period also produced an attitude of patronization and moral condemnation which stemmed from the Calvinistic heritage of Protestantism. Poverty was regarded as resulting from a defect in the character of the poor, probably from sloth. This attitude gave rise to the distinction between the deserving and the undeserving poor, which has been repudiated by modern social workers as repeated depressions and periodic involuntary periods of unemployment have shown that the masses are more sinned against than sinning in our day.

The characteristic person of the philanthropic period is the noble humanitarian, of which Jane Addams and Florence Nightingale will serve as exemplars. The world holds them up to our admiration, but they are remarkable not so much for the greatness they achieved as for the evident fact that they should have been saints, and probably would have been with the true faith and supernatural aims and aids. On the natural level their greatness could only peter out. Florence Nightingale, after the Crimean episode which made her famous, became a political agitator for military hospital reforms, some even dubious ones, to the extent of ruining one of her friends in Parliament. Kindly newspapers hid her growing querulousness from a doting public for long years until, at her death, they resurrected the lovely lady bending over the sick soldier's cot legend. Jane Addams was a pioneer founder of settlement houses. She suggests a comparison with Mother Cabrini because they were near contemporaries, both working among the poor in Chicago. The noble humanitarian's heroic efforts were on the natural level. Her Hull House, and she herself, were well-known to generations of college students, but are already passing into oblivion. The Italian saint led a hidden and obscure life, depending wholly on supernatural assistance in her work among the despised immigrants of the Chicago slums. She was not written up in the college sociology text books of her day. But she died leaving a religious community and a string of hospitals to carry on her earthly work, while she assists from heaven. As for her fame — she is obviously Chicago's (and New York's) most honored and leading citizen to date.

The change in the spirit with which the works of mercy were administered can be traced in nomenclature. Charity loves to call its institutions names like Holy Ghost Hospital, The House of the Good Shepherd, The Guardian Angel Adoption Home or The House of Calvary. The philanthropists went in for names like The Association for Helping the Deserving Poor, or The society for the Relief of Paupers. Lately, to get ahead of our story again, it has become the fashion to use colorless scientific words. An insane asylum (a beautiful word, Asylum) is a psychoneurotic institute or a hospital for the care of the mentally ill. When the private social work agencies in New York City consolidated a few years ago the late Alfred E. Smith had the simplicity and naivete to suggest the name of the new organization be The Friendly Neighbors. Of course he was overruled, and the name became The Community Service Society of New York, which is so nearly meaningless and so lacking in human warmth as to be difficult even to remember.

THE BREAKDOWN OF PHILANTHROPY

Here again a system of good works collapsed through no fault of its own. Philanthropy was a poor thing as compared with charity, but it was not given an opportunity to run its course. What happened was that our economic system collapsed. Industrial capitalism of its nature produced economic crises in the form of periodic depressions. The interval between these kept shortening, while the suffering they caused deepened, until the crash of 1929 was followed by a period of such depression that steps had to be taken in the direction of socialization. Philanthropic organizations had their resources diminished at a time of colossal want through unemployment. The problem of relief was so great that the government was forced to take it over.

THE THIRD PERIOD: SOCIOLOGY

A very curious thing happened when the state took over relief. That should have been the end of social workers (giving way to "investigators"), and it probably would have been were it not for the fact that the private social work agencies were still fairly handsomely endowed financially. They had the trained workers, they had the money, all they needed was a function.

At first the social workers became investigators for government relief, but this was a routine, high-pressure and pretty mechanical job, not worthy of their talents and training. If one reads the history of this period, it looks as though the social workers deliberately invented a function for themselves. They said, in effect, that people have other than material problems, and we shall help them solve these other problems. For some time the advance schools of social work have been fascinated by the theories of Sigmund Freud and trying to incorporate them into their case work. Gradually, then, these agencies have been transformed. Instead of prudent almsgivers, social workers have become the "professional" priestesses of the new religions of psychology and sociology.

The corporal works of mercy, so to speak, have passed on to the bureaucratic state, which dispenses relief, social security, unemployment insurance, and which threatens to control the practice of medicine and practically everything else. We have moved from love, to pity, to mechanization. We have regressed from God to man to animal or machine. All individual responsibilities are being absorbed into one gigantic centralization with its army of robots who administer the red tape with which the whole thing will be smothered. The government has its social workers, increasingly so, but the elite in the profession are still in the private non-sectarian (really atheist) agencies, where policies are formulated, methodologies are effected, and curricula are determined. The New York School of Social Work, controlled by the Community Service Society, is the exemplar of all graduate schools of social work, not excepting the Catholic schools, which have strained out the gnats and swallowed the camel.

It is probably only a matter of time before the private agencies will fall under government control; as it is they already influence government policies. It is beside our point to trace further the course of total socialization, and finally communism, which threatens. It is more useful to examine the philosophy (really the theology) which governs increasingly the whole "profession." It can be seen most clearly in its most advanced stage among the New York non-sectarian elite. Happily things are still more wholesome elsewhere, but this is the preview of the future, unless we can prevent it.

THE NEW RELIGION

Social work is now concerned with the *spiritual* works of mercy. In an age with dire spiritual problems everywhere, and of unprecedented religious decline, one can see that the very virtues of social workers would lead them to undertake the "spiritual direction" of their clients. Since the social workers themselves are singularly underprivileged, religiously speaking, it is no wonder that they have come up with a vicious new religion.

Language plays a very important part in the new social work. The essence of the language is that it removes everything from the moral order. You never say "good or bad," or "right or wrong," but "positive or negative," or "constructive or destructive." Beatitude has become "adjustment to one's environment." Spiritual problems are "emotional" problems. People are "clients" or "cases," and so on. Unconsciously, almost, they have introduced a new moral code, largely Freudian, in which the sins are "refusal to cooperate", being "different," or "suppressing instinctual desire."

The new social worker does not give the client money (except incidentally). She doesn't give the client assistance. She doesn't even particularly give advice any more. Most of her work consists in receiving confidences of the most intimate order and dictating enormous, detailed, and extremely dull, case histories.

The social worker does not give away all her worldly possessions for the love of God. She does not even give up her finery and make-up for the durable tweeds and flat heels of the humanitarian workers. She likes to dress well, for her clients' sake. She thinks they would feel slighted were she to come to them poorly attired. May God have pity on us, for there is truth in her contention. Even our tenement dwellers are now bourgeois.

THE DILEMMA OF THE SOCIAL WORKER

In our day we see the three periods, charitable, philanthropic and sociological co-existing. There is no doubt, however, that deterministic, Freudian, state-imposed sociology is in the ascendancy and that it will make the work of religious orders, and even that of private agencies, virtually impossible. Already the work of the Church suffers almost inevitable diminution of charity because of financial entanglements with state funds, governmental red tape, lack of a sufficient number of religious vocations and the like.

The more centralized and depersonalized the system becomes, the more demand there will be for social workers, and the more frustrating their work will be. Of their very nature social workers are intermediaries; they do not take defective or orphan children into their own homes, they arrange to have them taken into an institution or someone else's home. They diagnose cases of loneliness, but they do not become the personal friends of the lonely. They advocate good housekeeping, or arrange for the services of a housekeeper, but they do not themselves roll up their sleeves and do the dishes. They give not of their own money (in the professional capacity) but of the money of others. The most necessary function which social workers perform is their least exalted one: that of unwinding red tape, fathoming the intricacies of organized charity, and transferring bewildered moderns from the place of need to the place of remedy.

THE DIRECTION OF RECONSTRUCTION

Wholehearted personal and corporate charity is the only way to restore the works of mercy to a Christian framework. If social workers are to lead themselves and us out of the wilderness, their supreme need is for an intense supernatural life. Above all they need the training which is conspicuously absent from the present curriculum: spiritual training. Perhaps they must get it from the apostolic movement. When they get it, however, and their charity begins to overflow into their work, then the framework of organized charity will begin to crack and we shall see the birth of a new outgrowth of the works of mercy, at once Christian and suited to our times.

What will it be like? Who can foresee the loveliness of the institutions which the Holy Ghost raises for each age that is docile to His directives? There will be charity in superabundance (such is needed for an age grown so cold as ours). There will be a total instead of a half-giving. Those who have fallen down will be uplifted only in one direction — Christward. The workers themselves will be united closely in Christ. The chances are that many or most of them will in time cease to be social workers, abandoning their intermediary positions for direct action on problems as they gain wisdom to see the solutions necessary. They may or may not become religious. In our day we shall see the corporate work of dedicated lay people sometimes operating where formerly the work would have been done by a religious order. Secularism demands new modes of operation.

The modern world often is right in its general direction, perverse in its specific aim. Maybe the spiritual works of mercy will be of supreme importance, even as the social workers intuitively sense. (Perhaps the corporeal misery of our times will be so great that it can only be met by huge organizations.) Then it will be Christ versus Freud, man raised to God versus man reduced to machine, God's order versus annihilation. The future belongs to those who love. Indeed, if we do not restore the fullness of supernatural charity to act as the oil of society, there may be no future.

17
How Modern Man Became Merry
JULY 1948

RETRACING BRIEFLY THE HISTORY OF MODERN MAN, we find that the Acquisitive Society was superseded by the Leisure State, which in turn gave way to the great Age of Penance just ended.

It was during the early acquisitive age that the institutions of society gradually were oriented to money-making as a final end, refashioned from the old Christian pattern to the service of mammon. Not everyone swung over to the love of money, but the leaders of society did, and they exercised a sort of personal monasticism in the pursuit of that end.

Since we are concerned here chiefly with recreation rather than economics, let us pause to examine the leisure-time activities of the acquisitive man. The outstanding characteristic was secularization. The play of that period was no more related to God than was the work. The holidays were patriotic and bank holidays, not saints' days. Men golfed solemnly, with an awareness of the physical benefits to be derived from a day in the open air after a week at the office desk. They traveled much abroad during the intermittent periods of peace, for cultural and business reasons, engaging chiefly in sightseeing. They enjoyed the theatre, concerts, card playing, and what they used to call the "books of the month." This is the early acquisitive period, remember, when men still seemed able to hold to the good natural order, when it looked as though, having abandoned Christianity (except for occasional lip service), men could maintain a cultured pagan standard of life.

As the rich grew richer, but not happier, the poor were regimented increasingly, by the natural progress of an unnatural system of industrial mass production, into a property-less, proletarian condition in which they were virtually robots. It is unlikely that the masses of the people, with their Christian heritage, could have been persuaded (as the leaders were) that money could buy happiness. But they did discover that in an industrial society money can buy quite a bit of oblivion. The more industrialized society became, so much the more intolerable life became for the masses of the people. The more intolerable life became, the more industrial production was diverted from physical necessities (such as housing, basic clothing, and food) to instruments of entertainment and diversion. Men slaved monotonously to make the television sets which would make their monotonous lives tolerable. They sold themselves into the chain gangs of the automobile plants so as to earn enough money to buy an automobile. A sort of ratio persisted between the demands of a dehumanized population for escape and the sacrifice of mind, will, energy and talents which went into making the latest escape device; the former always running a little ahead of the latter. Naturally the majority of men did not realize that they were busy tightening the noose around their own necks. They looked to a paradise of pleasure just beyond their reach. It was called the Leisure State.

The theory of the Leisure State was exactly the opposite of the Christian theory of life and work. "Man is born to labor as the bird to fly," one of the contemporary Popes said. The Leisure State denied this, contending instead that man is made to play and will be able to do so almost all the time as soon as science has made work unnecessary.

It never did come about, as the supporters of the Leisure State anticipated, that the work week was reduced to five or ten hours. Instead it hit a brief forty-hour low and then rose again until it reached a seven-day week. However, leisure as an ideal was certainly enthroned. The entertainment industry ran into the billions of dollars. Huge amphitheaters, sport gardens, stadiums, gymnasiums, playgrounds, race tracks, provided the setting for spectator, professionalized sports on a gigantic scale. Movies, radio and television were ubiquitous. Escape literature flooded the newsstands. Although the work week did not decrease but increased, the invention of labor-saving devices made it possible for men to divide their time between mechanical office or factory work and sedentary amusements. It freed women from what they liked to call the "drudgery" of housework, so that they too could become parts of the machinery in offices and factories. Then they too had to escape from their dehumanized existence into the temporary oblivion of drink or lust or the movie house.

As long as it could, by fair means or foul, the Leisure State refused to recognize its major problem, but in the end there came about a sustained national crisis. People were bored. Everyone was bored. One could put the greatest mechanical wonder of science down in any man's home—say a machine by which he could pick up a chance conversation in the streets of Shanghai, or something that would transport a man to the Emperor's Palace in Tokyo in three minutes. Our good man would but yawn, or say, "Yeah, it's a nice color," or "What's this dial for?"

The government tried in every way to awaken people's interest in anything at all besides relaxation. There resulted a rash of things such as garden clubs ("Nature is the most fascinating thing on earth. Just wait until you have grown your own little radishes!"). But there were no takers, except for a few eccentrics who were so fascinated they began to worship nature and developed a ritual cult of the wheat germ. Again the government tried interesting the citizens in "worthy books," masterpieces of literature and philosophy beloved of other ages. No go! The majority were indifferent. A few intellectuals became sophists, and went around trying to tell people how much they had studied of other people's ideas without having attained to any major convictions of their own.

The breakdown of the Leisure State came about through some Catholics who decided one day to take the Church seriously and literally. There had been a lot of talk about doing penance and it finally occurred to one of the faithful that that might mean him. He managed to round up a small group to consider the matter. Right off they saw the difficulty. "If we stopped consuming so much, what would happen to the system?... It doesn't so much matter about us, but suppose it became a fad?... Suppose people lost their confidence in an ever-increasing standard of living?" But they decided to try it anyhow.

Following the theory (as they read in a spiritual book) that it is more humble to accept the penances God has sent one than to seek extraordinary ones, they decided to accept their monotonous work as penance. "Forgive us, O Lord, for we have forsaken Thee and sought after money," they repeated in their hearts as they set the screws in the radios or dropped the cookies into the designated places in the special fancy-assortment boxes. "Have pity on us, Christ, and make us men again," they chanted in unison, unheard by others over the din of the machines. "We offer our sufferings for the souls of this generation.... Accept them, O Lord," prayed seven young women in a Coca-Cola bottling plant, over the Musak in the background.

It naturally followed that the penitents abstained from the escapist joys of their co-workers in the evening. "If our work is going to be penance, then we must face the reality of it and not try to deaden the pain." They took to praying quite a bit at night and gathering in small groups (their number was spreading) for mutual support and encouragement. The more penance they did, the more they became aware of the need for penance. They began to see how wide was the gulf by which modern man had separated himself from God. They saw souls all around them in danger of everlasting fire.

"Let us fast for our fellow workers," they decided. So they did, limiting themselves to dry bread, fresh fruit, hash and boiled potatoes. And then a funny thing happened. "Have you noticed," said one penitent to another some weeks later, "how truly delicious are boiled potatoes?" "That's odd," said another, "I never liked hash in my life until now, and last night's meal was more delicious than ever I found the latest taste sensation in my days of culinary delight. My meals have a zest."

A similar thing occurred when the penitents started practicing custody of the eyes. All one Lent they went about with eyes cast down, abstaining from video, window shopping, advertisement reading, and even from viewing the budding trees, the floral displays in Radio City, the blue heavens by day or the starlit skies at night. "The single tulip I saw on Easter Sunday," testified one, "filled my whole being with its loveliness and the day with blissful joy."

So, too, with sound. Solitude and silence restored the power to appreciate delicate harmony (as opposed to the unmelodious imitation of factory noises of the latest symphonies and the maudlin sentimentality of popular crooning). Gregorian Chant for the first time had the power to lift their hearts to holy things.

Delight shone increasingly on the faces of the penitents, whose numbers had now swollen to the proportions of a minor movement. Quite a number of people were being jarred out of their lethargy. Then a new matter came up.

A middle-aged man spoke up at one of the weekly meetings of one of the original groups: I've been in this penitential movement three years, fellow Christians. I offer up the monotony of my work to Christ, same as all of you. You will remember we started doing this in order to make a virtue of necessity. Do you realize that we have inadvertently destroyed the necessity of our own slavery? Since we don't love automobiles, airplanes, television sets and three-inch steaks, we can live on very little. Must we continue to be robots or do you think God would be pleased to have us lead our fellowmen toward a more simple life, a more human work?"

That was the beginning of the end of industrialization as a pattern of society, and marked the death knell of the Leisure State. People began to form in small Christian communities and started to work at crafts, farming, and apostolic ventures. As their common Christian life and creative work grew, so their joy increased and overflowed into simple songs and dances. Sunday was again observed and men came to celebrate the holy days instead of the secular holidays. Where formerly there had been a military parade as the focal point of the day's festivities, now there was a religious procession, not so martial but twice as colorful, and inviting the participation of the whole community. Not the parade ground, the town hall, or the local tavern, but the parish church and especially the Cathedral, became the center of social activities. Tourism gave way to pilgrimages which united men of all nations not only in prayer and penance but also in an exchange of conversation and culture, in song, discussion and dance. People began to have fun in families. Parents found new delight in their children. Laughter rang out in the streets. Through the death of mortification came a life of new joy.

That's how modern man became merry.

18
The Impotence of Money Today
AUGUST 1948

R UST AND MOTHS AWAIT THE THINGS ON EARTH WHEN men cherish and accumulate them. Use prevents corrosion. It's the coat in the closet and not the one on the back that attracts moths. Similarly, good things are spoiled by misuse. The stomach that's pampered gets ulcers. Monetary disorders plague the societies which have put their confidence in money. Ours is such a society, now in its corrosive period. We have put our trust in money, so in the normal course of events money has failed us.

The most obvious failure of money is in respect to its most elementary function as a medium of exchange. Following the war in Europe money was of absolutely no use, and it still remains impotent for all except the very rich. This has not been wholly due to shortages, but rather to the opportunity which scarcity has provided for black marketeering. The destitute man of today is not necessarily penniless. Having money in your pocket is no guarantee that you can obtain a roof over your head; having a regular good-paying job doesn't mean you can buy meat for your family or get an automobile at list price.

These curious difficulties are familiar to everyone, but the failure of money to function normally is even more evident in respect to financial institutions.

SAVING IS ANTI-SOCIAL

We owe it to the Puritans to have developed a major virtue out of thrift. They made it respectable (with Benjamin Franklin's considerable help) to accumulate money for its own sake. "A penny saved is a penny earned." and so forth. Thrift became an end in itself. No one would ask you what you were saving for, and no one would question the fact that you were a wise and prudent man to do so. You would get rich (like John D. Rockefeller, Sr. who was niggardly with dimes to the end and commended those who patterned their financial conduct after him) and you would never be embarrassed by a "rainy day." Generations of American school children who were forbidden to learn about the Trinity were drilled in the virtue of thrift. Savings banks sprang up throughout the country, in whose accumulations school children were invited to participate in order to "get the thrift habit".

True Christianity never taught thrift for its own sake. It taught that frugality (as a way of life) was more conducive to virtue than luxury, but it also taught that a man's superfluous wealth (beyond what was necessary for his state in life) belonged to the poor. The money saved from fasting during Lent was for the poor box, not the savings account. A man was not forbidden to put money aside for the future if he didn't overdo it and if he had obligations, but his surplus was always to be tempered by charity. The Puritans, be it noted, frowned on begging as a corollary to their exaggerated ideas about thrift. They had to.

There is an irony in the way material things fail us when we fail God. Would Benjamin Franklin ever have imagined the day when it was considered anti-social for a citizen to put anything away? Yet that day is more or less upon us, although the compulsion in the matter is still for the most part hidden by a velvet glove. Nevertheless, we have so bolixed up the economic system that periodically we receive veiled threats about idle money (right now we are being urged to save as a temporary check to inflation but the mood will pass). Our fevered financial condition is dependent absolutely on a regulated flow of currency. It isn't how much money that counts, it's how often the same coins change hands. Factory workers are desirable citizens in a community because they spend every cent they earn. The conservative *bourgeoisie* is frowned upon. When a vulgar millionaire throws a pretentious wedding reception for his daughter, with champagne flowing and all the trimmings, people nod in approval and say, "Well, it's putting a lot of money into circulation and giving employment to a lot of people — a good thing."

WHAT IS A SOUND INVESTMENT?

Only simple people save money in a capitalistic society. Shrewd men *invest*, that is, they not only lay away money but they also expect it to generate more money. Here modern man's error was to expect too much of money. He wanted to have his cake and eat it too. He wanted absolute, or nearly absolute, security on the one hand and a handsome return on the other. The two are essentially incompatible. If you furnish the capital in a joint enterprise in which other men supply the skill and labor, then you have a legitimate claim to a share of the profits, if any, but you must take the risk of losing your capital to merit the rewards. On the other hand, if you want your money to be secure, hide it under the mattress, but don't expect it to grow small dollar bills.

The history of investments has been of one long effort to circumvent nature, to achieve profit without risk. It's curious to see how inevitably men focused their attention wrongly. Had they been interested in furthering worthy and sound enterprises with their capital surplus they would have examined Amalgamated Thus-and-So with an eye toward the common good. Since their primary (not at first their sole) interest was making money with money, they looked instead to the opportunistic angles of the enterprise (regardless of the common good) and built themselves a gambling house where the prices of stocks are determined by the speculation of traders. In this situation the tipsters and hunch-passers and fortune tellers who surround Wall Street were really as useful as anyone else in determining the day by day fluctuation of the market.

Everyone admits that the great Wall Street crash was not precipitated by any gross change in the country's real wealth. There wasn't a drought which ruined wheat, or a series or major fires in factories or a war which shut off supplies of natural resources in the Near East. Whatever the immediate cause (Was it because the banks called in their loans, so demonstrating their power to manipulate an economy built on credit and paper without organic relationship to real wealth?), it was generally agreed that the market had been heading for a well-deserved fall. Nowadays brokers are prevented by law from engaging in some of their more colorful deviations from right reason and honest practice, but speculation reigns king of the stock exchange nonetheless. Some men go to the races or bet on the numbers, others more respectable buy and sell stocks, but all fancy themselves prestidigitators, men who can make money fructify.

The books are now being balanced. Those whose chief desire and necessity is security are getting precious little interest on their capital. Thus, for instance, trust funds have fallen into some disrepute. Since trust companies are compelled by law to be ultra conservative in administering the estates left to widows and children (the heirs always are presumed to be widows and small children whereas often enough they turn out to be petulant and pleasure-loving adults now on their third marriage), their investments carry smaller and smaller interest rates. So much money is necessary now for a capital fund of this sort to yield an effectual annual income that few people will bother to aspire to it.

On the other hand, those whose chief interest is profit now find their only hope of security in giving their lives to following their money around. They are like men trying to cross a river with a rapid current by leaping from ice floe to ice floe as these are carried down-stream. The theory is that you can't trust any stock (investments all being precarious since they are no longer linked to real wealth or to virtuous management of companies), but that if you are deft you can realize a profit here, and then switch to a profit there, etc. Naturally, such a man never rests easily. He can't go fishing or read Plato or enjoy his family without keeping a weather eye out for the financial pages. Bernard Baruch, whose life has been spent in this fashion, planting and harvesting his fructifying dollars, once made a supreme act of renunciation by declining to transplant some of his budding dollars on a Jewish holiday out of respect to his mother. But few men have so much faith and courage.

INSURANCE

The insurance situation is a variation on the same theme, with peculiarities of its own. The Christian idea, of which modern insurance is a facsimile, is that it is useful for men to band together for their mutual assistance and security, so that the disasters which befall one member of a group ought to be met corporately by all members. Most modern insurance is based on self-seeking rather than mutual charity and rests not on an idea of the corporate good but on the sanctity of statistics. Men who should have looked to God's providence for their primary security, and to things like life insurance as secondary or tertiary instruments of providence and security, looked first to insurance and lost all practical trust in providence. (God became the specialist you called in on hopeless cases. The ordinary practicing Catholic today believes less in God's providence than in any other dogma.) The consequence is that in our day insurance is on one hand taking over the role of providence (as, for instance, the Metropolitan once was the largest farm owner in the country, and is now shaping the housing pattern in New York City, shaping it as though to the specifications of the Planned Parenthood Association, that is, in accordance with a dogmatic disbelief in God's care of His children) and on the other hand is proving a precarious and vulnerable providence. God's providence works this way: in return for faith and virtue practiced in the present, (Seek ye first the Kingdom of God and His justice) God gives His solicitous care in the future (and all these things will be added unto you—however much is necessary and however God chooses to give it, whether by gift or job opportunity or a fruitful crop, etc.). Insurance works otherwise: in return for certain definite sums now, a certain, definite, like sum later. The Achilles heel of insurance is inflation. If the $100,000 you contracted for is only worth $50,000 or $10 when you get it, then insurance has failed you. This is the disaster which hangs over all insurance in our day.

WHO WILL BE GOD OVER US?

Almost all financial enterprises, from insurance to international investment, are increasingly at the mercy of government-manipulated currency and so serve the interests of the omnipotent state or the omnipotent world government. Our fundamental dependence for bread and security is upon God. Money is merely one of the instruments of providence. Since we have put our trust in money, we have brought it about that money is no longer even a good instrument, at least for God's providence. It is becoming an instrument of a new and terrible omnipotence. The manipulation of currency value at will (the retiring of gold which has an intrinsic value, was one major step which made this possible) put everyone's fortune at the mercy of the government. The government, in turn, is not yet so debased that it manipulates currency for the sheer pleasure of destroying citizens. It is usually forced to manipulate the currency in order to prevent worse disasters (as when inflating currency disposes of a crushing indebtedness). Obviously, however, the manipulation of currency is a tremendous power in the hands of a tyrant (as the Russians currently are demonstrating in Berlin) and the power to manipulate also tends to produce tyranny. The man at the financial helm has to play the role of a provident God, he has virtually no other alternative.

NON SEQUITUR, AD ABSURDUM

It is currently proposed to remedy all our social ills with the almighty dollar. "Give so and so many millions and cure cancer!" "Let the state appropriate some several billions so we can have better and happier teachers." "The scourge of mental disease demands the utmost in our solicitude — financial of course."

Have we lost our power of reason? Will a dollar bill, when placed on the cancerous member, effect a cure? Is it some sort of relic? The theory is, of course, that the more money that is given to the cancer fund the more can be spent for research; the more spent for research the more likely the discovery of the cause and cure of cancer. This does not necessarily follow. What is needed is light and inspiration. There is nothing in the circumstances to indicate that a lone doctor could not see cancer for what it is if he is given the inspiration. Now the road to light on such matters, in addition to fundamental medical knowledge, experience and a certain intuitive gift, is prayer. Grace really lights up the mind and enables men to see syntheses which otherwise are obscured from them. But who among all these great doctors has even looked in the direction of humility? They are placing their confidence in IBM tabulating machines and vast sums of money contributed by a generous and too-trusting populace.

When the public school teachers of Rochester went on strike they, with the eager assistance of the newspapers, traced their discontent to low wages. The only children in the city who continued to be educated were the pupils of the nuns who receive a nominal salary of one dollar a day. There was a paradox that invited investigation, yet no one investigated. Certain it is we have bad education, rapidly worsening. Certain it is, too, that more and better-equipped school buildings are almost irrelevant to the question. The quality of the teachers is the key point. Our naive materialists fancy they can make better teachers by paying them more, saying, "You will attract a higher type person to the job." But will you? You might attract a lower type person, one who comes not sacrificing out of love of truth and teaching, but interested primarily in the monetary rewards. They also think they will improve the quality by extending the time spent in educational schools. But maybe the inferiority of teachers is due partly to having been subjected to inferior, nonsensical educational schools.

As for mental disease, is its increase not the most obvious manifestation of the disintegration of human beings? And are not religious truth, the observance of the moral law, and the healing and elevating effects of grace, the chief instruments by which men attain "wholeness"? Yet what experts are reported advocating spiritual reconstruction? They want only money: money for hospitals and attendants (that is, for the custodial care of the patients whom they expect to become increasingly numerous—showing that they really despair of reversing the trend); money for the psychiatrists who are finding this situation so lucrative. But what are the psychiatrists accomplishing? And which of any of them is working in harmony with the laws of human nature? And who has measured the harm they might be doing to souls?

MONEY AND THE APOSTOLATE

If money is impotent in the field of human health and happiness, it is infinitely more so in the field of the apostolate.

The sorts of apostolic enterprises which would greatly further the restoration of our country to Christ are fairly obvious. We need a Catholic daily newspaper, or several of them. We need Catholic movies, Catholic radio, Catholic care of (and cure of) the insane, a strong lay apostolate and schools that will turn out militant and integrated graduates. Money is not of the essence of any of these projects, yet when they are mentioned it is money which suggests itself to everyone.

Consider, for instance, the matter of a Catholic daily newspaper. It would certainly take a lot of money to start a Catholic daily, but is there in the whole country a handful of men at once competent and sufficiently Catholic in their mentality to initiate such a project? It would be much easier to raise ten million dollars than to find ten editorial workers who are fully formed and apostolic—and this despite the multitude of newspaper men in the country who are nominally, and even occasionally devoutly, Catholic.

Or consider the academic situation. Where are our great lay thinkers? Would it be possible to assemble enough real Catholic minds to form a beginning faculty for an adult education school anywhere in the country? If there were great minds and great teachers, hardly anything else would be necessary, and within a few years an intellectual ferment would begin to raise the level and Catholicity of thinking throughout the land. Meanwhile, some rich man has recently donated a million dollars to one of our Eastern colleges for the erection of a *business school.* Nothing could be more calculated to destroy what little Catholicity of thought remains among our young men.

A similar void exists in respect of mental disease. A recent conference of Catholic nurses seriously discussed the virtual absence of Catholic mental hospitals. This is not the first time the dearth has been noted. But what is a *Catholic* mental hospital, and are the existent ones strikingly different from secular institutions? That there are accidental differences is evident, but the chief obstacle in the way of Catholic mental hospitals is the absence of a personnel sufficiently Catholic in mentality, sufficiently holy and dedicated to meet the need.

THE POTENCY OF POVERTY

Paradoxically enough, there seems to be only one way to break the stalemate into which we have maneuvered ourselves, and that is voluntary poverty. If money is impotent, poverty (voluntarily embraced) is a touchstone of action. Religious orders continually bear witness to the world of poverty's power of accomplishment. All that is needed is two or three people dedicated to poverty and service for the love of God, and the wherewithal to carry out their projects follows. The several beginners need not be geniuses. It is the power of corporate dedication and the absolute incorruptibility that comes from a vow of poverty that counts.

Sooner or later (probably much too late) the world is going to come to the realization that its power of accomplishment must rest on love, not avarice. The balancers of the ever-more-difficult-to-balance books of hospitals are going to realize that the care of the sick can only be accomplished with the aid of dedicated nurses working for the love of God, and never with "professional women" who are paid as much as private secretaries or ditch diggers. Teachers are going to learn that truth is more to be cherished, and more stable in the long run, than tenure. Employers are going to learn that you can't buy loyalty with higher wages, handsome washrooms or public relations men — there comes a saturation point to man's self-disgust.

Must we wait until the world learns its lessons too late? Or shall we switch to a Christian economy right now?

19
The Age of Lay Sanctity
SEPTEMBER 1948

YOU CANNOT SAY, AS SOME DO, THAT MEN ARE GETting better and better with each succeeding age; history isn't like that. Nor can you say that men are getting progressively worse. What can be discerned is a pendulum movement. Temporal society moves toward Christ or away from Him. When it is moving toward Christ men's minds and men's institutions tend to focus more and more on Christ; the best artists take to painting Madonnas, the best architects work on cathedrals, and even the minor events of family life are marked by sacramentals. Such was the time of the Middle Ages.

The Renaissance brought about a sharp change and the pendulum started swinging in the other direction, away from Christ. Men didn't say so, they said they were going after the irrelevant-to-Christ, the secular; they wanted the wholesome, the healthy, the well-ordered, the just, the materially good. But that is impossible for fallen and redeemed man. We must either look above the natural order to the supernatural order (and when we do so the natural order is rectified and preserved), or we will fall below nature. When the pendulum swings away from the sacred, (as a term) it leads not toward the secular but toward the profane. That's where we are now, at the *bad* natural because we thought we could have the good natural without Christ. Our artists are busy painting lascivious girls for advertising posters, our architects are erecting temples to mammon in the form of skyscraper office buildings, and divorce is rampant.

TODAY'S CRISIS IS A SPIRITUAL CRISIS

It is because we have reached the end of the pendulum swing away from Christ that all our problems today are basically religious. It is folly to think that we can go from wars to peace without reference to Christ, or from no housing to adequate housing, or from economic disorder to economic order. Men are still trying but every time they try they fail. It is because we are fallen creatures who cannot hold to good except through our redemption in Christ. The most realistic program today is the Jocist program "to restore all things in Christ." The Jocists propose to reverse the trend or our times, to reorient society in Christ. That's the only thing that will work. The dreamers and wishful thinkers are those who place their full confidence in natural remedies, laws, leaders, science or psychiatry.

Since the world is sick for Christ, it is therefore the Church's moment. Wise men will look to the Church for the remedy. What does the Church propose? It seems (one cannot be certain) as though God is using this occasion for His Church to explore the means of sanctification in the lay state. The laity are caught in the hiatus between religion and life: God by perfecting them in sanctity will change them to bridges for the sanctification of the temporal order.

THE TREND TOWARD LAY SANCTITY

The evidence of recent history points to the sanctification of the laity as the major ferment going on in the Church. There is informal evidence at every hand: the surprising number of lay people who seem to desire a more than ordinarily holy life, the increase of interest in religion among Catholics and non-Catholics alike, the number of devoted lay people who don't seem to find their place in the religious life and yet desire an intense Christianity.

The testimony of the Specialized Catholic Action movements abroad is particularly telling. They have held out the highest ideals of sanctity to their members and have actually produced many contemplatives within the lay state. Records of the lives of the Jocists who died in concentration camps are being carefully preserved, against the day that the Church may want to investigate their causes.

There is also the testimony of the ordinary Catholic layman, especially the young one. He may not yearn for martyrdom or the heights of prayer. He may long for a quiet, bourgeois life in the suburbs supported by conventional religious practices. But unless he is blind he is beginning to see the handwriting on the wall: "It is no longer possible to be mediocre. Are you for Me or against Me?"

LAY AND RELIGIOUS LIFE

Religious life has always been regarded as higher in itself than the lay life, and rightly so, because the religious life is a way of perfection. Religious orders have set up integral conditions which of themselves conduce to sanctity: community life, the three vows of poverty, chastity and obedience, observation of silence, the Office and so forth. The laity are called to perfection too, but they are necessarily busy about temporal affairs and subject to multitudinous temptations and distractions. Lay saints do not besprinkle the missal as do religious saints, and many of the most promising laity of hagiography ended by repudiating their lay state—mothers going off to found convents over the prostrate bodies of their children, widowed queens retiring to the cloister, etc.

So there has grown up the feeling that the laity are inferior members in the Church, a feeling which is currently expressed by the remark, "If you want to be so holy why don't you go into the convent?" And indeed, a lot of lay people who do want to be holy are behaving like religious out of the cloister. They try to keep up religious practices in the lay state,[1] sometimes saying the Divine Office, or forming into semi-religious communities under a modified rule. Especially in Europe there are a lot of these groups of people who are sort of half-religious and half-lay. They may represent a temporary phenomenon in the Church, one which will later disappear as they themselves develop into real religious communities, or as the principles of sanctity in lay life are further worked out. But even if these institutes find a permanent place, they will not satisfy the demand for a path of perfection in the lay life because they are not susceptible of general application.

DIFFERENT APPROACH TO LAY SANCTITY

Ordinarily, the combination of the lay state with the practices borrowed from the religious life is extremely difficult. The two don't mix very well. The lay person hasn't time to say the Office, has duties of his state which interfere with silence or make it impossible to take on extraordinary penances. When he copies the practices of the religious life he is always seeming to withdraw and to lose his power of influencing his fellow laity.

May it not be that the path of perfection for the laity will, superficially at least, be radically different from that of the religious life? Is it not possible that the incarnation in the lay state of the essential likenesses in all roads of perfection will produce quite different means from those the religious use as their path? Laity shouldn't shrink from

---

[1] We do not wish to deprecate the piety of lay people who take on modified practices, as do Third Order members for instance, but we don't believe they represent today's main way to lay sanctification.

The Age of Lay Sanctity

the lay life but use it as a road to God. That does not necessarily imply worldliness, less so now that we must restore all things in Christ than at any other moment in history.

THE KEYNOTE IS APOSTOLICITY

It is the lay apostolate which is the keynote to lay sanctity. This is primarily so because it offers a magnificent opportunity for referring all our actions to Christ. You can't get very holy if you are pulled two directions at once, if your life is divided between two things which cannot be referred to the same end, if you are a business man during the week and a practicing Catholic on Sundays, if you are building a railroad days and doing spiritual reading evenings, if you are on the assembly line most of the time and taking the parish census on Saturdays. To advance in holiness you have to get the "single eye" the Gospel talks about. The religious does it by leaving worldly activities and substituting sacred activities. The lay apostle does it by transcending temporal activities with the lay apostolate.

The factory worker is no longer primarily the sixth man down in the second row, putting on a screw as the product passes. He is primarily another Christ, providentially associated with adulterous Stanley Lucas on his left and despairing, cynical Joe Pulaski on his right, who would not know about their marvelous dignity if he were not there to tell them. The monotonous movement he makes with his hands is merely the occasion for his being there, and the more tiresome it becomes the more grace he will win for his neighbors by bearing it patiently.

The young nurse no longer yearns for the excitement of the operating room or the ease of the supervisor's desk, but she turns willingly to the bedside, not only because Christ is in the bed and she is called to help Him, but because the other nurses don't see Christ and she must know and love them so that their eyes will be opened.

So it is, all the way down the line even to the advertising copywriter who declines to continue working against Christ and the student who wants to know the first truths first, because the world needs them. The apostolate gives the layman a single eye.

It also does something else which is conducive to sanctity. It sets up supernatural charity as the guiding principle of his life. He works for the love of God in the love of his neighbor. He chooses his associates for the love of God, singling out those who need him rather than the most pleasant companions. He gives up his sleep or his lunch or his leisure or his money for the same reason. He does not think always of the sanctification of his own soul. He thinks of others, even wanting to get holy because "you cannot give what you haven't got." And so indirectly he does become holy, whereas the pious, unapostolic lay person is very apt to turn in upon himself and fail to get holy despite hours spent in church and a grim determination to be a saint.

RENUNCIATION AND DEDICATION

The religious renounces all except a bare minimum of the things of this world for the sake of God. By doing so he helps detach himself from the love of these things. If the layman is to become holy he must also become detached, but he must ordinarily do it in the opposite way, by using the things of this world for God. It so happens that in our time this is an especially good channel to sanctity.

Take the matter of marriage. The religious foregoes the pleasure of marriage for God's sake. The layman who undertakes the full responsibilities of marriage today for God's sake is hardly in danger of forgetting God. First let him decline to limit his family and he will realize that he couldn't indulge in "gracious living" of the Jinx Falkenburg and Tex McCrary type, even if he wanted to. Then there is the little matter of the fact that our society doesn't go in for family wages, or provide family houses any more, or even give verbal encouragement to parenthood. Married people today have to practice heroic fortitude in respect to living arrangements. Many are their trials even when they are happily married. The unhappily married who refrain from divorce, and that with a cheerful countenance, are the modern martyrs.

Consider also the matter of talents. The religious often gives up the use of his talents for the sake of prayer or penance, or else he makes the use of his talents subject to the will of his superior. It is an antidote to pride. Here, too, the lay apostle is faced with the opposite action to achieve the same effect. He has to use his talents, *plus*. Lay apostles have to show a willingness to be used as instruments, and that usually means they will be used to do great things, greater things than they are able. That means they will be sustained by God's grace, and have to count on supernatural aid. Then if they get proud, God takes the props from under them and they are nothing again.

What is true of talents is true of riches and other things of the world. Within an apostolic context, material possessions become such a burden of responsibility that having nothing looks like a remote paradise by comparison, much in the way that the sick man's immaculately clean, white hospital bed looks inviting to the worker exhausted by a day on his feet and an hour's ride in a crowded subway. If Henry Ford II, for example, were to dedicate his life to undoing the accumulated ills he has inherited, the very process would lead to a sort of crucifixion, compared to which a hermit's cave and bread and water diet would look inviting.

In short, life in the world today is a heavy cross by its very nature. Most people are busy running madly away, jumping from one escapist pleasure to another. Anyone who turns around and picks up the cross probably needs, at least at first, the comfort of whatever incidental consolations come his way.

PENANCE IN THE LAY LIFE

Once the laity orient their lives to charity and apostolicity, the incidental and inevitable suffering involved becomes meritorious. The crowded subway becomes a hairshirt and the jibes of fellow-workers a sort of flagellation.

Religious often take a vow of stability, which helps keep them from being attached to a particular place. Today's laity are visited with chronic instability which is an opposite cross producing the same general effect. The family that moves around after seasonal work or searching for decent housing has but to remember the Son of Man Who had nowhere to lay His head, in order to have a certain peace without permanency. The lay apostle who travels (and apostles travel an awful lot) gets to feel more at home in any Catholic church than in his own home base, because it is the church that gives continuity to his wanderings.

It's paradoxical how many of the conditions of lay life are the opposite from the religious life and yet can be turned to similar uses. The silence of the cloister is an aid to recollection. The noise of the factory and the subway do not conduce to recollection but can be accepted as penances which will make it easier to recollect later. It is hard for the laity to practice custody of the eyes, but it is a mortification using the eyes to look at the ugliness and disorder that man has made of the modern city, if seen that way. The misunderstanding of parents is a common trial to lay apostles, and useful for their sanctification. Parents often object because their children don't wish to be worldly successes and make a lot of money. Some degree of poverty is an almost inevitable accompaniment of the apostolate, if only because the world doesn't reward handsomely those who go against its spirit.

The above are common mortifications which accompany the lay apostolate. They are usually followed by others voluntarily undertaken to promote this or that cause within the apostolate.

AIDS AND CONSOLATIONS

The center of the lay apostle's day is Mass and Communion, as it is for the religious. But with the laity Mass is the sole official sacred activity of the day and comes to be of even more relative importance than in the convent or monastery.

It is significant that dialogue Masses and much of the singing participation in the Liturgy is being promoted by lay apostolic groups. It is significant, too, that daily communion is encouraged and easily available today, because the lay apostle has to have his daily Bread if he is going to live by faith in an atmosphere which speaks of God only by His absence. It is a pity that our Catholic immigrants remained in the large cities and were sucked in by urban industrialism, but the churches they built every few blocks now serve as "power houses" for the present generation of the church militant whose apostolate is within the old order.

Next to the Mass, spiritual direction is of primary importance to the laity. Religious have the rule of their order and the counsel of their superiors to guide their lives, but the laity have neither a rule nor a Christian order in society, nor (usually) marvelously Christian parents to guide them, and it has ever been true that a man is not trustworthy as his own guide. It is hard to find a good spiritual director, especially one who understands the lay apostolate, but the laity have at least the advantage of being free to search far and wide in order to find one. Once found, a good spiritual director will give the laity a spiritual anchor and orientation.

Christ led a very active life during the time of his apostolate. It was only occasionally that He was able to retire alone to the mountains to pray. The laity lead a similar life, with only an occasional opportunity for a retreat. The retreat movement has anticipated this need. Now that retreat houses are fairly widespread, and whole religious orders have dedicated themselves to the task of making retreats available, there is a growing demand for retreats of greater spiritual intensity.

Those who are in the apostolate need solid and somewhat advanced doctrine. They want Saint Thomas and Saint John of the Cross rather than watered-down, minimum Christianity and pious exhortations. But they are beginning to get it here and there, even if they have to arrange for their own retreats and retreat masters.

COMMUNITY WITHOUT FORMAL BONDS

The most convincing evidence that the ferment among the laity is the beginning of something new rather than just a stimulation of Catholic lay life in general, is that it is uniting the lay members of the Mystical Body. Without direct formal compulsion, for instance, the members of Specialized Catholic Action come to a unity in Christ marked by an authentic spirit which is everywhere the same, and by an organization which is already nearly world-wide.

One curious thing is that the organization precedes the full development of the movement. It is international and cosmopolitan from the beginning, catholic as the Church. Even where there is no organization there is cooperation among apostolic groups and a feeling of mutual security and confidence which makes formal organization unnecessary. The unity is always an effect of the realization of oneness in Christ, rather than on selective natural grounds. Lay apostles meet, even for the first time, as old and dear friends. It is shocking by contrast to notice that fellow-members of a half-dozen years standing in an organization like the Holy Name Society or the Sodality, can yet be almost complete strangers to one another, each hiding his own sorrow, or shame, or ideals, and each conscious of superficial differences between them of wealth, position or beauty.

God wishes not only each man's salvation, but also the salvation of the whole body of the Church. We must grow to see ourselves not as isolated units, as self-sufficient as possible, but as parts of an organic whole which is increased or diminished by the actions of each one. We all have functional positions within the Mystical Body. If we can teach doctrine we must do so, but we need the cooperation of others to do it efficiently. If we have personality gifts, or can act, all those things are frustrated by an individualistic approach to religion. It is therefore a sure sign of ill health in the Body when each Christian works unorganized and alone, and a sign of good health when Christians can and do organize and cooperate. That is happening today. The Mystical Body is beginning to realize itself as one Body among the Catholic laity.

COOPERATION BETWEEN RELIGIOUS AND LAITY

If the laity are the front-line troops of the Church today, it does not follow that the importance of the religious life has diminished. Nor does it mean that vocations to the religious life will fall off. The lay apostolate usually increases them. It merely means (if our thesis is true) that the Church in growing to its fullness has now worked out the fundamental conceptions of religious life, that religious orders have been established and incorporated into functional positions into the permanent life of the Church, and that now the Church moves on to enfold the laity in a closer embrace than heretofore.

You frequently hear laity speak of the Church as though it did not include them, as though nuns and priests were somehow more surely Catholics than they. Indeed it has been a fairly widespread opinion among the laity that they were somehow outside the doors looking in. One unhappy consequence has been that they haven't felt any particular responsibility within the Church. Theirs to save their own souls (with minimum effort) and contribute money. Theirs not to know doctrine, beyond a catechetical level. Theirs not to apply Christian principles in daily life. Theirs not to talk religion or defend the Faith. As a consequence *all* the responsibility for the Church has been dumped into the hands of the clergy and religious and now lay Catholics are beginning to criticize the way "the Church" is doing things that they should be doing themselves.

The work of the laity is not to usurp or intrude upon the proper work of the religious, but to reorient the temporal affairs of society toward Christ, to concentrate on marriage, business, housing, politics, and the rest. They will need the direction of the clergy in varying degrees according to the nature of the projects, and some work will be shared necessarily by religious and laity, but once it is quite clear that the laity have their own proper work to do in the Church the relations between religious and laity will become closer and more harmonious. It will be easier for nuns to teach future lay apostles than future millionaires, easier for hospital nuns and lay nurses to understand each other when both lead dedicated lives according to their fashion. We shall all begin to see that the eye has need of the hand ... that there are many functions within the same body.

20
The Tragedy of Modern Woman
NOVEMBER 1948

IF YOU WANT TO TAKE THE MEASURE OF MODERN SOCIETY in terms of human happiness, watch the faces of the women. The female of our species is much more sensitive than the male to the things of the spirit, and whatever she feels, and is, will be written on her face after the age of twenty-five or thirty. We are so fashion-conscious that we seldom even look at the soul of modern woman as revealed by her eyes and the lines of her face. In this way we miss observing that most American women, those emancipated and lovely ladies of commercial fiction, either cry themselves to sleep every night or are past giving way to the sorrow and frustration that encompasses them.

WHAT WOMEN WANT

The nature of woman is a matter for philosophical and spiritual investigation. No Gallup poll is needed, or would even be useful, in finding out what women are made for. They are made as all human beings (men included) for God, both here and hereafter. But in a special way women are destined for love and service; love and service of God, usually in the person of another human being. It can be stated dogmatically that the key to any woman's character, and to her happiness or unhappiness, lies in discovering *whom* she loves, whereas a man, though he shares ultimately the same destiny, is frequently caught loving a yacht or a car or a corporation.

In respect to a woman's loves, she will be happy if they are rightly ordered and duly reciprocated, miserable otherwise. Rightly ordered means that God will get her first love and that all her other loves will be somehow in Christ. In this light one can examine modern woman and see that our society has betrayed her on every level.

THE TRAGEDY OF WASTED SACRIFICE

The tragedy of the aging woman with grown-up children today is the tragedy of wasted sacrifice. In God's plan marriage is intended to be the path of sanctification for most women, the altar of daily sacrifice made easy by love. Marriage is so natural a vehicle for dying to oneself that even today it is rare to see a married woman who is selfish unless she has refused through contraception to permit the ordinary fructification of marriage. A woman with a child immediately takes on dignity, a dignity which increases as the family grows and the sacrifices multiply. The normal woman, be she Christian or pagan, gives to her children before herself. They are well clothed while she gets shabbier; they attend school at the expense of new furniture or perfume. The normal woman does not even notice her sacrifices because she loves her children and is surrounded by their need for her.

So far it is all part of God's plan. It is all a prelude to joy unceasing. It is a sort of purgatorial stage of the spiritual life to act as a prelude to the joys of union with God. A Christian woman, while loving her husband and children, should grow increasingly eager for what popular psychologists, with their foolish terminology, call the "empty nest" period, when the house is deserted and the children all at college or married. She should be eager because she should be pretty well stripped of self-love and ready for a swift progress in the spiritual life once she is free for more prayer. She should be already far enough advanced spiritually to count past sacrifices as nothing and to hope she can soon live a more penitential, frugal, simple, and contemplative life than has been possible with a growing family around. Like the saint queens of hagiography she should be planning the personal service she will give to the sick or the needy when her hands are free to love Christ in His least lovable.

The tragedy of the middle-age American woman whom God intended thus to sanctify hits you with full force if you listen to "Queen For A Day" or any of the radio give-away programs. They represent a mountainous vulgarity, a truly shameful indignity. But slightly less vulgarity the same tragedy extends to the more refined suburbanites who waste their declining years in bridge, travel and gossip.

Everyone cooperates in making sure that the years of sacrifice do not fructify. "Now you can have your new Nash, your trip to Bermuda, your hair elegantly done and purple tinted, dishwashing machine and fine clothes!" scream the advertisements, seconded by public opinion. What they are really saying is, "Now that you have been at least partially stripped of self-love, you can learn to love yourself again, so that you may be able to lose your soul after all, and if you don't lose your soul you can at least have the opportunity of going through the stripping all over again, and in a much more painful way, in Purgatory."

Husbands only serve to heighten the tragedy, although for other reasons. Owing to a distorted ideal of married love (more about this later), it is considered today that a woman must hold her husband's affection by her physical charms. How cruel the world's way is, compared to God's? In God's plan a man and his wife would so have grown in spiritual unity by middle age that the most beautiful eighteen-year-old secretary, despite her evident charms, would fail to hold the husband's attention. In the world's scheme love never deepens. It's always superficial and physical. This imposes a torture on all middle-age women whose waistlines finally expand beyond all repressing and who look more and more pathetic in their determine youthfulness. They must always be dieting when they would otherwise (had they been nearing the goal of holiness) be fasting. They suffer doubly because they will not accept suffering. They are vastly more lonely for having turned away from solitude. The devil is a hard task master.

THE TRAGEDY OF HALF-GIVING

The tragedy of half-giving stalks the unmarried women who are not nuns. Perhaps the best way to see their plight is within an historical perspective.

The single state is, strictly speaking, unnatural. It is tolerable and significant (as will be shown) only within a Christian context where it can be raised to a supernatural role. Pagan societies never tolerated single women (as a class, that is; there were accidental special cases). They were pressed into concubinage or prostitution. One of the most notable social effects of Christianity was that it provided a status and function to unmarried women. They would be "brides of Christ," women who were impatient of reaching their final goal of divine love through the intermediary channel of human love and so chose a direct route of total and immediate self-giving to God, either in a life stripped of all but the barest necessary activities for the sake of contemplation or within the framework of a religious order devoted to the works of mercy. As brides of Christ these women were able to love as fully as possible and their love overflowed all over Europe in the service of the poor and the sick, the homeless, the leper and the ignorant. Peace and joy characterized their countenances and people said of them then as they say of them now, "You can never tell how old a nun is—they always look young."

The Protestant Reformation dispensed with nuns, totally in some countries, partially in others. But Protestantism couldn't erase the memory of the freedom not to marry, nor the ideal of free service in the works of mercy. The last several centuries have witnessed the progressive deterioration of the status of the single woman as she was divorced progressively from her role of Christ's spouse. We still have vestiges of the tail end of that regression in the "noble humanitarian" maiden lady who was popularly called an "old maid." Popular appellations are usually somewhat accurate, even if cruel. No one would ever have called a nun an old maid. It was the secular spinster who had withered up because she couldn't love fully and give her service wholly. And now we see the final decay of half-giving. Teachers, nurses and social workers, divorced from Christ except accidentally (where they are pious on the side but do not see Christ in the patient or the student or client, or if they do are caught up in a system which doesn't corroborate their findings), are sick of half-giving, of leading lonely if useful lives, and are capitulating to self-seeking. They are all asking for more money, not knowing that their frustration comes from quite another source and that they are but jumping from unhappiness to ruination.

CAREER GIRLS

Career girls are another facet of the unmarried woman problem, descended in an indirect line by way of the emancipation of women. They are not wholly the termini of the secularized nun but are caught up equally with the disgruntled wife. Without tracing their ancestry in detail, let us examine their present plight.

It can be said categorically that the career girl cannot be happy (that is as a career girl — she may accidentally be fulfilled because her career is secondary to the support of an aged mother or a brother studying for the priesthood, or because she only works for a little while and finds it exciting). You have only to ask one question to see why. *Whom* does a career girl love? As a woman she must love *someone* wholly.

She does not love God, not enough anyhow. That is apparent by definition. A career girl is one who is forging a place for herself in business, government, the arts — some secular activity. It does not involve a religious dedication. God, then, is out of the center of her life.

Most career girls try to go against their natures. They pretend that they can make themselves like men, impersonal, objective, happy in the pursuit of things. If they have love affairs, they try to make them seem casual, as though their hearts were not involved. The more glittering a woman's career (in the eyes of the world) the more apt the woman herself is to be distorted, unhappy and neurotic.

Then there are a multitude of career girls who love their bosses, knowingly or unknowingly, morally or immorally, with home-breaking effects or not. It is not in a woman to give her total service and dedication to the Amalgamated Pickle Company or National Horseshoes, Inc., without having a personal attachment involved. Business tends to exploit this fact because it is to the interest of the firm to have devoted workers, and if a roomful of girls is going to be asked to work late night after night it is useful to have a handsome personnel manager. The situation is especially acute in the case of secretaries, so aptly named "office wives." Night after night, from coast to coast, important Mr. Jones leaves the office early for golf and then cocktails and dinner, while Mary Jane Smith works on until 8:00 P. M. cleaning up the mail. Often enough she doesn't know why she does it, and most often too Mr. Jones is obtuse enough to accept the sacrifice without realizing its disorienting effects on Mary Jane's life.

The only way for a determined career girl to escape from the emotional disorders which beset her is for her to give all her love to someone whose interests are identical with her own, that is, herself. Needless to say, self-love is to the self's ultimate destruction, but it seemingly frees people from being hurt by others (the person you love always has the power to hurt you). When a career woman thus "frees" herself by loving only herself she becomes a ruthless creature who terrifies all around her. A calloused male seeking money or power is warm and human by contrast. And, needless to say, such a woman is in a far more perilous state as regards her soul, than the secretary she makes miserable and the comptometer operator who is secretly in love with the head bookkeeper.

THE LAY APOSTLE

Single women must again turn to Christ with a total love and service. It is easy to say that they ought to marry or enter the convent, but that is often not the answer. Neither is it the answer for them to continue their secular course and pile up novenas on the side. Today's answer to the problem of the single girl is usually the lay apostolate, some form of Catholic Action which will give her a Christ-centered life and a very important function within the contemporary framework of life. Wherever girls have turned to some vital form of the apostolate, the marks of frustration, neurosis, loneliness and unhappiness have indeed begun to disappear. Life is not really as difficult as it seems. God's way is easy and includes everyone.

THE TRAGEDY OF SUPERFICIAL UNION

The tragedy of the married woman today can be traced to a misunderstanding about the nature of human love. We are made, says the Church, in the image and likeness of God. The modern world contradicts this: We are made, it says, in the image and likeness of animals. The union of a man and woman in marriage, says the Church, is analogous to the union of Christ and His Church and can only be understood in that light. It is a spiritual union, expressed through the union of bodies. The union of man and woman in marriage, says the world, is like the mating of animals, to which is attached a little more delicacy and celebration because we are higher animals.

So the world prepares young people for marriage by teaching them physiology and the techniques of making love, and sends them into marriage (armed with contraceptive devices) physically mature but spiritually infantile.

As the marriage relationship becomes (as it must) progressively more intolerable, the publishers belch a mountain of books giving further instruction on the art of eroticism, and finally society shepherds the aggrieved partners singly onto the psychologist's couch, and on to the divorce court.

There virtually is no such thing as sexual incompatibility. The root trouble is the lack of spiritual harmony, and behind that a deficient spiritual development or a complete absence of spiritual orientation. How could marriage possibly succeed?

But let us return to the married woman. She has to love someone wholly. *Whom* does she love? She ought, of course, to love God and her husband as Christ's intermediary but most times she does not.

There is a natural tendency for women to love their husbands as though their husbands were God, as though they were indeed a woman's final end. This is owing to woman's great need to love and give herself wholly and it always leads to disaster. If the husband becomes her god the wife becomes subordinate to him in a disastrous way. She takes her standards from him (what is good is what pleases him, what is bad he doesn't like), whereas she is supposed to be the member of the family who preserves the moral standards which come from God. Her entire happiness hinges on him, and he is often a poor enough specimen. She becomes jealous, she demands much more of him in time and attention than he wants to give. Eventually the husband will be unable to tolerate this unnatural worship, accompanied as it usually is by frequent tears and emotional outbursts, and the woman will be driven to a nervous breakdown. Or else she will discover in one shattering blow that her god is a clay idol and be so disillusioned she will hate him.

If a woman doesn't love God supremely, and chances not to worship her husband, there is always the possibility of gross over-attachment to her children. Under the guise of maternal solicitude a vast multitude of woman are seeking a self-satisfaction in their children, making their sons over-dependent on them and robbing their daughters of real lives of their own. Enough evidence of this sort of thing is at every hand to omit any elaboration here.

Or the married woman, like the single woman, can love herself. All loves reduce in the end to self-love or love of God, but those who love anther during their lifetime have not yet settled in self-love even if they haven't attained God. Determined, premeditated self-love, as in the newly-married girl who loves clothes inordinately and wants no children, is like premature self-damnation. It's like making the final choice between God and self on the very threshold of life.

THE NEW PAGANISM

Paganism has always been marked by the degradation of women. Whether in cultured Athens or Hindu India or ancient or modern China, you will look in vain for the regard for women with which Christianity marked Western society. The degradation takes two forms: women are reduced to slave-like work and to objects of pleasure. We are returning to paganism with ever more swift strides in our society, and again it is marked by the two signs of women's degradation.

The emancipation movement has ended in women's slavery. The myriads of office and factory girls, regimented, depersonalized, with their every gesture prescribed and tabulated, are the armies of slaves on whom the new paganism is being built. Superficially it does not seem so because, for the moment at least, we encourage our new slaves to dress like Hollywood stars and we appease their appetite for life by the vicarious excitement of the movies, radio and pulp stories. We even pay them well, but it is a quarter of a century since Belloc reminded us that slavery is still slavery even if it is well paid — and cushioned about with television sets and double chocolate sundaes.

The moral debacle, plus divorce, birth control and other "enlightened" measures, has resulted in the reduction of women to a pseudo-prostitution, of which the wolf call (which so many poor ignorant women think flattering) is the symbol.

It is into this atmosphere, this post-Christian situation, that the young girl of today emerges from adolescence. For her it will be like starting all over again to work for the true emancipation which Christ came to bring her. She can no longer drain out the last dregs of happiness and dignity left by a residual Christianity, but has to forge a new path in the manner of Saints Agatha and Agnes. But not quite in their way because they were lone Christian martyrs, defying worldly parents and a pagan society. The modern Catholic girl has the opportunity of uniting with a multitude of others in the lay apostolate, not so much to defy an inevitable authority and suffer death as (through the lay apostolate) to take advantage of what freedom of action is left to bring Christ, purity and happiness to a dispossessed younger generation whose elders have not seen fit to pass on their residual Christianity. But like the early martyrs, the young woman of today may well be repudiated and cast out by her materialistic parents.

NOT LESS LOVE, BUT MORE

There is only one answer to the tragedy of the women who are making modern society quite literally a vale of tears, and that is an ordering and an increase in their love. It is pathetic to see the pseudo-solutions which the popular magazines hold out to women whose problems they often see quite clearly, and whose unhappiness has certainly not escaped them (as has not the potentialities of exploiting them for profit). How can they give any but superficial remedies? How can they suggest anything except what might deaden the pain (sometimes at the expense of virtue)? Bridge is no remedy. Helena Rubenstein does not hold the key to happiness. A new dress won't do it. Neither will an affair, a raise, a cruise or a good book.

Unlike the indifferent husband, Christ welcomes love and total devotion, and reciprocates a thousandfold. Unlike children, Christ does not outgrow His desire for our affection. Unlike the world,

Christ forgives us, no matter how far we have fallen. He can purify the impure, as He perfected the woman taken in adultery.

The central fact of the case is that women need to love tremendously and there is only one Person whom they can safely and satisfactorily love: Christ. And the more disordered their present loves the more whole-hearted will have to be their conversion to a love of Christ.

There is no remedy for modern woman's tragedy except Christ, and wherever Christ is introduced all human relationships begin immediately to straighten themselves out.

1949

21
The Two Enemies of the Church
JUNE 1949

ONE HEARS OF A PROPHECY THAT IN OUR DAY THE Church will be attacked by two great enemies: one from outside and one from within. If so, the prophecy is accurate. We do have two great enemies today: one of them is external and comprises the haters of Christ; the other is more subtle, it is the apathy that has descended on Christ's followers. The camp of the external enemy is in the control of the communists and most Catholics have been alerted to the terrible danger with which they threaten us. The interior enemy has no central authority, and is unorganized, because it is a negative sort of enemy. It is merely that much of the salt has lost its savor. Call it mediocrity, or secularism, or lukewarmness. If you wish to find an excuse, you can call it the residual effects of the near-death blow which was the Reformation. But there is no particular point in finding excuses or allocating blame. And it goes without saying that the Church remains inviolable, and holy, at all times, no matter how much the surface is scarred. But if a Trappist in China has to suffer terrible tortures before death because people in America have not used the graces God has showered on them (and such a Trappist did so suffer, it being revealed to him that it was for this reason); and if cruel martyrdoms in Europe are a reflection of the tepidity of the masses of Catholics, then we cannot take comfort in the thought that the gates of Hell shall not prevail. Rather it is for us to discover how they have been able to lay such a heavy siege, and to meditate how best to lift it.

THE RELATIONSHIP BETWEEN THE TWO ENEMIES

The enemy without is the Devil's answer to the enemy within. Our arch-enemy is merely moving seven new devils into a void which we have swept, but which we have neglected to fill with vital Christianity. He is but satisfying humanity's yearning for Christ with a caricature of Christ. We are told that those who are not with Christ will be against Him. Our sin has been not to attack Christ, but to try to remain neutral for all practical purposes, and it turns out now that everything we touch is against Him.

We can ward off the direct attacks of the communists with ever more hideous martyrdoms and with the prayers and penances of only God knows how many hidden souls. We can stall occasionally by turning an election or forcing a diplomatic issue. We can only conquer communism by filling the void of our daily lives with Christ. The only permanent remedy is for the salt to regain its savor. This is the Church's remedy, and although it is meant as a general call to a deeper, more sincere Catholicity, it is meant especially as a call to the apostolate, particularly the lay apostolate. If the salt has lost its savor, with what will the world be salted? It is a particular sort of recovery that we must make, a recovery of apostolicity and of the power of apostolicity. It is not a vague thing either. The purpose of this article is to discuss the general principles and technique involved.

THE INDEFENSIBILITY OF THE STATUS QUO

As a preliminary, let us make it quite clear that the status quo is indefensible. To champion mediocrity (under the name of prudence, of course), or the profit motive, or industrial capitalism or secularism, because these things are better than communism is like trying to fight pneumonia with a severe cold. All deep thinking economic philosophers agree that the economic platform of communism was provoked by the inherent injustices of the capitalist-industrial system (with its profit motive supreme). Karl Marx, the father of communism, said so. So did Max Weber, a brilliant German Protestant. So does Christopher Dawson, our outstanding Catholic historian. It is sad, then, to observe that so many Catholics think they defend the Church by defending liberal economics departed from fundamental Christian ideas about justice, property, usury and the common good, that it has sired such an unlovely child as Marxism. To an intolerable and unstable economic situation there are two alternative answers: either supersede the errors with worse ones which look like correctives (as Marxism does), or return to Christian principles (as is the platform of Christian "radicals"). So, for instance, the answer to a grossly unjust distribution of property, is either to eliminate all private property by the state taking over (as in communism) or redistribute private ownership on a small scale (which is roughly the distributist platform). These two solutions differ from each other as night from day; they have in common only their mutual distaste for the laissez-faire ideal.

So it is all the way down the line. Take the case of marriage. The proponents of divorce say that it is a hideous and intolerable thing for a man and a woman to live together in hatred. And so it is. But there are two alternatives: one is to loosen the marriage bond, and the other is to develop the spiritual union between husband and wife by religious reinforcements all along the line.

No Catholic would defend the communist view of marriage, but many Catholics fail to see that the situation is parallel in the economic, political, spiritual and every other order. They ought to think more deeply and read their own great writers. They ought also to cease calling fellow-Catholics "communists" because they try to realize Christian doctrine in practice. The only defense against communism is a Catholicity lived, and that would be radical (which is to say it would go to the roots) in our day.

We are witnessing a widespread revolt against lukewarmness. Christ said "be ye hot or cold." but He didn't say that hot was cold; they are indeed at opposite poles. However, He preferred even the cold to the indifferent. The lukewarm are the ones He is going to spit out. And lukewarmness is precisely the religious temperature of the status quo. It has its intensities in lust and avarice, and pleasure, but it thinks it is a dangerous thing to love God too much.

THE FUNCTION OF THE LAITY

Today's crisis centers around the laity for the precise reason that the enemy is secularism. Our problem is not that God is not in the churches, but that He is nowhere else. He isn't allowed in business, recreation, the professions, marriage, schools and politics. Christ has been thrust out of the *layman's* domain; hence the logical instrument by which He will be reinstated is the layman. That is the reason for the lay apostolate, which is not just another good thing, but is of supreme importance.

Because Protestantism denied the sacramental powers of the priesthood, the Catholic Church was forced to reemphasize the distinctive nature of the priest and for fear of misinterpretation laid no stress for centuries on the idea, which was current in early Christianity and is found in the Gospels, that the laity have a sort of participated analogous priesthood, deriving chiefly from the Sacrament of Confirmation. This doctrine is being revived by the Church in connection with the lay apostolate. It doesn't mean, of course, that there is not an essential difference of power and function between the laity and the clergy, but it does mean something. It means that the laity are capable of being formed into mature, apostolic responsible Christians who can participate *with initiative* in the Church's apostolate.

IS IT DANGEROUS TO GIVE THE LAITY INITIATIVE?

Many people fear the lay apostolate precisely because it does involve not a complete autonomy, but much more responsibility and initiative from laymen than in the immediate past. They say it will be dangerous to give the laity responsibility. It is true, I think, that it is dangerous to give the laity responsibility. Let us admit that, and then let us look at the problem more closely.

First of all, is it inappropriate to mention that life is dangerous, and particularly that Christianity is always courting danger? An army would not get very far if it never took chances or suffered casualties. We would never have any saints if everyone stuck to the first stages of the spiritual life because there are possibilities of self-deception in contemplation. "Playing safe" is hardly a Christian attitude. God Himself has set another pattern by giving us free will, which is supremely dangerous to our salvation. We shall someday know how many "casualties" God has tolerated in this respect for the sake of a higher good.

So the question is not so much whether it is dangerous to give the laity responsibility but whether or not it is necessary, whether or not it is the mind of the Church, whether or not they have the capacity to be fitted for it, despite the fact that some may not prove worthy.

Probably the reason that many are opposed to lay responsibility is that they imagine the disaster which would follow from giving responsibility to the type of lay person generally found in the Church today, dutiful and docile but immature in respect to his Catholicity. They remember the days of lay-trusteeship when lay people tried to dictate to the Church about matters belonging in the ecclesiastical jurisdiction, not realizing that the present situation is calling for laity to take *apostolic* responsibility in the *temporal* order, after they have been formed spiritually and intellectually under the clergy; without realizing too that the laity remain always under the *control* of and sometimes under the direction of the hierarchy (as in specialized Catholic Action where the laity exercise a limited initiative under general coordinating directives).

The Two Enemies of the Church

Again, it is not so much a question of whether the laity ought to be allowed to influence the temporal order or not; *they inevitably do so already.* The question is whether their influence will be for Christ or against Him, and, if for Him, whether or not it will be exerted in the most effective way. If you look around the United States you will see that almost everything has turned from Christ. The newsstands are crowded with trash, error and pornography. The stores are full of luxurious, poorly-made and immodest clothes. Almost all new housing invites the practice of contraception. The movie houses are full of movies which at best ignore Christ. None can deny that Catholics are involved in every step of this Christ-less civilization. Nor is it any longer possible to maintain that the Catholic contribution is a minor one, and that the thing to do is for Catholics to get in there at the bottom, work their way to the top, and then change things. There are Catholics at nearly all the tops, owning the greatest tabloids, controlling movie companies, directing newsstand syndicates, and being presidents of department stores. When is someone going to challenge their consciences? When are they going to learn what they must know in their hearts already, that as Christians they are bound by a higher law than current business ethics? Devotions won't teach them, and contributions to charities won't excuse them. If someone were to put the responsibility for restoring the temporal order squarely on their shoulders, where it belongs, then they would be challenged.

Another unfortunate effect of a passive laity is the temptation it presents to the clergy to step out of their spiritual domain. That is why trouble keeps popping up about priests "meddling" in politics, both here and abroad. That is why priests come up with solutions to the economic problem or get lost in a maze of secular administrative affairs. It hasn't happened often in this country yet, and it doesn't always end unhappily, but it is dangerous for a priest to be preoccupied with temporal problems. When a priest does so it is usually to do what the laity ought to have done but have left undone. It may seem strange to a future generation that we have seen a priest crusade against usury and other financial ills, yet we have had many Catholic bankers and a president of the stock exchange who have not even noticed any of these disorders.

The apostolate is the corrective for these troubles, because it develops a responsible, mature laity. The tragedy of most Catholics who are prominent in secular affairs is that they are spiritually midgets.

It isn't a question of good or bad will. It does the Church no good to have men of good will in high places if they have not also good sense and Catholic minds. Even though in the former case they may do the Church favors or give her money, this does not outweigh the harm they do by seeming to put the Church's seal of approval on the activities in which they are involved.

THE CONCEPT OF THE LEAVEN

Society must be redeemed from inside. You hear the Young Christian Workers talking about being a leaven. They hope to work like yeast in the lump of dough. As through kneading the yeast is everywhere present in the dough, so through their temporal activities they are everywhere; in factories, offices, hospitals, professions, sports and theatres. If they allow themselves to become leaven, by becoming instruments of Christ, the whole mass of people and institutions will be raised to Christ.

The idea of the leaven is pretty much common sense in the modern situation (the communists have it too but in a perverse way, "boring from within"). It is obviously suited to a lay initiative and it contrasts with the techniques used by the Church at the time of the development of the religious orders, the so-called "Dark Ages" during which the Church christianized Europe. Then Christians weren't everywhere as they are today; the mass of people were barbarians, waiting to be converted and civilized. So far from being excluded from temporal activities, such as economics and politics, the Church had even to supply these things, bishops sometimes being temporal as well as spiritual rulers. The Church's method was roughly as follows: it withdrew a Christian elite (the monks and nuns) for special spiritual and intellectual training; these religious established monastic centers from which flowed Christian instruction as well as practical and intellectual training. Some two-thirds of the cities of France were organized around such a nucleus of integral Christianity.

Today's situation is the opposite. The Church enjoys no particular prestige and has very little power to influence temporal society in an authoritative or ecclesiastical way. She cannot impose her principles of economics or politics and when she makes them known most of the world fails to listen (as witness the almost entire ignorance of papal encyclicals which prevails among non-Catholics, even in high places, not to mention among Catholics, or the failure of the U. N.

lately to heed the Church's plea for an internationalized Jerusalem). Catholics are everywhere today, as opposed to formerly, but they aren't very Catholic.

So instead of the Church's being the center of society and working its influence outward, the Church remains on the periphery and works as a leaven through the laity who will restore the central position of Christ as King of this world as well as the next. Whereas formerly the religious and clergy were the chief apostles, with the laity assisting, now the laity are in the forefront, with the clergy and religious forming the laity and controlling and directing them, not without, however, giving them the responsibility necessary to act prudently.

ERRORS TO BE AVOIDED

Since the laity must leaven society they must be in society, but if they conform to secular norms of conduct they will no longer be leaven. This dilemma is at the heart of the problem of the lay apostolate.

Some, seeing how much holiness is necessary to raise up a society as pagan as ours, have withdrawn the laity for intensive spiritual and intellectual training according to the great masters of the contemplative life. Almost invariably the laity so trained find themselves alien to their former environments and so unable to influence society from within. However, they are usually valiant Christians and their projects, while on the periphery of society, will probably be very valuable in the future; meanwhile, their own holiness, self-sacrifice and dedication are certainly pertinent to the salvation of America.

Those who go to the other extreme are less fortunate because they end up sacrificing their own holiness to a misguided zeal for getting along. They are the people whom Cardinal Suhard compassionates in one of his pastorals, who make sacrifice after sacrifice to win peoples' trust and friendship in order to bring them Christ, but find in the end that they have conformed so completely that they are empty-handed—they have only themselves to give.

The solution to the dilemma rests in formation. Anyone who ponders the Jocist method will be deeply impressed with its genius. In the first place the apostle does not seek his own perfection apart from his fellows. The see-judge-act inquiry technique is not an examination of personal conscience, but of social consciousness. It does not say, where have I sinned in a *formal* manner? It says, where have *we* sinned in a *material* way? Where are we unconscious pagans? It brings Christian light to bear on the immediate social circumstances. This method has the further virtue of insisting on action from the beginning, as this action is the occasion of the formation of the apostle himself in realistic charity. It manifests the need of a strong sacramental and prayer life, while not bottling grace up inside the soul. As Father [Donald L.] Hessler has said, speaking of receiving frequent Communion, "whoever eats such powerful food needs a lot of exercise." He meant the exercise of charity in an apostolic way. The first fruit of Catholic Action is the formation of the apostles themselves. It produces mature, responsible leaders who work on their environment, chiefly through a manifest charity.

THE NEW ELITE

For better or worse our society is in process of changing its leadership. On the side of worse we see the strong men of Europe, former house painters, soldiers or laboring men. Winston Churchill, the aristocrat leader, seems like the vestige of a former day, and there is no need to mention the dispossessed monarchs of Europe, for they have completely lost their leadership. Our own congressmen and senators cannot all be characterized as "gentlemen," and F. D. Roosevelt may have been our last president to come from the landed gentry (whom he, in any case, "betrayed"). If you go into even the most conservative American cities you will see that the "better people" (the cultured, the well-educated, those who have been wealthy for generations and Americans for a long time) no longer are really in control, or else their control is threatened.

The communists would say that this is merely evidence of the impending dictatorship of the proletariat, and a good thing too. The dialectical resolution of history has designed that the working man will reign supreme.

The Church, on the contrary, does not hope that all men will be reduced to the dead level of industrial wage-earners. She prefers a society with economic, intellectual, and functional differentiations because that corresponds to the nature of men.

That does not mean that Christianity favors the present social structure. It would be hard to hold that the high positions of men in our society are by and large filled by the most competent or deserving. After all, we have been through centuries of secularism, within which society became progressively more corrupt. It would not be too much of an exaggeration to hold that the people we honor most are the richest; money does not so much follow on position, as it buys position. Even many of the old families have unsavory beginnings, as have been exposed in many a popular biography. It can be further held, I think, that most of the old-line leaders have forfeited their right to leadership. They have been like generals who hid while the battle was on. When inflation threatened the bankers suddenly became very interested in farming and bought up most of the farmland in the country, as an ace in the hole. The men who built the great black factories which belch forth smoke on the children of their workers, have themselves long since moved to the suburbs where their own children are surrounded by greenery and solicitude.

To be a true leader of the people a man must first identify himself somehow with the people. No wonder Vito Marcantonio wins elections for he tells his constituents, poor tenement dwellers on the East Side of New York, that he and they share the same cockroaches. He reminds them that they don't have to go down to Wall Street to see him, as would be the case with his Republican opponent. No one is going to beat Vito Marcantonio by sitting around Tammany headquarters and accusing him of being a communist. Only another leader, a Christian who really is a leader, will be a serious rival.

What we need is not to sustain the old elite, but to form a new elite of Christian apostolic leaders. The "teams" who have gone into the slums around Paris first endeavor to "share the destiny" of the most underprivileged people and then to lead them from within. We must remember that Christ our Leader took on our human nature and shared our destiny in order to redeem us. In imitation of Him we must accept the temporal destiny of those we propose to lead. That means that if people are insecure we must accept insecurity, if they are threatened with the atom bomb, we must not run away.

THE MOBILE UNIT

Quality, not quantity, counts in this revolution. The modern world is not going to be won by horse power but by strategy, and although the aim is to win the masses (by force or conversion) the standing army will be small, mobile and will consist of highly trained leaders. If we are trying to hold up the strength of a society which was only slightly ailing it would be useful to give a little reinforcement everywhere. But we are trying to forge a new world quickly before the old one collapses and for that we need depth of vision, dynamism and key people who can lead the masses who are already too confused to think for themselves.

You do not get dynamism from watering down your doctrine to the level of the most complacent man. You get dynamism from the greatest possible fullness of truth and light, even if that is embodied in only a few people. Our Christian dynamism comes from Christ, of course, and it's better for gaining the world to have five people in a parish or town whose supernatural life is so intense that they really manifest Christ (especially in the market place, where it will always cause some sort of riot because it will confound ordinary business and social customs), than it is to have a whole township of mediocre practicing Christians.

The lay apostolate is always characterized by small, dynamic working units, no larger than free discussion size. In the Young Christian Worker movement they are called "cells." In this the lay apostles have copied the communists, who had the technique from Our Lord. Christ preached to the multitudes, but He gave most of His time to training twelve men who then set out in all directions to form other cells; and so Christianity developed, slowly at first, then spreading by geometrical progression until it took over the world. As long as the cells can grow organically, as through teams and more cells and teams, with an international superstructure and central committees, a movement using this technique will be effective, capable of swift action, and will develop a constant stream of loyal leaders.

The Communist Party is small, even in Russia, and prefers to remain so. It does not hope to win the United States or England by winning a national election but by gradually perverting the institutions of society to its uses (and crippling those which won't conform) so that communism has but to move in on what it has already won. Against such tactics old-line politicians and economists are virtually helpless. One reason is that they work with unwieldy groups. Observe how often our own Congress is rendered impotent to act by a simple manipulation of parliamentary procedure, even when it is only a case of partisan interest within the anti-communist body. Political meetings and labor union meetings today are always subject to communist disruption by a clever use of Robert's Rules, but note that the communist meetings are not conducted by the same method. Catholic labor schools are strong on teaching parliamentary procedure themselves to counterbalance the communists but that is a purely defensive tactic.

In the Church you see a parallel situation. Most church organizations are large and unwieldy, with the dose of Christianity appropriately watered down. They try to reach everyone, and that is probably why they end up having virtually no influence on anyone.

By contrast the lay apostolate uses the streamlined method of the cell movement. It is willing to start very small as long as it is free to be as dynamic as leadership development can make it. It is only after the leaders are trained that its influence multiplies—and then geometrically.

THE COMING MYSTICAL AGE

The six best-selling, non-fictional books in America today are on religious topics. Trappist monks rival the latest bathing suit obscenities for space in the pages of *Life* Magazine. Does this mean that America is turning Christian?

Not necessarily. What it means is that the great age of naturalism, rationalism and secularism is about finished and that men are ready to swing completely into the opposite camp. The opposite camp is mysticism. Mysticism doesn't mean natural law and ethics and social philosophy and apologetics, even though these are all good things. Mysticism means contemplative prayer, the supernatural life, the truths which are above reason, all those aspects of the Faith which have been hidden deep in monasteries and convents while life in the world was so barren, so unbeautiful, so scientific and statistical. The age of the eager beaver and the extravert is coming to an end. Men begin to turn envious and respectful eyes toward those who see what can't be counted and measured, toward those who love solitude and prayer rather than those who are good fellows at a party.

Mysticism is a much more lofty thing than reason, but there is a false mysticism which is below reason and which hits a depth of evil undreamed of by the simple sinner. This false mysticism with its murky depths has been winning adherents for a long time. One would be naive to suppose that communism is simply materialistic. Communism is materialism raised to a mysticism and given a soul. One sees it in the misty light that comes into eyes of those who dream of the classless society, of the perfect beatitude which they are going to establish here on earth. Freud raised sex to a mysticism. His lust is a transcendental lust, not like ordinary sex, but containing within itself the fulfillment of all joys.

Both communism and the lay apostolate put their appeal on a mystical plane. If communism simply appealed to self-interest it would only enlist the tentative support of the worst people, but it does in fact attract the best blood, the young idealists, and they are willing to sacrifice themselves completely and blindly for the cause, without hope of reward. Communism talks a lot about solidarity and this too in sort of a mystical way. And work is ennobled with an aura of holiness. And so on down the line.

In answer the Church must bring out its highest life and not just the rules of the minimum observance. The lay apostolate is eager for the best. It frankly hopes for (and has already achieved in not a few cases) action as an overflow of contemplation. It wants heroic virtue and the love which is supernatural charity. When Canon Cardijn speaks to his Jocists he always emphasizes the "mystique" of the movement. The most menial work is ennobled by its participation in Christ's redemptive campaign. And, of course, there is the living reality of Christ's Mystical Body, reemphasizing itself in the bond among apostles.

This then is the level of battle: two mystiques facing each other, one above and one below reason. Perhaps we shall soon be fighting with all the supernatural help we can summon against principalities and powers. It will be terrible, but it will be wonderful too, for there will then be only one enemy and the Church will be purged of tepidity, showing her glory before men.

22
The Problem of the Newman Club

SEPTEMBER 1949

THE PROBLEM OF THE NEWMAN CLUB

Every member of a Newman Club can rattle it off that the purpose of the club is to foster the spiritual life of students, their religious instruction and their social life, *in this order*. Nearly all of them will also admit (especially the distraught and discouraged chaplains) that in practice the order is reversed. The average Newman Club is overwhelmed with social events, has very little strictly spiritual activity (one annual Communion breakfast and one retreat, neither well attended) and does only fairly well with the religious instruction. Every year a few zealous students try heroically hard to shift the emphasis from social to spiritual and to awaken some vitality in the characteristically apathetic members. Similarly with the chaplains who are often bewildered at the small reward of their herculean labors. It is sometimes possible, because of great activity or large numbers to imagine that particular Newman Clubs are accomplishing much, but this apparent success should be considered in the light of the fact that the Newman Club is the sole organized instrument for reaching Catholic students in secular universities. A number of converts is not impressive if great numbers of Catholics lose their faith at the same time. Nor is it an achievement to have "sponsored" marriages amongst nominal Catholics if the marriages are not really Catholic, nor to have kept to the minimum observance of the Faith practical pagans who will almost certainly prove weaklings in the crises which they cannot help but face in our day.

Does this sound as though the Newman Club should be held responsible for all the evils of secular education? Certainly not. Yet if the Newman Club is destined to play a losing game (as, for instance, if it means taking the diocesan time, money and priestly services principally to sponsor secular recreational activities among nominal Catholics), then the effort might better be abandoned. On the other hand, maybe the Newman Club is missing real opportunities for lack of vision. Certain Newman Clubs in this country, as for instance at the

Universities of Iowa and Illinois, are extremely effective because they take a realistic view of the total university situation. It is time that all Newman Clubs took serious stock of their roles on their own campuses.

THE SECULAR DILEMMA

Newman Clubs have usually been suffered or tolerated by the Church rather than enthusiastically hailed, and this because they cater to Catholic students in secular institutions, and in theory the Catholics shouldn't be there at all. Indeed, it is more than a theory. Catholics are prohibited by canon law from attending secular colleges and universities without special permission. Furthermore, there is a basic conflict inherent in the very idea of secular education.

However, the fact of the matter is that hordes of Catholics do go to secular colleges and universities and that the Church in practice tolerates it, and even tolerates the presence there of considerable numbers of nuns and priests. It may be a bad idea but it is a *fait accompli*, so much so that New York University can claim to be the "largest Catholic college in the country."

Because of the Church's reluctance to seem to condone the presence of so many Catholics in non-Catholic schools, Newman Clubs have been step-children in the matter of chaplaincies. This is their primary disability. Many Newman Club chaplains are really parish priests taking on this one added responsibility, to which they can give very little time and for which they are often enough unsuited.

Another serious consequence of the secular problem is that the caliber of Catholic students is generally fairly low. The reason is that Catholics who attend secular colleges often do so for impure motives. Sometimes it is a snobbish appeal, oftentimes it is with a view toward worldly success. Usually the student is already secularized, or very poorly instructed, when he arrives. Some enroll under parental pressure or economic stress, and many, whether their motives are good or mixed, have never had a clear view of the Church as Christ. In consequence, it is likely that the more noble and sincere characters on campus will be found among the non-Catholics. We shall return later to the question which arises as a result of this condition.

TIMES HAVE CHANGED

When the Newman Club was founded around the turn of the century, secular education, though rationalistic and uncatholic, was not yet oriented against the natural law, against morality, and against God. It had some virtues and a Catholic could, by supplementing it with Catholic learning, come out fairly well-educated while remaining a good, even if not a spectacular, Catholic. Any present-day treatment of the Newman Club must take into account the tremendous recent worsening of the schools. The very principles of reason are being superseded by a systematized atheism. In the face of this it is impossible for even the Newman Club to play a supplementary or defensive role. It will have to join the intellectual battle and that means that its students (and teachers), or at least some of them, will have to be given sharp and sound and profound instruction, not only in doctrine but in theology integrated with psychology, science, history and the rest of the subjects.

EVERYONE GOES TO COLLEGE

Everyone goes to college today who has the time or money and the greater percentage are not real students. The general policy of the Newman Clubs has been to cater to the soft-headed majority of fun-loving collegians. It is true that it cannot neglect these, since they are in the majority and are likewise in spiritual need. Yet the intellectual is the rightful inhabitant of the campus and in the long run the person most likely to influence educational circles and through them the masses. He should be cultivated, and he should not be expected to accommodate himself to juke boxes and dances. Any effort to reach both the student and the collegian should be spiritual and liturgical, for here is their common ground. Otherwise let there be separate and suitable activities. The collegians can have preparation-for-marriage courses while the intellectuals study Saint Thomas. In this way the best in both groups can be cultivated.

THE SCARCITY OF TIME

Lastly there is the problem of time. Students are overwhelmed with extracurricular activities of which the Newman Club is just one. To our mind the Newman Club is usually too deferential in regard to the students' time. It should insist with the students, as does Catholic Action and the Legion of Mary in their activities, that nothing (except classes) takes precedence over the Newman Club. Christianity cannot play second fiddle to athleticism, or to other clubs or to dates. Naturally this insistence will have to be backed up with the good use of the students' time by the Newman Club. If there is not some way of cutting through the everlasting parliamentary procedural organizational red tape which characterizes Newman Club meetings, then let the club be run on different lines. Let it also simplify the planning of activities, preferably by cutting many of them out. Why, for instance, does the Newman Club have to sponsor so many dances (which, they say, the members demand) and then have to beg the students to buy tickets to said dances? The fact must be faced that the youth of today is already surfeited with pleasure, and that when the world is in the balance, even students must put away childish things. It is true that students are immature, but must the Newman Club help prolong their adolescence?

NEED FOR APOSTOLIC ORIENTATION

We should like to suggest that the key to the solution of the Newman Club problem lies in apostolic orientation, somewhat in the manner of the parochial apostolic orientation suggested by Abbé Michonneau and explained in *Revolution in a City Parish*. This would involve a profound change in thinking. Instead of seeing the Newman Club as a pathetic and rather hopelessly ineffectual *defense* weapon within the confines of a huge, godless educational factory we must learn to see the Newman Club as a mustard seed of the re-Christianized education of the future, the spark on the campus which can start a spiritual conflagration. We must realize that the only defense today is an offensive.

It is not necessary to point out that the secularists and neo-atheists of American campuses influence not just by their teaching but by the tremendously powerful atmosphere which they create. This atmosphere is the product chiefly of their unconscious presuppositions. The very air they breathe out (and the Catholics breathe in) is heavy with rationalism, secularism, and a sort of triumphant sensualism. The students are the heirs to a lot of false promises, but being young and innately idealistic they identify sincerity with feeling (hence free love and other moral aberrations in respect to sex). Since their rational faculties have only been superficially trained, they readily concur in a superficial intellectual synthesis which has an immediate plausibility.

It is to this atmosphere of glorious and triumphant paganism that Catholics have to bring the message of Christianity, see and make others see the perspective of eternity rather than the narrow confines of a few mortal years. They have to convince their fellows of the superior reality and value of the spiritual over the sensual and emotional life. They have to restore the objectivity of morals and truth.

This is not easily done, but it has to be done. Without it there is no possibility of success. The first necessity is to see that it has to be done and to realize with all due gravity that it is a whole atmosphere, reinforced by every campus activity and every class, that has to be combatted. It is almost a "mystique" one is up against, rather than a series of intellectual errors.

FAITH AS A WEAPON

The only way to combat this mystique is with an alternate mystique. The Christian lives by faith, which is a true mysticism and his view on the world should be colored by faith. As the pagan student approaches life and learning with his unconscious materialistic bias, so the Christian student should come upon the scene with a complete basic structure of principles in the light of which he makes all his judgments. It would not be necessary to stress this were it not for the habit Catholics have of clearing their minds of what they already know with certainty, in order to approach a problem "scientifically."

Newmanites would do well to read Newman's own sermons on faith and reason in order to correct this basic error. It will change their whole approach to their academic career. If the sociology professor demonstrates the necessity of euthanasia or birth control, the students who use their faith will not denude themselves of the truth on these matters to follow the teacher's "scientific" reasoning, nor will they argue that these measures are evil in themselves and therefore cannot be used, however desirable their use might be from the point of view of social welfare. No, instead the students will approach the question with their own *a priori* certainties. They will say to themselves: "Euthanasia and birth control are wrong, we know that with certainty (and we are not going to re-examine these questions again and again to see if they are true although we might demonstrate their truth to anyone who asks sincerely). We also know that God's laws are always in harmony with the common good (since He is the ultimate common good) and that these practices, being contrary to God's laws, are sure to make a social mess. The professor must be wrong either in his facts or his logic or his definition of the common good. Let us peacefully examine his argument to see where he is wrong and what the right developments would be."

Students who proceed in this way will get a Christian education in spite of the school and stand a much better chance of influencing their teachers and fellow students. It will gradually be perceived that they have a total view of the world, a view which explains the facts of history, science and experience in a much better way than does the materialist view. Their Catholicism will not appear as an occasional and unaccountable negation as it now appears to non-Catholics, and often to Catholics themselves.

We have stressed this basic intellectual approach (that is colored by, indeed saturated with, faith) because it is fundamental to the intellectual apostolate. It will mean a deep faith on the part of Newmanites, and we will come to the cultivation of that later, but it will mean primarily a *use* of faith, a refusal to hold faith in abeyance before the "scientism" of modern education.

THE PRIMACY OF CHARITY

The best attitude to take toward the enemies of the Faith in secular colleges is this: No matter how much they blaspheme, no matter how terrible their errors are, no matter how virulently anti-Catholic they seem, they do all these things chiefly out of ignorance of the Faith.

The main reason for assuming such an attitude is that it is almost always true, and where it isn't true the attitude of charity will still be appropriate.

If this attitude is taken it will prevent zealous students from fighting on the wrong plane. It is a good thing to know all the errors which are going around campus, and to keep Catholic students from being contaminated by them in so far as possible (by keeping, for instance, a list of the more harmful and less harmful teachers and steering Catholic students accordingly), but it is not a good thing to start a vicious sort of warfare on the level of mutual vituperation. It brings out the worst in the Catholics and often hardens non-Catholics in positions which they formerly held only superficially.

One thing which will help clarify a lot is the primary apostolic orientation of the Newman Club. Students who see themselves as the bearers of light are much more apt to be gracious than students who see themselves as a persecuted minority.

THE SICK AT HEART

Everything conspires in our world and on our campuses to hide the tragedy which lies just under the surface of people's lives. Our adolescents are sick at heart, especially the "pagan" ones. Nearly all of them come from broken or unhappy homes. They are confused. They have no one to confide in, no way of getting rid of the guilt of their accumulated sins. They have no vision and no goal (which is the main reason they are frantic for pleasure). Above all, their hearts ache for God because they were made for God. They are all in process of messing up their lives, just at the time when their lives should be full of promise and hope.

Newmanites should concentrate on this tragedy, which they know is just below the surface, rather than on the hard and seemingly happy surface. Their attitude should be one of compassionate kindness and respect. With charity they can break through the surface to the suffering on a thousand little occasions, especially if they are sincere about their own love of God, their own weakness and suffering and need of prayer. Catholics must stop pretending that they too are deliriously happy with the coke-and- drug-store world of Hollywood and college campuses. By admitting to depth they will attract those who long to extend their roots into the world of grace.

CHAPLAINS NEED LAY ASSISTANCE

All the above may seem highly theoretical, but actually it flows easily into practice, once the central idea is grasped.

The most important person is the chaplain, but that does not mean that chaplain has to carry everything himself. The strongest criticism which can be made of chaplains who are otherwise admirably suited to Newman Club work, is that they try to do everything themselves, thus limiting their effectiveness to their own intellectual and physical resources, while the students remain unformed for leadership, initiative and responsibility. On any campus the work of the Newman Club lies far beyond the capabilities of one or two, or even a score of chaplains. The situation is parallel to that of the parish. If parish priests work themselves to death and yet leave untouched the bulk of their missionary work, they are not doing an intelligent job because they could reach out much further and much more effectively if they planned their attack with the use of responsible lay people.

For instance, as in the parish so in the Newman Club, it would be very wise to divert a handful of members into a Legion of Mary praesidium, which would in an organized way work to uncover and retrieve lapsed Catholics, or would undertake to sell or distribute Catholic literature, or start a Catholic library—certainly essential activities.

Or again, a Catholic Action cell is a very good formation center for leaders, an excellent way of the chaplain's getting first-hand accurate information on campus morals and doctrines, and potentially furnishes a group which could take over certain activities—including social.

The chaplain who would encourage these two groups would be tremendously rewarded, at a great economy of his time for they together would take only two meetings and one session with a Catholic Action leader a week. Of course, both groups would bring lapsed Catholics and prospective converts to the chaplain, and so keep him busy, but at his proper priestly duties.

Both the Legion and Catholic Action (Y. C. S.) would be autonomous groups, of course, and not comprehended by the Newman Club. But the club could foster and house them and the chaplain would pretty much have to chaplain them too, and could so integrate all the campus activities.

THE SPIRITUAL BASIS

Any chaplain's primary job is going to be to set a spiritual framework, to begin his Catholic center around the Holy Eucharist. The ideal is a Catholic chapel catering especially to the campus, or at least daily Mass under some favorable circumstances. It is impossible to exaggerate the value of "ornamenting" this primary sacramental act, both for the Catholic students' sake and as an apostolic weapon. The chapel should be as liturgically beautiful as possible, the Mass sung or dialogued (a really good Gregorian choir is almost imperative); provision for breakfast after Communion if necessary; perhaps short homilies every day, certainly fitting sermons on Sunday. Tremendous importance should be placed on daily Communion and weekly Confession, for apostles in an alien atmosphere need every help from grace.

The highest ideals of the spiritual life should be held out to students in church and in Confession. A class in the spiritual life should be made available not only to Catholics but also to non-Catholics, and instruction and encouragement in prayer. Today's youth is more eager for prayer than is generally realized.

There has been some talk, but very little experimentation in regard to retreats for non-Catholics, say over weekends. The Newman Club ought to sponsor such, being very careful, of course, in the choice of retreat masters. Just the opportunity to visit a monastery or convent in a noncommittal way, and to hear about Catholicism from the spiritual angle (special stress on the lives of the saints would be good) might change whole lives. It goes without saying that such events should be announced with enthusiasm rather than apology on campus, with appropriate explanatory remarks.

THE INTELLECTUAL

The sort of catechetical instruction often necessary to give to Catholic students should be dispensed with efficiently and quickly. A good, solid, swift refresher course at the beginning of each year should put it out of the way. Then the Newmanites can go on to better things. But let them be things related to their problems, such as moral questions, the political philosophy of the Church, the lay apostolate, marriage, and "what shall I do with my life?" It is a terrible thing to water down any of these subjects to a worldly or a natural level. There is another general principle — that youth should be given the best and the highest, should be asked to give everything. As previously remarked, there is a sort of complacent mediocrity amongst the generality of Newmanites which would seem to make it imperative to water things down. The best way to attack this (in our opinion) is to reach over the heads of this semi-inert barrier to the best on the campus, that is, to reach over the Catholics to the non-Catholics. Without watering down, but with care in one's terminology, it is possible to talk to the whole student body (or as many of them as you can attract) about marriage, birth control, Church and State, etc. Let the Catholic students stir up enthusiasm and the chaplain concentrate on getting good talks.

There is another angle which can be tried in some colleges. That is politely but firmly to ask of the professor or college president that a Catholic priest or recognized authority be allowed to take over So-and-so's class for a day to give "the Catholic point of view" on communism or promiscuity or whatever it is that has recently been presented in an anti-Catholic manner.

It seems as though the best intellectuals on every campus steer clear of the Newman Club, with good reason. In order to start a strong Catholic intellectual ferment the Newman Club should form a group, or encourage a group to break off from it, in order to operate on a high intellectual level. There was such a group at the University of Chicago once, centering around the study of Saint Thomas and organized as Dominican tertiaries. Saint Benedict's Center in Cambridge worked on the appropriate level, and with amazing success amongst the highest intellectuals of the highest center of intellectuality in the country. Saint Benedict's Center came to an unhappy end, but not because of its intellectuality. It may in part have been due to an overly-strong reaction against the lukewarmness and loose thinking of other Catholic campus activities, including the Newman Club.

THE SOCIAL END

In reading about the foundation of the Newman Club one is struck by the fact that the social end not only comes third in the agenda, but was also intended to be more a consequence of the other activities than something especially calculated or planned.

It is now used as bait in a game which is getting harder and harder to play.

Wouldn't it be well to return to the founders' ideas and let it almost take care of itself? Then we won't hear any more laments of this sort, "We went to the Newman Club regional convention.... *Of course* we had to stay at a luxurious hotel, of course we had to wear formals and go to an expensive dinner dance. An awful lot of delegates didn't go to Communion, but showed up at the Communion breakfast. Hardly anyone would talk seriously and they would have thought you were crazy to mention God except at the appropriate places in the program." That sort of thing (which seems to be the *usual* case) is the natural result of baiting people with a good time.

Social life will take care of itself. It does with the Legion of Mary (or rather it is provided for by the Legion in small, appropriate doses). It does in Catholic Action. Comradeship in Christ is the natural overflow of apostolic activities. People who work together in this way form deep friendships. Then Communion breakfasts and special liturgical celebrations, or picnics, dances or trips in honor of Holy Days, are easily, simply and inexpensively arranged, and everyone will want to go.

WHAT SUCCESS CAN BE HOPED FOR

We said at the beginning of this article that the Newman Club should fix its sights on the noblest students, who would probably be non-Catholic, and that all, or nearly all, the activities should aim at reaching out to them, over the heads of, but with the help of, the ordinary Catholic membership. Newmanites should feel themselves apostles to the campus at large. The effects of such a program should be great in the long run: some conversions, surely, and more than now; a considerable dispelling of the general ignorance of Catholicism;

above all, an enormous increase in the prestige of the Church which will have repercussions for a long time.

But what of the ordinary Catholic students who will not be catered to in the sense of giving them what they want (i.e., fun)? It will probably turn out that these students will be confirmed and strengthened in their faith in the only way it could be done — as an indirect effect of the increased Catholic prestige. They will very unlikely leave the Newman Club if it becomes, as it easily could, the liveliest place on campus.

But it is the leaders who will really count and most of them will probably be converts. If this is the case (that is, if our analysis is correct), then an apostolic orientation is the only mold for the Newman Club of the future.

23
Christian Vocational Guidance

OCTOBER 1949

GOD MADE MEN DIFFERENT FROM EACH OTHER because they have different things to do, different functional positions to fill in an organic society. If we could read the mind of God we would know in each generation what the work of the world is and where each man belongs (John herding sheep in Asia, Mary praying in a convent in Spain, James starting a paper in Africa and George running an elevator in Chicago). We could tell everyone where to go and what to do, and everyone would be substantially contented because the round pegs would be in round holes and the square pegs would be in square holes, each man's work would correspond with his gifts and each man would see how necessary he was to the whole, the simple as well as the learned, the rich as well as the strong, the feeble-minded child as well as the statesman.

However, the men who have set themselves over us as gods (the psychiatrists, industrialists, personnel experts and socialist-statesmen) have a different and far inferior view of the world's work, and they are trying to crush us haphazardly into the pigeonholes of their systems. The result is much human anguish, especially in the young. Worse than that, the result is liable to be the loss of many souls, because, just as it takes heroic virtue to remain married to the wrong woman, so everything in a job for which one is unsuited tends to lessen rather than increase one's virtue. Most people realize this in a sort of way, which is why we have a rash of vocational counselors springing up. However, these vocational experts are trying to redistribute people within false systems, and so they can only make minor adjustments. The variety of human beings corresponds to the variety of functions in *God's* plan, not the want-ad columns of industrial capitalism or the forced labor of the servile state. In a word, our economic and political system does not reflect the divine plan. For every simple soul God made to man an elevator or tend some sheep, industrial capitalism wants a thousand robots. Furthermore, none of these man-made systems come out right. They have a lot of people left over (women over forty, aged and indigent parents, the insane, the feeble-minded, the grey men in the skid-rows of large cities, the unemployed). God, by contrast, makes no unnecessary people.

GOD'S PLAN FOR OUR GENERATION

If God's plan for our generation remains essentially a mystery there are nevertheless a few major directives from on high. God has not told us exactly how it will work out but He has said through His Church, that our work is the *restoration of all things in Christ*, that is, the reorientation of modern society to a Christian end. That means beginning new social forms, reforming old ones. It means a general and widespread personal reform, as the preliminary, the means and the end of the whole restoration. It means a whole new and intense spreading of the Good News, a "propaganda offensive" as the caricaturists of Christianity would say. So much we know in a general way, and this knowledge is particularized and supplemented by periodic directives from the Holy See. Using this as a guiding framework, today's Catholic has to set out to find *his* vocation. He will not, however, be able to deduce it from general premises. To find particular vocations you have to start at the personal end, and work up into the pattern. Since God makes both the people and the general plans, there corresponds to each one's duty a "call" to its performance. A vocation means precisely that the work is ready and waiting (if not in the physical circumstances, at least in the need), and that the person to do it (who is likewise always qualified, with God's help) has but to correspond to the signs leading to it. The idea of vocation (as we have said before in these pages) is diametrically opposed to that of job-hunting. One is a "call" within an organic, functional system, the other is a competitive pressure, or an aimless searching, to fit into a mechanized whole.

THE INADEQUACY OF SECULAR VOCATIONAL GUIDANCE

Clearly, Christian vocational guidance ought to be radically different from the prevailing secular efforts. It cannot adapt their general plan with minor modifications or additions. As long as Catholic schools, employment agencies and clubs continue to sponsor talks by representatives of the Bell Telephone Company, personnel managers of big department stores, and chemical manufacturing companies, they will be steering students into lifework which virtually renders them impotent to participate in God's plan for the renovation of society, thereby jeopardizing society *and* their soul's salvation. This is true even if guidance tests are able to route the students more or less according to their natural talents. Christianity is not something which can be super-added to society today, it can't be pasted on to a secular occupation as an ornament, but must act as the formative principle of a new order.

NEED FOR CHRISTIAN VOCATIONAL GUIDANCE COURSES

The religious instruction and formation of Catholics is largely nullified unless they are also enabled to make vital contact with society at a point where they can infuse Christ's life into the social organism. To help them to make this vital contact should be the work of Catholic vocational guidance and training. For the lack of it graduates of Catholic schools are floundering around or resigning themselves to subordinate positions within a mammon-centered economy in which they are powerless to effect radical changes and are themselves frustrated. Or else they succumb to the practical paganism around them.

There is a similar need in the Catholic Action movement among workers. Most of the workers themselves feel a need to progress into integrally Christian work after starting a ferment in their offices and factories, and there is no reason why they shouldn't do so, as others become trained to replace them. Furthermore, they need to lead those over whom they have influence into something fuller than personal or family Catholicism. To direct confused modern people into fruitful occupations in respect to the new order is a very great work of mercy. This could be done through setting up vocational guidance courses as "services," later following them with training schools and placement bureaus. What is all important is that such services be conceived in a Christian way and not patterned after the secular design.

The purpose of this article is to indicate what such a course might comprise.

THE COURSE
Requirements

If the course is given by a Catholic school all interested students can participate on the general supposition that their Catholic education has given them a desire for a worthwhile Christian career. This is usually the case too. The sort of hardened materialism that is so regrettably common among young working Catholics is usually acquired during the first year on a job. It has frequently been noted, in the Telephone

Company for instance, that girl graduates of Catholic schools have good will, some idealism and fairly good sense of values, when first employed, but that it only takes several months for them to fall into the groove of "monotony plus pay-check" from which it is difficult to arouse them again.

For this reason vocational guidance should be offered among workers only to those who are discontent with their jobs and not just because the jobs do not pay enough for clothes or luxuries. One effect of the Catholic Action ferment should be to create this discontent, to make workers hunger for more Christian and meaningful lives.

Those who are chosen for the course should realize that this is not an academic course, but one in which they should expect to discover their vocation, or the direction of it. This will not be done by magic, nor without a change in themselves. Therefore let them, in fact urge them, to take measures to attune themselves to God's will. There should be a regular program of prayer, fifteen minutes a day, Mass, and a little spiritual reading perhaps, that each agrees to follow, praying not only for light in his own case but for everyone in the class. Apart from their spiritual preparation there will be no "homework."

Method of Conducting

Probably the best way of conducting the course would be through a series of informal lectures to the whole class, followed by group discussion. There should be some personal contact from the beginning with each student by the teacher or the Catholic Action members. There should also be provision for a personal interview with anyone who wants it, with the teacher or other of the lecturers. The students should get to know each other also, since they are going to have to solve their problems jointly.

The number of lectures will depend on the resources of the group giving the course.

The Question of Ability Tests

Ordinary vocational guidance leans heavily on tests: personality tests, intelligence tests, manual dexterity tests, and so forth. These are just elaborate means of discerning general abilities and particular talents. There is nothing magic about them. In fact, rather than being an improvement on natural judgments they tend to be an elaboration of the obvious, or a less sensitive (because mechanical) way of estimating abilities. One reason they are generally used is because counselling is done in respect of strangers, by people who are trained to give tests rather than to estimate character. Since it is presupposed in this course that there will be warm, personal relationships established, and that everyone concerned is sincere, I consider it unnecessary to introduce tests, but this without entirely despising them.

Lecture 1: The Idea of Vocation

The idea of vocation must be made very clear at the outset. Spend several talks on it if necessary. Let every member come to realize that he has a vocation, that there is a lifework waiting for him to do. The ordinary modern youth has no preparation for his lifework, so that he cannot judge what he ought to be doing by what he can do now. He should be prepared to train as long and as patiently as necessary, once he has some idea where he is going. HE must be prepared to make sacrifices, with God's help. The longer he has been in an unsuitable rut the more sacrifices he will have to make, which is why it is so important to steer youth while they are still in school.

It would be well to make clear the difference between being patient and drifting. The drifter is always discontent, goes from job to job aimlessly working. The patient man sets goals for himself. He says, "I know it is God's will for me to be doing this now so I will do it as well as possible, even though I don't see where I go from here." Or he figures, "I'll stay at this dead-end job only six months longer, and meanwhile I shall take the following steps to discover my vocation."

But above all, in this first lecture, the students should learn that God has a plan for them and they are not just chaff to be blown around by the winds and whims of the work-a-day world which they know. They must have confidence that prayer and searching will lead them to a path which, whether pleasant or unpleasant, will be co-natural with them, so that their life can expand in God.

Lecture 2: Temperamental Directives

Some people teach today that you cannot classify people, that you cannot rightly say, for instance, that Mr. Smith is a phlegmatic type, but only that Mr. Smith is Mr. Smith, a rational animal but otherwise unique. There are others, with whom I agree, who say you can make rough classifications of people, and that these are very useful for self-knowledge and for finding one's vocation.

In this regard I prefer the classical division of temperaments to the modern efforts. The classical division is into sanguine, melancholic, choleric and phlegmatic, or a combination of these. I have often seen it happen that a person who comes to understand his temperament will suddenly have realizations like this: "So that's why I nearly had a nervous breakdown doing that stupid work, while Mary Jones was quite contented," or "Now I realize that I shouldn't be always urging John Smith to heroics or mortifications. Until he becomes a saint he needs a modicum of the world's goods, whereas it is not holiness so much as temperament which enables me to live in barren surroundings."

There are a number of good descriptions of the temperaments available. You will find one in the back of Tanquerey's *Spiritual Life*. A more understandable and popular summary is available in a small pamphlet *The Four Temperaments* by Conrad Hock (Bruce). The *Ligourian* magazine's issue had a very good article on the temperaments, relating them among other things to fitting occupations. Here is their view (these refer to the pure temperaments rather than the mixed).

The sanguinic temperament is best fitted for "athletics, acting, or salesmanship, and any work that requires meeting and mingling with people, without too much responsibility for details," whereas the melancholic temperament is admirably suited for "the fine arts: literature, painting, etc.; speculative study and research; teaching, preaching and writing on religion." The choleric temperament will best succeed in "executive positions, if faults are checked and controlled. Makes an excellent farmer, where energies can be directed to conquer the land, not other people," and the phlegmatic temperament does best "scientific and mechanical detail work, experimental research, the practical trades and occupations. Good for personnel work, because of clear judgment unclouded by emotion."

Some of these things, of course, are hard things to do in a Christian way these days.

The discussion of temperaments really ought to continue until everyone in the class knows where he fits in, at least roughly. However, students should not be urged to tell their temperamental discoveries to everyone, because these facts are very revealing.

Lecture 3: Talents

Temperament indicates a direction, whereas talents are more specific. Melancholic people in general may be suited to writing or painting, but a particular melancholic can only be a writer or a painter if he has the talent. Some general things can be said about talents.

In the case of genius, which means exceptional talent, there really is no difficulty. Anyone who can play Mozart at three has a lot of problems but no vocational problem.

Among ordinary people there is a certain transfer of abilities. One who is good in mathematics need not necessarily become a mathematician. He may become a bookkeeper but he may also become a theologian. Basic aptitudes are what vocational tests reveal, whether a person has a mathematical mind or a poetical mind, whether he has a good memory or can put alarm clocks together when they come apart. As aforesaid, most people know this about themselves already, and in any case it is not conclusive evidence of one's lifework. The secular counselor dovetails these talents with the fields of opportunity in the secular, un-Christian world. We have to know them too, but use them otherwise.

It would be well to stress that not all talents indicate the main work of one's life. Some are meant to ornament life. We have fallen into the habit of putting a price-tag on everything in a day when women sell their beauty to John Powers and men sell their personalities to advertising agencies, their voices to radio stations. But if a girl is a pretty good singer she should join a choir and praise God with her voice. If she is beautiful, and also modest, it will help preserve her marriage.

Students of the course should privately list their talents, developed or not. They should ask themselves what they do with their spare time, when they are under no compulsion. Hobbies are often an indication of frustrated careers. However, nothing specific can be deduced from talents (except where they are outstanding) unless something more is taken into account: circumstances.

Lecture 4, 5, and Etc.: Opportunities

These talks will be the Christian counterpart of the lectures by the Telephone Company, Macy's, International Business Machines, and the rest. They should preferably be given by people active in the field of the lay apostolate and should strive to give the Christian vision of reconstruction in major directions. Unlike I. B. M. these fields have little to offer in a concrete way yet. They are virgin terrain, waiting for pioneers. Nevertheless, since it is pioneers that God needs, one can suppose that the students, singly but more likely in groups, will themselves become pioneers. The talks should cover the whole field, tell the type of approach necessary, the abilities to develop, where and what training can be obtained, the projects which need to be started and what beginnings have been made. Here are a few suggestions for talks.

Writing and publishing. Here stress should be on the new Christian offensive, the type of magazine or paper that is being started, the type of writer and worker who is needed; the need for a distributing system for Christian literature, apostolic book stores, book barrows, etc. In short, a whole survey of the field.

The works of mercy. There should be a clear statement of the general problem (that is, the secularization of most works of mercy under the state) and then show the direction of the works of mercy done in a Christian way, whether by the laity or religious. Special stress (possibly special talks) should be given to peculiarly needed Christian action, such as in the care of the insane, houses of hospitality, and home nursing.

Farming and the land movement. Here a good talk would show the real picture, the difficulties, the possibilities, the need for farming and the possibilities of getting it. It would tell of beginnings already made by land groups.

The crafts. This should particularly center around problems like housing, and the possibility of Christians developing groups of different sorts of craftsmen who can break the deadlock in respect to basic living problems.

Education. A real discussion of the possibilities of teaching what is most needed—as in rural schools, Negro schools or in adult education amongst the confused intellectuals of Chicago or New York. Stress should be put not on degrees and accreditation but on truth, how to learn it and where to be able to teach with as little as possible preliminary exposure to the nonsense of Columbia Teachers' College.

These five suggestions are just a beginning. As anyone can see, this sort of thing could go on forever. The chief difficulty will be to get speakers who have the vision and are in the field. It would be better to describe these things at second-hand rather than run the risk of having them treated in the old secular way, which deaden the Christian ideal with human prudence.

The Concluding Lecture

It is unlikely that anyone's vocation will be clearly settled as a result of this course, but everyone should begin to see dimly the direction in which he must go. The final lecture should be, therefore, not only a brief recapitulation with special emphasis on the ideals and basic principles, but the beginning of the next step, which is training.

The ideal would be for the group to break down into small groups to arrange for training and further discussion. Thus a handful of would-be intellectuals can form a study group to pursue the subjects they think will give them necessary background. Some would-be carpenters can get a retired carpenter friend to instruct them or can volunteer as weekend apprentices on an apostolic housing project.

Besides training, the group should look forward to apprenticeship wherever it is available. Here is where the sacrifice will come in, because a job at which you learn, especially in the apostolate, will pay a lot less than the world will pay you for being its slave.

The Need for Courage

It takes a lot of strength to go against the current and those who try will not get much encouragement. That is one reason why they should stick together. Besides, groups are necessary. This is no age for individual achievements.

Most of all, a person will need the gift of fortitude, which must be fed by a constant cultivation of the interior life. We are not building a temple for mammon but a holy world for God.

24
The Unity of the World

DECEMBER 1949

ALL HUMAN BEINGS BELONG TO THE SAME SPECIES, but that does not mean that they live in peace and mutual love. On the contrary, they seem to be doing just the reverse; so much so that the species is now threatened with self-extinction. Under the dire threat of the atom bomb there is a lot of hard thinking going on about how to unite all peoples and countries in at least concord and order. We are reminded, for instance, that we are brothers, members of one great human family. But we knew that already, and the knowledge has not prevented fratricide.

There are many proposed systems for unifying all men. The most important, other than Christianity, is now communism. The communists propose a totalitarian world government obtained through force and deceit, maintained by terror. They would impose an unnatural economy based on technology, and would regiment men's thinking in conformity with their mystical materialism. Ultimately, communism is neither a political nor an economic system but a religion which absorbs all the political, social, economic and other functions of men.

Granted, as we are beginning to realize, that Christians have to oppose this global communism with a global Christianity, it is necessary to consider what, in fact, the Church does teach about the unification of the world.

A TRANSCENDENT UNITY

The Church teaches that there will not be any harmonious unity of humanity on the natural human level. In order for humanity to realize itself it will have to rise above itself. In a word, the unity of the world has to be based on the *supernatural* elevation of men. It is no more possible for the world to be unified on the natural level than it is for individual men without grace to accomplish the integration of their faculties and functions. The reason is to be found in original sin.

As in Adam there was a natural war of his faculties, body against soul, owing to the fact that he combined in his nature the spiritual and material orders, so in the world of men there are a multitude of conflicting interests and overlapping claims which avarice, greed, envy and the other sins have intensified over the centuries into wars, unjust systems, and traditional national hatreds. The corrective of Adam's native potentiality to self-discord lay in the gift of integrity which he had and lost and which is approximately regained only through grace and holiness, owing to the merits of Christ.

We are familiar with the effects of Christ's redemption in so far as they concern each man individually and his salvation. We are less familiar with the same doctrine as it applies to humanity considered as a totality, the human species. In this regard theologians point out that Adam is the father and head of the human race as the progenitor of all our flesh, but that Christ is the new head, through having taken on human flesh at the Incarnation. He took a particular human body, but actually engrafted the whole human race to His divinity at the same time, because we are all related to each other, and now to Christ, in the flesh. What Christ accomplished was the actual, though virtual, elevation of the whole human species to a share in His supernatural life. Everyone is included in that elevation, though in varying degrees. Unbaptized pagans are related to Christ through an unrecognized reflection of the divinity. They are potential members of Christ's Body. Then there are the actual members, the dead ones who through mortal sin have reduced their sharing to a minimum, and the active members who participate in the life of the Mystical Body in varying degrees.

Two things about this doctrine are important to us here. One is that at this level of incorporation in Christ the human species can attain a true unity. The other is that temporal history is precisely a record of the progress toward God of the totality of the human race.

THE CHURCH

The means of unification of the human race was established by Christ during his earthly life. The application of that unity and redemption is made in time, by Christ still, but by an extension of His life and His Human Body, called the Church. The Church really is a living body, an organism. Christ is its head, reigning visibly through His Vicar the Pope. We are its members (like the arms and the legs and the cells of a regular human body), living a supernatural life which comes to us from our head. It is a true unity for all members share in the life of the same person, Christ.

It is this Catholic Church which is intended to be the vehicle for the unification of men. That is the deepest reason why the Church has to go to the far ends of the world to seek membership. Men can be saved without officially belonging to the Church, although it is harder that way. Yet they should belong to the Church for there is a totality of creation to be unified and brought to God, as well as souls one by one.

EVERYONE IS MEANT TO BE A CATHOLIC

Does that mean that the world will have to become Catholic before it will successfully attain a world order? How reluctant people are (even Catholics) to subscribe to such an idea! We have fallen into the habit of thinking it is right, normal and satisfactory for the Indians to be Hindus, the Arabs to be Moslems, the Chinese to be Buddhists and our neighbors to be Protestants.

We persist in thinking this way, though even the partial good which really does exist in heretical and pagan religions has become so weak or corrupted that it scarcely serves its adherents at all and they are open prey for any strong force that comes along, probably communism.

But to get back to the question: does the world have to become Catholic before it will attain peace and order? It would be unwise to answer that question with a straight "yes" because that would conjure up all sorts of misconceptions. The truth is deeper and more radiant than a simple "yes" would suggest. It would be better first to clarify a few notions.

THE UNIVERSALITY OF THE CHURCH

The first difficulty is that Catholics themselves are not today very catholic. There is a lot of parochialism which colors the lives of the ordinary Catholic laity, giving the lie to the outsider in regard to the Church's claim of universality. The word "Catholic" often suggests the idea of "Irish Catholic," and scares off those of temperaments unsympathetic to the Celtic. Eastern-Rite Catholics in America have received (and still do in some places) precious little sympathy, or even toleration, from those of the Latin-Rite. Furthermore, missionaries in the past (not so much now) have taken not only Christ and His Sacraments to the heathen but also a slab of drab Western, nineteenth-century culture and customs as well, so that Catholic churches in the Far East often stand out as anachronisms and eyesores by comparison with the delicate grace of the pagan temples.

Happily a reform of this sort of parochialism has been under way in the Church for a long time. It was really a denial of the universality of the Church, much in the same way that the ordinary American Catholic stifles the apostolicity of the Church when he refuses to give Christ to his associates and neighbors.

Universality is one of the marks of the Church and it is the only true universality that the world will ever find. It consists in this: it unifies while preserving diversity. The Church gives the life of Christ to all people and this life is capable of infinite variety of material expression. Just as every saint has a unique and very marked personality, yet all saints alike manifest Christ, so Christianity can produce any number of cultures, each distinct, yet each Christian. It can produce an authentic Chinese Christianity which will preserve and bring to perfection all the essential characteristics of the Chinese. It can do the same with the Indian or the Japanese cultures — Christianize them without destroying them, indeed at the same time perfecting them. And not in a calculated way either, as something planned, or pasted on, but as an organic growth according to the spirit of the people. That is why the Popes insist on developing a native clergy everywhere as soon as possible. That is why there is the possibility of making Chinese a liturgical language. That is why certain far-seeing missionaries are asking for volunteer lay people to go to the Far East to plant themselves, as it were, in native society and fertilize the development of a Christian culture. What is asked of these laity is that insofar as is humanly possible they abandon their Western identity and clothe themselves with the mind and heart of the East so that Christ can use them as instruments for an indigenous Christian civilization.

The *unity* of the Church's universality lies in the person of Christ, Who is head of the Church and Whose life flows through all the members. The *diversity* of the Church's universality lies in the matter which this life infuses, with all the distinctions of temperament, function and ability which mark the human race.

All rival claimants for universality attain unity only at the price of uniformity. This is particularly true of communism which uses technology as its instrument of unification. It offers not one Life but one way of life, and in this respect capitalism has been its precursor. It was capitalism that introduced the business man into the non-Christian world where the Church had formerly sent missionaries. Now following on the ground prepared by the business man, is the

The Unity of the World

industrialization of these countries. The factory is the great source of uniformity—with its mass production all nations begin to dress alike, according to centralized designs, drive the same cars, build houses alike, etc. Accompanying this standardization of externals is a mass propaganda effort to create a uniform mentality through movies, radio and other technical instruments issuing the great doctrine that it is a sin for one man to be different from the next. Communism openly works toward a classless society in which individual differences will be obliterated. We Americans echo the same doctrine more politely. This is the era of the great leveling, with the Church the only hope of maintaining authentic diversity, the only instrument for preserving, while perfecting, the human personality.

ORGANIC UNITY

Is it necessary for the world to become Catholic before it can attain a global harmony? The answer is that the Catholic Church alone can unite the world without destroying it, and it seems as though in God's Providence the moment to set the foundation for that unity has come; there can be no retreat to more local and partial manifestations of Christian order.

This unification is more a matter of giving the world form than it is of numerical conversion. In the past the method of conversion was to convert one person after another, or possibly one family or one village, to make certain that the converts would support each other against relapsing. But over and above the catechetical effort, Christian missionaries have always brought some temporal benefit to pagans, both as a free act of charity and because the Church is interested in the temporal as well as the eternal welfare of all men. Sometimes the Church brought schools and hospitals, sometimes newspapers or rice, according to the needs of the people. What the people everywhere need now is not so much medicine or food or even education—what they need is *civilization*—a new one replacing (and salvaging the residual good in) the old ones which are everywhere vanishing. The Church today must bring the world a new social order, with legal systems, economic techniques, governmental modes, a daily culture, instruments of popular education—in fact, a whole new world. If it brings people this Christian structure of society, then the people themselves will be naturally channeled into the Church. If Catholicism does not bring this structure the communists will, and conversions will be almost impossible, so sharply will Christian morals go against the grain of everyday life.

So, to say that the world must be Catholic before it has unity means primarily that it must attain a Catholic structure, be Christ-centered in its institutions, and that this effort must be concomitant with the conversion effort, possibly even preceding mass conversions, at least in some places.

Take the United States, for example, because our own is one of the great missionary territories. Whether or not America goes Catholic will be more a result of a social ferment, of a realization of our principles in newspapers, schools, labor unions, etc. than it will be a result of proselytizing by the nearly-pagan Catholics that most of us are. It is a wonder that we somehow do manage to convince a few other people of at least the sacramental reservoir or the doctrinal truth of our faith.

The situation today is parallel to that of the Western world during the Dark Ages. Then, given a virgin Europe populated by rude barbarian tribes, the Church had at once to develop a civilization and Christianize the people. Today in the face of a world-wide crisis and of the tremendous developments of science and technology, the Church has at once to Christianize and civilize, or re-civilize, on a global scale. As the material circumstances of the two cases are radically different, so will today's solution be radically different from that of the Middle Ages.

LEGITIMATE DISTINCTIONS KEPT

To say that the world will, please God, become Catholic is not to say, of course, that the Pope will become king of the world, but that the Mystical Body will be conterminous with the human race. Just how civil and temporal affairs will be synchronized with the ecclesiastical Church structure remains to be worked out, but, from what is going on now in the Church and from what the Popes have said, it looks as though this harmony will be attained through the maturation of the laity in the Mystical Body. When the Church needed to bring men hospitals, schools, orphan asylums, and leprosariums, good things which are not precisely the work of the clergy, then the Church developed religious orders of brothers and sisters. Now that the work is to give the world *civilization*, to form and develop a new temporal order, this again cannot be done by the Bishops and priests. Neither does it fall within the province of religious orders. The Church's answer appears to be a mature and responsible, formed laity. When we do get formed lay leaders, docile to the hierarchy, but in a manner suited to adults, not infants, then strife like that between Church and State will vanish, because Christian statesmen will mold their lives and careers around the pursuit of the common good ordained to Christ. So it will be in every branch of life. The natural point of integration of the temporal and religious spheres is the Christian layman who by nature and vocation lives in both spheres and *has* to reconcile them.

THE SACRAMENT OF UNITY

When we talk about the laity and about politics, economics, and the temporal order, we are apt to forget what we stressed at the beginning of this article and what we shall stress again here, that men will be truly united with each other only on the supernatural plane, albeit this unity will overflow on and find expression in temporal institutions. Now the Church teaches that the chief supernatural instrument of unity is the Sacrament of the Holy Eucharist. By receiving the Blessed Sacrament men are progressively engrafted on Christ and therefore live ever more intensively the same life. We speak truly of receiving not "union" but "Communion."

It is therefore significant that the Church has urged the laity to receive frequent or daily Communion. Also significant is the increasing devotion of our day to the Blessed Sacrament and the fact that the Sacrament is present, even if hidden to ordinary eyes, everywhere in the world, even behind the iron curtain. It is like the seed of new life and harvest, still germinating in the dark ground.

If we are nourished by the same life and if the same Holy Spirit animates us all to the work of our day, then we have a right to expect startling results in the way of unification. We ought to see lay Christians working and cooperating together on the basis of their Christianity, regardless of their accidental differences of race, or color, financial and social positions. We see that in the lay apostolate. Lay apostles from all countries, even those which are warring against each other, meet for the first time as old friends and dearly beloved ones, plunge immediately into deep conversation about restoring the world to Christ, quite naturally pray together, share their goods, proffer joyful hospitality to each other, scarcely even noticing worldly distinctions. Soon people will begin to say again, "See those Christians, how they love one another," and we will know indeed that a new world is being born.

1950

25
Catholic Action and Responsibility

JANUARY 1950

CATHOLIC ACTION IS NOT JUST A MATTER OF STIRRING up the laity to activity rather than passivity, but it is a specific remedy for a specific disease of our time. The technique it uses is no more arbitrary than is the medicine prescribed for a sick person. The technique which most perfectly embodies the Catholic Action idea (according to Pius XI) is that evolved by Canon Cardijn for the workers (Jocists), which consists in a cell movement working with social inquiries (see, judge and act). The modern disease is *irresponsibility*, and it is the precise ill that Catholic Action seeks to remedy. In this article we shall endeavor to show how it does it, and also to make friendly criticisms of some of the ways that the technique is being worked out.

AN AGE OF IRRESPONSIBILITY

We are living in a great era of irresponsibility. Terrible things happen, one after another. Yet it is difficult to say exactly who is responsible for causing the evils, and even more difficult to find anyone responsible for correcting them. In this respect ours is a subtle age. Formerly there was a more direct correspondence between the evil that was done and the evil wills of certain specific people who caused it to be done. Also, to remedy the ills was a matter directly related to the changing of the wills of people. Now it is otherwise. People are not so much indifferent as they are helpless and confused. They cannot be inspired to an all-out effort at reform because it is not clear what path will bring about reform. There is a tremendous sea of good will which has yet to be tested, a great area of generosity largely going to waste.

Irresponsibility extends from the smallest to the greatest matters. A boy just out of college or high school finds himself afloat in an economy which tosses him here or there, and which he neither understands nor has the power to combat. It is useless to tell him to practice virtue, to work hard, save money, be honest, etc. (things which worked in another day). He realizes, as though by instinct, that he is not the master of his fate.

So it is with the factory or clerical worker of more mature years. It's useless to tell him to save money, to look forward to buying a home and setting aside money for his old age. He knows that his future is bound up with wars, unemployment, strikes of workers in remotely related industries, and other factors completely beyond his sphere of influence.

Or take marriage. A bride and groom today have two strikes against them to begin with, not so much because of their own shortcomings as because of the ills of society. The success of their marriage will be jeopardized by the housing shortage, the lascivious girls of the advertisements, the absence of family wage scales, the presence of television and by the terrible pressure of a social philosophy of luxury, pleasure, comfort, materialism and promiscuity which will surround them twenty-four hours a day. Can they fight all this by simply practicing personal virtues? They are often not even aware of their enemies.

The welfare state is our greatest testimonial to irresponsibility. Because the doctors have failed to guard our health (and yet, what can any one doctor do in the face of modern problems?), we shall have socialized medicine. Because the real estate men and the landlords and carpenters and builders and architects have failed to house us, we shall all live in great bee-hives or jails where sterility will prevail. Because parents have failed, psychiatrists will take over. Because statesmen have failed, tyrants will reign.

Yet who, precisely, has failed? Is it this doctor, or mother, or mayor? Is it all of us or none of us? And what can this one or that one do now? Anyone who tries simply to practice the virtue which worked in another age is likely to find it will boomerang on him.

There is a lot of ersatz responsibility around but that merely serves to camouflage our real state. It is true that we can choose between a number of unsatisfactory candidates for president or mayor, but are we not powerless to conjure up a saint-statesman such as is desperately needed? We may (as public opinion) interfere with the workings of Congress, for good or for evil, but we can't reform Congress. We may, with our study clubs and our reading of newspapers and news magazines, be well informed about the surface happenings of a world in agony, but does that mean we are doing one thing to save it?

THE PERSONALIST ANSWER

The most natural reaction against the impersonality and irresponsibility which is suffocating us is an heroic assertion of the fact of personal responsibility. The term "personalist" comprehends a variety of degrees and opinions, and the personalist movement crosses all religious borders. It can be embraced, though possibly without ultimate congruity by atheists as well as Christians. It believes in the supreme importance and sacredness of the human person. It measures things by what these things do to *people*.

Its practical motto is "do it yourself." If someone is hungry, feed him; don't wait for the state to do it. If your aunt is insane, take care of her; don't send her to an institution. If you need a house, build one. If factory work dehumanizes the individual, then factory work must go.

When, and if, personalism is taken as an ultimate remedy for the ills of society it implies gross errors. It is just an idealistic version of rugged individualism. It becomes a sort of cult of the person, by himself and in disregard of God. It does not have a true understanding of the common good. Ultimately, what's wrong with society is that it is not ordered to God, and not that it does violence to the human personality. It tends to destroy *us* precisely because it isn't ordered to God, and we will never fix society by concentrating on ourselves.

On the other hand there is a false common good on the horizon, which serves the collectivity at the expense of everyone. Against this threat it is necessary to shout to the heavens that we are not just helpless powers in the hands of politicians, that human minds and wills, infused by grace, still have the power to transform the earth. But the unit of reconstruction must be not just persons, but groups of people in organic units.

THE NEW DIMENSIONS

While society see-saws back and forth between the opposite errors of individualism and collectivism, the Church is re-discovering for society the truth that man is by nature a social animal, unable to work out his destiny alone. Man is only truly man when he is a functional part of a group, the family group or a working unit of society. Because they will be small groups, men will not be lost, be mere members, as in the modern states. Because the working unit is a group, not an individual, no man will be under pressure to be and do all things at once. Because the groups will be organic, as in living things, each man will make a different contribution, so each will be dependent on the others, and charity and the other virtues will necessarily flow between them.

CATHOLIC ACTION AND THE GROUP ANSWER

The first of the admirable features of Catholic Action, then, is the fact that it takes as its working unit a homogeneous group of twelve people or fewer, which is called a cell. Here it resembles the Communist Party which also works on the cell principle, and which took its inspiration from Christ and His disciples. Cells don't grow bigger, they multiply, and they are related to each other as parts of an organic whole, directed and coordinated by a head. As in the human body, the cells in Catholic Action are not stereotyped reproductions of each other but are functional units of a whole. There is a homogeneity within each cell, but a diversity in the whole.

The power of Catholic Action to transform the world rests in its vitality rather than in mere numbers, although the movement does provide for great numbers in its multiplication of cells. Now, in order to have vitality, the groups must be organic (that is, living) and where Catholic Action doesn't succeed it is often because the cells have a mechanical unity rather than a real homogeneity. You cannot arbitrarily choose your basis of uniting with others. Rather you have to discover the groupings that the nature of society itself demands. All members of the cell must share their most important problems and work on those. If a group of married men are all veterans, they would be unwise to inquire into their status as ex-soldiers while they have the much more pressing problem of how to Christianize marriage today. Men who are lawyers would be unwise to unite with journalists to consider the problem of recreation in the parish in which they all live, since the problems of the legal and journalistic professions are themselves so pressing.

One reason that many of the girl's cells of Catholic Action accomplish less than they should, is that their basis of homogeneity is often superficial. They take as their common problem *this* office, or office workers in general, while the underlying and gnawing problem of the unmarried or not-yet-married woman will always be her unsettled or unsatisfactory state in life. Until this matter is resolved, all inquiries should be related to it, at least indirectly. This could be done by seeing all surface problems in the light of the nature of women. So long as Catholic Action operates on the principle that "well, we are here, so that's probably where we belong, so let's start Christianizing the place," they will only use their zeal to perpetuate what may be a bad situation (i. e. girls in offices). An example of this is a recent effort of the Young Christian Workers to get female office workers to join the unions. That would seem to imply an acceptance of office work for women as good, or at least inevitable, without having inquired whether it really is or not.

A similar case would be that of advertising men. It would be a good idea to have a cell of advertising men but the inquiries would necessarily have to be made so as to allow the men gradually to understand the real nature of advertising, since this so-called profession is at least under the suspicion of being fundamentally un-Christian. This does not mean that the men would be told "bang-bang—your jobs are bad", but only that the inquiry should be free and fundamental. If it turns out that advertising really is un-Christian of its nature, we ought not to be afraid to let advertising men discover that. If we are afraid, then we do not trust God to have some other vocation for these men which they are currently missing. The timid policy of not daring to face the possibility of reorienting these men will only lead to superficial inquiries (about saying "good morning" to everyone in the office) and superficial reforms (like raising the neckline of a semi-nude picture girl a quarter of an inch). How could such Catholic Action renew society?

Or take the obvious instance of, say, Hearst newspapermen. They can either dare to inquire whether the framework of Hearst journalism is inimical to the Faith, or they can putter around with a thousand trivialities and technicalities.

On the other hand, where you have something that is fundamentally good, you still have to be basic, but you needn't tear the house down. Not every girl in nursing probably belongs there but you can assume that most of them do, and make your reforms, however drastic, within that context.

THE NEUROTIC PERSONALITY OF OUR TIMES

It is always easier to see other people's problems than our own—or their sins. Human nature is like that. In our day this characteristic is very much exaggerated by general neurosis. Whatever the causes of neuroses are, the effects are clear. They cloud up personal judgments with all sorts of emotional distortions. The neurotic is very warped in judging himself or circumstances which involve personal relations. The excellent mind he often has shows itself only in abstract, remote, or depersonalized matters. So a maladjusted student can be brilliant in mathematics. So a man who can't manage his own household can be a brilliant engineer. So thousands of young people who don't have the heart or understanding or power of personal relations to go into politics or farming communities, seek and find relief in working for the vast governmental bureaucracy, as clerks or as planners of a sterile society not erected on human incalculables. So also is it an exaggerated tendency of our times to study everything except what relates to us. Any man in the street will pass an opinion about Chinese or White House affairs, however bewildered he is about his own wayward son. Catholics, too, love to form study groups. The suburban women whose very hearts are being crushed by a prevailing spirit of keeping up with the Joneses, study the Marshall Plan or the errors of Protestants. Girls whose co-workers at the next desk may be thinking of blowing their brains out in despair, are very interested in the foreign missions.

HOW TO MAKE AN INQUIRY

The Catholic Action inquiry is a sort of guided investigation of the near-at-hand, of the area in which Mr. Jones and Mrs. Smith could really exercise a decisive influence if they could bring their united efforts to bear on it. If you like, it is to the social order what psychiatry is to the person. But just as a neurotic could (and often does) wander aimlessly and nearly forever, through his thoughts and feelings where his analyst or director has no real understanding of human nature or its purpose, so a Catholic Action group can investigate interminably and get hopelessly confused without strong and clear inquiries based on the fundamental structure of the problem.

Put it another way. It almost seems as though the person making Catholic Action inquiries must already know the answers. He must have some idea what the nature of the field is, but also some sense of where the modern situation goes off. That doesn't mean that nothing will be left to the Holy Ghost working through the cell members, for plenty will be left to them, and they may often have to correct and adjust inquiries as they go along. But it still holds that they need guidance from outside to keep their inquiry clear and basic. Who is this person?

It isn't, probably, the priest who is guiding the group. His special province is the moral and spiritual angle. The chances are he will be too remote from medicine, labor, nursing or whatever the field is, to have an idea of the basic problems in detail.

Perhaps this is where the intellectual comes in. Certain it is that there is a cleavage now between the intellectual Catholic and the man practically engaged in a business, profession or industry. Yet God made intellectuals and probably intended them to give the sort of guidance which they are capable of giving. Their specific gift is to be able to see things whole, and under a hierarchy of principles. They must learn from the practical man, but can't they also help him?

Take, for instance, intellectuals like Hilaire Belloc. Can't his great thinking on the servile state and on property help the workers to figure out their course in the face of the welfare state? Or consider Christopher Dawson and Christopher Hollis, who have done so much thinking and writing about capitalism, usury and other problems. Are Catholic Actionists going to ignore them? Could bankers and insurance men possibly do so with impunity?

Soon we are going to have to make some fusion between the practical and the intellectual men if we are going to reconstruct society. Perhaps the second or third-rate intellectuals (like us) could act as catalytic agents between the great brains and the leaven, not only through writing but also through aiding in making inquiries. At least it seems possible, and that is why we are printing some sample inquiries at the end of this article to show what we mean by an organic approach.

ACTION AND COMMITMENT

We said at the beginning of this article that Catholic Action had the answer to the irresponsibility of the age. Masses are irresponsible, single persons are impotent, but the organic small group is an opening wedge to the transformation of society. Then to be responsible you must have understanding, and the social inquiry is precisely an eye-opener into what the Christian answer is to the problem at hand.

But there is a third element in responsibility, and that is the sense of being irrevocably committed to a circumstance and a problem. This, too, should be the natural result of Catholic Action. The Gospel inquiries, the services, the whole gradual deepening of the spiritual life of those in Catholic Action will be a major contributing factor. But over and above that there is the insistent third part of the social inquiry, the *act*. With each slight advance in understanding there comes an increase in responsibility to do something about it. And each time something is done the person who does it gets more deeply involved in people and problems and circumstances. Almost without realizing it he will get a new set of friends (mostly people who need friendship or help) and be involved in setting up *services*.

When Catholic Action works in an organic way the natural result should be to entrench its members deeply into the social order (at the root of problems, in the midst of a throng of people whom they influence); in fact, the effect should be precisely to make that fusion with the world (they with the world, and Christ with the world through them) which will enable them to leaven it. After a time they should be so deeply committed that anything they do will affect the whole body.

This effect is partly evident in Catholic Action now, but not nearly so much as it should be. People explain that they lack the right leaders. But could it not be again that matter of organic inquiry? One way to test an inquiry is to see if *real* actions flow from it. Where the action tends to be over and over again "telling other people these ideas" or "talking about these things here or there," it probably isn't an organic inquiry. And spreading knowledge in this way does not deepen the commitment of the Catholic Action leader a bit.

THE FUTURE OF THE LEADERS

Catholic Action forms people. That is its great contribution. Yet when a person is formed he cannot go back to a lifework which he previously had patiently endured only because of his own underdevelopment. Now he needs something worthy of his new self. What we are beginning to see is Catholic Action leaders having to leave the youth movement because they are too old and so finding themselves, although formed, at loose ends. We also see Catholic Action students graduating from school, and consequently from the student movement, with finer and more apostolic characters than their fellows, but equally as lost as regards their future. This must mean that the Catholic Actionists were entrenched only in the movement itself and not in society. Ought they not to have committed themselves more and more as they went along so that finally they were at rest and expanding in the place to which God called them? Perhaps this is too much to ask of Catholic Action but we think it would flow naturally from inquiries which are basic and organic to the problem. In the long run it is in the transformation of society that the masses will find their way back to the Church.

26
It All Goes Together
FEBRUARY 1950

THE REPUBLICANS ARE GOING TO TAKE A STAND NEXT election against socialized medicine, which is one of the pet measures of the Truman administration. Let them argue the matter until doomsday, but the truth will not prevail. Or let one of the parties triumph, as will surely happen. Then we shall either have socialized medicine and a thousand ills following in its wake; or we shall not have socialized medicine, and the multitudinous troubles we now have will be intensified a thousandfold. Medicine is in a crisis, but it isn't that kind of crisis.

A doctor in New Hampshire has knowingly, deliberately, openly, and probably idealistically shortened the agonizing last days of a cancer patient by euthanasia. He seems to have the tacit sympathy of many in the medical profession, not to mention that of his friends and neighbors, including the victim's husband. By what process did the art of healing evolve into the science of killing? How did doctors become veterinarians? The whole matter is full of paradoxes, and to understand it means to undertake a philosophical study of the development of modern medicine.

I. HEALING IS AN ART

There is a whole nest of medical ills which can be traced to the fact that medicine, which is by its nature primarily an art (to which certain sciences are auxiliary) has by a shift of emphasis come to be treated as a science. The difference between an art and a science is that art has a practical end (healing the body) whereas science has an intellectual goal (understanding diseases). There is no necessary connection between the two things. Many scourges of the human race have been wiped out while their nature remained mysterious. The black plague disappeared with sanitation control, leprosy left Europe through quarantine and yellow fever vanished from areas where swamps were eradicated. To take the other case, knowledge does not necessarily lead to healing. One gets the impression that some physicians regard death as a minor incident which takes place between the final diagnosis and the autopsy. And what is one to think of the cancer researcher who has finally sliced a cancerous cell into minute particles and encased each one in a transparent plastic material for more careful inspection? Suppose he is finally able to observe every single feature of the diseased cell, will he then be able to cure or prevent cancer? Will he really know anything about it? Should his cleverness discover some substance which kills cancer cells without killing the people who have cancer, what reason would he have to suppose that a person thus cured would not develop other and even more interesting and unusual diseases as the direct result of a chain of bodily circumstances commenced by the previous medicine? In fact this sort of thing has been precisely what has happened in the case of chickens which developed diseases from the unnatural life forced on them by avaricious chicken-breeders, who resorted then to strange cures instead of mending their ways, and then had to have *new* cures for the *new* ills, and so on. Obviously something is radically wrong.

What's wrong is that we have forgotten that medicine is an *art*. That means simply *God heals*, we only dispose the body for His mysterious natural mending process. Sometimes the body is disposed by some natural process, like sleeping or exercise or a special diet. Sometimes it takes sterner measures, like a heart stimulant, or a purgative. The most drastic remedy is surgery which ought therefore to be resorted to last. But surgery also (normally) merely removes obstacles to the body's self-healing.

The art of medicine uses sciences, but in an auxiliary capacity. A certain amount of anatomy, physiology, and other sciences help the doctor to get the sort of background he needs. It is rather like the case of a man carving a statue. He needs to know wood, something about its grain and hardness. He needs to know how to use certain instruments. But he doesn't have to know all there is to know about wood and steel. He does not need to analyze them to infinity. His skill comes mostly from his natural gift, trained by imitation and practice to the skillful manipulation of his material.

More and More about Less and Less

As long as the sciences remained handmaids to the art of medicine they were useful, and their advances advanced medical progress. However, science somehow usurped the primary position with doctors, and having lost its initial restraint went hog-wild with intellectual curiosity.

A parallel thing occurred in education, agriculture and other fields. That is how it happened that "pure" scientists, merely following the direction of their own studies, ended up with atom bombs and long range bombers. Similarly other scientists ended up with chemical fertilizers, homogenized milk, inhiston and profrontal lobotomies. The really pure search of the mind for truth is for ever deeper and more comprehensive forms of truth—for primary causes, which is to say ultimately for God. This is the only kind of truth which legitimately can be pursued absolutely for its own sake. All other forms of knowledge are validly sought only within a context. The mind that wanders where it will, will wander down strange alleys according to someone else's will, by an unconscious bias, or it will strive for a totality of quantitative knowledge rather than for primary causes.

As you go toward an understanding of first causes, knowledge simplifies. If you keep to a superficial, facts multiply without ever getting more lucid. In the medical school of today, as indeed in all colleges and universities, an extraordinary memory is the student's greatest tool. He will have to learn every last muscle, fiber and bone by rote. He will have to know a thousand diseases along with their symptoms and remedies. He will have to know a great deal of a lot of sciences. He will be literally buried in books during his student years. When he gets practicing he will be expected to keep up with a torrent of new discoveries, experiments, chemicals, drug compounds and theories lest his practice become obsolete.

There are many who now say that even basic medical knowledge is beyond the capacity of the ordinary man. There is just frankly too much for him to learn, and then to keep abreast of. The only solution is to divide up the knowledge, with each one of a corps of doctors specializing in a particular part of the human anatomy. Some ideal of this sort is realized in the modern medical center. The patient is put on an assembly line for a series of routine tests and examinations, which reveal almost automatically the nature of his case, after which he is shunted to the proper specialist for treatment.

The Lost Art of Diagnosis

If human beings were automobiles the assembly line technique would be suitable to them. But since they are complex organisms they cannot be understood or treated mechanically. The highest art of the art of medicine is diagnosis, and it is this which is going by the board in the modern situation.

A certain amount of specialization in medicine is perfectly legitimate if it is grounded on good general knowledge and corresponds to a special skill in an intricate manner. The trend in specialization today is not precisely of this sort but wants to accomplish with a corps of doctors, supported by tests and measurements, what formerly rested in one doctor. It wants to take the guesswork out of diagnosis by the perfection of measuring and recording instruments. It tends to perfect the doctor's equipment and instruments rather than the doctor.

Diagnosis on the contrary is an art which presupposes a comprehensive knowledge and a trained sense of synthesis. The doctor takes his tests and makes his observations. All the facts and hints and suggestions are tossed around in his brain almost without conscious advertence, and out comes a piercing diagnosis. Doctors like this rise above their specialized knowledge. They are *artists*. They become more skilled and valuable with the years. They are not merely mechanical dispensers of wonder drugs. They have a sort of instinctive sense of synthesis. Crushing a man under a multitude of facts rather than familiarizing him with a few light-giving principles destroys his intuitive genius. There is no reason to suppose that a cancer cure will emanate, except by accident, from a research laboratory that uses IBM tabulating machines and that blindly tests one after another plant or chemical reaction.

While educators are scrutinizing medical schools they would do well to consider if a gifted man could flunk out because he couldn't press all that academic, scientific and factual knowledge into his brain. It would also be a good idea to consider if a young woman with almost a gift for healing could fail to qualify for a modern nursing school because she couldn't master in academic form the knowledge which she makes use of almost by instinct.

II. SECULARISM

Another root cause of confusion in medical circles is secularism, which took man out of his eternal context and made this world his be-all and end-all. Naturally this secularization took place gradually. What is more important, it came about by implication rather than by direct statement. Had the secularists said, "There is no life after death, so let's eat, drink and be merry," many would have opposed them. What they did rather was behave according to the diminution of their belief in immortality, which meant finally that this life and the things of this life became precious to them to the point of an obsession. To their frantic search for health no one could oppose a contempt for health because health *is* a good thing. Religious people could only say, "Yes, health is a good thing, but it is not the best thing; its loss is not an unqualified disaster. *Relative* to honor, sanctity and eternal life it loses some of its importance." But no one allowed them to say it. It was part of the unconscious strategy of the secularists to keep the discussion strictly *ad rem*, to circumscribe all discussions by their own narrow limits.

Life and Eternal Life

If we are to live forever, in Heaven or in Hell, then this life here on earth is a mere trying ground, an overnight stop in an uncomfortable inn. It is terribly important, but its importance rest entirely on how well we acquit ourselves. A long life is not necessarily an advantage. It is only advantageous if one is advancing toward sanctity at a steady but slow pace which needs ninety years to prepare one for Heaven without going through Purgatory. It is also advantageous for a wounded man in mortal sin to recover unconsciousness in order to repent, or a sick man to regain health in order to do penance. There is a story told of a saint who prayed for someone to recover from a severe illness, and whose request was granted; but God revealed to the saint that it would have been better for the person to die, because he would now save his soul with the greatest difficulty.

It is only God Who knows when a person may most advantageously die and it is not for us to go about trying to be clairvoyant on the subject. Our role is rather to do what is right according to the circumstances and our states in life and leave the rest in God's hands. We are not arguing that if a man sickens he should be left to die on the theory that now is God's time for him. This is what the pagan medicos like to insinuate that religious people advocate. But the shoes are on the other foot. It is they who are, in a paradoxical manner, taking eternal destinies in their own hands. They are the ones who have learned to prolong life by extraordinary means and under such difficult conditions that the strongest man is tempted to despair and suicide. They are the ones who now propose to cut life short according to their own sentiments. They are the ones who have decided that a grown woman has the right to live at the expense (murder) of her child.

It is interesting to note the case of infant mortality. One often hears modern medicine brag about the reduction of infant mortality as an absolute good. Ironically, when more children died in infancy the majority of children were baptized and so went straight to Heaven. Now they live on, but in a world which is oriented away from the salvation of souls. If their lives prove failures for eternity they might better have died, baptized, before they reached the age of reason. This is not to say that the medical profession is directly or even in this case indirectly responsible for the neglect of Baptism. It is merely to say that no one can brag about the decrease in infant mortality as an absolute good. It would be good if other things were equal. Medical progress of this sort cannot claim an absolute measurement of good. It cannot even say, "We've done our part, what is the matter with the priests and the ministers" (like the scientists who say, "We've invented all these fine things; it's not our fault that the moralists can't control the use of them"). Doctors, too, belong to the moral community and have a duty to rid society of secularism. Like the scientists they are perhaps more deeply implicated than other people in the worsening of society, if only because theirs was the graver responsibility neglected. After all, they deal daily with life and death.

When men lose belief in immortality they naturally tend to exalt this life as an absolute. If they forget about the soul which lives forever, they become terribly solicitous about the body which is the *sine qua non* of their living now. This is what happened to the secularized modern world. Life — not the *good life* which always looks beyond the grave — but just life under any conditions and at all costs became an absolute. The whole orientation of modern medicine was to the end of preserving life. The doctor, from having been a little higher than a veterinarian or a barber, became a sort of priest honored in almost a mystical way. It can hardly be accidental that great hospitals have a suggestion of the cathedral about them, or that the operating table is like a high altar.

We said before that the scientific element in medicine followed its own nose in its researches, and that that necessarily involved direction from an unconscious bias. Secularism is the main bias. Medical research tended naturally to fit into this philosophy and sought to discover ways of prolonging life (when it might otherwise, for instance, have been looking for ways of preventing disease by keeping an organic balance of elements in the body). So it developed surgery to a fantastic degree, and with it the fabulous and fabulously expensive operating rooms of the modern medical center. Great surgeons operate for six, seven and eight hours on one patient. Most of their patients would normally have died save for their ministrations. Besides the surgical advances there have also been developed extraordinary means of prolonging life under artificial conditions—the oxygen tent, intravenous injections and such.

With all this, which really did extend life under extraordinary conditions and extraordinarily difficult conditions, the amount of pain and suffering was increased and prolonged. So the inventive minds of medical research "naturally" tended to the discovery of all sorts of opiates and pain killers. This trend tends as a term toward the state in which men are kept alive in so maimed and/or doped a condition that the patients, relatives and doctors all wonder if it isn't better to put the wounded and virtually useless specimen of a disfigured humanity to a merciful end.

Not Life, but the Enjoyment of Life

When secularism had run its course and God was virtually eliminated from temporal life, it naturally came about that the more fleeting and intense pleasures of life became highly valued. Without God men despair, so they turn to the pleasures of the senses, or to great business and activity, to hide from their despair and these pleasures in turn bring despair in their wake. Such being the case men wanted to use their bodies intemperately. They wanted all the pleasures of eating, without the temperance of fasting or frugality. They had an unquenchable lust because they didn't know a satisfying love. They couldn't take time to rest or recuperate or slow their systems down to a normal pace. They were too busy making money, too afraid of the inactivity which would leave their minds face to face with the losing game they were playing.

So they demanded of the medical profession not so much life now as license. They wanted a drug which would keep them awake when their bodies craved the sleep necessary to recuperate lost strength. They wanted other drugs which would overwhelm a tormented mind with sleep. They wanted vitamins to compensate for the denatured food which their own avarice had foisted upon them. They wanted sundry pills to aid an overtaxed digestion. They wanted, as the advertisements so alluringly say, not to suffer the penalties of over-indulgence. But the penalties of over-indulgence and neglect are not just due retribution in the order of pain and spiritual cleansing, although they are also this and therefore of great merit if accepted with the proper dispositions. They are also nature's effort to heal itself by precipitating the conditions of recovery. Persistent neglect of root requirements of the body, possible because we can now be hepped up[1] with drugs acting more or less superficially, means an ultimate, premature and pretty devastating reckoning.

The Irony of the Modern Situation

The modern secular doctor is caught up in a set of circumstances which criss-cross with contradictions. Yesterday he was driving himself to keep alive human beings under practically test-tube conditions. Tomorrow he may deliberately kill these unfortunates, and a variety of others, with noble motives. Meanwhile the poor victim of either too long or too short a life is kept in an atmosphere almost hermetically sealed against the useful information that he soon may die. The one thing he is not given is an opportunity to put his soul in order. The only attitude toward death which is thoroughly lacking in the average hospital is a realistic one.

It follows as a corollary to secularism that suffering makes no sense. If there is no life after death, no possibility of gaining grace for oneself or others, suffering, as in animals, becomes an absolute evil. Euthanasia follows as a natural consequence.

III. MEDICAL MONEY AND SOCIALIZED MEDICINE

There are certain things which can only be done for love and not for money. The priest's work is one of these. So is a wife and mother's twenty-four-hour-day total service. So is nursing, which demands not only an aptitude but also a devotion, which cannot be successfully constrained within set hours and a strict routine. So also is medicine. We call it a profession to indicate that it transcends the commercial, but that word has lately been debased by using it to ennoble things like advertising and public relations which could be more exactly designated as rackets.

There is no point here in tracing the decline of medical ideals in detail. Suffice it to say that "for love" must mean primarily "for love of God," if it is to hold its own. The humanitarian motives which characterized the age of philanthropy just passed, are insufficient. If a doctor has to love his patients for their own sake rather than for the love of God, he is going to be disillusioned and find contempt and disgust creeping in. Or

---

[1] Invigorated or stimulated (colloquialism). —*Ed.*

sentimentality. It is false compassion springing from a sensitive nature not rooted in supernatural virtue that advocates euthanasia.

Two tendencies are noticeable among doctors who have lost the true spiritual ideal. The natural idealists who might easily have become saints are the ones who are transgressing Christian moral principles. They are the euthanasia and birth control advocates. Their ideas spring not so much from viciousness as from misdirected goodness. On the other side are the doctors who go after money and who see in the profession chiefly a means of enriching themselves. These doctors, too, would have found great strength in a strong, spiritual ideal, yet their sins seem more deliberately in the order of self-love than those of their idealistic colleagues. We tolerate, even respect, the rich medico. We are impressed by the thick carpets of his office. We are a little proud that our operation cost two thousand dollars (as though we had had the privilege of being sliced by some godlike creature). It hurts, but it also tickles our vanity that Dr. So-and-So, who is treating our heart murmur, demands twenty-five dollars for the very privilege of crossing his threshold. Very many doctors now love money, and we respect them for it as long as it is done with professional dignity. All our wrath is reserved for the contraceptive people, the therapeutic abortionists and the euthanasia advocates. This is right in a certain sense because no matter how lofty their motives, they are perverting the very foundations of medicine. But on the other hand, if these doctors could recapture true spiritual principles they could be counted on to restore the professional at great sacrifice.

Probably widespread avarice among doctors (and it is widespread; young boys now dream of medicine in terms of a Park Avenue practice), countenanced and sometimes encouraged by us, is the broad base of the road leading to socialized medicine. It has its counterpart in nursing, with unions and constant demands for higher wages and shorter hours. Nurses are generally discontent and someone has sold them on the idea that it is because they are underpaid, which it is not.

Health Comes in a Bottle

It is usually said that people have never been so healthy as they are right here and now in America. It is a disputable point. The great scourges which wiped out whole populations have at least temporarily abated, so there may be less serious sickness. On the other hand a good case can be made for saying that health has never been at such a low ebb under ordinary conditions. Americans keep going only with the constant aid of vitamins, aspirin, laxatives, cold medicines and sleeping tablets. They are not exactly sick, but neither have they a positive health, which is vital and energetic. Their bodies don't operate normally without the help of drugs. Drugs are expensive, especially vitamins. It costs money to remove the minerals and vitamins from our food by denaturing, and then it costs money to supply them in an artificial form. Moreover, something is lost on the way.

Degenerative Diseases

The major modern problem in medicine is concerned with degenerative or deficiency diseases such as cancer, tuberculosis, dental caries, heart ailments, and others, which have or may have their origin in some unnatural or inorganic food or mode of living. There is a growing protest from men who have faced these problems squarely and *wholly*, that such things as white bread from bleached flour, white sugar, pasteurized and diluted milk, and chemical fertilizers used in farming, bring about the disposing conditions for these diseases. (Like the weakened tissue in which cancer grows. Sometimes you hear, for instance, that pipe smoking "causes" cancer of the mouth, but it will only cause it by irritating already deficient tissue. That is why cancer removed from one spot often crops up in another. The pre-disposing condition remains. It does not seem that the main stream of cancer research is directed toward this weakened tissue, but toward the cancer cells and how to kill them.) God has given us the conditions for natural health within a wide latitude. The Eskimo can keep healthy largely on blubber, the Swiss mountaineer on dairy products, the Scotchman on grains and the man of the tropics on fruits and fish, so long only as all these are *whole*, that we take the elements of them in the living synthesis that God has made. A similar principle applies to drugs. Even primitive people have known by tradition and experience the curative effects of certain herbs. Some of the most striking modern drug discoveries are based on or are substitutes for this folk knowledge. It used to be the fashion of doctors to despise folk wisdom, but now they know that the old women who used foxglove for dropsy were applying digitalis in its natural form, that ma-huang, a herb used by the Chinese from ancient times, contains ephedrine. So too, penicillin is just a certain form of mold, or its chemical "equivalent." Sick dogs have always by instinct burrowed into the moldy earth of forests and lain there until they recovered.

It would be wrong to exalt the primitive unduly, but the herbal medication did have one advantage, that the specific remedy was found in natural combination with other subsidiary and often beneficial elements. The effects were generally milder and more diffuse than with the modern drug counterpart. Also they were found in organic matter. It is problematic whether synthetic drugs are really a substitute for the living elements, or only a reflection of them. With vitamins there is a vast difference in the effects of the chemical and natural ones.

Underlying all of these considerations there is a basic principle which is that God intends us to conform with the way he has set up the world. If we don't conform we get into subtle and mysterious trouble, and then if we won't mend our ways we have to try to set ourselves up as gods and order the whole universe on principles of our own devising. That's what is going on now. Besides being sinful, it is also very costly. We have mentioned our drug-store health. There are other much more expensive factors.

The modern diseases seem to be especially expensive ones to treat. Cancer is the occasion of very frequent and very expensive surgery. If the case is hopeless it nevertheless takes considerable time to run its course, with hospitalization, expensive dressings, expensive opiates. Tuberculosis needs protracted periods of specialized hospitalization. The national dentist bill is colossal. The price we pay for our sins of commerce, exploitation, luxury and sterility can be reckoned in dollars as well as pain. It raises the national hospital bill astronomically.

Research Foundations

Our generation is very concerned to find the prevention and cure of the modern scourges. To this end we have set up national foundations of various sorts to which all Americans have contributed generously, amounts in the millions. These foundations stand high in national health costs. The cancer foundation recently approached Congress directly for huge appropriations.

Questions have to be asked. What is the relationship between ten million dollars and the cure of cancer, if any? What is the relationship between Christmas seals and the cure of tuberculosis? What now, since it is the newest thing, is the raising of public funds going to do to prevent heart disease?

To take the last case first. Lots of people die of heart disease. It's a wonder more don't, with the stepped up pace of our society and the dog-eat-dog nature of our business world. Almost anyone would be qualified to diagnose the condition. He would recommend less anxiety (trust in God's Providence), less avarice, more walking and less rushing from coast to coast by plane. He would suggest a return to simpler desires and simpler modes of living. For those who have really great responsibilities from which they cannot withdraw, the remedy is undisturbed inner peace, another name for which is contemplation. If the heart disease association were to use its money for setting up classes on how to pray, or in helping finance rural communities or "back to the land" movements, one could see a long range attack on the problem. However, their aims are otherwise. They propose to use the money for "education, research and service." In as much as this means telling people that a lot of Americans die of heart disease, it does not seem very necessary. The papers could do it on their own initiative. If it is to go for research, it will at best stimulate laboratory men to find another safety valve for our over-indulgence, another reprieve so we can go on with high-tension living instead of learning that money isn't everything and that we rest wholly in God's loving hands. Sometimes these health and research foundations look very much like feather bedding, like soft berths for a lot of high-pressure publicity men.

The New York tuberculosis society says that T. B. thrives where there is dirt, poverty and undernourishment, so it *knows* what the root cause is and doesn't need to do research on the matter. But is any of the money they collect diverted to making clean what is dirty, to making the poor rich or giving food to the hungry? Or do they set up hospitals for the care of victims? No, in so far as these things are done they are done by Our Holy Mother the State. Even though most other local T. B. associations do care for victims of the disease, huge sums are still diverted to propaganda, thus fattening the purses of advertising and publicity men, plus a corps of sleek administrators. One would hesitate to accuse these people of deliberately creating occupations for themselves, yet one is reminded of the social workers in some New York hospitals who have invented the job of being middle men between the doctors and the families of dying patients, "to prepare the relatives to accept the fact that the patient won't live." This multiplication of unnecessary intermediaries is the bureaucratic spirit, a sort of organized device for receding from social realities, a national schizophrenia. And it costs money. Add a billion or so dollars to the national health bill for these foundations.

The High Cost of Hospitalization

It costs more per day to lie fairly neglected, eating nearly nothing, on an iron cot-like bed in a bare room with five or six other people in a hospital, than it does to take a nicely furnished room with private bath in a good hotel and have three good meals sent up to you in bed. Furthermore, the hospital is tax free, doesn't have to pay dividends, and never suffers from a shortage of guests, whereas the opposite is true of hotels. Yet the ordinary hospital shows a deficit. Why?

The ordinary voluntary hospital doesn't extend much charity. Even ward patients pay, or the city pays for them. Out-patient clinics get the doctors' services free and charge the patient what he can pay, which should cover materials. One eye-ear-nose-and-throat hospital in New York made forty thousand dollars profit on the glasses it dispensed patients in one year alone.

A major effect of the Blue Cross and other hospitalization plans is the guarantee of prompt payment of hospital bills. These plans have been of great financial advantage to the hospitals.

Another factor in hospital costs is that hospitalization is now the norm, even for childbirth. It seems better all around to have children at home, and it certainly costs less. Now babies cost a minimum of $150[2] in large cities, for no good reason except that we have been gradually forced into the hospital pattern.

If you add up all the extraordinary expenses of hospitals, such as the very expensive equipment in the operating room, the high cost of drugs and the increasing cost of personnel, it still remains somewhat of a mystery why hospitalization comes so high. And there let us leave it, as a mystery. Possibly it is one which should be investigated by proper authorities. It may be that large hospitals are by nature uneconomical. Perhaps it would be cheaper to keep the elaborate operating equipment in one or two hospitals in a city so that other hospitals can concentrate on nursing care without big investments for seldom-used equipment.

Howsoever that may be, staggering hospital bills are precipitating socialized medicine.

---

[2] Adjusted for inflation this is roughly $1,600 in 2021. The cost for delivering a baby today under normal conditions in a U. S. hospital ranges from $5,000 - $10,000 uninsured. — *Ed.*

The Socialization of Medicine

The pressure toward socialized medicine or socialized insurance or socialized anything else is the anguished need on all sides for a central authoritative disposing agent which can effect an equitable distribution of money and services. It responds to the hunger for God with a substitute god, the bureaucratic state. With God as the disposing agent, as formerly, men had but to follow His laws, natural and supernatural, and an harmonious relationship of all factors would be achieved through the instrumentality of the free wills of men (and involving, as God intended, the perfection of the men concerned). This substitute god, the welfare state, disposes all things deliberately by human reason, in *disregard* of men's perfection. It encourages human irresponsibility and graft. Men are (such is their nature) less solicitous about public property than their own. More people are unemployed when there is unemployment insurance, quite a few people went to the hospital every year "just for a rest" when the hospitalization plans went into effect.

Socialized medicine will be much more expensive than private medicine because to the same costs (enhanced by graft and waste) will be added the salaries of an army of bureaucratic administrators and their clerks. Furthermore it will not work; that is to say it will not even achieve the efficiency and equity that it promises. One has only to look at Soviet Russia to see that "each according to his needs" cannot be attained by legislation and that bureaucracies are hopelessly inefficient.

Religious people have special things to fear from socialized medicine. They see Freudian concepts invading hospitals. They see the ever-increasing pressure for euthanasia, sterilization and therapeutic abortions. They fear, rightly, that government control can force an anti-Christian mold on the whole medical field.

The Alternative

The opponents of socialized medicine, however, are ineffective. Merely to be against it is like being against the law of gravity. Socialization is that natural conclusion of a hundred converging trends in every branch of medicine.

The alternative to socialized medicine is a root and branch reform of the whole medical picture in accordance with natural and supernatural principles. Even those reforms which unbelievers and atheists can subscribe to with their natural intelligence, like the necessity of whole

It All Goes Together

foods and organic treatment, cannot be effected without a tremendous religious revival, because to accomplish them means that men (not just doctors, or even primarily doctors, but farmers, bakers, the lords of the drug business and the great food corporations) must be pried loose from their avarice, detached from their vested interests, and must make tremendous sacrifices before God for the common good.

Our sin, as Christians, would be to despair in advance of converting men, or at least a sufficient number of them to a reform and a new life.

Among doctors and nurses the reform will probably begin when they grasp the idea that medicine is essentially a labor of love. An analogy may help.

Suppose parents were to revolt against their voluntary services to their children. Let us imagine that fathers demanded a dollar an hour for walking the baby at night and that mothers wanted union hours and time and half for overtime. Also let us suppose that mothers were to specialize in nursery work and demand the services of cooks and other experts to prepare baby food. All this, of course, to be paid by the state which would also have to cough up a thousand dollars per baby as a bonus for maternity. Something of the sort happened in Russia when the State tried to take over the care of children. It failed of course. Things that God intended to be done out of love must be done on that basis. To try to do them otherwise involves fantastic costs (quite apart from more important ill effects). And God will see to it that the laborers are taken care of if they trust in Him and do things His way.

Medicine is not exactly like this case, but it is something like it. God intended the sick to be taken care of out of love as the chief motive, and in all sorts of informal as well as formal ways. The wherewithal necessary for doctors and nurses would follow. However, if you reverse the procedure and look *first* to the welfare of doctors and nurses, and to the financial stability of hospitals, you can expect neither prosperity nor health to follow.

27

The Rainmakers[1]

SEPTEMBER 1950

WE ARE BEGINNING TO HEAR THE RUMBLE OF legal controversy arising as a result of the use of artificial methods of rainmaking to fill New York City's reservoirs. Resort owners in the Catskills realize that their living is being jeopardized, and the farmers in Orange County say their crops have been greatly damaged. Pretty soon these legal problems will have to be faced. The purpose of this article is not to try to solve them but to suggest that the matter may go much deeper, into profound moral problems which no one seems to have raised. We should like to raise them, and we should also like to show why it is that in this and similar matters where many people feel vaguely there "is something wrong involved," no ready moral criterion for judgement is at hand.

In clarifying the matter it is necessary first to recall to modern minds two general truths, or perspectives.

THE HARMONY OF THE UNIVERSE

The natural created universe is a harmonious system made up of lots of other lesser harmonies, all synchronized in an orderly way. The planetary system, for instance, is so delicately balanced and rhythmic in its operation that men referred to the "music of the spheres" long before they got all their scientific facts straightened out. In seeing the harmony they were perhaps nearer the truth about the cosmos than the modern astronomer who is unable to see the design for being too preoccupied with the minutia. Or take the wonderful complexity and balance of the human body which not only grows and reproduces but repairs itself. Or the soil which follows a cycle of giving and taking nutrition, and which renews itself with the help of a myriad of micro-organisms, bacteria and worms.

The weather is one of these harmonies about which we shall go into more detail presently.

---

1 This article was co-authored with Ernst Florian Winter (1923–2014) an Austrian-American historian and political scientist who contributed several articles to *Integrity*. —*Ed.*

A few generalizations can be made about all of these harmonies. Although they are composed of simple elements, they are all complex in the way these elements are interrelated within each small harmony and the way they are synchronized with the elements in other harmonies. There is something very delicate about the harmony *as* harmony even if the individual elements in it are as gross a planet. We always think of the mechanism of the watch (which is a man-made harmony) as delicate, but these natural harmonies God has established are even more delicate. The planets "keep time" (their movements are the measure of our time) more accurately than the most delicate Swiss watch. And the influence of the soul over the body and vice versa is so subtle that we have not been able to pin it down.

Another thing, these harmonies are directed from within, so to speak. They have their own internal principle of operation which is God's law written in them. They do not depend on man for their working. It is because of this *internal* principle of operation that these harmonies tend to balance themselves. So, for instance, when the body is injured in one part the whole body tends to compensate for the injury and tries to restore balance. In neither Swiss watches nor Ford cars does a healthy part come to the aid of an injured part, nor do these mechanisms repair themselves.

MAN'S LORDSHIP

The second neglected truth concerns the nature of man's lordship of the universe. It is fairly evident that man is the top creature in the visible universe, but if he were not we would know it from God's telling us. "And he said: Let us make man to our image and likeness: and let him have dominion over the fishes of the sea, and the fowls of the air, and the beasts, and the whole earth, and every creeping creature that moveth upon the earth."

On the other hand we know that Satan is called "the Lord of the world," so our problem is to figure out in what way the world belongs to God, in what way it belongs to man, and in what way it belongs to the Devil, and then we must not mix the three up.

The world belongs to God absolutely. He has made it out of nothing and holds it in existence. He made all the laws of its operation and is therefore free to bypass them, as He does when He performs miracles.

The world belongs to man by delegated authority. He didn't create it and therefore does not have absolute jurisdiction over it, such as a creator would have. However it is for his use. It doesn't exist for its own sake, but for man. Man can use the world, but does he have a right to abuse it? He also has certain obligations. His first obligation is to serve God. If the world is made for man, so man is made for God, and if man does not serve God it will follow as a corollary that he will not know rightly how to use the world.

God has told man how to conduct himself and use the things of this earth. Man has the revealed moral law, and the natural law as made explicit by the Church. He is expected to figure some things out himself, applying his reason to the nature of things to see how God intended them to work. Some people hold, among them the foremost contemporary Catholic anthropologists, that man didn't learn about nature little by little but that he forgot it gradually, having had a certain basic plenitude of this knowledge given him in the Garden in Eden, where also all animals obeyed him. With the first sin, nature rebelled against man, but the knowledge he lost only gradually, and there are still some genuine primitive tribes on earth living in little "paradises." Not only do they live peacefully, happily and morally, but they have a wonderful "folk knowledge" of plants and animals and their uses.

Whether or not this theory is correct, it is true that man has a certain natural "discernment" about these things but one which can be lost by abuse. There are many Americans today who would see nothing wrong with, say, buying a fertile farm and "raping" the soil for twenty years for quick profits. Yet most people on earth at all other times would have abhorred this. What we have lost is a precious natural power of discernment.

Now as for Satan's lordship. Being an angel, Satan is much brighter than man and much cleverer as a scientist. He can't perform miracles but he can do wonders, and presumably he could mess up the natural universe a lot if God did not curb his efforts. Satan's one concern about the universe is to wreck man's soul. He probably does what God allows him to do in causing disease or disasters where it is to his advantage. His other avenue of approach is to get *man* to mess up the world, working through his pride or avarice or vanity, so the world won't serve him and will be an occasion of the loss of his soul. The prediction is that one day Satan will take over, ruling the temporal order as a pseudo savior through Anti-Christ. There is no reason why he should not at that time assume his own particular jurisdiction over nature.

RADICAL DEPARTURE OF MODERN SCIENCE

So much for the preliminaries. Man has to use the world. To use it he must know it, and how it works, whether he gets this knowledge from the memory of the human race or his own discernment or speculation. There is no reason why he should not order and refine and systematize this knowledge, both to extend it and to use it more efficiently. When he does this, common sense and folklore develop into the natural and physical sciences. This should be all to the good, and very useful. For instance, if man understands the elements that go into making weather, he will want to develop instruments to measure temperatures, detect wind direction and velocity, gauge humidity, barometric pressure, etc. Without precise reports on these and other factors air travel would be unsafe, weather predictions could not be made. But there is no point in multiplying instances of the value of scientific knowledge in which everyone concurs. Nor would we dispute the principle that these advances have been made (until recently) through an increase in knowledge.

However, of recent years science has gone off on a new track, a radically different one, which seems to result from an increase in understanding but which may represent quite the opposite. In almost every field new applications of this new science are being manifested. With the weather it is artificial rainmaking; with agriculture it is commercial chemical fertilizers and sprays; with the human mind it is lobotomies; with matter as such it is atomic fission; with our bodies it is vitamin pills; with facture it is (analogously) the assembly-line technique. We believe that there is hardly any thinking person who has not been troubled in his mind by these developments, but probably vaguely, not knowing quite why, and hesitating to express distrust of the great god science and the sacred principle that no curbs should be placed on man's knowing more and more.

THE RESULT OF IGNORANCE

Yet if we look at the situation clearly, it isn't in these instances a question of knowing more but of knowing less. In one sense, true, they know more. They know how to do all these things and that they have certain desired or desirable immediate effects, like destroying whole cities, making disturbed patients quiet, growing apples without worms, stepping up production and the like. But note—in no case do they know precisely what the long-term effects will be, or even what the less spectacular short-term effects are.

The atomic scientists *did not know* whether or not their atomic fission would set off a chain reaction that would destroy the world. They *did not know* all the secondary effects on unborn children, etc., which occurred at Hiroshima, and they still do not know much about them.

Vitamin pills sometimes have very odd effects, as occasionally does penicillin, and as frequently do the inhiston[2] drugs. The degree of dehumanization of man that follows on his being mechanically subordinated to assembly-line procedure is still not fully realized. Don't ask the lobotomy doctors what they are doing or how a lobotomy affects a person's intelligence. As for the chemical spray and fertilizer people, they are like children who go about setting the house on fire because they are cold and want to get warm. Let us not neglect to mention the DDT people whose ministrations have had such freak effects (one of which is to cause a hardier type of mosquito to arise in California, which is not only DDT immune but which also has the power to sting 200 times as poisonously as their relatively harmless ancestors).

Why don't they know what they are doing? Because they don't understand those harmonies we mentioned earlier. They are intruding their particular bits of knowledge, usually chemical and often accidentally discovered, into a complex of interrelated factors which is a mystery to them.

It is true that the harmonies are sick harmonies and scientists sense this. The harmonies are, so to speak, distended. The thing to do would be to help restore their balance. *Instead our scientists destroy the whole harmony, the whole system*, keeping only a semblance of it going (by artificial feeding) until the moment of awful reckoning comes. If we were to draw it, it would look like this:

---

2   As one amusing ad from a U. S. newspaper stated: "Inhiston is not merely another 'cold tablet'—not a salt, effervescent powder, aspirin or quinine compound. Inhiston is an *anti-histamine*, with an action based on a new, revolutionary concept of cold treatment. Nation-wide research on various anti-histamines has proved that *colds can be stopped*, in the great majority of cases, if anti-histamine treatment begins within an hour after the first cold symptom appears. This is truly wonderful news!" (*Toledo Blade*, Dec. 5, 1949)—*Ed.*

The Rainmakers

1) The harmony God made—nice balance of elements, serving man well.
2) Unbalanced harmony—still operating from an internal principle, but serving man less well.
3) Broken harmony—internal principle unable to operate.

THE RESULT OF IMMORALITY

In God's plan the natural law (how things work) and the moral law (how man should operate) are synchronized. They should work in concert automatically, so that a man who followed the moral law wouldn't necessarily have to know natural science in order to behave rightly in regard to creatures. If the farmer who raped the soil hadn't been avaricious he would naturally have tended to farm in a way that respected creatures and soils. And if the scientist were not proud, but truly humble as he claims to be, he would come out with better answers. However, this is not to judge anyone in particular, for when a society is very corrupted, as ours is, individual people can innocently take on what are in themselves nefarious practices.

Let us observe, though, that each of these things under consideration, has a background of some unrepented sins. With the farmer and the chemical fertilizer company it was largely a matter of avarice. They wanted a high yield so they wouldn't allow the soil to renew itself by slower and more organic methods. It was our spirit of luxury too. We wanted fruits and vegetables that "looked nice" in preference to less attractive but more nutritious ones. And of course we all wanted to live in the city where work is softer and canned entertainment is near at hand.

The assembly-line method was also born of avarice and was aided and abetted by everyone's sloth. The "necessity" for artificial rain-making is a natural consequence of all these sins. It is bound up with the inhuman concentration of populations in cities, with the wastage of water in manufacture, especially in the manufacture of synthetic goods, and with the rape of the soil.

Lobotomies are purely a matter of convenience for a society which has some troublesome characters on its hands which it is reluctant as yet to kill outright. It is the natural terminal of the type of thinking psychiatry is doing. Instead of examining society's conscience to see what we have done to destroy our brothers in Christ (and so perhaps to find a way back), we try only to make their care easier for us.

When one ponders long on how directly our social and personal ills are bound up in the seven capital sins, one gets new insight into Our Lady's messages. Unless we repent we cannot change the direction of our remedial work, and if we do not repent we are certainly going to jump right from the frying pan into the fire.

INVITATION TO TYRANNY

There is one other generalization which needs to be made about our new "radical type" of scientific direction. Since it breaks the harmonies which operate by God's wisdom, on the principles put in them, they will not operate at all now except from outside, but by whose wisdom? Our bodies will only function as sundry parts of a drug store are poured into them at the advice (guess?) of some doctor weighted down with the latest results of the latest tests pouring in from everywhere. People who spray orchards are now up to sixteen different sprayings a season and at the mercy of the chemists. Where is the politician who can be trusted with the atom bomb? Christ said we shouldn't fear the man who can kill our bodies, but him who has the power to cast us down into Hell. He meant we should fear God. But who, for similar reasons, would not be terrified to fall into the hands of the lobotomists, or the Freudian analyst, or the Soviet agents who can work their hideous wonders on the will with drugs?

Yes, every one of these radical new discoveries invites, though in varying degrees, a god-like power or wisdom or cleverness. But they do not invite God.

We shall return to this point. Let us stop generalizing and consider the specific case of the rainmakers.

WHERE RAIN COMES FROM

Rain is a factor in the weather harmony. The first thing to realize is that all the rain that falls was first evaporated from the earth's surface. It is drawn up by the action of the sun, more or less readily depending on the humidity of the atmosphere. Every woman notices this principle in operation in the time it takes to dry clothes on dry days and overcast days.

The weather pattern is not stationary but moves. In our latitude

The Rainmakers

it moves, at irregular speed, across the continent from west to east. A person living in New York can, for instance, check the Chicago weather and figure that in a day or two it will reach New York, somewhat modified, unless a cold front comes down from Canada or a hot blast sweeps up from the Gulf. It is because the weather moves that the water picked up in one place is dropped in another.

The water comes mostly from the oceans, lakes, rivers and streams. However some of it is ground water, brought to the surface by vegetation. Plants and trees sink their roots deep down into the soil and siphon the water up through capillary action, not only for their own use but also to bring it into the air where it is reabsorbed into the atmosphere, to continue the cycle. Where lands have been denuded of forests by ruthless lumbering or of grass by reckless plowing, the topsoil is blown away and a hard surface of clay forms. Rain water then runs off, as on cement, instead of sinking into the ground. The water remaining below the surface from happier days is sealed in.

Weather moves in a pattern of alternate high and low pressure areas. These have their ultimate origin in the fact that the sun heats the equatorial region more intensely than other parts of the globe. Heat causes the air to rise and expand, with new air then rushing in below and the expanded air circulating outward. A pattern has developed of a succession of pressure areas. The "highs" carry dry and usually warm weather, so they are more inclined to absorb moisture. The lows bring in cool air, with condensation of moisture and precipitation in the form of rain.

Atmospheric moisture tends to condense into clouds and is precipitated under certain conditions. One element is the contracting of the air in the low pressure areas. It is also precipitated when the clouds (which are unable to rise to a higher altitude) run into a barrier such as a mountain range. That is why one side of a mountain is often verdant and fertile, while the other side is barren.

A further important factor in precipitation is vegetation, particularly forestation. If clouds containing rain pass over a heavily planted area or a forest, they are likely to drop their moisture. It is not fully known why. One possible explanation is that a sort of moist column of air rises from the forest because water is in the process of evaporation. This may add just enough extra moisture to the passing cloud to carry it beyond the saturation point.

Precipitation is also affected by local conditions, in which case, of course, the rainfall is localized. In a natural way it is affected by small lakes and streams, and even small areas of vegetation. Unnaturally, it is affected by cities. The smoke of industrialism, rising above any manufacturing city, seems to have an irritating chemical effect on clouds which makes them disgorge their water. Of course this water is of no use to the concrete below, nor can it sink into the earth to replenish the underground water table. It is carried off and polluted by the sewerage.

ECONOMIC SINS AND WEATHER CHANGES

From the slight sketch above it is evident that the weather is bound up with factors under man's control, since it is intimately related to what he does with the earth's surface. Nature's tendency in virgin territory is to keep the water in circulation. There are natural forests and plain areas, and the elements working unrestrictedly tend toward conservation and increasing fertility and vegetation. These in turn tend to modify the extremes of weather. If man had respected the balances set up by nature, merely directing and maneuvering them for his own just use, he could have preserved fertility, modified the climate, enriched the already good soil, and improved the less fertile parts.

We all know that the history of mankind has not been one of solicitude for the natural laws in this respect. Christians have only to recall that Northern Africa, now a desert, was once the fertile home of many of our early saints. Most deserts are man-made deserts. The dust-bowl of America is a desert in the making, and it is the handiwork of almost our own generation. We are not concerned here to discuss the land but only to say that our abuses of land and forest have far-reaching repercussions on the weather. These abuses are well advanced now and their effects are being more and more intensely felt. Even so, the weather does not change because of them overnight. Natural processes move slowly, which is an advantage because it gives men time to adjust themselves.

As our sins have caused profound disturbances, with more and worse ones promised, so our repentance could repair the damage in a natural way, but that too will take time (although perhaps not as long as people think). It could be done with judicious reforestation, the right kind of planting, the return of organic matter to the soil, etc. If it is not done soon it will be completely too late. So far we are not disposed to do it. We prefer to cover up immediate ill-effects with artificial remedies which may put us in a mess far worse than any we have yet dreamed of.

ARTIFICIAL RAINMAKING

We hope we have made it clear that we can influence the weather in natural ways, involving a return to the natural moral law, to respect for God's gifts and creatures and their right use. However, we are determined on a course of expediency; we are going to make our own weather.

There seem to be two main ways of producing artificial rain. One, which has been chiefly used in the Catskills so far, is to work from the ground with silver iodide smoke. Trucks producing this smoke travel up and down the highways. Presumably this is a form of "irritation" similar to that of factory smoke in towns.

The other, and more effective means, is to seed the clouds with dry ice. This suddenly reduces the temperature and condenses the air, like a miniature low pressure area. They use this method in Texas, where huge ranches have their own airplanes which rush at every passing rain cloud, competing openly with the next ranch for the precious water, and naturally getting entangled in all sorts of quarrels among neighbors.

Superficially it might seem as though these artificial methods are not very dastardly, inasmuch as they imitate what's happening in the usual course. The trouble is that they are artificially induced into a system, a harmony, with which they have no organic relation. Even on a small scale it is apparent that rain dropped in place X cannot be dropped in place Y farther on, as had been its wont, and that the whole system has suddenly to readjust itself. With a whole lot of little interferences like this, rather than changes established permanently, and gradually (as a "natural" interference would be, such as the planting of a forest belt to protect the dust areas), but capricious or operating from an *outside* principle, the inevitable effect will be to *confuse* the weather harmony. It will no longer be a harmony, a balance of integrated elements operating according to an internal principle. It will be a whole lot of isolated natural effects being produced at will by human manipulators (who, be it remembered, do not know what dynamite they are playing with). Some political "doctor" will have to run the whole show, deciding when it will rain where, until nature takes its horrible revenge.

SCIENTIFIC PRAGMATISM

We must insist that this unnatural breaking of harmonies is not the only kind of sin that men can commit, but only a special kind of sin. One might call it an unnatural and immoral *means* to an end which may be good or bad.

We are not saying that naturally good means are always accompanied by a noble objective, although in these matters it is hard to use them immorally. It is authoritatively reported however that Russia has succeeded in doing so. That country followed and elaborated upon excellent suggestions that were made for our own country with respect to its dust bowl. Organic scientists here had proposed a 1300-mile strip of protective forestation for the dust-bowl area, along with certain revegetation plans. Russia took the idea and used it for the double purpose of redeeming its barren steppe country and at the same time as a means of deliberately stealing rainfall from southern and eastern Europe, so as to turn these latter areas into desert. The Russians planted 2600 miles of strip forest some years ago. By blasting a mountain top they redirected a river to the Caspian Sea, which had formerly flowed north. At the latitude of their operations the pressure areas move in a reverse direction from that of northern United States. Consequently the Russian experiments could hope to induce precipitation on their own steppes, of moisture formerly destined to fall on Europe. This experiment is nearing its completion. We mention it to show that bad men can use good natural means to do their evil, although it takes them longer. This project may prove very unhappy in its results for certain populations and civilizations, and it will drastically change the pattern of the weather cycle. Nevertheless a harmony will continue to exist and the principle of operation will still be from within, and according to natural laws.

However this sort of thing is not our temptation. We do not covet other nations' fertility and if we did we would probably be less patient about getting it. We are more likely to be tempted to try to do good with bad means (like the compassionate birth controllers). Our whole turn of mind is pragmatic, and this philosophy pervades our scientists. They will not ask whether it is moral, but only whether it will effect some immediate benefit. As soon as the experimental period is finished and the ways of making rain are perfected we can expect to be propagandized by some rosy picture of turning deserts into flower gardens, which will make any dissenters seem like bitter kill-joys who want everyone to starve to death.

THE TRUE AND FALSE WHOLES

The two major intellectual sins of the scientific mind (besides pride) are this pragmatism and a certain provincialism, or partialism. Men have been unable for years to see anything *whole*. That's why they couldn't see the harmonies.

Now the pendulum is swinging, but we would be naive to assume it will swing into the true course, since we do not intend to repent and change our ways. (How far we are from beating our breasts is revealed by an article on our water supply in an August issue of *Life* magazine in which water is treated explicitly from the point of view of its possible exploitation.) More likely it will swing into a worse error in the opposite direction.

Let us review the weather situation. First there was the disregard of the natural harmonies; then the abuses of avarice; then the problems (dust bowls and not enough water for New York City); then experimentation with the pragmatic, artificial remedy. The near future promises a chaos of little warring efforts to steal rain from the heavens. We can expect that to be followed by a "savior" who will come to the rescue of the common good, and insist on order, balance and equity in the distribution of rain. But *not* by a return to organic means and the natural harmony operating by the internal principle (God's law). It will have to be a new harmony artificially operated from without by scientific means and a *political* principle. The whole thing will be operated by a myriad of slave-scientists under the direction of a world tyrant who will consider himself wise enough to say who will have rain from his heaven and who will not.

Will there ever be a man that wise? God is that wise, and perfectly just. Anybody else who so sets himself up will be playing god. His name will probably be Anti-Christ.

28
The Servant Problem

SEPTEMBER 1950

ONE THING FREUD DID DISCOVER, OR AT LEAST reminded us of, is the fact of *symbolic* action. It amounts to this, that a person cannot help revealing the state of his soul, whether in his body, his motions, attitudes or actions. When Pilate washed his hands of the guilt of Christ's death, he deliberately symbolized his exact attitude toward the coming execution. Freud's idea is that neurotic modern man does the same thing indeliberately, and even unconsciously. We express what we are in our neurotic habits and our physical indispositions, for all to read who possess the key. The trouble with Freud was that he had the wrong key. It fitted the lock, but it turned in the wrong direction.

This is not an article on psychiatry, but a sort of socio-analysis of a particular modern problem. It presupposes that as a man's soul writes itself on his body, so society's soul writes itself on our streets, into the architecture of our buildings, in the way we organize our hospitals, in every institution. Only one of these manifestations is under consideration here. It is the servant problem.

THE SIMPLE FORM

The most obvious form of this problem is the difficulty that middle class women (many themselves parasitic) have in getting domestics. A generation ago domestics were very plentiful (at least Negro maids were). Now they are scarce, even though net wages are very high relative to those paid to industrial or office workers, and despite the shortened hours and even social security.

I suppose no one will shed a tear over the fact that a lot of more or less childless housewives have to do their own work. Nor will I. One wonders, however, if the disappearance of the servant class marks the dawn of a glorious era of equality, or whether it is a mark of our general decay. Its first meaning is that thousands upon thousands of young girls are now in factory and office environments, doing mechanical, stultifying work, whereas formerly they were in home environments exercising a lot of intelligence and skill, as well as brawn. They obviously prefer their new situation, but is their preference rooted in Christian ideas? They want nice clothes, easy work and a chance to meet boys (not necessarily synonymous with a chance to make a good marriage).

There are, of course, some servants available. One cannot help but observe how snobbish most of them are and how strong their preference is for work in very rich homes, where a chauffeur can drive them to town, where they do specialized work within stated hours, and where they have the companionship of the servant community.

The people who really need help, young married couples with lots of children, are almost invariably poor (because of the children) and no one would dream of working for them—with such long hours, in such crowded quarters, and for next to nothing. Instead of helpers they are offered labor-saving devices like automatic washing machines, electric thises and thats, and birth control. Presently the mothers will have to go to work in the factories too, and then the state or the factory will provide nursery care for children *en masse*.

It is hard to see how young women stand to gain anything by nursing machines and files instead of babies. Most of them make no conscious choice but act under very heavy social pressure from all sides, including home and school. It is part of a general direction in which the world is hastening. In countries where socialism has had a head-start on America, as in New Zealand and Australia, these conditions have prevailed very much longer. Everyone there is as good as everyone else, and is saved by the factory system from the necessity of personal service.

THE AUTOMATIC VENDOR

This is where Freud's symbolism comes in. Our revolt against serving each other is so profound that it unconsciously (neurotically, so to speak) projects itself into every phase of life. It accounts for the extraordinary (and otherwise nonsensical) crop of automatic vending machines and devices. From coast to coast the *preferred* way of purchasing is by sticking money in the slot or pushing around a tray or a little wire basket.

One of the early manifestations of our repugnance to service was the cafeteria, a place of ungracious eating. Then for years the Automat stood out as a kind of curiosity. There, as in some cafeterias, the good was much better than average. But to get it involved a scramble such as in a subway rush. Eating in the Automat means a few hurried moments of gulping down food at a table of very transient strangers, amid a fearful din and in full view of lots of dirty dishes. All this is to avoid only one thing, the personal service of waitresses. One wonders how much money is saved. I personally would be surprised if any economies are affected. There are still a lot of people needed to run the mechanical system, only their jobs are now duller.

There was quite a stretch of time between the Automat and the supermarket, but the same principle carried over. The same temptations, too. They always put the desserts first in cafeterias, so as to tempt people to eat, not wisely but luxuriously. It must be a very strong-willed housewife who can resist the more expensive and "prepared" foods in the supermarket, where they practically jump into your basket. What happened to all the clerks who formerly personally served and personally knew their customers in the little grocery stores? They must be behind the scenes some place making up the delectable packages. Supermarkets are glorified warehouses. All we have done is to eliminate the end-man, the grocer. Mechanizing things this way, you do not have to depend on *persons*. You do not have to worry about whether or not a clerk is bright or of sound judgment because nothing goes through his brain and he has no judgments to make. I remember how depressed I was when the meat counter disappeared from the local supermarket, and in its place were a lot of little packages of meat, temptingly wrapped and neatly priced. First of all I wondered what had happened to the butchers. They probably work at night now, cutting and wrapping, and caring not a hoot about whether Mrs. Jones has a nice dinner party or Mrs. Smith stretches her narrow income to the nourishment of all her kids. What depressed me especially was that I enjoyed getting meat by just picking it out of a bin. I don't know much about meat, and in this way no one could stare at me for my ignorance. I thought of all the modern young women who were possibly even stupider than I in these matters, and of how I (and probably they) had given in to "prepared this" and "prepared that," and of how I knew that every concession to time and mind savers was a concession to malnourishment and the relinquishment of a skill, or a potential skill, which meant freedom. Then I rationalized that it didn't matter about me because I don't have a family to care for, but if I were a young housewife I would certainly not make these concessions. But I probably would, and they probably do, because in the absence of personal service and neighborliness, we are all alike frantic in our efforts to get all the necessary things done somehow.

Anyway, after the perfection of supermarkets, self-service came in like a tidal wave. Cigarettes, nylons, cold drinks, hot drinks (coffee), contraceptives (in England), popcorn, handkerchiefs, stamps, are all available through slot machines. In California, gas stations are run on the self-service basis, which seems like a far cry from the all-service stations where young men fell over the car to check your oil and wipe your windshield. But it really isn't, since the love in both cases is for money, not you.

NON SERVIAM

With all this, what are we trying to say (consciously but most unconsciously) if it is not: I will not serve? That, of course, was the famous last statement of Lucifer. Are we really at the dawn of a beautiful democratic tomorrow or is the world perhaps a little less simple than that? I should like to suggest that the modern striving for equality is rooted in pride, that it has brought about a complete reversal of the Christian attitude, and that it promises a slavery more degrading than the world has ever known.

The idea of servitude as a noble thing came into the world with Christianity. Pre-Christian pagans had a lot of good ideas but this was not one of them. They despised slaves as they despised manual labor. Then God "took the form of a servant."

One of the Pope's titles is "The Servant of the Servants of God." Peter Claver, who came from a very good family, was granted the privilege of vowing himself to be "slave of the slaves forever." The theme runs all through Christianity. Religious orders have been formed a thousand times to *serve*, and in a menial capacity, everyone from lepers to sick poor, from slaves to children. To this Christian attitude we owe the now dying conception of a professional man, a lawyer, doctor, or statesman, as a *public* servant, with tremendous responsibilities, in honor, to the poor and the sick and the helpless.

THE CHRISTIAN HIERARCHY

It seems as though Christ intended to show us a sort of double hierarchy in society. The more important a man's position the more he is to be the servant of all. In this way power and position are not only rendered harmless to the little fellow, but sweeten all society by their charity.

A favorite saying today is, "Power corrupts, and absolute power corrupts absolutely." Of course there is some truth in it, but it misses the point. There is only one person who has absolute power and that person is God, Who is absolutely just and incorrupt. Insofar as we are god-like, that is, Christians and saints, we can be trusted with power and position because we will use it as God did. We will become the servants of all, and the higher we are, the more universal we will feel our responsibility to be.

We think we have to arrange society so as to modify everyone's power, because we are afraid to trust anyone. Perhaps our approach is wrong. If we regarded the idea of the dignity of really serving we could again begin to trust people. But the first step is down, not up.

FALSE EQUALITY

In the early days of Christianity slaves and nobles, simple and wise, rich and poor, mingled together in love and service of one another. There existed the true equality of free men in Christ.

Our sort of equality is something else. We are rapidly banishing cultural, educational and "good family" distinctions by our general leveling measures, such as free and compulsory education, the democracy of the subway, the radio and the army. It really is a leveling process, a forcing down of all excellencies to a common mediocrity.

Meanwhile there has arisen a much worse, because more mechanical, ladder based strictly on material considerations. The poor Negroes have been drawn into this. Instead of being welcomed into general society as our dear brothers in Christ they are being admitted to all good shops because "their money is as good as anyone else's." Young people everywhere, out of school and college, and too proud to do work which is dirty or menial, are selling themselves into the slavery of the office or factory assembly line (glamorized, of course, at the moment). The next step will be the tyranny of force (arms and the secret police) instead of money. The camouflage of slave labor will be removed and we shall all be more or less numbers on a chain gang. And it will all be ultimately because we have said, "I will not serve." God has told us that a Christian sort of equality comes as the result of beating our way to the lowest place, and we have not believed Him.

THE CHRISTIAN REVIVAL

It is almost an instinct with Christians to become servants. As their spirituality deepens they are inspired by grace to look around and see whom they can serve. The trouble today is that the instinct is little encouraged by fellow Catholics who have themselves fallen into mediocrity and the stupefying comfort of a bourgeois existence.

People sometimes say of *Integrity* that we have nothing *positive* to offer. We do offer positive things, but it is in the nature of the modern situation that positive solutions look uncompromising. We want Christ to come as a worldly success, and take over, and we are scandalized if He offers us the Cross. But it is the Cross that has saved the world, and it does it again in every generation.

So we say to young Catholics who are casting about for something to do with their lives: "Look around and see where you can best serve. But be realistic about it. See the need that is really being neglected. Don't go looking for lepers if the insane are close at hand. Don't teach women who don't know how to pray the best way to apply cosmetics. Teach schools in the neglected areas, not where teachers are highly paid and unionized. Be prepared to fill needs at a personal sacrifice." It sounds like vague advice, but anyone who is casting around will admit, if he is honest, that there are two clear-cut directions in which he can move. The first difficulty is not to find a place to dig in, but to make a commitment of the heart.

1951

29
Did We Never Have It So Good?

JANUARY 1951

BERTRAND RUSSELL, AT HIS AMAZINGLY POPULAR LECtures at Columbia University recently, said that unquestionably men as a whole are happier on the whole now than they were in the eighteenth century, and that this happiness is the fruit of modern science and industry. Lord Russell is an old man, more naive about progress than a comparable thinker would be today. The above optimistic statement seemed to be more a dogma with him than a judgment which could be substantiated by even the evidence elsewhere presented in his speeches.

But to consider his contention seriously for a moment, how would we go about discovering the relative happiness of different ages? Human happiness is hard to measure, though we have some indices to human *un*happiness. Extreme *personal* unhappiness expresses itself in suicide (the natural terminus of despair), and escapes from thinking, whether physical as with alcohol and other drugs, or spiritual as in the distraction of semi-meaningless entertainment. Unhappiness in relations with other people is reflected in divorce and war. The despair of the species manifests itself in the practice of birth control. On this negative evidence our age stands condemned without any necessity of inquiring further into the unpleasantness of the eighteenth century. It may be interesting, though, to note in passing that it is almost instinctive with apologists of modern times to cite the eighteenth century as the basis for unfavorable comparisons. It was then that the evil fruit of the Reformation was most evident. The Christian institutions of the Middle Ages had been destroyed. Yet nothing benevolent had yet arisen to replace them. There remained chaos and misery, while very harsh laws (death for petty theft and no mercy for children) attempted to suppress the widespread revolt against wholesale injustices.

THE BELIEF IN PROGRESS

It does not so much matter what Bertrand Russell thinks, but there are others. Even though one would have expected a general disillusionment of recent years, there still persists the commonly held idea that we are lucky indeed to live in this age and that it would have been an unspeakable darkness to have lived in another time, or place (for we are lucky to be Americans too). Those who tend toward communism probably explain away the fact that our globe is at present imperiled, by a mystical hope like Bertrand Russell's. His theory is that it is often darkest before the dawn, and that, just as a mountain climber might encounter terrific obstacles while nearing the summit, which is hidden from his view by overhanging rocks, so we may be without realizing it on the very threshold of a paradisiacal age. Note how this theory parallels, or rather caricatures, Christian mystery. Those who hope in Christ know that they will have to go down to the death before they live (and analogously, perhaps, with civilizations), and this is a mystery too, but not an irrational one. The eventual success of the Christian will be the fruit of his own virtue and Christ's redemptive sacrifice. The secular optimist expects good to come from nothing except more intense crises and the mere passage of time, although his belief is buoyed up by a superstitious trust that science and industrialism will produce happiness and peace, to which they are in fact completely unrelated.

The reason for people to be easily confused about our day is that there is evidence both of seemingly great good and seemingly great evil. We have television, and the Korean war, the U. N. and the atom bomb. Therefore many people say that the world has always been partly good and partly bad (an echo of "there's always been friction between parents and children"), so why get excited?

If it is true that there is nothing particularly unique about our age, and that we have an illusion of crisis from being too close to events and from the fact that some of us are temperamentally apocalyptical, then we ought to resort to sedatives. But if the "don't get excited" people are wrong, then they couldn't have chosen a worse time to make their error, because the stakes have never been so high nor our potential destructive power so great. Perhaps their own position of unconcern is more a matter of temperament than of judgment. Or likely a closer examination of their position and ours on particular points will show that we are farther apart than we think.

Did We Never Have It So Good?

We believe that there are very many people holding more or less the following views:

1. That there is less cruelty today than ever before; people are kinder.
Now this just isn't true. The first half of the twentieth century has seen cruelties which in intensity and extension rival or exceed anything in history. Forced labor, concentration camps, modern weapons of war, wholesale extermination of populations, torture chambers, dispossessed people, violation of women, religious persecution, all these things come readily to mind. We Americans want to think that they are crimes to be laid at the feet of our enemies or our erstwhile allies only, but it cannot be so maintained. We alone dropped the atom bomb. We sanctioned the dispossession of huge populations and the bringing down of the Iron Curtain in front of other peoples. We dallied until the Russians reached Berlin, so we share the responsibility for the Red Terror of looting and raping that took place there. Our soldiers also committed crimes but admittedly on a much smaller scale. Everyone credits America with good intentions but (as the book *The Twenty-Fifth Hour*[1] so frankly shows) that does not mean that people suffer appreciably less under our benevolent but mechanized rule than they did under the Nazi Germans. Furthermore, we should err in supposing that we are very far removed from the spirit itself of the S. S. guards, since it has been shown (for instance in the book *Hitler in Ourselves*[2]) that even the Nazis were very charming in many of their relationships. The modern evildoer is not an ogre, he is a man who can snuff out the lives of five hundred Jews in a gas chamber and then go home to play with his children and eat a hearty lunch. Our president, who is more typical of us Americans than he is an outstanding, distinguished leader, bubbled over with glee on hearing, aboard ship, that we had finally dropped an atom bomb on Japan and that it was the "big success" that had been promised. Modern man may find an advocate to plead for him on Judgment Day that he knew not what he was doing, because he was so shallow and immature, or because of the discontinuity of his nature, but it is unlikely that he will try to rest his case on kindness.

If we can avert our eyes for a moment from the towering savageries of our day, there is an area nearer our personal and domestic lives

---

[1] Written by the Romanian author and eventual priest, Constantin Virgil Gheorghiu (1916–1992). — *Ed.*
[2] Written by Max Picard (1885–1965), a Swiss priest and author. — *Ed.*

nearly smothered in "kindness." We see it in the "permissive atmosphere" created by the psychiatrists and social workers in their relations with young delinquents. We see it in the "compassion" of those who favor euthanasia and birth control. We see it in the "conscientiousness" of progressive parents who impose neither discipline nor doctrine on their children, in the "automatic passing" of students from one grade to the next in school, in the "mercifulness" of the divorce court, and the anxiety of the psychoanalyst to rid his patient of the burden of "guilt feelings."

If men were dogs this symposium of benevolence would rightly be labeled kindness. But is it kind to treat men as though they were animals? Is it kind to act as though they were irrational, to behave toward them as though they were incapable of making moral decisions and to deny that their souls are immortal?

2. That there is less ignorance today. Almost everyone is literate. A college education is within the reach of all. Children can have the whole world brought to their living rooms by television.

But literacy is a tool for learning, not a proof of wisdom. And whereas very many people now go to college, at least in the United States, this is more because college standards have been lowered, and public funds appropriated for tuition, than because young people have been elevated.

It can be shown that on every level, from that of the erudite down to the simple, the power of thinking has greatly declined in the last several hundred years. To take the common man, he once (before he could read or write) went wild over Shakespeare. Now it is Jack Benny, or a quiz program, or the comics. Which fare is more nourishing? On a higher level, Saint Thomas, written for the equivalent of high school students, is beyond the capacity much less the interest of most university graduates.

The end-term of the "education made easy and interesting" movement favored by progressives is the little child wide-eyed in front of the television set. The world is now in his living room. The only trouble is that it doesn't make any sense—or rather that it doesn't make anything except "sense." Television presents a kaleidoscopic multitude of phantasms, the raw material for thinking (but a garden or a sea shore or even a multiplication table and some elementary history books would be more suitable raw material for the child-mind). Where are the principles with which to order these facts? Everyone has forgotten them. And where are the intellectual virtues and disciplines with which to process the knowledge and digest it? Atrophied for want of development. All the information in the world is useless for those who cannot think. Worse than useless — they will get a great big headache from undigested facts racing through their imaginations. They would be a lot better off herding some sheep in a remote valley somewhere, with nothing but some memorized psalms and tales of local history to dwell on.

3. That there is more equality today. Class distinctions are not so rigid as formerly. There is more chance to get ahead.

The sort of equality people have vaguely in mind when they exalt our supposed "classlessness" really means "equally rich," or "equally well-dressed," or "equally able to stay at the Waldorf." We certainly do aspire to this sort of equality, and some barriers between classes have been broken down. For instance, in the aristocratic society of the past it was even forbidden by law for a common man to ape the dress of the nobility, though he were able to get the money to do so. In fact a man's trade was indicated by his clothing. Now everyone dresses at least in the styles of the upper classes even though the materials and workmanship allow all degrees of difference. It is true too that anyone can aspire to be president, or a millionaire, and although not many succeed to these positions, the determining factor is not birth, nor even brains.

It is not an accident that alongside this breakdown of barriers is a degradation of standards. Everyone can go to college only when colleges have lost all pretension to scholarship. Anyone can be a political leader when statesmanship no longer exists. Even a Brooklyn gangster can edge his way into society when society has become cafe society. We shall never all be rich, but very likely we shall hit a dead level of destitution not long hence.

Equality in the sense of "classlessness" is a false ideal because it does not correspond with reality. Men are different from each other and unequal in their gifts. Therefore a society which is according to nature will be functional and hierarchical. Men are content not in a competitive world but in a world where each can occupy his own niche. This contentment breeds stability, and the fraternity which modern men hope vainly to find in equality. It is said of the Middle Ages that they "sacramentalized the inequalities of men," and it was at this time that the lord and the servant were on familiar terms, and queens and ladies personally tended the poor. Our present lords and leaders are almost infinitely removed from the proletariat, and even members of the same income bracket, as in the suburbs, live side-by-side but as strangers or superficial acquaintances.

4. That we have more knowledge of the physical universe and sovereignty over it.

Let us admit that the above statement is true, at least the first half of it, and examine its fruits. The claims naturally fall into several categories.

a) Modern science has vastly increased man's power through the use of steam, electricity and other sources of energy. This increase in power means the productivity per man is multiplied many times. In effect, it makes industrialism possible.

Remember that we are examining the goodness of our age. What has industrialism brought us? We have many more *things* than formerly. More dresses, more automobiles, more pots and pans. Our life is softer and easier from the point of view of the energy we have to exert. On the other hand most men have lost their economic independence. Almost all men have been robbed of satisfaction and creativity in their work. We have been integrated into our own complicated machinery rather than having it subserve us. Although there are many schemes abroad for making our lives more tolerable in accidental ways, there is no promise held out for the de-mechanization of our jobs. Therefore it would not be unfair to conclude that on the altar of industrialism we have sacrificed our humanity.

b) We have conquered time and space, through radio, airplanes and television.

Yes, we have. The question is whether or not this is a good thing. We cannot avoid seeing that these inventions serve, prospectively and historically, the forces of evil and tyranny much more readily than the forces of good. Let anyone who fails to see this read Orwell's *1984* and the other prophetic books of our time. Now if this is true, or rather since this is true, would it not be more logical to regard these wonderful inventions as stepping-stones to total tyranny rather than as proof of the magnificence of our age?

As far as the ordinary citizen is concerned the immediate effect of these inventions has been to step up the tempo of his living. Now he is always in a hurry. He has a multitude of things to take care of. He does not have time to think, still less to contemplate. Anyone who wishes to be a philosopher, or a writer, or a man of prayer or even just to avoid ulcers or to keep sane, has to cut through the complications of modern life as through a dense thicket. Human beings have a considerable power of adaptation but their whole nature cannot be changed, even to synchronize with a bright and speedy new world. Man is the measure.

c) There are several corollary claims which follow on the scientific inventions. One is that we have *more variety and refinement* in our possessions now.

We do have a deceptive semblance of variety, really only mechanical variation. We have a lot more foods, but they taste more and more alike, and alike tasteless. We change our dress styles every year, but uniformity and drabness in dress is nevertheless becoming global. Architecturally a similar process goes on. True variety is in nature and in human creativity, both of which are being stifled.

The "refinement" argument is rather easily refuted. It rests mostly on white bread and refined sugar, two injurious foodstuffs.

Similarly, people claim that we have *more comfort and convenience* in this age. Now comfort is the summit of the bourgeois ideal and there is no denying that it is a sort of characteristic of our day, with its cushioned rubber everything (including kneeling benches), and its overheated houses and air-conditioned theatres. It has never been regarded as particularly compatible with the Christian life, since it is a sort of blanket refusal of asceticism.

Our conveniences are mostly to compensate for the inconveniences of modern living. It is convenient to have a car — if you live ten miles from your work. It is convenient to have an elevator — if you can't live in a private house. It is convenient to have a washing machine — if you have no one to help you with the wash.

DIFFERENT COLORED GLASSES

One could go on arguing these and similar points, but it would take up too much space, and is a little unfair because the opposition does not have an opportunity to defend itself. The important thing is to see that two people, even two Christians (or even daily communicants) can look at the same modern circumstance, yet one bless and the other curse it. We hope we have analyzed some of these points enough to show that the critics of modern society are not just being negative, that they do not have a perverse attachment to primitiveness. Something is gained when evil is seen for what it is and what is gained is more truth, a nearer view of reality. It is not necessary to come up with a plan to save the world in order to exercise the privilege of showing that it needs saving. However, it would be useful, and intellectually constructive, to explore the framework in which the Christian criterion of an age can be drawn up.

THE CHRISTIAN CONTEXT

We must first of all see the meaning of history. Time unrolls. It begins at the creation of the world out of nothing. Then there is the beginning of man, the fall, the selection of the Jews as the chosen race, and their history in preparation for the coming of Christ. The Incarnation and the Redemption are the center of history, not the middle-point in years, but the focal point in meaning. After them comes the application of the fruits of the Redemption to successive generations and to all nations *until the number of the elect is filled.* Then time comes to an end. We are in that last period now. We do not know, and have no way of knowing, whether we are midway, just beginning or nearly finishing it. We do know from revelation that at some point in this period Satan will apparently triumph over the earth, in the brief but terrible reign of Anti-Christ.

Note several things about the above outline of history. First of all, it is an entirely supernatural framework. Within it men do not proceed from a state of crude cavemen of little intelligence to being intellectual and cultural giants. We should wipe out of our minds the popular evolutionary ideas which most of us have unconsciously absorbed, whereby we anticipate some sort of superman race of the future. Neither is there anything in this supernatural framework to suggest that we have to tear the physical universe apart and reorder it to our own ends. There just is no direct or necessary connection between scientific achievement and the "fulfilling of the number of the elect." Superficially it *looks* as though there might be a connection between say, television and the conversion of the Chinese. The only thing one can say for certain, though, is that we have to preach the Gospel and therefore we have to have some means of reaching all peoples, not saying what means.

We can also say on the basis of the above that absolutely speaking the years 1 to 33 were the best time of history because then God

Did We Never Have It So Good?

walked the earth, and that the worst time absolutely will be the reign of Anti-Christ, when even the elect will be deceived except for God's special help. Of other times we can say that each has its chronological position and its special work, which is at least partly bound up in mystery. Civilizations rise and fall, but history is not cyclical for all of that. The twentieth century is not the thirteenth century any more than the man is still a boy.

Let us get back to the theory that there is good and bad in every age, ours included. There is a sense in which this is true, but I think that sense is not what is ordinarily meant. My impression is that these people are thinking on a natural, even a material level. They want to pick and choose from a jumble of *things*, sorting out the washing machine in the "good" pile, the H bomb to the left in the "bad" pile. They want to lift out selected "good" articles from current magazines, while disregarding the pornography and trash. Now the badness of our age (to my mind) is not of that sort. It is more like a rotten egg beaten up with the cake batter and making the whole thing inedible. Or like a stink bomb put in the ventilating system.

Our badness consists of huge driving forces going in wrong directions (Freudianism, saturating everything with sex, or industrialism, turning us all into robots, for example), a pervasive false sense of values (materialism and the bourgeois spirit), a general lowering of all standards (naturalism, mediocrity), with naked evil showing through more and more clearly, rising out of the east and out of the west and even filtering up through the floor boards under our feet.

Where then is the *good* to be found? Contrary to popular opinion it does *not* reside in clever inventions or luxurious material standards of life. Neither is there very much of it in the ocean of sentimentality usually mistaken for a sea of good will, which is largely the disordered compassion of the multitudes of the mediocre.

The good is Christ-with-us, and practically nothing else. It is the Blessed Sacrament, hidden and silent and ubiquitous, and more powerful by far than the atom bomb. It is the inestimable privilege of daily Communion, which makes us strong to see the spiritual truths written in daily events. It is the charity of Christ, more beautiful than the sunsets and the landscapes and the flowers and the homes which our sins have destroyed—the charity of Christ in people, little ones and unexpected ones and previously unlovely ones, almost all of them ignored by the councils of great men.

The goodness is also in opportunity, in that little time and freedom which remains before the darkness descends. At least here in America we still have some liberty, and this is why we are lucky to be Americans, which really is a matter of luck and isolation rather than superior virtue. The opportunity is useful for only one thing, for making Christ known, converting hearts, trying to form some Christian institutions; for penance and the apostolate. For this reason alone we can thank God, as Pius XI did, that He makes us live among the present problems. But only on condition that we believe the second part of his statement, "It is no longer permitted to anyone to be mediocre."

The opportunity is also open to enjoy one last bountiful Thanksgiving, one more pagan Christmas, one more sensual indulgence, one last wardrobe of new clothes, or to buy a television set on time payments. If we indulge in these things we shall at the very least soon become mediocre, unsalted.

When the darkness finally closes in on us, as it has already closed in on much of the rest of the world, there will be only one good left, the goodness of Good Friday.

30

About Television

FEBRUARY 1951

THERE SEEMS TO BE A LAW OF DIMINISHING RESIS-tance, whereby people corrupt easier and quicker as progressive barriers come down. For instance if someone were to institute nude bathing, I would be surprised to find much general disapproval. Certainly nothing to compare with the hullabaloo said to have been aroused when women's skirts were originally raised above the ankles. Or remember all those years of discussion, disapproval and hand-wringing about "necking"? Sexual immorality has now reached the stage of wifely infidelity and homosexuality, but the public does not burst spontaneously into righteous alarm. Its moral sensitivity has been so blunted that the nicest people merely cluck over dispassionate socialized statistics of depravity.

To my mind this law of our deterioration explains why the curious institution of television has moved into millions of American homes without perceptible friction on the part of the householders, why deluxe sets were dangled without misgiving before the chance-takers at church bazaars. After George Orwell's "1984" one would expect people to have premonitions of Big Brother every time a picture flashed on their screen. But no. People had neither shame nor fear in purchasing their sets.

Even now as I write I can imagine my readers being astonished at my audacity in presuming to criticize television. I can hear them say, "This is too much! Now *Integrity* is going overboard! This surely is Jansenism! How negative can you get?" Perhaps they will even be wondering what anyone could say against television except perhaps to criticize the décolleté[1] of its female stars.

This is not a diatribe against television. It is a weighing of its value in the light of social circumstance. It is a closer look at the television clichés. The perspective may be new in places, but the originality of this article consists mostly in calling nonsense by its true name. The wife of a drunkard would not think of setting up a well-stocked bar

---

1   A low neckline on a woman's dress or top. — *Ed.*

preliminary to putting her husband on rations. Yet a million mothers of small children seem to think the key to rationing their offspring's televiewing is to buy a set of their own.

This criticism of television may be unpopular but it is extremely easy to make. In its order television is just about as obviously harmful as nude bathing is in its order. True, the morality is not so clear cut, but that does not mean that the consequences cannot be even more disastrous.

Let us trace the genealogy of television in the hope of discovering whether it is a little monster or a little prodigy. On its father's side it is the child of technology, grandchild of capitalism. On its mother's side it was conceived in the womb of despair, ignorance and dehumanization.

First then as to the siring of television. This can be made clearer by contrast with radio. When radio was invented, by the chance discovery of a scientific genius, people thought it a clever toy. No one thought of *using* it with any universality until it was discovered that it could be turned into an instrument of money-making through commercially-sponsored programs. So radio belongs to the capitalistic era, where the final criterion is profit, even though it is in itself technologically wonderful. Capitalism and technology are accomplices anyhow, and the eras of their respective supremacy are not always easy to separate. We know however that we have passed through an age in which money was the be-all and end-all, and that during this time big business men even suppressed the use of inventions which were to the common good, if they threatened financial disaster to existing companies. Most people sense that we are now entering another period in which the finality belongs to technological perfection and scientific progress. We *have* to have jet-propelled airplanes, just because men can invent and make them and not because anyone is really in that much of a hurry. Once we get them we can justify them as being useful in war, but since the enemy has them too, the result is only a speedier version of the same deadly flight. We had to have atomic power for the same reason. Here the huge expense was more clearly related to warfare (modern warfare has its own causal affinities with technology, just as previous wars had with capitalism, but that is not the subject of this article), as it is doubtful if Americans would have allowed the government to spend the money without that excuse, but it was in the cards even if there had been a delay.

It seems to me that television belongs more to this technological orientation than to capitalism. It was deliberately developed by huge teams of technicians to bring to perfection all the potentialities of the radio-type instrument. If sound can be brought into people's living rooms, why not pictures? And if pictures, why not colored pictures? And if the process works one direction, why shouldn't it work backwards, bringing the sights and sounds of the living room to a central police bureau? But maybe that isn't scientifically possible, and we will not have the sort of spy system Orwell described. Or maybe it is possible but belongs to the next era when technology will be superseded by a tyranny which will direct its development to the ends of the tyrant.

It is true that television has, apparently, an enormous money-making potential because its advertising can be made so vivid, though it is also enormously expensive to produce. I would guess that television would have come anyhow regardless of whether it would make money in the same ratio as radio. It had to come (because it was technologically possible), and if it wouldn't pay its own way, there would have been found some other way of supporting it. Through shortages of materials, or socialization of industry, it may happen that advertising income will not be available to television. We shall see then if it withers and dies.

THE MATERNAL ANCESTRY

Now about television's mother. She represents the passive principle, the receptivity of society to this new institution.

There is no doubt but that television was received by the public with amazing enthusiasm. It sold itself like hot cakes. The recent high-pressure and illegitimate advertising of television sets was apparently related to an overstock of manufacturers' output in the face of threatened technological improvements. It was not needed to make people buy television so much as to make them buy now rather than wait until later.

We said above that the mother of television was despair, dehumanization and attendant ills. Modern man has universally certain characteristics. He has a dull, uncreative job, while his talents go undeveloped. He lacks that self-control and self-possession, the fruit of spiritual training, which would enable him to work his way out. He lacks an education which would have given him breadth or bearings. He has no home life, or a bitterly unhappy one. He takes no real part in community life. He is largely separated from the outdoors and wholesome participation in sports. He has no hope of essentially bettering his condition. If he saves money the government gets it. If he finds an apartment it is smaller than the last one. If he gets another job it is the same as the last one.

What does he want, then, more than anything else? Something to make him forget how unsatisfactory his life is. Something to dull the pain of his living. If it has a slight kick — if it titillates his senses, so much the better. In a word, television is made to order.

Does anyone seriously dispute this? The best concrete evidence is the irrefutable fact that television sold the best and the fastest and the earliest, not to those who could best afford it, or whose cultural interests were the greatest, but to those who could afford it least, *but needed it the most*, the urban proletariat, whose lives are the most dehumanized and deprived of all.

At the other extreme there is a small body of people who have a deep spirituality, or a creative occupation, or an intellectual or cultural interest, or whose family life is deep and satisfying, to whom it would never occur to get a television set. Where those who have sets lead, or come to lead, more human or especially more Christian lives, the sets are used only once in a while for particularly good programs. These people can take it or leave it. They are certainly not typical. The usual television family finds televiewing as necessary to the daily routine as eating and sleeping.

THE TRUE NATURE OF TELEVISION

In effect, the television is an opiate. It is spiritual dope for deadening the pain of modern living. It is the marijuana of the masses and the opium of the people.

Television has all the characteristics of a powerful narcotic, but it works on the spirit of man rather than on his body. That is fitting, for his intolerable pain is of his soul. First of all television is narcotic in that it is a pain-killer. Where there is physical pain the hurt can be stopped at wither of two places, the locus of the wound, or *the brain*, for bodily harm has in a sense to be understood, to communicate knowledge of itself to the higher centers in the brain, before it can be felt. This principle can be illustrated by the power deeply spiritual or strong-willed people have to endure pain. If they can divert the entire attention of their minds from their pain, the pain will cease, and in proportion as they succeed it will diminish. When Saint Lawrence said the heat of charity which consumed him kept him from feeling the flames, it was much the same thing on a supernatural level.

So some pain-killers paralyze or soothe the hurt place, others cut off the communication of hurt to the nerve centers of the brain. The general effect of narcotics is in the brain area. They induce a stupor, a sort of sleep, a dulling of the brain, which prevents the pain from registering. With television it is the same way. It does not make the unhappy marriage happy, or the job creative; it does not give hope, but it does give forgetfulness. This it does through its tremendous, almost hypnotic power of centering the attention of a person on the screen. It is like a huge distraction. It keeps pictures racing through the mind so fast that the power of *thinking*, the contact of the mind with reality, is virtually suspended through not being able to intrude on the person's attention.

Anything that magnifies or enchants the senses can be turned to this illegitimate use. Music can purify the emotions and subserve the intellect and the spirit, as good music does, or it can be like a siren, enslaving the higher faculties. A play or movie can give a deeper understanding of life, catharize the emotions and lift up the spirit, or it can deaden a man's discouragement by removing him from reality for a couple of hours. The contradiction that exists in the movie industry today is really because people want two mutually exclusive things from cinema-going. The critics and the moralists and the artists want the movies to show great pictures to stir the souls of men. But the masses of routine, undiscriminating movie-goers are without realizing it in search of oblivion. They want a lot of pictures which are mildly distracting and titillating, but they don't want to be lifted up, awakened and ennobled. They want stupor and their mass inertia makes a powerful impact on the heads of movie companies, who are New York financiers who care neither for art nor stupor, but only for money. The point about the movies is that they can be used as a narcotic, and because many people have used them this way the production of pictures has been profoundly influenced. As a result the routine production of Hollywood can be classed as dope.

Similarly radio is more in the nature of a narcotic than movies (and is so used by millions of soap opera fans), but is less powerful because it has only auditory appeal. Television has all the power of sound and sight, along with the advantage of being in the home and available at all waking hours. It is a "natural" for spiritual narcosis and in fact it fell at the psychological moment right into that opening that the decay of modern society provided.

Several other characteristics of narcotics have their parallel in television. Everyone knows that the Chinese opium smoker, seemingly so quiet and lifeless in his "den," is really having roseate dreams. Dope fires the imagination, greatly stimulating the natural power of day-dreaming. Some narcotics overwhelm the imagination so powerfully that the addicts commit crimes under their influence. So it is with television, especially with respect to children, who have nightmares, who cannot study, and to whom the real world looks endlessly prosaic by contrast with the television screen. The adolescent is also very much influenced, as he is also by the movies. He, or more likely she, imagines and desperately longs for the glamorous life brought in on the television screen. Nobody will deny that the standard of values actually reflected by television is incredibly base (to wear immodest clothes, to go to the Stork Club every night, is to live in a world of irresistible glamor), but few people realize that television is much better able to portray this false world than sound ideals of morality or sanctity. Spiritual goodness looks like folly to the worldly-minded, to those who have not passed through an asceticism of the senses. But even so it is more faithfully portrayed by books, which convey ideas, that by pictures.

Finally, narcotics are habit-forming, and so is television. Anyone who wants to hold that television is just a clever invention, useful for entertainment or education, will be hard put to explain why the usual television owner is drawn daily to his screen as the drug-addict is to his hypodermic needle. Why is it that Americans as a body virtually have abandoned the most elementary rules of hospitality and courtesy, and follow a pattern of beckoning their guests into a darkened room, there to ignore them for the rest of the evening. These same people would willingly put aside something which was merely pleasant. They would not turn away the Joneses because they had planned to go to bed early that night. "Pardon us if we don't ask you in, Mr. and Mrs. Jones, but Helen and I are pretty tired and we thought we'd go to bed early tonight." "Oh, it's you, Mr. Jones! How nice of you to come over. I'm sorry I won't be able to talk to you, as I'm in the middle of a very interesting book." Of course no one would say these things. But the compulsive-drinker won't stop getting drunk for the Joneses' sake and neither will the television addict abandon his screen. "My father is turning into a vegetable," one of our friends said. "He just sits watching that screen every night." A visit to the dens of Chinatown, if they still have any, or to those of Harlem, would reveal men and women in a parallel stupor.

It is because dope is habit-forming that money is no consideration. Narcotics are expensive and the money is always forthcoming, even if it has to be got by theft. So far as I know, no one steals to buy a television set, but certainly the majority of television sets cost out of all proportion to what families can afford. Mrs. Smith may not have been able to save enough money for a new dress (at $20), but she has to have television (at $200). Mr. Smith may be already heavily in debt, but he will get a set on time payments. Neither of the Smiths would have acted so imprudently in the purchase of a house or in getting money to educate their children. These last are desirable things, but not accompanied by a compulsive drive that overrides reason.

THE MORALITY OF TELEVISION

We have tried to show that television is by its nature an opiate, and if this is granted it follows that television is in about the same moral position as morphine, that is, dangerous for general usage. Of course you cannot press this comparison too far, and here the comparison breaks down. You can say that morphine is good when used medically as an opiate under appropriate conditions. You cannot say that television is ever good as an opiate because whereas it is good sometimes to dull bodily pain by stupor, the pain of the soul is best relieved in other ways, by prayer, consolation, absolution, music, hope, humor or distractions of an innocent and non-habit-forming nature.

The whole evaluation of television centers around this question of its nature. The argument is between those who hold, as we do, that television is an opiate and therefore essentially bad (though accidentally and occasionally it may have a good program of a stimulating nature—to be essentially bad doesn't mean to be totally bad), and those who hold that television is a neutral instrument which can be turned to good or bad uses.

In making our judgment we consider television to be a certain combination of men, material, money, talent and machines working together for a common end. For want of a better word we would call television an institution. Its nature, its essence is determined by the chief reason for the collaboration of all the diverse elements involved.

Is this the desire to spread truth? Obviously not. Is it avarice? That is the personal motive of many of the people involved, perhaps the majority, but there are gross, uneconomical or extra-economical factors involved in television. Is it technological perfection then? Technology is the inclined platform down which television is rolling, but in itself it is a mechanical impetus, sub-human, and therefore an insufficient explanation. The need for dope in a dehumanized society is a better explanation. This is the human situation that provided the inertia which is the major reason for television's growth. The promotors more or less unconsciously corresponded with the inarticulate demand.

Those who hold the "neutral" view regard television as a material gadget, a little box in the living room capable of wonderful things. But looking at television from this narrow material viewpoint you fail to account for most things about it. You cannot even explain how it got in everyone's living room.

This same difference in ways of judging modern society divides Catholics on a whole series of issues, including rhythm, industrialism and advertising. Our opponents are always divesting the subject under consideration of its meaning before examining its morality. They break rhythm down into isolated acts and omissions which can be attributed the sustained purpose of not having children. That purpose belongs to the series of acts and omissions, considered as series. Similarly, industrialism becomes machinery, rather than a particular *arrangement* of men and machines whereby the former is subordinated to the latter.

We are trying to discern the ordering principles of the configurations of society. It is not so much the *matter* of society that is undergoing change as it is the *arrangement* of the elements of society. And it is this ordering which has to be judged if we are going to prevent a bad order's being superseded by a worse one. As long as we decline to tangle with these essences and orders we will find a way to justify every new maneuver of the atheist synthesis, until the day that we wake up to find ourselves strangled.

* * *

Let us now approach the subject of television from other directions, taking as our springboard the usual arguments in favor of its use or reform.

THE "GROUND FLOOR" ARGUMENT

One hears it said that we Catholics must make haste to get into television on the ground floor, as we failed to do in radio. The supposition is that television is a powerful instrument of communication just standing there waiting for whoever is alert and clever enough to turn it to his own uses. It is assumed that, if television ends up making people more pagan instead of more Christian, the world will have been lost by default on our part. It is maintained that this is what happened with radio. Why, right now the Catholics can have any amount of time on television, if they will only take the trouble, etc.

Now if two men have very different purposes, even clashing ones, their sporadic co-operation is going to be an uneasy one. It's the same way with institutions. Let us take the case of radio, where the case is more clear-cut than with television because more in retrospect (although the case is probably even stronger with television). Radio as an institution has as its consuming interest the making of money. The Church's consuming interest is the salvation of souls. These two ends are unrelated, if not inimical to each other. The meeting point of the Church and radio is that radio-waves are considered to be in the public domain, so falling under federal regulation. Stations are expected to make a gesture at least of public service, which includes giving some air-time to religion. They were happier to do this in the early days when sponsors were scarce. Now they are trying to crowd the religious programs out. The working partnership of religion and radio will continue to be artificially sustained, but their tendency to destroy each other will also continue to exist under surface politeness.

What is true of radio is even more true of television. The programs on television are still under the auspices of the advertising business, even though their audience wants not so much now to be entertained as to be kept from thinking. Anyone who seriously tries to make a general secular program thought-provoking will be working against the grain. People do not look to their opiates for activation. Personally I don't think there is much hope of "cleaning up" television programs from within either. Anyone who removed the off-color stories and the V-necklines from television programs would be working against the best interests (that is the financial interests) of the sponsors, and so against his own professional advancement. Recent history shows that outside censorship, or the threat thereof, is a much more effective controlling factor.

Where we have failed in radio to a certain extent, and may fail in television, is in not making the best possible use of the time extended us through the courtesy of the stations under the pressure of the Federal Communications Commission. These little opportunities do not belie the fact that the orientation of radio is to money, television to narcosis, but show that there are small free areas reserved to the common good. We cannot hope in such isolated instances to outweigh or nullify the effect of the institutions as a whole, but we ought to make the most of what opportunity offers. The mistake to which we are tempted is that of watering down our message to mediocrity or secularism, in imitation of the general error of all mass-media.

THE OPPORTUNISTIC ARGUMENT

Back of many people's desire to make the best apostolic use of television possible, is an unconscious assumption that providence's designs will fit into man's master plan. We have a marvelous instrument of communication. It must follow that God plans to use it, with our help, to spread the Gospel. Why does it follow? Maybe He plans it and maybe He doesn't. But it is generally assumed that His ways are our ways. Once that assumption is made it follows as a corollary that we should strive to maneuver ourselves into "positions of influence," which means into the key positions for blaring forth the world's wisdom.

But let us examine the premise. God has specifically revealed to us that His ways are not our ways, and that furthermore His will generally manifests itself as a sign of contradiction to us. God, picking out a *spokesman* for Israel, chose a man who stuttered—Moses. Looking for someone to help along the missions, He singled out a sheltered young daughter of the French *bourgeoisie*, and then he put her in a cloistered convent in Lisieux. Our Lady wishing to communicate an important message to the human race chose a cloistered nun, a handful of children here and another handful there, making sure that the places were remote and inaccessible. To channel His message and the royal ancestry of Our Lord through His chosen people God used the branch that was exiled in Babylon and had to find its way back after many years, rather than those who remained in Palestine. If we take these and a thousand like examples into consideration, we will not be over-anxious about television. We will not feel that if we miss our chance here, God will be in a dilemma. Rather we should remind ourselves that God seems to have a predilection for foolish and unlikely instruments. We ought not to be surprised if He disregards the airplane and sends a crippled envoy around in a wheel chair. We should be prepared for Him to bypass television and radio, commentators, dictators and statesmen to single out, for instance, some unknown Finlander who speaks none other than his native language and communicates with the world by letter.

No one can understand God and we should perhaps be as presumptuous to exclude television as others are unconsciously presumptuous in assuming God will use it. Nevertheless there is one other thing which needs saying against the fittingness of television. Chesterton long ago pointed out that there is an inverse ratio between what contemporary men have to say and their power to say it. I doubt this ironical fact is mere chance. It is common experience that the more important one's message, the less need it has of artificial means of transmission. News of a good and important product passes rapidly from housewife to housewife, whereas bad and unnecessary stuff needs wide advertising. What saints have to say can be lost in a trunk for one hundred years or published obscurely and unattractively by a mediocre press in some remote corner — and sell a million copies. God's birth in Bethlehem had no fanfare, nor was it needed. His death on Calvary was hardly heeded by the Roman Empire. Yet it transformed the world. Holy men and women run away from the world, and the world beats a path to their door. Father Lombardi reaches and transforms hundreds of thousands of people, not because he uses radio or television, but because he spends five hours a day in prayer and practices heroic poverty — so having something to say.

We seem to have forgotten that holiness has a power of attraction unlike anything on earth. If we were preoccupied as Catholics with learning and living the truth and with doing what needs doing in the apostolate, we could forget about whether or not the world would know. In fact we would have to spend our time fighting off publicists. Many of us have become so preoccupied with how our good deeds will come to the attention of the general public that we can't concentrate on making these good deeds heroic acts of charity. We are so concerned to reach a nation-wide audience that what we have to say turns out not to be very exciting.

In other words, if we were better we wouldn't need television, the ordinary means of communication would be quite sufficient. It is only when men have little or nothing to say that they have to shout and vivify it. Radio and television bear witness to the world's emptiness. What are these things to us?

Yet the Holy Father uses radio and television and so can we legitimately use it when the occasion arises. But that does not mean we should put our hope in these things or unconsciously assume that God depends on them. It ought not to bother us if radio, television, airplanes and atomic power were wiped out tomorrow. God does not need them. A world tyrant certainly does. If would be very unfortunate if Catholics would fight to sustain the props of a coming world dictatorship, just because now and again these things have served to get a priest to a dying Eskimo or to bring the Pope's voice halfway around the world. Let us rather use these things as though we used them not.

THE CULTURE AND EDUCATION ARGUMENT

If radio had been just an invention and not a vehicle of the advertisers ordained to the end of making money, it would have been very useful as a tool of adult education. It could have taught people French at home. Housewives could have listened to the reading of great books while they did their ironing. The municipal station in New York, WNYC, is rather like this, and by far the best station in the country to my mind. But radio has failed ingloriously to fulfill its educational potentialities.

There are some people who do not agree that radio missed the boat here. Their attitude is well reflected in the public statements of the late Walter Damrosch, and centers around music. He said:

> I do not have to tell you of the miracle that radio has worked in this country. The results have been awe-inspiring. Beethoven and Bach as well as Wagner and Verdi have brought their music into the humblest and remotest dwellings.

Well there is some truth in this, and it is to the credit of the better radio stations that they have sustained symphony orchestras through a sense of public responsibility. Nevertheless the audience for serious music remains small, although of an elite nature. Nor is this accomplishment wholly a good thing.

Most people are confused about music. They think that because it is serious it must be good, which is like thinking that *New York Times* must be a good paper because it is so hard to read. A lot of modern serious music is discordant, offensive to the ears, and violates the "right reason" that there should be in music.

Many so-called music lovers are really idolaters. Their emotions are profoundly moved by music and they mistake this for religious fervor. "*Music* is my religion," one hears them say. This is an idolatry that Walter Damrosch shared. Listen to him:

> Realizing the joys that music can bring to men, I have done my utmost to spread its gospel. Today as never before the world stands in need of music. The machine age, with its opportunities for increased leisure, demands means of employing that leisure to advantage. Healthful sports are necessary but so also is something that will satisfy the spiritual craving. Music fulfills this desire.

Let the culture-vultures rejoice in their music. The ordinary housewife and working man who would have a desire for intellectual self-improvement if they were in normal circumstances, need a profound spiritual reconstruction. And this, I believe radio (with television) is quite unable to give them. A particularly good sermon will strike home to a few, but what people need especially is to shed their own *passivity*. Five housewives who form a group to discuss their common problems along the see-judge-act lines are beginning to capture the initiative in their own lives. Radio and television cannot give them this sense of community and responsibility, and all the brains and talent in the world cannot compensate for its absence.

IT'S HERE TO STAY

I've heard this said ("It's here to stay") about television in France, where it's just beginning to come in and therefore not "here" yet. I've also heard it said about industrialism under similar circumstances. And of course about industrialism in America. What people mean really is that television and industrialism and etcetera are inevitable and irresistible. Now if there is one thing that's here to stay in that same sense, it's artificial birth control.

Let Catholics dwell on that for a while, and they will see that there are some pressures which must be resisted even when they seem overwhelming.

As a matter of fact much of the power of the militant atheists today consists in nourishing a general belief that it would be useless to oppose them. In this way they often persuade people to lay down their arms before the attack is made. Or at least people are persuaded to make a bad peace with the new conditions. Industrialism is a very sad example. It has had the effect of dehumanizing people and destroying the vocational and creative nature of their work. Seeing this, nearly everyone is willing to accept industrialism and the world which it brings in its wake. Most Catholic leaders have also thrown in the glove, which is odd because it means that they have acquiesced to a world order which isn't the one God ordained. They think thereby to conserve their energy to compensate for the evil in accidental ways—like Walter Damrosch and his music. But instead they find themselves having to capitulate to a whole series of innovations. Television is one of these. Its hypnotic effect on people is partly the result of their dehumanized work-lives. Under the circumstances it is probably rightly thought that an all-out battle against the television soporific is liable to be a losing one. But in so far as it is a losing effort, so much the more inevitable and horrible will be the internal collapse that this entire unnatural order is building up for itself.

WHAT SHALL WE DO ABOUT TELEVISION?

When we ask this question we must realize that there is a sense in which it is meaningless. We don't own television so we are not in a position to dispose of it. People who ask, in a similar vein, "What shall we do about industrialism?" make the same unconscious mistake. They feel they ought to find an answer that would be useful if they owned all the factories—a master plan for transforming or reducing industry. It is from this false start that the ambition arises, on the part of lay apostles no less than, even if later than, on the part of the communists, to *get control* of industrialism, so that they can put the master plan into effect. What will the communists do with industrialism when they take over? Canonize it, use it to sustain their power and to enforce their own odd idea of beatitude, a materialistic paradise. What will lay apostles do with industrialism? Either they don't know yet, or they think they will decentralize and humanize manufacture, not realizing that it will then be too late.

Christianity doesn't have to get control of the world before it can start operating. It works the other way around, planting seeds, spreading charity, teaching and contradicting the world in little ways until it grows and fills the earth (allowing for setbacks from the powers of darkness). Christian social action should do likewise. If the plan can't begin now but must wait until it gets power, control and ownership, we ought to regard it with great suspicion.

It would be better to ask, "What shall we do *in the face* of television?" Then the answer is easy: RESIST IT.

As apostles we are in a position to do something directly about the conditions which make television possible. We have a way of treating the despair, the spiritual disorders and the uncreative work, even if only on a small scale for each of us or each group of us. It is difficult for us to do this work now, but it will be virtually impossible once the human pain has been deadened by the powerful new drug. To the extent that we resist television ourselves, so much the more apostolic zeal will we possess. To the extent we can persuade others to resist also, so much the more possible will it be to get through to them with the Good News.

Let no one say that the advice to resist television is being negative. The absence of television is no more a negation than sobriety is. It is more like the minimum condition of receptivity to the words of salvation.

31
Religious Fanaticism

APRIL 1951

How readily the accusation of fanaticism is made (most often by parents) against anyone who wishes to be more than perfunctorily pious or zealous in his religion today. It falls like a mechanical anathema upon those who practice voluntary poverty or otherwise seriously cross the conventions of worldliness. Lay apostles feel it even more than religious do because they, having more recently arrived on the scene, are less respectable. Fanaticism is the popular term. The more learned among the advocates of moderation are also more specific, intermingling charges of Jansenism, rigorism, and perfectionism with such colorful expressions as "crackpot."

It is against a background of this tirade, sometimes loud and close at hand, sometimes faint and muffled in the background of my work and association, that I approached Monsignor Knox's great book on *Enthusiasm*.[1] It is the long (600 pages) sad tale of the zealous who become zealots, of fanatics through the ages.

Thirty years, off and on, have gone into the writing of this book. It is impossible not to admire the result. Other men seem to have eaten their intellectual food raw and in haste by comparison with the manner in which Monsignor Knox has fed his mind. There is a maturity, a mellowness, a balance and an artistry about his scholarship which is delightful. Here is substance and truth and fairness from a man who knows his subject thoroughly. There is also a dry humor running through the pages. The writing is so lucid, so precise and effortless, that I can well imagine the book being used as a model for students of the English language (as it certainly ought to be as a model of historical scholarship).

One of the things that impressed me most was the mood of the book. Monsignor Knox is never beating some pet idea of his to death. He has the detachment of the scholar. Yet he is very much there too,

---

[1] *Enthusiasm, A Chapter in the History of Religion with Special Reference to the XVII and XVIII Centuries.* R. A. Knox, Oxford University Press. (It has been republished several times since it was first published in 1950 — *Ed.*)

nor is he afraid to say whether or not he admires some of the characters involved. Yet he never believes anything worse about them than the facts establish and he consistently refrains from final pronouncements, thus leaving many things unresolved. In the last chapter he says he is not concerned to *criticize* but to *interpret* enthusiasm. I felt that only a man of great charity and virtue could have delved so deep and judged so little, could have shown so much restraint. Certainly by temperament Monsignor Knox cannot be inclined towards fanaticism. The sympathy he evidently has for these ill-directed conflagrations can be better explained by his own confession (in *A Spiritual Aeneid*) that he has ever been attracted to the defense of lost causes. So it happens that he does not end up saying, in effect, "Isn't it a pity that the Church has had to suffer so much from people who went off the deep end," or that "The moral of this tale is to beware of too much zeal." The French quotation with which he finishes the book suggests rather the biblical injunction, "Be ye hot or cold, for the lukewarm I will spit out of my mouth."

Enthusiasm deals only with aberrations *in a certain direction*. The opposite direction from worldliness. It begins with the Corinthians whose wayward tendencies are mentioned in Saint Paul's first letter to them. Enthusiastic tendencies, it seems, have been with the Church from the beginning. Often the same errors, exaggerations and practices persisted for long periods, now dormant, now come again to life. The movements were largely underground during the Middle Ages. The Quakers and the Anabaptists, the Moravians and the Methodists are Protestant manifestations of enthusiasm. The great Catholic examples to which Monsignor Knox gives most of his attention are Jansenism and Quietism. This account largely closes around the year 1800 with only a few nineteenth-century references to show that enthusiasm didn't die suddenly. I was rather disappointed it wasn't brought up to date, but Monsignor Knox thinks that, at least in England, the phenomenon has most disappeared in the last century.

WHAT IS ENTHUSIASM?

Enthusiasm is a *tendency* and not a specific doctrine or mode of behavior. It is the opposite tendency from worldliness and laxity. It is hard to define but easy to discern (long after the event at any rate). Here is how Monsignor Knox attempts to express it.

> ...There is, I would say, a recurrent situation in Church history—using the word "Church" in the widest sense—where an excess of charity threatens unity. You have a clique, an élite, of Christian men and (more importantly) women, who are trying to live a less worldly life than their neighbors; to be more attentive to the guidance (directly felt, they would tell you) of the Holy Spirit. More and more, by a kind of fatality, you see them draw apart from their co-religionists, a hive ready to swarm. There is provocation on both sides; on the one part, cheap jokes at the expense of over-godliness, acts of stupid repression by unsympathetic authorities; on the other, contempt of the half-Christian, ominous references to old wine and new bottles, to the kernel and the husk. Then, while you hold your breath and turn away your eyes in fear, the break comes; condemnation or secession, what difference does it make? A fresh name has been added to the list of Christianities.

It is in the light of contemporary religious trends and problems that I should like to discuss only a very few of the many interesting subjects raised by this book. My selection is determined by my own mental meanderings and does not necessarily follow the relative emphasis placed on the subjects by Monsignor Knox.

ULTRASUPERNATURALISM

Monsignor Knox remarks that "If I could have been certain of the reader's good will, I would have called my tendency 'ultrasupernaturalism.' For that is the real character of the enthusiast; he expects more evident results from the grace of God than we others." A few paragraphs further he says, "at the root of it (enthusiasm) lies a different theology of grace."

In other words, the whole problem centers around the problem of the relationship between nature and grace. Lean too far to one side and you become a naturalist, too far to the other and you become an ultrasupernaturalist, wanting grace to do all the work. The Moravians, for example, with the New Testament precedent of one example of sortilege (choosing a successor to Judas) made drawing lots the rule rather than the exception. Even marriages and particularly elections were to be decided in this fashion. Again it shows itself in temptations to theocracy, the identification of Church and State, or the contention that Christians, being under a new law, are exempt from civil or parental authority and only obey magistrates or parents, when they do, as a matter of courtesy.

If there are aberrations on this point in the Church today I think they are likely to break out with respect to God's providence and the matter of vocation. It is easy to presume that God will take care of one as He does the lilies of the field and the birds of the air, without one's moving a muscle, especially a muscle of the brain. Yet God does take care of people who trust Him and who seek first the kingdom of Heaven and who are not necessarily efficient according to the world's standards. Furthermore, it *is* necessary to react strongly against the complete lack of trust in God manifested by a world maniacally intent on security.

With respect to finding one's vocation there is often an element of superstition. It is so difficult to gauge the times, so hard to find one's place in a chaotic world that people understandably prefer to consult fortune tellers or seek a mystic.

By and large the ordinary Catholic way of meeting the problem of the relationship between grace and nature today is to duck it. Sunday, grace—weekdays, nature. Or as in many Catholic papers and magazines, the solution is to juxtapose the two, serving up a potpourri of secular stories and articles along with a few pious meditations and maybe a question box. It is probably because *Integrity* meets the problem of nature and grace head-on that it is in some quarters suspected of "ultrasupernaturalism" or "exaggerated supernaturalism." As a matter of fact, we are following as clearly as we can the Thomistic line of reasoning on this matter, and so far as we know have not departed from it.

ANTINOMIANISM

Antinomianism is one of the many new words I learned from reading *Enthusiasm*. It is the doctrine that Christians are not bound by the moral law (being above it) and it appears with amazing regularity in the course of history. People get the idea that they are saved, or converted, or justified by faith, so they cannot sin any more. Ergo they need not take the precautions against temptation that other people take. Nudist cults are apt to grow up. As a matter of fact, contemporary secular nudists probably suffer from a non-religious version of antinomianism. It's a nasty business which often starts with a sort of angelism and ends with an orgy. Father Divine's followers, having been elevated to a new state, forego sex and live in brother's dormitories and sisters' dormitories. I am sure Monsignor Knox was not surprised when Father Divine ("God" himself) married. Of course it was a purely spiritual marriage, nothing carnal involved. An old, old story.

The reason I mention antinomianism here is not because I see it hovering around the lay apostolate (quite the contrary) but because in an extenuated way it seems to be a modern non-Catholic phenomenon. I do not say a Protestant phenomenon, though it is implicit in Luther's and Calvin's doctrines if they are pushed to their logical conclusions, and John Wesley fought hard against the possibility of it among his associates. However, I am thinking more of the wishful-thinking type of cult or the pseudo-mystical, such as Unity, Christian Science, and the Swamis. Are not these, apart from their doctrinal aberrations, unmoral, unethical? Do they ever talk about cheating in business or having one wife?

A religion which harps on morality all the time is not very attractive, and creates a yearning for contemplation. As a matter of fact, we are now entering a "mystical" period. All the more reason therefore to beware of thinking ourselves beyond the necessity of cultivating virtue, even or especially natural virtue, and falling into undisciplined habits. Incidentally poor Saint Augustine, who seems to have lent himself unwittingly to the self-justification of heretics so often, here furnishes a convenient slogan for misinterpretation: "Love and do what you will."[2]

CONVULSIONS AND CHARISMATA

After reading this book I felt very sympathetic toward people who have a horror of being religiously demonstrative, especially non-Catholics. This for the reason that I was reminded of how recent were their own unhappy experiences, or their parents', with revivalism of one sort or another. I can see why they are content with church services which, though dull, are dignified and why they are apprehensive when their children "get religion" with a fervor attached to it. The human race, it seems, inclines to be explosive and its favorite field for detonation is the religious one. The Church can usually contain and direct this dynamite. Outside the Church it is far less easily controlled.

---

[2] Often translated as *Ama et fac quod vis* or *Dilige et quod vis fac*—Homilies on the First Epistle of John; Tractatus VII, 8, *In epistolam Ioannis ad Parthos.—Ed.*

All the aberrations suffer from it sooner or later. The Quakers started with quaking and ended up conservative and soft-spoken. The Jansenists began in a dignified, intellectual, even aristocratic manner and ended up with the convulsions of the Cemetery of Saint-Médard, the nine-day wonder of Paris. Anyone could go see for himself "men falling like epileptics, others swallowing pebbles, glass, and even live coals, women walking feet in air... You heard nothing but groaning, singing, shrieking, whistling, declaiming, prophesying, caterwauling. Women and girls who played a great part in these exhibitions, excelled in capers, in somersaults, in feats of suppleness. Some of them twirled around on their feet with lightning quickness of dervishes; others turned head over back, or stood on their hands in such a way that their heels almost touched their shoulders." And so on.

A little later, and in England, convulsive phenomena accompanied the early Methodist preachers. John Wesley, who was very interested in preternatural phenomena and who recorded all this sort of thing in his journal, had convulsives in his congregations much more often than today's Methodists like to admit. He wasn't a wildly emotional speaker either. Yet it frequently happened that he had a few men or women (more often women, as usual) in a swoon at his feet, or shaking, with characteristic swellings of throat or intestines and possibly making interesting noises as well.

Monsignor Knox inquires only a little into the nature of these odd phenomena, it not being strictly on his point. Are they caused by hysteria, the Devil, charlatanry, or are they real religious experiences? Or are they a mixture, and if so, in what proportion? It's a fascinating subject but, as aforesaid, he doesn't go very deeply into it, though he does give enough facts to show how difficult the matter is to resolve. For instance, those who watched the Saint-Médard Cemetery goings-on described above, reported that they felt definitely elevated spiritually by the spectacle.

A number of enthusiasts had private visions, or revelations, or heard voices, or so they said. It is a private phenomenon not open to investigation. Occasionally but rarely there were claims of messiahship, even by women.

The Pentecost phenomenon "speaking with tongues" is one of those charismatic gifts like prophesy which was quite common among the early Christians, but very rare thereafter. Speaking with unknown tongues is one of the signs of diabolic possession, but the collective claim to such powers which crops up among the enthusiasts is not necessarily accounted for in this manner. An interesting point is that the strange languages spoken by Pentecostals of various sorts need not be an existent language. The claim is made that what is humanly unintelligible is one of the "tongues of angels."

Revivalism and the more spectacular charismatic phenomena have been diminishing in England now for quite a while. Monsignor Knox is aware that all sorts of religious curiosities continue to exist on this side of the Atlantic. Anything can happen in America. Here is where all the eccentrics and free thinkers have always come to roost. The "land of the free" was the refuge of every queer religion. Monsignor Knox doesn't press his point, but his occasional references are devastating enough. I am not disposed to argue with him. Ours is the land of the Mormons, the Pentecostals, the Jehovah Witnesses, a variety of utopian settlements, Father Divine, a million dollar business in astrology, Wall Street brokers who play the market according to the directives of their "mediums," and the rash of phony religious religions found in Los Angeles and elsewhere. Revivalism of the more unrestrained emotional sort was the childhood experience of many non-Catholics over fifty.

There is this to be said, however, and Monsignor Knox hints at it too. The fervor and emotionalism and fanaticism of today has moved beyond the orbit of Christianity almost entirely, and so does not really qualify as "enthusiasm." The people involved are of lower and lower intelligence, far less civilized. Their movements are on the borders of diabolism, of real degenerate paganism, with all its obscenities and superstitions. Huge numbers of people seem to be sinking into that hideous darkness from which Christianity over so many centuries raised men and purified them.

The Holy Father has warned us that we are entering a great age of superstition, a by-product of industrialism. There is thirst for the miraculous, an eager credulity abroad. Look what happened at Necedah.[3] The pendulum is swinging again. That cold unbelieving rationalism which would not admit the cures of Lourdes to be genuine, even though it saw them, has vanished, and people are ready to believe anything and everything at tenth hand on the basis of the flimsiest

---

[3] In reference to the so-called Marian apparitions given to Mary Ann Van Hoof (1909–1984) in Necedah, Wisconsin between 1949–1950. These were deemed false by the local bishop. —*Ed.*

rumor. Superstition can do a great deal of harm to the Fatima message by regarding it as a magic formula instead of realizing that, simple as it seems on the surface, it involves a real change of life. The danger is not here just from simple people but even more from what we could call "unintegrated" members of the upper classes whose vested interest in conformity to the world is very great, and who are unconsciously searching for a "devotion" on which to spend their energies.

I wonder if Monsignor Knox would agree with me that a lot of human ardor which formerly would have led to sanctity or, if warped, have resulted in religious fanaticism, now served communism. I suppose he would agree. The same intensity is there. The same impatience with mediocrity and temporizing. There also is the great vision of the New Jerusalem, the idealistic, the total sacrifice and dedication. The fact that the reform of the social order is the preoccupation of the communists lends their movement an earthly basis, seemingly incompatible with superstition, charismata, emotional orgies and the other more spectacular manifestations of enthusiasm. However, if we can learn anything from Monsignor Knox's admirable history, it is that the tougher they are the harder they fall. We ought not to be surprised then if the communists suffer a sudden change to credulity, if they start performing "miracles," if they have visions, and if they take to writhing on the ground in convulsions to honor unseen powers.

SILENT CHARACTERS AND BACKWASHES

There is one thing about *Enthusiasm* which makes it a difficult and sometimes disheartening book to read. The things that are omitted are conspicuous by their relevance. I do not say this in criticism of the book because it is not a history of the world or of the Church, but a study of people who were intense in their religion and went off the track. One has to supply a running commentary of one's own, on the successfully enthusiastic, the saints. This takes lively thinking while one reads, and to do it well one would have to supply hagiography on a level of scholarship comparable to Monsignor Knox's — obviously impossible for such as I. Nevertheless an effort of the mind in this direction is absolutely necessary. When one finds that disaster overtook someone because of taking the Bible very literally, or neglecting the most ordinary rules of natural prudence, or holding out too high an ideal of poverty, one *has* to remember Saint Francis who did these same things to an extraordinary degree. Otherwise the book induces a sort of despair. There were times in reading it when I wanted to buy a television set and get a job in advertising as a precaution against excommunication.

The other omission which begins to prey on one's mind is the background of worldliness against which the enthusiasts reacted. There is a sort of double backlash (the author points this out but calls only one movement backlash). It works this way: The Church gets lax and worldly (in particular Monsignor Knox cites the worldliness of the clergy as the remote occasion of all enthusiastic exaggerations), causing those who are zealous by virtue or temperament or both to strike out in the other direction. They end up as saints if successful, or as heretics if not. When they err and become "enthusiasts," the well-meaning people whom they have inspired become discouraged with the impossible ideal they hold up and react against it, finding themselves in unhappy league with worldlings. A sad situation.

WORLDLINESS

I wish Monsignor Knox had gone more into the problem of worldliness. In particular it would have been nice to have had some discussion of the fact that worldlings never seem to get into trouble. No one regards them as a menace to the Church even when they love money, become too respectable, too complacent, too bourgeois. They usually continue to enjoy honor and praise, and die peacefully in their beds with all the consolations of the last Sacraments.

It has always seemed to me unfair that the people who conform, or who water down the Christian message, should receive so little reprobation. Now I think I have been wrongly impatient in some respects, justifiably so in others. Worldliness is not an immediate threat to the unity of the Church as enthusiasm is, and therefore can better be tolerated, while the question of the just rewards and punishments can be left to God. On the other hand worldliness probably does incomparably more harm to the Christian cause in the long run than fanaticism. Would it be wrong to say that the American Church is heavy with the weight of the half-Christian or the half-hearted Christian today? I think not, and I think these do great harm, chiefly in acting as a smoke-screen for Christ in His Church before the eyes and yearnings of the tormented modern pagans. It is a commonplace that the main thing which keeps non-Catholics out of the Church is the Catholics — their avarice, their hypocrisy about birth control, their political chicanery, but most of all the fact that they are in the alleged flame without catching fire. How can this be His Church if so many practicing Catholics are so very tepid?

If the worldly will be accountable before God for scaring off the non-Catholic they also, and those who water down doctrine, have their responsibility for the exaggerations of the enthusiasts. Consider the case of who is damned and who is not, and how many. One of the recurring signs of enthusiasm is the underestimation of God's mercy in this regard. The Jansenists prematurely consigned numbers of people to Hell in a manner and tone strikingly similar to that of the Father Feeney group. How much of the blame for this error in either case rest with those who first erred in the other direction? I myself can remember that in recent years it was seriously debated in the most respectable quarters, under the influence of too much psychological determinism, whether it is *possible* for a person to commit a mortal sin. Those who raised the question leaned to the view that it is not. In those same circles there was great insistence on the fact that we cannot be sure of any one person's being in Hell. I am always reminded of that when Garrigou-Lagrange cites, as he frequently does, the case of Judas in Hell, as though it were obvious that he is there. It seems daring of him to say so. And what would happen to a Dante today?

Consider the psychological effect that such teaching as the above has on a person. My first reaction was, "If it's true that none of our contemporaries are in danger of Hell fire, we certainly are wasting our time in the lay apostolate." Then I thought of all the people I knew who seemed to be struggling for their soul's salvation, or jeopardizing it in a harrowing way. I remembered my own sins. I recalled the numerous private revelations about the dense population of Hell, and Our Lady's saying that more people will lose their souls through sins of impurity than any other sins today—and decided to stay in the lay apostolate. But the temptation is there, especially if one does not get out of hearing of the "laxists" to feel, by contrast, that almost everyone is heading for Hell. The pendulum again.

Evidently the Holy See is conscious of the watering down of doctrine and its responsibility for provoking rigorism, because in *Humani Generis* there stands out one statement, boldly and almost irrelevantly, the pointedness of which is unmistakable: "Some reduce to a meaningless formula the necessity of belonging to the true Church in order to gain salvation."

HOW TO STAY OUT OF HERESY

The problem for the enthusiastic type of person is not, as it might seem in reading this book, to hit a balance between ardor and worldliness, to bank the fires, so to speak. The problem is to be a successful enthusiast, a saint, rather than an unsuccessful one. Those who fail end way out on a limb someplace, openly defiant, or holding very unorthodox doctrines. Yet in most cases there was a time in the early part of their careers when they paused uncertainly, as the road to sanctity parted from the road to schism. What made them choose wrong? Is there some one point or virtue or idea that a person can cling to as a safeguard against deviation from the Faith? I would say "no," following, I think, Monsignor Knox's conclusions. Why? Because Christianity is a *balance* of elements delicately held. And because there isn't a single good thing which cannot be distorted, or about which there isn't the possibility of self-deception.

Christianity is dangerous, as life and love are dangerous, only more so. It feeds on daring and initiative. Also on obedience and self-abnegation but these last come to channel a flood or contain a fire. The first element is a vision, not a precaution. Security lies more in the direction of trust than in sloughing off of all uncertainties and risks.

One of the things I have observed, and that this book bears out, is that people who are overly anxious for official approval do not necessarily turn out to be the most orthodox or obedient. Take for instance the matter of *imprimaturs*. The Church requires this seal on certain writings, not on magazines like ours, incidentally. We are sometimes castigated for "not having an *imprimatur*" as though that fact invalidated everything we said, as it were magic-ally. Yet nine-tenths of *Integrity's* material is analysis of social trends which asks only that the reader think along with us to see if our conclusions do not recommend themselves as true.

Similarly in the lay apostolate there is a temptation to try to get the Church to bless all incipient projects and surround them with the mantle of ecclesiastical approval. Usually the people who thus operate do it from a conscientiousness. They think that to be a "better Catholic" lies in the direction of extravagant protestations of filial devotion. But there is no necessary correlation between all this elaborate show of obedience and real docility in a time of crisis. The reverse situation doesn't necessarily work either. The only point here is that this over-caution is not the major formula for staying in the fold.

Religious Fanaticism

Another favorite refuge is to undertake an obligation of obedience incumbent on one's state in life There are probably a lot of cases besides the obvious one of scrupulosity, where lay people do well to obey their confessors blindly, even taking a vow of obedience. But there are also a lot of cases where the temptation to do so stems from a reluctance to use the ordinary means of determining one's course, especially the use of the brain. The sort of obedience to a superior which is becoming to a religious, as part of his state in life, can easily make a lay person a prig. "My director says I can't do so and so, or I must do such and such" more often than not means walking out on a mess someone else has to untangle. How easy it is, also, to find a director to one's taste, or unconsciously to mold a director by supplying him with biased facts. One often hears it said, that if a director misdirects his subject the blame is on the priest's head. True enough, but with the lay apostle there is always the question of whether or not it is justified to shift the burden of the responsibility in this manner. We should not be trying to escape the responsibilities for things that go wrong but to direct them rightly. All that trouble at Port Royal, the center of the Jansenist fury, came through the Mother Superior's director who molded her wrongly.

But there is one virtue, surely, in which to take refuge. Is it not pride which has made enthusiasts obdurate in the face of authority? Therefore humility, the queen of virtues, must be a guarantee of orthodoxy and sanctity.

Consider then the case of Michael Molinas, a Spanish priest of the seventeenth century, who was sent to Rome to represent the cause of a priest from his district who had died in the odor of sanctity. For some unknown reason he was later relieved of his charge. In a letter written back to Spain he accepted this blow very humbly, in terms which most of us would envy. He had, he said, never wanted the job, but had done it out of obedience. Now he was discredited. "God be praised for this humiliation, a rich treasure if only he uses it properly!...Well, now he is free from any temptation to vain glory; *bonum mihi quia humiliasti me*," etc. I was in the very process of admiring these sentiments when Monsignor Knox's comment came like a dash of cold water. He detected in the letter an "hysterical humility" characteristic of the Quietists, one of the most infamous of whom poor Molinas became. Some years later this man (who had meanwhile become the most distinguished spiritual director in Rome) publicly admitted in the Church of the Minerva that he had taught a whole string of very odd doctrines; that he had engaged in indecent practices over a long period of time, and that he himself had not sacramentally confessed for twenty-two years. The Inquisition then sentenced him to life imprisonment. Throughout the whole proceedings Molinas remained impassive and Monsignor Knox wonders if he were truly repentant or if he perhaps resigned himself inwardly to the passive acceptance of a supreme martyrdom, in a complete caricature of the virtue of humility.

So, whereas it is true that the virtue of humility is fundamental and will save us from a thousand snares, it is also true that one can deceive oneself that one possesses it and possibly more easily than with other virtues.

CHRISTIAN EQUILIBRIUM

It is a balance then, and not a formula, that keeps the Christian center. Since it is a balance of a lot of elements, then it is wise not to throw out any of the elements in a wave of oversimplification. Spiritual direction, the frequent reception of the Sacraments, the cultivation of virtue, spiritual reading, theological study commensurate with one's state and education, docility to Church laws and teachings, respect for authority, the practice of mental prayer, association with other Christians in some recognized form of action (this especially, for the sandpapering effect), collectively will safeguard the Christian.

But there is another thing it is well to remember if and when things get difficult. The equilibrium that the Christian practices is not gross but extremely delicate. In a sense it gets more delicate the more one tries to walk in Christ's footsteps. It would ultimately be impossible to maintain if God had not provided us with a sure Guide.

When Saint Francis' order, already grown very large, fell into dissension between those of the strict and those of the lax observance they sent for the Saint to come back from Egypt to arbitrate. As he was nearing Assisi Saint Francis had a dream of a small black hen which was not large enough to shelter all her chicks. This he interpreted to mean that he was no longer powerful enough to protect the followers who were most dear to him and who desired to follow his rule most closely. So Saint Francis by-passed Portiuncula and went straight to Rome, where he placed the responsibility for the order on the Pope.

It seems to me that the lesson we learn from this is not just the obvious one, that the Church being divinely guided is wiser than we are and has to straighten out problems of great magnitude. The deeper lesson comes when one sees that from any human way of looking at it, the Papacy did a poor job of straightening out the Franciscan difficulties (except in the negative sense that the order didn't secede from the Church). Perhaps the world was not worthy of Saint Francis, so God let men have the mediocre way of their own choosing. Perhaps, perhaps, perhaps... but who is going to understand God?

The deeper meaning seems to be that we must not only accept the authority of the Church, but also the mystery of the Church, which like the Cross can be a sign of contradiction.

32
The Crisis
AUGUST 1951

WHAT IS THE NATURE OF THE WORLD'S PRESENT *crisis? Are we being attacked by that summation of all heresies which Anti-Christ is supposed to bring in his wake? Or are the good people of the world, who are in the majority and include most Americans, being harassed by a small number of human beasts whose chief inspiration is the blackness of their own souls? Or are we going through a natural, though painful, evolutionary process which will end in the rightful triumph of the working classes? Or are we paying for our sins, and painfully, because of their enormity? Is our lack of Christianity projecting itself into a caricature of Christianity which we have invited by our own subconscious efforts?*

I should like to call our crisis the *triumph of secularism*. The whole world is taking on a temporal finality, consolidating itself in a new way, on the basis of values which can be computed, ideals which can be realized, plans which can be accurately made and unfailingly carried through, of men whose all is this side of the grave.

Perhaps "triumph" is not the word, because the victory has not yet been won and may never be, but the secular synthesis is certainly in its final stages, with no adequate hindering force in sight. If secularism prevails, and even though it may have a brief reign (in the very nature of the case) it would be terrible beyond believing.

Yet it does not sound terrible, does it? "The reign of secularism" does not send cold shivers down one's spine like 'behind the iron curtain" does. Secularism appears to be a less formidable enemy than communism. Haven't we had it dinned into us that ours is a secular culture, a secular state? Yet we feel no pain, indeed we seem to be the most favored of nations.

I have called the evil "secularism" because I think that is its determining quality, and because this name helps us see danger where it exists, without waiting for it to be covered with the official political mantle of communism. Specifically it will help us to see how near we are in our own hearts and homes and country to capitulation from *within*.

The Crisis

For we in America, though superficially united (almost homogenized) are interiorly wandering in wastes, hesitating at remote crossroads, or setting off on journeys in diverse directions. We seem to belong to one culture, but we are beginning to have different ideologies.

Three women share the same room in a maternity hospital. One rejoices in her infant as a gift from God, will baptize it and rear it in holiness. Another hates the child she has borne because it interferes with her life of selfish pleasure, and she will alternately spoil and abuse her offspring until it is corrupted or becomes neurotic, or in any case revolts against its unfeeling parent. The third has planned and calculated this almost lone fruit of her womb. It will be brought up scientifically. Psychology will reign in the place of morality. Three women together in the same room, yet separated almost infinitely. Can they even find anything to say to each other? As for the children, they will grow up separated by universes—or, more likely, fighting to the death with each other for the possession of the universe.

These three women symbolically represent three distinct worlds in which Americans live. Some of us live in all three worlds at once, each world fighting with the others for the privilege of directing our lives. This battle within us is merely a reflection of a similar global battle for the possession of the earth. The first step in understanding this titanic struggle is to define and sort out the contendents so we can choose our sides. The division is not according to nations or political parties, not on the basis of democratic or totalitarian, but according to principles which are deeper still, dealing with ultimate things—whether men will obey Christ, love their own freedom as an absolute and vacillate forever, or shut themselves up in the prison of this world as the slaves of the Devil.

THE THREE IDEOLOGIES

The three contendents are Christianity, liberalism, and that dynamic materialism, that transcendent secularism, which is known in its political aspect as communism.

Christianity

For the most part our Christianity is residual. There are scraps of it left over from the Middle Ages, but daily fewer scraps. The cathedral used to be the center and heart of every town, but that is only of European memory. Kings used to be crowned by bishops and reminded of their responsibility to God for just and holy government. There is scarcely a king left and modern rulers, as rulers, defer precious little to the Deity. Crucifixes have vanished from the law courts and the law itself is shifting its foundations off the moral basis. The "holy crusade" which is going on for the separation of church and state aims to rid civil government of any traffic with religion or morality.

The crucifixes are gone from the school-rooms too, and secular education miniatures the struggle for ideas. Except in isolated localities it can truly be said that Christianity has vanished from education and the moral standards it upheld are on their way out too.

Economics is another area from which Christ has been banished. One cannot serve both God and money. The world chose money some time ago.

Christ lingered longer in family life, because a man could shut himself up with his wife and children and live holily, even if that often meant living in poverty. But of recent years the family has been attacked so strenuously that this last wall is down. The schools pulled the children into apostasy. The advertisements, the movies, the laws and the newspapers destroyed the chastity of the home and made everyone discontent with frugality. The neighbor's children did the rest.

It is fairly accurate to say that in America Christ has been thoroughly routed from society. But not from people. There are still Christians and there is, of course, still the Church. But since society has changed and no longer lives by laws harmonious with Christianity, the Christian is in a worse dilemma every day. That is why so many people are leaving the Catholic Church. They find it impossible to practice the moral law (even cut down to a few precepts) and be at peace with their times, so they compromise until they can compromise no longer, and then they leave. Or else they decide to stay in the Church and remodel the world to the Christian pattern. Those who make this last decision represent the new life in the Church. They are not necessarily holier than some of those who cling to a residual medieval Christianity, but they are, or promise to be, a dynamic force for Christ in the contemporary situation.

In looking for the orientation of the modern world which is toward Christ one will find very little social realization of it in existence. The Church with its parochial and diocesan structure is impressive and is more or less alive in different localities, but it is regarded as sectarian and usually is outside the mainstream of temporal events.

The Crisis

The institutions of the Church, such as schools, hospitals, and newspapers, are more or less in the same dilemma as individual Catholics are. There is a tremendous pressure on them to compromise with the worldly spirit, and where they do not, they are considered sectarian and some times do fall into a narrow groove, unable and unwilling to cope with modern problems. But here and there within them is a struggle to arrive at a new pattern, apostolic, intense, and dynamic.

Liberalism

The prevailing practical philosophy of Americans is liberalism. Since its spirit pervades the very atmosphere we live in it is not surprising that even most Catholics are practical liberals in their daily lives.

Think of liberalism as a vacuum, a chaos where men are guided by principles of expediency rather than absolute morality, as absence of order, as inconclusive and indeterminate, and you get its mark. It served to destroy the Christian order, not by contradicting it so much as by diluting and confusing it, by nullifying it at every turn. For the Christian absolute it did not substitute another absolute, but an absence of any absolute, an indeterminism, a tolerance of good and evil, truth and untruth, not in a prudential way, as allowing certain evils to exist rather than stirring up worse evils in trying to eradicate them, but as not really preferring one to another. Liberalism used good words ambiguously, so that gradually they were drained of their Christian implications and then gradually again were charged with meanings antithetical to Christianity. It enshrined *liberty, equality and fraternity,* but as ultimates, not as means and not as by-products of absolute things such as truth and goodness, not as related to morality but as isolated from God. It worshipped democracy, which is only a *means* of government, which depends on basic ideals for its real worth. It talked endlessly about freedom, and it was easy to persuade people that this was the same freedom that Christians cherish, but was it? Christ said, "You shall know the truth, and the truth shall make you free." His freedom is a *result* of knowing the truth — the result of what the liberals like to call "intolerance" and "dogmatism." The liberal's freedom is quite different. It is the freedom to search for truth. Of course, it is a good thing for the men who do not know the truth to be able to look for it. The trouble with the liberals is that they will not let anyone find it. If anyone claims to find it, he becomes an outcast from their society. They are, it turns out, dogmatists in their own curious way. They know there is no truth, or if there is, it's not knowable.

We have a liberal government, without any real principles, paying lip-service to God, and talking more and more about democracy and freedom, while both these are vanishing for lack of roots in something deeper. We have, or did have until a few years ago (things are rapidly changing), a system in this country of liberal economics, which meant free competition and the legal right to abuse the moral right of private property. It also involved freedom from sanctions against usury. Our system of free compulsory education is also, or was until recently, liberal. Liberal means undogmatic, which means remaining undecided about all the important truths (except that one is allowed his private opinion) while attaching an exaggerated importance and a thousand dogmas to matters of art, literature, science, hygiene, and civics.

The effect of liberalism, economic, philosophical and cultural, over a period of centuries, has been to destroy all norms. It has no moral code of its own and has endured only as long as Christian morals have survived to hold society together — not only Christian morals but Christian standards of all sorts. The end of liberalism had to be dog-eat-dog because the philosophy itself has no backbone, nothing wherein to construct a life or society. We are in the last stages of it now, and we find everything in ruins. Western society, indeed the whole world, has become one great big vacuum, one vastness empty of all positive content.

Transcendent Secularism

And nature abhors a vacuum. Mankind simply cannot endure without a pattern, a direction, a form, a stability. We have to have an order, or we shall disintegrate.

Now just as the soul is the form of the body, so something spiritual has to be the ordering principle of a society. One cannot sort out men and groups of men mechanically, the way the nineteenth century materialists tried to do. Their atomization will just continue despite the regimentation. To mold a society one has to have a central ideal that is transcendent, that will catch men's hearts and evoke their sacrifices. In other words, one has to have a religion or something not religious in itself which is raised to a religious level.

Men have worshipped many false gods, but it has remained for our day to see them make a religion of atheism. This probably would not have been possible in another day. To proclaim that there is no God and to expect men to become delirious with joy, one has to imply that now *we* have become gods, and this can only be convincing with modern science and technology and the vision that they present to men of their being able to control the universe, to explore all its secrets, and to create all by themselves the New Jerusalem.

This vision is the core of the new ideology. That is why we have called it supreme secularism. It is a caricature of the Christian thing on a this-world level. Like Christianity and unlike liberalism, it has the power to establish an order. This time it is not just Western society but the whole world which is going to be comprehended within a single system. In fact we are in the last stages of the completion of this synthesis. The men, many of them Christians, who are speeding the industrialization of India, of China, and of South Africa, seem not to realize that they are collaborating in the completion of a secular synthesis, not because machinery is in itself evil, but because the mechanization of all production under centralized control will be the chief instrument both for de-humanizing men and of tyrannizing them absolutely. Their very daily bread will depend on the god in Moscow, Paris, or New York rather than on the God in Heaven; on their complete enslavement rather than on their sweat. The case is similar with television. Those who defend it for the potentialities which the instrument itself has for giving vivid information about Christianity, mostly in its externals, are being unrealistic, for they fail to see the functional role of television in the materialistic synthesis. *Everyone* has to become a part of this new world order, and this subjugation of peoples involves not just their external enslavement but a crushing of their spirits, a regimentation of their minds. The generation which has known better things, whether the Christian vision or the liberal freedom to do and think what it pleases, is now being put to sleep while the secularists gain control. And once they have control, television will become a purely political instrument.

THE CENTRALITY OF POLITICS

The new ideology promises an order and a central ideal for which men can give their lives. Both are absolutely secular. Here we come upon an important twist. As the Christian order was centered in God, that is, in a transcendent end, all the different temporal functions took on relative rather than absolute importance. The political order, as governing, was the most important but could not claim an absolute finality, because men were destined for a higher life after this life. The new ideology has made absolutes of this life and this earth, and so the political order has taken on the importance and the finality fitting only to the supernatural order. Under the circumstances it cannot be anything except tyrannical and arbitrary. If there is no God to have power of life and death over men, then the state must usurp this power. If there is no God for us to love with our whole hearts and souls, then we have to give our total devotion to the state. Idealists and philosophers speak of "humanity" now reigning supreme, but this is a fiction because humanity as a person does not exist. There has to be a master brain whether it be a Hitler or a Stalin, or some future tyrant. Furthermore the role of absolute ruler of the bodies and souls of all mankind is too big and too terrible for any man, however proud or evil or gifted he is. Of its very nature it invites the co-operation of the netherworld.

RULES OF LIFE

It is because of this political absolutism that "right" or "wrong" takes on a political color in the new secular era. Christianity was a moral order in which the good and the true were the guides of doing and thinking. Under liberalism there was a confusion of standards. Since it was during this period that men's passions and avarice were allowed to develop virtually without hindrance, so-called "moral" judgments were usually mere expedients in view of an unexpressed bias toward money or pleasure as an end. Even good things were done because they "worked" or "paid." Honesty was the best policy, for instance. Toward the end of the period certain advanced thinkers shed even moral terminology and talked instead about "positive" or "negative," "constructive" or "destructive" conduct.

These last carry us into the new ideology as they are absolutely unmoral, and are ambiguous, not in the confused way of the liberals but in the deliberate way of the new masters. They are good enough explanations for the masses, but they are not the real "morality." The real standard is a political one, for the reasons outlined above. It is established in view of the absolute and arbitrary power of the dictator and his law, the ever-changing "party line." To "sin" is to *deviate*, to be "virtuous" is to hew the party line. "Truth" is what the party or the dictator says. See how exactly this caricatures Christianity. For the Christian, Truth is ultimately a person, *God.* For the secularist it becomes also a person, the dictator of the world, or ultimately Satan.

Our fury is already descending upon those among us who have accepted the communist gods. We can hardly imagine how a man, like Mr. [Alger] Hiss, could be so dedicated in his non-deviationalism, could abandon all standards of morality and truth for a mysterious (and mysteriously unrewarding) total service.

But how far is this really from our own hearts? He who is already in the liberal camp, in practice even if not in theory, is precariously near that new order which seems so very different. Let us take a particular case, the question of having babies.

BIRTH CONTROL

The Christian believes that God will send him a certain number of children, for whom He will then provide through His providence. This works out very well when a society is Christian because then the organization of temporal affairs follows God's laws. Providence has a clear channel, so to speak.

The liberals allowed the Christian order of society to disintegrate and a money-centered economy to arise in its place. By so doing they destroyed the harmony between personal morality and economic advantage. It became disadvantageous to have more than a very few children, and since God rarely sends parents just two offspring, the pressure for birth control began, increased and was finally legally sanctioned. Birth control is a very good example of the liberal mentality. The whole case for it rests on personal expediency, which in turn rests on a more or less unconscious basis of selfishness. No one asks (except the Catholic Church, a thorn in everyone's side) whether or not contraception is *moral*. That is not the criterion. It's a pragmatic question, a matter of expediency. ("If I have only two children, I can give them a college education." "The doctor says it isn't safe to have another baby." "John and I want to enjoy the first few years of our married life, before we start to raise a family.")

The thing that interests us now is the Catholic compromise — Rhythm. Here is a method of birth prevention which does not involve unnatural practices and which therefore shifts the question of morality from single acts to motives and attendant circumstances which can be, and often are, vaguely interpreted. Thus a Catholic is enabled for all practical purposes to think right along with the liberals, expediently.

"We are only going to have two or three children because if we had more we would have to live on a lower social plane, or forego a car, or my wife couldn't work, etc." This mentality, so widespread among Catholics, is undermining their faith and they are in serious danger of being swept into the new atheistic synthesis unawares, since they already belong to it in their sympathies.

Liberalism has turned out to be just an opening wedge for atheistic materialism, and Rhythm is an opening wedge for Catholics to become liberals. That is why we should persistently encourage families to take the alternate course, to have the children God sends and to trust that He will specially care for them despite unfavorable prevailing secondary causes. Such families should join with other like-minded families to start the reconstruction of society along Christian lines.

SCIENTIFIC POPULATION-PLANNING

Otherwise here is what will probably happen, for indeed it is already happening. Birth control will be superseded by "the scientific planning of population on a large scale." This is the new era. It already prevails in Soviet Russia and is being introduced in a very comprehensive, scientific way in Japan. No longer will a person be able to decide whether he wants children or not, or how many. All that nice arbitrary liberal stuff will be replaced by compulsion on the part of the state. Men and women will breed when they are told to, and use contraceptives when they are told to. It will still be a matter of expediency rather than morality, but not of personal expediency.

In Europe under the dictators it concentrated on breeding. In Asia it is starting with the imposed limitation of families. Japan is the experimental ground. A blanket plan for population-control was first made along "scientific lines." It was not accompanied with threats or sanctions, since it counted on the voluntary cooperation of the Japanese. Recently a Japanese writer advocated in a leading newspaper that certain compulsive measures be taken. He suggested "that a maximum of children for any one family be fixed by law and that fines should be imposed for every additional child born.... If the maximum is fixed at three, each family having more children should be fined 100,000 yen ($28) for the fourth child, 30,000 yen ($84) for the fifth, 100,000 yen ($280) for the sixth and 500,000 yen ($1,400) for the seventh." He bases his demand "on the alleged fact that in spite of the 'common knowledge' Japanese have of the urgent necessity of controlling births 'as the first economic policy of the nation,' there has been 'no decrease in the birth rate.'" He urges that "the first thing to do is to revise the existing criminal code so as to make abortion easy.... Birth control clinics should be established all over the country and instead of lecturing to girls in trouble or those wishing to limit the size of their families, abortion should be performed right away without questions being asked."

When scientific population-planning comes to America, I think it will start with encouraging births. Let us assume it will anyhow. Let us say the government will want to step up the population. It will probably pass a law making it worthwhile, even desirable, to have many children. There will be a bonus, say, for each new member of the family. There will be prizes given along with a lot of publicity and praise, to the parents of the most numerous brood. And does anyone think that many Catholics will not hail this as a sign that the United States is really becoming Christian, really seeing the light? I predict this will happen even if the government openly states that it acts for "scientific" reasons. Let us go a step further and watch the government suavely encourage illegitimate births, say by setting up maternity centers where girls in trouble can go to get the best of care, where their anonymity will be preserved, from where the babies will be placed in good homes, and the mothers given a new start. The measure will drastically reduce our shameful annual abortion rate.

All in all it will seem such a good measure that no one will be able to object to it. And indeed there is only one clear-cut criticism — *it does more or less the right thing for wrong reasons.*

OUR MORAL DILEMMA

Let us pause here for a moment and observe that people who wish to behave morally are always in a dilemma these days — a dilemma, not a temptation. In simpler days men were faced with simpler problems. "Shall I behave dishonestly and unjustly and so become a millionaire, or shall I be good and probably remain poor?" It may have been hard to make the right choice, but it was not difficult to figure out which choice *was* right.

But now we have dilemmas, and a dilemma is a different thing entirely. In a dilemma there are two choices, neither one of which is choosable. It puts the moral man in a state of paralysis. And indeed there is no way out of a dilemma through choosing. One has to slip through the horns of it in some other way, such as by backing off and approaching the problem differently or by transcending the alternatives.

The above-mentioned hypothetical dilemma is one in which we are asked to choose the right things that are being done for the wrong reasons. Under scientific population-planning an individual married couple relinquishes the control of the size of its family to the state, even when the state happens momentarily to be encouraging large families. For instance, the state will give bonuses for children from public funds — a good thing if the state were dedicated to God and the observance of the moral law, because then the state could be trusted with increased responsibility for the common good. If it is a scientific secular state, however, each seemingly benevolent measure deprives the citizen of the possibility in the future of making a personal moral judgment contrary to scientific planning. If the couple chooses to have children as they come, and *allows* the state to make this financially possible, it is at the same time acceding to and strengthening a system already against God and which may presently press married couples to commit mortal sin. The attack is indirect, of course. What the couple is first asked to do is *not* something that is a clear-cut sin, the practice of contraception, for example. Rather it is asked to surrender some more freedom. We have, I think, a strong moral obligation to consider to whom we surrender that freedom — and the likely consequences.

There seems to be a third alternative: to have children but *without* accepting the easement the state offers. Although this course will be open to an occasional favored person, it is hardly possible in the natural order since it calls for much sacrifice and for a great power of resistance to a proffered easier course. The genuine third alternative is to go above the state to God and count directly on His providence. The conditions He has set are these: "Seek ye first the kingdom of God and His justice, and all these things will be added unto you." And this means in practice that if couples, with prayer and heroic trust in God, band together to turn the world again to Christ (that is, work somehow in the apostolate), they can raise large families without disaster. But this third alternative is what I would call slipping through the horns of the dilemma by transcending the dilemma. It means breaking the bonds of secularism, and so necessarily of the dilemmas of secularism.

The Crisis

Then there is the housing dilemma. Do we want large-scale housing with government financial aid, or are we going to sit by and let veterans be homeless, marriages break up etc.? We have chosen the large-scale housing because we deplore homelessness, but along with our choice has come a *kind* of housing hardly calculated to encourage Christian families and we may soon find ourselves in an even more compromising position, but with rabbit warrens of apartment houses and chicken-coop suburban developments as *faits accomplis*.

Shall the native populations of the world have the right of self-determination (and so be presently swallowed up by the Russians at their borders) or shall they be kept unjustly subject to the Western colonial rule? Another dilemma.

Our big mistake is to choose at all when the world comes up with one of these dilemmas. Something else has to be done with a dilemma. It presents two unchoosable choices because it has the problem all wrong. The God's-eye-view of the world is complex, but not impossible. God wants us to choose the right thing but He does not expect us to crack our heads open trying to decide which wrong thing to do. Men can get in terrible spots but there is always an honorable way out — contrition, penance, prayer, the acceptance of death or suffering, poverty or bankruptcy.

Is it because the modern world rejects a priori certain alternatives that it comes up with its unsolvable problems?

I should like to give an example of Catholic thinking which is of the same order because it unconsciously accepts the secular context of a problem. I single out this instance merely because it is in the current news and not because it is necessarily worse than others.

Father Edmund Walsh, S.J., has just published a book about the morality of the use of the atom bomb. He finds that it is morally justifiable to drop an atom bomb in order to prevent a sneak attack. In other words we can bomb Russia so that she will not be able to come over and surprise us with a bomb. There is some curious (to me) reasoning back of this conclusion, but what is relevant here is that Father Walsh is arguing around a dilemma. In a time of danger of a surprise attack we have two courses: either we bomb Russia and disable her, or we "commit suicide" by waiting for her to destroy us. Having decided against suicide, Father Walsh attempts a moral justification of the first choice.

Now I, too, dislike the idea of "suicide." It is better to be killed than to kill unjustly, but just sitting around waiting for the enemies of Christ to take over the earth and destroy the souls of men does not seem very Christian to me. On the other hand, by what process of casuistry have we come to condone horrible mass killings as a precautionary measure?

It seems to me that Father Walsh and the rest of us would be relieved of making such unhappy decisions, if we remembered that one cannot choose in a dilemma and that the presence of two bad alternatives indicates *the matter has to be re-thought.*

Taking a second look at this thinking about the atom bomb one sees that a number of things are unconsciously presumed. For instance, that this is a secular crisis, the course of which is dependent upon the strategy of militarists, upon which side is quicker with the atom bomb, upon the diplomatic maneuvering of statesmen. Also, that miracles are not to be hoped for and that spiritual means are not be considered, or at least that they have no practical value. And finally, on what grounds do we believe that to forestall Russia in the dropping of the bomb, or even to destroy her, would resolve our international problem? What hope is there in it?

It is possible to hold very different tenets. With faith the evidence for them is almost blinding. One can suppose that the world tension is caused by the collective apostasy of nations from the rule of Christ, that this is in a certain sense a mystical war. One can further believe that even now we are being saved from complete destruction by the penance and holiness of obscure saints who persuade God to prevent our self-destruction. Would not the presence of ten just men have saved the city of Sodom? We can believe (the easier because Our Lady has said it) that penance is the key to peace and that, for instance, it might be more *practical* (and it certainly is more Christian) to get the inhabitants of New York and/or Cleveland, Detroit and Chicago, to spend the night praying the rosary together in the streets, than it would be to send an A-bomb of our own off in the direction of Moscow. What if the Russian flier is already en route? Is God powerless to destroy his plane and the bomb with it over the North Pole? Didn't God turn the battle of Lepanto?

Didn't He cause the walls of Jericho to collapse, and the Red Sea and the Jordan to separate their waters so the Jews could cross?

There is even another consideration. In the eternal view, God may be allowing the atom bomb threat *just so* our singularly obdurate generation will finally be brought to its knees. So whoever manages to wriggle us out of this tight situation may not be doing us a favor. If it takes the threat of an A-bomb to put the fear of God into us, what hope will there be that, having escaped by killing a few million of our fellowmen, we shall be disposed to penance thereafter? And if we are not going to repent, *collectively as well as individually,* why bother to save our skins?

Now if we really did have a strong faith, and if we did see the world's problems in the light of that faith, we should be able to slip through the horns of all the modern dilemmas simply by making the effort to see the Christian vision of the new world and then to have the courage and the self-sacrifice necessary to make our vision a reality.

Just because it is the habit or our generation to act as though God had no relevance to human problems is no reason why we should do likewise. We have let it seem as though huge new hospital buildings and vast federal appropriations were the key to the restoration of medicine, whereas it is obvious that the real problems are that the doctors have become avaricious and that medical thinking disregards the natural and moral laws. We shall not solve our medical problems until we see them for what they are; yet there is no Catholic medical society of any consequence in the United States. So it is, all the way down the line. The world is bankrupting itself, beating its brains out, exhausting all human resources, to solve problems L, M, N, O, P whereas the real problems are A, B, C, D and E. The first problem is not to *solve* but to *think on a different plane.*

THE CARE OF THE UNFORTUNATE

Before leaving the contrast of the three societies in which we are living simultaneously, it may be useful to show their manifestations in one more field, the care of the unfortunate. What does each of them do with the weak, the sick, the poor, the maimed, those unfortunates whom we have always with us?

It would seem at first glance that the Church has been outmaneuvered in taking care of the unfortunate. This was strictly her province in the Middle Ages and has been the occasion for the formation of countless religious orders. Men used to pay tithes to the Church, as they now pay income taxes to the state, and the Church assumed responsibility for a wide area that is now falling under the tender mercies of the welfare state. Though most of the Church's charitable institutions continue to exist, they are paralleling similar secular services and are all involved with them in money and methods. Consequently the institutional exercise of supernatural charity is almost stifled.

For the Christian however, there is always the possibility of exercising charity, because there are always some derelicts of other unfortunates around that the world cannot integrate into its system. There are also the spiritual works of mercy, more needed now than ever before and in nearly every milieu. Much of the best thinking in the contemporary Church has been in line with developing new approaches to the exercise of charity, suited to our day. The Catholic Worker with its houses of hospitality is a major example. The Young Christian Workers is another. Within the traditional institutions and religious orders themselves there is some ferment going on, a groping for a mode of adaptation to modern circumstances. The danger is that the adaptation will be a superficial one, a mere accommodation to public financing and scientism, rather than a new expression of an eternal charity.

If Christian charity is going through a crisis of adaptation and remolding, its liberal counterpart, philanthropy, is in a much worse condition, in fact on its deathbed. Liberalism here represents the bounty of the rich toward the poor, in human compassion. Take a look at the remains. Rich men's money has become all twisted up and has forgotten about compassion. The *last* thing it would be used for would be to feed a derelict or to see a T. B. patient through the final stages of his illness. Very rich men seem to feel not that they are obliged to help the less fortunate but that they are gods, with a control-of-the-universe position to maintain. The Henry Ford and Rockefeller Foundations do more than just dabble with a new world religion of their own invention. Howsoever interesting this may be, it is beyond liberalism and way over into that new era. One glance at the other end, at the immediate dispensers of mercy, shows that liberalism has failed here too. Nurses, social workers and school teachers become daily more strictly professional or more strictly mercenary. So let us be done with philanthropy, since it is no more. Men cannot love consistently and continuously unless their love be supernatural charity. That is the lesson we should have learned from philanthropy's failure. And now we are falling prey to a terrible idea indeed.

THE ATHEIST'S MILLENNIUM

The new technological society has created an illusion that it will wipe poverty and suffering from the face of the earth. There will no longer be an unemployment problem, an old age problem, a sickness problem. To begin with, these things will be taken care of through the bounty of the state with social security, compulsory insurance and state benefits. Eventually they will be wiped out entirely. Once a scientifically planned economy is under way, there will be no unemployment, no depression and inflation cycles, no arbitrary power in the hands of rich men. Medical research will bring about a state of permanent physical well-being. Scientific birth control will synchronize production and population, wonder-drugs will control scourges.

What of the insane, the old, the mentally deficient? They too will be scientifically cared for by euthanasia, eugenics, sterilization and contraception. It is still impossible to champion these last measures openly in America, but they form an integral part of the scientific control of human well-being. Their existence measures the margin of failure of the scientific planners, who characteristically make the facts fit the plans by lopping off residues.

If the leaders of the new society would admit that their calculations will never balance, which is the truth of the matter, they would be unable to perpetrate their mass executions of the unfit. However, they always explain that these massacres are incidental to the transitional period preceding universal beatitude (an explanation which satisfies men born and bred in the expedient philosophy). It is in the vision of the New Jerusalem that their strength lies. People are even willing to sacrifice their own generation, including themselves, for a millennium in which they will not participate. The communists have discovered how great the capacity for sacrifice is in human beings. They have succeeded in perverting the greatest of human virtues, charity.

The best way for Christians to combat this false devotion is to show that its object is illusory. That was how the communists attracted people away from Christianity in the first place. They called religion merely an opiate, and they talked about the folly of believing in "pie-in-the-sky." We ought now to turn the tables on them, but perhaps the reason we do not do so is because we share their illusions to a certain extent. We are against birth control as morally wrong, but we really do not trust God to regulate the population of the earth so that it will not outstrip the food supply. Christians and atheists alike take it on faith that India has to be industrialized to save its teeming millions from starvation. No one ever asks if industrialization will really relieve India.

But we have arrived at a point in this discussion where it is useful to discuss the secular synthesis in more detail, so we shall cease making the contrast of the three societies and proceed to the essence of our problem.

TRANSCENDENT SECULARISM

We have already said it several times. The essence of the new era is the usurpation by men of the prerogatives of God. We have made ourselves gods, and we are running the universe.

That is why there can be no more mysteries. Previously men placed their confidence in God Who controlled everything and Who was infinitely wiser than men. They trusted Him to know what He was about when He sent them babies, to control the movements of the planets and the activity of atoms. The more men learned about the intricacies of the universe, so much the more were they moved to admire God's handiwork.

Modern scientific atheism leaves nothing to a higher intelligence. Of course it denies the religious mysteries of the Trinity, the Incarnation, the workings of providence. But it also denies the "natural" mysteries. It allows nothing to happen in the universe that it does not know about and control, even if that knowledge is so vast and complex in extension alone that it cannot be held in the human mind and has to be stored in mammoth calculating machines.

Here is the real cause for grievance against modern science. Modern scientists are the theologians of the new religion, busily exploring the secrets of the earth so that their masters, the political rulers, will be omnipotent and omniscient. The truth of the matter is that scientists are not free to follow their own investigations wherever they lead, either in fact or in moral theory. Their supposed freedom is nothing more than a myth. They are enslaved in regiments—by the government for atomic research, by medical foundations to hunt for cures, and by huge corporations like General Motors and the Telephone Company to work out practical invention. Not only are they told what direction their minds are to take, they are most often, like the assembly-line worker, made to concentrate on a minute part of a whole which they do not understand or which is kept secret from them.

The Crisis

But even if it were true that scientific men had intellectual freedom of research, they would not be morally free to do what they pleased. There is a cliché to the effect that scientists have out-stripped morality, that their discoveries, like the atom bomb and poison gas, are good in themselves, and that the difficulty lies in the fact that morals have not grown proportionately so has to render these things harmless to humanity. Back of this naive theory is the supposition that scientists are above the moral law. Other men may have to direct their energies with respect to the common good but not the devotee of the test tube or the control man of the atom-smashing machine.

The liberals have done their propaganda work so well that when one mentions putting any restrictions on scientific investigation, the picture one gets is that of an arbitrary and bigoted censor crippling the intellectual life of great men. The true picture is otherwise. The ideal is the truly humble scientist, humble before God and His creation. Such a man, for instance, was the late Sir Albert Howard, who, because of his genius and his docility to facts, found out how to restore fertility to the soil of India through organic farming. Would that people would learn from him how to help the Indians rather than listen to the irresponsible voices of the mechanists.

Atheist scientists tend to pride and intellectual curiosity, two vices unrecognized by the materialist. We suffer not from their love or truth but from their vices, which pervert the direction of their search for truth. Our society does not know how to protect itself against these moral defects.

In this perspective the true significance of artificial rainmaking, for instance, can be seen. The weather is a natural mystery, not because any one factor in it is beyond human comprehension, but because the balance of elements which go to make it up is so very complex and delicate. God controls the balance of these elements, although our use or abuse of the soil has a long-term profound effect on the weather cycle. The artificial rain-makers destroy God's harmony of the weather elements for a direct control by men. If instead they had used organic methods of farming and refrained from deforesting the earth they would have improved and stabilized the weather without the necessity of all this elaborate probing. But this course would have involved moral reform.

At this point the rain-makers are irresponsibly interfering with things they are far from understanding. In fact, here as elsewhere, it is likely that the magnitude of involved elements is forever beyond man's comprehension. But if it were not, the man who would have to hold the control would have the power of life and death over the whole universe and then we should see if we rest easier in his whims than in the arms of God.

The new secularists have taken Christ's saying, "You shall know the truth, and the truth shall make you free," and have twisted it to their own ends. According to their interpretation it means that "We shall presently know all the secrets of the universe, and when we do, we shall be free to control our own destinies." No longer shall we fear "chance" happenings—bad weather, famine or cancer. Men will understand these things completely and so be able to prevent them. They will constitute their own providence.

The great intellectual illusion of our times is that we can know everything about the universe. Its corollary is that by knowing we shall be able to manipulate. This is not the illusion just of intellectuals, it has completely caught the public imagination. Witness how easy it is to raise astronomical sums of money, whether from private individuals or the government, for things like atomic or cancer research. These are great projects destined (so we think) to uncover the final secrets. It would not be nearly so easy to raise money to feed the poor or to give nursing care to hopeless cancer cases, even though these latter causes have a certain natural power of arousing compassion. Money spent for them is money down the drain according to the unconscious modern mentality. What is the relief of this pain or the feeding of that mouth compared to the vision of a disease-free, poverty-less world?

Superficially it seems that men are learning more and more about the universe, but they are learning less and less, because they are studying secondary, tertiary and even more superficial phenomena instead of fundamentals. It is true that the illusion of knowledge is tremendously seductive. The high priests are also secretive so it is not surprising that ordinary people are taken in.

We have not the space here to elaborate why it is that the hope to learn all about the universe is an illusion. Briefly, men have looked for facts in isolation (and accumulated mountains of them) instead of having looked for meanings. They have refused to study the harmony God put in the world and so have been led by their pride to the point of destroying it. Now they are going to concoct a harmony of their own.

THE ILLUSION OF ABUNDANCE

Man has at last discovered the secret of abundance. It lies in the technological reorientation of the world.

We wish with our whole hearts that this theory were held only by atheistic materialists, but such is not the case. There seems to be only a handful of people who think differently and by no means are all of them Catholic. Let us state the proposition for increased abundance in the words of Canon Jacques Leclercq (*Commonweal,* March 30): "Today we are approaching a stage where abundance is within reach of all." Canon Leclercq goes on to make another point about distribution. He does not even bother to prove the quoted statement. But is it true?

God has given mankind a certain amount (plentiful amount) of fertile soil, of forest, of air, coal, water, oil, iron, animals, etc. If organic matter is returned to the soil which is properly cared for in other ways, the fertility of land, that particular form of abundance, will remain constant or increase slightly. In some places this has happened. In other places improper use of the soil has turned large areas into desert or dust bowls. Taken as a whole therefore the abundance has declined. Of course there is still some virgin land, but to begin using that is not to increase abundance through technological means, although building railroads and such may make these lands more accessible and enable men to exploit their fertility. In this case technology is accessory to the exhaustion of abundance rather than to its increase. Our domestic agriculture has fared similarly under technology. Large scale farm machinery plus the lavish use of chemical fertilizers can transform and exhaust the soil much faster and more efficiently than was heretofore possible. During the period of exploitation the use of chemicals may produce deceivingly attractive results, just as certain medicines produce a temporary and artificial color or energy in persons of declining health.

Technological farming also produces an inherently inferior product which seems to be having very disturbing effects on human health, but apart from this it is also true, as the distributists have repeated *ad nauseam,* that chemical and mechanized farming produces more *per man* but less *per acre* that does organic, small-size family farming. Abundance is on the side of doing things the natural way.

What is true of farming goes also for livestock and their products. One can make chickens lay more eggs by unnatural methods, but it is questionable if the eggs are as good, and certainly the chickens are far from hardy. Just as sprayed fruit trees have to be sprayed more and more and more, so chickens living in sterile conditions under electric light develop diseases which are treated in ways that give rise to new diseases, etc. The case is not very good for abundance here, nor is it in the case of cows and milk.

So much for food. The technologists' case is even weaker when it comes to those natural resources which cannot be replenished. We are behaving like prodigals with our coal and oil and iron, not to mention our forests and water. All these things are being systematically exploited and fed into the hungry jaws of mass manufacture—waste, waste, waste. I suppose if we tried we could produce a television set for every family in the universe, or even a motor car, or a bomb or a gun, or some Kleenex, and create one splendid mirage of a materialistic paradise. But it would only mean that we have stepped up the rate of exploitation still further. The day of reckoning will be nearer and more painful when it comes. Where is the increased abundance?

The illusion of abundance used to be created largely by the exploitation of "primitive" (that is, unindustrialized) peoples. In the next stage it rested largely on the rape of the soil and the elements of the earth (along with some manipulation of national finances). Now it is true we have another piece of wool to pull over our eyes—new kinds of energy and synthetic products.

Synthetic products like nylon, bakelite, and all the new compositional materials, are again made out of *something* and that something is exhaustible in its turn, although it is true that it exhausts resources other than the traditional ones. Generally the old material is preferable anyhow, but apart from that it was usually available without elaborate processing and therefore without putting its user at the mercy of the system.

In a recent article in *The New York Times* the reporter rejoices over the United Nations counterpart of the Point Four program. Technologists are being dispatched to "primitive" places in the world where there are forests, just standing there, to show backward people (who have so far been stupid enough just to use the wood for fuel or building houses or making furniture) how systematically to cut down their trees and to sell the wood in the world market. In this way these countries will enter into the industrial abundance. Henceforth their chairs will come from Brooklyn and the material for their houses from Ohio and Bombay. Perhaps wood from Burmese forests will even have

The Crisis

the honor of rolling up First Avenue in New York City by the tons and tons all day long to feed the inexhaustible high speed presses of the New York *Daily News,* bringing the world-weary proletariat juicy bits about the latest domestic scandal or proclaiming imitation pearl necklaces to be available at ninety-eight cents.

Of the abundance that atomic energy promises I have little to say except, where is it? It must be a very odd type of mind which can look upon the splitting of the atom as having been a happy event for mankind, whether in the light of how we have used our knowledge in the past or in the prospect of how we are going to use it.

THE ILLUSION OF MAN'S PROVIDENCE

Now that we are setting ourselves up as gods the hardest job is to provide a universal providence, to synchronize the mechanical system we have set up in a shrunken world. One might say that the scheming and conniving of the communists is to bring about this new order almost as much as it is to gain power, or rather that the two go together.

The contrast between God's order and the new order is the contrast between the natural order and an artificial one. It is better to state it this way than to try to follow the maneuvering of Moscow, because our own planners and sociologists, time-and-motion-study men, and psychiatrists are in the overwhelming majority working to bring about this secular synthesis, many of them inadvertently.

Everything has to be changed, and everything has to be diminished to fit into a shrunken world, diminished and reoriented. The world itself has to become smaller, more centralized and more uniform, as the new rulers can neither control nor comprehend the breadth and diversity of the world God made. This is the real impetus back of the stepping up of time and the shortening of distances. The most clever modern inventions have been to the end of this speed-up: the airplane, the jet plane, television, radio and telegraph, the assembly line; and there are a thousand gadgets, little and big, for cooking roasts in three minutes, getting headache relief instantaneously, healing wounds, growing flowers in record time. Nearly everyone feels the odd psychological impact of these too-rapid changes. One gets it very clearly going from place to place by airplane. Visitors sense it in the hectic pace of life in New York City. The East hates the West for bringing it to them. Most people suffer from nervous tension.

The "natural order" of God placed man in a framework of time which was measured by the movement of the planets, reflected in the slow changes of season and the sequence of day and night. When man's life was synchronized with nature and natural things, his mind and his soul could expand and develop in their proper way. Under the new dispensation mellow thought has given way to fleeting impressions. Man's mental life is fragmentary and superficial. He has been so over-stimulated that his emotions are atrophied. There is no hope of restoring society to God's order without also destroying the maddening pace of modern life — unless one has the foolish hope of changing the nature of man too, so that he can be integrated into the new order. Such a hope men do have, which we shall discuss later.

The new providence, operating within its shrunken globe and controlling everything by its total power, will plan the size of families, the production output, assign each one of us to his life work, decide which areas of the earth will have factories and which will have factory-type farms. It will plan and build our housing, move populations from place to place at will, give us the entertainment and culture it sees fit, and subject us all to a "conditioning" type of education.

We are familiar with the pattern because it has been described to us by writer after writer. We are less familiar with the idea that it will be not so much a consequence of tyranny as of the consolidation of the world on a secular pattern. It is implicit in the secular idea worked out to its logical conclusion. Tyranny is a part of the pattern rather than the motivating force.

Naturally the hardest part of this synthesis to achieve is the reduction of man. Yet the atheists hope to create a new man. Let us examine him.

THE NEW MAN

We rarely get even a suggestion of the new man here in America yet. Fuchs and Hiss foreshadow him in ways, and we are puzzled to understand their psychology. We are uncomprehending too when we read some of the communist stories or about the Nazi war trials. Then we occasionally meet someone who has been psychoanalyzed and has reached a false peace that is rather frightening. It too is prophetic.

For the most part however, we see not the new man but the disintegrating old man. We observe the ill effects of a shrunken, secular, mechanical universe on the human race about us.

The Crisis

Men do not like being diminished. One of their first reactions is to turn the full force of their love, which properly belongs to God, on human beings, a mother, a father or daughter, a wife or a husband. This results in a great deal of human anguish, maladjustment, broken marriage, ruined lives, neurosis, etc., and it gives rise to the profession of psychiatry.

Early in the game men's creativity was smothered by industrialism and this has been the occasion of wholesale escapism and the widespread use of opiates. So the characteristic American man and woman is intellectually dull. Not only that, but more and more brutalized. More and more incidents reveal this. Only the other day a young man attempting suicide was poised at a great height and about to jump. A priest and a young girl were nearby trying to dissuade him. But the crowd below was impatient for its thrill. Housewives shouted, "Jump," and frenzied teen-agers hopped up and down, screaming, "Go ahead!"

Americans are also getting emotionally exhausted from the constant over-stimulation of their sensibilities, emotions and passions.

Culturally of course our contemporary man is bankrupt. Industrialism has destroyed culture. It is now busy destroying it all over the face of the earth. A Japanese who is one generation from the kimono, and secularized, has lost all the dignity of his people. He wears colorless Western clothes, practices birth control, has materialistic aspirations, has fed his mind on American movies, and behaves just like us, only worse. He has given up a real, if imperfect, culture for none at all. The Hindu from India can be uprooted just as quickly. Naturally it would not have been possible to uproot them if their roots had not been rotting, but it is very questionable if no culture at all is to be preferred to a decadent culture. In any case the uprooting is being done, and the consequent absence of traditional or religious ties is the first condition for making the new man.

What will the new man be like? We do not know, but we hazard the guess that he could be called "the hollow man." He will not operate organically from the inside, but mechanically from the outside, in response to external stimuli. He will be almost like a robot.

The way Fuchs explained his own psychology was that he practiced a sort of schizophrenia, never letting his traitor life cross his pleasant social life, even mentally. Fuchs liked his friends and found club life and the English code of honor in social relationships very pleasing. But within Russia there is no such life, and social codes of honor are disappearing everywhere. A man who had never known them would not have to split himself. A dictator in control of a whole generation could condition children. Instead of developing in them a delicate conscience and a sense of shame, they could be taught hygiene and a sort of stoicism. It will be easy to woo them from any sort of philosophical speculation, if our own schools are any criterion. Our public school students are no longer taught to *think* but are expected to memorize, or just to soak in ideological concepts. The typical graduate engineer is almost invulnerable to spiritual or philosophical ideas. He uses his mind a lot, but only with respect to practical, concrete problems.

It is useful, though depressing, to consider the role that psychiatry plays with respect to the changes in man. The whole mainstream of psychology and psychiatry is an amoral substitute for morality. Natural man belongs in the moral order, the new scientific man operates on deterministic principles. What he does he is conditioned to do by emotional ties beyond his control, or by traumatic experiences antedating the age of reason. The essentially atheistic nature of modern psychology is so clear-cut that it needs no arguing. As regularly as a moral problem is mentioned, in *The New York Times* for instance, an amoral, psychological solution is offered by some psychiatrist or official or social worker. Juvenile delinquency, dope addiction among high school students, job unhappiness, marital difficulty—it doesn't matter what it is. Yet Catholics are still confused on this subject, and the main reason is that most psychiatrists are very tolerant of religion, morality, confession, etc., *in a subordinate role*, for their therapeutic effect, and not as true.

When Satan tempted Christ the third time in the desert he offered Him lordship over the whole world in return for His submission, knowing that he had nothing to fear from good things which were subordinate. Atheism has nothing to fear from religion which will take second place.

The general method of psychiatry and psychology is the same as that used by physical scientists. It is to *explain away* higher things, like holiness, morality, self-sacrifice, or remorse, by giving an explanation in a lower order. It can even be a true explanation, although secondary or partial.

Another disservice which psychiatry does is to resolve problems on a low level which should be resolved on a high level. People whose lives are all awry, because of the diminution that is being pressed upon them on every side, are led to "adjust themselves," that is, to accept the mediocrity the world offers. It is precisely the opposite solution to that offered by Saint Therese of Lisieux to men deprived of the opportunity to do great deeds.

Psychiatry prospers because men really are mixed up, and many of them are beyond the direct assistance of moral and spiritual help. Some agent has to help them unwind. If it is going to be a psychiatrist, it will have to be one who is not only understanding and holy but also one who is intellectually capable of seeing the Christian truth which the atheists have perverted. Such a man should lead the maladjusted toward sanctity and apostolicity.

The new man will be very obedient but in a robot sort of way. We said before that God governs the universe according to nature. The nature of man is to have free will. God moves his will, but according to its nature, freely. The new rulers will disregard nature and will seemingly be able to go unheard-of lengths in moving men's wills *unfreely*, that is, by force. Orwell describes this in the case of his hero in "1984." What the tyrants wanted and got was not that the man should do their will, but that he should *will* their will; they wanted his complete allegiance. We see the same thing attempted with Cardinal Mindzenty and other leaders in Eastern Europe. What this shows us is that the term of the remolding of man is not slavery or death but eternal death, the destruction of his soul. This indicates clearly its diabolical origin because only the Devil can be interested in forcing a submission so profound that it will be eternal.

WAR

Modern wars are the violent accompaniment and necessary expression of the upheaval and transformation of the whole social structure. Most of the wars in history were comparable to typhoons, tornadoes, or other violent storms on the earth's surface. Now the very globe is heaving. We are having social earthquakes like those which raised up mountains and submerged great areas under newly formed seas. The pent-up violence of humanity has been let loose. No force is yet great enough to subdue the catastrophe which has been unleashed.

The old Christian world order is almost finished. The atheistic world order is rushing to its completion. What is at stake is an ordering of the world which is a continuing process to the materialists, who have the initiative. It goes on in one way during wars, in another way during respites from wars. That is why the Russians scarcely pause for the signing of a peace treaty before they undertake the "peaceful penetration" of the next country on their list. They cannot stop even if they want to, because there is no resting place in a half-completed synthesis. Half an order is no order, and things will not balance. We always want to stop after a period of fighting and sink back into luxurious unconcern for global order. That is, we Americans do. The Catholic Church behaves apostolically in a fashion parallel to but contrasting utterly with the Russian action. "Go ye to all nations and baptize them." It is a never-ending process until truth and love are brought to all men.

With a new synthesis there will be an order, and that will end the upheavals and the wars.

Here again we see what a dilemma the Devil has put us in. However unworthy contemporary Christians are, however much their own negligence has contributed to this crisis, it nevertheless remains that they (and other men of good will) are fighting against the completion of that synthesis, they are trying to prevent night's closing in on mankind. If they did not resist, the new order would be finished in no time, and all possibility of serving God or organizing any opposition would be cut off.

It is this resistance which causes wars. Of course it is really the Russians who are provoking wars by annexing territory, and stirring up revolutions where it is convenient to their cause, but they want a new order and war is only incidental to the getting of it. They used to be the revolutionaries trying to break down our system, but now we are the revolutionaries trying to interfere with their wave of the very near future. They can even make it seem as though we are standing in the way of peace, with some reason. Except that it would not be peace but a hideous caricature.

It is significant that although we (the side of residual Christianity) have won the last couple of wars it did us no lasting good. We could not win the peace, and in each succeeding war the margin of victory was less. It looks as though it does us no good to win wars. The reason is that we are fighting a new world order purely defensively, with no alternative scheme. The Christian new world order, which alone can conquer the atheists, is embryonic, barely conceived. Furthermore "our" side is still weakened by fighting under banners of nationalism, democracy, freedom, and the bourgeois way of life. There is no army for Christ.

The Crisis

A further irony is that every time we fight we become more like the enemy. Our warfare is technological, our men fight like engineers. Human virtue and compassion are almost irrelevant. We press all our national wealth and resources into developing A and H bombs. Therefore it becomes more and more clear that we are trying to cast out devils by the power of Beelzebub.

We rapidly approach the point where we have two absolute alternatives, neither of which can we choose. A dilemma again. We can decline to fight — and we are lost. Or we can fight and lose to the same enemy in a different way. Everyone is busy trying to figure out how to slip through the horns of this dilemma. The proposed solution is the United Nations, which seems to be only a forum for illuminating ideological differences. Back of the political efforts of the U. N. delegates to negotiate a peaceful settlement of problems, there is a lot of sociological study going on in an effort to work out a world plan along humanistic lines. It is supposed to be an alternative plan to the atheistic synthesis. It proposes universal regard for human rights, the elevation of the position of women, the sharing of scientific knowledge, the spread of education, etc.

This, I believe, is playing inadvertently into the hands of the Devil. The dilemma is Lucifer's handiwork. And so is this seemingly hopeful resolution of the dilemma, which will preoccupy vast numbers of intellectual workers and will add up to precisely nothing.

Mankind can only slip through the horns of this dilemma by transcending it, by seeking a solution on a higher plane, because this is no ordinary dilemma but the work of the Devil.

DIABOLISM

It would appear to be an inescapable truth that it is impossible for men, as the world now is, to become merely pagan, or to become evil in merely human measure. The only paganism possible for mankind now is some veiled form of Devil worship: the only kind of evil that a man can espouse is the evil of the beast. Redemption has made it possible for us to be like God. By way of consequence, it has involved that we cannot fall except by becoming like Satan *(God, Man and Satan,* by Bernard J. Kelly, C. S. Sp.).

We have arrived at the heart of the crisis. Men have invited Satan to become their master, not because men wished to do wicked things but because they wished to do good things without God. The humanitarians, the philanthropists, the literary people, and the artists for art's sake have pulled us down into Hell every bit as much as have the usurers, the adulterers and the purveyors of black magic.

To state that the world is secular is to state who is its master. We have invited him, and every day he becomes more clearly enthroned. In the order of creation the angels, good and bad, have a certain natural power over men. We only escape the demons by being elevated to an order above them.

In revelation the Devil is called the Lord of the World. And it looks as though in our times he is coming into his estate. Heretofore the Devil's influence has been localized or personalized. Now he is getting control of the social order, the physical order, and the political order of the world. Seemingly he is aiming at a system which will almost mechanically destroy men's souls, no matter which way they turn. The diminution of man is the first great step, then hunger, crowding, cold, dispossession, the horrors of war and torture and concentration camps, the perversion of education, the regimentation of life, the disappearance of individual initiative, the vulgarizing and confusing of minds through picture-opiates, the prevention of thinking through the ubiquity of meaningless noise and talk.

Once one sees the Devil as the instigator of the system, many things become clear. It explains how so many unrelated people and factors synchronize their efforts. A master mind is prompting and tempting and suggesting, playing on men's weaknesses. It explains also the spiritual nature of the new order. Since it is aimed at the destruction of souls, its work is sometimes accomplished without the least physical violence.

THE IMPOTENCE OF PURELY NATURAL ACTION

Because the Devil's synthesis destroys the natural order, it is tempting for Christians to look to the restoration of the natural order as the antidote, or at least as the primary and preliminary action demanded by circumstances. The fact that the natural law is binding on all men, not only on Christians, and that human reason is capable of being persuaded of its truth, is a further inducement to place emphasis on this level.

Reforms of various sorts are suggested: organic farming, return to a wholesome nutrition with "whole" food, banishment of usury from the financial world, the breakdown of large cities, distributism, folk dancing and culture, clean government, the re-appreciation of woman's nature and domestic role, credit unions, co-operatives, study groups of all sorts, creative work and recreation, housing reform. All these are good, most of them are also necessary, but none of them singly nor all of them collectively has the power to wrest the world from the Devil, as they stand and without being ordered to a higher end. Here is where the theology of nature and grace enters the picture again, to remind us that in one sense the "good natural" is just as far from the supernatural as is perverted nature—for they are both infinitely removed from it. "Without Me, you can do nothing."

There are several illusory positions to be dealt with.

THE "GOOD NATURAL" NOT THE CHRISTIAN

If it were possible to achieve all these natural reforms by natural action, which it is not, the result would not be a Christian society. We have to say this because many people confuse a Christian order with a naturally good order. They are as different as day from night. Christ's own life centered in the mystery of the Cross, so His society can be expected to bear an analogous resemblance. Christ's life was a contradiction, so His order can be expected to contradict the world too. Consider, as illustration, how different the humanist's "ideal man" is from the saint. He has culture, refinement, learning. His natural gifts are all developed. He is courteous and clean and interested in the common good rather than in his own advancement. Obviously it is an ideal which rests heavily on natural endowment, material and social advantages.

Sanctity, in contrast, can use any human base, wise or simple, rich or poor. It completely fulfills its subjects, even intensifying their natural gifts, but by ordering a man's whole life to charity. A certain transformation and elevation of his nature takes place within which the nature is perfected but not with the finality one finds in the humanist. Saint Francis of Assisi was a talented and charming youth before his "conversion." He gave up all promise of human development and achievement. Yet who can say that the saint lacked any fulfillment of his nature. His charm was still there, mysteriously magnified. He was a leader of men above anything he could have hoped for in war or politics. Furthermore what Francis became he could never have become by first perfecting himself in the natural order. The transformation and elevation of his faculties demanded as prerequisite their radical subordination to a higher principle. Francis the saint was so different from what would have been Francis the fully developed man that the quality of the two would have to be submitted to a different measure. One of the most striking contrasts would be in external appearance, that is, in the material aspect.

The same thing holds true with the social order. It is not only in the hearts of men that the difference lies between the naturally good man and the Christian, it is even more sharply evident in the temporal embodiment of the two ideals. We build housing projects and garden suburbs and fancy sometimes that we are making Christian communities, or at least communities waiting for and adapted to Christian groups. But these natural embodiments of natural standards, such as good garbage disposal, attractive houses and private garden plots turn out to be sterile and lifeless and to act as a natural constraint rather than encouragement of the life of mutual charity. It is not the goodness in these projects that condemns them, because Christianity incorporates all the good things like space and air and gardens and family-size units. But it does it in a different way and one which cannot be foreseen by merely technological considerations. Perhaps the best way to express it is to say that the naturally good thing is dead, like a corpse, or frozen, whereas the Christian thing is alive and vital and warm. Or maybe the difference is in the hierarchical structure of a community, a housing project, a political order. Or perhaps it lies in the fact that the naturally good scheme is "perfect" in a narrow, materially realizable way, whereas the Christian social order, being an embodiment in sinful mankind, is imperfect and perfect at the same time. Just as Saint Francis' clothes were beggar's rags and his body was sickly, so a Christian realization in a social order is unlikely to achieve new paint on all the houses or perfectly paved roads. But as Saint Francis lent a beauty to his very garments so these Christian things will take on a beauty which will transcend and transform the material element. Needless to say it will not be the beauty of the glass-brick kitchen advertised in the *Ladies Home Journal.*

SEEK YE FIRST...

This leads us to the second illusion, which concerns the order of precedence. It is an error to think that society can be given a Christian form except under the aegis of the supernatural. As far as the social order is concerned it is precisely in the matter of form, of arrangement, of juxtaposition of values, that Christianity manifests itself. This is similar to the case of the soul and the body. The matter of the body is in the material order, but it is the soul, the spiritual principle, which makes the body develop, and causes it to develop in a particular way. Undoubtedly the action of the soul in forming the body has to be proportioned to the limitations of the particular matter it has to work with, but the initiative rests with the spiritual.

Similarly in the social order it is spirit that develops institutions and projects, conditioned by the limitations and possibilities of the particular human situation. If that spirit is secular it will form certain institutions, and if it is impregnated with supernatural principles it will form somewhat different institutions. If we let the secular realize its own form in a society and *then* try to Christianize it, the secular forms will have to be displaced by other forms, some change will have to be made as well as an elevation. Where the secular forms have degenerated badly they will have to be entirely replaced.

FALSE HOPE IN THE NEUTRAL

Most of the naturally good reforms mentioned earlier are "neutral"; that is, they are good in themselves and standing alone. The question arises whether we ought not to try to put them into effect as soon as possible without waiting for the world to become Christian. It seems like a much more ambitious project to restore all things to Christ than to get young people to do folk dancing or to make and distribute whole-wheat bread to malnourished people. Besides, many non-Catholics, not ready to join the Church, are willing to co-operate on these naturally good projects. We also belong to this world, it is argued, and owe it to our citizenship to work for good temporal ends.

Now the illusion here is that it is easier to bring about a good natural order through natural efforts than it is to obtain the rectification of the natural order through the orientation of the world to Christ.

It is possible to obtain temporarily certain objects in the natural order, but by and large this naturally good world is impossible, and therefore unrealistic, whereas the ordering of the world to Christ is our mission and may perhaps be closer to realization in our day than it has ever been.

The reason the naturally good order is impossible is, theologically, owing to original sin. The naturally good society is impossible to fallen man.

But apart from theological considerations we should learn by our own experience and analysis. Our great hopes are always failing us.

We think we can create wonderful citizens if only everyone gets an education—but human virtue keeps declining. We think we can create good interracial relationships by non-religious means, but we do not succeed. We think we can clean up political corruption by the right use of our franchise, but the change is only momentary, or seeming, and the situation continues to worsen.

One difficulty with "neutral" means is that being neutral, they cannot sustain their indeterminism and will become an instrument of atheism, avarice or idolatry if we decline to impregnate them with Christianity. The communists use folk dancing to better advantage than we do, the British co-operatives are huge capitalistic enterprises, and lots of people worship wheat germs.

Another difficulty with naturally good and neutral projects is that in themselves they do not arouse enthusiasm. Man thirsts for the infinite, not the wholesome. He will only be wooed away from the dynamism of the Devil by Christian dynamism, and Christian dynamism comes from the supernatural. The failure of a lot of efforts by men of good will in recent years has to be attributed to lack of enthusiasm rather than anything else. And is it not just to reject a project in the temporal order if it has no power of arousing enthusiasm?

This qualification should be added. Since Christian dynamism comes from the supernatural, which comes from God, we cannot summon it to aid any project of our own devising. We shall have to choose the projects which grace and reason indicate as appropriate and timely.

Any widespread effort to bring about a good natural order by purely natural means has to fail for an obvious reason. It would involve a wholesale reform of manners and morals, and it would be sheer illusion to hope for this outside of an intensification of religious spirit.

Take the matter of nutritional reform. At a thousand places in the economic system something is done to our food which makes it less alive, less whole. The reason is always that making more money or technological efficiency lies in that direction. To reform food one would have to reform the economic system, which means one would have to cure the human race of avarice and pride, or at least reduce these vices to normal size and control them.

Take another case. Some decentralization, some landward movement, probably large scale, is an obvious necessity. But it involves sacrifice and a return to frugal living, which most people will not countenance

The Crisis

unless they are first freed from the concupiscence which the advertisers have visited upon them. The principle that purely natural reform, however good, can have only very limited and partial success in rectifying the social order is even more apparent when it comes to the more human type of problem. Political corruption, juvenile delinquency, the prevalence and increase in divorce, suicides and mental disorders are all problems that demand profound spiritual and moral reform at the most fundamental level. Yet the more desperate these problems become the more reluctant men are to trust in religious means, especially supernatural means. The fact that some little good can be done by counseling, by playgrounds, by stricter law enforcement and by electric shock treatments leads to false hopes and further neglect of root treatment. So we postpone the day when we shall have to face the fact that only Christ and Christianity undiluted (but not abstracted from daily life and social problems) can save us. Meanwhile catastrophe is at our heels.

We hope that no one will be tempted to conclude that because this "good natural" is impotent to transform the world that it is to be disregarded in favor of the bad natural. There is a sort of connaturality between rectified nature and grace, so long as proper order of precedence is observed. Whole food and a human tempo of life cannot call down faith, hope and charity, but charity can normally operate better in a person with good health than in a person whose nerves are frayed and whose endurance is slight. Reason does not call down faith, but faith is nullified where ignorance and error abound.

What we are advocating is not the abandonment of good natural means and projects for a sort of "angelism," a piety that refuses to incarnate itself. Rather we want action that is at once temporal and supernatural, that uses the good natural but at the same time transcends it.

Actually much of the good natural effort made by Christians is not merely on the natural plane (sanctified, remotely perhaps, by a morning offering). It is more than that, but it is still not enough. Sometimes the supernatural is extrinsic to the project itself, as in co-operatives where the accompanying adult education is Christian or the motives of the men involved are supernatural and point to a goal beyond the merely economic.

Or again, men have mixed motives. They give alms to a beggar partly for the love of God and partly to get rid of him.

Or again a man may work for purely natural reforms because he has a position of responsibility in a secular society, and the duties of his state in life demand this action. His conscientiousness in performing his duty may be inspired by Christian motives and so even the secular act participates remotely in a supernatural orientation. As far as individual consciences are concerned or even the well-being of small groups, some softening of the doctrine has to be allowed. It still remains that for large bodies, or mankind as a whole always, and particularly in today's crisis, only a deeply Christian initiative will be effectual.

CONCLUSION

Even if the secularists succeed in completing their world order, which would be the worst thing that could possibly happen to our globe, it would still be true that God is in absolute and effortless control of the universe. And it would also be true that He allowed the evil to happen in view of a greater good which He will bring out of it. Christians need to be reminded of this truth, not so that they will become passive spectators of a world in its agony, but so that they will become as children, working hard and peacefully, not as though everything depended on their prudence and strategy, but as trusting the providence of their Father in Heaven.

We must cultivate this sort of trust and, as a corollary to it, we must become spiritually detached from every temporal condition. The man who wants to behave morally and is prepared to do so *unless it involves the loss of his job* limits the operation of grace to the present economic structure. The family that prefers its material and social position to a real corporate holiness or to the establishment of social justice in its area, is like a wall in the path of the kingdom of God on earth. He whose honor stops short of preferring death or disgrace is like a straw in the path of political corruption or dictatorship.

It is hard to prefer God to everything whatsoever else, but it is the condition of turning the world to Him, as well as the requisite for our own salvation. That "he who loses his life shall find it" has a universal social application today. People are afraid to ask everything of the ordinary man (who is always some other man besides ourselves), but if they do not the Devil will. When the world is this way it is not charitable to relieve men of the necessity for heroism by casuistic reasoning. It is charitable to make them heroes and to give them a vision of a life which may not be long or comfortable but can be

The Crisis

glorious. Christ came not to find excuses for men's mediocrity and conformity but to spread fire on the earth.

If men will cultivate this combination of trust and detachment, they will necessarily lose their secular outlook. Their treasure will be in Heaven, and so their thoughts will naturally be elevated into a wider perspective. Their lives will become less superficial, which is the second absolute condition of becoming useful for Christ in the modern world. The daily lives of millions are now almost entirely meaningless, with the torrent of useless or erroneous facts, the thousands of fleeting impressions, the noise and time-killing distractions. As presented by newspapers, even political and military news does not make any sense but is a play-by-play account of the surface manifestations of changes which are really occurring at a much greater depth. Those who are influencing history, for good or for evil, have to be on a deep level. Getting down there has nothing much to do with formal education, which has capitulated to the superficial too. It means hard work, real thinking and studying, and for those on God's side, prayer and the Sacraments. It is hard to see how a person of really first-rate intellectual capacity could stay on the surface. But not all those who go to a deeper level are necessarily intellectuals.

Interestingly enough, at the level at which things really have meaning and are really influenced, mankind is being re-united and re-organized. The history of the communist movement shows how a handful of radicals with a common doctrine naturally fell into a unity which crossed national borders and language barriers and built up a political organization later superimposed on millions of people unaware of what was going on. A similar thing is going on with Christians. Below the level of perfunctory religious practice there is an international re-federation of apostolic people taking place, with a very close bond of unity to each other and to the hierarchical structure of the Church.

Below the level of superficiality then, and united with each other, we Christians must work as hard as possible, full time, to bring about Christ's kingdom on earth. But our program will be shrouded in mystery because God will save the world and bring about His order in His own way. We shall not be like the communists, meeting clandestinely to plot treachery and violence, to map out the best ways to cripple cities or cause work stoppages. We should not try to match their cunning by our more moral cunning. That would be like trying to outwit the insect pests which are destroying our orchards by inventing more and more sprays. We ought instead to act like the organic farmer, revitalizing society at the roots by giving it new life. In this way we shall gain the initiative in the world struggle and rebuild from within.

To say that we should not be cunning does not mean that we should not be wise, for Christ has said that we should be wise as serpents. But wisdom is profundity and takes into account the mysteries. It sees, without fully understanding, that simple acts of real charity have a transforming effect on the world, and that the faith which seems like folly to the world can really move mountains as one of the least effects. Wisdom comes from the Holy Ghost, Who can infuse light into a mind which opens itself to eternity but cannot operate on the level of human prudence and scheming.

Even many good people think in their hearts that holiness would be a real impediment to solving our crisis. They would welcome piety in the simple, but they would be afraid of it in statesmen, business men and "practical" thinkers. This view shows an unconscious secular presupposition. It is as though they said Christ cannot heal our society, only we can with our human cunning.

The truth of the matter is that God alone can help us, and the price of His assistance is our humility. We think we are fighting the Russians but we are really fighting human pride.

1952

33

Optimism

JANUARY 1952

SOME PEOPLE ARE OPTIMISTIC BY TEMPERAMENT, which means they have a natural disposition to look on the brightest side of things. In its extreme form this characteristic is light-hearted and superficial to the point of irresponsibility, never discerning obstacles, always disregarding the handwriting on the wall and the shadow of unpleasant things to come. People of an ultra cheerful turn of mind were as sure that Hitler would never gain control of Germany as they are that it is foolish to worry about the centralization of power in the welfare state, and that, in general, "it can't happen here." But perhaps I have already gone beyond the marks of the optimistic *temperament*, which is usually a blessing to oneself and one's associates, especially in the social sphere, to the optimist *creed*, which is not necessarily an out-growth of the temperament. The optimist creed is not a good thing. It holds that everything is ordered to the best in this best of all possible worlds, and, by an implicit denial of Original Sin, blithely trusts in the goodwill, and indeed goodness, of all men.

THE OPTIMIST CREED

We see the optimist creed today on two different levels. On the superficial level it is characteristically American and materialistic, but in a naive way. It is the cult of cheerfulness for its own sake. It brought in the era of the joke teller. It is responsible for the optimist clubs where men group together to reassure each other that business will be good and to exchange funny stories.

Because we Americans have a background of this sort of thing, we can easily slip into a much more dangerous type of optimism without being fully aware of what is happening. We can go from looking on the bright side of things to thinking that we can redeem the world and dry all its tears by the proper use of material things.

For this is precisely the new religion which is on the horizon, the global redemption of mankind by man through industry and science. It is the convergence of secularism, materialism and optimism.

Tomorrow shall the iniquity of the earth be abolished, says the gradual for the Vigil of Christmas, and then adds, *and the Savior of the world shall reign over us.*

Now the first part of this is precisely what is being said by the new type of glorified materialism and humanism. *Tomorrow shall the iniquity of the earth be abolished.* These complete atheists do not go on to say "and a new world tyrant (perhaps anti-Christ?) will rule over us." But they might as well have said it.

This hope of a temporal, secular redemption is the heart of the communist message, but it is also commonly held by the new liberals and in varying degrees by all those who are expecting to create a better world without reference to morality or grace. It is also held with modifications and inconsistencies by not a few Catholics. It is the most seductive, and it will soon be the most pervasive philosophy, or rather theology, we have seen in a long time. It is the official dogma in quite well-rounded form of the Unesco division of the United Nations.

THE DOCTRINE

Tomorrow shall the iniquity of the earth be abolished. The new secularism can be best understood as a caricature of this holy promise. It is a false redemption, but a promise of redemption.

First of all it promises to deliver us from our sins by removing the causes of sin. The causes of sin (which is not called sin of course), according to this doctrine, lie in a bad ordering of the world, or for the person, in a bad orientation of life. The reordering of the world is now taking place, and will be accomplished chiefly through technology which will relieve poverty, disease, want, etc. By scientific birth control, synchronized with scientific farming and industry, controlled by scientific distribution of produce, living standards everywhere will be equalized and raised. We can even hope that "technology, for all its perils, has the power to increase wealth, to provide for starving populations and in the end to reduce and *perhaps abolish social inequality.* This is a process that no sane man would wish to stop. Nor can it be stopped."

This quotation is from a Unesco broadcast commemorating the third anniversary of the Human Rights Declaration of the United Nations. Note that it is axiomatic that it is a good thing to abolish social inequality. This is the UN version of the Marxist classless society. With the advent of classlessness is expected a disappearance of greed, avarice, hatred and all the rest of men's vices, because the atheists regard these faults as provoked entirely by outward circumstances. As a matter of fact, virtually the opposite is true. Sins come from the will of man and have to be corrected there. Outward circumstances can and do aggravate and increase them, but not always or necessarily. In the wider perspective it is not so true that bad conditions make men bad, as it is true that bad men bring about bad conditions. Both social and moral changes are necessary, but they should go together with the emphasis on, and hope in, the moral rectification. I need not point out to the readers of *Integrity* that a classless society is in any case not the desideratum of a Christian social order and should it arrive, it would in fact have terrible consequences, since it does not correspond with the order of nature. The materialists' hope in this regard is simply superstition.

Let us look at another part of that quotation. It is held that the classless millennium will be brought about by technology. Now it is true that technology has a leveling effect on society but only in that it makes men more alike as it makes them less like men. It is not true that technology creates a community of love. Power and money hierarchies flourish more readily in factories and bureaucracies than ever they did in aristocracies. Here again the promise of redemption reduces to mere words. The end and the means are not merely disproportionate, they are unrelated.

One more factor must be mentioned in this central false promise: *Tomorrow shall the iniquity of the earth be abolished.* As far as persons are concerned, materialistic psychiatry will do for them what technology promises to do for the masses of men. It will remove the obstacles to the natural flow of goodness in the individual. Here we see clearly how optimism carries over into this false hope. The materialists are determinists. They pretend not to believe in good or evil since they do not believe in free will, but nevertheless they do implicitly believe that progress tends towards a beatitude of sorts and that human beings are essentially stainless and benevolent.

HEAVEN ON EARTH

This article does not pretend to be a full analysis of the secular synthesis. We have discussed it before and we shall discuss it again. Here I am only concerned to show certain characteristic fallacies in its reasoning.

I can't help mentioning the subject of peace. Mrs. Roosevelt said the other day on the radio in Paris that the Human Rights program will bring peace, because nothing is so destructive of Human Rights as war, so any effort to promote human rights will be a step in the direction of permanent peace. The reader can have his own fun disentangling the logic of this statement.

Peace is the tranquility of order. The only order that can be tranquil is the one God ordained for the universe. There is a regimentation that looks like order but is only uniformity and which, temporarily only, suppresses the passion of mankind. There is a kind of apathy that looks like tranquility but usually makes no pretense of seeming ordered.

Death looks like peace too. If secularists are successful this is probably the caricature of peace that they will achieve.

Besides peace, happiness is also promised modern man in the shining vision of a technological future. He will be happy because he will have a high standard of living, comfort, food and gadgets. This proposition can easily be refuted from our own personal experience, or St. Thomas' inquiry into what makes men happy. However, it does suggest certain things about the way men have been deceived into vain hopes, and it might be useful to consider these.

HOW TO CREATE FALSE HOPE

A friend once told me that almost all his adult life his work had been harried by financial difficulties and that he had dreamed of the bliss that would come of solvency and a well-ordered money life. Then it finally came about. "Do you know what it feels like?" he said. "Like nothing. It is the absence of feeling."

Herein lies an important truth. It is men who are sick who pin their hopes on health, men who are hungry who dream dreams of food, men who are bitterly and a long time cold who are ready to worship fire, men who are crippled who dream of walking, men thirsting who appreciate water, men suffocating who discover the rare value of air.

Chesterton said that we ought not to take so for granted the wonder of having legs or the miracle of speech, and this is true in a certain sense. But it is also true that these things are part of the normal equipment of men and that men are made to know, love and serve God, not to sit around glorying in ankles or ozone. Not that Chesterton meant that they should, but the evil genius behind what is happening to the world now has found that by depriving masses of men of the simplest necessities of life (thus bringing to their concentrated attention and longing what they would ordinarily take for granted), men can be made to forget about their eternal destiny and even their intellectual and aesthetic ambitions, and will pin their hopes on something materialistic.

Men could never have been brought to look for their redemption in the material order unless there had first been great material disorder and deprivation. This is the secret of the communist successes during hard times. This is, in fact, why the communists create hard times where they do not already exist. Since the secular heaven is a this-world heaven, it is important to *diminish* man's universe. But man is made for God and yearns for Him. Take away, therefore, some normal part of man's equipment, a roof over his head, or a job, or his daily bread, so that he will be acutely aware of what's missing, and he will forget about the higher things.

But food in your belly feels like nothing. It makes you forget your stomach. Health is a state of not noticing the body. The absence of a house is painful, but the presence of a house makes you forget about houses. Once a man has these basic necessities he again feels unhappy. They have not made him happy. They have just relived a pain which shouldn't have been there in the first place.

THE FALLACY IN AMERICAN BENEVOLENCE

Americans could learn a lesson from this in various fields. We spend billions of dollars helping starving and ill-clothed people in order to seduce them away from the communist ideology. Then we are surprised that we have not bought their loyalty for American ideals. But food and clothing will only take away a certain pain. They do not give meaning to life and American ideals are so nebulous at the moment that they amount to saying this: "A certain material standard of living will give meaning to life." But it will not, and the communists have a more dynamic, if erroneous, ideology to offer.

Or again, the laboring classes were discontent *and* economically exploited We have made the mistake of thinking that higher wages and other purely material concessions would satisfy the workers, whereas as a matter of fact, it has made them more dissatisfied because they no longer have to waste time thinking how they will eat and if they will hold their jobs. In short, you cannot satisfy a spiritual hunger with material food.

THE CATHOLIC INVOLVEMENT

Not a few Catholic minds have been sucked into the optimist pattern of thinking. This is not to be wondered, because in its extreme form the thesis is very dynamic. It has borrowed an apocalyptical aura from a nearly forgotten Christianity.

The key point is technology, for that is the means, the almost mystical means, by which the global paradise will be achieved. Beware then of Catholics who, brushing aside certain grave ill-effects of a technological society, glow with enthusiasm for the new world which they expect to follow as the direct result of greater and more comprehensive technology.

The late French personalist, Emmanuel Mounier, is an outstanding example. He was a man of apparently good will who became so sympathetic with the communists that he began to share their materialistic vision. In a recently published book of his articles he deals confusedly, but at length, with machine civilization. One thing is clear; he is very optimistic about the future, on the *basis of the promises of technology*. Hear him:

> We have still to ask whether the total effect of a machine civilization, once its teething troubles are over, is not in the last resort of capital importance to the ethical development of humanity and whether it is not, for a great number, an indispensable condition to the exercise of a really human existence.

Mounier thought that technology represents the advent of *maturity* in human progress. Instead of being at the mercy of nature, and subject to its rhythm, man is to be *liberated* from the natural law and from the natural rhythm, to make new laws and a new rhythm. Work is to become effortless and since God, according to Mounier, put a curse on man's work purely vindictively, it is right, just and clever that man should at least succeed in freeing himself from the hardship of toil. Mounier went so far as to compare the experts awaiting the results of the first atom bomb experiment in New Mexico to the medieval knight on the eve of his consecration, because the moment of the minority of man was ending and he was to become "within the limits of his range, the master of creation".

So far as I have seen, no one has ever successfully explained away the dehumanizing effects of machine-tending on man. The indisputable fact

Optimism

of dehumanization stands unanswerably in the path of the Christian embrace of technological society. But Mounier sweeps away this obstacle in one fantastic gesture. He says that after all we've been a long time in the so-called natural order, who knows but that in another 200,000 years we won't feel differently about the rhythm of the machine?

As even Leslie Paul, who did the foreword to his book, points out, Mounier was very close to Pelagianism and almost one with Marxism. Yet he wanted to keep his faith and to reconcile his faith with the new machine society. Had he been more clear and logical in his writing he might have realized the fundamental contradiction in which he was involved.

To a lesser degree many Catholic thinkers are attempting exactly what Mounier attempted.

New Life, a monthly magazine published by the English Young Christian Worker priests recently carried an article on *The Church and the Social Problem* by Very Rev. A. Dondeyne of Louvain University. I think it is not wrong to assume that the reasoning in this article is fairly representative of Jocist thinking about technology.

Msgr. Dondeyne starts by admitting the secular thesis that "viewed on the world scale and in its main lines, the history of civilization is basically the history of the progressive emancipation [from matter] of man and mankind." In fact, "the ultimate meaning of history is the history of man's progressive liberation." He goes on to say that the emancipation of man and mankind depends on three factors: "The progress of positive science and industrial technique, a more genuine recognition of man by man, and the education of man."

A little further on he says, "the workman ... knows that modern industry has the capacity of assuring the mass of people a more truly human existence." And still further on,

> At bottom, what is happening now is that mankind has realized that modern technical methods offer, or will offer in the near future, sufficiently developed possibilities to ensure the whole of mankind a more human existence consonant with man's dignity. For the first time in history, *the idea has arisen that access to the benefits of civilization and culture is possible for great numbers of people.* [His italics] A mass liberation of the human person is no longer considered a utopian vision, and it figures on a programme drawn up for fulfillment relatively soon in the future.

This is enough to show the thesis. Note that it is the *emancipation* not the *salvation* of mankind which is taken as fundamental to history and that this must be a material emancipation, a freeing from the natural order and rhythm of the universe, since positive science and industrial technique have finally made it possible. It promises to make, not saints, but truly human people and truly human people are, by inference, consumers. They are not people who will work creatively or holily, however humbly. They are not people who will determine their own work and follow their own bent. They are tenders of machines whose glory will be in the fact that they will be able to possess all the materially good things the machines will make.

Now I submit that this is not only to expect something from technology which technology will not, in fact, fulfill, but that the goal itself is a wrong goal entirely, not only irrelevant to, but inimical to, the Christian vision.

OPTIMISM AND HOPE

The problem that we are involved in here is not the problem of whether machinery is good or bad in itself. It has nothing to do with a desire to go back to cave dwelling or wooden plows. The question is: shall we put our *hope* in technology, or shall we put our hope where it belongs, in Christ, and let machines fall into their own relatively unimportant place.

If we put our *hope* in technology we shall bring about a world in which technology will absolutely rule us and we shall tremble at the thought of a broken pipe or the exhaustion of the electric power, or the breakdown of some giant machine, as though it would (and in fact it will) have the power to wipe us all out. If we had put our *hope* in a person it would be the same thing, that person would be able by a frown to wreck our happiness. Absolute hope is only rightly placed in God. Whatever we transfer this hope to becomes a god. Seen in this light we can realize that the inevitability of the technological society depends on our secularism and materialism and can be arrested only when we transcend it by placing our hope where it belongs. The new world in the making is only a projection of our own spiritual diseases.

But it is no easy job to convince a materialistic, amoral world that its real trouble is sin and that Christ has redeemed us from sin. It's rather like going to a dying agnostic's beside. His friends are all saying that he will surely get better, better in fact than ever, that he can have perfect confidence in medical science. And that's precisely what he wants to hear. How difficult it is to say that the important thing now is to make peace with God, to repent of one's sins, and yes, death may be near, but is in any case inevitable sometime and it behooves us to turn our eyes heavenward.

The really important thing is the salvation of mankind by Christ and not the emancipation of mankind by technology. To say so is not angelism but is a matter of putting things in their proper order. If we really did so, the world, including the material world, would rock with the consequences. What would a wave of penance do to the economic order? What would the application of the idea of vocation do to dislocate and reorient employment? What would true charity do to international peace? What would moral reform do to politics?

A palsied man was brought to Jesus to be cured of palsy and He said, "Son, thy sins are forgiven." Now the Jews were the opposite of us. They thought it blasphemy to forgive sins but possible to heal miraculously. Whereas we take for granted the absolution and consider the other hard. Maybe only after we fail to heal our own palsy, will we come asking God for a miracle in the material order. What mercy it will be if then we are absolved instead. Taking up our beds and walking will be an anticlimax.

34
The 100 Neediest Cases
FEBRUARY 1952

EVERY YEAR DURING ADVENT *THE NEW YORK TIMES* publishes "The 100 Neediest Cases," capsule case histories from the files of the private welfare agencies. The public is invited to contribute funds for the relief of these unfortunates, which it generously does—this year to the extent of about $300,000.

The short cases are written in a stereotyped fashion, with an almost exaggerated sensitivity to the human side of the problems, to the psychic and emotional elements. This is our heritage from Dr. Freud. (The case that received the most contributions this year was a young woman whose severe facial disfigurement marred her happiness and employability.) By contrast, there is no advertence to moral considerations at all, although only in two cases is there a suggestion of an immoral situation—once birth control and the other divorce.

It may be useful to observe some things about the 100 Neediest Cases, for they reflect a good deal about our society as a whole.

THE ROLE OF THE PRIVATE AGENCY

Nearly all the needy in these cases are in a financial jam. Mr. X has lost his job. Mrs. B, with three little ones, has been deserted by Mr. B. Miss Y needs clothes. Someone else needs hospitalization, or psychiatry. However, with the exception of incidentals, such as board while awaiting adoption, or a hearing device or some special training, money matters are not the substance of this appeal. Our Holy Mother the Welfare State already tides over the jobless, supports the fatherless, hospitalizes the ill and puts a roof over the heads of the old. In fact it is rather a surprise to find out how all-embracing this care is.

It may even be that many generous souls are moved to pity the 100-plus neediest cases for their material wants and to send money for relief of these without noticing that such have already been taken care of by public agencies. What the private agency uses the money for is usually found in the last sentence, which reads something like this: "Friendly counseling of a case worker is needed to help Mrs. L realize that there is much to anticipate, rather than fear, in a life with other old people whose interests are similar to her own," or, "But she will need help in re-establishing a healthy relationship with Roy and in dealing with his behavior problems."

Private agencies shifted over from the corporal to the "spiritual" works of mercy back around the time of the big depression when destitution soared way beyond the reach of private philanthropy. It was pretty much a case of trained social workers looking for a function, with the help of Freud, and that is why all the social work schools are so profoundly psychiatric. Here is how *The New York Times* put the situation this year:

> The State now assumes responsibility for providing the destitute with the material necessities—food, shelter, clothing, basic medical care. But these are not enough.... For there are other needs which cannot be met with financial aid alone. These are the needs of the spirit rather than the body, needs intensified by poverty, loneliness, dismay, despair, which only the warmth of friendly personal interest and the reassurance of wise counsel can remedy.

THE NEEDIEST ARE THE UNLUCKY

Nobody *has* to go to a private agency for help. And presumably nobody really wants to go. Nevertheless very many do go because they are hopelessly confused and bogged down by their own lives and have no one to turn to.

Who are they then, these unhappy creatures? As I read the cases I could see more and more clearly that they were ourselves, you and I, and the man next door, with this difference, that the "neediest" had a piece of bad luck. So often in their histories it mentions the precipitating incident. Mr. and Mrs. K, who were muddling along, though far from leading radiant lives (in a word, like everyone else) were (*un*like everyone else) hit by a car which jumped the curb onto the sidewalk, crippling and impoverishing them. Or Mrs. H slipped on the ice. Or Mr. X gave up and headed for Texas, leaving Mrs. X and the children. Or the O's apartment house was torn down and they couldn't find another place to live. Or Sally P. had a mental breakdown. Or Mr. Y got cancer and Mrs. Y had to go to work and the Y children became juvenile delinquents. An accident, a sickness, a housing crisis, one little burden too many on some frail shoulders, and the whole house falls down—because it is rotten anyhow.

These are the rootless, the relative-less, the property-less, the unskilled, the wage-earners, the readers of tabloids and seers of movies, the televiewers, the women who do not know how to bring up their children and have to do so in the most unnatural surroundings, the couples who come to marriage without traditions or understanding, the women who know nothing about cooking except for the instructions on the Birdseye packages and the recipes on the subway car cards, the old and alone.

Here, in a word, is modern man. He's not terribly much different if he's rich. Loneliness, dismay and despair, not to say confusion, neurosis and badness, flourish at least as easily among the rich who flock to the psychiatrists as the poor flock to the social workers.

IT'S A DEBACLE

The 100 neediest are then ourselves, our neighbors, everyone. They are not some special group of weak or simple-minded. They are not the poor we have always with us. They are average city people who have had a stroke of bad luck. Let some bigger stroke of collective bad luck come along and we'll all get bogged down.

It is important to see them this way because then one can see that our society is, in fact, disintegrating. The mechanization, the lack of order, the absence of roots, traditions, vital religion, property, skill and green trees, is screaming at us, and would seem to indicate how drastic the renovation has to be.

In his Christmas address the Holy Father stated clearly that we would be foolish to hope for a peaceful, stable world based on the present lack of order. A new, stable, right and Christian order has to be achieved everywhere. The "100 Neediest Cases" is a perfect example of what he meant. If these people had roots they would have relatives and neighbors, and if they had relatives and neighbors they wouldn't have to go to a social welfare agency to ask advice about a troublesome husband or child. A spool of red tape wouldn't be needed to get someone to cook a husband's supper on Thursday, or mind a few babies a day or two, or clean a house. If the neediest were trained for marriage they would make more suitable ones and know how to build a family. If they had a vital religion they would not have to have a case worker calm their fears every time the soul made itself felt in a life ruled by distractions, noise, clamor and materialism.

GLOBAL INDIGESTION

So what we are really dealing with is a disintegrating society and not a special problem within a framework which is solid enough. When you really look at the problems that social workers are coping with, they merge into the problems of humanity in general in a disordered age, being only specially acute because someone has given up trying or is becoming hopelessly confused.

It follows that these problems are not susceptible of real solution within the framework of organized social work. It is a wholly inadequate instrument at best and this quite apart from any consideration of the goodness or badness of individual social workers or of social work schools. What social workers can do and apparently have to do in this emergency is to unravel some of the red tape of a complex inorganic society for people who can't fathom the maze of social services which they have to use. This is a necessary evil, a palliative. It is not a highway to the reconstruction of the world.

But because social workers are daily meeting and trying to help solve all the problems of a humanity in anguish, they feel themselves under some obligation to be all things to all men, to spread themselves thin and alleviate everything. It is not by accident that case work, which bites off everything, finds itself chewing peanuts. In a way you might say that social work has shouldered all of God's problems and ends up hopelessly bogged down in trivia.

THINGS THAT ARE NOT FOR SALE

People need friends, advice, helping hands, spiritual instruction, education, all the things that the 100 Neediest Cases talk about, and more. But you cannot go on supplying these things artificially and inadequately. It won't work, and it's uneconomic.

It won't work because it can't be genuine. Take friendship. "There are a lot of people in the city who need a friend and don't have one," say the *New York Times*. But a friend is someone you have known for years, who shares your background, and interests, who will be around in time of need, whom you can call on. It is not someone who is paid to see you every Tuesday and who will never see you again if she gets a job in another agency. The greatest amount of good will on the part of the social worker will not overcome the fact that she cannot really fill the role of a friend. There is only one way of becoming a true friend without having the normal conditions and that is through an intensity of charity and complete giving of one's life to the service of people, feeling free, then, to see them when needed, and having no desire or obligation to desert them. But this is the method of Saint Vincent de Paul or the Catholic Worker Houses of Hospitality—simple, direct, total, and way beyond the tight little restrictions of social worker.

Now, besides being impossible, the reconstruction of society through organized social work is also uneconomic. The best things in life are free, or so God intended they should be. Just as no maid would do for money all the work a wife and mother does for love, so in the long run, priest, friends, neighbors and dedicated people have to do the counseling and consoling and the emergency housework and child care of this world. The harder and more disagreeable the task, the more astronomical the cost if not done for love. The world cannot afford it.

THE ORGANIC APPROACH

Since some social workers are needed to untangle red tape, this article is not to urge the premature dissolution of the profession. But is it not a mistake to channel the most heroic young women into a profession which will frustrate them? And it will, because it is an artificial framework, obliged to operate superficially.

Rather the concentration should be on primary services and on the restoration of the social order to what is natural and Christian—the restoration of marriage, neighborhoods, homes, roots, and the sense of vocation.

Actually the problem does become clearer, even though not simpler, if not constrained artificially within the organized social framework. Incidentally, what is said here of organized social work applies, many times magnified, to the welfare state. And when I have said that the social work view is simpler, I don't mean it is simpler to do because in fact it is impossible, but it looks simpler. In the 100 Neediest Cases the implication is always there that the K's family problems really will be solved by the counseling of the social worker and that Mr. X's threatened mental breakdown will in fact be warded off by seeing the psychiatrist. Yet people who are close to social work know these cases can drag on for years without being much influenced at all by the consulting, that any conspicuous success is rare and often can be traced to something like getting a job or finding an apartment rather than to the "spiritual" ministrations of the worker.

However, to return to the point, no real progress will be made in solving the problems of a disintegrating society unless we look at them in large. If people need friends and relatives then they must get roots again, which means owning their own houses and living and working in the same place most of their lives, not being industrial nomads. Yet look at all the energy and money that goes to build huge city housing projects which will always go against the grain of an organic society and which tend to aggravate all the ills of the Neediest Cases. Let us face the fact that there is no enthusiasm for a movement organic-wards and vocation-wards.

Or again, if there are certain things which God intended be done by neighbors then something has to be done to restore neighborhoods. The Catholic Church has an advantage here over non-Catholics because parishes are really potential neighborhoods regardless of the inorganic basis of the civic community, for the supernatural is a strong enough basis of unity to develop communal life on a higher level than the natural, where the natural unity is lacking. Some work is being done in this direction by Catholic Charities and by parishes but, considering the need, it does seem as though it is proceeding too slowly.

However, this article does not intend to indicate how society will be restored, but only to remind people that this work is the task of the whole Church. It has to be treated at its roots and on a long range basis. Furthermore, this reconstruction has to start wherever one can or is. It does not start with the neediest necessarily, or even probably.

NEW FORMS OF DEDICATION

However, there is another sort of effort which properly should begin with the neediest, and this seems to me to be where really dedicated young women should find their vocation, either instead of going into social work, or as a natural development of an effort at social work. There must be some reason why social workers are always writing papers on "The Destitution of the Negroes in Such-and-Such-a-Place," or "Dope Addiction Among Teenagers," but so seldom leave their profession to clothe and house these particular Negroes or take jobs in hospitals for drug addicts. It may be traceable to the bureaucratic mentality which seems always to be receding from the problems before it, a mentality which will set up a committee or write a report instead of renting a house and taking a couple of people in, or rolling up sleeves and scrubbing the floor. This is not so much laziness or lack of generosity as a sort of paralysis induced by the inorganic, mechanized nature of the system.

It would be natural, if social work were natural, for young women to progress from red tape to primary services, to go beyond giving advice to serving, perhaps in new and very dynamic ways.

Emergency housework and child care, done in a deeply religious and dedicated spirit, could bring more physical order into confused households, and give the doers the satisfaction that a red-tape, half-dedicated job lacks. Or again, if people who are cracking up need some place to go for a combination of physical and spiritual strengthening, why isn't such a place started?

The more regimented we become the harder it is to do anything in a small group and with personal initiative. Perhaps that is why, with so much generosity around, there are no new, adapted channels within which it can realize itself. But another fact seems to be a general capitulation of Catholics to the mechanized approach. If this is true, would that some courageous souls could shake themselves free and make a pathway into more fruitful meadows.

BOOK REVIEWS

OCTOBER 1946

ESSAYS IN RECONSTRUCTION
Edited by Dom Ralph Russel
Sheed and Ward, 1946

IT IS ALREADY OUT OF FASHION TO DENOUNCE OUR TIMES. What further need is there to expose the decay which assails everyone's nostrils? We can therefore turn our thoughts to the more fruitful task of rebuilding. There will probably be a lot of Catholic books on the subject of reconstruction. This, one of the first, is welcome because of its constructive thesis as well as for its several other excellencies. It is a collection of recent English essays on such subjects as science, literature, philosophy, economics and the spiritual revival.

What is most striking about the essays collectively is the intellectual competence of the authors. They usually start by presenting, tersely and precisely, the Church's teaching, or the history of the relevant heresies, or the policies of the government, or some other background information on the matter at hand. It is always excellently done. One recalls especially the comprehensive view of modern philosophical errors in Dom Illtyd Trethowan's *The Reconstruction of Philosophic Thought*, and Michael Fogarty's summary of the economic situation in England (as of 1943) in *Catholics and Economic Reconstruction*. Nevertheless, while one admires this intellectual competence, one cannot help hoping that never again will all this academic background material have to be waded through. It is not necessarily in this way that one arrives at the Christian truth about contemporary life. For instance, this same essay on economics does not ring true for all its learning. Analysis and conclusions cling depressingly to the natural order. They are neither so fresh nor so penetrating as Eric Gill's view based on personal experience, observation and intuition. Nor half so true, in our estimation. They also compare unfavorably, in the matter of depth of Christian understanding, with a recent parallel effort in England, Adam Doboszynski's *The Economics of Charity*.

The most interesting essays in the book are the first two, the last two, and the one on science. Dom Ralph Russell wrote the first two, which consider the general problem of reconstruction. He writes from the integral Christian point of view, with primary stress on the supernatural elements. The last two essays deal competently with Specialized Catholic Action movements. Their two authors, Lieut.-Col. Hon. Anthony Lytton-Milbanke and Father John Fitzsimons (chaplains of the Young Christian Workers of Liverpool) show penetrating understanding of their subjects. When they describe methods, as they often do, they go out of their way to show why the methods suit the problem at hand.

Catholicism and Science, by F. Sherwood Taylor, is the exploration of near-virgin territory. The author strongly condemns the attitude which regards science as "purely scientific" and without moral obligations saying:

> The principles of modern slaughter were elucidated by men who were concerned with problems unconnected with war, and are in no way responsible for the devastation of our world. Those who applied these principles to the armament industry had no more than a cool and scientific interest in a mechanical problem, but cannot be held guiltless. They were interested in science, not in killing; they abstracted their work from its whole consequences but this, of course, does not absolve them from responsibility.

Essays in Reconstruction makes no pretense of looking beyond the English scene, thus losing some of its value for Americans. However, it will prove useful until we can do as well.

Book Reviews

NOVEMBER 1946

JOY

By Georges Bernanos
Translated by Louise Varese
Pantheon Books

JOY MAKES MELANCHOLY READING. IT IS THE STORY OF one saint and a half-dozen or so very unprepossessing sinners. The saint is always joyful, but the author's mood is that of the sinners. The depression which creeps over the reader is not conducive to full appreciation of the joys of sanctity.

Chantal de Clergerie is the heroine. She is extraordinarily pure and innocent, as we are assured over and over again in the course of the book. She is a mystic who experiences ecstasies, but who is so pure and innocent that she thinks them manifestations of an hereditary nervous disease. Even the reader is not fully reassured on this point because of the almost maddening way the author has of talking around the subject. The book would be much improved by the addition of a few simple categorical statements. Everything said concerning Chantal's extraordinary gifts goes like this:

Chantal: "The secret of my..."
Anyone else: "Because of your..."

Joy would make a dull play but would be inexpensive to stage. Only three sets are necessary: the library, kitchen and Chantal's bedroom of Monsieur de Clergerie's country estate. Then a handful of actors, and almost no props. There is no action, other than an occasional walking to the door as though to leave. For the rest, interminable conversations. These are called "great dialogues which bare the secrets of souls" on the jacket blurb, but they seemed muddy to me.

In time it becomes evident that events, or rather conversations, are leading (the chauffeur keeps saying so) to a crisis of some dire sort. I couldn't discern the direction for a long time, and then I began to hope that Chantal's purity and innocence were going to save the souls of all the nasty characters; of her selfish and hypochondriac father, her avaricious, psychopathic grandmother, the miserable worm of a psychiatrist, the priest who had lost his faith and the very evil Russian chauffeur. I had especially hoped for the chauffeur, who seemed so taken with Chantal and had even foregone his daily ration of dope as a noble gesture of some sort. So the end was a rude shock and I still don't see the logic of it, but maybe that is my fault.

Joy will probably please Bernanos fans for all of that. It is not as good as his other works which have been translated but it is in the same turgid style. Bernanos must be a very unhappy man to radiate such gloom, and the wicked in Europe must be much more sickly and neurotic than the wicked here if Bernanos faithfully portrays them.

Perhaps the translator is partly responsible for the lack of clarity. Certainly it is startling to find such a heroine as Chantal exclaiming "My God," sometimes five or six times in as many pages. She probably only said "Mon Dieu," in the original.

For all that there are times when the book has power. The scene of the psychiatrist with his patient rings true, as does Chantal's charity for her grandmother.

WOMAN OF THE PHARISEES

By Francois Mauriac
Translated by Gerard Hopkins
Henry Holt & Company

PHARISAISM IS AN EASY TARGET FOR NOVELISTS. BESIDES being a fairly common failing, it has the advantage of readily winning the reader's contempt. What is rare and wonderful is a charitable presentation of a pharisaical person. Francois Mauriac has done it.

The woman, Brigitte Pian, is the second wife of a French provincial gentleman, and stepmother to his son and daughter. Pious and righteous, she habitually attributes her own meddlesome propensities to correspondence with the designs of God's Providence. She succeeds in introducing tragedy into most of the lives around her.

The story is told as the first-person reminiscences of Brigitte's step-son, supplemented by recourse to diaries and other sources. It is skillfully told, with restraint and deep spiritual insight. The characters are excellently drawn in the case of all the leading figures. But the most remarkable fact about the book is that it is an excellent Catholic novel. This is not only because it is set against a background of the Faith, but because the studies of character are really studies of souls, with the norm of sanctity always in mind. The treatment of them all is compassionate, stressing the workings of grace. A less spiritual man than the author could perceive the havoc wrought by a pious hypocrite. It takes some depth to see that no one can create havoc such that God is prevented through it from drawing souls to Him. It takes a greater depth of charity still to perceive that God loves even pious hypocrites and uses His own means to save them.

There are some beautiful spiritual passages in the book, especially in the Abbé Calou's diary and in Octavia Trombe's love letter to the indecisive Puybaraud.

THY FAITH HATH MADE THEE WHOLE

DECEMBER 1946

A CENTURY OF THE CATHOLIC ESSAY
Edited by Raphael H. Gross, C.PP.S
J. P. Lippincott Company

THIS BOOK CONTAINS THE CREAM OF THE CREAM OF CATHolic essays, culled from many years of discriminating reading on the part of the author. There is Mr. Sheed's magnificent piece on "Reading and Education." There is Christopher Dawson's "Christian Freedom," in which cosmic issues are explained lucidly, at a level a thousand times more profound than ordinarily. There is Msgr. Fulton J. Sheen at his very best, in "The Conspiracy Against Life." There is Hilaire Belloc, "On Lying,"; Chesterton, both facetious and scholarly, and Ronald Knox, and Father Gillis, and Padriac Colum, and Eric Gill and Alfred Noyes, and so on; forty-five essays in all. Congratulations to Father Gross and his publishers.

Book Reviews

FEBRUARY 1947

AUSTRALIA: THE CATHOLIC CHAPTER

By James G. Murtagh
Sheed & Ward

AUSTRALIANS AND IRISHMEN WILL APPRECIATE THIS BOOK especially. It is a pain-staking, well-documented account of the Catholic contribution to the growth of Australia, and it does not omit to trace the careers of the more colorful Irish figures involved. Others than Australians and Irishmen will be interested chiefly to contrast the position of the Faith there with its position here, especially in view of the economic situation. After early, and unsuccessful, efforts to build an economic system on small agricultural free holdings, Australia fell prey to capitalism and its abuses. Things happened faster in Australia than here. The country is now considerably socialized and highly unionized (they have a statute to the 8-hour day). All along the Church was involved, usually through vigorous bishops. There was an interesting controversy as to whether the socialization process was that which the popes were warning against. The presumption was (the same thing now going on in England) that this was a different socialism, somehow harmonious with the faith. One wonders.

Significantly, the strongest American influence on contemporary Australian Catholic social thought is, according to the author, that of Dorothy Day and Peter Maurin. There is an Australian *Catholic Worker*, and it is refusing to accept an economic goal which does not include a plan for redistribution of property into small holdings.

MAJOR TRENDS IN AMERICAN CHURCH HISTORY

By Francis X. Curran, S.J.
America Press

SOMETIMES THE HISTORY OF THE CHURCH IN THE UNITED States is written apologetically, the author inadvertently giving the

427

impression that it was a comedy of errors. Such an author is so lost in the welter of historical detail or so beclouded by an unconscious attitude of Protestant supremacy that he cannot see the blinding light of the Mystical Body of Christ. All thanks to Father Curran for having the simplicity and learning to coordinate our Catholic and Protestant religious backgrounds so that it synthesizes with the Faith. In this book, Protestantism is seen for what it is: a heresy with a troublesome present and an inglorious and intolerant past. Throughout, one senses the tremendous power, confidence, holiness and growing strength of the Catholic Church. All this is done not as a distortion of history, but as a restoration of true historical sense. The book is straightforward, dispassionate, charitable and precise. It is short (less than 200 pages) and so cannot qualify as a major historical work. It is more like an essay, but one which might well form the basis of a more detailed study.

THE CHRISTIAN HERITAGE IN AMERICA
By George Hedley
Macmillan

A SERIES OF SERMONS GIVEN AT MILLS COLLEGE ON THE different Protestant denominations, the Catholic Church, the Orthodox Church and Judaism. Much less substantial than other recent Protestant reviews of the religious situation, it is overlaid by the cosy, eclectic philosophy of benign indifferentism.

Book Reviews

APRIL 1947

MORALS IN POLITICS AND PROFESSIONS

By F. J. Connel, C.SS.R., S.T.D.
The Newman Bookshop

MOST OF THE CHAPTERS OF THIS BOOK HAVE ALREADY appeared in *The American Ecclesiastical Review,* and so may be familiar to priests. We rejoice that they are now available to the laity.

This is practical, hard-hitting, moral theology for doctors, lawyers, nurses, public school teachers, social workers, soldiers and sailors, judges, legislators and politicians. The book is filled with close reasoning rather than pious vagaries. It sets forth general principles and makes unqualified decisions. It talks not about abstract problems but very concrete, contemporary ones like artificial insemination, the "third degree," the atom bomb, and the distribution of prophylactics to men in the armed service.

On the whole Fr. Connell is of the strict observance. Anyone who thinks *Integrity* exaggerates the difficulty of leading a Christian life within the present framework of society should read this book. Without pulling any punches Father Connell flatly upholds moral principles wildly at variance with what everyone else is doing. Hear him on morals in politics:

> He says legislators must vote according to the common good, and that if they subordinate the common welfare to personal or political motives they not only sin but may also become liable in conscience to make restitution. He says that a politician who appoints an incompetent to a job is bound to make restitution to the public treasury for the damage resulting from the incompetency.

He says quite firmly that expediency is "out" as a basis for the conduct of public office.

This book is not the whole story, but it is an excellent statement of what is right and wrong in specific situations. The author has a very good sense of the actual situation in the professions with which he is dealing, especially in the realm of statesmanship. However, I doubt that he realizes the full extent of the difficulty that is involved in applying the moral law in some of the professions. Take nursing for instance. It is good to hear it firmly said that the dying must be warned they are dying. There are many hospitals where a nurse will immediately lose her job if she does not conspire to keep the patient ignorant of his imminent demise. This is not a situation which can be met simply by applying the moral law. It calls urgently for a Catholic Action type of spiritual revolution of the nursing profession. Nonetheless, you do have to apply the moral law, and begin now. It is no criticism of Fr. Connell that he sticks to his theology. It is the work of *Integrity* and other lay efforts to complement his teaching by an analysis of the temporal problems.

Book Reviews

MAY 1947

THINKING IT OVER

By Thomas F. Woodlock.
Declan X. McMullen Co.

THE LATE MR. WOODLOCK WAS FOR MANY YEARS AN EDItor and the daily columnist for the *Wall Street Journal*. This is said to be a representative collection of his columns, arranged according to subject rather than date.

What interests me especially in this book is to try to reconcile Wall Street with Mr. Woodlock, or vice versa. First let us consider Mr. Woodlock, who was nearly eighty at the time of his recent and lamented death. His life was without financial blemish and he was personally honored and respected on all counts. He took his Catholicity seriously, even writing a book, *The Catholic Pattern*, in witness of his faith. Just to see him, as I did on nearly his last Ash Wednesday, early approaching the altar at St. Patrick's Cathedral, was to realize that he was a man living very close to God.

What then, of Mr. Woodlock's Wall Street? As revealed in these essays it is the same old Wall Street at its best: Capitalist, conservative, bent on investment rather than speculation, terrified of Communism, scornful and fearful of government control, fighting mad at the packing of the Supreme Court, early alert to the menace of Hitler, and derisive of liberalism.

My disagreement with Mr. Woodlock's economic doctrine is not entire (but nearly so) and profound. That does not so much matter now. What literally astounds me is that there is hardly a single statement in these essays which differs from the "party-line" of a myriad of the more intelligent Republican Capitalists who were, and are, as regards their spiritual lives, poles apart from Mr. Woodlock. It is as plain as anything why Mr. Woodlock was popular with the men of Wall Street. What is not plain, at least to me, is why there was no apparent effort made to bridge the spiritual gap.

Let us put it this way. Mr. Woodlock was a man of prayer, writing for an audience composed largely of the spiritual underprivileged, yet not speaking to them of God. To be sure, he reduced all his arguments (via the Constitution and the Declaration of Independence) to the dignity of the human person, which he then predicated on a supreme moral law or some such (which meant to him the fullness of the Faith, but which, I am certain, conjured up precisely nothing to his largely non-Catholic audience). Aside from that, God is practically not mentioned. Christ is never named in the book that I could find, not even at Christmas. Goodness is advocated under the guise of the natural law rather than the Redemption. But is the Redemption irrelevant to Wall Street? Or even to the preservation of the natural law?

Similarly, there is that common habit of exposing the sins of absent brethren. It is perfectly safe to damn Communists on Wall Street. But what about the sins of avarice and luxury? Where is the prophet who will damn them on Wall Street?

It will be said that Mr. Woodlock was a columnist on a financial paper, not a preacher. He was not hired to save men's souls, but to clarify issues within the Capitalistic system. That is what Mr. Woodlock undoubtedly thought himself, for he was very apostolic, generous, and devout in his private life, and no one could suggest that he was any less than totally dedicated to work for the Church and the preservation of society.

Nevertheless, because I am most familiar with the state of the receiving end of his columns, I wish he *had* preached, and I cannot help but feel that he ought to have done so. Maybe he would have lost his job. Maybe on the other hand, he would have broken down the financiers' morbid embarrassment about discussing the things that really matter. The elder J. P. Morgan used to let himself into an empty church on weekdays because he liked to sing hymns. It is a pathetic little gesture, showing that a man may gain the whole world and not know what to do with his own soul. In the midst of such, where is one's duty? Mr. Woodlock sometimes gives the impression of a man tied in mental knots from trying to reduce the Apostle's Creed to the size of the Declaration of Independence.

It is easy, now that the Faith is on the *offensive* (and no one is any longer really awed at Wall Street) to say these things. It may have been impossible and imprudent to have said them in the era, so recent and yet so finished now, to which Mr. Woodlock belonged. In any case, my remarks are intended more as pricks to our own contemporary consciences than as condemnation of a man who was far better than I am. R. I. P.

Book Reviews

THE THREE AGES OF THE INTERIOR LIFE, VOL. 1

By Reginald Garrigou-Lagrange, O.P.
Trans. By Sr. M. Timothea Doyle, O.P.
Herder

THIS IS THE FIRST ONE TRANSLATED OF A TWO-VOLUME work on the spiritual life by the most eminent French Thomist. The entire work represents a summary of a course on ascetical and mystical theology which has been given in the Angelicum in Rome for the past twenty years, this volume ending after a consideration of the way of beginners. According to the author himself, this work treats in a higher and simpler manner the same subjects as covered in *Christian Perfection and Contemplation,* and *L'amour du Dieu et la croix de Jesus* and indeed it is much less controversial, and therefore easier, than the former work.

For those who are not familiar with Garrigou-Lagrange, we should say that he is a brilliant defender of St. Thomas' doctrine of grace and that he consequently holds (and keeps reiterating) that the path of the saints through the purgative, illuminative and unitive stages is the normal and inevitable path for all of us; and that most of us are bogged down somewhere on the outskirts of the spiritual life for lack of understanding of the path of holiness and because of resultant general ineptitude in our spiritual lives. So he undertakes to explain the why, wherefore and how. Most of this volume is given over to a general treatment of the life of grace and the spiritual organism. Only toward the end does it come to a specific consideration of the way of beginners.

Let learned men give the author the praise and appreciation owing from theologians. We are not competent to do so. All we can say is that we are abundantly grateful to and for Garrigou-Lagrange. He is *Integrity's* favorite theologian. He is simple enough for us. He is abundantly lucid. Reading this book you are alternately exclaiming, "Oh, *that's why* . . . " and finding yourself carried away by the greatness of the ideal sanctity.

The translation is excellent, as also is the typography.

THY FAITH HATH MADE THEE WHOLE
JULY 1947

WHAT AILS MANKIND?

By Gustave Thibon[1]
Sheed & Ward

THIS IS A SMALL BOOK OF ESSAYS BY ONE OF THE GREATest contemporary Catholic minds. The author analyses the disintegration and perversion into which modern society has fallen progressively since the French Revolution. Taken as a whole it contradicts all the current platitudes about democracy and the good life, with devastating logic and analysis.

One is tempted to demonstrate the excellence of the book by endless quotation, chosen almost at random. I chose the following on work not because work is his main preoccupation (it isn't), but because it makes a point that we have been trying to make in *Integrity*:

> The proletarian of today hates work. Even when he is well-paid, his dissatisfaction is not appeased. He suffers not so much from being an exploited worker as simply from being a worker, and his endless material demands are but superficial and misleading manifestations of this fundamental malaise. The reason for this malaise is that the proletarian's work is unorganic and inhuman. And the remedy proposed by the socialists is better distribution of profit, higher wages! As if this were all there could be to the labor problem.... Until working conditions in industry—and also in trade—change, it will but injure the proletarian to raise the wage level.... You cannot remedy the ills resulting from work which is inhuman by increasing the worker's economic well-being. On the contrary, this is a good way of aggravating his boredom and easing his decline.

Most of the book deals with the political structure of society, especially with the weaknesses inherent in democracy and the harm (in the form of envy and insecurity) which results from declaring all people

---

[1] Gustave Thibon (1903–2001), French Catholic philosopher, author of over twenty books and nominee for the Nobel Prize in Literature four times. —*Ed.*

to be equal when they are obviously not equal. The author shows that the breakdown of the traditional classes which were based on organic function and responsibility (even when the corresponding privilege was abused), has led to our present hierarchy of wealth with all its accompanying disorders. He proposes that a class system be reinstated on the basis of privilege and honor carrying in its wake responsibility, insecurity and asceticism, so that only selfless men will desire to gain high position. He does not suggest how this new order of things is to be brought about.

Does this book sound reactionary? It isn't. It is bitter realism. But it isn't a cheerful book, obviously. Every so often the author can't help remarking how like Hell modern civilization is becoming.

AUGUST 1947

A HISTORY OF THE CHURCH, VOL. III

By Philip Hughes
Sheed & Ward

THIS THIRD VOLUME DEALS WITH THE REVOLT AGAINST the Church, from Aquinas to Luther, that period which preceded and made possible the Reformation. It does not make pleasant reading for it is an almost unrelieved tale of men's betrayal of Christ in His Church. But it is fascinating and profitable reading, with constant present-day implications. What was then beginning is now finishing completely in our generation, attended by, on one hand, final horrible perversions and barbarisms, and on the other by the fruits of the purification of the Church, and new spiritual beginnings.

Father Hughes' treatment of Church history is impressive. Obviously a scholar, he is acquainted at first hand with all the researches on key questions and, where necessary, he can and does give detailed facts. He is completely objective, never betraying the slightest anxiety to color the facts. His chief concern is to show the origin and development of trends rather than to interpret events from an apologetical point of view, although he occasionally does that, as when he points out how Popes good and bad during this period rise to the defense of the autonomy of the Church against the threat of the princes. The author is a man of judgment, knowing what is important and what is not, and a man of charity, notable throughout but especially in regard to Luther.

He treats the history chronologically, by periods, with time out three times to discuss Christian life, thought and sanctity. Here is where most of his interpretation comes in. The only weakness the book has is that these philosophical and spiritual considerations are separated from, rather than integrated with, general history.

Two themes run through the history at this period, both culminating, in a way, in Luther. One is the struggle between Church and State and, although the author does not stress it unduly, it is quite clear that it is not a case of the Church trying to usurp temporal power as of the State trying to subordinate the spiritual power, which the

Book Reviews

revival of pagan ideas abetted. Luther, then, represents the capitulation of religion to the political arm with what ultimate results the daily papers bear witness. The other theme is the progressive departure from truth, first in opposing faith and reason, and so on down to the intellectual anarchy of Luther. Philip Hughes shows this as a movement away from and neglect of St. Thomas. He has an interesting discussion on the "Devotio Moderna," apropos of "The Imitation of Christ." Here the application to our own day is obvious. We have been the recipients of the tradition of devotions separated from theology, with Garrigou-Lagrange among other champions of a new return to St. Thomas.

Good will is what saves men's souls, but the reader of this history will learn the disease to which good will is liable in the absence of good understanding.

MEDIEVAL PHILOSOPHY

By D. J. B. Hawkins
Sheed & Ward

FOR A NEAT, CLEAR RESUME OF MEDIEVAL PHILOSOPHY, this is excellent. One senses an ease of mastery on the part of the author. What is important, what is new and what is relevant, is quite clear to him, and the whole is related, in an especially good final chapter, to modern philosophy and to present day philosophical needs. There are occasional lapses into humor and colloquialisms that make you wish the writer would bend yet further in the direction of the ordinary mind.

THY FAITH HATH MADE THEE WHOLE
SEPTEMBER 1947

MODERN CHRISTIAN REVOLUTIONARIES

Edited by Donald Attwater
Devin-Adair Company

IT IS HARD TO BELIEVE THAT A CATHOLIC EDITED THESE five little books, here bound in one volume. One has visions of a villainous, greedy publisher forcing upon an unhappy Donald Attwater all sorts of authors and subjects likely to catch the attention of this or that buying public. But this thesis breaks down when one reads the introduction, in which the editor professes to be happy about this babel of tongues, this potpourri of truth and error.

Be it on Mr. Attwater's head then. The result of his endeavors is utter chaos. Of his five subjects, only two are Catholic; of his five authors, only one, himself. The one study of a Catholic by a Catholic is the only really commendable section of the book. The subject is Eric Gill, whose very close friend Donald Attwater was, and it is admirably done. It is as neat and precise an analysis of Gill's thought as one could wish, and Gill was eminently qualified to be considered a modern Christian revolutionary.

I cannot find the heart to denounce the study of Chesterton with the wrath it deserves because F. A. Lea, who did it seven years or so ago, has already recanted in part, in appended notes, and has no doubt already had the wrath of Catholic England on his head. Suffice it to say that F. A. Lea is not a Catholic (and openly deplores the misfortune of Chesterton's conversion), was only twenty-three years old when the essay was written, and throughout it compares G. K. Chesterton unfavorably with someone named John Middleton Murry, a pantheist and Marxist.

The study of Nicolas Berdyaev is very competently done. Berdyaev is nominally a Russian Orthodox, philosophically really an existentialist. His biographer and critic, Eugueny Lampert, understands Berdyaev, understands Russian, understands the Orthodox Church and knows the position of the Roman Catholic Church, so his study is precise and intelligible. Those who are familiar with Berdyaev only through his study of the bourgeois mind will be surprised to see how far his thinking has strayed from Christianity. He is a revolutionary, in a sense, but is he Christian?

The same question arises in regard to the essay on Kierkegaard, Berdyaev's philosophical forebearer in existentialism. But apart from whether or not Kierkegaard really fits under the heading of a Christian revolutionary, it would have served some purpose to have made a penetrating study of his existentialism in the light of St. Thomas, inasmuch as the doctrine is causing a mild flurry at the moment. But this study by M. S. Chaning-Pearce only adds to the confusion. It is bad enough that a man who does not really understand should try to analyze another man who did not really understand (in their diverse fashions) and once in a while suggests a wild parallel between Kierkegaard's philosophical errors and the progress of the soul to God as described by St. John of the Cross. In the end all you can be sure of is that Kierkegaard was a profoundly melancholic man.

There is no point in detailed discussion of the fifth essay, as it is the same story. Nichol Macnicol, a vague Protestant, analyzes Charles Freer Andrews, another vague Protestant, in a worshipful treatise lacking key concrete facts. It is hard to see anything through the haze, but seemingly Andrews was a gentle and winning person who fell into ineffectual sentimentality from which Catholicism would have saved him. He went to India, where he was a friend of Gandhi and [Rabindranath] Tagore, and where he evidently lost his Christianity in a blur of universal brotherhood. He does not sound (for all that he worked against racial discrimination) either Christian or revolutionary, but he was probably very nice.

THY FAITH HATH MADE THEE WHOLE

DECEMBER 1947

THE DRY WOOD

By Caryll Houselander
Sheed & Ward

MEN ARE WEARY OF SEEKING TRUTH IN THE FULNESS OF factual information (they have reached the perfection of statistics and research, but their heads are still void of wisdom). Men are also weary of living on past glories or in the future of the "progress" myth. They are nauseated by the unrealities and fictions and sentimentalities with which they hide from the enigmatic reality of the here and now. They will give their allegiance only to those who can explain life in the intensity of the present moment. They are moved, therefore, by the pseudo-realists who say, "Here is *real* life—it is one vast sewer of despair," because that's what their own lives look like to their own superficial view. Or they will give their allegiance to a Christianity which can take the garbage can of contemporary life and show Christ present now, redeeming now, transforming now, the rich and the poor, old and young, Protestant and Catholic and Jews and pagan refuse of our own apartment houses and offices and parishes. This is Caryll Houselander's gift. She can see Christ behind the smoke screen of our human sins and limitations. She can cut through the camouflage of secularism to show men as they really are, desperately in need of God, and to show Christ dispensing Himself to humanity through His Church.

The Dry Wood is Caryll Houselander's first novel, set in a slum parish of London. It is a story of sanctity and sin and God's grace moving men's hearts, in a setting of intense ordinariness. Hundreds of little touches of ordinariness shield the novel from any slight falsification of facts, so that Christ may show through the more clearly. When the pastor hears Confessions, he is yet bothered by his rheumatism. The pious of the parish are often tedious and self-righteous. The rectory housekeeper is fittingly called "The Test of Faith." The parish church is a monument of cluttered ugliness and bad taste, and the author seeing that, yet sees that to some it looks beautiful even when it isn't, and that it is often in reality beautiful. She sees the candles like stars at a High Mass and the altar boys like little cherubim. There isn't a grain of sentimentality in the book, but it is filled with awe and compassion and love, and great deal of wonderful humor.

The story revolves around a central character and a thesis. The focal character is a seven-year-old who is crippled and mute from birth. The thesis is that twentieth century sanctity is child-like sanctity and that the sufferings of pure and innocent children are needed to redeem a world sunk in vice and pride.

The author's compassion and humor take the bitterness out of her sometimes very penetrating criticisms of such things as over-emphasis on liturgical reform, and youth movements which pour all their budding apostles into the same mold.

To my mind the best thing of all, in a book which is excellent throughout, is the charity and clarity with which Caryll Houselander views Solly Lee, the book's most despicable character. I doubt if there can be found anywhere as good an analysis of the destitution of the modern Jew.

VIPERS' TANGLE

By François Mauriac
Sheed & Ward

WHILE THIS PURPORTS TO BE A FIRST-PERSON ACCOUNT of an old man and his avarice, it is really, by reflection, a tale of complacent Catholicism hiding the face of Christ from those He came to save. It is a magnificent novel, beautifully and skillfully written. Although it first appeared some years ago, this is the first American edition.

The book is written with so much feeling that it must have some autobiographical origins. Mauriac was himself out of the Church for many years. The hypocrisy, pharisaism and mediocrity of "good Catholics" must have held him, too, at a distance from Christ. In this story his "good Catholics" are rich, well-bred, pious. They are educated at schools run by outstanding religious orders. But they do not really believe, to the point of resting their lives on it, the Christianity they profess. It becomes ever more evident that their lives are oriented to Mammon. The whole tragedy of making religion a thing of superficial practices is summed up by one of the characters, a young woman deserted by a worthless husband whom she adores. When it is suggested she turn to God, she cannot "see the connection."

The situation Mauriac describes in this book is not foreign to our shores. Many a pagan who takes refuge from his own despair in drink or lust, and who has no illusions about his own virtue, can nevertheless see the connection between Christ's teaching and the morality of daily life which is missed by ardent churchgoers. Indeed, mankind knows instinctively what ought to be done about a pearl of great price when he discovers it, and does not sell all he has. No one expresses these truths better than Francois Mauriac.

Book Reviews

FEBRUARY 1948

NATURE, KNOWLEDGE AND GOD

By Brother Benignus, F.S.C.
Bruce

AS THIS BOOK HAS OVER SIX HUNDRED PAGES OF SOLID philosophical matter, it might be well for this reviewer to admit at the start that [s]he has not yet read it all, and that even if [s]he had [s]he would not be competent to evaluate it as a Thomistic theologian, weighing it against all the other learned books which explain Saint Thomas with abbreviations or additions. This is not a scholar's review but a student's review—the judgment of a lay, would-be Thomist with apostolic rather than academic pretensions. For such, then, is Brother Benignus' book useful?

It is not only useful, it is a delight! It does with Saint Thomas' material what Saint Thomas himself probably would have done contemporarily. After explaining Saint Thomas' position clearly, he considers the relevant modern philosophical position and also the latest findings of science which are considered to bear on the subject (often they are irrelevant to the philosophical position and it is very useful to know that too). There is throughout the book an ease of development which shows what a thorough and deep understanding the author has of his material. Similarly, his explanations are extremely clear. And, like a good teacher, he repeats. He's always tying the new principle in with the old principle, or viewing a previously explained point from a slightly different angle. You get so you count on these repetitions to help your mind reach philosophical comprehension.

This book covers all of Saint Thomas except the moral theology and that part dealing with revelation. It is chiefly metaphysics and psychology. It's not a condensation of Saint Thomas; it's more an elaboration, with omissions. That's why it's so helpful. It goes over and over, for instance, the matter of hylomorphism (the relationship between matter and form) and the proofs for the existence of the soul. This is the material which is especially hard for modern man to grasp. On the other hand, he skips any detailed treatment of the passions, referring you the relevant parts of Saint Thomas' *Summa* (which cover some one hundred large pages in the new Benziger translation). That is wise, because there is nothing difficult about the passions if you read Saint Thomas with care. So it seems as though Brother Benignus has chosen his points of emphasis out of deference to the empty and difficult spots in the modern mind, always reinforcing the foundations doubly. He knows what doctrinal errors to combat today which are not always the same errors as in the thirteenth century. He knows also the state of modern science, which is very important. All this he synthesizes with such obvious ease that the reader takes courage: "Maybe it's not forever beyond me, either!"

Those who are searching Saint Thomas (or ought to be) for philosophical studies, or for the comprehensive world view that an educated lay apostle has to have to turn a secular society Christ-ward, will find a treasure in this book. Using it in connection with Saint Thomas you need only Garrigou-Lagrange's works on the anatomy of the supernatural life, and a lot of time to study, to become vastly more wise than, say, the President of Harvard.

THE LOVE OF GOD AND THE CROSS OF JESUS

By Reginald Garrigou-Lagrange, O.P.
Herder

THIS IS A WORK ON ASCETICAL THEOLOGY WITH A PRE-liminary discussion of some of the underlying doctrine. The second part deals directly with the spiritual life and in the author's usual excellent manner. He always gives the theological reason for things, citing Saint Thomas and Saint John of the Cross (showing, too, the harmony between the two), and yet applies them simply, with examples, so that they are readily understood. As usual, there is that extraordinary clarity with which Garrigou-Lagrange always treats of the relationship between the natural and the supernatural. He is dealing with the necessity of mortification and its relation to spiritual progress.

The first section is a doctrinal treatise on the problem of pure love (ought we to love God more than ourselves?). The ordinary reader will have difficulty following this through, not because the answer is not clearly made but because it is given only after the consideration and refutation of all non-Thomistic erroneous views of the subject.

Book Reviews

MARCH 1948

FRANCE ALIVE

By Claire Huchet Bishop
Declan X. McMullen

HERE IS A BOOK DESCRIBING THE NEW SPIRIT SWEEPING the Church in France. It belongs with *Fishers of Men* and *Priest-Workmen in Germany*, but, whereas these two describe from within specific apostolic adventures, *France Alive* is a reportorial survey of all the new lay and clerical movements in France, even touching on the Protestant, Jewish and Orthodox ones. It is immensely valuable for opening one's eyes to the spectacle of the Church contemporizing itself, and besides makes exciting reading.

"The torpor is gone" from the Church all the way down the line; "to be Christian is to astonish." The Jocist Movement, which was the first to astonish, is now some twenty years old. The author quotes the title page from their remarkable edition of the Gospel (*GOOD NEWS, or Infallible Method to be Happy and at Peace, brought by Christ Jesus*, etc.). The M. P. F. is the Popular Family Movement, busy with community affairs on a non-religious basis but with a spirit of sacrifice. (One said, after visiting a sick person: "Just think! She thought I was a social worker! Isn't that horrible? I told her I was a neighbor, a *neighbor!*") Most Americans haven't heard of the *teams*, small groups of three or five, priests or laity, who live in the midst of the people, sharing their life, work, insecurity, bedbugs, squalor and dirt, just to be *present*, following the example of Charles de Foucault. Then there are the missionary priests, who work sometimes in teams too. They work in the factories, say Mass at night in their tenement apartments, explain the Sacraments as they perform them. There is the splendid work of the J. A. C. (Young Agricultural Workers) who are breaking down the peasants' avarice and sending packages to the cities out of their own rations.

These are only hints of what the book contains. By all means buy it and read it.

Perhaps one other thing ought to be mentioned here. The book deals extensively with the reconstruction of the parish. Again and again there comes up this problem of money. The French proletariat was sickened by too much talk about money in the churches, and by the graduated scale of marriages and funerals according to price. To win back the people the forward-looking clergy have taken drastic measures. In some parishes the solemnity of the Sacraments is the same for everyone, paid pews are out, so are envelope collections. Indeed, there are no collections in some places, but only voluntary, anonymous contributions put in a box in the back of the church. Priests have reduced their scale of living to that of their least parishioners. These measures seem to be healing the breach between the clergy and the people who most need them.

PRIEST-WORKMAN IN GERMANY

By Henri Perrin
Translated by Rosemary Sheed
Sheed & Ward

A FRENCH JESUIT LEARNED FACTORY WORK AND VOLUN-teered to go to Germany as a French workman among others. He had with him one trained Jocist lay leader. This book is a diary of their apostolate.

It was not known generally that Father Perrin was a priest. Despite poor food and grueling work hours, he and his assistant, Jacques, set about organizing their entire region through weekend trips, saying Mass with, and speaking to, groups in other factories rounded up by other Jocists. How effective the trained leaders were, and how impotent the merely pious Catholics, is the lesson of this first part of the book. At one point Father Perrin says:

> Some days later, a wonderful letter form a seminarian told me how much Sunday's meeting had made him think. He had suddenly realized that he must be Christ in his camp, the living Christ, loving and making holy all whom He meets. After a pretty harsh criticism of his seminary, he told how he had got to work even in his dormitory. And there he was—he who up till then had thought only of his own pieties, whose apostolate had finished with rehearsing

plain chant for Sunday Mass—"daring" to suggest to his two working companions to pray with him for the sleeping Lager. The two others gazed at him, astounded, but he found words which hit the mark, and for the first time they prayed together. From then on they continued to make discoveries of friendship in the Christian community....

When the priest was discovered by the Germans and arrested, he continued his apostolate in a series of prisons, still assisted by Jacques from without. It is a fascinating story, but more than that, it is revealing. He transformed the atmosphere of one prison cell after another, changing hate to love, distrust to cooperation, bringing Christ in amongst His least brethren. Yet he heard only two confessions in all that time. Among those men (to what extent is it true among American neo-pagans?) one doesn't speak of making one's Easter duty. They have to learn Christianity all over again, starting with silent spread of charity as a prelude to the Good News. What stands out above all else is that where men are pulling against each other, Father Perrin and the Jocists start pulling them together again. The effort is toward harmony, cooperation, friendliness and love.

This is one of the most important books to come out of the new movements in the Church. Learn from it as Father Perrin learned from his suffering, that the masses are "de-Christianized, yes, but they are not against Christ. And the smallest thing will sometimes uncover Christ's face for them and by slow degrees awaken their love."

THY FAITH HATH MADE THEE WHOLE

APRIL 1948

GROWTH OR DECLINE? THE CHURCH TODAY

By Emmanuel Cardinal Suhard
Fides Publishers

THIS IS WHAT IS HAPPENING TO THE CHURCH; SOMETHING is dying, and something is being born. We are living in a period of convulsive transition.

That is the thesis of last year's Easter pastoral of the venerable Cardinal Archbishop of Paris. More than any other single document which has appeared, this one throws light, clarity and direction on the contemporary chaos.

The Church, says Cardinal Suhard, is a unity of two natures, as was Christ. It is divine and, as such, eternal, immutable and intransigent. It is also truly human and, as such, realizes itself (but never completely) in one temporal society after another, each time taking its complexion from the human conditions, which it transforms, perfects and turns Christward. Today the Church is shedding the temporal mold of a dead Western culture and beginning to inform, to give soul to, the modern world. The Mystical Body of Christ is not dying, as its critics like to hold, but is once more evidencing her eternal youth. Ours is not the old age of the Church, rather it is another springtime!

Using this thesis the Cardinal analyzes the two opposing errors in the Church today. Modernists, who neglect the intransigent, eternal aspect of the Church, want the Church to adapt itself to the modern world even to the point of accommodating her doctrine. The alternate error remembers the eternal and immutable in the Church, but forgets her power of successive incarnation. The Cardinal calls these people the "integralists," and among them includes those who want to run away from the world, or who condemn it wholly, or who cling to medieval institutions as the only possible realization of Christian principles. The error is the same in both cases: seeing only one nature of the Church to the exclusion of the other.

What is needed and what is being born is a new synthesis of religion and life suitable to our own day. That means complete intransigence

Book Reviews

in matters of revelation and tradition (including Saint Thomas, but not as having exhausted the application of revealed truth to the temporal order), combined with great daring and vision and novelty in realizing these principles anew. The preliminary work belongs chiefly to the intellectuals, who have to make a new *summa*, and to the lay apostles of Catholic Action in its various forms.

Speaking of a new Catholic synthesis, Cardinal Suhard says:

> The whole work will be of long duration and will not be the work of one man. The time has come when the greatest service that can be rendered the Church and her children is to make the "Christian summa" of the world in formation. The greatest error of the Christians of the twentieth century, and the one its children would not forgive them, would be to let the world take shape and unite without them, without God—or against Him; to be satisfied with recipes and tactics for their apostolate. It will perhaps be the great honor of our time to have started what others will carry through: a humanism in proportion to the world and God's plan. On this condition, and only on this condition, can the Church develop and become in a near future what she was in the Middle Ages for the West: the spiritual center of the world. The atheistic and anti-Christian civilization, which is spreading in our time, can give way to a sacred culture, to a Christian transfiguration of life.
>
> Need we add that this task is incumbent on the intellectuals, as it was in the time of the great Doctors of the Church. They must bend every possible effort to the "creation" of a Christian society in which the kingdom of God will be sought above all else. The first apostolate, at the present crossroads, is in the realm of Thought. The Church is at this turning point where she can lose all, or win all, according to the spirituality she offers mankind.

That is not the most important passage in the pastoral letter (one would want to quote it entire) but it is the one which sheds light on *Integrity's* task. Cardinal Suhard's whole letter serves to remind us of how poorly we measure up to the work to be done while it shows us the vision toward which we are groping. Everyone in the lay apostolate ought to get hold of this book, to use it as a measure and guide for his own efforts.

THY FAITH HATH MADE THEE WHOLE

JUNE 1948

THE IMAGE OF HIS MAKER

By Robert Edward Brennan, O.P.
Bruce

THE ONLY SOUND BASIS FOR THE STUDY OF MAN IS THE rational psychology of Saint Thomas Aquinas based on Aristotle's foundations. Nearly all modern secular psychological studies bypass this ancient wisdom in favor of some half-baked conjecture thought up yesterday by a professor or a psychologist ignorant of the past. Much, too, of modern so-called psychology is trivia or garnished physiology, or solemnly dished-up common sense; or else it is Freudian, which is a sort of modern perverse effort to get a framework of study such as Aristotle gave us. It can be said, categorically, that no true and great advance will be made in psychology except on a solid basis of Saint Thomas. Hence it is very important to study rational psychology and this is done increasingly in Catholic schools. The material is in the *Summa*. It is also in Father Brennan's earlier book, *Rational Psychology*, which is the text used by most colleges. But that was a scholarly book, using strictly philosophical and technical language, and was really difficult. *The Image of His Master* is rational psychology simplified and, so to speak, brought up-to-date, synchronized with the latest in scientific study and presented against a background of modern philosophical and psychological thought. This book is most welcome; seldom was a book so needed, and it is remarkably well done. The simplification has been possible only because of Father Brennan's profound understanding of his subject. He has concentrated on essentials and has always gone straight to the heart of each subject. This book is not a textbook, but it probably will be used as such by some schools and certainly the ordinary reader will find it necessary to study it, rather than just to read it, even though the text flows and no special academic training is presupposed. Since it is not a large book (only three hundred and some pages) it cannot be exhaustive in any way. It gives the high points, properly related to each other and to the modern world. It should be an introduction for many to rational psychology, and should lead them on to the *Summa*, where they will get the full picture from which they can begin working on some of the great modern problems of psychology.

THE HUMAN WISDOM OF ST. THOMAS
Arranged by Josef Pieper
Sheed & Ward

IN ITS SUBTITLE THIS BOOK IS DESCRIBED AS A BREVIARY of Philosophy. The compiler has taken significant principles from Saint Thomas and just set them forth in major categories but without comment. What emerges is, quite literally, a meditation book. We have been undernourished on spiritual maxims without sufficient sound theology and philosophy. Here is the solid substance. Anyone who has done any serious thinking on his own will find these principles to be like torches shedding great light.

JULY 1948

BODIES AND SOULS

By Maxence van der Meersch
Pellegrini and Cudahy

THIS IS A LONG NOVEL ABOUT THE MEDICAL PROFESSION. It was very popular in France where it appeared in two volumes, no under one cover in translation. Van der Meersch is a magnificent writer with a profound spiritual understanding. *Bodies and Souls* is not ostensibly a Catholic novel, but is based on a theme from Saint Augustine and has a spiritual orientation.

The setting of the book is a great European hospital, whose faculty and their families furnish the chief characters. Experiments in shock treatment, researches in T. B., autopsies, ward visits, laboratory experiments, and the latest philosophical concepts of medical theory, are the background against which the stories of men's souls are written. The medical background is minutely detailed and precisely accurate (a medical opinion, not mine).

There are a half-dozen or so major characters and many minor ones, whose stories form the interweaving plot of this book. The novel is a brilliant and penetrating analysis of souls, a fact quite missed by secular reviewers, one of whom complained of the "defect" of a pervasive moral attitude. The author shows, magnificently, the subtle and deadly temptations to vainglory and wealth which stalk the greatest of the doctors. There are also several poignant love stories, in which the children of the medical faculty are involved. But whether the character is being tried in his profession or in his domestic life, it is the same soul's struggle in either case. Some of the stories end tragically, some happily, but it is always a matter of spiritual defect or spiritual triumph. Therein Van der Meersch reveals his own greatness of soul. Success to him is not wealth, fame, or even humanitarian greatness, but ultimately the love of God, and his thesis is that all loves are reducible in the end (and indeed reduce themselves) to love of God or love of self. "Two loves have built two cities: self-love that despises God, the earthly city; the love of God that despises the self, the celestial city."

Michel Doutreval, the idealistic young doctor in the story, abandons a brilliant career to marry a tubercular for whom he has pity. A cheap novelist would end his story there, to the playing of "Hearts and Flowers." A mediocre novelist might have Michael turn to his poor patients for peace and fulfillment. Van deer Meersch shows Michael's love disappear, the fervor of his sacrifice grow cold, the poverty and ugliness become oppressive, the temptation to escape beckon. But Michael stays with his wife and gradually, when looking at her, begins to see another Face shine through. Of this love of God, then, is born a new and holy love for his wife and his work.

The love story of Michel's sister, Fabiene, even more clearly illustrates the same spiritual truth, that natural love can be preserved and purified only lifting it to God, to the sacrifice of self. Van der Meersch is a true realist who even goes so far as to portray the life of the soul as it is.

MY BOOK ABOUT GOD
By Julie Bedier and Louise Trevisan
Macmillan

FOR YEARS CATHOLIC PARENTS HAVE BEEN PLAGUED BY the problem of finding attractive Catholic religious books for their children. The really lovely books, with the most beautiful illustrations usually turned out to be Protestant, or even worse, ethical-culturish in content. It was to remedy this situation that two Maryknoll Sisters (the author and artist of this work) set up a project to furnish good Catholic books, colorfully illustrated, for children. This is the first fruit of their efforts and it is splendid, beautifully produced in beautiful colors. It is about how we are all children of God, rich and poor, black and white and yellow, young and old; God loves us all and we must love each other.

THY FAITH HATH MADE THEE WHOLE

AUGUST 1948

THE MEANING OF MAN

By Jean Mouroux
Translated from French by A.H.G. Downes
Sheed & Ward

THIS IS THE BEST BOOK I'VE EVER READ ABOUT THE NATURE of man. The author rests his matter soundly and profoundly on a Thomistic foundation, without being academic. He also sees, and is compassionate about, the depths to which modern man has fallen, yet knows also the power of Christ to heal and elevate the worst of us. This is the work not only of a splendid theologian but of a holy man.

One joy of the book is the simplicity and ease and clarity with which the very difficult doctrines are elucidated. Problems of human liberty, different sorts of love, the relationship between the body and the soul, the effects of the redemption and so forth, are handled with skillful competence. Everything is sharp, yet integrated. It is the balanced view of one who sees the totality because of help from the Holy Ghost and not from having wandered for many years through a maze of superficial detail.

The book is divided into three sections. The first, called Temporal Values, deals with man's relationship to the created order, and is a sort of panoramic view. The second, Carnal Values, deals with the body, its nobility, its misery, and finally its redemption. This part of the book is highly instructive and very interesting. The third and longest section, on Spiritual Values, is necessarily tougher going and some may flounder in the doctrinal parts. The author deals first with the human person, then spiritual liberty, Christian liberty, love, charity, and then the sacred character of man.

Jean Mouroux has the rare gift of seeing the synthesis that God has made between the natural and the supernatural in man. Natural man is a philosophical abstraction for there has never been any such. Fallen man is not the reality either, for we have been redeemed in Christ. So to see any living man actually as he is you have to see him in relation to Christ. This comes up over and over again in this book. To cite one example, among many, it is of the essence of the author's treatment of the reciprocal obligations of married people. That women should be subject to their husbands is a familiar if unpalatable dictum. Often enough people drop the ending because it means nothing to them. "Let women be subject to their husbands *as to the Lord*" is what the Church says. In this book you will find out why and also see why the truncated admonition is useless.

THY FAITH HATH MADE THEE WHOLE

SEPTEMBER 1948

AMERICAN HUMANISM AND THE NEW AGE

By Louis J.A. Mercier
Bruce

WHAT A CURIOUS AGE WE LIVE IN! PSEUDO-SCHOLARS and half-baked, ill-educated "experts" keep our printing presses busy hammering out their inaccuracies and sophisms, which are then solemnly reviewed by the leading newspapers of the country. It is a delightful shock, then, to discover an author who is educated, integrated, learned and charitable, who can write books dealing with fundamental problems clearly and truthfully against a background of exhaustive knowledge. Dr. Mercier is such a man. In this book he examines the contemporary state of higher education and liberal thought in the United States. You could not wish for a more admirable survey, for he discusses the leading figures, Irving Babbitt, Dr. Hutchins, Walter Lippmann, Lyn Harold Hough and Norman Foerster. He clearly delineates the underlying philosophical problems, and he describes the relevant educational experiments. All this is done in the light of his own avowed, uncompromising, but also unbelligerent Catholicism, which he describes as the philosophical position of Supernaturalized Humanism.

This book accentuates the positive. Dr. Mercier says there are two trends in American thought, which find their sharpest division in respect to the nature of man. He is not here concerned to trace in detail the aberrations of the naturalists, John Dewey et al, but discusses those who are struggling for the light and who have arrived philosophically at various degrees of the truth. They all see man as sprit as well as matter, and most of them see the existence of God and man's dependence on Him for help. Without embracing the Catholic doctrine of supernatural grace, they nevertheless leave the door open for the fullness of the truth. Dr. Mercier's description of the St. John's University experiment is especially interesting.

At the end of the book Dr. Mercier speculates on the possibility of an educational compromise on the position he calls Theistic Humanism, that is to say on the basis of philosophy and the natural law, following the Pope's own exhortation for cooperation among all men of good will. But in an epilogue written recently the author is less optimistic. Oddly enough, his compromise suggestion rests on interfaith cooperation, yet most of the men the book is concerned with have approached the Catholic opposition from agnosticism or irreligion rather than through the traditional Protestant sects. It would therefore seem that there is more hope that such men (either they themselves or others following the same trend) will help restore education on a fully Catholic basis than that a compromise can or will be reached. Insofar as there is residual truth in Protestantism it should be cherished, of course, but is it sufficiently dynamic for a world where the forces of error and evil are achieving a militant synthesis which threatens to sweep all before it?

THY FAITH HATH MADE THEE WHOLE

OCTOBER 1948

THE SEVEN STOREY MOUNTAIN

By Thomas Merton
Harcourt Brace

AT THE LAST JUDGMENT IT WILL NOT BE EMBARRASSING to have our sins made public, nor will the revelations about our neighbors have the savor of scandal. For it's not going to be a case history of us (we are nothing and by that time we shall know it) but a testimonial to God's merciful grace. We shall not even see ourselves or each other, for being lost in the contemplation of Him.

You have to be very close to God's perspective to see your own life that way while you are still on earth. Saint Augustine's *Confessions* is the classical example. And now all of a sudden we are blessed with another record of God's dealings with a human soul, and this time in a setting as contemporary and close as the Seventh Avenue Subway. *The Seven Storey Mountain* is the autobiography of Thomas Merton who is not yet thirty-five years old and who, from having (as the book jacket says) lived a full and worldly life, is now "beyond humiliation." He is a Trappist monk, and now a priest, at the Gethsemani Abbey in Kentucky. He writes with the simplicity and honesty and objectivity of one who is really writing God's story and not his own.

One hears all sorts of stories about Thomas Merton's past. It is said that before his conversion he was a communist, an editor of the *New Yorker*, a Quaker, but he was never any of these things. One useful accomplishment of this book is to get the record straight.

Thomas Merton was born in France of a New Zealand father and an American mother, neither of them with a specific religion. His mother died while he was quite young (the book contains a number of descriptions and meditations on the modern pagan way of dying and being cremated) and his father (who was a good artist, a cultured man and a spiritual one) died when Tom was an adolescent.

Father and son spent considerable time together in France, and then Tom was educated in England up through one year in Cambridge. Between times and afterwards he lived with his maternal grandparents in Douglaston, Long Island, from which base he attended Columbia

Book Reviews

College and University, where his best friends were a handful of Jews and Mark van Doren. His grandparents were as American and bourgeois as Mary Pickford and Douglas Fairbanks (whom they greatly admired) and had fifteen secular magazines on the living room table.

As Thomas Merton advanced in manhood the spiritual and moral disorder within him increased. It is the same sorry tale of modern youth which we see thousands of times in this irreligious age, only in this instance the caliber of the human being was exceptional. This particular prodigal had intelligence and insight and a zest for life and tremendous energy. He also had what is rare today, a solid educational background, or at least an intellectual discipline, and sound set of cultural values. He never loved money. But he laid waste his life with bad reading, movies in sickening quantity, several packs of cigarettes a day, hot jazz, sitting up all night in bars, a succession of amours, and all of those things which make modern life so very much like hell. He also had a series of spiritual adventures and insights, graces which were resisted but which finally overwhelmed him. He was baptized in Corpus Christi Church up near Columbia toward the end of his studies and then spent several years restoring the order of his nature through grace. He ended up at Gethsemani at the age of twenty-six.

All sorts of important people like Evelyn Waugh and Clifton Fadiman, Graham Greene and Clare Boothe Luce, have hailed this book, on its flyleaf, as a great and lasting spiritual treatise. I agree with them heartily. It may not be another *Confessions*, but one certainly is ready to hail it so in the enthusiasm of first reading. Or again, it may really be of that caliber, and it has the tremendous advantage of being set in the experiences and heartaches of our own sorry generation. Not even the man next to you in the subway, or the bright young intellectual on the library steps, or the girl having a cocktail after work, could say, "I don't know what he's talking about." They could only say, "Why, I never saw it from that angle!"

THE PRIEST AND THE PROLETARIAT

By Robert Kothen
Sheed & Ward

THIS SMALL BOOK (VERY SMALL) IS A SERIES OF QUOTAtions, with comments, on the idea of priest-workmen. In France some priests have been going down into the factories, working and living with the de-Christianized masses in order to start new parishes among them. The thing is not advocated for the clergy in general but has been approved in exceptional cases in France. The fundamental reason is that it has become in France "more difficult for a parish priest to speak to a worker than it is for a missionary to get in touch with a native." This book doesn't take sides, it just gives some descriptions and comments. It's always running over with the idea of the lay apostolate. Perhaps if a few priests descent to the depth of modern industrial life, their example will draw the masses closer to the clergy. No one recommends the general practice. This is a good little book for anyone who wants a condensed view of the modern problem of the separation of the Church from the people.

THE MASS OF THE FUTURE
By Gerald Ellard, S.J.
Bruce

WHY WOULD A MAN WHO IS SYMPATHETIC TO THE USE of the vernacular in the Liturgy write a book in which every paragraph is introduced by a Latin phrase in bold face, a Latin phrase which usually comes from an obscure source, as far as the layman is concerned, and which is not translated? This unnecessary erudition in what purports to be a semi-popular book about all the radical restorations (to simplicity) in the Liturgy that might take place in our day, causes Father Ellard to lose the sympathy and often the patience of his reader. At least it does if I am the reader. There are not only Latin phrases, but there are also Latin footnotes, and some Greek is thrown in, and some Hebrew, and some scholarly biographies and a lot of historical minutia about the origins of the Mass. The sprightly title and even more sprightly chapter heads simply do not conform to the substance the book contains.

Now that that is said, be it noted that there are many little interesting bits which everyone will like, and that the special student of the liturgical movements will find it a treasure-house of reference material. But it is more a compendium than a survey.

Book Reviews

DECEMBER 1948

YE GODS

Written and Illustrated by Ed Willock
Sheed & Ward

A COUPLE OF DOMINICAN TERTIARIES WERE RECENTLY moved to protest against the sharp and harsh manner in which the editors of *Integrity* have represented the contrast of modern life with Christian principles in the pages of the *The Torch*. The protest went something like this: "Now that they have a magazine of their own why don't they confine their writing to its pages? We have plenty of good nuns and priests to tell us these things. Do the laity have to enter the arena?" The complaint of these two good women started a controversy in the pages of *The Torch* which I do not propose to continue here, save to chide them gently on their clericalism.

Ye Gods is a collection of some of the nasty stuff they were complaining about — which appeared in *The Torch* under the title of *The New Mysticisms*. It's a series of illustrated chats about the household gods, the graven images and golden calves of modern American people. It speaks of such things as Variety, Efficiency, Money, The Regular Guy, Bigness, Popularity, and the excuse "I Only Work Here." Its thesis is that men who do not really worship God will worship something else as though it were God, and that modern man does indeed invest everything he touches with a sort of mystical absolutism.

Just as the good women said, it's a horrid business. The drawings are anything but pretty (the one for "I Only Work Here" shows Pilate washing his hands) and the copy plows right into the subject ("As it is generally used, success is a nice word for something nasty"). I like the one about The Regular Guy best:

> The Regular Guy is the man facile in all those fields that require neither courage nor initiative. He is the man maidens fancy and wives despise. He has all the lovable virtues of the child, but none of the virtues of the man. He is a man of leisure. He knows how to have a good time, likes to be called by his first name, dances well. He is charming.

He dresses with studied carelessness. He practices nonchalance before his mirror. To preserve his gaiety of manner, which with him is in the nature of a vocation, he avoids responsibility. He is at home among women.

The Regular Guy is the hero of the easily satisfied. He satisfies the desire of a girl who wants in a man a mirror to reflect her own vanity. He satisfies the desire of the man who wants to remain a gay young blade — indefinitely. He satisfies the desire of the layman who expects in his priest nothing more than a smiling hail-fellow-well-met who goes around like Pollyanna doing good and clucking his tongue at evil. He satisfies the doting mother who would prefer that junior should never grow up. He satisfies the citizen who thinks it fine to be able to call the President of the United States "Harry." He lightens the lives of all those people who choose to think that life is just a bowl of cherries with whipped cream on top.

Anyone who has developed a strong stomach for reality through reading *Integrity* will like *Ye Gods* and find it profitable. It will serve the useful function of helping you see your contemporaries not as the irreligious matter-of-fact people they fancy themselves to be, but as the devoutly religious members of the world's most superstitious and idolatrous generations.

Book Reviews

JANUARY 1949

YOU CAN CHANGE THE WORLD

By James Keller, M.M.
Longmans

THIS IS THE HANDBOOK OF THE CHRISTOPHER MOVEMENT, and it deserves some careful attention—if only because the Christopher movement has, through its ready appeal and the enthusiastic lecturing of its founder, Father Keller, captured the zeal and idealism of thousands upon thousands of American Catholics. The book is very much like Father Keller's speeches. Its framework and most of its matter consists in stories, beginning "A young Negro...," "Two business men in a restaurant in Chicago...," or "A young man who once studied for the ministry in California..." Of almost equal importance are the quotations; Father Keller quotes rabbis, ministers, Dr. Gallup, labor leaders, editors, manufacturers, presidents of broadcasting companies, editors of Protestant (and anti-Catholic) newspapers, columnists—nearly anyone and everyone. With all the stories and quotations there is little room for anything else, and there is very little else. In parts there is quite a bit of pedestrian research data, about such things as the number of people murdered annually in the United States or the kinds of agencies that take trained social workers. Father Keller does not argue from principle, so do not expect a reasoned, philosophical analysis of the times. Such principles as the book contains are chiefly to be found in the headings, either gratuitously assumed or derived from case histories. In general tone and makeup, as well as in the burden of its message, *You Can Change the World* has a strong odor of Dale Carnegie about it. And as with Dale Carnegie too, it is a little hard to pin the author down to any particular thesis. There is hardly a modern cliché or pious slogan that does not appear in the book some place. All that a reviewer can do is to take the all-over thesis that the book conveys to him, and examine it in the light of the lay apostolate. If some people object to this interpretation, pointing to this passage or that (which they easily can because the book touches on nearly everything, even where some of the things contradict each other) the reviewer has no defense against them, save to say he was trying to be fair according to the light of his knowledge.

Let me say, then, that with Father Keller's most fundamental thesis I agree. We both think the laity should be apostolic, that they should go into the market place (although we differ in our interpretation of this) and that they should widen their vision and think big. The Christopher theory is that each one of us should become a "Christ-bearer," that we should accentuate the positive, that lay people should get into the jobs which count most in terms of influence (education, government, labor management and publishing) even at a financial sacrifice. Father Keller seems to imply that no organization is necessary for the apostolate. At any rate, Christophers are unorganized although they are urged to join existent organizations in order to influence them.

My chief grievance against the Christophers is that they shy away from the implications of being Christ-bearers. The appellation ought to imply the fullness of the doctrine that we are *other Christs*, according to which we must become instruments by which Christ continuously reconquers the world through grace. As the supernatural virtues and gifts progressively increase in us, and sanctify us, Christ is manifested to the world and draws men to Him. Our role is to be crucified in the process, losing our lives to gain life, and becoming the instrumental cause of the conversion of our neighbor, and the sanctification of the temporal order. Seen this way effective Christophers are rare, as saints are rare, and the real change of the world a very difficult process, founded on a succession of calvaries. That does not mean a multitude of people are not called to the apostolate; in our day that seems exactly to be the case. But it does mean that the essential struggle is the same as always and it would be wrong to minimize the sacrifice involved.

There is another sort of "good work" which is much easier than the way of the cross through supernatural grace, and this is the way of natural virtue, activity and enthusiasm—a little kindness here, some cheering words there, some letters to congressmen, an apt word at a labor meeting. It is one of the Christian mysteries that whereas all these things are good, they can add up to just so much sound and fury, changing precious little, unless they have deep roots in a higher life. Surely Father Keller knows this better than I. Yet this book seems to cling to the natural level of goodness and to place undue hope of real accomplishment therein. Occasionally the supernatural life is mentioned, but not very often, and there is no real stress put on frequenting the Sacraments. The Declaration of Independence seems almost interchangeable with the Ten Commandments, and the defense of American democracy nearly synonymous with the defense of the Church. It is not made at all clear that *you* can change the world is true if by it we mean Christ can change the world if we allow Him to act through us.

In view of the above it is not surprising that this book seems superficial. It is written with a lot of exclamation points and emotionalism, so you're liable to find a lump rising in your throat because young Henry Ford says "Good Morning" to some of his least employees. Now it's nice that he does so, but neither Henry Ford nor Father Keller is even thinking in terms of the major problems of industrialism. In fact, here is one of the points where Father Keller's prejudices show. There's nothing wrong with industrial capitalism, according to him. There are selfish capitalists but it's always a personal sin which has not been incorporated essentially into the system. On the other hand there is nothing too awful to be said against the communists. They are "the subversives," and they must be driven back at all costs. Father Keller never sees them as God's scourge for our sins, as Our Lady implied at Fatima.

Besides sticking pretty close to the natural and the superficial, it cannot escape one's notice that Father Keller's plan is a little naive. I have felt this for a long time, as I listened to the glib advice he has been giving the young, and now I am sure of it. Father Keller's knowledge of the fields he recommends his Christophers going into does not come from experience, much less from wisdom. He describes job opportunities in these fields in the book. It's an unenlightened research job, without any real understanding of what goes on. In publishing he is particularly naive. Because virtually all secular publishing is oriented to profit, much of the material spewed out by the presses is either pornographic or atheistic. How can a Catholic cooperate in spreading this error and obscenity? This problem, which shrieks at anyone entering the publishing field, is not even touched on by Father Keller. Furthermore, in advising young writers, he tells them that the majority of editors definitely do want good material to be submitted for publication. Although "good" is not defined, still and all one gets the impression that *The Ladies Home Journal* and similar large magazines are aching for some idealistic young writer to write something godly. One suspects that Father Keller's knowledge of publishing is limited to expensive lunches with well-heeled executives whose pious chatter he has been taken in by. In this same chapter, incidentally, we are told that Hollywood is crying for decent scenario material (one studio found only six manuscripts out of two hundred submitted to have even faint screen possibilities) and that leading Hollywood studios never open unsolicited manuscripts. The chapter on social work is again naive. It's about a thousand light years removed from coming to grips with the real problems of the field such as we of *Integrity* (I say this without boasting, but by way of contrast) tackled in an issue about six months ago. One interesting note is that Father Keller avoids attacking Freud. Freud is never mentioned by name, though his teachings are once adverted to as a materialistic philosophy which can lead to Marxism. For Father Keller and others of the sweetness and light school there is only one enemy: communism.

Conspicuous by its absence in this whole book is any mention whatever of the lay apostolate other than the Christopher movement. Now it happens that holiness and prayer and sacrifice and souls' struggles have gone into the understanding and launching of the modern lay apostolate. Yet Catholic Action, the Legion of Mary, Friendship House, the Catholic Worker, and other organizations might just as well have never existed for all that Father Keller pays no attention to them. All these have found it very hard to bring Christ to the modern world, because it required the transformation of the lay people themselves, the working out of a proper technique, and the laborious business of attaining to harmony of action in their own organized groups. But Father Keller has suddenly found that the whole thing is easy and no organization is necessary. Whoever has worked in the modern situation has discovered the necessity of organization, which also has strong papal support. It will be a pity if Father Keller whips up the enthusiasm of the nation (and he undoubtedly does whip up enthusiasm) only to have it quickly burn out for lack of spiritual substance and because of unrealism in viewing the modern world.

Book Reviews

APRIL 1949

FRANCE PAGAN?

By Maise Ward
Sheed & Ward

OVER THE WEEKEND OF JANUARY 15, 1944 THERE DIED in a tenement in Paris (of fumes from a disordered coal stove) one of the most famous of contemporary French priests. He was Abbe Godin, who headed the so-called "mission priests" (priest workmen) who were to begin their work in the Paris slums and factories on the Monday following this death. His had been the greatest responsibility for the work that was beginning and he had the day before prophetically said that now he could vanish.

Abbe Godin was a remarkable priest with a remarkable insight into his time. Let us take his life first, on which Mrs. Sheed has done an inspiring job and which occupies the first section of the book. Godin asked God to take away his vocation to the priesthood rather than let him become a complacent, ordinary priest. He didn't just drift into a seminary and then go along with what training offered. He was always figuring out what it means to be a priest in our time, and how he could acquire the necessary assets. One of his resolutions: "Negative rules: not to be a priest-photographer, or a priest-beekeeper, or a priest-spectator. Simply to be a priest. You don't become a priest for your family, or for your mother, or for your sister, but only for God. The priest's employment is not gardening or entertaining his fellow-priests agreeably. It is saving souls." Another time he made up a litany to Our Lady, which begins:

> From becoming a bourgeois priest, deliver me, Mary.
> From forgetting that I am poor,
>   that I have always been poor;
> From forgetting those who suffer;
> From spiritual selfishness;
> From the ecclesiastical spirit;...

After he was ordained Abbe Godin became a Jocist chaplain and worked out for Cardinal Suhard (and with the help of another priest) a report on the condition of the now very famous *France, Pays de Mission*, here translated and edited as Part II of *France Pagan*?

Now we come to Abbe Godin's observations and theories. He found three types of areas in France. In the first type he placed active Christian communities, not perfect, and suffering from lukewarmness, but still Christian. In the second category he placed areas where the culture and civilization remain Christian but where Christian practice is limited to small groups, relatively isolated from the rest of the community. There is still a Christian base here for rejuvenation.

The No. 1 problem of the Church in France was (and is) the third category: the areas which have lapsed into paganism, with neither Christian tradition nor Christian practice remaining, where the mores and customs have sunk to a very low moral level.

Abbe Godin's thesis is simply this: for rechristianizing the pagan areas the Church cannot use ordinary conversion methods, much less exhortations to "return" to something which is by now foreign to the mentality of the people. The Church must adapt the methods it has developed of evangelizing new pagan territories. It must send missionaries to live among the people, win their confidence and gradually teach them the Faith. It must, moreover, not accept individual isolated conversions *but build up new communities of Christians.*

This last is all important. Apropos of it Godin says that very much of the heroic work of the Jocists has ultimately proved fruitless because their converts could not be integrated into the existing parochial system of the Church. Parish societies are composed of nice, well-mannered boys and girls. The Jocists brought in hordes of hoodlums, marvelously zealous and heroically attached to Christ, but ill-clothed, uncouth in speech and sometimes retaining some shocking habits for a while. They needed a long catechumenate such as the Church gives the Eastern pagans. They would not be respectable parishioners within several generations. Yet zealous as they were they could not hold to the Faith individually, they needed a community. So many lapsed, and their last condition was worse than the first. Others were killed in battle before their zeal waned, and Godin was glad that they were. Until such time as the ordinary parish could accommodate itself to the task of incorporating these new members Abbe Godin and the other missionaries planned to set up new communities where these Christians could gain a foothold in the Church.

The Americans' problem is, "To what extent can Godin's finding be useful to us in analyzing our own situation?" My opinion would be as follows:

There are very few areas in America which ever were Christian, or at least Catholic in their orientation, for our country was pretty secular from the beginning. Most American environments are areas of desultory religious practice combined with a secular mode of life. There are an increasing number of thoroughly pagan sections, where religious practice is ridiculed, both among the depressed proletariat and the intellectual and café society circles. However, in America where one's financial and social standing can change overnight and classes aren't fixed, it is a small matter to put on at least the externals of respectability. It would only take a few weeks to integrate a former prostitute, say, into the parochial sphere, and not much longer into parish societies, if she cared to join them. Our difficulty is that our parish societies are usually as dull as dishwater and have, over a period of years, screened out all except the most patient and complacent members of the Church. We can't integrate our converts, because we haven't anything exciting, vital, contemporary and above all apostolic to offer them. Our parishes live pretty much in the past, when their duty was to gather the faithful around in as large numbers as possible (watering down the "dos" of Christianity accordingly) to exhort them to remain firm. Now it would be better if they went in for training select groups of shock troops according to one of the new techniques of Catholic Action or the Legion of Mary, and used these as spearheads into a secular world to turn it to Christ. Maybe this is what the Abbe wanted in France too. One gets hints. Certainly the dynamism which is welling up in the Church will have to be channeled soon if it is not to be scattered and ineffectual.

TRANSFORMATION IN CHRIST

By Dietrich von Hildebrand
Longmans Green

THE CHURCH CHARACTERISTICALLY CLOTHES ITS MYSTICAL ideas in rich imagery derived from the terminology of human love. Here is a man of great learning and wide culture, writing about the spiritual life in at least a semi-mystical vein, who characteristically uses the barren, abstract language of philosophy and sociology, speaking of "respond to value," "inter-personal situations," "tensions" and using words like "signalize" and "happify." By pointing these out I do not mean to disparage the book or its author but rather to identify the sort of spiritual book it is. Throughout I was tempted to call it mystical *philosophy* rather than mystical theology. This is at once its merit and its shortcoming.

To speak first of the merit, Professor von Hildebrand really goes far in integrating true philosophy with spiritual experience. To my mind his most successful chapter is that on "True Simplicity" in which he shows the contrast between the over-simplification of experience that characterizes fools and the unity and harmony of life which one experiences as he draws near to God Who is Himself Oneness. Here, as in most of the chapters, the author makes a careful, analytical study of the problem and with good psychological insight describes types of people who miss true spirituality. He sees pretty clearly the aberrations of the mildly neurotic in this regard.

One reason I particularly liked the chapter on simplicity is that it not only enlightened my mind but also moved my heart, this latter being something that the rest of the book usually fails to do. Here we come to the drawbacks of the philosophical emphasis. It is too much on the level of human reason, whereas theology, without denying reason, always centers about the mysteries of faith and therefore calls faith into play in understanding it (or should). So Garrigou-Lagrange, whose theology is very analytical and just bare bones, nevertheless raises your heart and mind to God pretty consistently. The reader of this book by von Hildebrand will usually find himself dropping back into culture and learning. At least this is what I found.

Most disappointing to me is his chapter on "Recollection and Contemplation" where he fails to emphasize, at least with proportionate

Book Reviews

stress, the utterly transcendent and supernatural character of Christian contemplation. I would quarrel with him too about the relationship between contemplation and action, as he doesn't seem to grasp the Thomistic view of contemplation flowering into action, a point which is fundamental to the lay apostolate. Therefore we find him picturing a lay life which is devout and recollected (von Hildebrand is certainly a good antidote to activism) but apart from the main stream of life today. It is the sort of life possible to a cultured intellectual, but not the sort open to a cultureless modern barbarian riveter or truck driver. But then it will probably be another generation before the genesis of Catholic Action is realized and before it will be generally understood that grace, using the lay apostolate as its vehicle, can raise up other Christs in the very centers of all that is unlovely in the modern world.

RICH AND POOR IN CHRISTIAN TRADITION

Edited by Walter Shewring
Burns Oates & Washbourne

ANYTHING THAT HAS EVER BEEN SAID ABOUT POVERTY (to my memory) by *Integrity*, *The Catholic Worker*, or any other so-called radical publications of today, seems pretty pale when stacked up against the thundering voice of Mother Church on the subject down through the ages. Or perhaps I do *The Catholic Worker* an injustice. Certainly it has written beautifully on poverty, and Peter Maurin's expression for beggars, "The Ambassadors of God," is in the most orthodox tradition.

Be that as it may, the English editor of this book has translated and brought together the writings of famous ancient doctors of the Church, of the modern social Popes, of Saint Thomas and Saint Catherine of Siena, Bossuet and others (with the notable exception of Saint Francis—perhaps he did not write anything) and topped it off with a magnificent introduction of his own. The book contains some pretty strong statements, such as Saint Jerome's "Every man of riches is either a rogue or a rogue's heir" and Saint Peter Damian's

"No festering wound stinks more unbearably in God's nostrils than the dung of covetousness." The ordinary tenor of the book is only slightly less vigorous. The position consistently taken is certainly at variance with modern practice and attitudes of Catholics. What is even more impressive is the absolute unanimity of the writers in respect to their subject.

It does not say in this book that it is all right to be rich if you use your money right (you have to earn it honestly, which is barely possible, or inherit it from someone who did and anything superfluous belongs to the poor by right). Nor does it say that the eye of a needle through which the rich have to go is a mountain pass, nor that the Church needs the rich (the Church is the Church of the poor, and the rich are only allowed in it to relive the sufferings of the poor). There is nothing from the first to the last page which would in any way comfort or justify or encourage the thousands of contemporary young Catholic men and women who are breaking their necks to become rich.

Let the poor read this book to learn of their eminent dignity and cease trying to better their material lot. Let the rich and the avaricious read it if they dare — and see what it does to them.

Book Reviews

MAY 1949

THE FAILURE OF TECHNOLOGY

By Friedrich Georg Juenger
Henry Regnery Co.

LAST MONTH WE REPRINTED THE FIRST TWO CHAPTERS OF this book in *Integrity*, and we intend to reprint nearly all of the rest of it in the coming months. Those who cannot wait are urged to buy the book. In our opinion it brings more real understanding to bear on modern problems in the economic and technological order than any other single work we have read. The author is a poet, one of the great literary figures of contemporary Germany. He is not a Catholic. Perhaps we ought to point out right away that Juenger misses the truth in a couple of his chapters, places where he comes right up against philosophy, and betrays a confusion resulting from having been educated with Kant and other moderns (what wouldn't his mind have accomplished if he had been nurtured on Saint Thomas!). Specifically, he is wrong about free will and time, yet in neither case does he give the simpleton's view and in neither case does his error penetrate his total analysis.

Probably it is because Juenger is a poet that he can see the significance of technology. His is the mystical, the contemplative view, in which all the pieces fall into place once you grasp their unifying principle. Do not suppose that because he is a poet he is vague and dreamy. He knows scientific principles and industrial methods, so that the book is filled with concrete examples.

What he sees, briefly, is that technological science has become an end in itself, been deified, and that what is happening in the modern world is that everything, the economy, our daily life, the state, and all human considerations are being systematically subordinated to the technological rationalization. The process is now nearing its end and revealing its true character; it is demoniacal.

Anyone who wants to be as wise as a serpent would do well to meditate on this book. It gives one a sense of having hit rock-bottom truth, and on such a basis one can have dove-like simplicity, without danger of waking up tomorrow to find one has played the enemy's game after all.

THY FAITH HATH MADE THEE WHOLE

CROSS AND CROWN

Quarterly edited by
Dominican Fathers of River Forest, Illinois

ONE THING AMERICAN CATHOLICISM HAS REALLY BEEN needing is a good spiritual magazine—nothing erudite or academic, but on the other hand something very different from a pious, inspirational journal. It would have to be rooted in the most orthodox mystical and ascetical theology, in the tradition of Saint Thomas and Saint John of the Cross. It would almost have to be edited by priests, although the writers should include the laity. One would hope to see such a magazine deal especially with contemporary spiritual problems, of which lay spirituality is certainly one of the foremost.

Such a magazine has now appeared. Called *Cross and Crown*, its first issue has a leading article by Father Garrigou-Lagrange, and it includes Fathers Gerald Vann and Walter Farrell among its contributors. It bristles with Thomism and orthodoxy. It is not erudite or academic. It makes many little efforts to relate its doctrine to the concrete, materialistic world of today, thus indicating that it proposes to deal with contemporary spirituality. Although this first issue is a trifle heavy, it is full of promise for a more lively future, now that the foundations are solidly laid.

The important thing is that the magazine has appeared and that it gives promise of practical enlightenment to laity as well as religious.

It is interesting to note that the English Dominicans have been editing a spiritual magazine (*The Life of the Spirit*) for two years or so. Theirs started out, probably of necessity, reprinting little-known spiritual treatises and such. Already it is deep in matters of contemporary spirituality, especially lay spirituality. We hope *Cross and Crown* will develop in similar fashion. We regret a little that it is a quarterly rather than a monthly, as the latter might make for livelier discussion.

Book Reviews

THE CURE D'ARS
By Abbe Francis Trochu
Newman

HERE IS A NEW PRINTING OF THE DEFINITIVE BIOGRAPHY of Saint Jean-Marie-Baptiste Vianney, the holy parish priest of Ars, who is certainly one of the most remarkable and interesting of modern saints. This life is based on the canonization proceedings and therefore is both comprehensive and accurate.

The Cure of Ars lived in the nineteenth century a life so penitential and austere as to demonstrate that the tales of the Desert Fathers are not exaggerated. He had a poor little parish, but he set out to win it entirely to Christ, with first of all his own penances and prayers, then hour-long sermons which were much to the point, and finally by a battle to the death against dancing and against taverns. He won: the dancing ceased, the taverns closed. The people of Ars became model Christians, who prayed while they worked, gathered each evening in the church for night prayers and exemplified Christian virtue. Into this model town then poured hordes of pilgrims and penitents, drawn to the Cure's confessional where he healed souls in a fabulous fashion. For years Saint Jean Vianney spent sixteen to seventeen hours a day in the confessional, beginning at 1:00 A. M. During the two or three hours he allowed himself for sleep, he was frequently kept awake the Devil's antics, this especially if a big sinner were due on the morrow.

It was just about the time of the American Civil War that this great saint died. Some three hundred priests and five thousand laity were in his funeral procession, while much of Europe sorrowed. All our secular school children know and venerate Abraham Lincoln, a great and noble man. That they never even hear of this contemporary who was far, far greater indicates the radical misdirection of their education.

475

THY FAITH HATH MADE THEE WHOLE

WHAT IS THIS CATHOLIC ACTION?

By Rev. Francis B. Donnelly
America Press

THIS IS A PARTICULARLY VALUABLE LITTLE PAMPHLET. IT consists of papal quotations arranged and explained so as to bring out the providential nature of Catholic Action in our times. It contains line drawings which are also very useful in making the points clear. It begins with secularism and goes on to show that Catholic Action is essentially a program of integration, with the laity in the forefront and the hierarchy in control. One thing that is usually not understood about Catholic Action, but which is made very clear here, is that the laity must have full *executive* responsibility for the fulfillment of their apostolate. Even people who have been working at Catholic Action for some time will profit from reading this work.

Book Reviews

JUNE 1949

COMMUNISM AND CHRISTIANS

By six authors, from the French
Newman Press

TOO MUCH SUPERFICIAL CRITICISM IS MADE OF COMMUnism. It is wrong philosophically, yes. It is wrong economically, yes. It will never work, of course not. It can't last, or flourish or spread—but it does. Here is a book which goes much deeper. It is a symposium of essays by Francois Mauriac, Pere Ducattillon, O.P., Alexandre Marc, Nicholas Berdyaev, Denis de Rougement, and Daniel-Rops, examining the success of communism against the background of the failure of Christians; not the failure of Christianity, but the failure of Christians.

There does not seem to be any comparably informed or profound discussion of communism here in America. Douglas Hyde in England has recently done a splendid pamphlet and book, very clearly written (simpler and clearer than some of the philosophical parts of this collection), but the thing is much plainer against a Christian background, as here. These essays are especially frank and penetrating. They are very sharp in their repudiation of capitalism, for one thing, but they don't make the mistake of going along with communism unconsciously. You will not find them accepting the communist platform point by point until they are virtually in the Marxist camp. They avoid this by always seeing the problem on the spiritual level, where it really rests. Daniel-Rops (whose essay I liked best of all) sums up the general point of view when he says:

> (communism) destroys the unity of man, of human society; it monstrously opposes masses of men one against the other. And the very effort it proclaims towards a classless humanity, towards a union is, as it were, the inverted image of Christian unity in charity, the demoniacal projection in the mirror of hatred of the Christian effort to establish unity.

THY FAITH HATH MADE THEE WHOLE
NUTRITION AND THE SOIL
By Dr. Lionel James Picton, O.B.E.
Devin-Adair

THE SIGHT OF A PASTY-FACED ADOLESCENT MEMBER OF Our Lady's Sodality sipping Coca-Cola and munching Ritz crackers should jar upon the integral sense of Christians. So should "boughten" white bread on the hospitable table of convents and monasteries. Food robbed of its vital elements is the counterpart in a lower order of spiritual life without grace.

The crusade against denatured food is beginning to break out in the open, after many heroic years in near-obscurity. The American Medical Association will some day have to answer for its silence. So will our legislators for their acquiescence. So will the publishers and newspapers which conspired to keep exposés on the semi-secretive level, privately printed or issued by little-known institutes. It's so easy to label as "crackpot" ideas which do not circulate in popular arenas. Meanwhile Pepperidge Farm Bread which *really* is bread becomes phenomenally popular on the East Coast while our corrupt economic ways keep up the elaborate pretense that it doesn't even exist. Meanwhile, too, women have miscarriages, or quarrel with their husbands, because they lack the vitality to cope with circumstances of modern life, and another hundred thousand Americans slip into mental disease because their frayed nerves and exhausted bodies can't stand up against the strain of work or family life any longer. What a reckoning there will be in heaven.

Nutrition and the Soil is the latest in a series of books exposing the truth about positive health (the sort that does not have to take vitamin pills and patent medicines). Those who have read the others will find this very interesting. Those who have never tackled the subject had better begin, and here is a better place than most.

The thesis is that if we were really healthy we would have a natural immunity to most diseases. This vital health depends chiefly on a proper balance of elements in the body, which in turn depends on the eating of whole (unprocessed) foods grown in soil which has been organically fertilized.

Dr. Picton's book is full of examples, illustrations, experiments, stories, and recipes. Since he is a medical doctor it stresses the medical aspects, particularly in relation to child-bearing. It makes fascinating reading and is a good rounded presentation of the subject.

Book Reviews

JULY 1949

PEACE OF SOUL

By Fulton J. Sheen
Whittlesey House

HEARTY PRAISE IS OWING TO MONSIGNOR SHEEN FOR the clarity with which he sees modern man's spiritual dilemma and the courage with which he points it out. This is the sort of insight that abounds in his latest book:

> An overemphasis on temporal security is a compensation for a loss of the sense of eternal security. When the soul becomes poor through the loss of its wealth, which is virtue, its owner seeks luxury and riches to atone for his inner nakedness.

Yet despite the frequency of his penetrating remarks, this book doesn't quite come off. Perhaps it would be better to say that it does a lot of good things but not the good thing it set out to do.

We can fairly assume, I think, that Monsignor Sheen set out to give the Christian version of *Peace of Mind*, that bit of rubbish (sentimentality and diluted Freudianism) written by the late Rabbi Liebman, which has been enormously popular because it promises an answer to the mental torment of almost everyone. It is a good example of people's given a stone when hungry for bread. Man's trouble today is really spiritual. It needs a Christian to give the right answer. That is what Monsignor Sheen tries to do. It is this reviewer's opinion that it doesn't quite succeed. It's a matter of not quite making the synthesis, of seeing the disintegration of the moderns on the one hand, and Christianity on the other, but of not quite fusing the two. What should be a synthesis turns out after all to be a very close juxtaposition. At the risk of arousing much ire, it may be pointed out that this is the chief difficulty at present among Catholics trying to make the psychiatric integration. A very conspicuous example is Dom Verner Moore who, with full psychiatric training and experience, and intense Christianity, never succeeded in seeing the two fields in one focus. His books are chiefly medical, with the religion superadded.

Monsignor Sheen approaches the problem in this way: first he shows what a mess we are in and that it has spiritual roots; then he abruptly switches to a sermon based on a Gospel reading or to a philosophical explanation of a doctrine, say original sin, in typical classroom presentation. Somewhere in between is a hiatus. Take his first chapter, where he states the general thesis that we are in a state of frustration. He ends up that by saying our situation is parallel to the young man named Legion from whom Christ cast out the devils in the Gospel, and concludes that we will be healed of our neuroses when we are restored to peace with God and our fellow men. But Christ *exorcised* that young man in the Gospels, who possessed of devils *literally*, so if the case is parallel (which is a perfectly good thesis to my mind) let Monsignor Sheen advocate exorcism literally as a cure for neuroses, which he does not do. Again, Monsignor Sheen too often fails to carry out his own advice to start with the confused modern mind and work back to the central Christian notion, proceeding psychologically and not according to the order of philosophy. Most often he switches to an ordered philosophical presentation, so that one has the overall impression at the end that the book is basically apologetical, with the analysis of the modern mind (while often well done) essentially an embellishment.

Throughout its pages, too, the book carries on a running argument with modern psychiatry. Most people will criticize Monsignor Sheen for not going along with modern psychiatry far enough. My criticism would be that he does not take a strong enough stand against it. The book is full of qualifying, hedging statements, like the following:

> Some mental disorders, however, refuse to be ignored, even after guilt as a cause and examination of conscience as a cure have been applied. There remain many mental ills which have a purely psychological and neurological, even a physiological, basis; these only a good psychiatrist can cure.

But Monsignor Sheen never says what mental disease is or what a "purely psychological" ill is.

Our particular concern here, as usual, *is not with either psychiatry or the psychoanalytic method, both of which are valid in their spheres.*

What are their spheres? He does not say.

Monsignor Sheen has no quarrel with psychiatry as such, which is fine because psychiatry deals with organic mental ills, among others.

He also, however, approves of some psychoanalysts and also some Freudians (who do not give Freud a twist he didn't intend—says Monsignor Sheen—that is, toward a deification of sexuality). I think he makes too many concessions. The psychoanalytic field is absolutely dominated by Freud, though there are variations on the theme by different members. Furthermore, anyone who has read Freud will find him quite obscene enough. A good case can be made for those who hold that their consummately obscene theories are just the making explicit of what was implicit in Freud.

Monsignor Sheen also treats the concept of the "unconscious" with a little too gingerly respect, especially since, after much talk and footnotes, no real definition of it is given. I await an explanation of the unconscious in Aristotelian-Thomistic terms. Was there a field of the inner life of such importance, as this is purported to be, which these great minds missed?

When prominent members of the analytic field agree with him, Monsignor Sheen quotes them to add weight to his own argument. He does this several times with Karen Horney. But why? If he does not respect her general position, why should her occasional concurrence be of value?

Monsignor Sheen knows a lot about modern psychiatry from reading (no doubt also from testimony of persons). While (in my view) he often concedes too much to the conclusions derived in that field, he sometimes misses the kernel of fact in psychiatry. Most often secular psychiatrists give a false analysis to a problem which really is there. On the other hand Monsignor Sheen dismisses with a wave of his hand the idea, for example, of a man's being in love with his mother (so-called Oedipus complex), but there remains the great problem of "momism," which the psychiatrists have tried to explain and Monsignor Sheen has not explained.

If this review is critical, it is not because the book is not good; certainly it is not meant to disparage the great good it will do. It is more a regret that it failed to accomplish a particular job which it set out to do and which very much needs doing.

THY FAITH HATH MADE THEE WHOLE

AUGUST 1949

THE CATHOLIC REFORMATION

By Pierre Janelle
Bruce

THIS IS A MORE INTERESTING BOOK THAN IT WOULD SEEM to be at first glance. It is one of those historical works, the fruit of conscientious scholarship, which contains a lot of detailed and accurate information, not yet simplified into a comprehending thesis. The thesis it does have seemed to me to be gratuitously tacked on. Even from the factual information the author gives I was tempted to analyze the circumstances differently. Nor would it be merely an intellectual exercise. The problems here dealt with have progeny in our own times.

Pierre Janelle describes the decadence in the Church preceding the Protestant revolt. The major obstacle to reform was anarchy in the Church organization. The major abuses were directly traceable to the Renaissance: luxury, superficiality, worldliness, elegance, moral decay and extravagance. The author's thesis is that a reform could not be accomplished until Christians found a way to take what was good in Renaissance culture without what was bad, to take the forms of classical paganism without the content. He also holds that this was the accomplishment of Christian humanism (particularly as embodied in Jesuit ideas and education) which finally accomplished the Catholic Reformation. It is, I suppose, a popular thesis. Yet even the book does not bear it out.

For about a hundred years before the Protestant revolt there were abortive efforts at reforming the Church. They all failed because the people were too attached to the Renaissance way of life. Only after the terrible sack of Rome did the reform begin in earnest, and then it was too late to salvage Christendom. This reads like modern history. We too have seen, and continue to see, all sorts of attempts at reform, but they seem impotent in the face of such things as The American Way of Life—material splendor, television, cars and the rest. After the atomic bombing of New York and other places we can expect that those who are left (if any) will be sufficiently chastened to cooperate with widespread reform. The major difference between the sixteenth and the twentieth centuries is that whereas formerly people were attached to artiness and elegance, now they are attached to comfort, science and industrialism. And just as people would have agreed in the sixteenth century that they wanted chastity in high prelates and a cessation of extravagant spending, only they didn't want to give up luxuriousness to attain it, so people will agree now that they don't like divorce or birth control or juvenile delinquency, but they are unwilling to part with country clubs, advertising, gadgets and the rest of the things which some people consider to be the occasions of the common modern sins. Can you take the forms of paganism without the content? Can you study Ovid for his literary excellence without noticing that he deals with pagan gods and goddesses, whose doings were often obscene and are under the suspicion of diabolism? Can you have television without escapism and masses of morons?

It seems to me that Pierre Janelle makes a poor case in defense of his thesis. He rests it too heavily on a humanist named Sadolet, a classical scholar who wrote an ode to celebrate the finding of the Laocoon (of which sculptural group Adrian VI, who was one of the unsuccessful reformers, said merely "here were statues of pagan gods again"). Sadolet advised many of the popes of that time, but his worth to the Church might have been because of his other excellencies rather than his humanism (just as it might be held that Thomas More was canonized for losing his head in a matter having nothing to do with his interest in humanism, so that the matter of his humanism has to be justified on other grounds than those of the martyr's sanctity).

The Church is always reformed by saints and it seems to me that if Janelle had used this as his major thesis then the thesis about humanism wouldn't precisely have fitted, even secondarily. You could hardly, for instance, have called Saint John of the Cross or Saint Teresa humanists.

It is true, though, that the reform was tempered by humanism, in fact by a fairly considerable residue of Renaissance culture. The Council of Trent has its proceedings written up elegantly and the Ratio Studiorum was certainly based on the study of the classics. Janelle considers there to have been a happy synthesis made of Renaissance culture and Christianity, but would it not be possible to hold instead that a compromise was made — a compromise not strong enough to prevent a considerable reconstruction of Church life, yet insidious enough to prevent a total restoration?

One thing that has to be accounted for is that, despite the counter-reformation (and without underestimating its tremendous accomplishments) the Western world has been quite steadily worsening until today it seems to be at its very lowest point, in art, literature, music, economics, politics, morality and indeed every phase of temporal life. This is as true in the Catholic countries as in the Protestant countries, although in a different way. In this light it looks as though the Catholic Reformation was only partially successful and that its weak point was precisely its failure to detach itself from pagan culture. An alternate thesis would regard the Middle Ages (for all their shortcomings, in regard to which I think Janelle is unjust) as the high point of Christian society, and the problem would be to account for the decay and corruption of a civilization so essentially ordered to Christ. It could be held that it was precisely the reintroduction into Europe of ancient pagan culture, through the accidental instrumentality of the Crusades, that set in motion the successive attacks on Christianity which are culminating in our day. With the classics came the glorification of the purely natural (as opposed to the supernatural), the exaltation of culture rather than holiness, or as preliminary to holiness instead of subsequent to it, the over-refinement of manners along with the perversion of morals. All these things had certain splendor in the Renaissance, and all of them too are still with us, but now far from splendid. If you hold, as Janelle does in this book, that a humanistic synthesis was made in the Catholic Reformation, how then will you account for the utter corruption of our own day?

SEPTEMBER 1949

MAKERS OF THE MODERN MIND

By Thomas P. Neil
Bruce

IF I WERE YOUNG AND JUST FINDING OUT HOW DISEASED the modern world is, I would devour this book. It would fill me with joy to learn that Calvin is the one who gave us our respect for money and business, that Freud was an extremely proud man who could not get along with anyone, and that, indeed, all the bum ideas that are going about are not traceable to the Church but to the enemies of the Church. I would consider it my great good fortune to find essays on Luther, Calvin, Descartes, Locke, Newton, Rousseau, Kant, Bentham, Darwin, Marx and Freud, which simplify and clarify their ideas better than I could do in twenty-five years of research and present them in a popular manner along with fascinating biographic details.

It must be because I am getting old that such a treasury of information and personal tit-bits palls a little. What I want is something simpler and more penetrating. As Mr. O'Neil treats these men they don't seem quite real. Yet I would not accuse him of pulling his punches, certainly not of watering down his moral or doctrinal judgments. Yet he is too "balanced" in talking about people who are probably not balanced. Luther is not so much a mixture of good qualities and bad qualities as he is an apostate priest, who probably was, as Mr. O'Neil sort of hints, diabolically possessed. If one saw Luther in the light of this fundamental living sacrilege, maybe everything would become clearer. Then we would not talk about "this doctrine" or "that belief" of Luther's, because they probably weren't doctrines or beliefs in the sense of rationally held conclusions. It would be more to the point to show how Luther's "ideas" served the Devil in attacking the Church. Similarly with Freud. We treat him as though he were a man with some bad faults. But can a man who wrote so many evil things be explained so ordinarily?

THY FAITH HATH MADE THEE WHOLE
SOCIAL ETHICS: NATURAL LAW IN THE MODERN WORLD

By Johannes Messner
Herder

THIS IS A MONUMENTAL (1000 PAGES), COMPREHENSIVE (everything from the nature of man to a study of world peace), and expensive (ten bucks) book. Add to that the fact that it is translated from the German, and you cannot help but say, "It had better be good."

It is good. It is more than worth any six social ethics books I can recall having seen, and so (to overcome the most obvious barrier to its purchase) is really comparatively cheap. That it is worth its price in size, weight and sheer abundance of material will be immediately obvious to anyone who glances through it.

To me the most impressive thing about Messner's book is the weight of its scholarship and the depth of its treatment. Without being "heavy" it is the opposite of all the word "superficial" suggests. It would be unthinkable, for instance, that Messner would not know the Aristotelian-Thomistic teaching on usury, and equally unthinkable that he would not be cognizant with all the great modern theories and operations in respect to finance. Throughout the book there is on one hand constant analysis and delineation of principles, and on the other a constant reference to modern conditions and problems, to the highest authority in technical and scientific fields for facts of the market or psychology or biology.

The other impressive thing about the book is that it makes an integration. It relates the philosophical principles to the biological data, to the experiential testimony and the social theory all the way down the line. And although Messner deals with natural law and temporal situations, the supernatural is not entirely missing, and certainly he is constantly aware of a higher law. The Catholic Church and her teachings often enter the pages of the book.

Messner works not just on theory but toward solutions in the practical order. I would not always agree with his solutions. Furthermore, I do not think that he is the most profound thinker on the problems of the modern world, but he is the best scholar I have found within the broad area of ethics. The disagreements are not a serious matter for Messner is engaged more in analyzing the problems than in fitting them into pet theories.

Book Reviews

OCTOBER 1949

THE MYSTICAL EVOLUTION IN THE DEVELOPMENT AND VITALITY OF THE CHURCH

By Very Rev. John G. Arintero, O.P., S.T.M.
Herder

THIS IS A GREAT MODERN WORK ON THE MYSTICAL LIFE, with emphasis on theological orthodoxy according to Saint Thomas Aquinas and Saint John of the Cross. The author writes not only to inform but also to correct errors about the spiritual life which have crept in though Protestantism.

Father Arintero, who died in 1928, was a great Spanish Dominican whose lifework changed from natural science to mystical theology. He was quite a famous spiritual director and himself very holy. His work is much like Garrigou-Lagrange's, or rather it is the other way around, for Father Garrigou-Lagrange learned from Father Arintero. They cover the same general ground, but the Spaniard's work is rather less "scientific" in presentation. He has tried to stay on the level of theological mystery, solicitous not to corrupt the doctrine by reducing it to the level of our understanding. Of the two there seems to be but little choice, but if I were to make a choice I think I would favor Father Arintero, as being less polemic and therefore somewhat more inspiring.

BARBARA CELARENT

By Thomas Gilby, O.P.
Longmans

IT CANNOT BE ACCIDENTAL THAT MANY OF MY FRIENDS and I feel an increasing desire to study logic. It may be because, in a world which overwhelms us with factual material, we sense that the failure to arrive at truth is an intellectual inability to sort and distinguish. There is, in fact, hardly anyone who does not smell something funny in the reasoning of his friends, the advertisers, the politicians and the would-be savers of the world. A sense of logic is innate in the human person, but it can, like the conscience, do with some polishing up.

Here, then, is a book which deals not only with logic in the narrow sense, but with the scholastic dialectic of Saint Thomas Aquinas, which reaches out to all the subtleties and pitfalls of the human reason. I must confess that I had never encountered dialectics before, and that it was the intention merely of sharpening my powers of deductive reasoning that I began to read this book. Instead of a narrow science I found an enlargement and enrichment of all my thinking processes. I found, too, confirmation and elucidation for the types of approaches to the truth which I had been groping for out of necessity in my own work — things like Saint Thomas' use of analogy.

So it is a rich book of its nature. But it is very condensed, so you have to strain your brain to read it. Furthermore, the author has a wealth of cultural knowledge which he introduces, to make it richer and also a little harder. He has a keen, but English, humor, which means the addition of a few blind spots. In fact, the book is like the title all the way through — deceptively beguiling. *Barbara Celarent* is not a girl's name, but a device for remembering syllogisms.

Among the most useful parts of the book are the sections on induction, deduction and the method of the sciences. Also there is the recurring emphasis on the fact that Saint Thomas does his reasoning in respect to the real, concrete universe and, owing to his doctrine about universals, does not have the problem that has plagued modern philosophers, of relating their abstractions to a material world.

The author is an English Dominican priest who wrote it on board the ship he chaplained in the late war.

Book Reviews

NOVEMBER 1949

CATHOLIC ACTION LITERATURE

SPECIALIZED CATHOLIC ACTION IS DIFFICULT TO DESCRIBE in a few minutes, or even a few hours. When someone hears about it for the first time and wants to know more, I am at a loss. There is no point in plunging into a description of the technique (you learn early not to do that, for no one sees any sense in the technique unless he understands that the whole role of the laity in the Church is changing). On the other hand, if you lead off by talking about the need for laity who feel responsible and take initiative, you go on and on and can't hope to get at the technique that evening. So you usually end up saying, "Go read about it, but there aren't any books around that cover the subject though there are some pamphlets if you know where to go to get them and I forget their names and which ones are good."

From now on I shall say, "Look, there's a book, go buy it. It's *Studies in Catholic Action*, by some anonymous Australian Catholic Actionists. It's distributed by Fides in South Bend (that's a Catholic Action publishing house) through Catholic bookstores." It's a good book, too, not terribly profound, but easy and informative and has the spirit of the movement in it. It tells *why* Catholic Action and *how*, describes the procedures and gives a lot of practical advice, derived from experience, on what works and what faults to avoid. It's written by lay people but I would have thought it written by a priest. It's certain to be helpful to priests anyhow, whether they are first learning about the subject or having difficulties with their own C. A. cells.

If I were not so glad to see this book I might quibble a bit with its minor points. On one of the very first pages it says the modern situation parallels the decline of Rome, at which former time some few people couldn't stand the corruption of society and fled, but most Christians stuck around and built Christendom out of the ruins of the Roman Empire. That's not how I heard the story. According to my version hordes of the best people fled (The Desert Monks), and it was these people who developed religious orders and the religious orders in turn which settled, educated, developed and Christianized Europe.

It's an academic point though, because I don't think the situation is exactly parallel today, but it presages in this book occasional digs at anyone who wants to remove himself from the industrial system or anything else in modern life. The consequence of this type of thinking is that you accept life as it is, then you tell the worker that work is a *vocation*, and presently he's getting mystical about selling Mickey Mouse toy wrist-watches, or adding another bolt to a television set coming down the assembly line. As is well known to our readers, *Integrity* doesn't accept the institutional structure of the modern world *carte blanche*, but that doesn't mean we are retiring to caves in the Arizona desert. However, this book concerns chiefly the mass movement of young workers, whose cooperation in the system is only material and whose chief work and glory is the transformation of their friends and neighbors, which they do with admirable charity and without too much necessary advertence to the system.

Fides has also published in mimeographed form a report of the second Catholic Action Study Weekend for Religious Assistants (nuns and brothers). The subject this year was *The Problem of Spirituality for Students*, with the chief talks by Patricia Groom, Sister M. Madeleine Sophie, S. S. N. D. and Father Putz. It's very good. The type of spirituality they are talking about is integral to the students' lives as students, not pious practices appended thereonto. Sister Madeleine Sophie's talk is very entertaining, and rather devastating. Here is her description of a teaching sister with a split personality:

> Here is a Sister, may her name not be legion, who is desperately concerned with what she rather primly terms "the development of my interior life." She swallows John of the Cross avidly, and plants her seeds of contemplation in every free minute she has. She moans heavily about the opposition between her "spiritual" and her "apostolic" life in the classroom. Teaching is so demanding on one's time — and so distracting! She tries so hard to keep recollected during her teaching day but "it's so hard to think of God when you're doing such worldly things as counting money, or noses, or marks. Thank God, retreat is just around the corner and I'll be able to get away from it all."

That may seem harsh, but it isn't so in the context of the talk. Sister Madeleine Sophie knows that Dom Chautard and others insist on the primacy of a deep interior life. She brings up that objection but does not, to my mind, fully answer it. She and the others in this book are right that nuns and students and priests have got to live single, simple lives oriented to charity, and that the work of the apostolate itself helps to sanctify, but it remains to be shown when and how and at what point the active life becomes an overflow of contemplation.

At the end of this report are some student Catholic Action programs for the current school year, on college and high school level. To my mind these plans are far below the level of the preceding discussion. They fall into naturalism, preoccupied with the health, living conditions and study habits of the students. Progress toward sanctity will have to be added as a side dish. I think that's because the inquiries don't go deep enough. In fact, I would go so far as to suggest that the students are in the same boat, although on the opposite side of it, as the Sister whose name we hope is not legion. Neither will be able to lead a single-directed life without examining the *contents* of the courses given and taken to see if the matter itself is focused on God.

THY FAITH HATH MADE THEE WHOLE

DECEMBER 1949

DESERT CALLING

By Anne Fremantle
Henry Holt

NEXT TO SAINT JOAN OF ARC, CHARLES DE FOUCAULD IS the most-talked-of and popular religious figure in France today, especially among the new apostolic groups. He is very little known here, although occasional and exciting references have been made to him for years in the apostolate. How wonderful it is that we should first get real knowledge of him from a book which is, simply, about as good as you could possibly imagine. It is thick and full, clear and detailed, beautifully written and absorbing.

Charles de Foucauld (born 1859) was a French nobleman who lost his faith in childhood and entered into manhood enjoying to the full the material pleasures of his class. He was a glutton, writing home to his grandparents about the choice wines he wanted during his holidays, and finally smoking only cigars made especially for himself. He was fat, slothful and not brilliant in his studies. He was a contemporary of Henri Petain at the famous military school of St. Cyr. Then he served a short time with the French forces in Africa where he was the enfant terrible of his regiment, and was finally released because he declined to give up flaunting his mistress in public. By this time he had squandered most of his patrimony and had been put under legal structures by his family.

Here is the man who may become one of the most influential of modern saints. He had a gift for exploration and geographical precision which led him to a careful and daring tour of the then completely closed country of Morocco. He went through it disguised as a poor Jewish rabbi, accompanied by another who was really such. His observations form a still-famous book studied in military academies. The African silence, the study of Moslem and Jewish holy books, plus the experience of chastity from which he developed a taste for it, led him to a holy priest and back to Christianity. His subsequent life was an ever more perfect imitation of Christ in His hidden and hard life at Nazareth. It led him through the Trappists to the desert again, where he was a famous marabout (holy man) living alone among the Touaregs, the least of the African tribes. By them he was murdered in 1916, as a consequence of the German effort to wrest North Africa from France. The White Fathers are promoting his cause.

De Foucauld seems to have been raised up to point a new way of evangelization in our day. He represents "Christ simply present." His idea was to go among those remote from, and almost pathologically antagonistic to, Christianity, simply to bring Christ there, both in the Blessed Sacrament and in Charles' own presence and charity. He led a contemplative life. He mixed with his neighbors and helped them, but in an informal way. He didn't make one single convert. He wanted followers, but didn't get any real ones until 1933, seventeen years after his death. Now there are several hundred of his brothers and sisters in France and Africa carrying out his ideas. They live and operate in very small groups of five and six. They earn their own living in some humble way, and live frugally among the poorest. Their spirituality is rooted in contemplation. They dress more or less like ordinary people. It is part of a new ferment in the Church, and Charles de Foucauld is its chief inspiration.

THY FAITH HATH MADE THEE WHOLE

JANUARY 1950

THE MATURE MIND

By H.A. Overstreet
W.W. Norton & Company

THE INNOCENT CHRISTIAN WILL APPROACH *THE MATURE Mind* by H.A. Overstreet (currently topping the best-seller, non-fiction lists) thinking that the author is going to say, "It's a pity more people don't grow up, here how to get them to do it...." Be it known, therefore, that Mr. Overstreet substitutes maturity for sanctity. Although it is never entirely clear what this new type of holiness is (as a true religious concept it is shrouded in mystery), nevertheless one can piece together a composite picture of the mature man, the *saint*. He is a person without free will who is conditioned by enlightened modern education to a possession of the supreme virtues of racial tolerance and cooperation. He is never irritable. He solves all problems by the *scientific method*, which is sort of a parody of the gift of faith, both in being supreme and in not being quite clear in our minds. He loves group discussions and has a passion for research. (Note this extraordinary statement to account for the shortcomings of Buddhism: "No one in Buddha's time knew how to set up the conditions for a research project.") The mature man and his wife have "creative" sex experiences, but do not let creative suggest babies to you, because it means something vague in the emotional order. The saint (the mature man) is the finest flowering of the evolutionary processes. He is strictly secular. He is atheistic. Science is his God—not the science of gadgets but the science of psychology and human relationships.

Therefore let the innocent Christian who reads this avert his eyes from the best-seller lists, cancel his membership in book clubs. Then let him buy a nice substantial book like *The Imitation of Christ* or *The Waters of Siloe*. Seriously, this is the sort of book which no one should read unless it is in the line of duty. Even then (for it seemed in my line of duty) it leaves one with a headache for a day or so.

This book is not an attack on Christianity directly, even though it contains some shocking anti-Christian passages, at once blasphemous and (oddly enough) childish. Instead we have maturity as the new substitute for Christianity. It is filling the vacuum left by the de-Christianization of Western society, and filling it with seven devils. Often the book says the right thing, but about a lower order. There are whole passages where you can substitute "spiritual" for "psychological" and the statement will be perfectly orthodox. Or again "insight" substitutes for "principle." We are not used to this sort of attack (although we are going to see plenty more of it) and therefore it could be very detrimental to one's faith.

Mr. Overstreet has a very good and penetrating (mature?) mind up to the point where it goes to pieces. His weakest area is religion, where he completely misrepresents every dogma he challenges. Catholics would spot his errors about original sin (we hope). Would they catch, however, the ultimate emptiness of his doctrine? Here the book resembles *Peace of Mind*, to which it is otherwise superior because Mr. Overstreet is much brighter and deeper than the late Rabbi Liebmann. In the end of both these best sellers we find that the mountain has labored and brought forth a mouse. For all the condescension of the authors toward Christianity, they end up advocating nice manners for third graders, compared to which the Sermon on the Mount is the thundering of God for the benefit of giant men, amid a chorus of a million angels.

COLLECTED LETTERS OF SAINT THERESE OF LISIEUX

Translated by F.J. Sheed
Sheed & Ward

THESE ARE ALL THE EXTANT LETTERS OF SAINT THERESE, 238 of them. Knowing this, I expected to be bored, at least part of the time, to encounter repetitions and trivialities. It turned out that the longer I read the more closely I read. Not once, but several nights I missed a few hours sleep for not being able to put the book down. Somewhere along the line I began praying to Saint Therese regularly.

The letters start when Saint Therese was only three (she had some help with this letter) and go up until within a few days of her death at twenty-four. Most of them are to her relatives, especially to her sister Celine, with whom she was particularly intimate. It was Celine who remained with their father until he died, caring for him during his long illness, and she then entered the Lisieux Carmel where Therese was her novice mistress. At about this time the saint was given, secretly, two priest-missionaries to aid in their apostolate with her prayers, her sufferings and her encouragement, so her correspondence did not diminish, but was transferred to these two.

Perhaps the most immediately impressive thing about the letters is their style, for which we are obviously greatly indebted to Mr. Sheed. Saint Therese's letters are very warm, and spirited, but with a great spiritual strength and reserve. All the warmth is there in the translation, and all the clarity, with not a grain of sentimentality, though it is easy to see how that might have crept in with a mediocre translation.

All the virtues of Saint Therese stand out in these letters. Her great simplicity reveals itself throughout, sometimes rather pointedly, as in a postscript telling a friend about a raffle the Carmel is going to have and the price of the chances. Here, and other places where she writes something she has been told to say which probably is distasteful to her, it is done very simply without a hint of her own feelings. Again she has that simplicity in what she writes the missionaries and the way she tells unpleasant truths when necessary. Coupled with this simplicity is a tremendous charity. She is always saying encouraging things to people, yet without deception or flattery.

Since I was preoccupied with the idea of maturity while reading this book I could not help but see how mature Saint Therese was from her earliest years. One gets the impression that she took up all her personal troubles with God from the beginning, so that she was free in her relations with other people to feel responsible for *them* and not intrude herself. Her reaction to seeing the Pope was very interesting in this regard. The episode was a disappointment. She told him she wanted to enter the Carmel at fifteen, but someone intruded to sum up her case to the Holy Father, somewhat brusquely and unsympathetically. She regarded the whole episode as something that happened according to the will of God, and in which she had done the best she could. It didn't seem to occur to her to be annoyed at the intruder, for she didn't see things from that human standpoint. Her quality of objectivity is especially marked during the suffering of her last illness, which she never reflects in her correspondence. Sometimes the letters are notably gay when the suffering was at its height.

Book Reviews

The letters are arranged by years, each prefaced by a brief biographical sketch of that year. This correlation between the life and the letters is carried out further in footnotes. The footnotes are really a joy. They tell what happened to all the main characters, how events turned out, and lots of other pertinent facts. They piece out, for instance, the remarkable story of the infamous Hyacinth Loyson, an apostate Carmelite priest about whom Therese writes and for whom she prayed until her death.

At the end of the book there is a calendar of the important posthumous dates of Saint Therese' intercessory life in Heaven as evidenced here on earth. From it one gets the impression that her apostolate is still growing.

SAINTS ARE NOT SAD
Assembled by F.J. Sheed
Sheed & Ward

The title of this book, though appealing in itself, has little relevance to the contents. The forty biographies of saints here assembled were all written within the last twenty-five years and it is that, not the gaiety of the saints, that marks the collection. Here we have a cross section of modern hagiography. Overwhelmingly it is interpretive biography. In genre it is remote from the simple, objective relation of facts (and fabrications) of ancient and medieval hagiography, although that is represented here by Saint Perpetua's own story, because it happened to be translated lately by Walter Shewring.

These sketches of saints are virile and their lives make sense to the modern precisely because their biographies see them against the perspective of the modern mind and scene. Some of the sketches have much more editorializing than fact. Some are just meditations about the saint—"What could God have meant by raising this one up?" I have no objection to this type of treatment; in fact, I think it is more or less inevitable, and very useful in our day. It makes interesting reading too. However, the interpretive element is so strong that it frequently focuses the saint's whole life and purpose to a meaning of the author's choosing which could be wrong. As a result you may be getting larger doses of Father Steuart or Father Martindale or

Archbishop Goodier than of Bernadette or Peter Claver or Camillus. What struck me was the impression of the saint was sharply at variance often with the one I had previously held, and correspondingly, different facts were singled out for emphasis. Father Martindale and the producers of *Monsieur Vincent* ought to get together on Saint Vincent de Paul. Archbishop Goodier and I see Saint Augustine quite differently apropos of the same *Confessions*. But if I were to write about Saint Augustine I would frankly fit him into my interpretation, so I have no complaint.

The biographies are all short, some very short. They are varied and the book is most attractive. It's a good sort of thing to have around a family, or a guest room, or to give as a present.

FEBRUARY 1950

THE SOUL

By Saint Thomas Aquinas
Translated by John Patrick Rowan
Herder

THIS IS A TRANSLATION OF SAINT THOMAS' *DE ANIMA*. IT contains twenty-one questions about the soul (such questions as whether the soul exists everywhere in the body, whether we have one soul or several, and what sort of existence our souls lead after death). The questions are treated in the manner of the Summa, with objections first, then discussion and then the answers to the objections. Nothing is added to the original except a few footnotes and an index. The format of the book is excellent and the cover-jacket is beautiful.

Here then, in one place, all translated, is the basic knowledge that is lacking to nearly all the men of today who are struggling with problems of the soul or of the relationship between the body and the soul. Let us fervently hope that some psychologists, psychiatrists, doctors and brain surgeons will have the courage to tussle with the scholastic discipline and terminology to see if they can find the key to their own most perplexing problems.

PSYCHIATRY AND ASCETICISM

By Felix D. Duffey, C.S.C.
Herder

FATHER DUFFEY HAS DEDICATED HIS BOOK TO SAINT BERnadette in reparation for the presumptive absurdity of a woman psychiatrist who analyzed Bernadette's "hallucinations" to find them the result of extensive infantile regression. This particular analysis and some other choice bits of nonsense from the psychiatric camp are quoted in the book. It is refreshing to see someone show a little honest indignation at the psychiatric mysticism and also to have him show up such a thing as the way practitioners think they have made a great contribution just because they have described some lurid life details.

The main contention of Psychiatry and Ascetism is that we all suffer from original sin, which is the root cause of our emotional disturbances, and that the remedy for the original lack of integrity is asceticism and prayer. All of which is true. However, what Father does not explain is how you unwind a person once he is neurotic. For this, I think something has to be added to the prescription for the normal case.

The book is uneven and has too many and too long quotations. Where the author deals with Catholic teaching it is presented in the usual way, condensed and theological. It needs to be re-stated to appear fresh. A non-Catholic would be pretty lost in it. Near the end of the book Father Duffey weakens and makes a few vague remarks to the effect that "of course modern psychiatry does many wonderful things and we wouldn't want to deprecate..." Some day I hope someone will write a book telling what these wonderful things are.

Book Reviews

MAY 1950

THE HOLINESS IN THE CHURCH

By Raoul Plus, S.J.
Translated by Mother Mary St. Thomas Newman

AN APOLOGY IS OWED TO OUR READERS FOR NOT HAVING sufficiently stressed in our pages the excellence of Father Raoul Plus, S.J. as a modern spiritual writer who is especially adapted to the apostolate. In France he has had great influence. Most of his works are now available in English. The most widely known is probably *Radiating Christ* but he has written many small volumes, including *How to Pray Always*, *How to Pray Well*, and *The Folly of the Cross*.

Father Plus' particular gift is well illustrated by the present volume. He *contemporizes* eternal principles and doctrines. That means defending the Church against its most formidable and influential opponents, using their own accusations as a starting point. It means opening our eyes to the ways in which grace works in our day. He is at an opposite pole from the secular journalists who see what is happening only in the realms of finance, economics, and politics. He also stands in contrast to those theologians who will give the principles but never the modern adaptation, or who play so safe that they ignore everything which is not ancient history, duly canonized.

Father Plus holds that not only does the Church produce saints in our day, as always, but that the crop is even more abundant the last hundred years or so, owing to the evil times. Without anticipating the Church's judgment he cites example after example of Christian heroism, only a few cases of which are generally known. His heroes include priests, soldiers, missionaries, Carmelites, parents, children, martyrs, workmen, hidden souls and eminent citizens. The total effect is almost overwhelming, and tremendously inspiring. And it is not accidental. The author agrees with Jacques Maritain that "Christian heroism will one day become the one and only solution of the problems of life." Has not that day come?

THY FAITH HATH MADE THEE WHOLE

STORM OF GLORY

By John Beevers
Sheed & Ward

IF THERE ARE STILL PEOPLE WHO SHY AWAY FROM DEVO-tion to Saint Therese because they think she is a saint sticky with sentiment, this is their book. It is written expressly to show the heroic strength of the saint's character. This it does not only by a direct effort of emphasis, but also by incorporating some new material, heretofore unpublished. Mr. Beevers has done a nice job. It is a virile book, and interesting reading.

Book Reviews

JUNE 1950

MENTAL PRAYER AND MODERN LIFE

A Symposium of articles, translated from the French "Cahiers de la Vie Spirituelle"
Kenedy

"NUNK" IS A COLLOQUIALISM OF THE LAY APOSTOLATE designating someone who "is neither a nun nor a monk but wishes it were." It is not meant unkindly. The trouble with nunks is that, wanting to become holy in the lay state, they have no other pattern for holiness than that devised for religious. It is not their fault if they become "little religious," always hurrying to church services, using every tiny interval of the day to get on with the divine office, and engaging in spiritual practices like custody of the eyes. The working out of a practical road to holiness suited to the lay state has lagged behind the thirst for holiness on the part of the laity. Therefore this symposium of articles is most welcome. It deals with modern prayer in general, converging on the problems of lay spirituality. There is a long introductory historical article, and then a discussion of methods of prayer centering around the *spiritual exercises*. The last practical section is directly on lay spirituality. Two articles interested me most.

"Making One's Life a Prayer," by J. M. Perrin, O. P., takes up what the author calls *the prayer of life*. Everyone has to withdraw for formal prayer sometimes, even busy laity, but where the time available is limited this prayer of life must be developed. It means establishing vital contact with Christ in every life situation, not as withdrawing from daily events, but as seeing and acting in them with an eternal perspective. The whole doctrine of the Incarnation is underlying, since through it the whole earth was redeemed and is no longer enemy territory. Very pertinent is Saint Catherine of Siena's answer to someone who complained of how hard it is to strive for perfection in the press of temporal affairs: "It is you who make them temporal." *The prayer of life* is not simple to attain. It involves using one's whole life for God and achieving a profoundly Christian mentality.

The other article that strikes me particularly is "Putting the Gospel in Our Midst" by a leader of a girls' white-collar Catholic Action section. She talks about *the method of the Gospel lived*, which is familiar to all those in the Jocist-type movements. It uses the Gospels as a basis for regular discussion of "how does this action or saying of Christ apply to my life?" and is followed by application in one's daily life.

The method of the Gospel lived has many advantages. It is a return to the primary source. It is suited to all people from the simplest to the most learned. It necessitates a supernatural approach to life and a high heroism, because that was what Christ taught and lived. It cuts right through all the casuistry and the neat distinctions, carefully misapplied, with which even practicing Catholics are wont to delude themselves. Recently I heard of a Catholic college student in New York City who argued seriously that it wouldn't be right for her to give away one pair of the thirty-five pair of shoes she owns because she has to have matching shoes for each outfit, because she has to dress becomingly for her state in life (which is rich bourgeois). Just the act of taking the Gospels as the standard, rather than social custom, legalities or advertising, is the preliminary to a Catholic renewal.

Book Reviews

JULY 1950

I LEAP OVER THE WALL

By Monica Baldwin
Rinehart

IT HADN'T OCCURRED TO US TO REVIEW THIS BOOK UNTIL lately. When it came out we bought it, enjoyed it, and were rather interested in what the reviewers would say. What moves us now is the rather scornful nature of the Catholic criticism, exemplified by the announcement of a forthcoming article in *The Catholic World* called "I *didn't* leap over the wall," by Sister Disgusta.

Everyone knows by now that Monica Baldwin was nun in a strict cloister in England for twenty-eight years, and then returned to the world early in World War II, perfectly legitimately and with the permission of the Holy See. The book is about her period of adjustment to the modern world, with a discussion of convent life by way of contrast. It is not an attack on convents, but an apology for them and for the contemplative life, written for the sophisticated educated pagan. It is not a personal history, although her own peculiar case necessarily intrudes.

Miss Baldwin was prevented from spending her first night out of the convent at her sister's apartment in London because her sister's roommate had "a conscientious objection to people who come out of convents." This same sort of minor persecution recurs from time to time in the book, mostly from relatives, and treated as briefly and as charitably as possible by the author. Since her problem is not that of making any sort of adjustment, but an adjustment so difficult that it involves her whole economic, spiritual and mental well-being, this is certainly the cruelest of torture. Furthermore, those who have conscientious objections to people who come out of convents are being "holier than the Pope," because the Holy Father freely released Miss Baldwin. In a transitional age great charity ought to be exercised toward the many, many people who cannot find, or have great difficulty finding, a place to take root. We Americans have lately, and quite rightly, begun to show compassion for fallen-away priests, instead of treating them as hopeless pariahs. Yet these priests, however sinned

505

against, also sinned gravely. Monica Baldwin's case involved not the slightest moral culpability. Why, then, should she be derided?

Alongside of this general disdain one sometimes finds a little name-calling, with "crackpot," or "misfit." Now I, and most of my good friends have been called "crackpot" on so many occasions that we have begun to regard it as a compliment. A "crackpot" is someone who doesn't operate according to Wall Street business principles. A "crackpot" is a religious idealist. A "crackpot" is someone who doesn't wear lipstick. A "crackpot," above all, anyone who is different in a society of rigorous conformists. So Monica Baldwin is a "crackpot," mostly because she has unusual ideas and finds herself in unique situations.

One other related matter that people bring up is this: if Monica Baldwin knew after ten years that she had no vocation, why did she wait eighteen more years to leave? But she answers this in the book. She didn't leave because she had made solemn perpetual vows to stay, and she didn't think the fact that she had made an awful mistake changed the situation. Then as things got harder she had great difficulty getting any authoritative advice about what to do (hence her somewhat acid remarks on Bishops and their visitations). She finally got information and petitioned to leave, because she thought her sanity was involved.

Miss Baldwin has been called snobbish, on the ground that she knew important people (her uncle is the former Prime Minister) and mentioned it, and because she made some disparaging remarks about the lower classes. Yet to me it seemed that she exemplified that sort of "classlessness" which characterizes Christianity. The unity of men in Christ, their possibility of being so united if they are not already, prevents the Christian from taking the natural inequalities of men too seriously or absolutely. They are there, but they can be transcended by love. They are useful for the functioning of the social organism, but we will be judged not by our states in life so much as on how we acquit ourselves in them. The modern secular idea of equality is quite different. Here natural inequalities are felt to be shameful. There has to be a leveling of everyone to the same mediocrity, stupidity and spiritual deadness. When Monica Baldwin came out of the convent she was sympathetic with socialism and prepared to feel warmly about the common man. She spent most of the first few years working and living with the lower classes, and she was disillusioned, not because the people were simple and ignorant, or even dirty, but because they did not love God or each other and because they resented anyone who was superior to them in any way, all this with a few exceptions. She didn't find all those wonderful traits which are supposed to characterize the common man and she said so. This is mere honesty. What she did do was work and live among them, in unbelievably awful and hard conditions. Let those who cry "snobbish" take on the lot of the poor as she did. She cannot be condemned either, in my opinion, for not having seemed one of them. Just to read books is to set yourself apart from most ordinary environments. Anyhow she was different, but she certainly shared their hardships, and she certainly didn't go about behaving like the landed gentry.

One other common criticism puzzles me. Monica Baldwin has been taken to task for indecent or immodest talk, mostly on the basis of her opening description of convent underwear (which in that convent was really archaic). It is true that she is by nature an outspoken, frank person, but the implication is that her remarks are lascivious, which they certainly are not.

In New York they write about Question Mark brassieres in the sky with airplanes, and the magazines, cigarette ads, etc., etc., etc., verge on the pornographic. Yet these things go unremarked by the sort of Catholics who are offended by the frank remarks in this book. We would not believe that there was this double standard except that we have heard people who regularly subscribe to *Life* and the national women's magazines say that *Integrity* is the sexiest magazine they have ever seen. And we are literally dumbfounded.

We hope that Monica Baldwin, who writes superbly, will find her vocation as an author, and that she will use her pen tellingly in the apostolate.

SELECTED WRITINGS OF SAINT TERESA OF AVILA

By William Doheny, C.S.C.
Bruce

AN ANTHOLOGY OF MYSTICISM

Edited by Paul de Jaeger, S.J.
Newman

THESE ARE BOTH ANTHOLOGIES OF CLASSICAL SPIRITUAL writings. Father Doheny's book, which has very attractive format and type, has short excerpts from Saint Teresa's writings, arranged by subject matter, using the Peer's translation. They will make you very impatient to get at the full text, as these bits are just teasers, and seem to stop just as you are getting really interested. Still, many people will probably have to go to Saint Teresa through this route as this book has the immediate appeal which the three-volume original lacks.

The excerpts in the mysticism anthology are more self-contained and very well chosen. The editor is a wonderful spiritual writer in his own right. He takes his selections from twenty-one of the great mystical writers, including Saint Teresa, Saint John of the Cross, Louis Lallemant, Saint Catherine of Siena, de Caussade, Surin, Saint Francis de Sales and Saint Angela of Foligno. This book is not for the casual Catholic, but is suited for anyone seriously striving for holiness.

Book Reviews

NOVEMBER 1950

NO POSTPONEMENT

By John La Farge, S.J.
Longmans

THERE ARE SEVERAL WAYS OF APPROACHING THE PROBLEM of our injustice to the Negro. Quite a bit is to be said for the noisy way which keeps flinging the inhumanity and irrationality of the situation into the faces of people who like to think they are respectable and good. There is also a great deal to be said for the quiet, persistent effort which works at the sources, as quietly as possible, and without fanfare. Father La Farge is the exemplar of this second way. He is a gentleman. He is uncompromising. He has a universal charity. He has worked in the interracial apostolate the better part of his priestly life.

Father La Farge's chief instrument has been the Interracial Councils, which he founded. They are local groups of Negroes and whites who meet to discuss interracial problems, who go to Mass and Communion together and have retreats together, and who do what they can to better race relationships and the lot of the Negro. There are Councils in thirteen cities. The fact that they do not call the attention of the general Catholic body to themselves is no indication that they are ineffective. One example will suffice to show what good work they do.

The American Negro is congenitally anti-Catholic, having absorbed an unthinking prejudice from his Protestant masters. The prejudice was automatically reflected in the Negro Press (200 newspapers and magazines at present). The Interracial Councils undertook to instruct, correct and inform the editors about Catholic affairs through friendly correspondence. Over a period of ten years they have succeeded in changing the whole attitude of the Negro press and dispelling the prejudice.

No Postponement is not just about the Interracial Councils, but contains Father La Farge's reflections on the interracial apostolate as a whole. Some things may particularly interest those who have not followed interracialism too closely.

Take the matter of prejudice in Catholic colleges. Manhattanville's decision to admit Negro girls is described here. I remember hearing about it at the time, for it had its dramatic aspects. First of all, the decision was taken on strictly religious rather than secular grounds. The exclusion of Negro girls was not compatible with the Church's teachings on the Mystical Body, and that was that. The Catholic Action students drew up some resolutions on the subject. The students and the alumnae were queried. The former were all for admitting a Negro girl. The alumnae protested. Reverend Mother Dammann stood firm, and justice prevailed. Similar action has been taken by other colleges since.

Then there is the question of the communist approach to interracialism. Superficially they seem to do much better than we because, quite obviously, they mingle freely with Negroes and practice no discrimination. Oddly enough, the official Kremlin program is not anti-segregation (which is the Catholic program) but the establishment of a "Negro nation" somewhat parallel to Israel for the Jews, and presumably to be situated in the South of the United States. American communist leaders have not pushed this program too enthusiastically, feeling it will be unpopular with most Negroes, but so far the Kremlin has refused to change the party line.

Another thing, Negroes are sick of being domestics. The fact that they have been limited largely to this field has meant in practice that wives have gone out to work (and then came home and did their own housework) while the men loafed because they could not find work, and the children, neglected, fell into delinquency.

The beginning and the end of this book may throw one off for they are dull. In them Father La Farge deals mostly with politics and national ideals. When he finds a ringing tribute to the deity at the end of a presidential address the patriotism in him is stirred. Perhaps I belong to a more cynical generation for I see in my mind's eye some tired, irreligious ghost writer mechanically appending a hackneyed bit of political piety.

THE SPIRITUAL LEGACY OF SISTER MARY OF THE HOLY TRINITY

Edited by Rev. Silvere Van Den Broek, O.F.M.
Newman

THE REASON FOR THE DELAY IN REVIEWING THIS BOOK (publication date, June 13th) is simply that I couldn't finish reading it. It provided me with so much material for meditation that the harder

I tried, the slower it went. Now that I'm finally through I would be quite happy, and find it profitable, to begin it all over again, were it not for the waiting line of prospective buyers.

What is so remarkable about the book? Perhaps it just happens to be to my taste and would not be to yours. However, I prefer to think that it is in a special way a guide to *contemporary spirituality*, as I shall presently try to show. Meanwhile, let me say something about the nun whose spiritual legacy it is.

Sister Mary of the Holy Trinity died as a Poor Clare in Jerusalem (in the convent where Charles de Foucauld was once the gardnerer) in 1942, when she was 41 years old. She had only been there four years. Her whole life centered around her religious vocation. A French-Swiss, she was the daughter of a Protestant missionary in Africa, but reared in Europe by relatives. Outwardly her life wasn't very exciting: A great affection for her family, from whom she was separated most of the time, her conversion, a succession of positions as governess or companion, recurrent tuberculosis, and vain efforts to enter seemingly hundreds of convents, also three false tries at the religious life. She was sent away from one place on account of her health, from another for reporting its irregularities to the superiors, and she left the third (a secular institute) of her own volition, in search of the cloister. Inwardly her life was one long effort to fulfill a vocation presaged by a vision in her girlhood. She was literally drawn into the Church by the power of attraction of the Eucharist, and guided to Jerusalem by a thousand detours and uncertainties (but when she finally arrived and went to the Poor Clare convent to pray, a nun came out and asked her to join the community, as though it were prearranged). Christ spoke to her interiorly almost from the time of her conversion (she was so uninstructed and naive that she thought it happened to everyone). In the Poor Clares Christ had her write down what He said, which is the spiritual legacy. This book is edited by her spiritual director in Jerusalem.

The revelations are most about practical, everyday affairs of the spiritual life. Christ tells Sister Mary how she will become holy and what she has done wrong and why, and how to bring harmony into the convent. You don't have to be a nun to transfer the advice into your own life.

Recurring emphasis is on being an instrument of God's work. Christ keeps saying to her, "Let *Me* direct your life." Once He points out that many people give all their time and energy and zeal to God, but they serve Him according to their own plan, rather than giving Him the whole direction of their lives so that He can act in them. He says these people will be rewarded for their generosity, but that their lives will not bear the fruit that His work would have.

It is this that I think is the characteristic note of the new spirituality. Of course it has always been a part of the Church's teaching, but it needs re-emphasizing in our day.

Sister Mary of the Trinity took a special vow of Victim, which meant not only that she offered to suffer for souls, but that she abandoned herself in a special way to the direction of Christ. He said to her:

> I desire these victims to be everywhere: in the world and in the cloisters; in every occupation, in every station of life, in the fields and in the factories, in schools and in stores, in families and in convents, in business and in the arts, everywhere ... so that their fidelity may bear witness to My words.

At another time He summed up what He asked of those who bind themselves in the Vow of Victim. These points seem to me to be a sort of *summa* of apostolic spirituality.

1. To listen to Me more than to speak to Me (which must mean that we are to be contemplatives and not just pious people reciting a lot of prayers).
2. To strive to reproduce My actions—My way of acting rather than My words (here is the concept of "bearing witness," as opposed to apologetics).
3. To be before men as they are before God, in a state of poverty that begs—not in a state of spiritual wealth that gives alms of its superfluity.... (this seems to be in the spirit of A.A.'s slogan, "There but for the grace of God...." People are so discouraged that they will only turn away from someone who finds temperance easy, knowing it is not for them. But if they see a person as weak as they are, or weaker, whom God protects, one day at a time, against drunkenness, they will be inspired to beg for grace. This doesn't apply only to alcoholism. Take marriage, for instance. The "perfect marriage" which has health and house and security

is not the one which inspires, but the one which has everything against it and succeeds none the less because God holds it together.)

4. To confine their efforts to spreading My Spirit, My gentleness, and My kindness which does not dwell on evil, but overcomes evil by good. By being exacting with no one but themselves, they will help souls, by their alliance and their respect, to receive the graces which their fidelity and their sacrifices will obtain from God. (This is the hard lesson that the world will be won by love and there is no other way to elicit good will. In another place Christ said that you cannot be too kind to people, the only way you can fail them is by not asking them what God asks. Perhaps we need this last reminder in America where it isn't so much kindness that is lacking sometimes, but the realization of the person's destiny — take for example the euthanasiasts.)

Sister Mary of the Holy Trinity died, as Christ said she would, suddenly and quietly, without any agony. Our Lord also said that she would die when she was ready, that is, perfected. The fact that she had some faults is reassuring to the reader. Certainly Christ gave her no reason to be proud, although He constantly reminded her of His great love. Here is a characteristic statement:

> Yes, you are the most unworthy in the convent, when I consider your sins; you are the least capable of all, when I consider what you do. Nevertheless I speak to you more than to the others: your unworthiness has attracted Me; I wish to save you from yourself.

As a matter of fact, Sister Mary of the Holy Trinity's life in itself is an example of a beggar before God. She seems not to have sinned seriously ever, but she did a lot of fumbling and some of her decisions with respect to her family seem to have been, though heroic, ill-advised and harsh. God not only guided her for many years with all the meanderings up blind alleys, but He also pulled a lot of her chestnuts out of the fire. It fortifies one's faith in God's guiding hand in our own lives, despite all the ruts and detours.

THY FAITH HATH MADE THEE WHOLE

THE SUN HERALD, NATIONAL EDITION

Kansas City, MO
A Catholic Daily Newspaper

SEEING THE FIRST ISSUE OF *THE SUN HERALD*[2] (WHICH really was published on the promised date of October 10th) was like a witnessing an incarnation. All those long-debated ideas about what a Christian newspaper really is, finally took a body, or rather took a daily, 8-page (will be twelve when machines get working right), tabloid-size expression. On the basis of the first three issues we can definitely say that the ideas have come to life. The paper is a personality, not just a hodge-podge of borrowed ideas. It's something new, and very interesting.

Critics of the project always feared *The Sun Herald* would slant its news in an illegitimate way. Well, it doesn't slant the news at all. There is not a suggestion of that biased type of reporting so often (alas!) found in diocesan papers. On the other hand, it is a frankly Christian paper, making no bones about the values it cherishes, putting up no elaborate pretense of not knowing good from evil. I think it is the welcome sense of values and meaning that gives so much warmth and friendliness to the paper. Secularism has really been banished, along with commercialism. The mood of the paper is good-humored and light. The editors take the world seriously, but not themselves. They are frank, but not heavy with a crusading spirit.

Another pre-publication false impression was that a Christian newspaper should be quite a bit like the *Christian Science Monitor*, though why anyone should think so is a mystery. Anyhow it isn't.

The national edition is understandably rather heavily dependent now on one of the large news services, but special articles by their own correspondents and their foreign editor, Isabel de la Vega, have already taken the edge of unintelligibility off some of this news. The editorials are excellent. So are the special articles. We are glad to see that *The Sun Herald* is going to plunge into that never-never land of the commercial newspapers (how they do defer to their advertisers!) and report on federal investigations of the fraudulent claims of patient medicines and processed foodstuffs. They are also frank on the subject

2   *The Sun Herald* was one of the first Catholic daily newspapers but for a myriad of reasons only lasted for six months. — *Ed.*

of race relationships. In this connection I remember hearing of a blatant anti-Negro incident in Chicago which even the intercession of prominent Catholic newspapermen couldn't force into the daily papers.

It is the features of the new daily which will probably do the most for its circulation in the beginning. They seem to be habit-forming. "Herself at Home" is a daily column by Peggy Wink, familial and interesting. It's a sort of Catholic version of Edgar Guest—simple and homey like his stuff, but instead of being sentimental it has deep spiritual insight. Then there is a marriage advice column, which is good but needs loosening up. Running serially is the autobiography of a Negro girl, a convert. Marion Mitchell Stancioff is doing a series of good articles, philosophizing on life in general. John C. Hicks, who also writes for us, has some very clever short satirical bits.

As always with a new publication, there's lots of room for improvement. We understand they are having quite a bit of trouble with some of the mechanical details and the mailing department, most through being understaffed. We hope that will be ironed out by the time this appears, and/or that some of our readers in the neighborhood will go around and help them.

We know the staff of *The Sun Herald* personally and we know the paper was born of prayer, of sacrifice and of faith. So we can vouch for the sincerity of the front-page editorial of their first issue, which read in part:

> ...We hold ourselves responsible to you and to God for telling the truth in this paper—the truth at all levels and at all costs. Please pray that we will always do this, and that you and all our other readers will be given grace to profit by it. We will be praying for you.

THY FAITH HATH MADE THEE WHOLE

DECEMBER 1950

ALL THINGS COMMON

By Claire Huchet Bishop
Harpers

MRS. BISHOP HAS HERE ASSEMBLED FIRST-HAND, DETAILED, documentary-type information of the communitarian movement, a new and most interesting effort to revitalize the social order. As the decay of capitalism has gone much further in Europe than here, so new ideas and experiments are also more evident there, especially in France. That is why it is very useful to have a report on these efforts, and valuable to those who are prepared to profit by it.

To my mind the momentum of communitarianism comes from the swing of the pendulum of contemporary feeling *away* (with a growing revulsion) from individualism, isolationism and avarice, *toward* cooperation, community and idealism. Many of the teachings of the Church, especially of the papal encyclicals, can be cited in favor of the movement, so it is not surprising that Catholics are numerous in it. On the other hand, the Communists are very prominent in the movement too, and understandably, because it follows a natural development of some of their ideas. But fundamentally there is a tremendous impulse to gather together the dispersed human atoms of a disintegrated society into little living groups that will grow and multiply. It's a matter of picking up the pieces and making a new world. Whether the communitarian movement, which is organized and has universal principles, is directing these seedlings of the new society toward Christianity or Communism can be disputed. But first we have to recognize that those who are unwilling to admit that there will be changes and drastic changes in the organization of production are not in a position to argue the question since they have not yet seen the natural situation which gives rise to the problem. This goes for the big-time planners, unionists and socialists as well as for the capitalist-individualists.

What is communitarianism? Think of it, if you like, as the lively great-grandson of the cooperative movement, for it stresses cooperation rather than competition. As the cooperatives were separately formed but bound together by common principles, so the communitarian movement consists of a group of autonomous Communities of Work, related by common principles and central headquarters. The communities are *economic* units. The exemplar community, Boimondau, in France, is a group of watch-case makers who commonly own and commonly govern their factory. Domain Ott is an association of wine growers. The Sociocratic Society of Bilthoven is really a school for children, but run on communitarian principles. There are dozens of these communities, all quite small — in fact communitarianism won't work in units larger than 100 families although there are groups within large companies, as for instance a community of milkmen within a large milk cooperative. Within the general principles the movement is extremely flexible. One community will be very different from the next, yet reflect the same spirit, a combination of practicality, personalism and idealism. There is always a strong emphasis on spiritual values. In fact, here is one of the points where I would query Mrs. Bishop, for "spiritual" is weasel word. If it suggests God to you, keep it in mind that it can as easily suggest Bach to the communitarians, and that Mrs. Bishop usually uses it in this latter sense.

It helps me in understanding Communities of Work to picture them as neither businesses nor religious orders, but participating a little in the nature of both.

They are like businesses in that they are groupings around a common work. Most often they form because the founders realize that together they can do what they can't do singly. For instance, several young farmers will pool their capital for the joint purchase of farm machinery, merging their land and working in a group. Or a manufacturer who consistently fails to stimulate his employee's interest or loyalty despite pension plans and the usual incentives, will relinquish his ownership of the factory to the workers. This is usually done gradually, with reimbursement to the owner and after indoctrination of the workers with the principles of communitarianism. It will surprise some how often the impulse toward forming these communities comes from the owner rather than the workers. Marcel Barbu[3] (the founder of Boimondau) was the pioneer here and has done more than anyone else to spread the ideas. But it would be wrong to think of the communities as joint-profit enterprises. The profit motive is

---

3   Marcel Barbu (1907–1984) was also a French politician who ran unsuccessfully for the presidency in 1965. — *Ed.*

definitely out, with returns limited and surplus often going to help start other communities. It is this rejection of the profit motive which makes the movement so revolutionary and sets it apart in spirit from the sort of solidarity for corporate gain that marks the usual trade union. There is a change of heart involved in communitarianism, not just a change of method.

Now we come to the resemblance the Communities of Work have to religious orders. Primarily it is in their spirit of corporate dedication and idealism. Very few of the communities have a dogmatic religious basis and in fact they are not allowed to be exclusively any particular religion, within the principles of the movement. They take as their first aim the achievement of a fuller life for their members, the "whole life" as they put it, and the first fruits of cooperation are increased leisure (by taking turns with the children and animals, farm wives get their first Sundays off) and education (like the cooperatives the communities regard study and group education as a first and compulsory essential).

Naturally the members are not celibate as are religious. Family life is the foundation of the communities and it is an advantage to be married. Housekeeping is considered a useful work and the women are paid for it, not through an increase in their husband's wages, but directly. Children are also paid—for growing.

Nor is there the "obedience" of a religious community—in fact the opposite is true. There is no compulsion beyond being held to the "common ethical minimum" of the group which everyone first freely endorses. At the most there is a sort of non-directive counseling. A cardinal principle of communitarianism is that all important decisions have to be *unanimously* agreed on (of course the daily decisions are taken care of by unanimously elected officers). Even in the children's school referred to above, one child holding out can prevent the director and the whole faculty from pursuing a course of action. It is argued that no one ever holds out just to be difficult, because in a communitarian atmosphere one's own self-interest lies in cooperating.

The most striking resemblance to the religious life lies in the degree to which the community concerns itself with the moral and spiritual worth of its members. Each man is judged and rewarded according to his *total value*, which means not only how well he works but how cheerful, amusing, self-sacrificing and agreeable he is. Communitarians must be prepared to face the equivalent of "chapters of faults" and to find that their whole lives, and particularly their characters, are subject to scrutiny. Of course they are anyhow in our own society, but no one dares comment except behind peoples' backs or in a fit of anger. It seems to me that this attitude to one's character is nobody's business is the real citadel of individualism (mixed up with some genuine justification for it). It will be much harder to win men to this feature of communitarianism than to woo them from the profit motive (which is getting rather unprofitable anyhow).

I have tried to give some general idea of the movement without citing many specific instances and without listing the principles in an ordered way. All this is done in Mrs. Bishop's book most admirably. One cannot help but pay tribute to the accuracy and detail of her reporting. She visited all the communities she describes and she has a sympathy and enthusiasm impossible to duplicate. It is quite useless even to try to condense the material that is it in the book. For that reason I strongly recommend reading it. You may like communitarianism or not, that isn't the point. What the book does do, through its excellent reporting, is to describe a concrete method of salvaging our economy. It will take a lot of discussion out of the realm of high-flown theory, right down into the practical order.

Personally I am very happy to have the arguments about economics moved into this living, concrete field. It will seem strange to some that this should be so when I admit that communitarianism is the most seductive argument I have ever seen *against* some of *Integrity's* basic positions. (Some of the seductiveness lies in Mrs. Bishop's warm enthusiasm which must certainly add a rosy glow to the movement—but even making allowance for that, it is an attractive thing.)

Here is what communitarianism does: it banishes capitalism (the profit motive) while retaining industrialism (the mechanization of work). I'm speaking now not of what may be made of the Communities of Work but in fact of what is held by the communitarian movement, which is an official sort of thing. Its dogmas are comparable to the Rochdale principles with respect to the cooperative movement. Communitarianism, then, explicitly rejects capitalism ("money doesn't make money," they say, reviving the argument against usury), though they are not necessarily against the use of capital. For them, as for all the major Catholic thinkers as well, capitalism means in practice the rationalization of production and distribution according to the profit motive.

Yet communitarianism makes no effort to guard itself against the technological rationalization of work. They want "the maximum of technology and science allied to a vivid sense of the whole man." They expressly state that "the economic expression of a Community of Work is not an artisan enterprise." That means in practice that they will sacrifice individual responsibility in the work itself, and try to compensate by responsibility elsewhere. They do not object to assembly lines and even now at Boimondau have the Bedaux System and music while you work for fifteen minutes out of every hour. They also favor large-scale farming machinery.

It seems to us at *Integrity* that the world is fast moving from the idolatry of money to the idolatry of applied science. And just as no amount of philanthropy could compensate the proletariat for the loss of property, so now no amount of security and culture and responsibility *outside of work* is going to compensate men for becoming machine parts. The question that keeps coming into my mind is whether or not communitarianism *has* to wed itself to industrialism and technology (I'm not talking now against machines as such). However it is too long a subject to go into here, and the fact is that they *do* choose industrialism. Nevertheless we ourselves and other groups have already begun to borrow some of their organizational ideas, which can certainly be transposed to apostolic ventures.

One last serious question. Is the spirit that animates communitarianism implicitly Christian (although sometimes explicitly Communist) because of its emphasis on human dignity and fraternity? Or put the question another way. We Catholics are used to saying that only Christ can renew the face of our scarred earth. Are we wrong then? Will the earth be renewed by "spiritual Catholics, Protestants, Humanists and Materialists" working together under the inspiration of communitarianism? (Incidentally, this concept of a spiritual materialist runs through the book. It means someone idealistic and generous, who probably like Bach, but who doesn't believe in God.)

Personally, I think you have to label the prevailing spirit of communitarianism "Mystical Humanism." It has an exaggerated idea of the importance, dignity and perfectibility of men apart from God. It does not see the need of grace. It seems to substitute "humanity" for the deity. It is a "mystique." Concepts like those of the "total man" (where we would say "the saint") come straight out of Marxism. Here again, does it have to be this way? Its members have a very legitimate desire to include all men of good will, and in so far the spirit is good. However, if Christ and not this "mystique" of humanity were at the center of these communities I should think there would be a profound change in the present spirit of the movement. And at present I should judge that the movement has not yet crystalized for or against Christ. Let us hope it does the former.

CHRIST THE SAVIOR & REALITY: A SYNTHESIS OF THOMISTIC THOUGHT

By Reginald Garrigou-Lagrange, O.P.
Herder

THESE TWO RECENT TRANSLATIONS OF THE WORKS OF the greatest contemporary commentator on Saint Thomas illustrates the range of Father Garrigiou-Lagrange's theological genius. *Christ the Savior* (700 pages) is an elucidation in strict scholastic form of the third part of the *Summa*; *Reality* (400 pages) a comprehensive survey of Saint Thomas' synthesis from the point of view of the essential doctrine.

The first book deals with the mysteries of the Incarnation and Redemption, plus a short compendium of Mariology. All the way through it compares Saint Thomas' teaching with that of other leading theologians who hold contrary views, and in the light of the leading interpreters of Saint Thomas. The book is obviously of major importance for theologians. It is very rough going for amateur theologians like myself. Because the subject matter is very important as a background to modern problems, it is worth the struggle, but even so the book serves us laity better for reference purposes than for straight reading in the hope of educating ourselves.

With *Reality* the situation is quite different. One is reminded of Saint Thomas himself who, after years of deep and detailed study, wrote the *Summa Theologica*, his crowning work, as a synthesis for *beginners*. This book is written with an ease that makes you marvel as you read it. It is an effortless reduction of Saint Thomas' teaching to its essentials. Precision comes without effort; you know that selectivity is there, but you don't feel it. There is the simplicity of the master rather than the beginner, a beautiful thing, making the work easy to understand yet profound at the same time. It is not a polemical work, yet here, as always, Father Garrigou-Lagrange writes with a consciousness of the critics of Saint Thomas. One can see the stress he lays on controverted points, especially those disputed by the "new philosophies," and subject to the warnings issued in the latest papal encyclical *Humani Generis*, yet there is an aura of benevolence about this work as though the author wrote it from the vantage point not of great knowledge alone, but of wisdom and charity. In the beginning he stresses the fact that Saint Thomas was not just a genius but also a saint, that he sought in prayer and before the Blessed Sacrament for the light he needed. Then Father Garrigou-Lagrange shows how, through the gifts of the Holy Ghost, sanctity is a direct aid to theological understanding. Certainly he himself must have relied heavily on contemplation for his own theological studies. The fruits of the gifts are more evident in this book than in any other of his I have ever read. The power of synthesis itself, here so clearly illustrated, certainly participates in wisdom.

Reality is a book I would recommend for beginners. It's much easier reading than most college textbooks on philosophy or theology. It's a good introduction to Saint Thomas, for it begins way back at the beginning with "these are the philosophical books Saint Thomas wrote, these the theological, and here are the names of his major commentators." Then he shows that the several thousand theses of Saint Thomas can be reduced to a few major ones, and in turn he elucidates these. This synthesis is a study of Saint Thomas in his essence, but against the background of other schools of theology and of modern errors. It is called *Reality* because realism characterizes Saint Thomas' philosophy. It is divided into eight parts as follows: The Metaphysical Synthesis of Thomism, The Blessed Trinity, Angels and Man, Incarnation and Redemption, The Sacraments, Moral Theology and Spirituality. This book would be a good foundation stone for any thinking Catholic's intellectual life.

Book Reviews

FEBRUARY 1951

SUCH LOVE IS SELDOM

By Anne Cawley Boardman
Harper

IN MY PARISH THERE ARE TWO SMALL COMMUNITIES OF nuns (teaching sisters and the Dominican Sisters of the Sick Poor). One or the other group is often at the seven o'clock Mass. The communion rail is long, and the nuns sit on either side of the center aisle. From time immemorial the laity have waited for the religious to go forward at Communion time and from forever the sisters have knelt in the middle of the rail. The rest of us filled in on either side. That always posed a neat problem for the priest. Should he give Communion to the sisters first, and then return at the beginning of the line? Or should he sacrifice courtesy to efficiency? Some did one thing, some the other. Then one morning the Dominican Sisters of the Sick Poor got up and marched themselves way off into right field where the communion rail begins. It was an obvious solution, but unexpected. Why is it one never expects nuns to change their customs? Anyhow, more or less during this same period the Dominican Sisters of the Sick Poor changed from starched to soft veils and they go quietly about our tenements one by one instead of two by two, so it's apparent that their order is unusual.

To my mind the most unusual thing about the order is that it does the works of mercy simply, without specialization, fanfare, red tape, inquisitions, referrals or institutions. The sisters are nurses who take care of the sick poor in their own homes—also clean, take care of the children, cook the husband's supper, render spiritual aid and bring in food and supplies where necessary, not to mention arranging for funerals. They correspond with the human need in a society that's trying to get human beings to correspond with mechanical systems.

The book is about the foundress of the Dominican Sisters of the Sick Poor, a Mary Walsh who came over from Ireland nearly a century ago and became a laundress. That was in the vicinity of this parish too. Between the Dominican Fathers, who first gave her spiritual direction and whose Tertiary she became, and the Paulists who really saw her through the years of her work and directed the formation of her institutions, she was guided from spontaneous charitable acts to serious group work and finally to the formation of a religious order. Those early years were filled with laundry, sick calls, hunger, cold, T. B., rats, and tenement stairs. And disappointments, monumental disappointments and discouragements. Also trials and misunderstandings. All borne with a patience, humility and hope that make me suspect that Mary Walsh is a saint who may some day be canonized. I hope so. She's just precisely the sort of model we need in this neighborhood where many of those old tenements still stand, rotting among the new deluxe apartment houses, but where rich, poor, and parishioners alike think they are on an escalator headed for an earthly utopia. A plain-faced, raw-boned Irish servant-girl with chapped hands might rectify our sense of values.

Book Reviews

APRIL 1951

PERSONALLY I CAN GO ON READING TESTIMONIAL STORIES for quite some time. The latest one is *Roman Road* by G.R. Lamb (Sheed & Ward), an Englishman born during the first World War and so belonging to my own generation. Two things impressed me especially. One is that in a messy world it is the misfits, if they escape suicide and insanity, who are most likely to come to roost in Catholicism, if only because they keep on looking. The other is George Lamb's honest view of the futility of climbing social ladders. He came from a Manchester slum, son of the working class. Just by the accident of being rather bright, he went to a middle-class school which made him a snob, and then to Cambridge where he was polished off. With each step he became more uprooted and in the end belonged nowhere. By the time he looked squarely at the fact that his poor widowed mother had been working in a factory all the years he had been acquiring his futile culture it was within several months of her death.

Simplicity is another one of Father Raoul Plus' little books, especially nice because it's an especially nice virtue. It's a sort of anti-neurosis virtue, bringing one's life into harmony by unifying it. The key to its cultivation is to concentrate on the one thing necessary, the will and glory of God.

Léon Bloy is still a mysterious figure, even to his admirers. I read with great interest a book of essays about him by E.T. Dubois (*Portrait of Léon Bloy*, Sheed & Ward). The author is a highly-educated European woman, who seems to know thoroughly all the subjects needed for a study of this man. She discusses his life, his ideas, his literary caliber, his spirituality, his ideas about the Jews, etc., and makes her judgments. They seemed like good judgments to me. Bloy is the great melancholic, with a passion for poverty. The author does not deny that he may have had, as he himself supposed, a very singular prophetic mission. She takes his ideas very seriously and shows their profundity, especially remarkable for the time in which he lived. Was he a saint? Could he have been a saint and still have uttered those terrible anathemas? Elfride Dubois is not ready to canonize Bloy. Had he a director, stood a little less on his own judgment, been rather more docile to the Church, he might have reached those heights he so passionately wanted to scale. The author thinks his greatest reward lay in bringing a few choice souls to the Church.

525

THY FAITH HATH MADE THEE WHOLE

MAY 1951

THE LOVE OF GOD AND THE CROSS OF JESUS, VOL. II

By Reginald Garrigou-Lagrange, O.P.
Herder

ABOUT A DOZEN OF GARRIGOU-LAGRANGE'S BOOKS HAVE been translated into English and published by Herder in recent years. I am not qualified to give a theologian's appreciation of this great contemporary Thomist, but I should like to express my gratitude as a layman. Most lay people who want to serve the Church come up against the necessity of having some sort of theological foundation for their thinking. Either their schooling has not carried them beyond the catechism, or has been concentrated on apologetics. They cannot just start reading Saint Thomas, nor are they attracted to seminarians' textbooks. Furthermore they will discover that not all philosophical or spiritual books contain explicitly or implicitly very solid or very accurate theology. Father Garrigiou-Lagrange is their man. He is lucid. He does not delight in the superficial embellishments of theology but sticks to essentials. He is repetitious, but in the sense that he always returns to central truths, so that the reader begins to take on the author's mind. He sees Thomism in contradistinction to modern errors inside and outside the Church, which is helpful. Finally he practices what he preaches, seeing truth as related to holiness and not aridly intellectual.

Three of his great works are on the spiritual life: *Christian Perfection and Contemplation*, *The Three Ages of the Interior Life* (2 vols.) and *The Love of God and the Cross of Jesus* (2 vols.). They are not just alike, but they are parallel works and the ordinary person will need only read one of them. I recommend the second work, the one on the three ages.

It is the second volume of the third work which is to be reviewed here. It deals with the passive purifications of the senses and the soul, the life of union and certain special subjects which will be mentioned below. It is written for spiritual directors and souls advanced in the spiritual life (the first volume was for beginners), but I think everyone can learn something from it. The description of the passive purifications of faith, hope and charity is a good reminder of how much *natural* dross is mixed with the supernatural motives for these virtues. During the purifications the natural reasons which uphold these virtues are withdrawn. We are allowed to be tempted, and if we come through unscathed hold the virtues much more firmly but our faith will be tested, and it will be like being plunged into darkness, until finally in the darkness itself a galaxy of stars will appear and we will hold our beliefs in the security of a higher mode of understanding. It seems to me that the whole Church is likely to be plunged into this purgation of faith today. All natural reinforcements to our beliefs may be swept away by scientism, by the apparent overcoming of the Church against whom Hell was not to have prevailed. So we should beware especially of the temptation to rest our higher truths on experimental grounds, to think that the cultivation of virtue is more clearly necessary because some psychiatrist has said so or that free will has been established because some psychiatrist has proclaimed the behavior of atoms to be capricious in the later analysis.

One thing Father Garrigou-Lagrange keeps saying is that the course of the spiritual life, so clearly marked in the case of contemplative religious, is less concise in the apostolic life (which would include the lay apostolic life) and is bound up with the sufferings and trials of the apostolate: "... in the injustice of men we find the justice of God for the purgation of our hidden sins."

Saint Thomas and Saint John of the Cross teach the same doctrine of the spiritual life but from different perspectives. Father Garrigou-Lagrange frequently quotes Saint John of the Cross and in this book takes time out to reconcile the two great teachers and to summarize briefly the whole teaching of the Carmelite doctor on the narrow road that leads to perfection.

One of the final chapters of the book is on the unity of the apostolic life, showing the synthesis of contemplation and action. Naturally the author takes the usual Dominican position that the apostolic life is the highest and consists in contemplation as an end in itself, but overflowing into action, "to give to others the fruit of our contemplation." He would include preaching and teaching on the subjects of contemplation, the administration of the Sacraments and spiritual direction, as types of action which can be considered into this apostolic sphere. The corporal works of mercy as such fall into a different category.

When I read this it occurred to me that most of the action in the lay apostolate could and should be the overflow of contemplation since it deals with souls, attracting and converting them, even counseling them, in addition to the lay form of preaching and teaching.

There is another chapter on Christ the King. Here the author quotes Cardinal Mercier as saying, "The principal crime that the world is expiating at the present time is the official apostasy of nations." No society has a right to be secular, or to treat one religion as though it were as good as another.

There is also a treatment of the Priesthood of Christ, of Mary, Model of Reparation, of Saint Joseph, Model of the Hidden Life, of the love of the Mass, and a treatment of free will and Christ's impeccable liberty.

The last of these mentioned could, as the author points out, provide matter for contemplation in a liberal society. God to whom sin is impossible is absolutely free; similarly with Christ, and also with Mary. In a certain way it is true of the saints. When they reach the unitive stage of the spiritual life they are not confirmed in grace, but almost. They are almost *committed* to doing the will of God, yet they have tremendous freedom. Obviously the liberals have it all wrong. True liberty is in following our nature and our goal, not in being able to sin. Those who mistake the idea of liberty end up enslaved to their passions within and to tyrants without. Which is exactly where we have ended up today as the result of liberalism.

So thanks to Father Garrigou-Lagrange for this and others of his books. May many in the apostolate seek their formation in his works.

Book Reviews

JUNE 1951

COMMUNISM, DEMOCRACY AND CATHOLIC POWER

By Paul Blanchard
Beacon Press

ON THE EVENING OF MAY DAY THIS YEAR A MASS RALLY was held at Carnegie Hall in New York, sponsored by an organization called "Protestants and Others for the Separation of Church and State." Its purpose was to discuss the Catholic threat to democracy. The two major speakers were a Presbyterian minister named Poteat (a missionary to Latin America) and Paul Blanchard. I attended the meeting to see what was up.

Carnegie Hall was filled, except for the top gallery. The most surprising thing to me was the nature of the audience. Perhaps I had expected a section of the communist parade to come to Carnegie Hall to finish off the day. I looked for workers in their shirt-sleeves, social workers from the New York School, long-haired intellectuals and labor organizers. I expected most of the audience to have arrived from Europe within the last generation or two, with visible and audible traces of the fact. Not at all. This assemblage was strictly 100% American in the most flattering sense: nice people, backbone of the nation, upper middle-class, professional, educated, respectable, sober, conscientious; not nouveau-rich, not radical, not vicious, not vulgar, but fair-minded, intelligent, good people, the graduates of America's best colleges.

Mr. Poteat and Mr. Blanchard said more or less what one would expect, only sometimes more suavely, sometimes more frankly. The content of their speeches did not interest me as much as the effect of their speeches on the audience. It soon became clear that all these people had gathered together for the first time in response to radiating postcards to friends of friends. They came to investigate, and with more or less open minds. I kept putting myself in their place (which was easy because I come from exactly the same background, was a non-Catholic, went to one of their colleges), struggling along with them to see if we could see through the speakers' arguments on their own face value. When the Popes were quoted in their encyclicals (out of context or in truncated form) there was a graciousness about the words of the Holy Fathers which could not be concealed. Did those people catch it? I do not know. But there were three moments when I thought the whole audience turned against the speakers, or at least stopped short in their thinking. Once was when Mr. Blanchard said angrily, "The trouble with the Catholic Church is that it thinks error has no rights against truth!" Did I imagine that all the examples of the "unreasonableness" and "unfairness" of the Church suddenly came into focus in their minds? The second time was apropos of censorship, when one of the speakers (Blanchard, I think) made the mistake of saying, "And the Catholic Church has the nerve to say it is the only body fighting for public morality." A couple of things seemed to fall into focus there too. The last time was when Mr. Blanchard got talking about sex and mocking the idea of purity, especially the idea of the celibacy of the clergy. He lost his composure, became vehement and vulgar. He also lost his prestige with the audience.

The people who streamed out of Carnegie Hall later that evening were obviously not "sold," but I could not reassure myself that they had not taken the first step. "... but still you have to grant that it is an agent of a foreign power," I heard one of them remark, and I suppose that was the typical reaction. Like lambs being led to the slaughter, I thought. They are intelligent people who have already been robbed by the liberal colleges of intellectual competence except within narrow technical fields. They cannot hold out very long.

But what do Blanchard and these others want of them?

This problem has been revolving in my mind ever since. Blanchard's new book is evidently part of the same campaign and adds further evidence. Here is more or less the line of reasoning I have followed.

In that meeting at Carnegie Hall the obvious immediate purpose was to *confuse* the audience. The object was to make them anti-Catholic, but by confusing them, and not by leading them to some positive position other than Catholicism. That was what was so sad. There is no one easier to confuse than a liberal. The liberal erects indeterminate things into absolutes. Freedom becomes a state of suspended judgment forever. Horrible is the man who dares to believe that he's got hold of a piece of truth. He is thereby a bigot, a dogmatist, a totalitarian. The only nice people are intellectual jellyfish.

"Democracy" is a word I never want to hear again. As Mr. Blanchard uses it, it is usually synonymous with "the most high god," or "social perfection with divine attributes." As I walked home that night I said to myself, "As a Catholic I have the freedom to like monarchy as a form of government—a freedom which obviously is disappearing everywhere." Well, that's the first point, the immediate object is to confuse. Why?

The second obvious thing is that the meeting at Carnegie Hall was like a textbook example of communist tactics. "Protestants and Others for the Separation of Church and State" sounds like a caricature of all communist-front organizations, and acts like it. Certainly the people on the platform did not seem to be believing Christians, even of a dilute sort, and I gathered that the audience did not believe much either (why should they, after graduating from Yale, Harvard, Vassar, etc.?). However the speakers were a little over-confident about the lack of religious sensibility on the part of the audience and made the mistake of mocking the "supposed virginity" of Our Lady. A man in the orchestra got up and furiously shouted that "the Protestants believe that too." My neighbors whispered, "A spy of Cardinal Spellman," but I think he was a believing Protestant.

I have finally reached this hypothesis. The communists are desperately trying to prevent any collaboration of the United States and the Catholic Church against communism. Maybe their main objective is to cut off the Church in Europe and the Far East from American support, the better to destroy Her. Maybe their objective is to make America atheist and communist from within and they want to discredit the American Catholic Church, the main obstacle to this accomplishment. Maybe they are as interested in one objective as the other. The reason they are going after the 100% American liberals is that this body stands in their way. They do not hope to convert them to communism (the communists have their own intellectual converts in the colleges) because they are, as a body, too decent and respectable. When communism takes over, these people will all be liquidated. What they want to do meanwhile is to turn them against the only strong moral and anti-secular ally they have.

My analysis may not be correct, but it satisfies me as a continuing explanation of what I see going on. I find it possible to hold this hypothesis even in the face of Mr. Blanchard's latest book in which he uses the American hatred of communism to incite Americans to hatred of Catholicism, which he says is the same thing.

In *Communism, Democracy and Catholic Power*, Mr. Blanchard is playing two ends against the middle. He has discovered that certain things have a parallel relationship, and other things have contrasting relationships—only he blurs the parallel's into identity most of the time. Let us take a few abstract examples to show how he reasons. Marriage and concubinage are alike under one aspect; marriage and friendship are contrasting under the same aspect; therefore friendship is different from marriage but concubinage is the same thing as marriage. Or again, monarchy and dictatorship are both rule by one man, who is not elected by the people, as contrasted with democracy where the rule is divided among many men elected by the people; therefore the Pope and Stalin and Mussolini and Hitler are all alike and all nefarious. (The reader can see that this is not only crooked reasoning, but that I have skipped a number of steps—like Mr. Blanchard.)

Communism and Catholicism are alike (according to Blanchard) because they both are totalitarian. They both are world-wide organizations with an intricate structure. They both have agents and sub-agents in all countries. They both "deify" their rulers, and in similar ways (here Mr. Blanchard goes into all the Vatican ceremonies—I would have thought a more obvious parallel could be drawn between Presidents of the United States with their armed bodyguards, and Hitler, Mussolini and Stalin with theirs, as contrasted with the Pope who goes unarmed among the people). They both engage in "thought control," putting their followers in intellectual strait-jackets. Both their organizations have strict discipline. Both manipulate the truth, both have a strategy of penetration of the whole world. The American answer is to fight against totalitarianism in all its forms, etc.

I find it impossible to believe that Mr. Blanchard has good will. His book is filled with distortions, evasions, crooked reasoning, emotionalism, calumny and vilification.

His greatest weapon is in the misuse of words, which makes quite the interesting study. In his Carnegie Hall address (where he was more frank than in his book) he kept calling the Pope's decrees and power "arbitrary," quite gratuitously. In the book I was amused to find the following about the Kremlin: "What kind of power structure has come out of this unique social revolution? On the whole it is tyrannical and cruel, but it is also *fluid* and *adaptable*." "Fluid and adaptable" is a synonym for "arbitrary" when used in connection with one's friends.

Is Mr. Blanchard a communist or a conscious collaborator of the communists? I do not know, and I cannot tell from his book. Superficially it seems that he is not, since much of this book is devoted to an exposé (on the whole without qualification) of the communists. He does a thorough, seemingly enthusiastic job of it, not revealing anything that is not generally known however. Yet a communist could write against communism if it served his purpose, so this is no guarantee that Mr. Blanchard is an enemy of the Soviet. Still, I did not have the impression that he is a believer in communism.

On the other hand most of the communist social doctrines are favored in the book one way or another. The sacred doctrine of self-determination is brought up in exactly the same way I heard it used by the Soviet puppets on the U. N. in their speeches. The passion for "leveling" society crops up now and again. In the last chapter there is a sort of special plea to Americans to concede to socialism as an expedient measure. And larded through the book, without direct advertence, is the accusation against the Church that it is "unscientific," which is a major communist point of attack at the moment. Miracles are "unscientific." The doctrine of the Assumption and the manner of arriving at it are "unscientific." The Church's objection to contraception is "unscientific," etc.

One cannot help asking, What does Mr. Blanchard believe? Certainly not in democracy — at least not in any recognizable form. He is an atheist. He hates and does not understand anything supernatural. He disbelieves, a priori, in miracles. He believes that there is no "moral" province which belongs to religion. He believes in the absolute subordination of Church to State. He believes all children should be forced to attend secular, state schools and the parochial school system should be forbidden (this came out more clearly in his speech than in his book). He believes in divorce, and that the Church should have no jurisdiction over marriage. He wants no moral regulation of sexual conduct. He wants the medical profession to be freed from any moral concepts.

Mr. Blanchard is not stupid, so it is hard to believe that he is playing into the hands of the communists inadvertently. On the other hand I am sure that if he is supporting them they will liquidate him for his trouble. He is not very discreet. It was when he discussed sex at Carnegie Hall that he seemed most himself; he was vulgar; he made crude and rather indecent remarks. Yet he did not seem like a man who had a weakness for sensuality. I got the impression of cold, intellectual hatred for purity and morality. Frankly, I was rather terrified by Mr. Blanchard.

THY FAITH HATH MADE THEE WHOLE

THE SONG AT THE SCAFFOLD

By Gertrud von Le Fort
Sheed & Ward

THIS IS A SHORT NOVEL BASED ON A REAL INCIDENT which occurred during the French Revolution. A house of women Carmelites near Paris fell into the hands of the Revolutionary forces and all the nuns were taken to the guillotine—except one who had previously fled the convent out of terror, and another. The runaway reappeared at the last moment to share her sisters' martyrdom.

Gertrud von Le Fort has undertaken, while telling the story indirectly (as though related to her by the one who survived), to explain the psychological and spiritual reasons for the defection through fear and the sudden surge of final courage. Those who have read her other books know that she is a master of such profundities.

The story is gripping, and spiritually very moving.

Book Reviews

JULY 1951

THE CASE OF THERESE NEUMANN

By Hilda C. Graef
Newman

THIS IS THE FIRST WORK IN ENGLISH TO QUESTION THE authenticity of Therese Neumann, the German stigmatist. There have evidently been doubts expressed in other languages, but how serious they have been I still cannot tell after reading this book. I doubt if anyone will learn the truth about Therese from reading Hilda Graef's account either. If Therese Neumann's stigmata are genuinely of supernatural origin, and if she is acting in accordance with God's will, then some of the facts in this book must be misrepresented and the author is liable to a serious charge of calumny. On the other hand, if Therese Neumann is a fake there are a lot of things that have to explained better than they are here explained. As an examination of the case, this book is essentially incomplete. It is also biased, although unintentionally. The discernment of spirits is the way to determine the truth about Therese Neumann and this has to be done by a holy priest learned in mysticism, who has the particular gift necessary. Probably a number of qualified priests have visited the stigmatist but possibly they have not made public their opinions; anyhow their opinions are not given here. The author mentions that Father Bruno, the Carmelite, was a visitor, but she complains that Therese did not wish to receive Communion from him, although he was present when she received Communion from another priest. Hilda Graef disapproves Therese's conduct on this occasion, but it is not clear that Father Bruno thought the preference of her own pastor significant, nor does the author say what Father Bruno's general conclusions were.

Here is what Hilda Graef has done. Basing her thinking on Saint John of the Cross and other unimpeachable sources, she has produced an hypothesis about what stigmatists should be like, and then she has tried to show how Therese falls short of this ideal.

Before examining the thesis I should like to point out the general inadequacy and unfairness of her method. One cannot escape the impression that she is selective of her material in a prejudiced way.

Objectivity would have demanded that she quote the strongest evidence against her point, which she does not do. For instance she tells in detail how a commission of observers failed to see any considerable flow of blood during the suffering of the Passion. Yet thousands of people have witnessed this phenomenon. Have none of the others seen blood flow? Furthermore her attitude is far from generous; it is not only suspicious, but almost malicious. It is so vehemently unfavorable that it perverts the argument. A few times the author slips from (1) having said that such-and-such could possibly be laid to hysteria, to saying (2) "the *hysteric* said or did...."

Here then is the thesis stated in a general way. It is true that exterior mystical phenomena are given for the benefit of others and do not necessarily presuppose high sanctity on the part of the recipient. Nevertheless the stigmata are in a somewhat different category historically and according to what is fitting. True stigmata should accompany only the state of union. Therese Neumann does not seem to be in this state because she does not seem to practice heroic humility and obedience. Thus stated it sounds as though the book is about the shortcomings of Therese's character, but actually it questions throughout the mystical phenomena themselves. I wish a better picture had been given of Therese's character. There seems to be nothing very damning in the evidence here (apart from that connected with the stigmata). She lied on at least two occasions when she was a child, therefore her reputation for unquestioned veracity is suspect. She does not mortify herself! (But she suffers the Passion, if she does; she never eats and hardly sleeps.) She talks a lot, and enjoys simple pleasures. She is not humble, as she is always justifying herself; she is not respectful because she interrupted a conversation between two bishops once, to say she recognized the language they were speaking; she is not obedient because she will not go to the hospital to be examined again, or her father will not let her. Now it may be perfectly true that Therese lacks humility and obedience but this book did not convince me because I found other possible explanations for each incident. I also thought a much clearer picture of her spirituality could have been given. Does she practice the moral virtues to a high degree? Is she responsible for love and harmony in her family and neighborhood?

I question Hilda Graef's whole hypothesis that God would give the stigmata only to those in a very advanced state. Isn't it presumptuous to say what God would do? Or isn't it possible that the stigmata could be genuine and that Therese was chosen to suffer in a special way before she was extraordinarily holy, and that she might even have taken pride in her favors and lost grace since?

Now if one is going to hold the thesis taken in this book, one has to account for the stigmata in another way. The explanation here given is psychological. Therese is an hysterical person, not a deliberate fraud, not diabolically possessed, but psychologically unbalanced.

When Therese was a young woman she suffered multiple physical ills, following on great exertion during a fire, and these ills (including blindness, deafness and paralysis) seem to have been of hysterical origin. She was healed of them at various times, but quickly. Thorough investigation of these cures was made by the medical expert of the Sacred Congregation of Rites, Dr. Poray-Madeyski. He rejects the idea that the cures of these diseases were miraculous, and attributes their original appearance to "very grave hysteria," which would also account for the nature of their disappearance.

I got the impression that the non-organic of Therese Neumann's early troubles was too easily carried over as an explanation of the seemingly mystical phenomena. Once hysterical, always hysterical. Yet Saint Thérèse of the Child Jesus (on whose anniversaries this Therese was cured and to whom the stigmatist attributes the cures) had a very mysterious illness when *she* was young, and a mysterious cure.

It is not my intention to defend the supernatural character of Therese Neumann's stigmata. I hope the stigmata are genuine and that she is pleasing to God. Yet the book gave me misgivings in spite of its own faults. There is no possibility of resolving the problem academically. And I agree with the author that we Catholics should not be ready to lose our faith over the genuineness of any particular mystic.

Nevertheless I think the reverse is also true and even more pertinent at the moment. We Catholics ought not to abandon mystics at the clink of a test tube. The secular religion which is brewing will explain away all miracles and mystical phenomena as "unscientific." That is, it will show that what credulous people thought to be supernatural or preternatural can really be explained naturally. And "naturally" in the case of mystics means "psychologically."

As far as I am concerned Hilda Graef has substituted still greater mysteries for the ones she wants to dispel. She has found that Therese's inedia (prolonged fast) is not necessarily supernatural because some non-Catholic in the nineteenth century was said not to have eaten for years. Hilda Graef is perfectly willing to accept this "natural mystery." There is some further implication that Therese probably does eat secretly, but the only evidence is that she will not go to the hospital (she once submitted to a two-week close surveillance at home).

Where do the stigmata come from? Hysteria is, I think, the reason given. It appears that Therese also has bedsores which have behaved in much the same way as the stigmata.

Mental telepathy explains many things to Hilda Graef. Therese says in her "ecstacies" what is suggested to her mentally by sympathetic bystanders, especially by her pastor. Now, I submit that mental telepathy, especially on the scale that Therese would have to practice it, is more mysterious than a charismatic gift or a diabolic suggestion, notwithstanding the studies at Duke University—which did not seem to me very world-shattering in their findings. We ought not to attribute to supernatural or preternatural causes things which can be explained naturally, but what right have we to give preference to things which are naturally mysterious but for which we have only names—like telepathy?

Clairvoyance is another case in point. Is it simpler and more reasonable to suppose that Therese can read the contents of closed envelopes because she is clairvoyant than because she is possessed or supernaturally gifted? It is true that certain magicians seemed to have possessed this power, but what is the evidence that they did not have help from some friendly devils?

It is alleged in this book that Therese is like a puppet, and assumes a childish, irresponsible personality during her ecstacies, and that this shows not that she is a great mystic but that she has a split personality. This is to explain one mystery with another mystery, because if there is anything that baffles the psychologists it is the phenomenon of a real "split personality." The obvious explanation is diabolism. No one seems to want to accuse Therese Neumann of being possessed but in this connection the question is finally raised. Her states of "elevated rest" are considered reminiscent of diabolical or *psychological* possession. And just what is psychological possession? Who does the possessing?

Toward the beginning of the book there is talk (taken from the French Carmelite studies) about parapsychological, paraphysiological, diapsychological and diaphysiological phenomena—which are in effect intermediary between physical and spiritual states, or combination states, so to speak. I plan to keep a healthy skepticism with respect to the scientists of the nervous system and the glands, lest they miss seeing the Devil for being intent on observing his subtle effects on the body. Actually I am more mystified by Hilda Graef's explanations than I would be by either the supernatural ones or the diabolical.

There is one instance I should like to cite as being very curious. Perhaps it is unfair to generalize from it, but here it is. Therese Neumann came to the priest one day and asked to receive Communion. She could barely stumble into the church and to her chair behind the altar. Two priests approached her from different sides of the altar, one with the Hosts. But Therese was already seated and calm. She opened her mouth to show a Host already on her tongue. Hilda Graef tries to make her out a smarty and show-off because of the dramatic elements in the story. The whole thing is dismissed as a conjuring trick.

At the end of the account I was still wondering where the Host came from, since there were elaborate protestations that implied that any conscious deception was played. On second reading I find the implication clearly there that Therese brought the Host with her. Well maybe, but there is no evidence given that this is so, and if it is so let's call Therese Neumann a fraudulent character dealing in sacrilege and be done with all these psychological pseudo-excuses.

* * *

Someone was good enough to bring to my attention a book called *The Physical Phenomena of Mysticism*, published by Barnes & Noble, but originally published in England. It is by Montague Summers who was not a Catholic but ordained, I think, to the Protestant Ministry.

Dr. Summers seems to have made a life study of witchcraft (about which he has written another book) and mystical phenomena. This book is mostly about stigmata, although it also treats ecstacy and other phenomena. I was very impressed by it, for it is a thorough, scholarly study, heavily documented. It is not at all rationalistic in its approach but defers always to the authority of the Church, recognizes her full teaching on these subjects and her powers of discernment.

Whereas Hilda Graef has obviously very little knowledge of these phenomena in general and counts a lot on the evidence of the few cases that have come to her attention by hearsay, otherwise referring to the most prominent of the stigmatic saints, Dr. Summer knows the whole subject thoroughly. There are over three hundred known genuine stigmatists and he is familiar with every listing of them, every document concerning them (especially the official documents which he generally uses). He also knows all about the diabolical stigmatists and the fraudulent ones (those who mutilated themselves to impress people with their sanctity). His approach to the whole subject is scholarly and deeply religious, balanced, objective in a very true sense. He is not afraid of the subject, nor is he anxious to jump on any bandwagons. He believes in being ultra-cautious about proclaiming a stigmatist as genuine, but is not afraid to try to find out. In the case of one Dominican nun who was declared a fraud and punished, he believes that she was the victim of malice and political corruption.

Dr. Summers agrees with Hilda Graef's theory that true stigmata are concomitant only with high sanctity. On the other hand he dismisses the possibility of "hysterical" stigmata. He examines the whole idea (on which she bases her hypothesis) that stigmata can be produced by hysteria because hypnotists have approximated the phenomena in likely subjects, etc. He refers to every known experiment of this sort. His conclusion is that whereas hysteria can produce some odd effects, the stigmata are completely out of the realm of the purely psychological. Wherever hypnotists have succeeded in producing by suggestion more than a slight redness or irritation, their activities are suspiciously involved with the diabolical.

Except for self-mutilation, which has occurred but which is easily detected, there are only two sources of the stigmata, according to Dr. Summers—the supernatural and the diabolical. He cites many cases of each kind and here his knowledge of diabolism in general is obviously a great help.

Dr. Summers does not treat of Therese Neumann in detail because her story is so well known. He gives a bibliography and the outlines of her story. He says the blood from her stigmata has been tested and found definitely to be human blood (which would contradict the one instance given in Hilda Graef's book). He mentions that Pius XI had her privately investigated and then sent his blessing to her and to her pastor. He also mentions the caution of the local authorities. He does not pass on her genuineness one way or another.

He is more detailed in his treatment of Padre Pio, possibly because he is not widely known. He also points out the evident sanctity of this Capuchin. Hilda Graef too (in an incidental statement) makes it clear that she has no doubts about the supernatural character of Padre Pio's stigmata and considers him very holy.

Dr. Summers also says that he knows personally of several stigmatists now living who are undoubtedly genuine, but about whom he will say nothing at all because he has been pledged to secrecy.

I am grateful to Dr. Summers for clearing the air from the muddled pseudo-scientific thinking of Hilda Graef. It's good to be back in a world where God operates very mysteriously on His chosen ones, and where Satan lurks, and where human nature is carried to the heights and brought to the depths. It is much better than a world in which everything can be explained away by the latest findings of the Ph.D's.

THY FAITH HATH MADE THEE WHOLE
OCTOBER 1951

THE MYSTICAL EVOLUTION IN THE DEVELOPMENT AND VITALITY OF THE CHURCH, VOL. II

By John G. Arintero, O.P., S.T.M.
Herder

WE ARE LIVING IN A GODLESS AGE, SO WE SEE AND judge accordingly. Like owls, we are blinded by the daylight (in this case the daylight of spiritual reality) and can see only at night (the night of superficial and sensual reality). What we see is really meaningless. A baby is born, of rich or poor parents, wanted or unwanted. He grows up, not in wisdom and grace, but in height and weight, literacy and sophistication. He marries this person or that, lives here or there, makes money or does not, is more or less violently unhappy, dies and is buried. So ends meaninglessly a meaningless life. Yet in spite of our blindness even such a life has meaning, hidden from ordinary eyes. To the Christian there are the great sacramental events. For everyone exists the great spiritual and moral crises which we prefer to ignore—the temptations, the graces, the terrible choices for or against God, the last struggle of the soul on his deathbed, however camouflaged to the beholders by the scientific impersonality of the medical attendants, the drugs administered, and the radio which continues playing beside the next bed. Furthermore, life continues in the now separated soul—searing self-knowledge, eternal or temporary punishment, perhaps glory.

Not only is the meaning of our lives essentially spiritual, it is essentially mystical, which means concerned with grace, if only to reject it. A soul progresses toward God and away from God. Here is the core of life. Daily events are the material with which the soul works out his salvation or damnation.

All the above is clear enough to any serious Christian. But project it to humanity at large, and it will be evident that some of the best Catholics are wearing bifocals. Yet this is true, that just as individual lives take their meaning from each person's relationship to God, daily events being the medium of the struggle, so the world takes its meaning from Christ (that is, the Church) and secular history is the

Book Reviews

material and background thereof. Or, to put it in stark form, history we call "B. C." was a preparation for Christ. Everything A. D. is ultimately measurable and meaningful only in relation to the developing and perfecting of the Church. When the number of the elect and the perfecting of the Mystical Body is completed (and only God knows when that will be) human history will cease and the end of the world will come, precisely because there will be no more reason for them to continue. Furthermore human events in any time in history take their real meaning from the building up of the Body. So, for instance if there are great wars and disasters, and the Church is persecuted, this is likely caused in the first place by Christians who have allowed themselves to become unsalted, who have let the Body become seriously diseased. But also these evils are a means of purifying and revivifying the Body of Christ because of the saints who come to its rescue.

I do not mean to oversimplify here, in the manner of certain sectarians who claim to interpret all the daily news apocalyptically. God's providence and the development of His Church are mysterious to us and will remain so, beyond certain general principles and private revelations. I merely wish to re-establish the Christian perspective in opposition to the progress theories which the secularists hold. True progress is not the progressive exploitation of natural knowledge in science and technology. True progress is not more bathtubs or more money. True progress is not more and more secular education. True progress is not more and more socialism. True progress is the fulfillment in sanctity and numbers of the Body of Christ in His Church.

This is a long preliminary to a book review. But the book has a long title, The Mystical Evolution in the Development and Vitality of the Church, a title which will become more clear in the light of the above. The author has written against the rationalists and the progressivists, but not with so much reference to the general secular situation as I have made. I have projected his ideas into a sociological context, whereas he sticks to the religious realm — nevertheless the implications are there.

Father Arintero was a Spanish Dominican with a considerable reputation for holiness and spiritual direction. The book is so heavily loaded with footnotes (very interesting ones, often citing particular cases of saints or holy people of the author's acquaintance) and chapter appendices (excerpts from holy writings) that only about half of it is text proper. Most of the space is given to "The Mystical Evolution of the Individual," which is a description of the three stages of the spiritual life in the dark nights. It is rather similar to the treatment of this matter by Garrigou-Lagrange (who learned from Father Arintero), but more discursive.

It is the third part, on "The Mystical Evolution of the Entire Church," which is particularly interesting. Father Arintero gives, one after another, graphic descriptions of the solidarity of Christians. He makes you see the Church as a living body always partly diseased, and sometimes ulcerous to the point of disfigurement, by unworthy members. But, he says, "... it is sometimes necessary to act with greater consideration toward sinners than toward the just," simply because they *are* the weak members of an ailing body, and to save the whole, also so that those of them who have necessary functions will continue to operate imperfectly rather than not at all.

Father Arintero shows brilliantly also how, because of the unity of the Mystical Body, each member can only aid the progress of the whole in his own functional role and in proportion to his sanctity. First place among vocations is given to victim souls because they are constantly restoring the whole body to health.

Book Reviews

DECEMBER 1951

GOD AND MAN AT YALE
By William F. Buckley, Jr.
Regnery

THERE IS SOMETHING RATHER IRONIC ABOUT THIS BOOK. Hordes of Catholic students are attending secular colleges throughout the United States. What the secular colleges are teaching is about as remote from, and antagonistic to, the Catholic faith as possible. The Newman Clubs whose duty it is to protect the Catholic students in these unfortunate circumstances, by and large adopt an official policy that looks very much like compromise. This means that instead of facing up to the *intellectual* situation, so as to meet the challenge at its roots, they cater to the mediocrity and the considerably-less-than-noble motives of the average student and arrange an exhausting program of predominantly social activities. Because they try for numbers instead of working with the nature of the problem, in the end even the numbers escape them. Certainly the first great loss, which they hardly notice, is that of serious and gifted students, of the young men and women who come to college searching for truth, who have the generosity and the nobility of heart to make every sacrifice for an ideal, but who are not the slightest bit interested in a watered down approach or a round of picnics and dances.

Father Feeney tried the intellectual approach at Harvard with phenomenal results which stand, in some respects, as a permanent good and a lesson despite the subsequent tragic failure of his group. St. Benedict's Center attracted the highest caliber of students, was responsible for many conversions, many vocations, and the strong Catholicity of a lot of young men and women who might well otherwise now be outside the Church. Newman Clubs should have the humility to learn from Fr. Feeney that they ought to dare great things. If instead they conclude smugly that it is better not to enter any intellectual arenas, it will be very unfortunate because for one thing the harm they do by their sins of omission, though hard to measure exactly, may be tremendous. And for another thing, someone is going to challenge the colleges even if they aren't, so they will

545

have missed an opportunity for leadership which they may regret.

Which brings us back to *God and Man at Yale*. Although the book doesn't indicate it, I understand that the author is a Catholic. He was graduated from Yale in 1950. Apparently quite on his own, he has undertaken to challenge the current Yale curriculum, fearlessly and brilliantly. As I write this, only a week or two after publication, the first edition is already sold out.

Mr. Buckley is an ultra-conservative, which (so he says) is the new radicalism. He has a keen, logical, and accurate mind. He was the editor of the Yale Daily News, and writes forcefully. His thesis is this: Traditionally, and in the minds of the alumni, Yale upholds Christianity and individualism (along with capitalism). The present bias at Yale is anti-Christian and socialist-collectivist. The alumni ought to be informed because the university is accountable to them. By right, and because they hold the purse strings, they control Yale's policies.

No defense of Christianity or capitalism or individualism as such is made in the book. It is not an apologetical treatise. With respect to religion the author merely shows that there is precious little, if any, championing of Christianity at Yale but that agnosticism and atheism are openly applauded by some teachers. He gives names and courses, citing especially the case of the late Professor Kennedy who taught Basic Sociology and Anthropology and openly mocked religion.

Mr. Buckley's plea for conservative economics is longer and more eloquent even than that for Christianity. Mr. Buckley is a rugged individualist and private enterpriser. The teachers at Yale are Keynesian socialists and the official textbooks are very biased toward government ownership. It is interesting to see an unpopular cause (in fact, a dead cause) so brilliantly defended, even though the atmosphere gets a bit stuffy now and then. There is no evidence whatever that Mr. Buckley ever read any Chesterton or Belloc, knows anything about the problem of usury, the subject of the common good, or has read the social encyclicals of the Popes. Consequently he makes a few bold statements which are patently erroneous in the light of Catholic philosophy. Nevertheless his negative criticisms mostly stand.

God and Man at Yale will find great favor with capitalists, republicans, conservatives of all sorts. There is very much good in it. However, it just isn't true that colleges are ultimately accountable to alumni. They are ultimately accountable to God. Truth *is*, and Mr. Buckley doesn't quite push this idea to its logical consequences. If he did, Yale

Book Reviews

would be seen to be in need of even more drastic repairs. But as it is, although his book seems drastic it is still on the superficial level. To give one curious instance, Protestant Episcopalian Bishop Henry Knox Sherill is a member of the Yale Corporation. He is presumed by Mr. Buckley to represent one of the forces for Christianity. Yet the Protestant Christians are themselves in an indeterminate position and this ought to be taken into account. Bishop Sherrill has just (Nov. 1st) been authorized by the National Council of Churches to head the Protestant protest against the appointment of an ambassador to the Vatican.

If Mr. Buckley's ardor had been focused on championing Christianity as such rather than on conservatism (presumably he would have been so-focused if he had fallen under strong Catholic intellectual and spiritual influence), I doubt that he could have written this precise book. Which would have been a pity — or wouldn't it have been? He might have left Yale for the Trappists, or just have left Yale, or have made a less popular type of criticism and been classed as a fanatic. As it is I see him rapidly rising to the chairmanship of the Board of Directors of General Motors or U. S. Steel.

THE REVOLT AGAINST REASON

By Arnold Lunn
Sheed & Ward

I WISH I HAD READ ARNOLD LUNN EARLIER. HIS NAME was very familiar to me from the time of my conversion but by some inopportuneness I never happened to read his books and gradually I came to feel almost as though I had from hearing about them, or at least as though the moment that they would have been helpful had passed. How wrong I was.

Mr. Lunn does one thing superbly. He is a master controversialist and logician with respect to the popular errors of the day. His special field is scientism and within it the doctrine of evolution. For at least twenty years he has been arguing and studying and thinking about evolution, so what he says on it is authoritative, up-to-date, lucid and brilliant. Most talk on this subject is muddled or over-solicitous of the good will of the atheists, or deals with some minute consideration. The general prevailing attitude (or at least so I have found) is that science has proved the evolutionary theory beyond a doubt, therefore we must bow down before facts, and anyhow we can salvage the Book of Genesis because we only have to believe that man's *body* evolved. Chesterton's quip that the only thing we know for certain about the missing link is that he is missing, is considered amusing but inaccurate.

Now Arnold Lunn does not entirely disavow the evolutionary theory, at least in a modified form, but he does show what tremendous difficulties stand in the way of accepting this hypothesis. Not theological difficulties, but logical difficulties based on the scientific data or lack of it. His book is rich in excellent quotations, including a number from leading contemporary scientists who have discarded the theory. Evolution continues to be taught in all the schools not because the best scientific minds still hold it but because academic appointments still require belief in it.

Evolution is just a major case in point. What Mr. Lunn really exposes is the *irrationality* of modern secular so-called scientific thinking. There are degrees. The "rationalism" of the eighteenth century used reason within too narrow a field, but still used reason. The final degradation is Logical Positivism which is just about a complete perversion of man's rational nature. The favorite word of the logical positivists is "meaningful," which crops up more and more with American writers. It's a particularly repellent evasion of clarity and, for that matter, of meaning.

The Revolt Against Reason is a complete revision of *Flight from Reason* which appeared twenty years ago and is considerably longer. I particularly recommend it for college students in secular schools because it will answer their questions. But it will also rid them overnight of their inferiority complexes, apologetical attitudes and defensive positions. Such a book as this could make a vast difference in a person's life if it came his way at the right time.

Book Reviews

JANUARY 1952

WAITING FOR GOD

By Simone Weil
Putnam

SIMONE WEIL HAS BEEN HAILED BY SOME NON-CATHOLICS, including Leslie Fiedler[4] who did the introduction to this book, and some Catholics too, as the Outsider Saint, the Saint of the Unchurched—proof that you don't have to declare your allegiance to the Church in order to be a saint. On the other hand, she is denounced by some reviewers for holding unorthodox views and indeed talking against the Church.

There are a lot of things that have to be accounted for about Simone Weil. She practiced unusual and heroic virtue. When she was *five* she refused to eat sugar as long as the soldiers at the front were not able to get it. (This in a solid bourgeois agnostic family.) The same sort of compassion marked her whole life. Although an intellectual, trained to teach, she worked in an automobile factory, sharing all the hardships of the workers until she broke down, and subsequently did the same thing among agricultural workers. She died, at 34, in England and could have been saved had she not declined to eat more than the ration of those in occupied France.

Simone Weil had mystical experiences of Christ's presence which there seems to be no reason to question. I am certainly not disposed, from reading about them, to doubt them.

She suffered from the age of thirteen almost constantly from migraine headaches. In the beginning she was tempted on their account to commit suicide. When she had her mystical experiences she was transported beyond the headaches, which continued nevertheless. To this special affliction has to be added the hunger, cold, dirtiness, ugliness, and utter exhaustion she frequently felt.

Simone Weil was an intellectual with a pretty good knowledge of theology. When she discussed the faith she did so in the light of profound doctrine and of its sacramental life.

---

4   Leslie Fiedler (1917–2003) was an American literary critic who applied psychological theories to American literature. — *Ed.*

549

Yet she refused to be baptized — on the grounds that she did not think it was the will of God for her — at least yet. She proposed just to wait (hence the title of this book) until God did something further about it. She thought perhaps she was meant to remain just outside the compassion with all the other non-Catholics. Yet she loved the Church almost fiercely and in no way superficially. She loved Christ and the Blessed Sacrament.

So what shall we make of Simone Weil? The best hypothesis seems to be that she was a person favored by God, of an heroic stature, who was in process of conversion but fighting against it. She probably would have come into the Church had she not died prematurely. There is no sign that God had ceased to pursue her because of her resistance. There is no sign of a death bed conversion, although there might have been one. And who knows the mind of God and why He allowed her to die at that particular time?

The above hypothesis does account for most of the problems about Simone Weil. There is no need for denying that she was more favored mystically than most of us and heroic enough to put us to shame. But neither do we need to say she was perfect. She was ugly and apparently ultra-sensitive to an unhealthy degree, even scrupulous (which may be the explanation of her refusal to be baptized). Her essays are a collection of brilliant and true ideas mixed with errors and insufficiencies. Most of the essays in this book fall under the general title "Forms of the implicit love of God," and these cannot be read, to my mind, without being on one's guard.

Simone Weil stayed awhile at the farm of Gustave Thibon who became her very good friend and preserved her manuscripts. But at first he couldn't stand her because she talked incessantly — about ideas, of course. She was carelessly dressed and conspicuously awkward about her gestures. But inside she had a soul delicate, extremely gentle, and charitable.

This very beautiful soul of hers is expressed most clearly in her letters to Father Perrin, a Dominican priest-worker whom she loved and to whom she exposed her soul. She said she had never really trusted anyone else in her life because she was afraid of being hurt, but she trusted him because of his great charity. The letters are the heart of this volume and very moving.

Where sin abounds, grace is poured out more lavishly than usual. Our days are very evil so we can expect much grace. Simone Weil's story adds to the growing evidence that we are living in one of the great spiritual ages.

Book Reviews
FEBRUARY 1952

S.O.S.: THE MEANING OF OUR CRISIS

By Pitirim A. Sorokin
Beacon Press

HARVARD SOCIOLOGIST PITIRIM SOROKIN IN THE 1930'S did some analyses of the modern crisis which were quite accurate and have stood the test of time despite his use of rather barbarous terminology of this own invention. This lately published sequel is a sad illustration of what can happen to prophets without roots. Professor Sorokin has taken to ranting. Most of the book consists of one long verbose torrent of invectives and accusations against all the people who have messed up the world. The culprits include virtually everyone.

Although Sorokin appeals to the Divinity he doesn't like churches much. He seems obsessed with the idea of pacifism and by implication smiles only on gentle people who love instead of hate, and who wouldn't hurt anyone. But as so often happens with people whose benevolence comes from a softness in the head or a weakness in temperament rather than from the burning charity of a Saint Francis, Professor Sorokin is almost a monument of hatred, as witness this book.

Besides the tirade the book contains an analysis of his Law of Polarization, which states heavily some fairly obvious truths—that crises produce extremists in both directions and that the extremes peril, attract and slip into one another. There is truth here but far from the most important truth the world is awaiting. One the level of this sort of sociology men can only burst their brains for a very meager understanding. I commend Professor Sorokin to dogmatic theology as a more fruitful source of understanding of the world, also a more peaceful and hopeful one.

THY FAITH HATH MADE THEE WHOLE

OUR SAVIOR AND HIS LOVE FOR US[5]

By Reginald Garrigou-Lagrange, O.P.
Herder

THOMIST SCHOLAR GARRIGOU-LAGRANGE IN THIS, THE most recently translated of a long line of impressive theological works, employs the Angelic Doctor's treatise on the Incarnation as his principal source from which to extract the stepping stones to the fact that "God so loved the world that He gave His only begotten Son..."

In his preface the author speaks of two pitfalls to be avoided in such a presentation. One is the over-attention to minutiae that clouds the stairway to faith which is, after all, as he points out, "far superior" to theology. The other is the lack of solid doctrinal foundation that mars (indeed, often results in misrepresentation) the so-called pious books, the "popularizations" found among best-sellers.

In cutting a straight path between the two, Garrigou-Lagrange puts forth his purpose as one "to invite interior souls to the contemplation of the mystery of Christ."

I do not think his success is to be doubted. Part I is a consideration of our Lord's interior life in relation to the mystery of the Incarnation. Part II is concerned with that life in relation to the mystery of the Redemption. Through them both, attentive readers will be aware of doctrinal wealth as well as incentives for pause and reflection. This is particularly true in the chapter which reconciles Christ's freedom of will and His absolute impeccability.

Probably the most interesting chapter in light of present day events that saw the coming and going of Simone Weil and of simultaneous raised eyebrows and "I saw her with my own eyes" assertions on Therese Neumann is the last, "Mystics Outside the Church."

Can there be mystics outside of the Catholic Church? What is the foremost prerequisite? The answer to the first question — yes — and the answer to the second — the state of grace — point up another bit of dogma that the author labored to be explicit: the state of grace, inside or outside the Church, is no half-way measure. Every rational creature chooses either to face God or turn his back on Him. The former disposition is the state of grace, the other is the state of mortal sin.

---

[5] Review written under the pseudonym, Carol Davis.

In other words, even the major mystical graces (as described by Saint Teresa) can attend to those outside the Church. But does such a thing happen often?

Well, says Garrigou-Lagrange,

> Let us not forget what Saint John of the Cross says even of the most restricted Catholic circles. "God does not raise up to contemplation properly so-called all who desire to attain it by following the way of the spirit. He does not take even half of them." "Why do they not reach this lofty state?... [Many souls], as soon as God tests them, flee suffering and refuse to bear the slightest dryness and mortification." If this is true within the visible Church, how much truer must it be on the outside! (Chapter XXXI)

As for the minor mystical graces, it is encouraging to note, considering the state of half the world today, they "can occur rather frequently... as a means of making up for the indigence of the environments where God's children find so little help."

Those who consider themselves students on the temperaments will find the chapter "Our Participation in the Mysteries" colorful fuel in their discussions. Holiness, says the author, takes three rather distinct forms, based on the temperaments of the individual. They are personified by three Apostles, Peter, John and James. They are manifested by the duty to know God, the duty to love Him and the duty to serve Him.

Peter represents those who would trip over themselves in showing love, who would be crucified head downward for Him. Their pitfall if not docile to the Holy Ghost can be rigidity, tenacity and obstinacy. "Their zeal is not sufficiently enlightened, nor patient and gentle enough. Some of them may turn too much to active works at the expense of prayer."

John represents a second group made of those in whom the intellect, rather than the will, dominates. "Their spiritual flame produces more light than heat." Their pitfall is to be content with knowledge rather than conform to the truths.

Then there is James who represents the majority of Christians faithful to daily duty. Their pitfall is in becoming too attached to practices that are good in themselves but do not lead direct to God. They like vocal prayers.

THY FAITH HATH MADE THEE WHOLE

The author did not go into the fact that John was the disciple whom Jesus loved; nor that the keys to the Kingdom went into impulsive hands.

THE SPIRIT OF PRAYER OF CARMEL[6]

By Francois Jamart, O.C.D.
The Newman Press

WHAT IS CARMEL? TO MOST OF US IT IS A MONTAGE OF unusual persons and vague, romantic scenes. Contributing to such a picture have been a biography here and there of its great mystics, a well-proportioned drama of the martyrs of Compiegne, an ever-present statue of the Little Flower, and interesting program notes like Edith Stein. All generate an interest and a certain awe, but they are not Carmel *in toto*. After all, there are innumerable Carmelite houses in Europe and America (not to mention mission fields) and there have been Carmelites to fill them since at least the 12th century. Not all have been Saint John of the Cross, Saint Teresa, Saint Thérèse, Sister Constance, Sister Elizabeth of the Trinity or even Father Gracian.

In a booklet that anyone can read in a couple of hours, Father Jamart has coordinated this loosely-joined series of impressions into one clear close-up of Carmel's aim, spirit and kind of prayer. Brief though it is, it leaves a concrete idea, and although the saints are certainly the star performers, one is very much aware of, in Hollywood parlance, the great army of bit players. (And as every student of Hollywood knows, some bit players make the grade and some don't.)

The Spirit of Prayer of Carmel sets forth the ultimate aim of the Order (with its two branches, Calced and Discaled) as infused contemplation. As this is purely a gift of God to give to whom He chooses, it looks on the surface as sort of a precarious goal. But, says Father Jamart, the Carmelite knows the value of correct disposition. He knows, in the words of Raoul Plus, "God never allows Himself to be outdone in generosity." Creating that correct disposition, then, is Carmel's immediate aim.

Father Jamart is not the most inspiring of writers, but he is clear-cut

---

6   Review written under her pseudonym, Carol Davis.

Book Reviews

and uninvolved. He quotes Holy Father John of the Cross and Holy Mother Teresa (as the Carmelites refer to the founding mystics of the Reform) with true filial fidelity and gleans from them, principally, seven acts in the Carmelite method of prayer. For the benefit of those interested in prayer methods (the author has a thesis that the word "method" has scared many away from anything but pure petition) those acts, or steps are: Preparation, reading, the meditation, contemplation (not to be confused with infused contemplation), thanksgiving, petition and conclusion.

But it is Holy Mother Teresa herself who wraps it all up neatly with, "In any case, the important thing is not to do a lot of thinking, but to love much!" (The exclamation mark, naturally, is hers.)

WHAT CATHOLICS BELIEVE[7]

By Josef Pieper and Heinz Raskop
Pantheon

NOT ONLY THE CREED BUT THE WHOLE CATHOLIC CHURCH is reeled out in slow motion in this little publication of which Father Gerald B. Phelan of the University of Notre Dame in his introduction calls "a simply beautiful and a beautifully simple book."

Its emphasis is on the Church in its primary essence, an organism, rather than in its secondary, an organization, upon which so much, too much, emphasis is put these days.

The result is a tendency to say: "Here it is. Here it is in a nutshell. This is what I've been trying to tell you about the Church!"

But such exuberance doesn't fit in with the quiet assuredness of the writers, one of whom, Josef Pieper, is Germany's leading lay apostle. With deft precision they "strip" for their readers not only the Creed, but the seven sacraments, the theological and cardinal virtues, scripture, Church history—well, everything, in little more than a hundred pages.

Here's a sample:

> Nor, we must admit, has there ever been a time in the life of the Church when she did not also show the effects of the human element in her... There have always been, and always will be, weeds among the wheat, chaff mixed with

---

7 Review written under her pseudonym, Carol Davis.

555

the grain; but the Christian does not let this confuse him. He knows that in the future as well as in the past these things are possible: unworthy popes, unworthy bishops and priests, an unworthy body of Catholics undeserving of the name of Christian. But all this does not threaten, let alone destroy, the holiness of the Church, in which "the Holy One of God" (Mark 1:23) continues to dwell. At the same time, our Lord's warning still stands: "It must needs be that such hurt should come, but woe to the men through whom it comes!" (Matthew 18:7).

You see? It is such calm conviction that rules the book from beginning to end. Every Catholic can learn from it; even if only its spirit.

Book Reviews

APRIL 1952

THE FLIGHT FROM GOD

By Max Picard
Regnery

MAX PICARD IS A GERMAN SWISS OF JEWISH ANCESTRY, a convert to the Catholic Church. He is a wise man, with a penetrating, intuitional view of the world. His books contain insight rather than ordered analysis or argumentation.

What Dr. Picard wants to show is what is really happening to the world below the level of surface events, and to the universality of this catastrophe. *The Hitler in Ourselves* is the title of the first book of his published here, and gives the clue. Hitler was not one evil man threatening to destroy us innocents. He was the personification rather of our own vices. In *The Flight from God*, similarly, the diagnosis of a sick world applies to us all. We are running away from God and rationalizing the flight. Everything is caught up in this tremendous fleeing, or soon will be. Within such an analysis there is no place whatever for singling out individual scapegoats, for arguing Europe versus America, East versus West, one nation versus another, or democracy versus some alternative form of government, not to mention the remote and rarefied arguments about Church and State, or minor election issues.

In Dr. Picard's view, it is this mass flight from God that explains everything. In the ages of faith individual men fled from God, but society continued to be ordered to Him, and therefore to have stability, certainty and other qualities of being. Today it is as though the whole world had become mobile, had suddenly entered a current of relativity and flux, had set out in great devouring masses and at an accelerating pace, toward its own destruction. How can a man stand still and *be* in a world of total *becoming*? Dr. Picard shows the application of his thesis to many fields, including art, economics, the modern city, the human face, language.

Sometimes the book is a little difficult. There are two introductions (one by Gabriel Marcel) which are helpful. I personally think the author beats his thesis to a near pulp sometimes.

According to Dr. Picard, the hope for a world fleeing from God lies in the flight itself. He takes his clue from Saint Augustine, who fled God only to encounter Him at every turn, but "The Hound of Heaven" also keeps suggesting itself. I found this resolution of the problem unconvincing. A world in flight from God, which has ordered itself to that flight (that is, which has secularized itself) is not in precisely the same situation as is a soul fleeing grace. And even in the case of a soul fleeing grace, it would be presumptuous to assume that God will continue to chase indefinitely.

Book Reviews

MAY 1952

SATAN

Edited by Bruno de Jesus-Marie, O.C.D.
Sheed & Ward

THE FRENCH CARMELITES PUBLISHED A SPECIAL FAT VOLume of articles on the Devil and various of his activities several years ago. Sheed and Ward has done a very great service in translating into English and publishing the bulk of this work. One has first of all to express this gratitude.

The next duty is to point out that *Satan* is in the nature of a *summa* about the Devil. There are thirty-two different articles. Some of them are solidly theological. One or two are so scholarly as to be understood only by specialists. Most are of general interest. There is only a very little space given to actual "case histories," and these were badly chosen. The longest one, "The Confessions of Jeanne Fery," may have been fraudulent. Readers would have been better served to have had a good description of a genuine case of possession. The other two cases are "The Confession of Boullan," which is not given, but merely commented on, and an odd account of a 17-year-old girl convicted of witchcraft. Odd because key facts seem missing and the viewpoint is (to my mind) biased. So anyhow, there is virtually nothing sensational in this volume, but there is a vast amount of solid information and learned speculation for serious thinkers. No, there is one thing sensational — the pictorial dust-jacket. It has a picture of Satan which is loathsomeness made graphic. A second conservative just-jacket also accompanies the book, and a good thing too.

There are five parts to *Satan*. Section I is theological, giving an excellent treatment of the Devil's own nature and the scope of his possible activities with respect to us. Section II, on the place of the Devil outside Christianity, has four pretty scholarly articles on pagan concepts. Section III, on possession & diabolism, is the longest and probably the most interesting. Section IV is on the Devil in art and literature, Section V on deicide. In the first section, the article on the Devil in Saint John of the Cross' writings stands out for its spiritual wisdom. According to Saint John, faith and humility are the two great weapons against Satan. The last section, on deicide, has only two articles, both excellent and both dealing with modern German trends. "Satan in Our Day," written by a Benedictine who died immediately afterwards, shows that Hitler's National Socialism was diabolical because it possessed the two main marks of diabolism — murdering and lying.

But the section on possession interests me most, and probably will interest most other people. The whole is written against a preoccupation with the relationship, if any, between psychology and diabolical activity. The editor, Father Bruno, leans heavily on the side of psychological explanations and so do most of his writers. In fact several of them are skeptical beyond what seems becoming to a Catholic. An English Jesuit, Herbert Thurston,[8] now dead I believe, writes of the Church and witchcraft almost as though he were trying to explain away, or at any rate minimize as much as possible, any concern the Church ever had with such a shameful (in the light of modern science) matter. Father Thurston is always the authority most quoted by those who want to escape from preternatural and supernatural explanations. Another famous authority on the skeptical side is Joseph de Tonquedec, S. J., who has done the article called "Exorcism and Diabolical Manifestation" here and who quotes heavily from Dalbiez, the unimpeachable Catholic reference for psychologists, and another, perhaps a worse skeptic. As a matter of fact de Tonquedec quotes Dalbiez but modifies his views. The burden of this article is that people must not be considered possessed, and be exorcised, unless all possible natural explanations of their conduct have been eliminated. This is Church teaching. The difficulty arises about whether a given psychiatric explanation suffices or is so much verbiage. The author credits psychiatry with being more of an exact science than seems to be the case.

Charles Moeller has done an excellent introduction to this volume, in which he suggests the reconciliation of the psychology-possession quarrel, based on an article by Msgr. F. M. Catherinet called "Demoniacs in the Gospel." It is perhaps the best article in the book. It will be well to end this review with a quotation from Msgr. Catherinet:

> We shall have to infer with the theologians that all true diabolic possession is accompanied, in fact and by a

---

[8] Herbert Thurston (1856–1939) also assisted with the revision of Alban Butler's *Lives of the Saints* published in four volumes. — *Ed.*

quasi-necessity, by mental and nervous troubles produced or amplified by the demon, and yet having manifestations and symptoms which are practically and medically identical with those produced by neuroses. The psychiatrist, therefore, is free to study these symptoms, to *describe* these mental troubles, and to indicate their immediate causes. There he stands on his own ground. But if, in the name of his science, he pretends to exclude *a priori*, and in all cases, any transcendent cause of the anomalies in question, then he trespasses beyond the bounds of his special competence. Precisely by confining himself to his own methods he automatically foregoes any inquiry of this kind. Never will he find the Devil at the term of his purely medical analysis, any more than the surgeon will find the soul at the point of his scalpel, or any more than the dog, seeing his master in anger, can estimate the moral or immoral character of these strange gesticulations: all that belongs to another order. But the doctor who wants to remain a complete man, above all if he enjoys the light of the faith, will never exclude *a priori*, and in some cases may well suspect, the presence and action of some occult power behind the malady. He will hand over its investigation to the philosopher and the theologian, allowing himself to be guided by their methods and he will have enough modesty to remember that where his medical science, brought to bear on a woman who cannot hold herself up straight, will see nothing but a partial paralysis of eighteen years' standing, the penetrating and infallible glance of Jesus discerned and asserted the presence of the Devil putting forth all his hatred against a daughter of Abraham.

THY FAITH HATH MADE THEE WHOLE

JUNE 1952

THE NEED FOR ROOTS[9]

By Simone Weil
Putnam

After Simone Weil's *Waiting for God* was published some months ago, a frequently asked question was, "Why didn't she become a Catholic?" Theoretically she was a Christian and there seemed to be no doubt in her mind that the Christian Church is the Church of Rome.

In *The Need for Roots*, the work of the last months of her life, there are some answers. On the surface it would appear that her reasoning takes an old, old line—the conduct of Catholics, from early Roman times through the Spanish Inquisition, on to and beyond the era of French anti-clericalism. There seems to be that chasm that only faith can bridge, that difference between the Church that is the living, vital, and often mutilated Body and the Church that is an organization of the sons of Adam.

But Simone Weil is not a superficial reasoner. She is a paradox, a complex soul, at one and the same time all French, all Jewish, all Christian. This should be remembered in reading *The Need for Roots*. The important thing, as T. S. Eliot says in his preface, is that we "expose ourselves to the personality of a woman of genius, of a kind of genius akin to that of the saints."

The book is the result of the request, in 1943, of the Free French authorities in London for her to write a report with recommendations for the renovation of the educational and governmental system in France after the war. It is as comprehensive an essay on, to colloquialize, "What's wrong with the world and what to do about it," as any on the contemporary market. And it puts a fearful awe in the reader to realize, nearly ten years later, how little, if anything, has been taken to heart.

In pedantic order the book lists the needs of the soul. Then, in Part II, with forensic skill, it lays bare the uprootedness of our time. Part III deals with recommendations for remedy.

---

[9] Review written under her pseudonym, Carol Davis.

The needs are, according to Miss Weil: order, liberty, obedience, responsibility, equality, hierarchism, honor, punishment, freedom of opinion, security, risks, private property, collective property, and truth — in way of appearance and not, we trust, importance.

We, as individuals, as social groups, as nations, lack these basic needs and, says the author, "Four obstacles above all separate us from a form of civilization likely to be worth something: our false conception of greatness; the degradation of the sentiment of justice; our idolization of money; and our lack of religious inspiration."

With irony she adds, "We may use the first person plural without any hesitation, for it is doubtful whether at the present moment there is a single human being on the surface of the globe who is free from that quadruple defect, and more doubtful still whether there is a single one belonging to the white race. But if there are one or two, which, in spite of everything, is to be hoped, they remain hidden."

No military conquest, no social movement, no civilization, and very few great names pass by her pen unnoted. Simone Weil had read a great deal; she thought even more and it is obvious that her bases of comparison for the deeds of history are the gospels. Therefore it is necessary for her to use the scalpel so very deeply with even her beloved France that German schoolboys will get no inferiority complex in reading her resume of French political development.

Except for a few spiritual bouquets tossed at the feast of the Jocists, castigation is the general rule. No one with half a conscience can avoid seeing that the shoe fits universally.

This summary of *The Need for Roots* is indeed an inadequate condensation of more than three hundred pages of impact, of philosophical meditation of a most unusual woman, albeit a young one (she was thirty-three when she died), one who never deliberately attempts to charm her reader. She is all seriousness.

But of special interest to us of the faith, who know her near-saintliness, her mysticism, her devotion to moral principal, are her criticisms of Catholicism. The work is liberally sprinkled. Here are two:

> But as for the churches, they offer us the supreme scandal of clergy and faithful asking God at the same time, with the same rites, the same words, and it must be supposed, an equal amount of faith and purity of heart, to grant a military victory to one or other of two warring camps.

In all the arguments in which religion and science appear to be in conflict, the Church displays an intellectual inferiority that is almost comic, for it is due, not to the force of the arguments adduced by the other side, usually of a very mediocre order, but solely to an inferiority complex.

These need no comment; there is truth there, but not all truth; there is error but not all error. We would wish for a Chesterton to deftly remold the facts, but it remains that Simone Weil, also of a superior mind, did not.

The secret may be that she, a Jew who bumped over the usual barrier to her kind to embrace the divinity of Our Lord, was never convinced of the divine mission of the Jews. As that is the foundation of the Christian Church, it is as if she were building beautiful castles in the sand — earnestly, with constructional perfection, with indeed, supreme charity, but not the chemical element that changes sand into concrete.

SEPTEMBER 1953

SELECTION I

Edited by Cecily Hastings and Donald Nicholl
Sheed & Ward

THIS IS THE FIRST OF A PROPOSED SERIES OF YEARBOOKS comprised of outstanding contributions of contemporary thought in fields ranging from anthropology to theology. The editors' particular preoccupation is the relation of sciences to theology and to each other, so they have tried to find experts with a universal view.

This first volume is very scholarly and scientific. The effort at universality is there, but not too successfully realized. I found several of the articles very difficult to follow because they were so technical. These were precisely the ones where a real synthesis was attempted, but a synthesis which leaned, in my view, far too heavily on the findings of experimental science as a basis. One of the articles, "Factors in the Stages of Moral Development," by Charles Baudouin, accepts the Freudian anatomy of the soul and tries to build it into a moral framework reconcilable with Christianity. This sort of thing leads to abstruse distinctions between the primary super-ego and the secondary super-ego, and finally leaves me far behind—and skeptical. Surely the synthesis that we are looking for will be far more lucid, broader, and deeper than this.

"The Reign of Anti-Christ," by Josef Pieper, was by far the most interesting article to me, though there were a number of excellent ones. I wonder why Pieper's article was placed last in the collection, with one of the very technical ones first.

There is an explanatory preface by the editors but it is inadequate. Next year I hope they tell more about articles and authors.

THY FAITH HATH MADE THEE WHOLE

OCTOBER 1954

NATURE AND GRACE

By Matthias Joseph Scheeben
Herder

WHEN EARNEST CATHOLICS DISAGREE AND START CALLING each other names, the usual epithets are: "You Jansenist," or "You Pelagian." The Jansenists are all those suspected of an exaggerated supernaturalism, too much emphasis on grace and not enough on nature. Their opponents are, of course, the naturalists. Now this is precisely the quarrel that Matthias Joseph Scheeben (1835-1888), a German theologian of the last century, examines in his first great work *Nature and Grace*, only recently translated. Scheeben was writing against the rationalists of his own day.

The difficulty of this problem lies in the fact that the Church seems to say contradictory things. On the other hand, she seems to picture nature as helpless when reproving the naturalists. Scheeben shows that the solution lies in making a clear distinction between nature and super-nature, between our natural life as given by God and the elevated life to which we are drawn by grace—also by God, of course, but in a different way. He shows that the Church in her various statements, and St. Augustine, depending on whom he's attacking, doesn't always specify the level of human action under discussion. Nature can do absolutely nothing of itself which is meritorious of eternal life or in the domain of the divine. In other words, it cannot do what God has destined us to do. That doesn't mean nature can't do good things in the natural order. It can, and not just in building houses or keeping accounts, but in knowing God as He can be known through creatures and loving Him as the author of creation.

Having given full credit to nature, Scheeben goes on to exalt grace, to show that it is a real participation in the divine life, a new order of knowing and loving. He emphasizes the connection of grace with the divine mysteries, a theme he later developed more fully in *The Mysteries of Christianity*. Then he deals with the relationship between nature and grace. We are used to hearing it said that grace builds on nature, but taken alone this is a kind of glib phrase, which can even give quite wrong impressions. It is not Scheeben's expression. He always emphasizes the distinction between the two orders. But a harmony between them exists in virtue of their operation with the same faculties, and the fact that they have the same Author. Grace does not destroy nature and neither does nature grow by itself into grace.

Nevertheless grace pervades nature, and in heaven there will be a fusion, a marriage between the two. Nature will not thereby be destroyed, but having been crucified, will be glorified. The analogy is with the Incarnation.

Though difficult, this is an interesting book, especially because the error Scheeben combatted is now virtually all-pervading. Not only do men think they can do all good things by their own efforts, but they have very odd ideas of what those good things are—their own glorification, Scheeben would say.

INTRODUCTION TO THEOLOGY

Theology Library, Vol. I
Edited by A.M. Henry, O.P.

AFTER READING THIS BOOK, AND THEN THINKING AND thinking, and then re-reading the introduction, I'm still not sure I have grasped the idea of the Theological Library, but I *think* I have.

There are going to be four volumes (six eventually), of which this first is only the introduction; a sort of comprehensive survey of the field. But what field? Not the field of theology as most people think of it. If it were called the field of religious scholarship I would be less puzzled. What this volume contains is ten articles or essays on fields of scholarship which contribute to, or reflect, dogma. It deals with the Liturgy, Canon Law, the Ecumenical Councils, Tradition in the Oriental Churches, Holy Scripture, Religious Art, and other things. It even has a nice little several-page discussion on revising the calendar, some interesting sociological reflections, and what I would call "101 Suggestions for Graduate Theses." These last are contained in a kind of list, by A. M. Henry, O. P., of subjects not sufficiently investigated yet; subjects like "The Theme of the 'Breath of God' in the Bible," or "The Prayer Life of the Incas."

Now my idea of an exciting subject for a graduate thesis in theology is something like: "The difficulties occasioned in modern medical research by the neglect of Teleology." I mention this just to point up the difference between what I would naturally expect to flow from a further study of theology and what the editor evidently expects to flow from it.

I would also have expected this volume to be something like a fatherly and encouraging talk about what theology is and how to approach St. Thomas. But the theology I had in mind only comes in for treatment in the last chapter, as the Science of the Faith. And here nobody gets much time. For instance, what did St. Bonaventure write and what of his is available in Latin and in English? I would like to have known and I thought certain I would find out because the rest of the book is full of references to, and bibliographies of, sometimes very obscure works. Anyhow I didn't.

The last chapter introduces the coming next three volumes (their chapter heads are also given elsewhere). Volume II, III and IV will be studies of doctrine, following the order of treatment of St. Thomas, but contemporized, both as to style and content. I can hardly wait to see what they will be like. For one thing, they will be not so simplified as the catechism, and not so difficult as seminary manuals. For another, they will not presuppose any philosophical underpinnings on the part of the reader, leaning instead on "the historical development of doctrines." They will be meant for earnest lay people, for religious who want to go deeper into doctrine, and (especially) for priests who wish to continue to grow in the subjects of their specialties.

It's a neat trick if they can do it. I remain full of curiosity.

Meanwhile I am glad to have this volume, which I shall use as a sort of encyclopedia of religious sources. It was sometimes very heavy going in the reading; at other times surprisingly light. The chapter on "The Echo of Tradition in Art" deserves some sort of medal as the only treatise on art (to which I am rather insensitive) which has filled me with delight and entertainment. I am sure it is pure coincidence that it is the only chapter in the book by a layman.

Shame on the publishers for allowing some gross errors in translation. There is a completely meaningless paragraph on page 44, and on page 189 we are told that the Council of Chalcedon "condemned and defined the existence of two perfect natures in Christ."

FEBRUARY 1956

JUSTICE

By Josef Pieper
Pantheon

JOSEF PIEPER IS A THOMIST PHILOSOPHER, NOT A THOMIST popularizer, and in the field of Thomistic philosophy he feels that "originality is of scarcely any importance." What is important is "to partake of and grasp the already established true knowledge of man which is not to be set at nought by the advance and march of time." His approach is particularly interesting in view of all the talk today about St. Thomas' inadequacy or incompleteness with respect to the modern situation. Not that Pieper says anything about the controversy or is at all concerned to exalt St. Thomas. His preoccupation is with the matter itself, and the proof of its inadequacy, at least on this present topic, lies in the powerful light it shed on contemporary history as it emerges from a really great mind. This book is obviously the fruit of deep study in the whole of philosophy, great love and respect for St. Thomas, the light which comes from truths really meditated, and keen knowledge of the modern world.

Justice is one of a series on the cardinal virtues. As usual Pieper follows the Thomistic development; first defining justice, then treating the prior subject of rights, then showing the relation of justice to the other virtues, as preliminary to discussing the three basic forms of justice. It's a compact, clear, instructive treatment, with concise applications to everything from liquidation and collective guilt to totalitarianism and Anti-Christ. However, it is the last several chapters, especially apropos of distributive justice, that Pieper waxes eloquent (in a philosophical way) and hits hard, St. Thomas and Aristotle swinging the hammer with him. In distributive justice common goods are allotted in a proportional equality decided by the ruler (and the laws) *alone*. If there is an unjust distribution, then what? Pieper insists that there is no higher third party which can arbitrate. Injustice simply will reign. It is not that Pieper disallows personal refusals to obey or other forms of protest. He is merely insisting on the immeasurable importance of the virtue of justice (and prudence) in rulers, after which he goes on to show how modern social and political conditions (with particular application to democracy) militate against the possibility that rulers will, in fact, have these virtues. His suggestion is that we take measures to restore authority to its dignity instead of continuing the downward trend through liberalism and chaos to tyranny. For, though St. Thomas thought monarchy the best of the tolerable forms of government and its opposite, tyranny, the worst, he considered that tyranny more often is the result of democracy gone bad than of the abuse of monarchy.

The last pages of the book go beyond justice, showing its insufficiency and why. Here it is barely a sketch, but again wonderfully exact.

All in all a splendid book for election year reading, preferably by politicians.

EDITORIALS

EDITORIALS

After Ed Willock (co-founder and illustrator) suffered a stroke on September 16, 1951, Carol Robinson was thrust into the position as sole editor of Integrity—*a position she would retain until being replaced by Dorothy Dohen in the April 1952 issue. We include all the editorials she wrote until that time so the reader can get further insight into her intellectual outlook.*

OCTOBER 1951

DURING THE NAZI REGIME A BOOK WAS PUBLISHED WHICH in a special way served as an epitaph for a dead Christianity. It did for charity what Malthus did for providence. It rationalized something which should have remained rooted in the mysteries of a higher than human order. Let us recall what Malthus did. He did not invent contraceptives. He did not advocate artificial birth control. All he did was figure out that if people continued to procreate in a normal manner, we would all presently starve because the resources of the earth would rapidly be outstripped by the population. He presumed to calculate a matter which he should have trusted to God's judgment, since God is the creator of the resources as well as the souls, and it might be assumed that He knows what He is about. After Malthus, birth control followed as a natural consequence.

The author of the Nazi book rationalized about the care of society's weak. He figured that if old and insane people, the mentally retarded and incurably diseased, the crippled and the misfits were allowed to drain the physical and financial resources of a country, the others would suffer, the whole state would be weakened, and the nation would finally be overcome by other less "sentimental" states, so that all its citizens would end by losing everything. The author was unwilling to follow his thesis through to its bitter conclusion of murder (under a variety of pretty names) but he might as well have done so, as others have or will. He merely said: "You people will shrink from the consequences of this truth, but don't be surprised then at what happens to you and your country."

People shrink less and less. The dictatorship countries do not hesitate to dispossess or liquidate whole areas of populations. Anyone in their borders who is a burden may well tremble for his continued existence.

In the democratic countries it looks superficially as though the opposite course were being followed. Never in history have public funds on so large a scale been used for the weak. Yet in the very shadow of the Welfare State we see arising euthanasia, sterilization, compulsory labor and other measures not unlike those of the Nazis and Russians.

So here, as in the matter of birth control, Christians have an opportunity to contrast their lives and ideas with those of secularism. In fact there are so many dispossessed and disinherited in the contemporary world that helping them in Christian charity ought to be the most important problem that society has, more important than war and atom bombs, more important than the American Way of Life and the advance of technology.

The Nazi author's calculations are wrong. It does not weaken a people to care for the unfortunate. It strengthens them. It strengthens them because it fosters their spiritual growth. The strength of individuals and nations is measured in virtue, not in automobiles. However, the carnal prudence of a materialistic generation cannot grasp this truth and it is even somewhat mysterious to Christians. If we could see that Christianity "pays," no faith would be involved. And, in fact, it doesn't "pay" in a humanly calculable sense. Prosperity, culture and peace are the by-products of goodness, but almost accidental and unexpected ones.

The Christian has to operate on another plane. He has to see that Christ shows Himself to our generation as dirty, homeless, covered with spittle and twisted almost out of a human pattern by sufferings and indignities which are beyond our imagination. Only faith and love will see the face of Christ in today's outcasts and only charity will resurrect them. He who sees the unfortunate on some lower plane, as numbers on a relief roll, or broken citizens, or human wrecks, will be unequal to the job of helping them. Or perhaps it is the other way around—he who does not accept the invitation to help Christ in His agony (whether He presents Himself as a D. P., an insane wife, a senile grandfather or a Negro neighbor) cannot be helped by Christ. The truth of the matter may be that our own moral sickness is so great that only some such great cross can save us. What seems to us to be a yoke may be the lever of our own salvation.

Editorials

NOVEMBER 1951

THIS ISSUE IS LIKELY TO BE SOMEWHAT OF A SHOCK TO our readers. First of all because it looks different. Ed Willock (who is getting better, and who thanks our readers for their prayers) will be unable to draw for a while, so Nell Sonnemann has done the cover and the cartoons. Nell is a convert and it is fitting that she should do her first art work as a Catholic for *Integrity* because its two editors were her sponsors at Baptism.

But the article to which this issue is given over may also surprise our readers, so we wish to give a few words of explanation in our editorial.

The Cult of the Common Man hits at the central idea of communism, that society must be *leveled* into one classless mass of men acting as a unit. Since this idea is also pretty clearly developed in socialism and is pervading democracy like a poisoned gas, the author, Aurel Kolnai,[1] doesn't talk about communism much, just about this false idea of equality, this *equalism*, with emphasis on its roots in liberal democratism.

Americans have been nourished on the doctrine that all men are created equal, which is sound enough as long as it conjures up images of escape from tyranny, of equality before the law, and of a spiritual order which transcends the often unjust lot of men on earth.

The doctrine that all men are created equal was never intended as a denial that men are conspicuously unequal. But today it is being pushed into that interpretation by the equalists, and we are gradually absorbing their interpretation. In fact there is a psychological social pressure bearing down on all of us to be ashamed of any excellencies we may possess, to desire nothing more for our children than that they be normal (that is, average), to boast of being unexceptional (that is, "regular"). Everyone has to go to college, but colleges have to lower their standards to make it possible. In a thousand ways we are being standardized, regimented, leveled.

This passion for leveling, this cult of the common man, has a religious flavor about it, a faint odor of a Christianity half-forgotten. We are in danger of being persuaded that it is, in fact, Christianity finally and triumphantly realized.

---

[1] Aurel Kolnai (1900–1973) was a Hungarian philosopher and political theorist. He converted to the Catholic Church in 1926 partly through the influence of G. K. Chesterton. His 1938 book, *The War Against the West*, was one of the first systematic critiques of Nazism. —*Ed.*

Mr. Kolnai's article is a vigorous reaction against this equalism, which he considers to be ersatz Christianity and contrary to the natural order, wherein men actually are unequal. He considers that an organic society must allow for these inequalities, must be hierarchical.

The biblical quotation which begins his article is the eleventh verse of the 14th chapter of Saint Luke. In the Gospel it immediately follows this parable:

> When any man invites thee to a wedding, do not sit down in the chief place; he may have invited some guest whose rank is greater than thine. If so, his host and thine will come and say to thee, make room for this man; and so thou wilt find thyself taking, with a blush, the lowest place of all. Rather when thou are summoned, go straight to the lowest place and sit down there; so, when he who invited thee comes in, he will say, My friend go higher than this; and then honor shall be thine before all that sit down in thy company.

Our cover drawing inspired by these verses, pictures the social utopia of the equalists. Christ likened society to a dinner table with high and low places. He admonished us not to fight for the head chairs, but to seek seats at the foot of the table. By contrast the equalist society is like a round table with neither high nor low places. We asked Nell to put a Lazy Susan in the middle of the table because in a classless society there will be no servants.

DECEMBER 1951

OUR LORD CAME AS A LITTLE CHILD TO SAVE A WORLD

hopelessly sunk in iniquity. Later He redeemed us on the Cross. But his first condition was infancy, and we who may expect the cross too, would do well to learn the lesson of childlike simplicity.

The modern world is a mad house. Anyone who doubts this the rest of the year, learns it again each Christmas. Everything is too fast, too much, too many, too exhausting and too complex. Holidays are just added burden and Christmas holidays are the most burdensome of all, financially, spiritually and physically. Something has to be done.

The thing to do is to become as little children, to simplify our lives, but in a Christian way. We must avoid false simplifications. For instance, we must not believe, with respect to reading, that we *have* to be well-informed, that the more printed matter that rolls off the presses the more obliged we are to read it. People are taking courses so that they will learn to read superficially a dozen books, scan six daily newspapers, or cover all the trade journals. This is not the answer. God does not expect us to keep pace with the presses and, if we are overwhelmed with undigested ideas, surely a stripping to fewer, more fundamental books is in order.

If the list of those to whom we have to give Christmas presents or send cards has become fantastically long, expensive and meaningless, that does not indicate that we should spend Advent becoming slick shoppers. It more likely means that we should stop dead in our tracks and refuse to conform to the convention that started this hypocrisy, and then begin again in quite a different way, from different principles.

However, there is one thing worse than complexity and that is a false simplicity, undertaken for worldly motives, such as lack of generosity with self, or stinginess with money, or the inability to summon up joy over the birth of Christ. This is the spirit of "let's not have a Christmas tree this year, because the prices are so outrageous and all it does is mess up the house." A materialistic simplification of life destroys all its savor, leaving us petty and empty.

There is another kind of simplicity which comes from depth and principles and enables us to do twice as much work with half the energy, and with joy.

With Christmas, simplicity is simple, because the liturgy indicates what should be done. Once we concede the point that Advent is Advent, a preparation for Christ's coming and a time of quiet, prayer, and mortification, a preparation of the spirit, then the frenzied crowds of shoppers seem very remote, and simple, home-made gifts suggest themselves. Advent wreathes, Christmas trees, cribs, special cooking, all of these things will be seen to be appropriate, satisfying and peace-giving.

The theory of simplicity is that if one puts first things first, second and third things fall into place naturally. But since most of the noise and nonsense of our almost entirely pagan Christmases ought not to exist at all, then those who put first things first will find a multitude of cares just simply dropping out of their lives.

There is another truth involved here, which is that the amount of work a person can do who is rooted in grace is incomparably greater than what is accomplished by natural energy. That's why, for instance, Father Garrigou-Lagrange says it is fitting for a bishop to be in the unitive stage of the spiritual life. He has so much work to do, such a large area to supervise and such a heavy responsibility, that somehow the work has to be unified in a wisdom higher than human. To be properly done such a work has to be the overflow of contemplation. Now natural prudence would dictate the opposite. It would say, this man is too busy to spend much time in prayer, therefore he will be excused from the necessity of cultivating a deep spiritual life.

What goes for bishops goes for busy lay people analogously. We too have a multitude of worldly cares. We too are, or should be, responsible for the apostolate. If we pore over books on efficiency and become brisk go-getters, whatever we accomplish will be so much fanning of the air anyhow. But if we start with simplicity, and as little children put our lives and affairs in the hands of God, Our Lord will accomplish much through us.

Often the beginning is hard and means a sharp break. No better time than Christmas season for making it.

We wish all our readers simplicity and peace and a very holy Christmas.

JANUARY 1952

WE WISH OUR READERS A HAPPY, A HOLY AND A *HOPEFUL* New Year. Hope seems to be precisely the virtue to practice in 1952, when ominous clouds are gathering and men everywhere are tempted to despair.

So fittingly, we have treated the subject in this issue. Dorothy Dohen's article on "Hope" is one of her best, we think. For the benefit of new readers, Dorothy has a gift of presenting sound theology in a simple manner with telling illustrations. Sheed and Ward has published a collection of her previous *Integrity* articles under the title, *Vocation to Love*.

Dr. John C. H. Wu ("Hope and Despair") is our friend (of which we are proud), author of *Beyond East and West* (of which Sheed and Ward is proud), translator of the Bible into Chinese, former ambassador from China to the Vatican, father of thirteen children, presently teaching law at Seton Hall College. His is the mystic's view of our subject.

R. C. Douglas' article ("A City Called Heaven") might seem to be off the subject, but it isn't. She is an American who has lived a long time abroad. Seeing her native land with fresh eyes, she says its hope lies in its contemplative life.

"Melancholy" and "Optimism" are diseases related to despair and hope. Father Keenan, an English Franciscan, has introduced the psychiatric angle. Peter Michaels of our staff, has taken the large social view.

Finally there is Friedrich Georg Juenger, the German poet, whom we reprint from time to time. The "Vengeance of the Fettered Elements" is one of those stabs into the heart of materialistic technology that should carry over for at least a month's invulnerability to propaganda about our brave new world.

Good reading!

FEBRUARY 1952

POVERTY OF SPIRIT IS THE ANTIDOTE FOR THE SPIRITUAL poverty of our age. And spiritual poverty is our disease, not material poverty. Or rather only material poverty is a consequence of a dying spirit. Even in the so-called underdeveloped countries of the near and far East, where economic and social life stagnates, it is an infusion of spirit that is needed far more than an introduction of technological equipment and know-how.

Quietly and modestly—almost unnoticed amid the clamor of propaganda and under the superstructure of giant organizations, poverty of spirit is expressing and radiating itself.

Most of the articles in this issue describe gropings and beginnings in this order. Although very different from each other they share certain characteristics. For one thing they do not have concrete, practical, measurable programs in the temporal order. They are not going to wipe out poverty, solve the Negro problem, restore family life or convert all the non-Catholics in the parish. They work toward all these things, but by opening up channels so that God's grace can work on the situation, in His own and partially mysterious way, rather than by depending on their own zeal or intelligence.

These beginnings are like seeds, small but powerful. It is always the little group, large enough to be like a family, few enough to fade into the environment. But deep—contemplative and sacramental—so that the roots may reach the waters of grace.

Our Lord, speaking to Sister Mary of the Holy Trinity, said, "Listen, you must not attach great importance to natural activity. *Without Me you can do nothing.* It is easy to make a stir, to work in a visible outward manner; it is very difficult to renounce oneself and to let Me work. And yet that is the only fruitful activity, which lasts throughout eternity."

MARCH 1952

NOW IT'S THIS WAY. IF YOU WANT CHRISTIANITY WITHOUT the Cross, and take instead to do-gooding or mystical feelings (whether in the name of Christ or not) the whole world will become obsessed with the need of redemption—like the child with a calcium deficiency, who takes to eating the plaster off the wall; or the sinner who will not face guilt and cannot wash his body enough; or the tense man with the superficial control, who breaks out all over in a rash; or the proletarian masses whose very humanity is denied them and who are ready any day to break out in mob violence.

We forgot man had to be redeemed, that is ransomed, that he'd got himself in a mess from which he was really powerless to arise. We knew it was a mess he was in, but we thought he could pull himself out—by education, by hygiene, by national self-determination, by a higher standard of living, by trade unions, by wonder drugs and atomic energy. Suffering increased. We redoubled our efforts to eliminate it (tomorrow), or deaden it (today).

Science and technology will not save us, but suffering can if it becomes not simply suffering, but the Cross. Both hurt, but one is rejected (and so embitters), the other is accepted in union with Christ (not just stoically) and so becomes a part of His Passion, a bit of the ransom of the human race.

This issue of *Integrity* is about the Cross, but naturally not all about it. Lent and penance is part of the subject. Suffering is a great bit of it. What may puzzle our readers at first is the relevance of humanism. But humanism is a doctrine of the self-redemption of man, of salvation without the Cross.

In a book by Arthur Koestler there is told how the very mention of a special torture chamber in a Soviet prison made the bravest men tremble. Yet no one could tell what went on there. It turned out that in this room each man met what he hated and feared most (an open attack by a rat, in the case of the hero of this book). It might be a little thing in itself, but it was the worse possible torture for the victim. Koestler's torture chamber is like a caricature of the Cross. Each man's cross is made to measure. It is the thing he dreads most, because it is the instrument by which alone he can die to himself, so as to find a higher life. For some it is humiliation, for others material deprivation, for still others the patient acceptance of a physical deformity, or the pain of illness, or the loss of someone loved, or the life-long gracious endurance of a marriage too hastily contracted. Lesser sufferings and voluntary penances strengthen us for our own crucifixion, but it is in our crosses that we shall find our redemption.

And so it will be with the modern world. There is plenty of suffering that goes along with material ambition and secularism (like having your hair pulled while getting a permanent wave or riding the subway to a plush job or enduring the delay in the coming of color television). It won't help. But the hardship attendant on having too many children (as the world figures), or of trying to live in the country for the sake of a more spiritual life, or of poverty endured for a Christian cause or in imitation of Christ, or the labors of the apostolate, all these mean something. And there will come a time when some sort of collective change of heart will have to take place, when we shall have to shoulder national crosses of our own making. Then if we do it as a penance and in retribution a new day will be dawning.

COLLECTED WORKS

Breaking the Chains of Mediocrity:
Carol Robinson's Marianist *Articles* (1947–1948)

The Eightfold Kingdom Within:
Essays on the Beatitudes and
the Gifts of the Holy Ghost (1962–1963)

Designs for Christian Living (1947)

This Perverse Generation (1949)

FORTHCOMING

An Embattled Mind: In Defense of St. Thomas
(The Wanderer Years: 1971–1987)

The Salt of the Earth:
The Lone Star Catholic *Articles* (1958–1959)